LEGAL FOUNDATIONS

LEGAL FOUNDATIONS

Keir Bamford

Kevin Browne

Judith Embley

Lesley King

Anthony Morgan

Lisa Rawcliffe

Published by

College of Law Publishing,
Braboeuf Manor, Portsmouth Road, St Catherines, Guildford GU3 1HA

British Library Cataloguing-in-Publication Data
A catalogue record for this book is available from the British Library.

ISBN: 978 1 911269 82 3

Typeset by Style Photosetting Ltd, Mayfield, East Sussex
Tables and index by Moira Greenhalgh, Carnforth, Lancashire
Printed in Great Britain by The Irongate Group, Derby

Preface

This book is divided into five Parts, the first four each dealing with one of the topics which pervade the syllabus of the Legal Practice Course. These topics are: Revenue Law, Professional Conduct, EU Law and Human Rights. Part V deals with the core subject, Probate and Administration. The material contained in this book is intended to be an introduction to the pervasive and core topics, and is designed for those with little or no previous knowledge of the subjects. It has been written primarily to support and complement the Legal Practice Course undertaken by trainee solicitors. The approach taken to the subjects is essentially practical and is enhanced by worked examples showing the application of the topics in a practical context.

For the sake of brevity, the masculine pronoun is used to include the feminine. To refer to 'he or she' on every occasion when such a reference was necessary would have added many extra pages to an already lengthy book.

The law is generally stated as at May 2017.

KEIR BAMFORD
KEVIN BROWNE
JUDITH EMBLEY
LESLEY KING
ANTHONY MORGAN
LISA RAWCLIFFE
The University of Law

Contents

Table of Cases

A

B

C

Table of Primary Legislation

Table of Secondary Legislation

Table of Abbreviations

ABS	alternative business structure
AEA 1925	Administration of Estates Act 1925
AEA 1971	Administration of Estates Act 1971
AIM	Alternative Investment Market
APR	annual percentage rate
ATP	authorised third person
CGT	capital gains tax
CJEU	Court of Justice of the European Union
COB Rules 2001	SRA Financial Services (Conduct of Business) Rules 2001
COFA	compliance officer for finance and administration
COLP	compliance officer for legal practice
COREPER	Committee of Permanent Representatives
CPR	Civil Procedure Rules 1998
CTM	Community trade mark
DPB	designated professional body
EAT	Employment Appeal Tribunal
ECA 1972	European Communities Act 1972
ECHR	European Convention for the Protection of Human Rights and Fundamental Freedoms 1950
ECJ	European Court of Justice
ECSC	European Coal and Steel Community
ECtHR	European Court of Human Rights
EEA	European Economic Area
EEIG	European Economic Interest Grouping
EFTA	European Free Trade Agreement
EIS	Enterprise Investment Scheme
ESC	Economic and Social Committee
EurAtom	European Atomic Energy Community
FCA	Financial Conduct Authority
FPO 2005	Financial Services and Markets Act 2000 (Financial Promotion) Order 2005
FSA	Financial Services Authority
FSMA 2000	Financial Services and Markets Act 2000
HMRC	HM Revenue & Customs
HRA 1998	Human Rights Act 1998
ICTA 1988	Income and Corporation Taxes Act 1988
IHT	inheritance tax
IHTA 1984	Inheritance Tax Act 1984
IP	intellectual property
I(PFD)A 1975	Inheritance (Provision for Family and Dependants) Act 1975
IPDI	immediate post-death interest
ISA	Individual Savings Account
ITA 2007	Income Tax Act 2007
ITEPA 2003	Income Tax (Earnings and Pensions) Act 2003
ITTOIA 2005	Income Tax (Trading and Other Income) Act 2005
LASPO 2012	Legal Aid, Sentencing and Punishment of Offenders Act 2012
LCS	Legal Complaints Service
LCT	lifetime chargeable transfer
LeO	Legal Ombudsman for England and Wales

LPA 1925	Law of Property Act 1925
MCA 2005	Mental Capacity Act 2005
MEP	member of the European Parliament
MEQR	measure having equivalent effect to a quantitative restriction
NCA	National Crime Agency
NCPR 1987	Non-Contentious Probate Rules 1987
NSNDI	non-savings, non-dividend income
OEICs	open-ended investment companies
PAYE	Pay As You Earn
PEP	Politically Exposed Person
PET	potentially exempt transfer
PR	personal representative
QLTT	Qualified Lawyers Transfer Test
RAO 2001	Financial Services and Markets Act 2000 (Regulated Activities) Order 2001
RPI	Retail Prices Index
Scope Rules 2001	SRA Financial Services (Scope) Rules 2001
SRA	Solicitors Regulation Authority
TA 1925	Trustee Act 1925
TA 2000	Trustee Act 2000
TEU	Treaty on European Union
TFEU	Treaty on the Functioning of the European Union
TLATA 1996	Trusts of Land and Appointment of Trustees Act 1996
VATA 1994	Value Added Tax Act 1994
VCT	Venture Capital Trust

REVENUE LAW

VALUE ADDED TAX

LEARNING OUTCOMES

After reading this chapter you will be able to understand:

- the circumstances that give rise to a VAT charge
- the current rates at which VAT is charged and supplies that are exempt from VAT
- the penalties for failing to comply with the VAT legislation.

1.1 INTRODUCTION

1.1.1 Sources of VAT law

The main charging statute relating to value added tax (VAT) is the Value Added Tax Act 1994 (VATA 1994), as amended by later Finance Acts and certain statutory instruments. Detailed provisions implementing the Act are to be found in the VAT (General) Regulations 1995 (SI 1995/2518) and other statutory instruments. In addition, HM Revenue & Customs (HMRC) issues VAT Notices which, although lacking legal force, express its views on the law. Value added tax was introduced in 1973 in order to harmonise UK law with European Community law, therefore EC Directives 67/227 and 77/338 are also relevant. The standard practioner's work is De Voil, *Indirect Tax Service* (Butterworths, looseleaf).

1.1.2 Charge to tax

In the current tax year, the standard rate of VAT is 20%.

Generally, VAT is charged whenever a business supplies goods or services. The business charges the customer VAT at 20% on the value of the goods or services. This is known as 'output tax'. The business deducts from the output tax which it collects any VAT it has paid ('input tax') on goods or services received and pays the difference to HMRC.

	Value of goods (£)	VAT charged to buyer (£)	VAT paid to HMRC (£)
(a) A manufacturer buys raw material costing £200 plus VAT from a producer	200	40	
Producer pays to HMRC			40
(b) The manufacturer sells finished article to a retailer for £1,000 plus VAT	1,000	200	
Manufacturer pays to HMRC			160 (200 – 40)

	Value of goods (£)	VAT charged to buyer (£)	VAT paid to HMRC (£)
(c) The retailer sells the finished article to a consumer for £2,000 plus VAT	2,000	400	
Retailer pays to HMRC			200 (400 – 200)
Total paid to HMRC			400

Note: (i)   VAT does not cost the business anything as any VAT paid is recouped from VAT charged.

(ii)   Each business accounts for VAT on the 'value added' to the goods whilst in the possession of the business. The value added by the manufacturer is £800 (£1,000 – £200). Twenty per cent of £800 is £160, the sum paid to HMRC.

(iii)   The ultimate burden falls on the consumer, who pays £2,000 plus £400 VAT for the product. The £400 VAT has been paid to HMRC in three stages.

1.2 CHARGE TO VAT

1.2.1 Definition

Value added tax is 'charged on any supply of goods or services made in the United Kingdom where it is a taxable supply made by a taxable person in the course or furtherance of any business carried on by him' (VATA 1994, s 4(1)). Tax will be charged on the 'value of the supply' (VATA 1994, s 2(1)). The elements of this charge are defined widely, in order both to prevent avoidance and to comply with the Directives, and are dealt with in outline below.

1.2.2 Supply of goods or services

1.2.2.1 Supply of goods

Any transfer of the whole property in goods is a supply of goods (VATA 1994, Sch 4). As well as more obvious transactions like the sale of consumer goods, this includes a supply of power or heat, the grant of an interest in land, and even a gift of goods.

1.2.2.2 Supply of services

Anything that is not a supply of goods but which is done for a consideration is a supply of services (VATA 1994, s 5(2)). This includes the provision of a solicitor's services for a fee, but not a gratuitous supply of services.

1.2.3 Taxable supply

Any supply of goods or services (other than an exempt supply) is taxable (VATA 1994, s 4(2)). Exempt supplies are listed in VATA 1994, Sch 9 and include supplies of residential land, insurance, postal services, education and health services.

1.2.4 Taxable person

A taxable person is a person who makes or intends to make taxable supplies and who is or is required to be registered under the Act (VATA 1994, s 3(1)). A person is required to register if he makes taxable supplies in a defined period which have exceeded a limit, which is set each year, or will exceed that limit. Currently, a person must register if the value of his taxable supplies in the preceding 12 months exceeded £85,000.

Any person who makes taxable supplies is entitled to be registered if he so requests (see 1.3.4). A person who makes only exempt supplies cannot register.

Once registered, a taxable person (individual, partnership or company) receives a VAT number which is issued for all businesses operated by that person.

1.2.5 Course of business

'Business' includes any trade, profession or vocation (VATA 1994, s 94). A supply in the course of business includes the disposal of a business or any of its assets.

1.2.6 Value of supply

Value added tax is charged on the value of the supply of goods or services. This is what the goods or services would cost were VAT not charged and is often shown as part of the price. For example, a television may be advertised as costing '£400 plus VAT'; £400 is the value of the supply.

If the supply is shown as being for a VAT inclusive amount (eg, a television costs '£240'), the value of supply is 'such amount as, with the addition of the tax chargeable, is equal to the consideration' (VATA 1994, s 19(2)). In the case of the television, the value of supply would be £200 and the VAT £40. A price is deemed to include VAT unless the contrary is stated.

If the supply is not for a consideration in money, the value of supply is taken to be its market value (VATA 1994, s 19(3)).

1.2.7 Rate of tax

The standard rate of VAT is 20%. However, there is a large category of supplies which are taxed at 0%. 'Zero-rated' supplies are listed in VATA 1994, Sch 8 and include food, other than food supplied in the course of catering, water, books and newspapers, transport and construction of dwellings. A reduced rate of 5% is applied to certain supplies, including domestic fuel, installation of energy-saving materials and child car seats (VATA 1994, Sch 7A).

1.2.8 Time of supply

A taxable person must account for VAT one month after the end of each quarter (see **1.3.1**). The time of supply (tax point) determines the accounting period within which a supply of goods or services falls.

In the case of goods, the basic tax point is the time goods are removed, or the time they are made available to the person to whom they are supplied. In the case of services, the basic tax point is the time the services are performed (VATA 1994, s 6).

The basic tax point can be varied in a number of cases. For example, it can be brought forward, if the supplier issues a tax invoice (see **1.3.5**) or receives a payment, to the time when the invoice is issued or payment received. It can be delayed, if the supplier issues a tax invoice within 14 days after the basic tax point, to the time when the invoice is issued. Thus the time for accounting for VAT may be brought forward or delayed.

1.3 TAX PAYABLE TO HM REVENUE & CUSTOMS

1.3.1 Introduction

A person who is registered for VAT must send a return to HMRC showing the VAT payable by him, together with a cheque for this amount, generally within one month after the end of each quarter.

The amount payable is the VAT he has charged on all supplies of goods and services in the course of his business ('output tax'), less any VAT he has paid in the course of his business ('input tax'). If input tax exceeds output tax, the person will receive a rebate.

1.3.2 Zero-rated and exempt supplies

Zero-rated and exempt supplies are similar to each other, in that the customer does not pay any VAT. However, a person who makes zero-rated supplies will be able to reclaim the VAT he has paid from HMRC. A person who makes only exempt supplies cannot register (see **1.2.4**) and so cannot reclaim VAT.

> **EXAMPLE**
>
> A baker and a doctor in private practice are converting premises into a shop and a surgery respectively. They will both pay VAT on the cost of their conversions. The baker, who makes zero-rated supplies of food, will be able to reclaim the VAT; the doctor, who makes exempt supplies of health services, will not be able to do so.

1.3.3 Taxable and exempt supplies

Where a person makes both exempt and taxable supplies, for example a doctor in private practice who also acts as an expert witness in personal injury claims, only part of his input tax will be deductible from the output tax charged on the fees for acting as an expert witness (see the VAT (General) Regulations 1995, SI 1995/2518).

1.3.4 Voluntary registration

A person who makes taxable supplies of £85,000 or less per annum is not required to register and charge VAT. This can be an advantage as such a supplier may be able to undercut larger rivals who are obliged to charge VAT.

However, only those people who are registered can reclaim any input tax they have paid. For example, a builder with a small business who bought a van could not reclaim VAT payable on the purchase of the van if he were not registered.

When deciding whether to register voluntarily, people in business must weigh up the advantage of being able to reclaim VAT against the disadvantage that customers might be put off by higher prices.

1.3.5 Tax invoices

A person making a taxable supply to a taxable person must provide him with a tax invoice. A tax invoice is an ordinary invoice or bill which contains specified information about the transaction, such as the VAT number, the tax point, the value of supply and the rate of tax charged.

The tax invoice is important because a person who is claiming to deduct input tax must have tax invoices in respect of all the tax claimed.

1.4 PENALTIES

1.4.1 Introduction

A person who fails to comply with the VAT legislation is liable to a range of criminal and civil penalties in addition to being required to pay any unpaid tax with interest. There are very few defences to these provisions, although, apart from the default surcharge (see **1.4.4**), the civil penalties may be mitigated. A number of these penalties are dealt with in outline below.

1.4.2 Fraudulent evasion of tax

A person knowingly concerned in the fraudulent evasion of tax is liable, on conviction on indictment, to an unlimited fine and imprisonment for a term not exceeding seven years (VATA 1994, s 72).

1.4.3 Breaches of regulations

Regulations impose many obligations on taxable persons. Breach of a regulation will lead to a civil penalty. There is a penalty of £500 for failure to keep certain records. Other breaches attract a penalty calculated at a daily rate over the period of the breach (VATA 1994, s 69).

1.4.4 The default surcharge

A person who fails to send a return (see **1.3.1**) is regarded as being in default. If he is persistently in default he becomes liable to a surcharge rising to 15% of the tax for any period in which he was in default (VATA 1994, s 59).

INCOME TAX

LEARNING OUTCOMES

After reading this chapter you will be able to:

- identify chargeable income
- identify allowable reliefs
- identify the appropriate personal allowance for a taxpayer
- understand the difference between income (except savings and dividend income) and savings and dividend income
- identify the tax rates applicable to taxable income
- complete a full income tax calculation.

2.1 INTRODUCTION

2.1.1 The importance of income tax

Income tax is the tax which produces the greatest revenue for the UK Government. For example, in the most recent year for which figures are available (2016/17), total tax revenues collected by HMRC reached over £566.7 billion, of which nearly £176 billion was generated by income tax (source: ONS: HMRC Tax & NIC Receipts, March 2017). Income tax is, therefore, a vital source of revenue from which public services such as health, education, welfare, transport and defence can be funded. Income tax is collected by HMRC (see **2.9**).

2.1.2 Sources of income tax law

2.1.2.1 Statute

The charging statute for income tax is the Income Tax Act 2007 (ITA 2007) as amended by later Finance Acts. Also of importance are the Income Tax (Trading and Other Income) Act 2005 (ITTOIA 2005) and the Income Tax (Earnings and Pensions) Act 2003 (ITEPA 2003).

Income tax is an annual tax renewed each year by Act of Parliament.

2.1.2.2 Case law

The meaning and extent of the statutory provisions are decided by the judiciary.

An appeal by a taxpayer against an assessment to tax is heard by the First-tier Tribunal. Appeals from the decision of the First-tier Tribunal are made to the Upper Tribunal (Tax and Chancery Chamber). There is a right of appeal from the Upper Tribunal on a point of law to the Court of Appeal and, with leave, to the Supreme Court.

2.1.2.3 Official Statements

There would be an impossible workload if all questions as to the meaning and extent of tax legislation were taken to court. Official Statements made by HMRC are therefore an important source of information. The two most important types of statement are Extra-Statutory Concessions and Statements of Practice.

Extra-Statutory Concessions

These are published by HMRC in a booklet. If a taxpayer satisfies the terms of an Extra-Statutory Concession, HMRC waives its right to collect tax which would otherwise be due.

Statements of Practice

These are announced by press release and published in the professional journals. They indicate what view HMRC will take of particular tax provisions.

Note that these Official Statements do not bind the courts.

2.1.3 What is income?

There is no statutory definition of 'income' and the courts have failed to impose a judicial definition. A distinction must be made between income and capital profits: the former is subject to income tax; the latter are subject to capital gains tax. Generally, money received will be income if there is an element of recurrence, for example, a salary or partnership profit share received every month, or interest paid on a bank or building society account every quarter.

2.1.4 Who pays income tax?

The following are liable to pay income tax:

(a)   individuals;

(b)   partnerships (partners are individually responsible for the tax due on their share of partnership profits);

(c)   personal representatives (who pay the deceased's outstanding income tax and income tax chargeable during the administration of the estate); and

(d)   trustees (who pay income tax on the income produced by the trust fund).

Companies pay corporation tax (see **Business Law and Practice**).

Charities are generally exempt from paying tax. There are tax-efficient ways of giving money to charities, for example, Gift Aid.

2.1.5 The tax year

Income tax is paid with reference to the 'tax year' or 'year of assessment', which runs from 6 April until 5 April the following year. It is referred to by the calendar years which it straddles: for example, the tax year beginning on 6 April 2017 is referred to as the tax year 2017/18. So, in the simple tax calculation below at **2.1.8**, Amy's salary received between 6 April 2017 and 5 April 2018 will be charged to tax in the tax year 2017/18.

2.1.6   Anti-avoidance legislation

Income tax is one of the taxes subject to the 'general anti-abuse rule' (GAAR) introduced by the Finance Act 2013. The GAAR is an addition to the existing anti-avoidance legislation in this area and is designed to allow HMRC to counteract 'abusive' tax avoidance schemes intended to exploit loopholes in the legislation covering the rules for calculating tax.

2.1.7   How much income tax is payable?

Income tax is a 'progressive' tax, ie a tax where the rate of tax increases as the income of the taxpayer increases, with the result that taxpayers with higher incomes pay a higher average rate of tax than those on lower incomes.

Tax is payable on taxable income, which is calculated by deducting any available reliefs and allowances taxed at the appropriate rate or rates. The allowances and rates are different for the various types of income. Therefore, before a final calculation is made, the different types of income must be separated from one another into three categories. The categories are:

(a)   non-savings, non-dividend income ('NSNDI'), comprising all sources of income except income derived from savings and dividends;

(b)   savings income, which is interest from various sources, for example building society accounts, most National Savings accounts, unit or investment trusts and corporate or government bonds and gilts; and

(c)   dividend income.

The steps to work through to calculate the amount of tax payable are as follows:

Step 1:   Calculate the total income

Step 2:   Deduct any allowable reliefs

           The resulting sum is net income

Step 3:   Deduct any personal allowances

           The resulting sum is taxable income

Step 4:   Separate NSNDI, savings income and dividend income, and calculate the tax on each type of income at the applicable rate(s) (starting rate, basic rate, higher rate and additional rate)

Step 5:   Add together the amounts of tax from Step 4 (to give the overall income tax liability)

Note: As explained below, income tax is charged on an individual's taxable income for 2017/18 at a variety of rates ranging from 0% to 45% (depending on the amount and type of income).

2.1.8 Simple income tax calculation

The five steps may be used to carry out a simple tax calculation. For example, Amy has the following income for 2017/18: £62,000 share of partnership profits, and £9,240 from writing learned articles. She is liable to make interest payments of £2,000 per annum on a qualifying loan. Amy is a single person. Amy's income tax may be calculated as follows:

			£
STEP 1	Calculate the total income		
	Partnership profits		62,000
	Learned articles		9,240
	TOTAL INCOME		71,240
STEP 2	Deduct any allowable reliefs (interest)		(2,000)
	NET INCOME		69,240
STEP 3	Deduct any personal allowance		(11,500)
	TAXABLE INCOME		57,740
STEP 4	Calculate the tax at the applicable rate(s)		
	£33,500 at 20%		6,700
	£24,240 at 40%		9,696
	£57,740		
STEP 5	Add together the amounts of tax from Step 4		
	OVERALL INCOME TAX LIABILITY		16,396

The calculation above indicates the principles used to establish an individual's liability to income tax. The remainder of this chapter will consider each step of the calculation in more detail.

2.2 TOTAL INCOME

Total income is the aggregate of the taxpayer's income from all sources which is charged to income tax.

2.2.1 What income is charged to income tax?

2.2.1.1 The chargeable sources of income

Income is charged to income tax if it comes from a source specified by the ITTOIA 2005 and the ITEPA 2003. The most important sources are listed below.

Location	Source
ITTOIA 2005	
Part 2	Trading income (Profits of a trade, profession or vocation. Part 2 therefore charges the self-employed and applies to sole traders, trading partnerships, sole practitioners and professional partnerships)
Part 3	Property income (Rents and other receipts from land in the UK)
Part 4	Savings and investment income (Interest, annuities and dividends)
Part 5	Certain miscellaneous income (Annual income not otherwise charged)
ITEPA 2003	Employment and pensions income (Income arising out of employment and including social security payments such as sick pay and maternity payments)

2.2.1.2   How do the chargeable sources of income work?

If income is shown to be derived from one of the sources, it will be charged to income tax. For example, if an individual receives rent from land, he will pay income tax under Part 3 of the ITTOIA 2005. Income not having a chargeable source cannot be charged to income tax at all.

2.2.1.3   Why is it divided into chargeable sources?

Each Part of the ITTOIA 2005 and the ITEPA 2003 has its own rules for calculating the amount of income. For example, under Part 3 of the ITTOIA 2005 (which taxes income from land) the charge is on rents and other receipts, but the landlord may deduct expenses such as repairs on the property, ie expenses of an income nature. This means that income tax is charged on the profit element rather than the gross income. Note that, from April 2017, HMRC has been phasing in measures to restrict the tax relief that landlords of residential properties get for finance costs, such as mortgages, to the basic rate of income tax.

Further details of how the ITTOIA 2005 and the ITEPA 2003 operate can be found in **Business Law and Practice**.

2.2.2   Exempt income

Certain items are free of income tax. They include:

(a)   certain State benefits;

(b)   interest on Savings Certificates;

(c)   scholarships;

(d)   interest on damages for personal injuries or death;

(e)   income from investments in an individual savings account (ISA) (see **5.3**);

(f)   gross income up to £7,500 a year from letting a furnished room in the taxpayer's home;

(g)   annual payments under certain insurance policies, for example, where insurance benefits are provided in times of sickness; and

(h)   premium bond winnings.

Most of the above items are set out in the ITTOIA 2005, Part 6 (Exempt Income). In addition, a number of items are exempted from tax because of Extra-Statutory Concessions (see **2.1.2.3**).

2.2.3   Calculating the total income

It should now be possible to calculate the total income.

The total income is the aggregate of chargeable income computed according to the rules of the various chargeable sources. To work out the total income of a taxpayer it is necessary to find out what sources of income he has, calculate the income arising under each source and then add all the 'gross' income together. For example:

Most types of income are received by the taxpayer without any tax having been deducted prior to receipt. These types of income are said to be received 'gross'. Trading, property, interest and dividend income are received gross.

2.2.3.1 Tax deducted at source

For most taxpayers, their main source of income will be employment income, from which tax will have been deducted at source. The payee receives the net amount, not the gross amount. This is to ensure a steady flow of tax to HMRC and then on to central government to fund public services throughout the year.

Any sum received after deduction of tax at source must be grossed up to find the original sum from which the tax was deducted. This gross figure must be entered into the payee's calculation of total income. This is because the tax calculation is a way of checking that, overall, the taxpayer pays the right amount of tax.

At the end of the tax calculation, the tax that has already been paid will be credited to the taxpayer so that he will owe HMRC only the outstanding amount.

Salaries and other employment income are assessable under ITEPA 2003 using the Pay As You Earn system (PAYE). Under the PAYE system, the employer deducts from the employee's salary and then pays to HMRC income tax at the appropriate rate at the time the salary is paid. The PAYE system also takes account of personal allowances.

Gross amount £100

Employment income cannot be grossed up using a simple formula because deduction at source may not be just at one single rate. Under the PAYE scheme, income tax at various rates and National Insurance contributions will be deducted from salaries by the employer using tables and information supplied by HMRC and taking into account the employee's personal reliefs. A certificate of tax paid (P60), showing the gross figure, is given by the employer to the employee on a yearly basis and he can put this figure into his tax return. A taxpayer must complete a tax return if he has other sources of income.

2.2.3.2 Savings and dividend income

The Summer Budget of 2015 introduced new rules for savings and dividend income. Historically, interest was paid net after deduction of income tax at 20%, and dividends after deduction of a notional 10% tax credit. From April 2016, both interest and dividends are paid gross, and both savings and dividend income will have the benefit of annual tax-free allowances (see **2.5.1** and **2.5.2**). Both savings and dividend income still form part of Total Income, and must be aggregated with other income at this stage

2.3 ALLOWABLE RELIEFS

Total Income
Less
Allowable Reliefs
=
Net Income

2.3.1 Net income

Net income is total income less certain specified commitments known as allowable reliefs, for example interest on qualifying loans. Allowable reliefs remove sums of money from the income tax calculation.

2.3.2 Interest payments on qualifying loans

Most interest payments receive no tax relief at all, for example ordinary bank overdrafts, credit card interest and hire purchase interest payments. The borrower pays the interest out of taxed income.

However, in certain cases, tax relief may be available for interest paid on money borrowed. A taxpayer obtains income tax relief for certain interest payments by deducting them from his total income as an allowable relief. To obtain tax relief, interest must be payable on a 'qualifying loan'.

Qualifying loans include the following.

2.3.2.1 A loan to buy a share in a partnership or to contribute capital or make a loan to a partnership

> **EXAMPLE**
>
> Dawn, a partner, has total income of £25,000. She borrows £10,000 to make a loan to the partnership to be used wholly and exclusively for partnership business. The interest rate on the loan is 7% per annum. Dawn's net income is:
>
> | | £ |
> |---|---|
> | Total income | 25,000 |
> | Deduct any allowable reliefs | |
> | (interest on qualifying loan) | 700 |
> | Net income | 24,300 |

There is a cap of £50,000 or 25% of 'adjusted total income' on the amount of relief that can be claimed under this provision. 'Adjusted total income' is taxable income less allowable pension contributions. See *Business Law and Practice* for further details.

2.3.2.2 A loan to invest in a close trading company

See *Business Law and Practice*.

2.3.2.3 A loan to personal representatives to pay inheritance tax

See **30.6.3.5**.

2.4 PERSONAL ALLOWANCES

Personal allowances are deducted from net income to obtain the taxpayer's taxable income. This means that a certain amount of income is free each year.

The availability of allowances depends not on the type of income involved but on the taxpayer's personal circumstances, for example disability or the amount of income received each tax year.

The taxpayer must claim his allowances each year in his tax return. The principal allowances available and deducted at this stage are as follows.

2.4.1 Personal Allowance

Net Income
Less
Personal Allowance
=
Taxable Income

The Personal Allowance available for 2017/18 is £11,500. This is, however, subject to an income limit of £100,000 (see below). It may be set against income of any kind. It is applied in this order: first against NSNDI; then, if there is a surplus, against savings income; and finally any remaining surplus is applied against dividend income. For most employees, their Personal Allowance will be used up by their employment income, unless such income is below £11,000.

If the Personal Allowance exceeds the net income of the taxpayer, the surplus is unused and cannot be carried forward for use in future years (subject to the Marriage Allowance – see **2.4.2**).

This allowance may be claimed by taxpayers resident in the UK, male, female, adult or child, married or single. Husband and wife are treated as separate single people. Each spouse is independently liable for tax on his or her own income, and each has his or her own Personal Allowance (but see **2.4.2**).

The Personal Allowance is reduced where the taxpayer's income exceeds the income limit of £100,000. This reduction applies irrespective of age. The Personal Allowance is reduced by £1 for every £2 of income above the £100,000 limit. The effect of the reduction is that for a taxpayer with income of £123,000 or more, no Personal Allowance will be available. In order to calculate the adjusted Personal Allowance for a taxpayer with a net income in excess of £100,000 but under £123,000, a formula may be used:

$$£11,500 - \frac{(\text{net income} - £100,000)}{2} = \text{adjusted Personal Allowance}$$

The adjusted Personal Allowance should be rounded up to nearest £1.

EXAMPLE 1

Jo has a net income of £50,000. Jo is entitled to deduct the full Personal Allowance of £11,500 from her net income of £50,000 to obtain a taxable income figure of £38,500.

EXAMPLE 2

Miriam has a net income of £110,000. Miriam is not entitled to deduct the full Personal Allowance as her net income exceeds the £100,000 income limit. Using the above formula, Miriam's adjusted Personal Allowance can be calculated.

$$£11,500 - \frac{(£110,000 - £100,000)}{2}$$

$$£11,500 - \frac{£10,000}{2}$$

$$£11,500 - £5,000 = £6,500$$

Miriam is entitled to deduct £6,500 from her net income of £110,000 to obtain a taxable income figure of £103,500.

2.4.2 Marriage Allowance

From April 2015, a transferable 'marriage allowance' has been available to married couples and civil partners. Where one spouse or partner does not have enough income to use their Personal Allowance fully for that tax year, they may transfer £1,150 of their Personal Allowance to their spouse or civil partner. The recipient must not be a higher or additional rate taxpayer.

2.4.3 Blind Person's Allowance

A taxpayer who is a registered blind person receives an allowance of £2,230. If a husband and wife are both registered blind, they can each claim the Blind Person's Allowance.

2.5 PERSONAL SAVINGS AND DIVIDEND ALLOWANCES

The Personal Allowance must be distinguished from the new Personal Savings and Dividend Allowances, which were introduced by the Summer Budget in 2015 and took effect from April 2016.

2.5.1 Personal Savings Allowance (PSA)

The PSA can be set against savings income, so that up to the first £1,000 of savings income will be tax free.

The amount of the PSA to which a taxpayer is entitled depends on whether the taxpayer is a basic or higher rate taxpayer. This is calculated by reference to the taxpayer's taxable income, as calculated at Step 3. (Allowances will be made for allowable pension contributions and gift aid.) Additional rate taxpayers do not receive a PSA. (Contrast the Personal Allowance, where both basic and higher rate taxpayers receive the same (£11,500 for 2017/18) and additional rate taxpayers receive a reduced allowance (see **2.4.1**).)

The table below sets out the amounts of the allowance.

Tax rate	Income band (Taxable Income)	Allowance
Basic rate taxpayer	£0 – £33,500	£1,000 tax free
Higher rate taxpayer	£33,501 – £150,000	£500 tax free
Additional rate taxpayer	£150,001 and above	No allowance

Table 2.1   PSA

Until interest rates start to rise from their current level of 0.25% (as at April 2017), it is unlikely that interest from bank or building society account will exceed the allowance, so, realistically, only the additional rate taxpayers will now pay tax on their savings. The Government estimates that a basic rate taxpayer would have to have £50,000 of savings attracting an interest rate of 2% before they exceeded the allowance. However, loans yielding a higher rate could be caught, for example peer to peer loans.

> **EXAMPLE 1**
>
> Asaad has a salary of £22,000, and receives interest of £750 a year. (He has no relevant allowable reliefs.) For the purposes of calculating how much PSA Asaad is entitled to, Asaad is a basic rate taxpayer, as his total taxable income is below the basic rate threshold. He therefore has a PSA of £1,000, which will be set against his savings income, and so he will not pay any tax on his savings income.

> **EXAMPLE 2**
>
> Janine has a salary of £61,000 and receives interest of £550 a year from her bank and building society savings accounts. For the purposes of calculating how much PSA Janine is entitled to, Janine is a higher rate taxpayer, as here taxable income is above the basic rate threshold (and below the additional rate threshold). She therefore has a PSA of £500, which will be set against her net savings income, leaving £50 taxable savings income to be taxed at 40%.

> **EXAMPLE 3**
>
> Eleanor has a salary of £200,000 and receives interest of £500 a year. (She has no relevant allowable reliefs.) For the purposes of calculating how much PSA Eleanor is entitled to, Eleanor is an additional rate taxpayer as her taxable income is over £150,000. She therefore has no PSA, which means that the whole £500 is taxable savings income and will be taxed at 45%.

2.5.2 Dividend Allowance

The Dividend Allowance can be set against dividend income, so that the first £5,000 of a taxpayer's dividend income will be free from tax. All taxpayers (whether basic, higher or additional rate taxpayers) are entitled to the £5,000 allowance. (Contrast the Personal Allowance, which is adjusted for higher rate taxpayers.) Taxpayers who receive less than £5,000 a year will pay no tax on their dividends, even if they are higher or additional rate taxpayers.

2.5.3 Nil rate bands

Although described as allowances, it seems that HMRC does not regard these as exemptions for the purposes of calculating total taxable income, but rather as a nil rate for each of these two types of income:

> ... higher rate income is income on which tax is charged at the higher or dividend upper rate, or would be but for the operation of this new savings nil rate or the dividend nil rate (which will also be available from 6 April 2016). Additional rate income is income on which tax is charged at the additional or dividend additional rate, or would be but for the savings or dividend nil rates. (Source: HMRC: Personal Savings Allowance: Update, 1 April 2016)

The result is that these allowances are not set off at this stage with the Personal Allowance to reduce taxable income. *Only* the Personal Allowance is relevant for calculating Taxable Income. The new allowances are relevant for arriving at and calculating the amount of the Personal Savings Allowance (if relevant) that the taxpayer is entitled to and the rates of tax that will be applicable to savings and dividend income (see **2.6.4**).

2.6 RATES OF TAX

2.6.1 Types of income

The taxable income is taxed at the appropriate rate or rates. We have seen that income tax is a progressive tax. The rates of tax increase as the taxpayer's income increases. In addition, the rates are different for the various types of income. Therefore, before the rates can be applied, the different types of income must be separated from one another (see **2.1.7**).

To find out how much taxable income is comprised of NSNDI and how much of savings and dividend income, the savings and dividend income are deducted from the Taxable Income figure arrived at in Step 3.

Taxable Income
Less
Savings and Dividend Income
=
Taxable NSNDI
This is amount of NSNDI which will be subject to tax at the relevant rate(s)

(This calculation ensures that the taxpayer gets the maximum allowed benefit from any deductions of any allowable reliefs and the personal allowance, as NSNDI is taxed at a higher rate than savings and dividend income.)

2.6.2 Order of taxation

Income is taxed in 'slices'. The first slice is the NSNDI. The next slice is the savings income, and the top slice is the dividend income (see Table 2.2). The rates are different for each slice. These rates are fixed annually.

Historically, there was a main rate for all income except dividend income, which was taxed at the dividend rate. The March 2015 Budget has now separated out the main rate into three distinct groups: the main rate for NSNDI, a savings rate for interest and other savings income, and a default rate that will apply mainly to trustees and non-residents.

Table 2.2 shows the order in which income is taxed, and the different rates for the tax year 2016/17.

Any savings and dividend income is taxed after NSNDI. Savings and dividend income are therefore treated as the top slices of taxable income (see Table 2.2 below).

Top slice	Dividends: taxed at the dividend rates	Dividend ordinary rate: 7.5% Dividend upper rate: 32.5% Dividend additional rate: 38.1%
Next slice	Interest: taxed at the savings rates	Starting rate for savings: 0% Savings basic rate: 20% Savings higher rate: 40% Savings additional rate: 45%
Taxed first	NSNDI: taxed at the main rates	Basic rate: 20% Higher rate: 40% Additional rate: 45%

Table 2.2   *Order and rates of taxation*

2.6.3 NSNDI

NSNDI is taxed first. Once the NSNDI has been calculated, it is taxed first at the basic rate, higher rate and additional rate. These rates are fixed annually, and the rates for the tax year 2017/18 are set out in Table 2.2.

> **EXAMPLE 1**
>
> Timothy has a taxable income of £180,000, of which £20,000 is savings and dividend income. Timothy's NSNDI amounts to:

Taxable income	£180,000
Less savings and dividend income	£20,000
NSNDI	£160,000

Timothy's NSNDI will be liable to tax:

(a)   at the basic rate of 20% on the first £33,500;

(b)   at the higher rate of 40% to the extent that it is above the basic rate limit of £33,500 but falls below the higher rate limit of £150,000. Therefore, £116,500 (£150,000 – £33,500) will be taxed at 40%; and

(c)   at the additional rate of 45% on the income in excess of the £150,000 limit (£10,000).

The tax liability in respect of his NSNDI will be:

£33,500	@ 20%	£6,700
£116,500	@ 40%	£46,600
£10,000	@ 45%	£4,500
£160,000		£57,800

The savings and dividend income is calculated separately (not shown here).

2.6.4   Savings and dividend income

Any savings and dividend income is taxed next, savings income first and then dividend income.

2.6.4.1   Rates of tax for savings and dividend income

Savings and dividend income are taxed at different rates, so it is necessary to separate out these two types of income. As we have seen, the rates for both types of income are calculated without making an exemption for the relevant allowances, so appropriate adjustments must be made for the fact that the 'first slice' of each type of income is taxed at 0%, before working out how much remains to be taxed at the appropriate rate.

2.6.4.2   Taxing savings income

First, the PSA must be deducted from the savings income figure to give the amount of savings income which will be taxed at the savings rates set out below.

Savings Income
Less
PSA (taxed @ 0%)
=
Remaining Taxable Savings Income
This is the amount of savings income which will be subject to tax at the relevant rate(s)

The remaining savings income after deduction of the PSA is taxed at the savings starting, basic, higher and additional rates. For the tax year 2017/18 the rates are as follows:

Starting rate for savings of 0%	£0–£5,000
Savings basic rate of 20%	£5,001–£33,500
Savings higher rate of 40%	£33,501–£150,000
Savings additional rate of 45%	over £150,000

As the PSA is treated as the 'first slice' of savings income, in order to work out whether an individual will pay start to tax on the remaining savings income at the savings basic, higher or additional rate, the amount of the PSA is added to his taxable NSNDI. Any remaining savings income after deduction of the PSA which falls below the starting rate limit is taxed at 0%. If it falls between the savings starting and basic rate limits, it is taxed at the basic rate of 20%; if it falls between the savings basic and higher rate limits, it is taxed at the higher rate of 40%; and any excess over the higher rate limit is taxed at the 45% additional rate. (For a summary of the calculation see the table below.)

Tax PSA @ 0%			
Add PSA to taxable NSNDI (This establishes the relevant rate(s) of tax)			
Remaining taxable savings income at the appropriate rate(s)			
If the taxable NSNDI *plus* PSA is less than £5,000, the remaining taxable savings income will be taxed at the starting rate for savings.	If the taxable NSNDI *plus* PSA is less than £33,500, the remaining taxable savings income below £33,500 will be taxed at the savings basic rate (and at the higher and additional rates as appropriate above £33,500).	If the taxable NSNDI *plus* PSA exceeds £33,500, the remaining taxable savings income below £150,000 will be taxed at the savings higher rate (and at the savings additional rate above £150,000).	If the taxable NSNDI *plus* PSA exceeds £150,000, the remaining taxable savings income will be taxed at the savings additional rate.

EXAMPLE 1

Eric has a taxable income (after allowances and reliefs) of £3,880, of which £2,380 is NSNDI and £1,500 is interest. Eric is a basic rate taxpayer, and so will be entitled to an allowance of £1,000, which is taxed at 0%. After deduction of the PSA, all of his remaining savings income falls within the £5,000 starting rate. He will be liable to tax:

(a)   at the basic rate of 20% on the first £2,380 of NSNDI (£476); and

(b)   at the savings starting rate of 0% on the remaining 'top slice' of £500 of savings income (£0).

EXAMPLE 2

Morven has taxable income (after allowances and reliefs) of £6,000, of which £4,500 is NSNDI and £1,500 is interest. Morven is a basic rate taxpayer, and so will be entitled to a PSA of £1,000, which is taxed at 0%. All of her remaining savings income, after deduction of the PSA, falls within the basic rate. (Taxable NSNDI plus PSA = £5,500.) She will be liable to tax:

(a)   at the basic rate of 20% on the first £4,500 of NSNDI (£900); and

(b)   at the savings basic rate of 20% on the remaining 'top slice' of £500 of savings income (£100).

EXAMPLE 3

Deka has taxable income (after allowances and reliefs) of £43,500, of which £41,500 is NSNDI and £2,000 is interest. Deka is a higher rate taxpayer. She will be entitled to a PSA of £500, which is taxed at 0%. All of her remaining savings income, after deduction of the PSA, falls within the savings higher rate band. (Taxable NSNDI plus PSA = £42,000.) She will be liable to tax:

(a)   on the NSNDI:

    (i)   at the basic rate of 20% on the first £33,500 (£6,700); and

    (ii)   at the higher rate of 40% on the remaining £8,500 (£3,400); and

(b)   at the savings higher rate of 40% on the remaining 'top slice' of £1,500 of savings income (£600).

EXAMPLE 4

Josh has taxable income (after allowances and reliefs) of £160,000, of which £140,000 is NSNDI and £20,000 is interest. Josh is an additional rate taxpayer. He is not entitled to a PSA. He will be liable to tax:

(a)   on the NSNDI:

    (i)   at the basic rate of 20% on the first £33,500 (£6,700); and

    (ii)   at the higher rate of 40% on the remaining £106,500 (£42,600); and

(b)   on the interest:

    (i)   at the savings higher rate of 40% to the extent that it falls below the higher rate limit of £150,000, so £10,000 (£150,000 − £140,000) will be taxed at 40% (£4,000); and

    (ii)   at the savings additional rate of 45% on the remaining £10,000 (£4,500).

2.6.4.3   Taxing dividend income

Dividend income is treated as the top slice of taxable income, above both NSNDI and savings income.

First, the Dividend Allowance must be deducted from the dividend income figure to give the amount of dividend income which will be taxed at the dividend rates set out below.

Dividend Income
Less
Dividend Allowance (taxed @ 0%)
=
Remaining Taxable Dividend Income
This is the amount of dividend income which will be subject to tax at the relevant rate(s)

The remaining dividend income after deduction of the Dividend Allowance is taxed at the dividend ordinary rate, upper and additional rates. For the tax year 2017/18 the rates are as follows:

Dividend ordinary rate of 7.5%	£0–£33,500
Dividend upper rate of 32.5%	£33,501–£150,000
Dividend additional rate of 38.1%	over £150,000

As the Dividend Allowance is treated as the 'first slice' of dividend income, in order to work out whether an individual will pay tax on dividends at the dividend ordinary, upper or additional rate, the amount of the Dividend Allowance is added to his total taxable NSNDI and total savings income. So, to the extent that dividend income falls within the basic rate limit, it is taxed at 7.5%. To the extent that dividend income falls between the basic rate limit and the higher rate limit, it is taxed at 32.5%; and any excess over the higher rate limit is taxed at 38.1%. (For a summary of the calculation see the table below.)

Tax Dividend Allowance @ 0%		
Add Dividend Allowance to taxable NSNDI plus total savings income (including PSA) (This establishes the relevant rate(s) of tax)		
Remaining taxable dividend income at the appropriate rate(s)		
If the taxable NSNDI *plus* total savings income *plus* the Dividend Allowance is less than £33,500, the remaining taxable dividend income below £33,500 will be taxed at the dividend ordinary rate (and at the dividend upper and additional rates as appropriate above £33,500).	If the taxable NSNDI *plus* total savings income *plus* the Dividend Allowance exceeds £33,500, the remaining taxable dividend income below £150,000 will be taxed at the dividend upper rate (and at the dividend additional rate above £150,000).	If the taxable NSNDI *plus* total savings income *plus* the Dividend Allowance exceeds £150,000, the remaining taxable dividend income will be taxed at the dividend additional rate.

EXAMPLE 1

Arthur has taxable income (after allowances and reliefs) of £10,000, of which £4,500 is NSNDI and £5,500 is dividend income. (He has no savings income.) Arthur is a basic rate taxpayer. He is entitled to a Dividend Allowance of £5,000, which is taxed at 0%. All of his remaining dividend income, after deduction of the Dividend Allowance, falls within the basic rate (Taxable NSNDI plus Dividend Allowance = £9,500.) He will be liable to tax:

(a) at the basic rate of 20% on the first £4,500 of NSNDI (£900); and

(b) at the dividend ordinary rate of 7.5% on the 'top slice' of the remaining £500 of dividend income (£37.50).

EXAMPLE 2

Sanjay has taxable income (after allowances and reliefs) of £51,500, of which £41,500 is NSNDI and £10,000 is dividend income. (He has no savings income.) Sanjay is a higher rate taxpayer. He is entitled to a Dividend Allowance of £5,000, which is taxed at 0%. All of his remaining dividend income, after deduction of the Dividend Allowance, falls within the higher rate. (Taxable NSNDI plus Dividend Allowance = £46,500.) He will be liable to tax:

(a) on the NSNDI:

    (i) at the basic rate of 20% on the first £33,500, (£6,700); and

    (ii) at the higher rate of 40% on the remaining £8,000 (£3,200); and

(b) on the remaining 'top slice' of dividend income (£5,000), at the dividend upper rate of 32.5% (£1,625).

EXAMPLE 3

Carrie has taxable income (after allowances and reliefs) of £160,000, of which £140,000 is NSNDI and £20,000 is dividend income. Carrie is an additional rate taxpayer. She is entitled to a Dividend Allowance of £5,000, which is taxed at 0%. Part of her remaining dividend income falls within the upper rate and part falls within the additional rate. (Taxable NSNDI plus Dividend Allowance = £145,000, leaving £5,000 of the higher rate available.) She will be liable to tax:

(a) on the NSNDI:

  (i)   at the basic rate of 20% on the first £33,500 (£6,700); and

  (ii) at the higher rate of 40% on the remaining £106,500 (£42,600); and

(b) on the remaining dividend income (£15,000):

  (i)   at the dividend upper rate of 32.5% to the extent that it falls below the dividend higher rate limit of £150,000, so £5,000 (£150,000 – £145,000) will be taxed at 32.5% (£1,625); and

  (ii) at the dividend additional rate of 38.1% on the remaining £10,000 (£3,810).

2.6.4.4 Taxing both savings and dividend income

The examples above illustrate the position where the taxpayer has either savings or dividend income in addition to taxable NSNDI. The example below shows a simple calculation where the taxpayer has both savings and dividend income, as well as taxable NSNDI (and see **2.8**).

EXAMPLE 1

Ben has taxable NSNDI of £17,500, savings income of £1,250 and dividend income of £10,000. Ben is a basic rate taxpayer and is entitled to a PSA of £1,000 and a Dividend Allowance of £5,000.

(a) Ben will be liable to tax on the NSNDI at the basic rate: £17,500 at 20% (£3,500).

His NSNDI will use up only £17,500 of the basic rate band, leaving £16,000.

The savings income is taxed next. To decide what rate applies to his savings income, the £1,000 PSA is added to his taxable NSNDI and treated as the first slice of his savings income and taxed at 0%. The remaining taxable savings income all falls within the £33,500 threshold, and is taxed at the savings basic rate.

(b) Ben will be liable to tax on the remaining savings income at the savings basic rate: £250 at 20% (£50).

This has used up a further £1,250 of the basic rate band, leaving £14,750.

The dividend income is taxed last. The £5,000 Dividend Allowance is added as the first slice of Ben's dividend income, and taxed at 0%. His remaining taxable dividend income all falls below the £33,500 threshold.

(c) Ben will be liable to tax on the remaining dividend income at the dividend ordinary rate: £5,000 at 7.5% (£375).

		£33,500 Basic rate threshold
Unused basic rate band	£4,750	
Remaining taxable dividend income	£5,000 x 7.5% = £375	
Dividend Allowance	£5,000 x 0% = £0	
Remaining taxable savings income	£250 x 20% = £50	
PSA	£1,000 x 0% = £0	
NSNDI	£17,500 x 20% = £3,500	

Note that the treatment of these allowances as nil rate bands has the potential to take a taxpayer into a higher tax band, increasing the amount of tax payable.

EXAMPLE 2

Assume now that Ben has taxable NSNDI of £27,500, savings income of £1,250 and dividend income of £10,000. Ben is a higher rate taxpayer and is entitled to a PSA of £500 and a Dividend Allowance of £5,000.

(a) Ben will be liable to tax on the NSNDI at the basic rate: £27,500 at 20% (£5,500).

His NSNDI will use up £27,500 of the basic rate band, leaving £6,000.

The savings income is taxed next. To decide what rate applies to his savings income, the £500 PSA is added to his taxable NSNDI and treated as the first slice of his savings income and taxed at 0%. The remaining taxable savings income all falls within the £33,500 threshold, and is taxed at the savings basic rate.

(b) Ben will be liable to tax on the remaining savings income at the savings basic rate: £750 at 20% (£150, as opposed to £50 in Example 1, where Ben was entitled to a PSA of £1,000).

This has used up a further £1,250 of the basic rate band, leaving £4,750.

The dividend income is taxed last. The £5,000 Dividend Allowance is added as the first slice of Ben's dividend income, and taxed at 0%. The Dividend Allowance has used up all of the remaining basic rate band.

(c) Ben will be liable to tax on the remaining dividend income at the dividend upper rate: £5,000 at 32.5% (£1,625 as opposed to £375).

(Hypothetically, were HMRC to allow deduction of these as true allowances in order to calculate taxable savings and dividend income, all of Ben's remaining taxable savings and dividend income would (just) fall within the basic rate band, thus reducing his tax bill.)

		£33,500 Basic rate threshold
Remaining taxable dividend income	£5,000 x 32.5% = £1,625	
Dividend Allowance	£5,000 x 0% = £0	
Remaining taxable savings income	£750 x 20% = £150	
PSA	£500 x 0% = £0	
NSNDI	£27,500 x 20% = £5,500	

2.7 CALCULATING THE TAX DUE

The five steps described above will enable a taxpayer to calculate his overall tax liability for a tax year. However, deductions can be made for any tax deducted at source.

Salaries and other employment income

Tax is deducted at source using the PAYE system (see **2.2.3.1**). The amount of tax paid (shown in a taxpayer's P60) is deducted from the taxpayer's overall tax liability. If the tax paid exceeds that liability, a refund will be due.

2.8 A FULL INCOME TAX CALCULATION

Frederick carries on a business in partnership and his total income from the partnership's trade for 2017/18 is £35,165. However, to buy his share of this partnership he took out a loan from the Blankshire Bank, and the interest on that loan is £1,165 per annum.

Frederick also has an account at the Guildfleet Building Society on which he receives interest of £4,500 in 2017/18. He also owns shares in a company and receives dividends of £10,000 net in 2017/18.

To calculate Frederick's tax bill for 2017/18:

	£
Step 1: Calculate total income	
Trade profits (ITTOIA 2005, Part 2)	35,165
Interest (ITTOIA 2005, Part 4)	4,500
Dividends (ITTOIA 2005, Part 4)	10,000
Total Income	49,665
Step 2: Deduct allowable reliefs	
Loan interest to Blankshire Bank	(1,165)
Net Income	48,500
Step 3: Deduct personal allowances	
Personal Allowance	(11,500)
Taxable Income	37,000

Step 4: Separate NSNDI and savings and dividend income and calculate tax at the applicable rate(s)

(a) NSNDI

Taxable income	37,000
Less savings income	(4,500)
Less dividend income	(10,000)
= NSNDI	22,500

This element of Frederick's taxable income falls £11,000 short of the £33,500 basic rate threshold and so is taxed at the basic rate of 20%:

£22,500 @ 20% = £4,500

(b) *Savings income*

The total of his NSNDI and savings income (£27,000) falls £6,500 short of the £33,500 basic rate threshold.

As Frederick is a higher rate taxpayer (his taxable income exceeds £33,500), he is entitled to a PSA of £500, which is taxed first at 0%.

The remaining savings income after deduction of the PSA (£4,000) all falls within the basic rate band, and so is taxed at 20%.

£500 @ 0% = £0

£4,000 @ 20% = £800

£800

(c)   Dividend income

The total of his NSNDI, savings and dividend income (£37,000) exceeds the £33,500 basic rate threshold by £3,500.

Frederick is entitled to a Dividend Allowance of £5,000, regardless of whether he is a basic or higher rate taxpayer. This is taxed first at 0%.

To the extent that the remaining dividend income after deduction of the Dividend Allowance (£5,000) falls within the remaining basic rate band (£1,500), it is taxed at the dividend ordinary rate of 7.5%; the excess over the basic rate threshold (£3,500) is taxed at the dividend upper rate of 32.5%.

$$\begin{aligned}
£5,000 @ 0\% &= £0 \\
£1,500 @ 7.5\% &= £112.50 \\
£3,500 @ 32.5\% &= \underline{£1,137.50} \\
& \underline{£1,250.00}
\end{aligned}$$

Step 5: Add together the amounts of tax from Step 4

OVERALL INCOME TAX LIABILITY (£4,500 + £800 + £1,250)   £6,550

There are no relevant deductions, as none of Frederick's income was deducted at source.

Income tax to pay   <u>£6,550</u>

2.9   COLLECTION OF INCOME TAX AND DATES FOR PAYMENT

2.9.1   HM Revenue & Customs

Before considering the collection of income tax (see **2.9.2**), it is worth noting that HMRC is also responsible for:

(a)   administering corporation tax, capital gains tax, petroleum revenue tax, inheritance tax, stamp duties, VAT, customs duties and excise duties;

(b)   collecting National Insurance contributions;

(c)   advising on tax policy;

(d)   advising on valuation policy and providing valuation services;

(e)   enforcing the National Minimum Wage; and

(f)   recovering student loan repayments.

2.9.2   Collection of income tax: deduction at source

There are two methods of collection of tax: deduction at source and the self-assessment regime.

As explained above (see **2.2.3**), for certain types of income, tax is deducted at source. The payer of the income acts as a tax collector by deducting from the payment the appropriate amount of income tax and handing it to HMRC. The taxpayer therefore receives the payment net of income tax.

2.9.3   Collection of income tax: self-assessment

The self-assessment regime covers all income tax due. There is a set of payment dates for all sources of income and a single tax bill for the year. However, where income tax has been deducted at source, the taxpayer will declare this income on his tax return and his overall tax liability will be reduced by the amount of income tax already paid.

Examples of when income will be declared on a tax return and the appropriate amount of income tax collected under the self-assessment regime are:

(a)   Trading profit (ITTOIA 2005, Part 2). Any income profits of a trade which a taxpayer has made will be assessed under ITTOIA 2005, Part 2 and collected under the self-assessment regime.

(b)   Rent (ITTOIA 2005, Part 3). A landlord (taxpayer) receiving gross rent from the tenant will be assessed to tax under ITTOIA 2005, Part 3 and any income tax payable will be collected under the self-assessment regime.

The self-assessment method assumes that the taxpayer has actually received the sum on which he is to pay tax and can send part of it to HMRC to satisfy his income tax liability. There is a risk that the taxpayer will spend the income received before HMRC can claim its share.

2.9.3.1   The tax return

Under the self-assessment regime, the taxpayer completes an annual tax return, which includes computation pages to enable the taxpayer to calculate his own income tax. Tax returns are issued soon after 5 April. There are different returns for different types of income. HMRC now encourages taxpayers to use an online tax return.

Even if a taxpayer does not normally receive a tax return, there is a statutory obligation to notify HMRC that he has income that is liable to tax. This must be done within six months of the end of the relevant tax year. There is a penalty for default.

2.9.3.2   Dates for payment

The online tax return and any payment must be filed by 31 January following the tax year to which the return relates. If the taxpayer would rather send a paper return, this must be submitted no later than 31 October.

The taxpayer is automatically required to make two payments on account towards the income tax due for any year, and then a third and final balancing payment to meet any tax still outstanding. The first payment on account is due on 31 January in the tax year in question. The second payment on account is due on 31 July after the end of the tax year. Any balancing payment is due on the next 31 January.

Each payment on account should be approximately one half of the income tax liability for the year. They are calculated by reference to the previous year's income tax liability, and are reduced to give credit for tax deducted at source. No payments on account are required if this 'relevant amount' is below a certain limit. This limit is set at a level that ensures most employees and pensioners (and others who receive the bulk of their income after deduction of income tax at source or who have relatively small outstanding tax liabilities) do not have to make payments on account.

EXAMPLE

Josie's income tax liability for 2016/17 came to £15,000, of which £7,000 was deducted at source. Her return for 2017/18 will be issued in April 2018 and a paper return must be submitted to HMRC by 31 October 2018, or an online return by 31 January 2019 at the latest. For 2017/18 she will make interim payments on account of ½ × (£15,000 – £7,000) = £4,000 on 31 January 2018 and 31 July 2018. Her final adjustment for 2017/18 is due on 31 January 2019.

Taxpayers have the right to claim a reduction or cancellation of payments on account where they have grounds for believing that payments based on the tax liability for the previous year will lead to an overpayment of tax in the current year.

2.9.3.3 Penalties for default

Interest is charged on any amount of tax unpaid at the due date for payment whether that tax is due as a payment on account or as a balancing payment. There are also fixed penalties for late or non-payment.

Throughout the self-assessment regime the onus is on the taxpayer, and there is a statutory requirement to maintain adequate records to support the return, backed up by a penalty for default. HMRC has extensive powers, for example random audits and specific enquiries, to check the accuracy of any return. Appeals against assessments and determinations are made to the First-tier Tribunal.

SUMMARY

There is no statutory definition of income but income payments and receipts have an element of recurrence.

Income tax is payable by individuals, partners, PRs and trustees.

Income tax is payable on income only if it derives from a source specified in either ITTOIA 2005 or ITEPA 2003. Income, which does not derive from one of these sources, is not taxable and some income is specifically exempted from tax.

Income tax is paid on income received during a tax year. The tax year runs from 6 April to 5 April.

There are five steps to be used to calculate a taxpayer's income tax liability.

Step 1: Calculate total income

This is achieved by adding together all the taxpayer's *gross* income arising under each source. Some income (eg interest received and dividends) is received net and will have to be grossed up before being added to the gross income from other sources.

Step 2: Deduct any allowable reliefs to give net income

Interest on a qualifying loan is an example of a payment which may be deducted at this stage.

Step 3: Deduct any personal allowance to give taxable income

Generally, the only allowance which may be deducted at this stage is the personal allowance of £11,500. This allowance is subject to an income limit of £100,000.

Step 4: Calculate the tax at the applicable rate(s)

Before applying the tax rates, separate the income (except savings and dividend income) from the savings and dividend income. This is achieved as follows:

	Taxable income
LESS	Savings and dividend income
	Non-savings, non-dividend income

First, tax the income (except savings and dividend income) as follows:

Basic rate	£0–£33,500 @ 20%
Higher rate	£33,501–£150,000 @ 40%
Additional rate	over £150,000 @ 45%

Next, having made adjustment for the Personal Savings and Dividend Allowances, tax the savings and dividend income, starting with any interest received.

To the extent that the starting rate for savings, basic rate and higher rate bands remain available after taxing the income (except savings and dividend income), interest received is taxed as follows:

Starting rate for savings	£0–£5,000 @ 0%
Savings basic rate	£5,001–£33,500 @ 20%
Savings higher rate	£33,501–£150,000 @ 40%
Savings additional rate	over £150,000 @ 45%

Finally, tax any dividend income element of the savings and dividend income.

To the extent that the dividend ordinary rate and upper rate bands remain available after taxing the non-savings, non-dividend income, dividends are taxed as follows:

Dividend ordinary rate	£0–£33,500 @ 7.5%
Dividend upper rate	£33,501–£150,000 @ 32.5%
Dividend additional rate	over £150,000 @ 38.1%

Step 5: Add together the amounts of tax from Step 4 to give the taxpayer's overall tax liability

Having calculated the taxpayer's overall liability, reduce that liability by any income tax deducted at source (and therefore paid direct to HMRC). The resulting figure is the income tax which the taxpayer is obliged to pay to HMRC.

The taxpayer will submit a tax return to HMRC by 31 January following the tax year to which the return relates. The taxpayer will make payments on account on 31 January in the tax year in question and on 31 July after the end of tax year in respect of his income tax liability. Any balancing payment must be made by 31 January after the end of the tax year.

CAPITAL GAINS TAX

> **LEARNING OUTCOMES**
>
> After reading this chapter you will be able to understand:
>
> - the circumstances that give rise to a capital gains tax charge
> - the method for calculating a taxpayer's chargeable gain(s) for the tax year
> - the means by which the taxpayer can claim tax relief on his capital losses.

3.1 INTRODUCTION

3.1.1 Sources of capital gains tax law

The principal charging statute is the Taxation of Chargeable Gains Act 1992.

3.1.2 The charge to tax

Capital gains tax (CGT) is charged on the chargeable gains made by a chargeable person on the disposal of chargeable assets in a tax year (6 April to following 5 April).

3.1.3 Chargeable assets

All forms of property are treated as assets for CGT purposes, including such things as debts, options, incorporeal property and property created by the person disposing of it. Sterling is excluded from the definition so disposals of cash do not attract CGT liability. The legislation does provide for a limited category of non-chargeable assets, the main example being private motor vehicles. The legislation also provides that certain assets which are not non-chargeable shall be wholly or partly exempt from CGT – see **3.4**.

Who pays CGT?

Chargeable persons are:

(a)   individuals;

(b)   partners (each partner is charged separately for his share of the partnership gains when there is a disposal of a chargeable partnership asset);

(c)   personal representatives (who pay CGT when there is a disposal of the deceased's chargeable assets);

(d)   trustees (who pay CGT when there is a disposal of a chargeable asset from the trust fund).

Companies pay corporation tax (see **Business Law and Practice**). Charities are generally exempt from paying tax.

3.1.4   How much CGT will an individual pay?

The steps required to calculate the amount of CGT payable are as follows:

3.1.4.1   Step 1: Disposal of a chargeable asset

It is first necessary to identify the disposal of a chargeable asset, for example the sale of land.

3.1.4.2   Step 2: Calculation of the gain

This, in basic terms, will be the consideration received when the asset is sold less cost.

3.1.4.3   Step 3: Consider reliefs

Various reliefs may be available (see **3.4**). Early examples assume that none of these apply for the sake of simplicity.

3.1.4.4   Step 4: Aggregate gains/losses; deduct annual exemption

An individual does not pay tax on all the gains he makes. There is an exemption for the first £11,300 of total net gains made by an individual in the current tax year (2017/18).

3.1.4.5   Step 5: Apply the appropriate rates of tax

When calculating the appropriate rate(s) of tax, gains are treated as if they were the top slice of the taxpayer's income for the tax year. There are four possible rates:

(a)   Subject to paras (c) and (d) below, if an individual's gains and taxable income added together do not exceed the threshold for basic rate income tax (£33,500), the rate of tax on the gains is 10%.

(b)   Subject to paras (c) and (d) below, if an individual's gains and taxable income added together exceed the basic rate income tax threshold, any part of the gains below the basic rate threshold is taxed at 10%, but the rate of tax on the gains that exceed the threshold is 20%.

(c)   Any gains made on the disposal of residential property (which is not exempted by the principal private residence exemption (see **3.4.2**)) are subject to an 8% surcharge on the normal rate, which means that such gains falling below the basic rate threshold will be taxed at 18% and above the threshold at 28%.

(d)   Any gains that qualify for entrepreneurs' relief (see **3.4.8**) are taxed at a flat rate of 10%.

Where an individual has gains that qualify for entrepreneurs' relief and other gains that do not, the entrepreneurs' relief gains (taxed at a flat rate of 10%) will be added to his income first with the result that his other gains will be treated (for the purpose of calculating the appropriate rate) as the very top slice of his income and so be more likely to be taxed at 20% (or 28% on residential property).

It makes no difference to the overall tax liability if residential property gains are taxed next or taxed after non-residential property gains; ie whether residential property gains are taxed at the basic rate or the higher rate, the additional 8% surcharge will always apply.

Note: All examples in this chapter assume that entrepreneurs' relief is not available. Please refer to **Chapter 28** of **Business Law and Practice** for a detailed explanation of how entrepreneurs' relief is applied in practice.

Gains realised by trustees and personal representatives are taxed at a flat rate of 20% (or 28% on residential property).

EXAMPLE

In August, Sarah sells shares for £91,300. The shares cost her £70,000. It is her only disposal during the tax year. Sarah has a taxable income for the tax year of £50,000, which means that all of her gain is taxed at 20%.

Step 1:   Identify the disposal
           Sale of shares

Step 2:   Calculate the gain
           Proceeds of disposal   £91,300
           Less: Cost   (£70,000)
                                        £21,300

Step 3:   Consider exemptions and reliefs   Nil

Step 4:   Gain   £21,300
           Deduct annual exemption   (£11,300)
           Chargeable gain   £10,000

Step 5:   What is the rate of tax?
           CGT at 20% on £10,000 is £2,000.

3.1.5   Assessment and payment of CGT

Capital gains tax is assessed on the aggregate net gain of the current tax year and so it is necessary to consider all the disposals made during the tax year. Tax for individuals is payable on or before 31 January following the end of the tax year (or 30 days from the making of an assessment if later).

The above example shows the principles used to establish an individual's liability for CGT. The remainder of this chapter will consider each step of the calculation in more detail.

3.2   DISPOSALS

3.2.1   The sale or gift of a chargeable asset

There must be a disposal of a chargeable asset. Disposal is widely defined and includes a sale or a gift. If a gift is made then HMRC taxes the gain the taxpayer is deemed to have made on the disposal. This is done by using the market value of the asset at the time of the gift instead of consideration received.

EXAMPLE

In September, Barbara makes a gift of a Ming vase worth £271,000. She had bought the vase for £180,000. It is her only disposal during the tax year. Barbara's taxable income for the tax year is £60,000.

Step 1:   Identify the disposal
           Gift of vase

Step 2:   Calculate the gain
           Market value of vase   £271,000
           Less: Cost   (£180,000)
                                        £91,000

Step 3:   Consider exemptions and reliefs   Nil

Step 4:	Gain	£91,000
	Deduct annual exemption	(£11,300)
	Chargeable gain	£79,700
Step 5:	What is the rate of tax?	
	CGT at 20% on £79,700 is £15,940.	

3.2.2   The disposal of part of an asset

A sale of part of an asset or a gift of part of an asset is a disposal, for example the sale of part of a field. This is considered in detail in **3.8**.

3.2.3   The death of the taxpayer

On death there is no disposal by the deceased, so there is no charge to CGT. The personal representatives acquire the deceased's assets at the market value at the date of death (the probate value). This has the effect of wiping out gains which accrued during the deceased's lifetime so that these gains are not charged to tax.

> **EXAMPLE**
>
> Christopher dies owning shares worth £150,000. He had bought the shares for £60,000. Since death is not a disposal, there is no charge to CGT when Christopher dies. His personal representatives will acquire the shares at the market value at his death, ie at £150,000. The gain of £90,000 is wiped out and is not charged to tax. The £90,000 is the difference between the cost of the shares and the market value of the shares at the date of Christopher's death.

3.3   CALCULATION OF GAINS

The basic aim is to tax the gain in value that the asset has realised from the date of acquisition to the date of disposal. Consequently, the gain is generally the consideration for the disposal (or market value if the taxpayer gives away the asset) less any of the following expenditure incurred by the taxpayer:

Initial expenditure

(a)   The cost price of the asset (or its market value at the date of acquisition if the asset was given to the taxpayer; or the probate value if the taxpayer acquired the asset by will or intestacy) plus incidental costs of acquisition. Examples of incidental costs of acquisition are legal fees, valuation fees, stamp duty.

(b)   Expenditure wholly and exclusively incurred in providing the asset. An example is the cost of building a weekend cottage.

Subsequent expenditure

(a)   Expenditure wholly and exclusively incurred to enhance the value of the asset, which is reflected in the value of the asset at the time of disposal. An example is the cost of building an extension to a house. The cost of routine maintenance, repairs and insurance, on the other hand, is not deductible.

(b)   Expenditure wholly and exclusively incurred in establishing, preserving or defending title to the asset. An example is the cost of legal fees incurred to resolve a boundary dispute.

Incidental costs of disposal

Examples are legal fees and estate agent's fees.

Note that expenditure which is deductible for income tax purposes cannot be deducted when calculating a capital gain.

EXAMPLE

Paul sells his holiday cottage (chargeable residential property) for £184,800. He bought the cottage for £50,000 and spent £700 on a survey and £1,300 on legal fees when he purchased it. He spent £7,600 improving the cottage. Legal fees when he sells the cottage are £800 and the estate agent's commission is £3,400. For the current tax year Paul has a taxable income of £23,500.

Step 1:   Identify the disposal
           Sale of holiday cottage

Step 2:   Calculate the gain
           Proceeds of disposal   £184,800
Less:
Incidental costs of disposal
    Legal fees   £800
    Estate agent's commission   £3,400
                                                                                  (£4,200)
Net proceeds of disposal   £180,600
Less:
Initial expenditure
    Cost   £50,000
    Survey fee   £700
    Legal fees   £1,300
                                                          £52,000

Subsequent expenditure
    Cost of improvements   £7,600
                                                                                 (£59,600)
GAIN   £121,000

Step 3:   Consider exemptions and reliefs   Nil

Step 4:   Gain   £121,000
           Deduct annual exemption   (£11,300)
           Chargeable gain   £109,700

Step 5:   What is the rate of tax?
           CGT at 18% on the first £10,000
           (ie amount of gain below the basic rate threshold) =   £1,800
           CGT at 28% on remaining £99,700
           (ie amount of gain above the basic rate threshold) =   £27,916
           Total CGT   £29,716

3.3.1 The indexation allowance

For gains realised before 6 April 2008, an indexation allowance was used when calculating the gain on an asset which had been owned for any period between 31 March 1982 and 5 April 1998. The purpose of the indexation allowance is to remove inflationary gains from the CGT calculation so that a smaller gain is charged to tax. Inflation is measured by reference to the Retail Prices Index (the RPI). The indexation allowance is calculated by applying to the initial and subsequent expenditure the percentage increase in the RPI from the date the expenditure was incurred to the date of disposal (or April 1998 if earlier). Tables published by HMRC express this information as an indexation factor for ease of calculation.

The allowance still has some relevance to gains, the charge to which has been deferred before 6 April 2008 by the use of various roll-over or hold-over reliefs – see **3.4**. This is because, on a subsequent disposal after 6 April 2008, the rolled-over or held-over gain will be reduced by the appropriate amount of indexation allowance, provided the relevant assets were owned for some time between 31 March 1982 and 5 April 1998.

The same point applies to inter-spouse disposals made before 6 April 2008 – see **3.9**.

3.3.2 Assets owned on 31 March 1982

Where a taxpayer disposes of an asset which he owned on 31 March 1982, special rules are applied. The aim of these rules is to exclude from the tax calculation the part of the gain that accrued before 31 March 1982, so that no CGT is paid on that part of the gain.

As a result, the gain on such assets is calculated by using the market value of the assets on 31 March 1982, rather than actual expenditure.

3.3.3 Losses

The formula 'consideration received (or market value) less cost' can produce a capital loss.

EXAMPLE

Christine bought shares for £10,000 three years ago. She sells them for £10,300 but her incidental costs of acquisition were £250 and her incidental costs of disposal were £200.

Step 1:	Identify the disposal	
	Sale of shares	
Step 2:	Calculate the gain/loss	
	Proceeds of disposal	£10,300
Less:		
Incidental costs of disposal		
	Broker's commission	(£200)
Net proceeds of disposal		£10,100
Less:		
Initial expenditure		
	Cost	£10,000
	Broker's commission	£200
	Stamp duty	£50
		(£10,250)
LOSS		£150

The treatment of losses will be considered at **3.6** and **3.7**.

3.4 RELIEFS

After calculating the gain, the next step is to consider whether any reliefs apply. Generally, reliefs may be available due to the nature of the asset being disposed of. The majority of reliefs are aimed at smaller businesses, to encourage investment in this sector of the economy.

The following is a non-exhaustive list of CGT reliefs.

3.4.1 Tangible moveable property

Wasting assets (ie assets with a predictable life of less than 50 years) are generally exempt. Most consumer goods will fall into this category, for example televisions and washing machines.

Not all items of tangible moveable property are wasting assets. Some will go up in value, for example antiques. However, they will be exempt from CGT if the disposal consideration is £6,000 or less.

3.4.2 Private dwelling house

A gain on the disposal by an individual of a dwelling house, including grounds of up to half a hectare, will be completely exempt, provided it has been occupied as his only or main residence through his period of ownership (ignoring the last three years of ownership).

For most people, their home is their most valuable asset. The effect of this relief is that the house can be sold (or given away) without CGT liability being incurred.

3.4.3 Damages for personal injury

The recovery of damages or compensation may amount to the disposal of a chargeable asset; however, the receipt of damages for personal injury is exempt.

3.4.4 Hold-over relief

Hold-over relief enables an individual to make a gift of certain types of business assets without paying CGT. However, if the donee disposes of the asset, the donee will be charged to tax not only on his own gain but on the donor's gain as well. Because hold-over relief defers the charge to tax until a disposal by the donee, there must be an election by donor and donee to claim hold-over relief.

3.4.5 Relief for replacement of business assets ('roll-over' relief)

This relief encourages expansion and investment in qualifying business assets by enabling the sale of those assets to take place without an immediate charge to CGT, provided the proceeds of sale are invested in other qualifying business assets. The charge to CGT is postponed until the disposal of the new asset.

3.4.6 Roll-over relief on incorporation of a business

This relief again defers a CGT charge. It is applied (subject to conditions) when an individual sells his interest in an unincorporated business (sole trader, partnership) to a company. The gain is rolled over into the shares received as consideration for the interest being sold to the company. The CGT charge is postponed until the disposal of the shares.

3.4.7 Relief for re-investment in certain unquoted shares

To encourage investment in small company shares, it is possible for an individual to defer payment of CGT on any chargeable gain provided the proceeds of sale are re-invested in certain shares in an unquoted trading company. This is dealt with in **5.4**.

3.4.8 Entrepreneurs' relief

From 6 April 2008, relief (in the form of a reduced rate of tax) is available on gains made by individuals on the disposal (ie on a sale or a gift) of certain assets, including:

(a) all or part of a trading business the individual carries on as a sole trader or in partnership;

(b) shares in a trading company, subject to certain conditions, including that the individual's holding is at least 5% of the ordinary voting shares of the company (ie, it is his 'personal' trading company);

(c) assets owned and used by the individual's personal trading company or trading partnership.

The detailed workings of this relief are set out in **Business Law and Practice**.

3.5 THE ANNUAL EXEMPTION

The annual exemption is applied to make exempt the first slice of the taxpayer's net capital gains for the tax year. Unlike the reliefs referred to in **3.4**, it is not applied to any particular disposal but is rather a general deduction from the total net gain. However, where someone makes gains on several disposals in a tax year and those gains are liable to CGT at different rates, the taxpayer is permitted to apply the exemption first to the gains that would otherwise attract the higher rates (see **3.6**).

As explained in **3.1.4.4**, the amount of the exemption for tax year 2017/18 is £11,300. If a taxpayer's net gain is smaller than the annual exemption the unused part of the exemption cannot be carried forward to the following tax year.

Personal representatives and trustees of settlements are also entitled to an annual exemption; see **Part V: Probate and Administration**.

3.6 CGT CALCULATION WHERE THERE IS MORE THAN ONE DISPOSAL IN A TAX YEAR

As explained in **3.1.4.5**, different rates of tax apply to disposals, not only depending on the taxpayer's income tax position but also due to the type of assets disposed of. In this respect, chargeable assets fall into three categories – residential property, other assets not qualifying for entrepreneurs' relief and assets qualifying for entrepreneurs' relief. Because of the different rates that apply, gains made on assets within each category must be aggregated in separate compartments.

Where the taxpayer realises gains in two or three of the categories, any losses and the annual exemption can be deducted from gains in the best way possible for the taxpayer (ie to the gains that would otherwise attract the higher rates), so from residential property gains first, then non-entrepreneurs' relief gains and, finally, entrepreneurs' relief gains.

As previously stated, the following examples deal only with disposals that do not qualify for entrepreneurs' relief.

EXAMPLE 1

Gordon made the following disposals during 2017/18. Gordon has a taxable income in the tax year of £40,000.

On 17 July 2017, he sold his 3% shareholding in Pibroch Ltd for £11,600. He bought it for £4,000 on 16 April 1997.

On 12 August 2017, he sold his holiday cottage, 'Landseer Lodge', for £190,000. He acquired it on his mother's death on 11 January 1990, when its market value was £30,000.

On 8 January 2018, he sold his units in TVT Unit Trust for £5,000. He had purchased them on 16 May 2001 for £9,000.

Note: For the sake of simplicity, the example ignores incidental costs of acquisition and disposal on all of the transactions and it is assumed that no reliefs are available on any of the disposals.

	Pibroch Ltd	Landseer Lodge	TVT
Step 1: Identify the disposal	Sale of shares	Sale of holiday cottage	Sale of unit trust units
Step 2: Calculate the gain. Proceeds of disposal	£11,600	£190,000	£5,000
Less: Acquisition expenditure	(£4,000)	(£30,000)	(£9,000)
Gain/(Loss)	£7,600	£160,000	(£4,000)
Step 3: Consider exemptions and reliefs	None	None	None
Step 4: Aggregate net gains/ losses	Non-entrepreneurs' relief gain	Residential property gain	
	7,600	160,000	
Deduct current year loss		(4,000)	
		156,000	
Deduct annual exemption		(11,300)	
Chargeable gains	7,600	144,700	
Step 5: What are the rates of tax?			
CGT at 20% on £7,600 gain on Pibroch shares is		£1,520	
CGT at 28% on £144,700 gain on Landseer Lodge is		£40,516	
Total CGT		£42,036	

3.7 UNABSORBED LOSSES

It is, of course, possible that a taxpayer's CGT losses in a tax year may exceed his overall CGT gains. If so, setting the losses against the gains will wipe them out completely and the taxpayer will have no CGT to pay. In such a situation, the setting-off of current year losses to wipe out the gains entirely means that the taxpayer loses the use of his annual exemption. The exemption cannot be carried forward to use against gains of future tax years.

If, after setting losses against gains, there are still unabsorbed losses, these may be carried forward to future years and then used to the extent necessary to reduce gains to the limit of the annual exemptions available in those future years. Unabsorbed losses can be carried forward indefinitely. The approach should be:

(a) work out the gain or loss on each disposal made during the tax year;

(b) deduct any losses of the current year from gains;

(c) deduct any losses brought forward from previous years to reduce any remaining gains to the limit of the annual exemption;

(d) deduct the annual exemption from any remaining gains.

Note: As previously stated, the losses and annual exemption should be applied in the most advantageous way for the taxpayer.

EXAMPLE 2 (CONTINUED FROM 3.6)

Year of loss

In 2016/17, the year before the **3.6** scenario, Gordon made gains of £30,000, and losses of £70,000. He had no unused losses from previous years.

Gains for the year	£30,000
Less: losses for the year	£70,000
Net loss for the year	£40,000

The £30,000 gain is wiped out, and the unused loss of £40,000 is carried forward to the next year.

As there is no net gain for 2016/17, the annual exemption cannot be used in this year and it cannot be carried forward to later years.

Year following year of loss

In 2017/18, Gordon's loss of £40,000 carried forward from 2016/17 would be set against the gain on Landseer Lodge (as this is residential property which would otherwise be taxed at the higher rate of 28%) after the deduction of the current year loss of £4,000. The annual exemption would also be applied against the remaining gain on Landseer Lodge for the same reason.

Step 4: Aggregate net gains/losses	Non-entrepreneurs' relief gain	Residential property gain	
	7,600	160,000	
Less current year loss		(4,000)	
Less previous year loss		(40,000)	
		116,000	
Deduct annual exemption		(11,300)	
Chargeable gains	7,600	104,700	

Step 5: What are the rates of tax?

CGT at 20% on £7,600 gain on Pibroch shares is	£1,520
CGT at 28% on £104,700 gain on Landseer Lodge is	£29,316
Total CGT	£30,836

FURTHER EXAMPLE

If Gordon's unabsorbed loss in 2016/17 had been greater, eg £180,000, it would be carried forward and used in 2017/18 as follows:

As the available losses are greater than the aggregate gains for 2017/18, these will be wiped out altogether and so there is no need to consider the order in which the taxpayer might like to apply the losses. In this situation the losses would simply be deducted from the total gains of £167,600. First, the deduction of the current year loss of £4,000 would mean that the aggregate net gains for the current tax year are £163,600. The brought-forward loss of £180,000 would then be set against this figure until the gains are reduced to the limit of the annual exemption of £11,300. The balance of the loss (£27,700) remains unused and can be carried forward to set against gains of future years.

	Loss carried forward	2017/18 gains
	£	£
2016/17 loss	180,000	
2017/18 aggregate net gains/losses		7,600
		160,000
		(4,000)
Use part loss	(152,300)	(152,300)
		11,300
Deduct annual exemption		(11,300)
2017/18 taxable gains		nil
Balance of loss to be carried forward	27,700	

3.8 PART DISPOSALS

Where the disposal is of only part of the asset the initial and subsequent expenditure are apportioned when calculating the gain.

EXAMPLE

Anna bought a large plot of commercial property for £100,000 in 2000. She sells part of it for £90,000 in October 2017. The remaining property is worth £360,000. This is her only disposal in the tax year.

Anna's taxable income for the year is £28,500.

Identify the disposal: sale of part of commercial property.

Calculation of the gain on the land sold:

The consideration received is £90,000.

What is the cost of the part sold?

The total value of the two pieces of land is £450,000, ie £90,000 plus £360,000.

The part sold is worth $\frac{1}{5}$ of the total value, ie £90,000 is $\frac{1}{5}$ of £450,000.

Therefore, take $\frac{1}{5}$ of the cost as the relevant figure for the calculation, ie $\frac{1}{5}$ of £100,000, that is £20,000.

	£
Proceeds of disposal	90,000
Less:	
Apportioned cost	(20,000)
Gain	70,000
Deduct annual exemption	(11,300)
Chargeable gain	58,700
What is the rate of tax?	
CGT at 10% on the first £5,000	
(ie amount of gain below the basic rate threshold) =	£500
CGT at 20% on remaining £53,700	
(ie amount of gain above the basic rate threshold) =	£10,740
Total CGT	£11,240

3.9 HUSBAND AND WIFE

3.9.1 Disposals between spouses

Where spouses or civil partners are living together, a disposal by one to the other is treated as being made for such a consideration as to provide neither a gain nor a loss. This means that a spouse (or civil partner) can dispose of property to the other without paying CGT on the disposal. The donor's gain is not wiped out but merely deferred. If the donee disposes of the asset, the donee will be charged to tax not only on the donee's gain but on the donor's gain as well.

EXAMPLE

David gives a portrait to his wife Jane. David will not pay CGT on this disposal.

The portrait was worth £100,000 at the time of the gift. It cost David £80,000 three years ago.

Usually, when a gift is made the acquisition cost of the donee is the market value at the time of the gift (£100,000) but because the portrait was a gift from her husband, Jane will acquire it with a value of £80,000, ie the amount David paid for the painting.

If Jane disposes of the asset, she will have a lower acquisition cost to set against her gain and she will be charged to tax on both her own gain and her husband's gain.

Assume Jane sells the painting for £150,000, five years later.

The calculation will be:

Consideration received	£150,000
Less: Cost	£80,000
	£70,000

If Jane had not acquired the painting from her husband, so that the ordinary rules applied, the calculation would have been:

Consideration received	£150,000
Less: Cost	£100,000
	£50,000

A comparison of the above calculations shows that a larger gain is produced on Jane's disposal where she acquired the portrait from her husband; but, of course, David avoided any CGT charge at the time of the gift to Jane.

3.9.2 Tax planning point: making full use of annual exemptions and lower rate of tax

The fact that that both spouses are entitled to a separate annual exemption in each tax year can lead to tax-planning opportunities. By way of example, assume that the wife wishes to dispose of a number of assets in the tax year and that these disposals would realise gains that use up all of her annual exemption and leave some of the gains chargeable. On the other hand, the husband would not be making any disposals and so would not use his annual exemption at all. In this situation, it may be beneficial for the wife to transfer some of the assets to the husband (remember that this is a disposal that would not create a gain or a loss – see **3.9.1**), so that they both make gains and both can use their own annual exemption to make exempt gains up to £22,600, rather than £11,300.

Also, if the asset-holding spouse would be taxed on gains at the higher rate of 20% (or 28%) but the other would be taxed at the basic rate of 10% (or 18%), it would again be sensible to make an inter-spouse transfer so that the disposal is made by the spouse who is subject to the basic rate.

INHERITANCE TAX

LEARNING OUTCOMES

After reading this chapter you will be able to:

- understand the overall structure of inheritance tax
- explain how a person's death estate is taxed
- explain how certain lifetime transfers are taxed
- appreciate the rules on liability, burden and timing of payments of inheritance tax.

4.1 INTRODUCTION

This chapter explains the basic principles of inheritance tax (IHT). Some form of death duty has existed in the UK since the 19th century and has varied in name and approach over that period, beginning with estate duty then capital transfer tax and now IHT. Inheritance tax is governed principally by the Inheritance Tax Act 1984 (IHTA 1984). Despite its name, the tax does not apply only to death estates but can also catch transfers made during life.

There are three main occasions when IHT may be charged:

(a) on death;

(b) on lifetime gifts made to individuals within seven years prior to death;

(c) on lifetime gifts to a company or into a trust.

4.1.1 Death

Inheritance tax is intended primarily to take effect on death. When an individual dies, IHT is charged on the value of his estate (broadly, his assets less his liabilities) subject to various exemptions and reliefs.

4.1.2 Lifetime gifts made to individuals within seven years prior to death

If IHT were limited to a charge on death, one way to avoid tax would be to reduce the size of one's estate by making lifetime gifts; IHT is therefore also charged on certain lifetime gifts or 'transfers' if the donor dies within seven years after making them. Such gifts to individuals are called 'potentially exempt transfers', because at the time when the transfer is made no IHT is chargeable; the transfer is 'potentially exempt'. If the transferor survives for seven years, the transfer becomes exempt. If he dies within that period, the transfer becomes chargeable.

4.1.3 Lifetime gifts to a company or into a trust

Inheritance tax might also be avoided by the use of a trust or corporate entity. At present a lifetime gift to a company or into a trust is immediately chargeable to IHT at the time when it is made, unless the trust is for a disabled person.

4.1.4 Anti-avoidance legislation

As with income tax and capital gains tax, IHT is one of the taxes subject to the 'general anti-abuse rule' (GAAR) introduced by the Finance Act 2013, which is designed to allow HMRC to counteract 'abusive' tax avoidance schemes intended to exploit loopholes in the legislation covering the rules for calculating IHT.

4.2 THE MAIN CHARGING PROVISIONS

Inheritance tax is charged on 'the value transferred by a chargeable transfer'. The term 'chargeable transfer' is defined as 'a transfer of value which is made by an individual but is not an exempt transfer' (IHTA 1984, ss 1, 2).

This charge may apply in any of the three situations outlined above, because the term 'chargeable transfer' may refer to:

(a)   the transfer on death; or

(b)   a lifetime transfer which is potentially exempt when it is made but becomes chargeable because the transferor dies within seven years; or

(c)   a lifetime transfer which is immediately chargeable at the time when it is made.

In each case, the method by which tax is calculated is broadly similar, and may be approached by applying a sequence of logical steps.

4.2.1 Step 1: Identify the transfer of value

A lifetime transfer of value is any disposition which reduces the value of the transferor's estate. On death, tax is charged as if the deceased had made a transfer of value of his estate.

4.2.2 Step 2: Find the value transferred

For a lifetime transfer, this is the amount of the reduction in the transferor's estate.

On death, it is the value of the estate.

4.2.3 Step 3: Apply any relevant exemptions and reliefs

Various exemptions and reliefs exist for public policy reasons which can reduce or eliminate the IHT charge on any given transfer.

Some exemptions apply both to lifetime transfers and to the transfer on death (eg transfers to spouse or civil partner). Others are more restricted, and many apply only to lifetime transfers (eg annual exemption).

The main reliefs are business and agricultural property relief, which may apply both to lifetime transfers of such property and to the transfer on death.

4.2.4 Step 4: Calculate tax at the appropriate rate

Rates of tax

A range of tax rates apply to IHT, the lowest being zero per cent. There are two bands for which this is relevant:

(a)   the nil rate band (currently £325,000) – available for all transfers of value;

(b)   the residence nil rate band (currently £100,000) – available only on a transfer on death where there is a 'qualifying residential interest'.

The rate of tax that applies in excess of the nil rate band and the residence nil rate band (where applicable) varies according to the type of transfer (details are given in context below).

Cumulation

The nil rate band will not necessarily be available in full (or at all) for any given transfer. In order to calculate the available nil rate band on any transfer, whether during lifetime or on death, one must first look back over the seven years immediately preceding the transfer. Any chargeable transfers made by the transferor during that period must be taken into account in order to determine how much of the nil rate band remains available. This process is known as 'cumulation' and is used solely to calculate whether the nil rate band is available for any chargeable transfer.

As the residence nil rate band is not available for lifetime transfers, it will be available in full on death, subject to any adjustments in relation to estates over £2 million (see **4.3.6**). Cumulation is not relevant.

This chapter will consider the detailed application of the steps outlined above to each of the three types of transfer in turn. Note that, for ease of reference in the examples provided, any mention of the nil rate band assumes that the band has always been £325,000. In fact, it has increased over the years to its current level. In real calculations one may have to identify the previous bands.

4.3 TRANSFERS ON DEATH

The steps outlined at **4.2** above apply as follows.

4.3.1 Step 1: Identify the transfer of value

When a person dies, he is treated for IHT purposes as having made a transfer of value immediately before his death, ie there is a deemed transfer of value. The value transferred is the value of the deceased's 'estate' immediately before his death.

4.3.1.1 Definition of 'estate'

A person's estate is defined by IHTA 1984, s 5(1) to mean all the property to which he was beneficially entitled immediately before his death, with the exception of 'excluded property'.

Property included within this definition falls into three categories, as set out below.

(a)   *Property which passes under the deceased's will or on intestacy.*
      The deceased was 'beneficially entitled' to all such property immediately before he died.

(b)   *Property to which the deceased was 'beneficially entitled' immediately before his death but which does not pass under his will or on intestacy.*
      This applies to the deceased's interest in any joint property passing on his death by survivorship to the surviving joint tenant(s). In most cases, the deceased will be taken to have owned an equal share in the property with the other joint tenant(s).

(c)   *Property included because of special statutory provisions.*
      By statute, the deceased is treated as having been 'beneficially entitled' to certain types of property which would otherwise fall outside the definition. These rules apply to
      (i)   certain trust property; and
      (ii)   property given away by the deceased in his lifetime but which is 'subject to a reservation' at the time of death.
      Each of these categories is explained further below.

4.3.1.2 Trust property included in the estate for IHT purposes

In certain circumstances, a person who is entitled to the income from a trust is treated for IHT purposes as 'beneficially entitled' to the capital which produces that income. This means that where a beneficiary who is entitled to all the income from such a trust dies, the trust fund is taxed as if it were part of the beneficiary's estate.

The type of beneficial interest covered by these provisions is known as a 'qualifying interest in possession'. To be an interest in possession, it must be an interest under which the beneficiary is entitled to claim the income from the trust property (or enjoy trust property in some equivalent way, such as living in it) with no power on the part of the trustees to decide whether or not he should receive it. An interest in possession arising before 22 March 2006 will be a qualifying interest in possession. The rules changed on that date and where an interest in possession arises on or after 22 March 2006, it will only be a qualifying interest in possession in limited circumstances. The main example is where the interest is an 'immediate post-death interest' (IPDI). An IPDI is, broadly, an interest in possession arising on the death of the settlor under his will or intestacy.

EXAMPLE 1

Gina died in January 2011. In her will, she left all her estate to her executors/trustees, Tom and Tessa, on trust to pay the income to Gina's son, Simon, for life with remainder to Rose absolutely. Both Simon and Rose are over 18 years old.

Tom and Tessa must invest the property to produce income. Simon is entitled to the income during his life. Tom and Tessa must pay it to him. Thus Simon, the life tenant, has an interest in possession.

When Simon dies, his rights under the trust cease. Under the terms of the trust instrument (Gina's will), Rose is now entitled to the trust fund, and Tom and Tessa must transfer all the trust property to her.

For IHT purposes, Simon had a qualifying interest in possession by virtue of it being an IPDI. Although he was entitled only to the income from the trust property and had no control over the disposition of the fund on his death, he is treated for tax purposes as 'beneficially entitled' to the whole trust fund. The fund is taxed on his death as part of his estate. The tax on the trust property will be paid from the trust fund.

EXAMPLE 2

The facts are as in Example 1, except that Gina did not die in January 2011. Instead, she created the trust on that date by transferring the funds to Tessa and Tom and signing a declaration that they were to hold on trust for Simon for life with remainder to Rose. While the beneficiaries' rights under the trust will be exactly the same as in Example 1, the trust will not be an IPDI. Instead it will be taxed under the 'relevant property' regime. Details of this regime are outside the scope of this chapter.

4.3.1.3 Property subject to a reservation

The Finance Act 1986 contains provisions designed to prevent people from avoiding tax by giving property away more than seven years before death but continuing to enjoy the benefit of the property. The rule applies where the deceased gave away property during his lifetime but did not transfer 'possession and enjoyment' of the property to the donee, or was not entirely excluded from enjoying the property. If property is subject to a reservation at the time of the donor's death, the donor is treated as being 'beneficially entitled' to the property.

> **EXAMPLE**
>
> In 2009, Diana gave her jewellery, worth £100,000, to her daughter Emma, but retained possession of it. Diana dies in 2017, when the jewellery (still in her possession) is worth £120,000. Although the jewellery belongs to Emma, tax is charged on Diana's death as if she were still beneficially entitled to it. The jewellery, valued at £120,000, is taxed as part of Diana's estate. The tax on the jewellery will be borne by Emma.

4.3.1.4 Property outside the estate for IHT purposes

From the above, it can be seen that the definition of 'estate' turns on whether the deceased was (or was deemed to be) beneficially interested in property immediately before his death. Property in which the deceased did not have such an interest falls outside the definition. Two common examples of property outside the definition are a life assurance policy once it is written in trust for a named beneficiary (because the proceeds are no longer payable to the deceased's estate) and a discretionary lump sum payment made from a pension fund to the deceased's family (because the pension trustees are not obliged to pay it to the deceased's estate).

4.3.1.5 Excluded property

Certain property which would otherwise be included in the estate for IHT purposes is defined in IHTA 1984 as 'excluded property'. Excluded property is not part of the estate for IHT purposes. One example of excluded property is a 'reversionary interest'. For IHT purposes this means a future interest under a settlement, for example an interest in remainder under a trust, created before 22 March 2006.

> **EXAMPLE**
>
> In 2005, Faith created a settlement placing £500,000 on trust for Guy for life, remainder to Hazel absolutely. Whilst both Guy and Hazel are alive, Guy has a qualifying interest in possession and Hazel has a reversionary interest (that is excluded property).

4.3.2 Step 2: Find the value transferred

4.3.2.1 Basic valuation principle

Assets in the estate are valued for IHT purposes at 'the price which the property might reasonably be expected to fetch if sold in the open market' immediately before the death (IHTA 1984, s 160).

This means that the value immediately before death of every asset forming part of the estate for IHT purposes must be assessed and reported to HMRC. Some assets, such as bank and building society accounts and quoted shares, are easy to value. Others, such as land, may be more difficult, especially where it was jointly owned (in some cases it may be possible to reduce the value of the share of the deceased to reflect the difficulty in selling a share in a jointly-owned property). Negotiations may be required (in the case of land, with the district valuer) in order to reach an agreed valuation.

The value of an asset agreed for IHT purposes is known as the 'probate value'.

4.3.2.2 Modification of the basic valuation principle: s 171

The IHTA 1984, s 171 provides that, where the death causes the value of an asset in the estate to increase or decrease, that change in value should be taken into account.

> **EXAMPLE**
>
> Brian has insured his life for £50,000. The benefit of the policy belongs to him (ie the policy is not written in trust). Immediately before Brian's death, the value of the policy to him is its 'surrender value' (ie the value if he surrendered his rights back to the insurance company in return for a payment). This will be considerably less than its maturity value of £50,000. Under s 171, the effect of Brian's death on the value of the policy is taken into account: its value for IHT purposes is £50,000.

4.3.2.3 Valuing quoted shares

The value of quoted shares is taken from the Stock Exchange Daily Official List for the date of death (or the nearest trading day). The list quotes two prices. To value the shares for IHT, take one-quarter of the difference between the lower and higher price and add it to the lower price.

> **EXAMPLE**
>
> John died owning 200 shares in ABC plc. On the date of John's death the quoted price per share is 102p/106p. The value of each share for IHT is 103p, and so the value of John's holding is £206.

4.3.2.4 Debts and expenses

Liabilities owed by the deceased at the time of death are deductible for IHT purposes provided that they were incurred for money or money's worth (IHTA 1984, s 505). Thus debts such as gas and telephone bills may be deducted. In addition, the deceased may not have paid enough income tax on the income he received before he died; this amount may also be deducted.

Reasonable funeral expenses are also deductible (IHTA 1984, s 162).

4.3.3 Step 3: Apply any relevant exemptions and reliefs

The main exemptions applicable on death depend on the identity of the beneficiary. Reliefs depend on the nature of the property in the estate. Thus it is important to see who is entitled to the property on death and whether the property qualifies for a relief.

4.3.3.1 Spouse or civil partner exemption

Section 18 of the IHTA 1984 provides as follows:

> A transfer of value is an exempt transfer to the extent that the value transferred is attributable to property which becomes comprised in the estate of the transferor's spouse or civil partner.

Any property included in the estate for IHT purposes is exempt if it passes to the deceased's spouse or civil partner under the deceased's will or intestacy or, in the case of joint property, by survivorship. (But note that under s 18(2), if the transferor is domiciled in the UK but the transferee is not, the level of the exemption is limited to £325,000. Alternatively, the transferee can elect to be treated as UK-domiciled for IHT purposes and so receive the full exemption.)

The rule applicable to qualifying interest in possession trusts is that IHT is charged as if the person with the right to income owned the capital (see **4.3.1.2**). This rule applies for the purpose of spouse exemption, both on creation of the trust (whether by will or on intestacy) and on the death of a life tenant.

> **EXAMPLE**
>
> In his will, Dan leaves his estate worth £300,000 to trustees on trust for his wife, Jane, for life with remainder to their children. Although Jane only has the right to the income from Dan's estate for her lifetime, the trust is treated for IHT purposes as if Jane owned the capital. On Dan's death, his whole estate will, therefore, be spouse exempt.

Note that this exemption does not apply to co-habitees.

4.3.3.2 Charity exemption

The IHTA 1984, s 23(1) provides as follows:

> Transfers of value are exempt to the extent that the values transferred by them are attributable to property which is given to charities.

Any property forming part of the deceased's estate for IHT purposes which passes on death to charity is exempt. The exemption most commonly applies to property which passes to charity under the deceased's will. However, if the deceased had a life interest in trust property which passes under the terms of the trust to charity, the charity exemption applies.

A similar exemption applies to gifts to certain national bodies and bodies providing a public benefit, such as museums and art galleries, and to political parties.

When large charity gifts are made by the deceased, not only is the transfer itself exempt, but it may affect the tax rate on the rest of the death estate (see **4.3.4**).

4.3.3.3 Business and agricultural property relief

Business property relief applies to reduce the value transferred by a transfer of 'relevant business property' by a certain percentage, provided that the transferor owned the property for the two years immediately before the transfer.

The reduction is 100% for:

(a) a business, or an interest in a business (such as a share in a partnership); and

(b) unquoted shares.

The reduction is 50% for:

(a) quoted shares which gave the transferor control of the company; and

(b) certain land, buildings and machinery owned by the transferor but used in his company or partnership.

Agricultural property relief applies in a similar manner to reduce the agricultural value of agricultural property.

Further details of these reliefs are given in **Business Law and Practice**.

4.3.4 Step 4: Calculate tax at the appropriate rate

4.3.4.1 Nil rate band

Generally, the position is that, if the deceased has made no chargeable transfers in the seven years before death, the rate of tax on the first £325,000 of his estate (the 'nil rate band') is 0%. If his estate exceeds the nil rate band, IHT is normally charged on the excess at 40%. In a small number of cases, provisions introduced in the Finance Act 2012 may apply. These provisions are aimed at increasing charitable giving and will apply a 36% tax rate in place of the normal 40% rate when at least 10% of a defined 'component' of a person's net estate (after deduction of other exemptions, reliefs and the available nil rate band) passes to charity. The provisions will rarely apply as most people will not want to give anything close to 10% of their net estate to charity, whereas those that do want a charity as their main beneficiary (often because they have no close family) tend to leave the vast majority of their estate to that charity with any other gifts falling within the nil rate band. For further details, see *Private Client: Wills, Trusts and Estate Planning*.

If the deceased died on or after 9 October 2007 having survived a spouse or civil partner, the nil rate band in force at the date of death of the survivor is increased by whatever percentage of the nil rate band of the first to die was unused by them (subject to a maximum increase of 100%).

> **EXAMPLE**
>
> Emily, a widow, dies on 21 August 2016. Her husband Guy died 10 years earlier leaving all his estate to Emily. There was no tax to pay on Guy's death as his whole estate was spouse exempt, and his nil rate band was not used. Emily's estate benefits from a 100% uplift in her nil rate band, so that the rate of tax on the first £650,000 of her estate is 0%.

Cumulation

If the deceased did make any chargeable transfers in the seven years before death the cumulation principle outlined at **4.2.4** will apply. The effect is that the lifetime –transfers use up the deceased's nil rate band first, reducing the amount available for the estate. Most lifetime gifts are potentially exempt from IHT and become chargeable only if the transferor dies within seven years. Less commonly, the deceased may also have made gifts in the seven years before death which were immediately chargeable to IHT at the time they were made, eg a gift into a trust. The cumulation principle applies to both types of transfer.

The 'values transferred' by such transfers must be aggregated. This means that any lifetime exemptions or reliefs which operate to reduce the value transferred are taken into account.

> **EXAMPLE 1**
>
> In 2014, David made a gift to his daughter. The value transferred (after exemptions and reliefs) was £175,000.
>
> In August 2017, David dies, leaving his estate, valued at £200,000, to his son. The estate did not include a qualifying residential interest.
>
> (It may help you, when calculating cumulative totals, to draw a timeline showing the relevant transfers. An example is given below.)
>
>
>
> The 2014 transfer was potentially exempt from IHT but has now become chargeable. David's cumulative total is £175,000.
>
> | The nil rate band applicable to David's estate on death is | £325,000 |
> |---|---|
> | less cumulative total | £175,000 |
> | = remaining nil rate band | £150,000 |
>
> Tax on David's estate:
> | £150,000 @ 0% = | nil |
> |---|---|
> | £50,000 @ 40% = | £20,000 |

For further details of the effect of the cumulation principle, see **4.6**.

4.3.4.2   Example of the application of IHT to an estate on death

Facts

Veronica dies intestate on 3 August 2016 survived by her partner William (to whom she was not married) and their children Brian (19) and Carla (22). She holds the following property:

	£
House (in joint names with William): value of share	90,000
Bank account (in joint names with William): value of share	5,000
Life assurance policies:	
(1) payable to estate: maturity value	195,000
(2) written in trust for William: maturity value	30,000
Unquoted shares: 15% holding in a trading company (held for 10 years)	15,000
Building society account	19,000
Car and chattels	15,000

There are various debts, including funeral expenses, which total £4,000.

Two years before her death, Veronica made a gift of £211,000 in cash to William.

She made no other substantial lifetime gifts.

Step 1: identify the estate

Property to which Veronica was beneficially entitled immediately before death:

Passing on intestacy (to children):	life assurance policy (1) unquoted shares building society account car and chattels
Passing by survivorship (to William):	interest in house interest in bank account

(Life assurance policy (2) is not included in the estate for IHT purposes because Veronica was not beneficially entitled to it immediately before her death.)

Step 2: value the estate

	£	£
Passing on intestacy:		
life assurance policy (1) (full maturity value)	195,000	
unquoted shares (market value)	15,000	
building society account	19,000	
car and chattels	15,000	
		244,000
Joint property:		
interest in the house	90,000	
interest in the bank account	5,000	
		95,000
		339,000
Less debts (including funeral expenses)		4,000
Value of estate (before reliefs)		335,000

Step 3: apply exemptions and reliefs

No exemptions apply to Veronica's estate as she had no spouse
and left no property to charity.

The unquoted shares qualify for business property relief at 100%:

100% of £15,000	<u>15,000</u>
Value of estate for IHT	<u>320,000</u>

Step 4: calculate tax at the appropriate rate

Cumulate the value transferred by chargeable transfers made in the seven years before death.
The gift to William was a potentially exempt transfer which has now become chargeable.

	£
Value of gift	211,000
Less two annual exemptions (see **4.4.3**)	<u>6,000</u>
Value transferred	205,000

Only £120,000 of Veronica's nil rate band remains available on her death.

Calculate tax on the estate of £320,000:

on £120,000 @ 0%	nil
on £200,000 @ 40%	£80,000

4.3.4.3 Residence nil rate band

The nil rate band will remain at £325,000 until April 2021. However, for deaths occurring after
6 April 2017, the new residence nil rate band (RNRB) will be available in addition to the nil
rate band. This will be £100,000 for the tax year 2017/18, rising gradually to £175,000 by April
2021. The allowances are as follows:

2017/18	£100,000
2018/19	£125,000
2019/20	£150,000
2020/21	£175,000

From 2021, both the nil rate band and the RNRB will increase in line with the consumer price
index.

For the RNRB to apply, the deceased must die owning a 'qualifying residential interest' which
is 'closely inherited':

(a)   A qualifying residential interest is an interest in a dwelling house which has at any time
      been the deceased's residence and which forms part of the deceased's estate.

(b)   For a property to be 'closely inherited', it must pass to:

    (i)   a child, grandchild or other lineal descendant of the deceased outright or on
             certain types of trust. Lineal descendants are defined as children, step-children,
             adopted children, foster children, or children where the deceased had been
             appointed as a guardian;

    (ii)   the current spouse or civil partner of the deceased's lineal descendants; or

    (iii) the widow, widower or surviving civil partner of a lineal descendant who
             predeceased the deceased, unless such persons have remarried or formed a new
             civil partnership before the deceased's death.

The RNRB will apply only up to the value of the deceased's residence. You cannot claim for
more than the property is worth. When calculating the tax, the RNRB is taxed first at 0%,

reducing the amount of the total chargeable estate, then, subject to cumulation, the nil rate band is taxed next at 0% and finally the remaining death estate at 40%.

Where the estate is valued at £2 million or more, the RNRB is reduced by £1 for every £2 over the £2 million threshold. To calculate the adjusted RNRB for an estate over £2 million, for the tax year 2017/18, the following formula may be used:

$$£100,000 - \frac{(\text{value of estate} - £2 \text{ million})}{2} = \text{adjusted RNRB}$$

If the deceased has not used all of his RNRB, like the nil rate band, any unused RNRB may be claimed by a surviving spouse, even if the first spouse died before 6 April 2017.

EXAMPLE

Angela dies on 4 September 2017, leaving her entire estate to her two children in equal shares. The value of her estate, after payment of debts and funeral expenses, is £1,750,000 and includes a house worth £1,250,000. Her husband, Richard, died four years earlier, leaving all his estate (worth less than £2 million) to Angela.

On Richard's death, the whole estate was spouse exempt, and the RNRB was not available to Richard's executors. As Richard has not used any of his RNRB, the amount transferred to Angela is an additional 100% of the RNRB, but at the current rate.

Therefore, when Angela dies, her executors can claim her own personal RNRB of £100,000 and Richard's unused RNRB of £100,000 (£200,000). This is the amount of RNRB current at the time of the death of the second spouse. If, for example, Angela had died in September 2018, her executors would be able to claim £250,000 (2 x £125,000). This is in addition to the £650,000 nil rate band (2 x £325,000) from which Angela's estate will also benefit (see **4.3.4**).

The Finance Bill 2016 introduced a downsizing allowance to prevent (particularly older) people from hanging on to unsuitable properties in order to claim the full benefit of the allowance. If, after 8 July 2015, the deceased has downsized prior to death to a less valuable property, or sold his property in order, for example, to move to a care home, the personal representatives can still claim the RNRB to which the deceased would have been entitled, provided the property would have qualified for the RNRB had it been retained, and the replacement property or other assets of an equivalent value (where the property had been sold) is left to lineal descendants.

4.3.4.4 Example of the application of IHT to an estate on death which includes a closely inherited qualifying residential interest

Facts

If we take the facts from the example above, Angela, who died on 4 September 2017, left her entire estate to her two children in equal shares. Her husband, Richard, died four years earlier, leaving all his estate (worth less than £2 million) to Angela.

Angela's estate includes the following assets:

	£
House	1,250,000
Bank and Building Society Accounts	25,000
Quoted shares	455,000
Chattels, including a car	25,000

There are various debts, including funeral expenses, amounting to £5,000. Angela has not made any lifetime gifts.

Step 1: Identify the transfer of value

Property to which Angela was entitled immediately before death

Step 2: Identify the value transferred

House	1,250,000
Bank and Building Society Accounts	25,000
Quoted shares	455,000
Chattels, including a car	25,000
	1,755,000
Less debts (including funeral expenses)	(5,000)
Value of estate (before reliefs)	1,750,000

Step 3: Apply exemptions and reliefs

No exemptions or reliefs apply on the facts

Step 4: Calculate the tax at the appropriate rates

Cumulation is not relevant as Angela did not make any lifetime gifts.

Calculate tax on estate of £1,750,000, remembering that Angela benefits from both the nil rate band (NRB) and the RNRB transferred from Richard:

(1)	Tax Total RNRB @ 0%:	£200,000 @ 0% nil
(2)	Tax Total NRB @ 0%:	£650,000 @ 0% nil
		£850,000 (leaving £900,000)
(3)	Tax remaining £900,000 @ 40%	£360,000

Note that both the RNRB and the NRB operate to reduce the amount of the *total* chargeable estate.

4.4 LIFETIME TRANSFERS: POTENTIALLY EXEMPT TRANSFERS

The definition of a potentially exempt transfer (PET) includes any gift made by an individual to another individual or into a disabled trust (IHTA 1984, s 3A(1A)), to the extent in either case that the gift would otherwise be chargeable.

This means that all lifetime gifts to an individual are 'potentially exempt' to the extent that no immediate exemption applies.

4.4.1 Step 1: Identify the 'transfer of value'

The term 'transfer of value' is defined to mean any lifetime disposition made by a person ('the transferor') which reduces the value of his estate (IHTA 1984, s 3(1)). In principle, therefore, any lifetime gift falls within the definition.

Certain dispositions are excluded from the definition, such as a transfer for the maintenance, education or training of the transferor's child under 18, or over that age if still undergoing full-time education or training, or for the maintenance of a dependent relative (IHTA 1984, s 11). Such dispositions have no significance for IHT.

4.4.2 Step 2: Find the value transferred

The second step is to find the value transferred by the transfer of value. In the case of a lifetime transfer, this is the amount by which the value of the transferor's estate is 'less than it would be but for' the transfer (IHTA 1984, s 3(1)). In other words, the value transferred is the loss in value to the estate of the transferor brought about by the transfer. The transferor's 'estate' is the aggregate of all the property to which he is beneficially entitled (IHTA 1984, s 5).

In practice, the loss to the estate will usually be the market value of the property transferred, although this does not follow in every case.

> **EXAMPLE**
>
> Vanessa owns a pair of matching bronze statuettes. The market value of the pair together is £80,000, but individually each one is worth £25,000. If Vanessa were to give away one statuette to her son, the loss to her estate would be calculated as follows:
>
> | | £ |
> |---|---:|
> | Value of pair | 80,000 |
> | Less value of remaining statuette | 25,000 |
> | Loss to estate | 55,000 |

Related property

The related property rules are designed to prevent tax avoidance in relation to a group or set of assets. The rules apply most often to property transferred between husband and wife.

> **EXAMPLE (CONTINUED)**
>
> Suppose Vanessa gives one of the statuettes to her husband Boris (an exempt transfer to spouse). Without the related property rules Vanessa and Boris would each then own one statuette worth £25,000.
>
> However, the two statuettes owned by Vanessa and Boris are related property. Under the related property valuation rule, the value of each statuette is the appropriate portion of the value of the pair, ie half of £80,000 which is £40,000. If Vanessa was then to give away her statuette, the value transferred would be £40,000.

4.4.3 Step 3: Apply any relevant exemptions and reliefs

As seen at **4.4**, a gift is potentially exempt only to the extent that it would otherwise be chargeable. At the time when a lifetime gift is made it may be clear that an exemption applies. Some lifetime exemptions, however, may apply to only part of a lifetime transfer, so that the excess is potentially exempt.

The main exemptions and reliefs applicable on death apply also to lifetime transfers. In addition, there are some further exemptions which apply only to lifetime transfers.

4.4.3.1 Spouse or civil partner and charity exemptions

These exemptions, outlined at **4.3.3**, apply to lifetime transfers as well as to the transfer on death. So any lifetime gift to the transferor's spouse or civil partner or to charity is exempt, even if the transferor dies within seven years.

4.4.3.2 Business and agricultural property relief

The reliefs set out at **4.3.3** apply to reduce the value transferred by transfers of business or agricultural property made during lifetime as well as on death. However, if the transferor dies within seven years after the transfer, the relief will generally be available only if the transferee still owns the property or qualifying replacement when the transferor dies (see **4.6.2**).

4.4.3.3 Order of application of exemptions and reliefs

Spouse or civil partner and charity exemptions are applied before reliefs, since their effect is to make the transfer wholly exempt. If, for example, a transferor gives relevant business property to his wife, business property relief is academic – the transfer is exempt.

The 'lifetime only' exemptions, however, may apply to only part of a transfer. Since the reliefs apply to reduce the value transferred, they should be applied before such exemptions are considered.

4.4.3.4 Lifetime only exemptions

The annual exemption (IHTA 1984, s 19)

The annual exemption applies to the first £3,000 transferred by lifetime transfers in each tax year. Any unused annual exemption may be carried forward for one year only, so that a maximum exemption of £6,000 may be available. The current year's exemption must be used before the previous year's exemption can be carried forward.

> **EXAMPLE**
>
> On 1 May 2015, Annie gives £3,000 to her son Ben. The transfer falls within Annie's annual exemption for 2015/16 and is exempt. Annie does not make any further gifts until 1 May 2017.
>
> On 1 May 2017, Annie gives £7,000 to her daughter Claire. Annie may apply her annual exemption for 2017/18 and may carry forward her unused annual exemption for 2016/17. Thus £6,000 of the transfer is exempt at the time of the gift. (The remaining £1,000 will be 'potentially exempt', as explained below.)

If a transferor makes more than one transfer of value in any one tax year, then the exemption is used to reduce the first transfer. Any unused exemption is set against the second and any further transfers until it is used up.

> **EXAMPLE**
>
> Sarah gives £10,000 to Jessica on 30 April 2017 and £10,000 to Kirsty on 1 May 2017. She has made no previous transfers. The annual exemptions for 2017/18 and 2016/17 will be set against the transfer to Jessica and reduce it to £4,000. (The remaining part of Jessica's gift and the whole of Kirsty's gift will be 'potentially exempt', as explained below.)

Small gifts (IHTA 1984, s 20)

Lifetime gifts in any one tax year of £250 or less to any one person are exempt. This exemption cannot be set against a gift which exceeds £250.

Normal expenditure out of income (IHTA 1984, s 21)

A lifetime transfer is exempt if it can be shown that:

(a)   it was made as part of the transferor's normal expenditure; and

(b)   it was made out of the transferor's income; and

(c)   after allowing for all such payments, the transferor was left with sufficient income to maintain his usual standard of living.

> **EXAMPLE**
>
> Andrew, who is a highly-paid company director, has a niece at drama college. He sends his niece £100 each month (paid from his income) to assist her with her living expenses. These transfers are exempt as normal expenditure out of Andrew's income (provided Andrew's remaining income is sufficient to support his normal standard of living).

Gifts in consideration of marriage (IHTA 1984, s 22)

Lifetime gifts on marriage are exempt up to:

(a)   £5,000 by a parent of a party to the marriage;

(b)   £2,500 by a remoter ancestor of a party to the marriage (eg, a grandparent); and

(c)   £1,000 in any other case.

4.4.3.5 Potentially exempt status

As long as the lifetime transfer is not immediately chargeable (see **4.5**), any value remaining after exemptions and reliefs have been applied at step 3 is potentially exempt. The transfer will become chargeable *only* if the transferor dies within seven years. The transferor does not need to take any action at the time when such a lifetime transfer is made, and if he survives for seven years it will automatically become exempt. However, if the transferor dies within the seven-year period, the transfer becomes chargeable and must be assessed as such. (For further explanation of the effect of death within seven years, see **4.6**.)

EXAMPLE

On 1 March 2017, Jane gives £130,000 to her brother, Brian. She has made no previous lifetime gifts. The disposition is a transfer of value because the value of Jane's estate is reduced. The value transferred is £130,000, the loss to Jane's estate.

	£
Value transferred	130,000
Less: annual exemptions for 2016/17 and 2015/16	6,000
Potentially exempt transfer	124,000

No tax is payable at the time of the gift. Jane has made a PET. If Jane survives until 1 March 2023, the PET will become completely exempt. If Jane dies before that date, the PET will become a chargeable transfer.

4.5 OTHER LIFETIME TRANSFERS: LIFETIME CHARGEABLE TRANSFERS

Any lifetime transfer which does not fall within the definition of a PET (see **4.4**) is immediately chargeable as a 'lifetime chargeable transfer' (LCT). The main example is a lifetime transfer made on or after 22 March 2006 into any trust (other than a disabled trust) or to a discretionary trust or company (whether made before, on or after 22 March 2006). The charge to IHT on lifetime creation of trusts is part of a wider regime under which further charges to tax arise during the existence of the trust and on its ending. The details of these further charges are beyond the scope of this book. The examples below refer to transfers into trusts: in each case it is assumed that the trusts are not disabled trusts.

4.5.1 Calculating tax on a lifetime chargeable transfer

Where an individual makes an LCT, the IHT calculation begins with application of the first three steps as described at **4.4.1**, **4.4.2** and **4.4.3**. Once relevant exemptions and reliefs have been applied (except the small gifts exemption which is not available to LCTs), the balance is chargeable to IHT and tax must be calculated by applying step 4.

The rates of tax applicable to LCTs are:

(a)   0% on the first £325,000 (the nil rate band); and

(b)   20% on the balance of the chargeable transfer (this rate being half the rate for transfers which are chargeable on death).

4.5.1.1 The effect of cumulation

Chargeable transfers made in the seven years before the current chargeable transfer reduce the nil rate band available to that current transfer. In other words, the value transferred by chargeable transfers made in the seven years before the current chargeable transfer must be 'cumulated' with that transfer (whilst the transferor is alive, any PETs made by him are ignored for cumulation purposes because they may never become chargeable).

EXAMPLE 1

In this example, it is assumed that Venetia has used up her annual exemptions in each relevant tax year.

On 1 May 2017, Venetia transfers £50,000 to the trustees of a trust.

She has previously made the following lifetime chargeable transfers (after applying relevant annual exemptions):

1 May 2009   £100,000
1 May 2012   £280,000

She has made no other lifetime transfers (and makes no more in the current tax year).

To calculate the IHT due on the chargeable transfer of £50,000, the values transferred by any chargeable transfers made in the seven years prior to 1 May 2016 must be 'cumulated'.

(Remember that it may help you when calculating cumulative totals to draw a time line, showing the relevant transfers. An example is given below.)

Venetia's cumulative total consists of the £280,000 transferred on 1 May 2012 (less than seven years before the present transfer).

The transfer of £100,000 was made more than seven years ago and can be ignored.

	£
Nil rate band	325,000
less cumulative total	280,000
= remaining nil rate band	45,000

Tax on current chargeable transfer of £50,000:
£45,000 at 0% = nil
£5,000 at 20% = £1,000

Note that only chargeable transfers are relevant for cumulation. If the May 2012 transfer had been an outright gift of cash, it would have been a PET and not chargeable (as Venetia is still alive). It would not have been relevant for cumulation purposes, and the whole nil rate band would be available in relation to the 2017 gift to the trust.

Remember that each transfer has its own cumulation period. If a new transfer is made, it is necessary to re-calculate the cumulative total.

EXAMPLE 2

On 1 May 2018, Venetia makes a further transfer of £100,000 to the trustees of the trust. Assuming that the rates of IHT remain the same as for 2017/18, her position for IHT would be as follows:

Nil rate band exhausted by transfers of 1 May 2012 and 1 May 2017.

Tax on current chargeable transfer of £100,000:

£100,000 at 20% = £20,000

EXAMPLE 3

Venetia makes the following further transfer to the trustees of the trust:

1 July 2019   £200,000

Assuming the rates of IHT remain the same as for 2017/18, Venetia's position for IHT would be as follows:

The transfer on 1 May 2012 was made more than seven years ago and can be ignored.

Venetia's cumulative total consists of the £50,000 transferred on 1 May 2017 and the £100,000 transferred on 1 May 2018.

	£	£
Nil rate band		325,000
less cumulative total		
1 May 2017	50,000	
1 May 2018	100,000	150,000
= remaining nil rate band		175,000

Tax on current chargeable transfer of £200,000:
£175,000 at 0% = nil
£25,000 at 20% = £5,000

Note that the effect of death on lifetime chargeable transfers is considered at **4.6.3**.

4.6 EFFECT OF DEATH ON LIFETIME TRANSFERS

4.6.1 Introduction

The death of a transferor may result in a charge (or additional charge) to IHT on any transfers of value which he has made in the seven years immediately preceding his death, whether those transfers were PETs or LCTs when they were made. First, PETs made in that period become chargeable and the transferee will be liable for any IHT payable. Secondly, the IHT liability on LCTs made in that period is recalculated and the trustees will be liable for any extra tax payable. In either case, as the liability arises on death, the rate of tax, once the nil rate band and, if relevant, the RNRB are exceeded, is 40%.

Once the transfers that must be (re)assessed have been identified by checking the seven-year period before the transferor's death, each of those transfers must be analysed chronologically, starting with the transfer furthest back in time and working through the transfers (ending with the calculation of death on the death estate). If a transfer was originally a PET, the rules are those set out at **4.6.2**; if it was a LCT, the rules at **4.6.3** are used.

4.6.2 Effect of death on PETs

Potentially exempt transfers are defined and explained in **4.4**. There is no liability on a PET at the time of the transfer, and it will become wholly exempt if the transferor survives for seven years after the transfer. Many gifts will thus escape a charge to IHT.

A PET will become chargeable *only* if the transferor dies within seven years of making the transfer.

4.6.2.1 Steps 1–3

As seen at **4.4**, the first three steps are applied to determine the size of the PET. Business property relief and/or agricultural property relief may apply to reduce the value transferred, provided that the transferee still owns the business or agricultural property (see *Business Law and Practice*).

4.6.2.2   Step 4: Calculate tax at the appropriate rate

The final step is to identify the rate or rates of tax applicable to the transfer in question. In order to do this, one must first establish the transferor's cumulative total of transfers at the time of the PET, as this will reduce the available nil rate band. The cumulative total will be made up of:

(a)   any LCTs made in the seven years *before the PET being assessed* (even if the LCT was made more than seven years before the transferor's death – therefore a taxpayer who makes an LCT may have to survive for 14 years before it ceases to have any impact); and

(b)   any other PETs made during the seven years *before the PET being assessed* which have become chargeable as a result of the transferor's death.

The rates of tax applicable to chargeable transfers made within seven years of death of the transferor are:

(a)   0% on the available nil rate band; and

(b)   40% on the balance (the lower 36% charity rate is not applicable).

EXAMPLE 1

On 5 May 2015, Adam gives quoted shares worth £356,000 to his daughter, Emma.

On 21 September 2017, Adam dies, leaving his estate (consisting of quoted shares and bank deposits worth £200,000) to his son, Matthew. He made no other significant lifetime gifts.

The transfer on 5 May 2015 was a PET which has now become chargeable as the transferor has died within seven years.

(1) Tax on the PET	£
Loss to estate	356,000
Less annual exemptions 2015/16; 2014/15	6,000
	350,000

Adam had made no chargeable transfers in the seven years preceding 5 May 2015, so his nil rate band was intact.

Tax on £325,000 @ 0%	Nil
Tax on £25,000 @ 40%	£10,000 (payable by Emma).

(2) Tax on the estate

The cumulation principle means that Adam's nil rate band has been used up by the chargeable transfer made within the preceding seven years.

Tax on £200,000 @ 40%	£80,000 (payable by Adam's PRs from the estate passing to Matthew)

EXAMPLE 2

Gina gave the following gifts of cash to her children:

1 September 2011	£200,000 to Claire
25 June 2015	£200,000 to James

Gina died on 30 August 2017 leaving her estate (consisting of her house and bank accounts worth a total of £400,000) to the two children equally. She had made no other significant gifts.

Both gifts were PETs which have now become chargeable as Gina has died within seven years.

(1) Tax on the 2011 PET	£
Loss to estate	200,000
Annual exemptions 2011/12; 2010/11	6,000
	194,000

Gina had made no chargeable transfers in the seven years before 1 September 2011 so her nil rate band was intact.

Tax on £194,000 @ 0%	Nil

(2) Tax on the 2015 PET	£
Loss to estate	200,000
Annual exemptions 2015/16; 2014/15	6,000
	194,000

Gina's cumulative total of chargeable transfers made in the seven years up to 25 June 2015 was £194,000 (the 2011 transfer to Claire). Only £131,000 of Gina's nil rate band remains.

Tax on £194,000	
£131,000 @ 0%	Nil
£63,000 @ 40%	£25,200 (payable by James)

(3) Tax on Gina's estate: The house is a qualifying residential interest which has been closely inherited, so Gina is entitled to the RNRB of £100,000. Gina's nil rate band has been used up by the two chargeable transfers in the last seven years.

Tax on £100,000 @ 0%	
Tax on £300,000 @ 40%	£120,000 (payable by Gina's PRs from the property passing to the children)

4.6.2.3 Tapering relief

Where a PET has become chargeable, tapering relief is available if the transferor survives for more than three years after the transfer. The relief works by reducing any *tax payable* on the PET.

Tax is reduced to the following percentages:

(a)   transfers within three to four years before death: 80% of death charge

(b)   transfers within four to five years before death: 60% of death charge

(c)   transfers within five to six years before death: 40% of death charge

(d)   transfers within six to seven years before death: 20% of death charge

EXAMPLE

1 January 2011	Leonora makes a gift of £96,000 to Isadora
	Leonora's cumulative total before the gift is made is £325,000
1 July 2017	Leonora dies

Effect of death:	£
Transfer of value	96,000
Less: Annual exemptions 2010/11; 2009/10	6,000
PET (which is now chargeable)	90,000
Rate of tax: Cumulative total £325,000 so all £90,000 is in the 40% band	
£90,000 @ 40%	36,000
Tapering relief applies. Leonora died within six to seven years of the PET so 20% of this figure is payable	
Tax payable by Isadora 20% of £36,000	7,200

4.6.3 Effect of death on LCTs

If a transferor dies within seven years of making an LCT, the IHT payable must be recalculated and more IHT may be payable by the trustees. The tax bill may be increased not only because the full death rate of IHT will now apply, but also because PETs made *before* the LCT may have become chargeable. They will increase the cumulative total and so reduce the nil rate band applicable to the LCT.

4.6.3.1 Steps 1–3

As described at **4.5.1**, the first three steps apply to find the value transferred by the LCT that is chargeable to tax. It will be necessary to check whether any reliefs claimed at step 3 when the LCT was made (such as BPR or APR) are still available.

4.6.3.2 Step 4: calculate tax at the appropriate rate(s)

Inheritance tax is recalculated in accordance with the rates of tax in force at the transferor's death if these are less than the rates in force at the time of the transfer; if not, the death rates at the time of the transfer are applied (the lower 36% charity rate is not applicable).

The cumulative total relevant to the LCT will determine how much (if any) of the nil rate band is available. The cumulative total is made up of:

(a)   any other LCTs made in the seven years *before the LCT being assessed* (even if such earlier LCTs were made more than seven years before the transferor's death); and

(b)   any PETs made during the seven years *before the LCT being assessed* which have become chargeable as a result of the transferor's death.

Remember that each transfer that becomes chargeable or rechargeable has its own cumulation period, which means that a taxpayer who makes an LCT may have to survive for 14 years before it ceases to have an impact.

EXAMPLE 1

Jasmin dies in November 2017. During her lifetime, she made the following gifts. In December 2010, she gave her son £100,000 in cash and, in January 2004, she transferred £300,000 to a discretionary trust for the benefit of her grandchildren. (Assume that Jasmin used her annual exemption each year.)

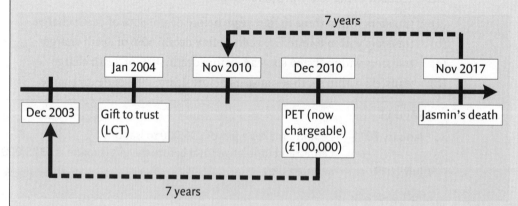

The December 2010 PET is just within 7 years of Jasmin's death, and has now become chargeable. As a result, it now has its own cumulation period, so you must look back 7 years from December 2010, when the PET was made, to see if any *chargeable* transfers were made during that period. The January 2004 LCT is just within the 7 years from December 2010 and must be cumulated. As a result, there is only £25,000 nil rate band left for the December 2010 PET.

Notes:

(a)   As Jasmin survived for more than 7 years from the January 2004 LCT, it is not rechargeable. It is only relevant for cumulation purposes.

(b)   Had the January 2004 transfer been a PET, as Jasmin survived for more than 7 years, it would never have become chargeable, and so would not be taken into account when calculating the cumulative total.

(c)   The cumulative total for the death estate, looking back 7 years from November 2017, is £100,000, ie the amount taken by the PET which has become chargeable. The January 2004 LCT has no effect on the death estate as it is outside the 7 years before Jasmin's death.

4.6.3.3 Tapering relief and credit for IHT already paid

Once the IHT on the LCT has been recalculated, and if more than three years have elapsed between the transfer and the subsequent death, tapering relief applies to reduce the recalculated tax (using the rules set out at **4.6.2.3**). Credit is then given for any IHT paid on the LCT at the time it was made but if the recalculated bill is lower than the original amount paid (which may occur if tapering relief is available) no tax is refunded.

EXAMPLE 1

On 1 May 2014, George transferred £381,000 into a trust on condition that the trustees must pay the IHT. He had made no other lifetime gifts.

(a) On 1 May 2014, George made an LCT.

	£
Value transferred	381,000
Less: Annual exemptions 2014/15; 2013/14	6,000
	375,000
Calculate tax.	
£325,000 @ 0%	0
£50,000 @ 20%	10,000
Tax payable by trustees	10,000

(b) George dies on 1 September 2017, within seven years of the LCT.
Recalculate tax at death rates.

	£
£325,000 @ 0%	0
£50,000 @ 40%	20,000
	20,000

George died between three and four years after the transfer, so apply tapering relief

	£
80% of £20,000	16,000
Less: tax already paid (see part (a))	10,000
Further tax payable by trustees	6,000

EXAMPLE 2

Drusilla dies on 1 August 2017. During her lifetime she made only the following transfers of value:

1 July 2011   Gift of £150,000 to Rukhsana
1 July 2014   Gift of £332,000 on discretionary trusts

The consequences are as follows:

(a) On 1 July 2011, Drusilla made a PET:

	£
Value transferred	150,000
Less: Annual exemptions 2011/12; 2010/11	6,000
Potentially exempt transfer	144,000

(b) On 1 July 2014, Drusilla made an LCT:
Charge to tax on 1 July 2014:

	£
Value transferred	332,000
Less: Annual exemptions 2014/15; 2013/14	6,000
	326,000

Rate of tax	Cumulative total zero	
	£325,000 @ 0%	0
	£1,000 @ 20%	200
Tax payable by trustees		200

(c) Recalculation of tax on PET following death: Drusilla has died within seven years after 1 July 2011, so the PET of £144,000 to Rukhsana has become chargeable. There is no IHT on the transfer as it falls within Drusilla's nil rate band, but her cumulative total is now £144,000.

(d) The tax on the LCT of 1 July 2014 must be recalculated.

Rate of tax: Cumulative total £144,000 so £181,000 of nil rate band left

	£
£181,000 @ 0%	0
£145,000 @ 40%	58,000
£326,000	58,000

Tapering relief applies. Drusilla died between three and four years after the LCT so the recalculated tax is reduced to 80%.

	£
80% of £58,000	46,400
Less: IHT already paid	200
Tax payable by trustees	46,200

(e) Effect on Drusilla's death estate. In the seven years before her death, Drusilla made two chargeable transfers. Her cumulative total at the time of her death is:

	£
1 July 2011 PET (now chargeable)	144,000
1 July 2014 LCT	326,000
	470,000

This means that, when calculating tax on Drusilla's estate on death, her nil rate band has been used up. Assuming that her estate did not include a qualifying residential interest, tax on her estate will be charged at a flat rate of 40%.

4.7 LIABILITY AND BURDEN OF PAYMENT

4.7.1 Meaning of 'liability' and 'burden'

The rules that follow concern the question of who is liable to account to HMRC for the payment of IHT and who bears the burden of the tax. HMRC is concerned with obtaining payment of the tax (ie liability). Payment will usually be obtained from people who are not beneficially entitled to the property but who hold property in a representative capacity (ie PRs and trustees). Those who ultimately receive the property are concurrently liable with such representatives, but in most cases tax will have been paid before the beneficiaries receive the property. The concept of 'burden' concerns who ultimately bears the burden of the tax.

4.7.2 The estate rate

The term 'estate rate' means the average rate of tax applicable to each item of property in the estate for IHT. When tax on the estate has been calculated, it may be necessary for various reasons to work out how much of the tax is attributable to a particular item of property in the estate. For example:

(a) since tax on certain types of property, such as land, may be paid in instalments, the personal representatives (PRs) must calculate how much of the tax relates to that property;

(b) the PRs may not be liable to pay all the tax on the estate. If the estate for IHT purposes includes trust property, the trustees are liable to pay the tax attributable to that property;

(c) the will may give a legacy 'subject to tax' so that the recipient has the burden of tax relating to that legacy.

The principle is that tax is divided between the various assets in the estate proportionately, according to their value. This may be applied by calculating the average rate of tax on the estate as a percentage, ie the 'estate rate'. For example, if the deceased's nil rate band was completely used up by lifetime transfers, the 'estate rate' would normally be 40%. However, it is not always necessary to calculate the estate rate as a percentage; instead, the amount of tax on a particular item of property in the estate may be calculated by applying to the value of that property the proportion which the total tax bill bears to the total chargeable estate.

EXAMPLE

Graham, who has made no lifetime transfers, leaves a house, valued at £210,000, to his brother, Henry, subject to payment of IHT, and the rest of his estate, valued at £190,000 net, to his nephew, Ian.

Tax on Graham's estate: £325,000 @ 0%   nil
                           £75,000 @ 40%   £30,000

The 'estate rate' is:

$$\frac{£30,000 \text{ (total tax bill)}}{£400,000 \text{ (total chargeable estate)}} \times 100 = 7.5\%$$

Henry pays tax on the house: £210,000   × $\dfrac{£30,000}{£400,000}$ =   £15,750

Ian pays tax on the residue: £190,000   × $\dfrac{£30,000}{£400,000}$ =   £14,250

The same result would be achieved if the estate rate of 7.5% was applied to the value of the house and residue respectively.

4.7.3 Liability for IHT on death

4.7.3.1 The PRs: tax on the non-settled estate

The PRs are liable to pay the IHT attributable to any property which 'was not immediately before the death comprised in a settlement' (IHTA 1984, s 200). This includes:

(a) the property which vests in the PRs (ie the property which passes under the deceased's will or intestacy); and

(b) property (other than trust property) which does not pass to the PRs but is included in the estate for IHT because the deceased was beneficially entitled to it immediately before death (eg, joint property which passes by survivorship).

Thus the PRs are liable to pay the IHT on joint property even though that property does not vest in them. Their liability is, however, limited to the value of the assets they received, or would have received but for their own neglect or default.

Concurrently liable with the PRs is 'any person in whom property is vested ... at any time after the death or who at any such time is beneficially entitled to an interest in possession in the property' (IHTA 1984, s 200(1)(c)). This means that tax on property passing by will or intestacy may in principle be claimed by HMRC from a beneficiary who has received that property. Similarly, HMRC may claim tax on joint property from the surviving joint tenant. Such tax is normally paid by the PRs and it is relatively unusual for HMRC to claim tax from the recipient of the property.

4.7.3.2   The trustees: tax on settled property

If the estate for IHT purposes includes any property which was 'comprised in a settlement' immediately before the death, the trustees of the settlement are liable for IHT attributable to that property. This principle is relevant where the deceased had a qualifying interest in possession under a trust (see **4.3.1.2**). Again, any person in whom the trust property subsequently vests or for whose benefit the trust property is subsequently applied is concurrently liable with the trustees.

EXAMPLE

In 1996, Ruth's father died leaving shares now worth £300,000 on trust for Ruth for life with remainder to Arthur. Ruth dies leaving property worth £200,000 which passes under her will to her niece, Tessa. The trust fund is taxed as part of Ruth's estate as she had a qualifying interest in possession for IHT purposes. She had made no lifetime transfers.

Tax on Ruth's death:

on	£325,000 @ 0%	nil
on	£175,000 @ 40%	£70,000

The trustees are liable to pay the tax on the trust fund (calculated according to the estate rate):

$$£300,000 \quad \times \quad \frac{£70,000}{£500,000} \quad = \quad £42,000$$

Arthur, the remainderman, is concurrently liable if any of the trust property is transferred to him before the tax has been paid.

Ruth's PRs are liable to pay the tax on Ruth's free estate (the remaining £28,000).

4.7.3.3   Additional liability of PRs

Property which the deceased gave away during his lifetime is treated as part of his estate on death if the donor reserved a benefit in the property which he continued to enjoy immediately before death (see **4.3.1**). The donee of the gift is primarily liable to pay tax attributable to the property. However, if the tax remains unpaid 12 months after the end of the month of death, the PRs become liable for the tax.

4.7.4   Liability for IHT on PETs

Where a person dies within seven years of making a PET, the transfer becomes chargeable and IHT may be payable. The transferee is primarily liable but, again, the PRs become liable if the tax remains unpaid 12 months after the end of the month of death.

The liability of the PRs is limited to the extent of the assets they actually received, or would have received but for their neglect or default. However, PRs cannot escape liability on the grounds that they have distributed the estate and so they should ideally delay distribution until IHT on any such lifetime gifts has been paid.

4.7.5 Liability for IHT on LCTs

4.7.5.1 Trustees pay

The transferor is primarily liable for IHT, although HMRC may also claim the tax from the trustees. In practice, the trustees often pay IHT out of the property they have been given.

EXAMPLE

Ahmed transfers £146,000 cash into a trust. His cumulative total is £285,000 and he is entitled to two annual exemptions. Ahmed stipulates that the trustees must pay any IHT.

		£
Value transferred		146,000
Less:	Two annual exemptions	6,000
		140,000
Rate of tax:	Cumulative total £285,000, so £40,000 of the nil rate band is left	
	£40,000 @ 0%	0
	£100,000 @ 20%	20,000
Tax payable by trustees:		20,000

4.7.5.2 Transferor pays: grossing up

If the transferor pays, the amount of tax will be more than it would be if the trustees paid.

This is because IHT is charged on the value transferred, ie the loss to the transferor's estate brought about by the gift (see **4.4.2**). If the transferor pays, the loss is increased by the amount of tax he pays.

EXAMPLE

Henrietta transfers £80,000 in cash to trustees of a trust. Earlier in the tax year, she gave them £331,000 in cash. She has made no previous chargeable transfers.

The annual exemptions for this tax year and last have already been used by the gift of £331,000 and her cumulative total stands at £325,000. All the current transfer will be taxed at 20%.

If trustees pay IHT:

The loss to her estate is £80,000. Tax payable is 20% of £80,000, which is £16,000.

If Henrietta pays IHT:

The total loss to her estate (ie the value transferred) is £80,000 plus the IHT payable on that transfer.

Therefore, in order to ascertain the value transferred, it is necessary to calculate what sum would, after deduction of tax at the appropriate rate (ie 20%), leave £80,000 (ie the transfer must be grossed up).

Gross up £80,000 at 20%

$£80,000 \times \frac{100}{80} = £100,000$

The gross value transferred is £100,000.

Calculate tax on £100,000:

£100,000 @ 20% = £20,000

> The tax payable by Henrietta is more than the tax payable by the trustees.
>
> However, if she pays, the trustees are left with the full amount of the property transferred, £80,000, as opposed to £64,000 if they pay.

4.7.5.3 Additional liability following the transferor's death

If additional IHT becomes due on a LCT following the transferor's death, the rules for those liable for the additional tax are set out in IHTA 1984, s199 (as summarised at **4.7.4** above).

4.7.6 Burden of IHT

Unlike liability, the question of where the burden of tax should fall is one for the transferor to decide. For example, the burden of tax could fall on the transferees of any gifts (including PETs and LCTs) or the transferor could choose to relieve them of that burden by paying any IHT himself on lifetime gifts and directing that any IHT arising following his death be paid from the residue of his estate. Further details of the default rules that apply when administering the deceased's estate are contained in **31.8**.

4.8 TIME FOR PAYMENT

4.8.1 Death estates

4.8.1.1 The basic rule

The basic rule is that IHT is due for payment six months after the end of the month of death (although PRs will normally pay earlier in order to speed up the administration of the estate as any IHT due must be paid before the grant of representation can be obtained; see **30.6**).

If the tax due is not paid on time, interest runs on the outstanding amount.

4.8.1.2 The instalment option

Some property, such as land and certain types of business property, attracts the instalment option. Any tax attributable to instalment option property may be paid in 10 equal yearly instalments, the first falling due six months after the end of the month of death. The tax on the estate is apportioned using the estate rate to find how much tax is attributable to the instalment option property.

The instalment option applies to:

(a) land of any description;

(b) a business or an interest in a business;

(c) shares (quoted or unquoted) which immediately before death gave control of the company to the deceased;

(d) unquoted shares which do not give control if either:

    (i) the holding is sufficiently large (a holding of at least 10% of the nominal value of the company's shares and worth more than £20,000); or

    (ii) HMRC is satisfied that the tax cannot be paid in one sum without undue hardship; or

    (iii) the IHT attributable to the shares and any other instalment option property in the estate amounts to at least 20% of the IHT payable on the estate.

4.8.1.3 Interest

Where the instalment option is exercised in relation to tax on shares or any other business property or agricultural land, instalments carry interest only from the date when each instalment is payable. Thus, no interest is due on the outstanding tax provided that each instalment is paid on the due date.

In the case of other land, however, interest is payable with each instalment (apart from the first) on the amount of IHT which was outstanding for the previous year.

4.8.1.4 Sale

If the instalment option property is sold, all outstanding tax and interest becomes payable.

4.8.2 PETs

Any IHT on a PET that has become chargeable is due six months after the end of the month of death. The instalment option outlined above may be available depending on the circumstances (IHTA 1984, s 227).

4.8.3 LCTs

4.8.3.1 At the time of the transfer

Any IHT on LCTs made after 5 April and before 1 October in any year is due on the 30 April in the following year. Inheritance tax on LCTs which are not made between those dates is due six months after the end of the month in which the LCT is made.

4.8.3.2 Following subsequent death within seven years

Any additional IHT on the reassessment of a LCT following the transferor's death is due six months after the end of the month of death.

Again, the instalment option may be available (IHTA 1964, s 227).

4.8.4 Example of the rules on liability, burden and timing

> **EXAMPLE**
>
> Xander, who was divorced, dies on 4 May 2017, leaving an estate on which the total IHT due is £150,000. His taxable estate (of £800,000) comprises instalment property (a house) worth £240,000 and non-instalment property worth £560,000 (of which £200,000 is Xander's share of a joint bank account held with this brother, Zak). Xander left a valid will, leaving the residue of his estate to his nephew, but which makes no mention of the burden of IHT.
>
> **Liability**
>
> The executors of Xander's estate are liable for the entire IHT due of £150,000.
>
> **Burden**
>
> As the will makes no contrary provision, the default rule is that the IHT on the share of the joint bank account is borne by Zak as the surviving joint tenant:
>
> $£200,000 \times \dfrac{£150,000}{£800,000} = £37,500$
>
> IHT on the property passing via the will is paid from the residuary estate as a testamentary expense:
>
> $£600,000 \times \dfrac{£150,000}{£800,000} = £112,500$
>
> **Timing**
>
> The house qualifies as instalment option property:
>
> $£240,000 \times \dfrac{£150,000}{£800,000} = £45,000$

This tax can be paid in 10 equal annual instalments, with the first instalment of £4,500 payable on 30 November 2017 (six months after the end of the month of death).

The remaining IHT of £105,000 is all due no later than 30 November 2017, but if the executors submit the IHT account before that date, they will have to pay the tax at that time. They will have a right of recovery from Zak for the £37,500 in respect of the joint bank account for which they have liability to HMRC but for which he bears the burden.

SUMMARY

The main occasions of charge to IHT are:

(a)   on death on the value of an individual's estate;

(b)   on lifetime gifts made by one individual to another made within seven years prior to death;

(c)   on lifetime gifts to a company or into a trust.

Lifetime gifts to an individual are only chargeable to IHT if the donor dies within the seven years after making the gift. At the time such a gift is made it is a 'potentially exempt transfer' (PET). It becomes exempt if the donor survives for seven years or chargeable if he dies during that period.

Lifetime gifts into a trust or to a company are immediately chargeable to IHT at the time they are made. They are known as 'lifetime chargeable transfers' (LCTs).

There are four steps to be used to calculate liability to IHT.

Step 1: Identify the transfer of value

On death this means the value of the estate, ie all the property to which the deceased was beneficially entitled.

For lifetime transfers this means any transaction which reduces the value of the transferor's estate. This includes any gift or a sale at an undervalue.

Step 2: Find the value transferred

On death this means the value of the property in the estate, valued at open market value.

For lifetime transfers this means the amount by which the transferor's estate has been reduced as a result of the transfer.

Step 3: Apply exemptions and reliefs

Transfers to spouse or charity are exempt whether in lifetime or on death.

Some exemptions apply only to lifetime transfers. These include annual exemption (£3,000 pa), small gifts, marriage gifts and gifts made as normal expenditure out of income.

Business property relief applies to reduce the value transferred by a transfer of certain types of business property by 100% or 50%. This may apply to transfers made in lifetime or on death.

Step 4: Calculate tax at the appropriate rate

If the estate includes a qualifying residential interest which is closely inherited, tax is charged at 0% on the first £100,000 (the residence nil rate band).

Tax is then charged at 0% on the first £325,000 of other transfers (the nil rate band).

In order to calculate IHT on any transfer, chargeable transfers made during the preceding seven years must be taken into account. Such transfers will reduce the nil rate band available for the current transfer.

The balance of the transfer in excess of the nil rate band is taxed at 40% (or, rarely, 36%) if the transfer is on death or 20% for LCTs.

Potentially exempt transfers (PETs) made within seven years of the transferor's death become chargeable as a result of his death. The rate of tax is 40%, but the amount of tax is tapered if the transferor survived for more than three years after the transfer.

If a transferor dies within seven years of making a LCT, tax must be recalculated at death rates, applying taper if the death was more than three years after the transfer.

TAX-EFFICIENT INVESTMENTS

LEARNING OUTCOMES

After reading this chapter you will have a basic understanding of the different forms of tax relief available on a range of investments.

5.1 INTRODUCTION

An individual with high levels of income or capital gains can reduce his exposure to tax by making tax-efficient investments. Depending on which investment vehicle is chosen, it may be possible to:

(a) obtain income tax relief on the investment (and so pay less income tax in the current year);

(b) ensure that future income or capital gains escape tax;

(c) avoid paying CGT on a capital gain by re-investing it.

The rest of this chapter introduces the main features of some investments which meet these objectives. However, no investor should allow a tax advantage to cloud his judgement as to the merits or risk of any particular investment. The list is not comprehensive, but gives examples of the opportunities available. Fuller treatment of these complex matters can be found in *Simon's Direct Taxes* (LexisNexis Butterworths).

5.2 INVESTMENTS ELIGIBLE FOR INCOME TAX RELIEF

5.2.1 Enterprise Investment Scheme (EIS)

This relief is designed to encourage investment in smaller (and riskier) companies. An individual is allowed to subscribe up to £1 million each tax year in the ordinary shares of qualifying unquoted companies. Broadly, this means trading companies that are not listed on The Stock Exchange, so there is no ready market for their shares. Certain asset-based activities, for example share dealing, property development, farming, shipbuilding and coal and steel production are excluded. During the two years before and three years after the subscription, the individual must not be 'connected with' the company. Thus, the combined shareholdings of the investor and his 'associates' (which includes spouse and close family) must not exceed 30%; neither he nor his associates are normally permitted to be paid employees or directors, although there are exceptions to this rule.

The relief is given by deducting a sum equal to 30% of the amount invested from the shareholder's income tax liability for the tax year of the investment (the maximum deduction is, therefore, £300,000), provided he continues to satisfy the personal qualifying conditions throughout the next three years. A further attraction is that gains on disposal will be exempt from CGT; conversely, if the enterprise fails, the investor's loss on his shares may be set against his income or capital gains.

5.2.2 Seed Enterprise Investment Scheme (SEIS)

This relief is similar to the EIS, in that the qualifying conditions are broadly similar, but it is aimed at small start-up companies with less than 25 full-time employees and assets of up to £200,000. The maximum qualifying investment is £100,000 and the rate of income tax relief is 50%. Subject to certain restrictions and provided the SEIS shares are held for more than three years, a gain on the sale of SEIS shares is also free from capital gains tax.

5.2.3 Venture Capital Trust (VCT)

A VCT is a quoted company run by professional fund managers as a vehicle to hold shares in a range of unquoted trading companies which match the EIS criteria. Smaller enterprises are thus given access to funds and the investor buying shares in the VCT can invest indirectly in smaller businesses, at the same time reducing the risk attendant on investment in a single unquoted company.

Such VCTs carry tax advantages similar to EISs, but to qualify the shares must be held for five years and the maximum investment each tax year is £200,000. A sum equal to 30% of the amount invested can be deducted from the investor's income tax liability (so the maximum tax deduction in any one tax year is £60,000). Gains on disposal are also CGT exempt. The added feature is that dividend income from a VCT is exempt from income tax.

5.3 INVESTMENTS PRODUCING TAX-FREE INCOME OR CAPITAL GAINS

5.3.1 Individual Savings Account (ISA)

Two types of ISA have existed since they were introduced in 1999: the Cash ISA and the Stocks and Shares ISA. A third type of ISA, effective from tax year 2016/17, is the Innovative Finance ISA (IF ISA). As the IF ISA relates to a particular method of investing, outside the usual requirements of the ordinary investor, this section describes the Cash ISA and Stocks and Shares ISA only.

In each tax year, an individual aged 18 or above (or 16 for a Cash ISA) and resident in the UK can put money into either or both types of ISA. If both types are used, they can be held with different providers.

A Cash ISA resembles an ordinary savings account and deposits are generally held in bank or building society accounts.

A Stocks and Shares ISA is a wrapper that can be put around a wide range of investment products, including unit trusts and investment trusts.

The ISA investment allowance for the current tax year is £20,000. This can be held in any mix of cash or stocks and shares and the funds can be freely moved between these categories, so giving the taxpayer the option of investing the whole ISA allowance in cash, stocks and shares or any combination of the two.

The tax benefits of ISAs are as follows.

(a)   No income tax liability on income produced by the ISA.
(b)   No CGT liability on gains arising from ISA investments.
(c)   Tax relief is not forfeited when money is taken out of the scheme.

Up until the current tax year, although money could be withdrawn from either type of ISA at any time without losing the tax benefits, contributions would remain the same for the purposes of calculating the available allowance for that tax year. So, if an individual who had invested £7,000 in an ISA in a tax year, subsequently withdrew £2,000 of that investment, the maximum additional ISA investment for that year would be based on the maximum allowance less £7,000 (not £5,000). As from April 2016, however, provided investors have what is called a 'flexible ISA', they will be allowed to dip into their current year investments, then replenish the balance in the same tax year without the transaction affecting any unused portion of their annual allowance. Taking the above example into the current tax year, that would mean that the £2,000 withdrawn could be reinvested as part of the original £7,000 investment, leaving a further possible £13,000 ISA allowance available in the tax year.

5.3.2 Enterprise Investment Scheme (EIS) and Seed Enterprise Investment Scheme (SEIS)

Capital gains are CGT exempt (see **5.2.1** and **5.2.2**).

5.3.3 Venture Capital Trust (VCT)

Both income and capital gains are exempt (see **5.2.3**).

5.4 INVESTMENT TO ESCAPE A CGT LIABILITY

5.4.1 Deferral relief on re-investment in EIS shares

Unlimited deferral of capital gains arising on the disposal of any asset is available where an individual subscribes wholly for cash for shares in a company which qualifies under the EIS. (As the shares must be acquired for cash, this relief will not usually be available to a partner or sole trader who transfers his business to a company, as the shares acquired following such a transfer are usually in return for the non-cash assets of the business.)

(a) This deferral relief is available where the shares acquired meet the requirements of the EIS (see **5.2.1**).

(b) The relief is complex but, in general terms, the individual's chargeable gain on the disposal of the asset (up to the subscription cost of the shares) is deferred until he disposes of the shares. The deferred gain is taxed at the rate applicable to the taxpayer in the tax year of the disposal of the EIS shares.

(c) The relief is available where the EIS shares are acquired within one year before or three years after the disposal.

(d) As regards the 'true gain' on the disposal of the EIS shares themselves, a slightly different relief applies. Such gains will be exempt from CGT if held for three years, but only if the investor is not 'connected' with the company (see **5.2.1**).

EXAMPLE

Shares in X Co Ltd (not EIS) have been held by Andrew for two years. He sells them and realises a gain of £60,000. This gain is deferred when he subscribes for shares in Y Co Ltd (an EIS company) for £100,000. Andrew holds the shares in Y Co Ltd for four years and then sells them for £120,000. His deferred gain of £60,000 is now chargeable to CGT. The 'true' gain of £20,000 on the disposal of the shares in Y Co Ltd will be exempt if all the qualifying conditions are met.

A similar relief on reinvestment in VCT shares was withdrawn in the 2004 Budget.

Tax Rates Summary

SUMMARY OF RATES AND ALLOWANCES FOR 2017/18 FOR INDIVIDUALS

Value Added Tax

Rates:	Standard rate:		20%
	Lower		5%
	Zero		0%
Registration threshold:			£85,000

Income Tax

Rates for non-savings, non-dividend income

Rates:	Basic rate	£0–£33,500	20%
	Higher rate	over £33,500–£150,000	40%
	Additional rate	over £150,000	45%

Rates for savings and dividend income			Interest	Dividends
Rates:	Starting rate	£0–£5,000	0%	7.5%

Note: the starting rate for savings income of 0% does not apply where the taxpayer's non-savings income exceeds the starting rate limit of £5,000.

	Basic rate	over £5,000–£33,500	20%	7.5%
	Higher rate	over £33,500–£150,000	40%	32.5%
	Additional rate	over £150,000	45%	38.1%

Income tax allowances:

Personal Allowance	£11,500
Income limit for full Personal Allowance	£100,000

Personal Savings Allowance:

Basic rate:	£1,000 (taxed @ 0%)
Higher rate:	£500 (taxed @ 0%)
Additional rate:	£0

Dividend Allowance:	£5,000 (taxed @ 0%)

Capital Gains Tax

Rates on gains:

Gains below the basic rate income tax threshold	10%
Gains above the basic rate income tax threshold	20%
Gains qualifying for entrepreneurs' relief	10%

Note: An 8% surcharge applies to gains made on the disposal of residential property.

Annual exempt amount:

Individuals	£11,300

Inheritance Tax

Rates:

£0 to £325,000	nil %
over £325,000	40%

Note 1: For estates, where 10% or more of a person's net estate is left to charity, transfers exceeding the nil rate band of £325,000 are taxed at 36%.

Note 2: A surviving spouse or civil partner may claim the unused proportion (or percentage) of the nil rate band of an earlier deceased spouse or civil partner. The unused proportion is based on the amount of the nil rate band available at the time of the death of the second spouse or civil partner.

Note 3: From April 2017 an additional nil rate band applies when a main residence is passed on death to a direct descendant. This will be:

£100,000 in 2017/18
£125,000 in 2018/19
£150,000 in 2019/20
£175,000 in 2020/21

It will then increase in line with the Consumer Prices Index from 2021 to 2022 onwards. Any unused nil rate band will be able to be transferred to a surviving spouse or civil partner. For estates valued at more than £2 million, the additional threshold (and any transferred additional threshold) will be gradually tapered away.

Transfer on death

Full rates apply.

Lifetime transfers

(a) Potentially exempt transfers

Gifts to individuals, and gifts into trusts for the disabled.

(i)   On or within seven years of death

On death, the full rates apply with a tapered reduction in the tax payable on transfers as follows:

Years between gift and death	Percentage of full charge
0–3	100
3–4	80
4–5	60
5–6	40
6–7	20

Note: the scale in force at date of death applies

(ii)   More than seven years before death – gift is exempt therefore NIL tax payable

(b) Chargeable transfers

Gifts into and out of most types of trusts and gifts involving companies.

At the time of gift, half the full rates apply. If the gift also falls within seven years of death, (a)(i) above applies but the lifetime tax (paid at the time of the transfer) will be credited against tax due on death.

REVENUE LAW

Chapter 2: Income Tax

Topic	Summary	References
Occasions of charge	Individuals, partners, personal representatives and trustees could all incur IT liability on the receipt of taxable income.	
Income or capital?	Income receipts must be distinguished from capital receipts. Only income can be subject to IT; capital gains may be subject to capital gains tax.	2.1.3
Chargeable income	To be chargeable, the income must come from a specified source and not be exempt.	2.2.1 and 2.2.2
	In practice, most income receipts are chargeable. In each tax year, all chargeable income from the different sources are added together to find the taxpayer's total income.	2.2.3
Deduction at source	Employers are obliged to deduct the recipient's basic rate IT liability, before payment, and send this direct to HMRC under the PAYE system. In such cases, it is necessary to gross-up the payment received by the taxpayer, in order to find his true income from that source. The grossed-up (as opposed to the net) income will be added to his total income.	2.2.3.1 to 2.2.3.2
Reliefs	The taxpayer may deduct allowable reliefs (eg interest on loans to invest in his business) from his total income. The resulting figure is his net income.	2.3
Allowances	The taxpayer may deduct relevant personal allowances (eg the personal allowance and/or the blind person's allowance) from his net income. The resulting figure is his taxable income.	2.4
	Taxpayers are also entitled to a Personal Savings Allowance of up to £1,000 on interest and a Dividend Allowance of £5,000. These allowances operate as nil rate bands for the relevant type of income, and are taxed at 0%.	2.2.3.2 and 2.5
Savings and dividend income and non-savings, non-dividend income (NSNDI)	Interest and dividends are savings and dividend income. All other income is non-savings, non-dividend income (NSNDI).	2.1.7 and 2.6.1

Topic	Summary	References
Rates of tax	Generally, taxable income falls into three bands – the basic rate band, the higher rate band and the additional rate band. Within these three bands, however, different rates apply, depending on whether the income is classed as NSNDI or savings and dividend income. NSNDI is taxed first, followed by interest and then dividends.	2.6.2
Tax credits	Once the taxpayer's total IT liability is worked out, credit is given for any tax deducted at source (eg by his employer). The remaining balance is then sent to HMRC, to meet the taxpayer's outstanding liability.	2.7
IT – liability and time for payment	In general terms, the recipient of taxable income must pay the balance of his tax liability to HMRC by 31 January following the tax year in which the income was earned. Special rules apply to the self-employed.	2.9

Chapter 3: Capital Gains Tax

Topic	Summary	References
Occasions of charge	Individuals, partners, personal representatives and trustees could all incur CGT liability when they dispose of chargeable assets.	
Disposals	For CGT to arise there must be a disposal of a chargeable asset. Disposals include gifts, as well as sales, but do not include property passing on death.	
Chargeable assets	Most forms of property are chargeable. The main exemption is sterling. In general terms, depreciating assets are also non-chargeable. This prevents the taxpayer from setting losses on these types of assets against his other chargeable gains.	3.1.3
Calculation of the gain	In basic terms, this is the sale price less allowable expenditure. The main element of allowable expenditure will usually be the acquisition cost of the asset but other expenditure is also deductible.	3.3
	To work out the notional gain made on a gift, the asset is deemed to be disposed of at its market value on the date of the gift.	3.2.1
Reliefs	Various reliefs are available, depending on the circumstances. Most of the reliefs available are aimed at encouraging business investment. Otherwise, a major relief for the ordinary taxpayer is the principal private residence exemption.	3.4.1
Disposals between spouses (and civil partners)	These are treated as being for such consideration as to provide neither a gain nor a loss. On a subsequent disposal by the donee spouse, the gain will be assessed by using the donor spouse's acquisition cost.	3.9.1

Topic	Summary	
Losses	Losses can be set against gains of the same t the net chargeable gain. Unabsorbed losse forward to set against gains of future tax ye way that the taxpayer does not lose the us exemption in future years.	
Rates of tax	(a) On normal gains, after deducting an annual exemption from an individual's net aggregate gains, the balance is added onto his taxable income. After doing this, if any part of the gains is below the basic rate income tax threshold it is taxed at 10% (or 18% on residential property), while any part of the gains above the threshold is taxed at 20% (or 28% on residential property).	3.1.4.5
	(b) Gains qualifying for entrepreneurs' relief are calculated separately from other gains and are taxed at a flat rate of 10%.	
	(c) Gains realised by trustees and PRs are taxed at a flat rate of 20% (or 28% on residential property).	
Liability and time for payment	Any taxpayer still having net aggregate gains after applying his annual exemption, is liable to pay CGT on them by 31 January following the tax year in which the gains were made.	3.1.6

Chapter 4: Inheritance Tax

Topic	Summary	References
Occasions of charge	A charge to IHT can arise on transfers into most types of trust or to companies, on other lifetime transfers made within seven years of the transferor's death and on property passing on death.	4.3 and 4.4
Transfer of value	IHT is charged on the value transferred by a chargeable transfer. A chargeable transfer is a transfer of value made by an individual but which is not an exempt transfer. A transfer of value is any disposition which reduces the value of the transferor's estate.	4.3 and 4.4
Value transferred	This is the amount of the reduction in the transferor's estate. On death, it is the value of the estate.	4.3.2.1 and 4.4.1
Exemptions applying to all types of lifetime transfer	Any property passing to a spouse (or civil partner) and to a charity is exempt. Business property relief (and agricultural property relief) may be available on relevant business (and agricultural) property, to reduce the value transferred by either 50% or 100%.	4.3.3
	In addition, lifetime transfers may be exempted by a number of other exemptions, including the small gifts exemption, gifts in consideration of marriage and the annual exemption.	4.4.3.4

Topic	Summary	References
Transfers into most types of trust	To the extent that exemptions are not available, these are immediately chargeable to IHT and are referred to as lifetime chargeable transfers (LCTs).	4.5
Rate of tax on LCTs at time of transfer	All amounts above the available nil rate are charged at a flat rate of 20%.	
Other lifetime transfers	The main example of these is a transfer to an individual. To the extent that other exemptions are not available, the transfer is a potentially exempt transfer (PET). As PETs, they are exempt from any IHT charge at the time of the transfer and will become unconditionally exempt if the transferor survives for seven years after the transfer.	4.4
IHT – effect of death of transferor within seven years of any type of lifetime transfer	To the extent that they do not fall within the nil rate band, LCTs made within seven years of the transferor's death must be re-assessed at the death rate of 40%.	4.6.3
	Any PETs made within seven years of transferor's death become chargeable transfers (failed PETs) and, to the extent that they do not fall within the nil rate band, are then chargeable at the death rate of 40%.	4.6.2, 4.6.2.1 and 4.6.2.2
IHT – cumulation	To assess the rate of tax on any individual transfer, it is necessary to take into account the value of any other chargeable transfers made within the seven years before the transfer being assessed. The nil rate band is applied to transfers in chronological order, so chargeable transfers within the previous seven years will have taken up some or all of the nil rate band, leaving only the balance for the transfer being assessed.	4.2.4, 4.3.4, 4.5.1 and 4.6.2
IHT – tapering relief	If any lifetime transfer (LCT or failed PET) was made between three and seven years before the death of the transferor, any IHT charge to which it is subject is progressively reduced by between 80% and 20% of the full liability.	4.6.2.3
IHT – transfers on death	The deceased is deemed to have made a transfer of value immediately before death. The value transferred is the value of his 'estate' immediately before death. The estate includes all property to which the deceased was beneficially entitled. Property held by the deceased on trust for others does not form part of the estate.	4.3
	Although property held by the deceased as a beneficial joint tenant passes automatically by survivorship to the remaining joint tenant(s), the value of the deceased's share in the property will form part of his estate for IHT purposes. Also included in the estate is property, which the deceased transferred in his lifetime but which he continued to have the use of until his death (gifts with a reservation of benefit).	4.3.1

Topic	Summary	References
	Liabilities of the deceased at the time of death and reasonable funeral expenses are deductible from the value of the estate.	4.3.2.4
IHT – exemptions applicable to death transfers	Any property passing to a spouse (or civil partner) and to a charity is exempt. Business property relief (and agricultural property relief) is available on relevant business (and agricultural) property, to reduce the value transferred by either 50% or 100%.	4.3.3
IHT – rate of tax on death transfers	Amounts falling within the residence nil rate band or nil rate band (subject to cumulation) are charged at 0%. The excess is taxed at 40% (except where a large enough amount passes to charity to trigger the lower 36% rate).	
IHT – liability and time for payment	Primary liability for IHT falls on the donee of a failed PET, the transferor of a LCT and the personal representatives of the deceased's estate.	
	In the case of lifetime transfers, if the transfer was made between 1 October and 5 April, the date for payment is six months from the end of the month in which the transfer was made. Otherwise, the payment date is on 30 April following the date of the transfer. On death, the general rule is that IHT is payable six months after the end of the month in which the death occurred. However, in the case of certain assets, such as land and shares, the tax may be paid in 10 yearly instalments.	

PROFESSION.

Author's notes

- This Part has been compiled from the S
  available at the time of writing.

- This book is not intended as a definitive

- This book is not intended to constitute legal advice. The publisher and author are not
  responsible or liable for the results of any person acting (or omitting to act) on the basis
  of information contained within this publication.

- The examples given in this Part are intended to illustrate a point only, and not as model
  examination answers.

THE LEGAL PROFESSION

LEARNING OUTCOMES

After reading this chapter you will be able to understand:

- what is meant by 'professional conduct'
- the role of The Law Society and Solicitors Regulation Authority
- different aspects of practice.

6.1 PROFESSIONAL CONDUCT

'Professional conduct' is the term that is often used to describe the rules and regulations with which a solicitor must comply. Solicitors, like every other person, must comply with the laws of the country. However, additional requirements are placed upon solicitors due to the nature of their job.

A solicitor is said to be a member of a profession. Other examples of members of professions include doctors and accountants. The public must be able to place a great deal of trust in such professionals due to the work that they carry out. For example, on a simplistic level, both solicitors and accountants often handle large amounts of clients' money. A client must be able to trust that this money will be safe in the hands of those professionals.

In addition to holding client monies, solicitors must be able to be trusted to act in the best interests of clients. Clients often seek advice from solicitors concerning transactions worth millions of pounds. With that amount of money at stake, the client must be certain that the solicitor will provide honest advice and take every step to protect that client's interests. Equally, clients often seek a solicitor's advice on sensitive matters. The client must be reassured that whatever the matter, the solicitor can be trusted to keep the information confidential and not, for example, sell it to third parties like the press.

Law firms, like any other commercial organisation, must comply with general regulatory requirements such as the Bribery Act 2010, which came into force on 1 July 2011. The Act creates a new offence under s 7, which can be committed by commercial organisations that fail to prevent persons associated with them (including employees) committing bribery on their behalf. It is, however, a full defence for an organisation to prove that, despite bribery having occurred, it nevertheless had in place adequate procedures to prevent bribery by persons associated with it. Guidance about such procedures has been published by the Ministry of Justice, and firms will need to ensure that they comply with this.

In addition to the general law, the Solicitors Regulation Authority (SRA) publishes a number of rules and requirements with which the solicitor (and those who work with solicitors) must comply at all times. These rules and requirements apply to the entire profession, including trainee solicitors and student members. The aim of these rules is to ensure the protection of the public and to uphold the integrity of the profession itself.

Breach of these rules and requirements can have severe consequences. For example, where a solicitor breaches certain requirements relating to the service provided to clients, he may be ordered to pay the client compensation of up to £50,000. The ultimate sanction for breach of the requirements of professional conduct is to be 'struck off'. This effectively ends the solicitor's career and prevents him from acting as a solicitor.

6.2   THE LEGAL SERVICES BOARD

The Legal Services Board was created by the Legal Services Act 2007. It supervises the 'approved regulators' of the legal profession. These regulators include the SRA (for solicitors), the Bar Council (for barristers), the Institute of Legal Executives (for legal executives), the Council of Licensed Conveyancers (for licensed conveyancers), the Chartered Institute for Patent Attorneys (for patent attorneys), the Institute of Trade Mark Attorneys (for trade mark attorneys), the Association of Law Costs Draftsmen (for law costs draftsmen), and the Master of the Faculties (for notaries public).

6.3   THE SOLICITORS REGULATION AUTHORITY

The SRA was established by The Law Society in January 2007 to take over the regulation of solicitors from The Law Society itself. The SRA also controls matters such as training and admission to the profession.

The SRA's own literature states that it is independent and regulates in the public interest. The SRA is governed by a board of 15 members. This board comprises seven solicitors and eight lay members. The current Chair is Enid Rowlands, who is the board's first lay member Chair. Details of the members of the SRA's board can be found at www.sra.org.uk.

The headquarters of the SRA are at The Cube, Birmingham, and there is an office in central London. Its budget is funded from the practising certificate fee (see **18.2**).

The regulation of the profession is considered in detail in **Chapter 7**.

6.4   THE LAW SOCIETY

6.4.1   Introduction

The Law Society is the representative body for solicitors in England and Wales. It was founded in 1825 to raise the reputation of the profession. Today it fulfils a number of roles.

The Law Society represents solicitors within England and Wales. For example, The Law Society lobbies the Government in respect of changes in the law, and campaigns for better working conditions for solicitors, particularly on behalf of solicitors undertaking publicly funded work. The Law Society also seeks to improve the reputation of the profession as a whole, and to promote the benefits of using a solicitor to the general public.

6.4.2   Membership

After admission, membership of The Law Society is voluntary. However, all members of the profession are bound by the requirements of professional conduct whether they are members of The Law Society or not.

6.4.3 Governance

The Law Society is governed by the Council of The Law Society. The Council delegates many of its powers and decision-making responsibilities to various Boards, such as the Management Board and the Regulatory Affairs Board.

6.4.4 Local law societies

There are approximately 120 local law societies throughout England and Wales. These often provide representation, training and facilities (such as law libraries) to local firms within their area. They also help to provide a link between The Law Society and local solicitors. Local law societies do not have any disciplinary powers.

6.5 DIFFERENT ASPECTS OF PRACTICE

The legal profession is made up of a number of different types of organisations. Within these organisations there are a number of roles that a solicitor may fill.

The SRA Practice Framework Rules 2011 set out the ways in which legal services may be provided to the public, and these are detailed below.

6.5.1 As a recognised sole practice or the employee of a recognised sole practice

A sole practitioner is a solicitor who chooses to practise on his own. He almost certainly will employ administration staff, such as secretaries, etc and may also employ other solicitors or paralegals. However, he will own, and therefore be responsible for, the firm in its entirety.

Whilst sole practitioners used to be fairly common, there is a general trend for solicitors to practise in larger organisations. There are a number of reasons for this. One prominent reason is cost. In recent times, a solicitor's practice has become more reliant on information technology. Solicitors' firms use such equipment for researching legal issues, for running sophisticated accounts programs, and for the day-to-day management of clients' files. Both the hardware and software required to perform these operations are expensive. Accordingly, it is easier to share this cost out amongst a number of partners, rather than for one person (ie the sole practitioner) to cover the entire cost.

Another reason is practicality. When a partner, or other fee earner, in a law firm goes on holiday, his clients' matters may temporarily be taken over by another solicitor within the firm. The sole practitioner may not have this option. Accordingly, the sole practitioner may have to arrange for a locum solicitor to supervise his absence from the office.

There is also a growing trend for solicitors to specialise in one particular area of law, for example family law or insolvency. Unless the sole practitioner is running a niche practice, this option is not open to him.

From 1 November 2015, sole practitioners will be authorised under the same authorisation rules as other types of firm. Accordingly, their organisation will be authorised by the SRA as a 'sole practice' rather than recognising the individual as a sole practitioner.

6.5.2 As a manager, employee, member or interest holder of an authorised body

6.5.2.1 Introduction

The term 'authorised body' means a body that has been authorised by the SRA to practise as a recognised body or a licensed body (SRA *Handbook* Glossary). This is perhaps the biggest change brought about by the reforms introduced by the Legal Services Act 2007.

A recognised body may take the form of a partnership, a limited liability partnership (LLP) or a company. These forms will be discussed below. Licensed bodies include ABSs (see **6.5.2.4**). Authorisation for authorised bodies is granted by the SRA and enables them to undertake certain aspects of 'reserved work', such as conducting court proceedings, the preparation/

lodging of documents relating to the transfer or charging of land, the preparation of probate documents and also immigration work, or as specified in the authorisation by the SRA in the case of licensed bodies (SRA Practice Framework Rules 2011, Rule 8).

The requirements relating to applications for authorisation and the conditions of such authorisation are set out in the SRA Authorisation Rules for Legal Services Bodies and Licensable Bodies 2011, which came into effect on 6 October 2011. These include a requirement that a manager or an employee of an authorised body or a related authorised body (as defined in the SRA *Handbook* Glossary) is designated as its compliance officer for legal practice (COLP), and one is designated as its compliance officer for finance and administration (COFA). These officers took up their roles on 1 January 2013.

6.5.2.2   Form of a recognised body

A recognised body may take the following forms:

Partnerships

Most solicitors' firms operate as partnerships. The firm is owned and run by the partners, who then employ other solicitors and administration staff to work for them. As the partners own the firm, they are entitled to share the profits generated by the firm between them.

Some large firms have two types of partners – 'equity' partners and 'salaried' partners. A salaried partner is the first step on the partnership ladder. A salaried partner may not be entitled to share in the profits of the firm, but he will receive a salary from the firm in excess of that paid to other non-partner fee earners. After a number of years, a salaried partner may be promoted to an equity partner, whereupon he will be entitled to share in the profits of the firm.

Limited liability partnerships

An LLP is an incorporated partnership. Instead of partners, LLPs have members. The members will share in the profits of the LLP.

Companies

A solicitors' practice may be incorporated as a company registered under the Companies Act 1985. The company will have directors and shareholders like any other company.

6.5.2.3   Requirements for a recognised body

Each recognised body must comply with a number of requirements under Rule 13 of the SRA Practice Framework Rules 2011. The detail of these requirements is beyond the scope of this book, but a brief summary of some of the key issues follows.

Eligibility criteria

To be eligible to be a recognised body, the partnership, company or LLP must have at least one manager who is a solicitor, registered European lawyer (REL) or (in the case of a partnership or an LLP) a body corporate as further defined in the Rules. In addition, all of the managers and interest holders (eg, a person who holds shares in the body) have to be lawyers and legally qualified bodies. The term 'lawyer' includes solicitors, barristers, legal executives, licensed conveyancers and notaries public.

Services requirement

The business of a recognised body is limited to:

(a)   professional services of the sort provided by individuals practising as solicitors and/or lawyers of other jurisdictions; and

(b)   professional services of the sort provided by notaries public, but only if a notary public is a manager or an employee of a recognised body.

6.5.2.4 Licensed bodies

The provision of legal services in England and Wales has changed radically with the introduction of alternative business structures (ABSs), a concept introduced by the Legal Services Act 2007. These structures allow non-lawyers to offer legal services alongside non-legal services. They also, for the first time, allow non-lawyers to own and invest in firms that provide legal services.

The first ABSs were licensed in early 2012 and so became 'licensed bodies' for the purposes of the SRA Authorisation and Practising Requirements. The SRA is a licensing authority for this purpose and licensed its first three ABSs in March 2012, including Co-operative Legal Services. A register of ABSs can be found on the SRA website.

Eligibility criteria

Under Rule 14 of the SRA Practice Framework Rules 2011, for a body to be eligible to be a licensed body there must be at least one manager who is a solicitor, an REL, a lawyer of England and Wales who is authorised by an approved regulator other than the SRA, eg the Council of Licensed Conveyancers (see **6.2**) or a European lawyer who is registered with the Bar Standards Board. It also has to be a 'licensable body'. A body ('B') will be a 'licensable body' if a non-authorised person (ie, someone not authorised by the SRA or another approved regulator):

(a)   is a manager of B; or

(b)   is an interest holder of B (eg, a person who holds shares in it or is entitled to exercise any voting rights).

Alternatively (or in addition to the above), a body ('B') will be a licensable body if:

(a)   another body ('A') is a manager of B, or is an interest holder of B; and

(b)   non-authorised persons are entitled to exercise, or control the exercise of, at least 10% of the voting rights in A.

Authorisation

Applications for authorisation to operate as a licensed body are governed by the SRA Authorisation Rules 2011. Under these rules, an application may be refused if, for example, the SRA is not satisfied that the applicant body's managers and interest holders are suitable as a group to operate or control a business providing regulated legal services, and/or that its management or governance arrangements are adequate to safeguard the regulatory objectives of the Legal Services Act 2007.

6.5.3   As a manager, employee, member or owner of an authorised non-SRA firm

Lastly, a solicitor may practise for a non-SRA firm. A non-SRA firm means a firm authorised by one of the other 'legal' regulators (see **6.2** above).

However, a solicitor practising for such a firm can only provide services to the public of a sort that the firm is authorised to carry out by the relevant regulator. For example, a partner in a firm regulated by the Council for Licensed Conveyancers could not carry out litigation services for clients, as the Council for Licensed Conveyancers is not authorised to regulate this type of work.

6.6   EMPLOYED SOLICITORS

An 'employed solicitor' is a solicitor who is employed by a non-solicitor employer. He may also be referred to as 'in-house counsel'. A number of large companies have in-house legal departments to advise on issues that arise from their business activities. Law firms often second their solicitors to work for their larger clients on a temporary basis. It is not uncommon for these solicitors to leave their law firm and go on to work for these clients on a full-time basis as employed solicitors.

Employed solicitors are subject to the same rules and regulations as solicitors in private practice. They will also be subject to the additional requirements of Rule 4 of the SRA Practice Framework Rules 2011 ('In-house practice').

6.7 LAW CENTRES

Law centres are run by solicitors, other legal advisers and community workers, to provide free legal advice and case work to disadvantaged individuals within local communities. There are 45 of these centres in England, Wales and Northern Ireland. The Law Centres Federation acts as a co-ordinating body for law centres nationally.

A solicitor who works for a law centre must still comply with all of the requirements of professional conduct. He will also be subject to the additional requirements of Rule 4 of the SRA Practice Framework Rules 2011.

6.8 LEGAL ADVICE CENTRES

A legal advice centre is a place where the public may attend for legal advice but where no case work is undertaken. In many parts of the country legal advice centres are operated by the Citizens' Advice Bureaux and solicitors will attend to give free legal advice either as honorary legal advisers, or on a rota scheme. The University of Law itself runs legal advice centres, staffed by its students under the supervision of a qualified solicitor.

6.9 DUTY SOLICITOR SCHEMES

The police station duty solicitor scheme aims to provide advice and assistance to people at police stations who otherwise would not be legally represented.

The court duty solicitor scheme aims to provide emergency legal representation at magistrates' courts on a rota basis to those who are not otherwise represented.

In both cases, the scheme is staffed by contracted solicitors on a rota basis, with fees being paid by the Legal Aid Agency.

SUMMARY

(1) A solicitor is said to be part of a profession. Accordingly, a higher standard of behaviour is expected of him than of a member of the public.

(2) The Solicitors Regulation Authority regulates the legal profession. It publishes rules and regulations with which a solicitor must comply in addition to the general law.

(3) These rules and requirements must be obeyed by all solicitors, whether they are members of The Law Society or not.

(4) The Law Society represents the legal profession.

(5) The legal profession is made up of a number of different types of practices.

REGULATING THE PROFESSION

LEARNING OUTCOMES

After reading this chapter you will be able to understand:

- how the profession is regulated
- how complaints against solicitors and those who work with/for them are dealt with
- the sanctions for breaches of professional conduct
- the role of the Solicitors Disciplinary Tribunal.

7.1 INTRODUCTION

The previous chapter looked at the legal profession and the fact that a higher standard of behaviour is expected from the profession than from an ordinary citizen. This is because solicitors are often trusted with large amounts of client money and/or a client's confidential information.

This chapter will consider who is responsible for specifying the rules and requirements which ensure that this higher standard of behaviour is met, and also how these rules are enforced.

7.2 HOW THE PROFESSION REGULATES ITSELF

7.2.1 The Solicitors Regulation Authority

As was noted in **Chapter 6**, the Solicitors Regulation Authority (SRA) was created by The Law Society in January 2007 to deal with the regulation of solicitors in England and Wales. Following the introduction of reforms brought about by the Legal Services Act 2007, the SRA now regulates solicitors, the firms in which they operate and all those working within those firms. However, a separate organisation, the Legal Ombudsman, is often the first point of contact for the public when complaining about solicitors (see **7.5**).

The SRA was created in anticipation of the Legal Services Act 2007. As we have already seen, the Legal Services Board supervises the SRA's regulation of the profession.

The SRA can publish and enforce rules governing how solicitors behave and conduct their business. As mentioned in **Chapter 6**, since early 2012, alternative business structures (ABSs) have enabled lawyers and non-lawyers to share the management and control of businesses providing legal services. In anticipation of this, the SRA decided to undertake a complete review of the regulation framework, and it subsequently formulated and put out proposals for consultation. The result is the SRA *Handbook*, which underpins the regulation of both traditional law firms and ABSs.

The SRA Code of Conduct 2011 contained in the *Handbook* replaces the Solicitors' Code of Conduct 2007 and came into force for all firms on 6 October 2011.

7.2.2 The SRA *Handbook* and approach to regulation

The *Handbook* sets out the standards and requirements which apply to everyone regulated by the SRA, so it covers not just traditional law firms and in-house practice but also the new ABSs. The current approach to regulation taken by the SRA is that it should focus more on the quality of what a solicitor is delivering to the client, rather than prescribing how the solicitor reaches that stage, and this is known as 'outcomes-focused regulation'. The responsibility for meeting the requirements in the *Handbook* and operating effective systems lies with the firms, and the SRA believes that this form of regulation will enable firms to devise and implement systems and processes that are right for their clients and the size and type of practice. This is likely to involve a greater degree of judgement on the part of firms than perhaps was the case under the more prescriptive 2007 Code.

The structure and content of the *Handbook* is as follows.

7.2.2.1 Principles

There are 10 Principles that are mandatory and apply to all those regulated by the SRA and to all aspects of practice. They underpin all of the *Handbook* requirements.

7.2.2.2 Code of Conduct

The Code is divided into five sections:

- You and your client
- You and your business
- You and your regulator
- You and others
- Application, waivers and interpretation

Each section is divided into chapters dealing with particular regulatory issues, for example: client care, conflicts of interests, and publicity.

Rather than containing prescriptive rules supported by guidance, as was the case with the Code of Conduct 2007, the current Code comprises Outcomes and Indicative Behaviours.

Each chapter sets out the 'Outcomes' required by the SRA. These Outcomes are mandatory and, when achieved, will help ensure compliance with the Principles. The SRA recognises, however, that these Outcomes may be achieved in a variety of ways depending on the particular circumstances, and they are supplemented by non-mandatory 'Indicative Behaviours'. These provide examples of the kind of behaviour which may establish whether the Outcomes have been achieved and the Principles therefore complied with. The Indicative Behaviours are not designed to be exhaustive and the SRA is clear that the Outcomes can be achieved in other ways. The SRA may ask a firm to demonstrate how it has met an Outcome if the relevant Indicative Behaviours have not been followed. In such cases, it would be prudent for the decision on how the Outcome has been/will be met to be recorded.

The provisions of the current Code are considered in detail in the following chapters. As there is no longer any guidance in the Code, reference will be made to the guidance contained in the 2007 Code as an aid to interpretation and application where relevant. However, it remains to be seen to what extent the SRA will place any weight on such guidance in the current regulatory regime.

7.2.2.3   The SRA Accounts Rules

This section contains rules for the protection of client money.

7.2.2.4   Authorisation and Practising Requirements

This section sets out various rules and regulations, including those relating to the training and admission of individuals intending to become solicitors, exercising higher rights of audience, firms setting up in practice and a Quality Assurance Scheme for Advocates (Crime).

7.2.2.5   Client Protection

This section contains the key elements for the financial protection of clients such as the SRA Indemnity Insurance Rules.

7.2.2.6   Disciplinary and Costs Recovery

This includes the SRA Disciplinary Procedure Rules.

7.2.2.7   Specialist Services

This section contains provisions which are applicable only when certain services are being provided to clients, for example the SRA Property Selling Rules. It also includes the SRA Financial Services (Scope) Rules 2001 and the SRA Financial Services (Conduct of Business) Rules 2001 (**see Chapter 17**).

7.2.2.8   Overseas Practice

The SRA Overseas Rules 2013 were introduced on 1 October 2013. They apply to regulated individuals established outside England and Wales, and to regulated entities which have operations under their control outside England and Wales. The rules are a starting point for the conduct of SRA regulated individuals and authorised bodies 'practising overseas' (as defined in the *Handbook* Glossary), and contain the Overseas Principles that are a modified version of the SRA Principles (see **Chapter 8**) to take into account the different legal, regulatory and cultural context of practice in other jurisdictions. Failure to meet the obligations set out in the Rules may result in regulatory action being taken by the SRA, including limiting, or removing, the right to practise as an authorised body or individual regulated by the SRA.

7.3   THE PERVASIVE NATURE OF CONDUCT

Conduct is said to be a pervasive subject – it cannot be viewed in isolation. It pervades all aspects of a solicitor's life and work, regardless of the area of work in which the solicitor chooses to practise. The topics covered in this book are of general application.

7.4   COMPLAINTS AGAINST SOLICITORS, AUTHORISED BODIES AND THOSE WHO WORK FOR THEM

A solicitor must ensure that clients are informed in writing at the outset of their matter of their right to complain and how complaints may be made (Outcome 1.9 of the Code of Conduct).

Clients' complaints must be dealt with promptly, fairly, openly and effectively by the solicitor (Outcome 1.11). Although having a written complaints procedure is not mandatory and the content of a procedure not prescribed, Indicative Behaviour 1.22 provides that it may tend to show that the Outcomes have been achieved and the Principles complied with where a solicitor has a written complaints procedure which:

(a)   is brought to clients' attention at the outset of the matter;

(b)   is easy for the clients to use and understand, allowing for complaints to be made by any reasonable means;

(c)   is responsive to the needs of individual clients, especially those who are vulnerable;

(d)   enables complaints to be dealt with promptly and fairly, with decisions based on a sufficient investigation of the circumstances;

(e)   provides for appropriate remedies; and

(f)   does not involve any charges to clients for handling their complaints.

The Legal Ombudsman (see **7.5**) has also produced a 'Guide to good complaint handling' which sets out how it expects lawyers to deal with complaints.

A copy of the firm's complaints procedure being provided to a client on request and, in the event that a client makes a complaint, the solicitor providing him with all necessary information concerning the handling of the complaint are both further Indicative Behaviours (1.23 and 1.24 respectively).

The firm must also inform the client of his right to challenge or complain about the firm's bill, and the circumstances in which he may be liable to pay interest on an unpaid bill (see **11.9.2**).

Clients must be informed in writing, both at the time of engagement and at the conclusion of the firm's complaints procedure, of their right to complain to the Legal Ombudsman and the time frame for doing so, and be given full details of how to contact the Legal Ombudsman (Outcome 1.10 and see **7.5**). As a result of the implementation of the EU Alternative Dispute Resolution Directive (2013/11/EU) in the UK in July 2015, clients must also be informed of the name and address of an ADR approved body which would be competent to deal with the complaint (ie, other than the Legal Ombudsman) should both parties wish to use the scheme, and whether the firm intends to use that approved body. The Chartered Trading Standards Institute (CTSI) has approved a number of ADR entities that will be able to provide ADR services. The obligation is to provide information about an ADR approved body, and so firms are not required to submit complaints to the body unless they wish to. Additional information must be provided by solicitors who come within the definition of an 'online trader' under a separate EU regulation on online dispute resolution.

7.5   THE LEGAL OMBUDSMAN

The Legal Ombudsman for England and Wales ('LeO') became operational on 6 October 2010. It was set up by the Office for Legal Complaints under the Legal Services Act 2007 and is based in Birmingham. It deals with complaints made not only against solicitors, but also against barristers, legal executives, licensed conveyancers, notaries and patent attorneys, claims management companies (amongst others), and it replaced the Legal Complaints Service (LCS) so far as complaints against solicitors are concerned. It therefore brings all legal service complaint handling under one roof for the first time.

The Scheme Rules provide that only certain types of client can complain to the LeO, including individuals, 'micro-enterprises' (broadly speaking, an enterprise with fewer than 10 staff and a turnover or balance sheet value not exceeding £2 million), clubs and associations with an annual income net of tax of less than £1 million, and personal representatives or beneficiaries of a person's estate. The complaint must relate to an act/omission by the lawyer and must relate to the services which the lawyer provided. The LeO also accepts complaints in relation to services which the lawyer offered, or refused to provide, to the claimant.

Ordinarily, the complainant cannot use the LeO unless the lawyer's complaints procedure has been used, and a maximum of eights weeks is given for the complaint to be resolved in this way.

The complaint should be brought no later than:

- six years from the act/omission; or
- three years from when the complainant should reasonably have known there was cause for complaint.

When the LeO accepts a complaint for investigation, it aims to resolve it by whatever means it considers appropriate, including informal resolution. If the LeO considers that an investigation is necessary, both parties will be given an opportunity to make representations. A hearing will be held only where the LeO considers that the complaint cannot be determined fairly without one. A recommendation report (an 'assessment') will then be made, with a time limit for response. If neither party indicates a disagreement within that time limit, the LeO may treat the complaint as having been resolved by the recommendation report. If, however, any party disagrees within that time limit, the LeO will issue a final decision (a 'determination'). The details of the procedure are set out in the Scheme Rules.

The LeO's determination may direct the lawyer to:

(a)   apologise;

(b)   pay compensation (together with interest) for any loss suffered and/or inconvenience/ distress caused;

(c)   ensure (and pay for) the putting right of any error or omission;

(d)   take (and pay for) any specified action in the interests of the complainant;

(e)   pay the costs of the complainant in pursuing the complaint;

(f)   limit the lawyer's fees (including that all or part of any amount paid is refunded, with or without interest, or that all or part of the fees are remitted).

The determination may contain one or more of the above directions. There is a limit of £50,000 on the total value that may be awarded in respect of compensation and the costs in respect of (c) and (d) above. The limit does not apply to (a), (e) or (f) above, or to interest on compensation for loss suffered.

If the complainant accepts the determination, it is binding on the parties and final, and neither party may start or continue any legal proceedings in respect of the subject matter of the complaint. It may be enforced through the High Court or county court by the complainant, and the report may also be published. If the complainant rejects the determination, both parties remain free to pursue other legal remedies (such as suing for negligence).

Although the LeO has the power to adjudicate on acts/omissions as a result of which the complainant has suffered loss, in the event that the LeO considers that the resolution of a particular legal question is necessary in order to resolve a dispute, it may refer that question to the court.

Lastly, where the LeO receives a complaint which discloses any alleged professional misconduct, it will inform the relevant approved regulator. In the case of a solicitor, this will be the SRA.

The LeO has published an online list of lawyers or law firms involved in complaints which have led to a formal decision by the LeO since April 2012. The list is updated quarterly.

More information about the LeO may be found at <www.legalombudsman.org.uk>.

7.6   BREACH OF PROFESSIONAL CONDUCT

7.6.1   Professional misconduct

'Professional misconduct' primarily concerns breaches of the SRA's Code of Conduct. For example, if a solicitor gave an undertaking (see **Chapter 14**) to post his client's witness statement to another solicitor on 1 May and then failed to do so, he would not achieve Outcome 11.2 of the Code and so would be said to breach the requirements of professional conduct.

7.6.2   The Solicitors Regulation Authority

Although all complaints from the general public are received through the Legal Ombudsman, complaints primarily concerning a breach of professional conduct will be dealt with by the SRA.

The role of the SRA is to protect the public. Accordingly, having received a report of a breach of the Code, the SRA must assess the risk to the general public posed by the solicitor. The SRA will write to the solicitor setting out the allegations or potential breaches of the SRA Principles (see **Chapter 8**) and seek a written explanation. If the SRA decides that further action is necessary, it may conduct a formal on-site investigation. This investigation will result in a factual report being made, detailing whether any breaches were found. If serious breaches were found, a more detailed 'desk-based' investigation may take place, requiring a written explanation from the solicitor before a final decision is made. The SRA may then decide that no further investigation is necessary or, if it considers that it is reasonable for those involved to remedy the decision, it may issue a letter of guidance. If the SRA decides that the Principles have been breached, there are a number of possible outcomes depending on the gravity of the breach and the status of the individual/body in question.

7.6.3   Outcomes – professional misconduct

The powers of the SRA following a finding of professional misconduct depend upon the subject of the complaint. Some of these powers are detailed below.

7.6.3.1   Firms and regulated individuals

The SRA may do the following:

(a)   *Make a finding with or without a warning about future conduct*

The SRA may make a finding about the conduct and/or warn about future conduct and recover the costs of the investigation.

(b)   *Impose a fine or rebuke*

The Legal Services Act 2007 gave the SRA new powers to rebuke and/or direct a firm and/or a regulated person to pay a penalty of up to £2,000 for law firms or up to £250 million for ABSs, and up to £50 million for individuals within ABSs. The details are contained in the SRA Disciplinary Procedure Rules 2011. As from 1 January 2008, the SRA has made its regulatory decisions public. This allows the general public to search under the name of the solicitor they propose to use, to establish whether he has been subject to any regulatory sanction.

(c)   *Control how the firm/regulated person practises*

The SRA could impose conditions on, or suspend, a practising certificate or the registration of a firm. It could also impose conditions on, revoke, suspend or modify the terms and conditions of authorisation of a firm.

(d)   *Refer the matter to the Solicitors Disciplinary Tribunal*

In some cases, the SRA does not make a final decision but refers alleged misconduct to the Tribunal, where it is responsible for prosecuting the matter. The Tribunal is independent from the SRA (see 7.7 below).

(e)   *Intervene into the practice*

The SRA can close the practice. The practice monies vest in the SRA, and the SRA takes possession of the practice documents, including client papers. An agent appointed by the SRA carries out the intervention and the practice is liable for the costs of this.

(f)   *Enter into agreements with the firm/regulated person*

These are regulatory decisions made by the SRA, the terms of which are accepted by the firm/regulated person. These agreements will detail the allegations made and the sanctions agreed, and are published on the SRA's website.

(g) *Revoke/suspend authorisation of the firm or withdraw approval of/disqualify an individual*

The SRA can revoke or suspend the authorisation of the firm or withdraw approval of or disqualify an individual from acting in certain capacities within the firm (eg, as a COLP or a COFA – see **6.5.2.1**), withdraw approval of a person being an owner of a licensed body, or impose conditions on the holding of an interest.

Note that the SRA's powers extend to non-solicitors if they are employed by a recognised/ licensed body/solicitor. The SRA may also decide to refer the conduct of employees or managers of a licensed body to an individual's appropriate regulator. There is a right of appeal against some of these outcomes.

7.6.4 Distinction between complaints about professional services and negligence

A solicitor owes a duty of care to his client in the law of tort. Where the solicitor breaches this duty and the client suffers loss as a result, the solicitor may be sued by the client for negligence (see further **7.10** below).

The client does not have to suffer any loss for the Legal Ombudsman to make a determination against the solicitor arising from a complaint about the services provided by him. The mere fact that the solicitor has provided services which are not of the quality reasonably to be expected of a solicitor is enough. For example, a solicitor may miss a deadline in respect of issuing proceedings, which would then deprive his client of the opportunity to pursue the matter in court. The service provided would clearly be below what it is reasonable to expect from a solicitor. However, it would also constitute negligence, as the solicitor has breached his duty of care to his client and as a result the client has suffered a foreseeable loss (ie, he will not be able to pursue his matter in court and recover damages).

The Legal Ombudsman and the SRA have no power to adjudicate upon issues of negligence in a legal sense, ie they are not courts and so do not have the power to adjudicate on legal issues. However, where there is an overlap between negligence and complaints about professional services, the Legal Ombudsman may adjudicate on those services where its powers of redress would be adequate to compensate the client.

7.7 THE SOLICITORS DISCIPLINARY TRIBUNAL

7.7.1 Introduction

The Solicitors Disciplinary Tribunal hears and determines applications relating to allegations of unbefitting conduct and/or breaches of the requirements of professional conduct by solicitors, RELs, recognised bodies, managers of recognised bodies and employees of recognised bodies/sole practitioners. Since 23 December 2011, the Disciplinary Tribunal has also dealt with appeals made in relation to ABSs and licensing rules. Most applications to the Disciplinary Tribunal are made on behalf of the SRA. However, except where the Solicitors Act 1974 expressly provides otherwise, any person may make an application directly to the Tribunal without first making a complaint to the SRA.

The Disciplinary Tribunal was established by s 46 of the Solicitors Act 1974 and is independent of The Law Society and the SRA. The members of the Disciplinary Tribunal are appointed by the Master of the Rolls. There is no statutory maximum on the number of members, and at the time of writing it comprised about 60 members, of whom two-thirds are solicitor members and one-third lay members. The solicitor members must have been admitted for at least 10 years, and the lay members must be neither solicitors nor barristers. The Disciplinary Tribunal sits in divisions of three members, each made up of two solicitors and one lay person. The decisions of the Disciplinary Tribunal may be delivered by a single member.

7.7.2 Tribunal procedure

The Disciplinary Tribunal has power, exercisable by statutory instrument, to make rules governing its procedure and practice. These rules are made with the concurrence of the Master of the Rolls. The SRA maintains a panel of solicitors in private practice who prosecute applications before the Disciplinary Tribunal on its behalf. In most cases, either the SRA's own advocates or the panel solicitor will present the case before the Disciplinary Tribunal. In complex cases, counsel may be instructed to present the case.

7.7.3 Application to the Tribunal

An application to the Disciplinary Tribunal must be made in the prescribed form, supported by evidence (this will be prepared by the panel solicitor, or the SRA's advocate where the applicant is the SRA). The Disciplinary Tribunal will consider the application and, if satisfied that there is a case to answer, will fix a hearing date. Either party may be represented at the hearing by a solicitor or counsel. Evidence is given on oath and witnesses may be called.

The decisions of the Disciplinary Tribunal are called 'Judgments' and 'Orders'. The Order itself, together with brief reasons for the decision, is made available at the end of the hearing. The Order takes effect once it is filed with The Law Society. A detailed written Judgment containing reasons, findings and repeating the Order is made available to the parties, The Law Society and The Law Society's *Gazette* after the hearing (usually within seven weeks of the hearing).

Where (unusually) an application is made directly to the Disciplinary Tribunal, the Tribunal may refer the matter to the SRA for investigation before proceeding with the application. Where in such a case the SRA investigates the complaint and finds it to be substantiated, it may take over the application on the applicant's behalf (or deal with the matter by using the powers of the SRA discussed at **7.6** above).

7.7.4 Powers of the Tribunal

The Solicitors Act 1974, s 47 gives the Disciplinary Tribunal power to make such order as in its discretion it thinks fit, including the following:

(a) striking a solicitor off the roll;

(b) suspending a solicitor from practice or imposing restrictions upon the way in which a solicitor can practise;

(c) imposing an unlimited fine payable to HM Treasury;

(d) reprimanding the solicitor;

(e) requiring the payment by any party of costs or a contribution towards costs.

7.7.5 Restoration to the roll

Once struck off the roll of solicitors, the Tribunal may also restore a solicitor to the roll.

7.7.6 Appeals

Appeal from a substantive decision of the Disciplinary Tribunal is made to the Administrative Court.

7.8 OTHER POWERS OF THE SOLICITORS REGULATION AUTHORITY

7.8.1 The investigation of accounts

In order to monitor a solicitor's compliance with the SRA Accounts Rules, the SRA may require a solicitor to produce his financial accounts, and any other relevant documents, to the SRA.

7.8.2 Intervention

Where the public is at risk, the SRA may take control of a solicitor's files and client monies. This is generally referred to as an 'intervention'. The SRA appoints another firm of solicitors to act as its agents to close down the practice. Intervention may also occur where a sole practitioner is unable to continue his practice through ill health, an accident or death.

7.8.3 Delivery of files

In order to investigate complaints of misconduct, the SRA has the power, under s 44B of the Solicitors Act 1974, to serve a notice on a solicitor requiring the delivery of a file or documents in the possession of the solicitor to the SRA. Outcome 10.9 of the Code also requires solicitors to produce documents and information to the SRA pursuant to a written notice.

7.9 POWERS OF THE COURT

A solicitor is an officer of the court. Accordingly, the court has jurisdiction to discipline the solicitor in respect of costs within any matter before the court. The court may order the solicitor to pay costs to his own client, or to a third party (see CPR, rr 44 and 45).

7.10 NEGLIGENCE

7.10.1 Introduction

In addition to or instead of the actions that the SRA or Legal Ombudsman may take, a solicitor may be sued by his client in the tort of negligence. A solicitor owes his clients a duty of care. Where a solicitor breaches this duty, and the client suffers loss as a result of that breach, the solicitor may be sued in negligence. A solicitor may also be sued for breach of contract in these circumstances. Firms must carry compulsory indemnity insurance against such actions (see **18.4**).

7.10.2 Steps to be taken on discovery of a claim

Outcome 1.16 of the Code provides that if a solicitor discovers any act or omission which could give rise to a claim by a current client against him, he must inform the client.

In circumstances where the client notifies the solicitor of his intention to make a claim, or where the solicitor discovers an act or omission which might give rise to a claim, it may tend to show that the relevant Outcomes have been achieved if the solicitor considers whether a conflict of interests has arisen or whether the client should be advised to obtain independent advice (Indicative Behaviour 1.12). It will be very rare that a conflict of interest does not arise in such situation.

However, The Law Society's guidance states that solicitors should respond to complaints even if they believe the allegations concern negligence and a referral to the firm's insurance provider will be necessary.

Where the solicitor does cease to act for the client, and is asked to hand over the papers to another solicitor who is giving independent advice on the merits of a claim, the solicitor should keep copies of the original documents for his own reference.

7.11 THE SRA COMPENSATION FUND

The SRA Compensation Fund is maintained by the SRA under ss 36 and 36A of the Solicitors Act 1974. The Fund is governed by the SRA Compensation Fund Rules 2011, which are accessible on the SRA's website and contained in the *Handbook*.

The Fund exists to make grants to persons who have suffered loss as the result of an act or omission of a defaulting practitioner (as defined in the *Handbook* Glossary, including a solicitor or the employee, manager or owner of a defaulting practitioner).

Applications to this Fund may be made where an individual/organisation has suffered loss due to a defaulting practitioner's dishonesty, or where the individual/organisation is suffering hardship due to a defaulting practitioner's failure to account for monies he has received. Eligibility criteria setting out those applicants that may be able to apply for a grant are set out in the SRA Compensation Fund Rules 2011.

Individuals/organisations are not automatically entitled to a grant from the Fund (they have to apply and their claims will be assessed). The Fund does not pay out sums of more than £2 million per claim.

Where payment is made from the Fund, the SRA will seek to be subrogated to the rights of the applicant and can therefore take proceedings against the defaulting solicitor to recover the amount paid out of the Fund.

The client may be asked to exhaust any legal remedy before applying to the Fund.

It may tend to show that the outcomes of Chapter 1 of the Code have been achieved where clients are informed if they are not entitled to the protections of the SRA Compensation Fund (Indicative Behaviour 1.11).

From October 2012 the SRA Compensation Fund is also to provide cover for claims made against uninsured firms (see **18.5.1**).

SUMMARY

(1)   The SRA is empowered by the Solicitors Act 1974 to publish rules and requirements for the regulation of conduct of solicitors, recognised/licensed bodies, members of recognised/licensed bodies, and employees of recognised/licensed bodies/sole practitioners.

(2)   These rules and requirements are enforced by the SRA and the Legal Ombudsman.

(3)   The SRA deals with breaches of the requirements of professional conduct, whereas the Legal Ombudsman primarily deals with complaints about services provided by legal practitioners, including solicitors.

(4)   The Legal Ombudsman deals with complaints relating to an act/omission by a legal practitioner and which relates to services provided by him. The client does not need to suffer any loss as a result of the service provided in order to raise the issue.

(5)   The SRA may impose disciplinary sanctions for a breach of the requirements of professional conduct, or in serious cases may refer the matter to the Solicitors Disciplinary Tribunal.

(6)   The Legal Ombudsman has numerous sanctions at its disposal. These include directing the solicitor to limit his fees, or directing the solicitor to compensate the client up to £50,000. The SRA/Legal Ombudsman has no power to pay compensation to the client itself.

(7)   The Solicitors Disciplinary Tribunal may fine a solicitor, suspend the solicitor or, as an ultimate sanction, strike the solicitor off the roll.

(8)   A solicitor will be negligent if he breaches a duty of care to his client and foreseeable loss results as a consequence of that breach. Where the solicitor has been negligent, he may be sued by the client for damages.

(9)   The SRA Compensation Fund is maintained by the SRA. Payment may be made from the Fund when a client has suffered loss as a result of a defaulting practitioner's act or omission or to cover claims against uninsured firms.

CHAPTER 8

THE PRINCIPLES

LEARNING OUTCOMES

After reading this chapter you will be able to understand the essentials of professional conduct.

8.1 INTRODUCTION

The profession is regulated by the Government (eg, the Proceeds of Crime Act 2002) and by the Solicitors Regulation Authority (SRA) itself. As was noted in **Chapter 7**, the SRA *Handbook* contains all of the SRA's regulatory requirements, including a Code of Conduct.

The starting point for the consideration of the regulatory framework is the 10 Principles. The Principles are all-pervasive and underpin all of the *Handbook* requirements. The chapters of the Code of Conduct show how the Principles will apply in certain contexts through mandatory provisions ('Outcomes') and non-mandatory provisions ('Indicative Behaviours').

8.2 THE PRINCIPLES

The notes to the Principles in the Code state that:

> The Principles embody the key ethical requirements on firms and individuals who are involved in the provision of legal services. You should always have regard to the Principles and use them as your starting point when faced with an ethical dilemma.
>
> Where two or more Principles come into conflict, the one which takes precedence is the one which best serves the public interest in the particular circumstances, especially the public interest in the proper administration of justice.

The Principles are mandatory and apply to all individuals and firms regulated by the SRA, whether traditional firms of solicitors, ABSs or in-house. Breach of the Principles may constitute professional misconduct. In the introduction to the *Handbook*, the SRA indicates that its approach to enforcement is proportionate, outcomes-focused and risk-based, and so how it deals with failure to comply with the Principles will depend on all the particular circumstances of each case: 'Our primary aim is to achieve the right outcomes for clients.'

Where an individual or a firm is practising overseas, the Overseas Principles will apply instead (see **7.2.2.8**).

8.3 PRINCIPLE 1: JUSTICE AND THE RULE OF LAW

Principle 1 provides that a solicitor must uphold the rule of law and the proper administration of justice. The SRA's notes to the Principles in the *Handbook* state that a solicitor has obligations not only to clients but also to the court and to third parties with whom the solicitor may deal. A solicitor's obligations to the court and third parties are discussed in **Chapter 16**.

8.4 PRINCIPLE 2: INTEGRITY

This Principle provides that a solicitor must act with integrity in all professional dealings with clients, the court, other lawyers and the public. A solicitor is in a position of trust, and so must behave in an appropriate manner to reflect that position.

8.5 PRINCIPLE 3: INDEPENDENCE

A solicitor must not allow his independence to be compromised. 'Independence' in this context means a solicitor's own and his firm's independence, and not merely his ability to give independent advice to a client. The notes state that a solicitor should avoid situations which might put his independence at risk, eg giving control of his practice to a third party which is beyond the regulatory reach of the SRA or other approved regulator.

8.6 PRINCIPLE 4: BEST INTERESTS OF CLIENTS

This Principle provides that a solicitor must act in the best interests of each client. The notes further provide that '[y]ou should always act in good faith and do your best for each of your clients'. In particular, the solicitor should observe his duty of confidentiality (see **Chapter 12**) and obligations with regard to conflicts of interest (see **Chapter 13**).

This Principle derives from the common law, as a solicitor is said to be in a fiduciary position in relation to his client. This fiduciary relationship is considered further in **Chapter 10**.

8.7 PRINCIPLE 5: STANDARD OF SERVICE

A solicitor must provide a proper standard of service to his clients. This duty extends to providing a proper standard of client care (see **Chapter 11** generally) and also a proper standard of work, ie the solicitor must ensure that he exercises the appropriate competence, skill and diligence, and taking into account the individual needs and circumstances of each client. Meeting the competencies set out in the Competence Statement forms an integral part of this requirement (see **18.2.8**).

This Principle is linked to the concept that a solicitor must act in the best interests of a client (see **8.6** above).

For example, imagine that a client is seeking to instruct a solicitor in respect of a complex dispute regarding a contract of insurance. If the solicitor in question knows very little about insurance law then he will be unable to act in the best interests of the client. The best interests of the client in this case would be for the solicitor to refer the client to an expert (ideally this would be a colleague, or alternatively someone in another firm) in the relevant field of law.

Equally, a solicitor must consider whether he has the capacity (in terms of work volume) to take on a particular matter. If a solicitor was to take on work when he did not have the capacity to deal with it effectively, he would not be acting in the client's best interests and would be unlikely to be able to provide a proper service to that client.

8.8 PRINCIPLE 6: PUBLIC TRUST

Both The Law Society and the SRA are keen to improve the reputation of the profession in the eyes of the general public. Accordingly, this Principle provides that a solicitor must behave in a way that maintains the trust the public places in the profession and in the provision of legal services. The notes state:

> Any behaviour either within or outside your professional practice which undermines this trust damages not only you, but also the ability of the legal profession as a whole to serve society.

For example, if a solicitor were to use money from his client account to fund the purchase of a new car then he would not only breach the SRA Accounts Rules, but he would almost certainly harm the public's trust in the profession and breach Principle 6.

A solicitor may harm the public's trust in the profession by behaviour outside of his solicitors' practice. For example, conviction of a criminal offence would lead the solicitor to breach Principle 6. Where a solicitor is convicted of an offence involving dishonesty, it is likely that he will be struck off the roll of solicitors.

8.9 PRINCIPLE 7: COMPLIANCE WITH LEGAL AND REGULATORY OBLIGATIONS

This Principle obliges a solicitor to comply with his legal and regulatory obligations, and to deal with his regulators and ombudsmen in an open, timely and cooperative manner. This will include dealings with the SRA and the Legal Ombudsman (see **Chapter 7**), and in relation to the reporting and notification requirements set out in the Code.

8.10 PRINCIPLE 8: EFFECTIVE BUSINESS MANAGEMENT

A solicitor must run his business or carry out his role in the business effectively and in accordance with proper governance and sound financial and risk management principles. This includes meeting the Outcomes set out in Chapter 7 of the Code ('Management of your business').

8.11 PRINCIPLE 9: EQUALITY OF OPPORTUNITY AND RESPECT FOR DIVERSITY

A solicitor must run his business or carry out his role in the business in a way that encourages equality of opportunity and respect for diversity.

In addition to complying with all anti-discrimination legislation, including the Equality Act 2010, a solicitor is under a much wider duty not to discriminate in his professional dealings with clients and others in relation to any group listed in Chapter 2 of the Code ('Equality and diversity'). Accordingly, a solicitor must not unlawfully discriminate against any person on grounds of age, disability, gender reassignment, marriage and civil partnership, pregnancy and maternity, race, religion or belief, and sex or sexual orientation. He should also not victimise or harass anyone in the course of his professional dealings (Outcome 2.1). A finding of unlawful discrimination outside practice could also amount to a breach of Principles 1 and 6.

The Outcomes in Chapter 2 of the Code require firms to provide services to clients in a way that respects diversity, and to make reasonable adjustments to ensure that disabled clients, employees or managers are not placed at a substantial disadvantage compared to those who are not disabled, without passing on the costs of such adjustments to these individuals (Outcomes 2.2 and 2.3 respectively). Having in place a written equality and diversity policy which includes the features set out in Indicative Behaviour 2.1, may tend to show that a firm has achieved the Outcomes of Chapter 2 of the Code and therefore has complied with the Principles.

8.12 PRINCIPLE 10: PROTECTION OF CLIENT MONEY AND ASSETS

This Principle provides that a solicitor must protect client money and assets belonging to his clients that have been entrusted to him or his firm. The term 'assets' in this context is defined as including money, documents, wills, deeds, investments and other property (*Handbook Glossary*). This closely links to Principle 4 and the duty to act in the best interests of clients.

8.13 EXAMPLES

EXAMPLE 1

Question   You are asked to act for Mr Monks, who wishes to sue X Co Ltd for a substantial amount of money. The case, if successful, would also generate a substantial amount of bad publicity for X Co Ltd, which would result in fewer sales for that company. You hold a significant number of shares in X Co Ltd. Should you act for Mr Monks?

Answer   You need to act in the best interests of your client (Principle 4), and you must also ensure that your independence is not compromised (Principle 3). If the case is successful, this may well lead to a substantial reduction in the share price of X Co Ltd, and you would stand to lose out financially in respect of your shares.

In these circumstances, could you act in the best interests of your client (when these interests conflict with your own) and provide unbiased and objective advice?

For these reasons you must decline to act.

EXAMPLE 2

Question   You are a sole practitioner who specialises in patent disputes. You are considered an expert in your field. However, you are already overworked and are struggling to keep up with your existing caseload.

You are approached by a large American company, which wishes to bring an action for a breach of one of its patents. You consider that this work would be very lucrative for your firm. Should you take on this work?

Answer   You must provide a proper standard of service to your clients (Principle 5). Your expertise is not in question. However, it would appear that you do not have the capacity to take on the work. Therefore you should decline to act, even if you would lose out on this lucrative work.

SUMMARY

(1)   The SRA sets out standards and requirements concerning professional conduct.

(2)   The starting point for consideration of the Code of Conduct and the other regulatory requirements is the 10 Principles.

(3)   The Principles set out the fundamental requirements which all individuals and firms regulated by the SRA must satisfy in practice.

(4)   Breach of the Principles may constitute professional misconduct.

OBTAINING INSTRUCTIONS

LEARNING OUTCOMES

After reading this chapter you will have learned about:

- the general principles of obtaining instructions
- advertising
- referrals of business
- fee sharing
- introductions to third parties.

9.1 INTRODUCTION

A solicitors' firm is a business, and has much in common with any high street store. Obviously a firm of solicitors sells services rather than goods, but just like a high street store it needs a regular supply of customers to survive. Without clients, a solicitors firm cannot generate income to pay staff salaries, the rent on premises, or for the upkeep of the office equipment. Accordingly, just like a high street store, a firm of solicitors must take steps to try to maintain and increase its market share. The two most common ways of trying to achieve this are through advertising and referrals.

9.2 GENERAL PRINCIPLES

As noted above, a solicitors' firm must take steps to try to maintain and increase its market share in order to prosper as a business. However, no matter how urgent these financial pressures may be, a solicitor must at all times comply with the requirements of professional conduct, and in particular with the Principles (see **Chapter 8**). A solicitor's primary duty is to his client. Accordingly, a solicitor must not do anything that would compromise his independence. Therefore a solicitor must not do anything, or enter into any arrangement, that would restrict him from acting in the best interests of his client.

For example, a firm of solicitors may be offered a large financial incentive to refer all clients requiring advice on financial services to a particular firm of brokers. However, the firm must not accept this offer if it would prevent the solicitors acting in the best interests of their clients.

9.3 ADVERTISING

9.3.1 Introduction

In the past, it was common for solicitors to rely on their personal reputation to obtain work. For example, a solicitor would earn a reputation for a certain type of work (eg, family law) by word of mouth in a town or city. This method of obtaining work is still valuable today. One of the best ways of attracting clients is by personal recommendation of a friend or colleague who has experienced similar problems. There are also publications, such as the Legal 500, which list the names of the 'top' solicitors in a particular legal field and geographical location.

However, in recent times firms have invested a lot of money with a view to attracting new clients through different means. For example, firms will advertise their services in local newspapers, on their websites or through promotional literature. The use of radio and television advertisements has become more frequent in recent years (particularly in the area of personal injury). The use of social media is also increasingly being embraced by the profession in order to engage with current and potential clients and to market its services.

The aim of these advertisements is to increase the general public's awareness of the firm in question, and of the services that the firm offers (ie, how the firm could help the potential client). Therefore, when a potential client needs the services of a solicitor, he will know which firm to contact.

Another purpose of advertising is to improve the reputation of the profession in the eyes of the general public. For example, during September 2004, The Law Society launched an advertising campaign entitled 'My hero, my solicitor', to remind the general public of the benefits of using solicitors, rather than unqualified individuals, when they have problems in their lives. The current campaign is entitled 'Use a Professional. Use a Solicitor.'

Solicitors are generally free to publicise their practice, provided that they comply with:

(a)   the general laws on advertising and data protection in force at the time. These include:

    (i)   the UK Code of Non-broadcast Advertising and Direct and Promotional Marketing (CAP Code),

    (ii)   the Data Protection Act 1998, and

    (iii)   the Privacy and Electronic Communications (EC Directive) Regulations 2003 (SI 2003/2426);

(b)   Chapter 8 of the Code of Conduct.

9.3.2 Chapter 8 of the Code – Publicity

9.3.2.1 General

Chapter 8 of the Code of Conduct is concerned with the manner in which a solicitor publicises his firm or practice, or any other business.

The SRA considers that there is an imbalance of knowledge between the general public on the one hand and the solicitor providing the service on the other. Accordingly, publicity in relation to the firm, practice or any other business must be accurate and not misleading, and not likely to diminish the trust the public places in the solicitor and in the provision of legal services (Outcome 8.1). The term 'publicity' is very widely defined and includes all promotional material and activity, including the name and description of the firm, stationery, advertisements, brochures, websites, directory entries, media appearances, promotional press releases, and direct approaches to potential clients and other persons, whether conducted in person, in writing or electronic form (*Handbook* Glossary). It does not, however, include press releases prepared on behalf of a client.

Publicity relating to solicitors' charges is also covered by these requirements. Any such publicity must be clearly expressed and identify whether VAT and disbursements are included

(Outcome 8.2). Examples which may tend to show that a solicitor has not achieved these Outcomes and therefore not complied with the Principles in relation to such publicity are:

(a) advertising an estimated fee which is pitched at an unrealistically low level (Indicative Behaviour 8.7);

(b) describing overheads of the firm (such as normal postage, telephone calls and client due diligence under Money Laundering Regulations 2007 – see **Chapter 15**) as disbursements in advertisements (Indicative Behaviour 8.8);

(c) advertising an estimated or a fixed fee without making it clear that additional charges may be payable, if that is the case (Indicative Behaviour 8.9).

9.3.2.2 Unsolicited visits or phone calls

A solicitor may wish to 'cold call' individuals in order to promote his business. As mentioned above in **9.3.1**, a solicitor must comply with the general law applicable to such marketing. This means that the solicitor must have all consents required by the relevant data protection legislation for the type of marketing he intends to carry out.

The Data Protection Act 1998 also permits all individuals to request that their details are not used for direct marketing purposes, and therefore if a solicitor receives such a request, it should be taken seriously and complied with.

In addition, Outcome 8.3 prohibits a solicitor from making unsolicited approaches in person or by telephone to members of the public to publicise his firm, in-house practice or other business. Accordingly, approaching people in the street, at ports of entry, in hospital or at scenes of accidents are examples of behaviour which may tend to show that the solicitor has not achieved the Outcomes, as will approaching people to conduct a survey which involves collecting contact details of potential clients or otherwise promotes his firm or in-house practice (Indicative Behaviour 8.5). However, the term 'members of the public' for this purpose does not include a current or former client, another firm or its manager, an existing or potential professional or business connection, or a commercial organisation or public body (*Handbook* Glossary). Even in circumstances when such visits or calls are permitted in this way, solicitors should be mindful of complying with the provisions of the relevant legislation.

9.3.2.3 Letterheads, websites and e-mails

As mentioned in **9.3.2.1**, a letterhead, a website and e-mails are considered forms of publicity. The SRA specifies that clients and the public must have appropriate information about the solicitor, his firm and how he is regulated (Outcome 8.4). Accordingly, letterheads, websites and e-mails must show the words 'authorised and regulated by the Solicitors Regulation Authority', and either display the firm's registered name and number if it is an LLP or a company, or, if the firm is a partnership or sole practitioner, the name under which it is licensed/authorised by the SRA and the number allocated to it by the SRA (Outcome 8.5).

9.3.2.4 Social media

Whilst there are no specific provisions in the Code that apply to the use of social media by solicitors and firms, regard must still be had to the Principles and the relevant Outcomes, including those in Chapter 8, when using social media as a marketing tool. For example, if a relationship with a client is established and continued via social media, the solicitor must still comply with Chapter 1 of the Code on client care (see **Chapter 10**) and Chapter 4 of the Code with regard to confidentiality and disclosure (see **Chapter 12**). A Law Society practice note on social media gives as an example a solicitor commenting on Twitter that he is in a certain location at a certain time which may result in him unintentionally disclosing that he is working with a client, so breaching the duty to keep the affairs of clients confidential (Outcome 4.1).

Where a solicitor is using social media for personal use, he must still be mindful that he could be associated with views expressed, comments and activities that are available to view by a wider audience online, and so should consider compliance with, for example, Principle 6, ie behaving in a way that maintains the trust the public places in the profession (see **Chapter 8**).

9.3.3 Responsibility for advertising

A solicitor may instruct a third party, such as an advertising agency, to deal with certain aspects of his advertising campaign. However, allowing any other person to conduct publicity for his firm in a way that would breach the Principles may tend to show that a solicitor has not achieved the Outcomes (Indicative Behaviour 8.6).

9.4 REFERRALS OF BUSINESS

9.4.1 Introduction

In addition to targeting the general public, a solicitor may also enter into an agreement with a third party to refer clients to the solicitor. For example, a solicitor could enter into an arrangement with a local estate agent, so that the agent will 'introduce' to the solicitor's firm any potential house buyers looking for a solicitor to complete their conveyancing. Any such arrangement must comply with the Principles, the most relevant being Principles 2, 3, 4 and 5 (see **Chapter 8**), and the Outcomes in Chapter 9 of the Code.

9.4.2 Chapter 9 of the Code – Referrals

As the relationship between a solicitor and his client should be built on trust, it follows that any referral arrangement should not jeopardise that trust. Accordingly, a solicitor should ensure that his independence and professional judgement are not prejudiced by virtue of any arrangement with another person (Outcome 9.1). Accordingly, allowing an introducer to influence the advice a solicitor gives to his client may tend to show that the Outcomes have not been achieved (Indicative Behaviour 9.11). The term 'arrangement' is defined to mean any express or tacit agreement between a solicitor and another person, whether contractually binding or not, and the term 'referral' includes any situation in which another person, business or organisation introduces, refers or recommends a client to the solicitor's business, or otherwise puts the solicitor and a client in touch with each other (*Handbook* Glossary).

A solicitor must also ensure that the clients' interests are protected regardless of the interests of an introducer (defined in the *Handbook* Glossary as any person, business or organisation who or that introduces or refers potential clients to the firm, or recommends your firm to clients, or otherwise puts the solicitor and clients in touch with each other) or the solicitor's own interest in receiving referrals (Outcome 9.2).

In entering into any arrangement, clients must still be in a position to make informed decisions about how to pursue their matter (Outcome 9.3). Clearly, accepting referrals where a solicitor has reason to believe that a client has been pressurised or misled into instructing him may tend to show that the Outcomes have not been achieved (Indicative Behaviour 9.12). Indicative Behaviour 1.4 ('Client Care') also provides that it may tend to show that the Outcomes have been achieved by the solicitor explaining any referral arrangements which are relevant to the client's instructions.

Entering into arrangements only with reputable third parties and monitoring the outcome of those arrangements to ensure that clients are treated fairly may tend to show that the solicitor has achieved the necessary Outcomes (Indicative Behaviour 9.1), as will advising a client if the arrangement with an introducer is not in his best interests (Indicative Behaviour 9.2) and terminating any arrangement that causes a solicitor to breach the Principles on any requirements of the Code (Indicative Behaviour 9.3). Being satisfied that any client referred by an introducer has not been acquired as a result of marketing or other activities which, if done by a person regulated by the SRA, would be contrary to the Principles or any requirements of the Code (see **9.3**) is also an Indicative Behaviour (9.4). Entering into any type of business relationship which places a solicitor in breach of any of the SRA Authorisation Rules or any other regulatory requirements in the *Handbook* may tend to show that the outcomes have not been achieved (Indicative Behaviour 9.10).

9.4.3 Referral fees

During March 2004, the Master of the Rolls lifted the ban on solicitors paying referral fees to third parties introducing clients to solicitors. These arrangements have been used mainly in areas such as personal injury and conveyancing. For example, in April 2005 it was reported that Shoosmiths had agreed to pay a referral fee to the Automobile Association (AA) in respect of the parties' deal that Shoosmiths would act as the exclusive provider of legal services to the AA's customers.

After some uncertainty as to their future, the SRA announced in December 2007 that referral fees would continue to be permitted. However, with effect from 1 April 2013, the Legal Aid, Sentencing and Punishment of Offenders Act 2012 (LASPO 2012) prohibits the payment or receipt of referral fees in claims for damages following personal injury or death. As a result, an Outcome has been added to the Code to provide that those governed by the Code must ensure that any payment (as defined) made for services, such as marketing, does not amount to a 'prohibited referral fee' (as defined in the *Handbook* Glossary with reference to the relevant sections of LASPO 2012) (Outcome 9.8). Firms are also obliged to retain records and management information to enable them to demonstrate that any payments made are not prohibited referral fees (Indicative Behaviour 9.9). The Outcomes are further supported by Indicative Behaviours 9.7 and 9.8.

The SRA has warned solicitors that they should only deal with claims management companies that are appropriately regulated. It is envisaged, however, that the ban on referral fees for personal injury work will result in a steep reduction in the claims management company industry and so result in a loss of client leads which firms previously derived from this source.

A solicitor must ensure that clients are informed of any financial or other interest which an introducer has in referring the client to him (Outcome 9.4), and that any financial arrangements are in writing (Outcome 9.7). Accordingly, it may tend to show that the relevant Outcomes have been achieved where a solicitor draws the client's attention to any payments he makes or other consideration provided in connection with any referral (Indicative Behaviour 9.5); and if he ensures that where any information needs to be given to clients, this is clear and in writing or in a form appropriate to the client's needs (Indicative Behaviour 9.6).

9.4.4 Limitations

A solicitor must not make any payments to an introducer in respect of clients who are the subject of criminal proceedings or who have the benefit of public funding (Outcome 9.6).

9.5 FEE SHARING

Fee sharing would occur if a solicitor made a payment to a third party in respect of a percentage of fees earned on a particular matter, or a percentage of the solicitor's gross or net fees for a particular period.

The provisions of Chapter 9 of the Code relating to referrals of business apply equally to fee-sharing arrangements. Accordingly, a solicitor must ensure that independence and his professional judgement are not prejudiced by virtue of any such arrangement (Outcome 9.1), and that the client's interests are protected regardless of the interests of the fee sharer or his own interests in receiving referrals under such an arrangement (Outcome 9.2). The client must be informed of any fee-sharing arrangement that is relevant to his matter (Outcome 9.5; see also Indicative Behaviour 1.4). The other provisions are as set out in Chapter 9 (see **9.4**).

9.6 INTRODUCTIONS TO THIRD PARTIES

9.6.1 Introduction

In circumstances where a solicitor wishes to refer a client to third parties, such as another lawyer or a financial services provider, the duties of the solicitor are set out in Chapter 6 of the Code. In making such a referral, the solicitor must ensure that his recommendation is in the best interests of the client and does not compromise the solicitor's independence (Outcome 6.1). A client must also be fully informed of any financial or other interest which the solicitor has in referring the client to another person or business (Outcome 6.2) and must be in a position to make informed decisions about how to pursue his matter (Outcome 6.3).

With effect from 1 April 2013, the payment or receipt of referral fees in claims for damages following personal injury or death is prohibited (see **9.4.3**). A 'prohibited referral fee' (as defined in the *Handbook* Glossary) must not be paid to those governed by the Code (Outcome 6.4). This is supported by Indicative Behaviours 6.3 and 6.4.

9.6.2 Financial services

A solicitor who carries out a regulated activity without being authorised by the Financial Conduct Authority or exempt will commit a criminal offence. A regulated activity would include giving advice on a specified investment such as stocks and shares. There are a number of exemptions and exclusions of which a solicitor may take advantage when carrying out a regulated activity (see **Chapter 17**).

However, it may tend to show that the Outcomes of the Code have not been achieved where a solicitor enters into any arrangement, eg with a financial services provider, which restricts his freedom to recommend any particular business (Indicative Behaviour 6.5). An example of this would be where a solicitor enters into an agreement with Monks and Co Financial Advisers to refer all clients seeking financial advice to that firm, as this would restrict the solicitor's ability to refer clients to another suitable firm within the area. The only exception to this is where the advice concerns regulated mortgage contracts, general insurance contracts or pure protection contracts (as defined in the *Handbook* Glossary). However, even where this exception applies, it may tend to show that the Outcomes have been achieved where any arrangement entered into by the solicitor provides that referrals will be made only where this is in the best interests of the particular client and where the contract is suitable for his needs (Indicative Behaviour 6.1). Where any referrals are made to a third party that can offer products from only one source (ie a tied agent), it may tend to show that the Outcomes have been achieved where the referral is to be made only after the client has been informed of this limitation (Indicative Behaviour 6.2).

Lastly, a solicitor must properly account to clients for any financial benefit (eg commission) he receives as a result of his instructions (Outcome 1.15 and see also Indicative Behaviour 1.20). This would include a referral to a financial services provider (see **11.13**).

The topic of financial services and solicitors is considered further in **Chapter 17**.

9.7 EXAMPLES

> **EXAMPLE 1**
>
> Question　Your firm is conducting a marketing drive. Your marketing department has identified a number of former clients who have not used your firm for a number of years. The marketing department suggests that the firm telephones these former clients to try to convince them to use the firm again.
>
> Your marketing department also suggests approaching people in the street to conduct a survey about legal services which would involve collecting their contact details as potential clients.

Can your firm do this?

Answer   Your firm must comply with the general law concerning advertising/publicity and also with Chapter 8 of the Code. A firm must not make unsolicited telephone calls to members of the public (Outcome 8.3). However, the definition of 'members of the public' does not include the former clients of the firm. Therefore the firm can cold-call former clients as long as it complies with the provisions of the Data Protection Act 1998 and the general law. The firm should have given its clients (and former clients) an opportunity to refuse to receive direct marketing, such as cold-calls. If this process has been carried out, the firm must not call those former clients who have withheld their consent.

Conducting the survey in the street would be an example of behaviour which may tend to show that the solicitor has not achieved the Outcomes in Chapter 8, and therefore has not complied with the Principles (Indicative Behaviour 8.5).

EXAMPLE 2

Question   You are contacted by a local firm of insurance agents who offer a wide range of financial products, but only those developed and provided by one particular insurance company. The firm proposes entering into an arrangement whereby you refer all clients seeking financial advice to it. In return it will pay you a modest commission for each client referred.

Can you accept this proposition?

Answer   In accordance with the Outcomes in Chapter 6 of the Code, any recommendation that a client uses a particular business must be in the best interests of the client and must not compromise your independence (Outcome 6.1). The proposed arrangement here would restrict your freedom to recommend any particular business to clients for the purposes of seeking advice on financial products, and so may tend to show that the Outcomes have not been achieved (Indicative Behaviour 6.5). However, an exception would be if the arrangement was only in connection with advice concerning regulated mortgage contracts, general insurance contracts or pure protection contracts (Indicative Behaviour 6.5). In taking advantage of such an arrangement, it may tend to show that you have achieved the Outcomes by informing the client beforehand that the firm in question is a tied agent (ie offers products from only one source) (Indicative Behaviour 6.2), and, in relation to regulated mortgage contracts, general insurance contracts or pure protection contracts, if the referral is in the best interests of the particular client and the product is suitable for his needs (Indicative Behaviour 6.1). You must inform the client of the financial interest you have in referring him to the firm, ie the commission (Outcome 6.2), and account to the client for this (Outcome 1.15).

SUMMARY

(1)   Solicitors should always be independent when giving advice to a client and ensure that their clients' interests are protected.

(2)   Solicitors are free to publicise their practice, provided that they comply with the general law on advertising in force at the time and with the Outcomes in Chapter 8 of the Code.

(3)   A solicitor's promotional material must not be misleading or inaccurate.

(4)   Solicitors may enter into a financial arrangement with an introducer and enter into fee-sharing arrangements, provided that they comply with the Outcomes in Chapter 9 of the Code.

(5)   A solicitor may introduce clients to third parties, such as a financial services provider, provided he complies with the Outcomes in Chapter 6 of the Code.

THE RETAINER

LEARNING OUTCOMES

After reading this chapter you will have learned about:

- accepting and declining instructions
- the duties owed to the client
- ending the relationship.

10.1 INTRODUCTION

The contract between a solicitor and his client is often referred to as a 'retainer'. As with any other contract, the relationship between the solicitor and the client is governed by the general law. However, in addition to considering the general law, a solicitor must also comply with obligations placed upon him by the requirements of professional conduct.

10.2 ACCEPTANCE OF INSTRUCTIONS

10.2.1 Terms of the retainer

As noted above, many of the terms of the retainer will be implied into the contract either by the law, or by the requirements of professional conduct. Some of these terms are considered below. However, the solicitor must ensure that the more basic terms of the retainer are understood by the client. One such critical issue is to ensure that the client understands exactly what work the solicitor has agreed to undertake. Although not required by the Code, it would be good practice for a solicitor to send a letter to his client at the start of the transaction, confirming to the client exactly what he understands his instructions to be (and also what action, if any, the client must take), along with certain other information to show compliance with the Outcomes in Chapter 1 of the Code ('Client Care') and the Principles (see **Chapter 11**). This will help to avoid any misunderstandings at a later date, such as where a client makes a complaint against the solicitor for his failure to complete a certain task which the solicitor was unaware he had been instructed to complete.

It is important that a client's expectations are managed at an early stage of the solicitor–client relationship. If the client knows what the solicitor will and will not be doing for him, there will be less scope for problems to arise at a later date.

10.2.2   Identity of the client

Equally, the solicitor must ensure that he clarifies the identity of his client. For example, a solicitor may be instructed by a director of a company concerning the debts of that company. The solicitor will be obliged to clarify whether he is being instructed by the director in her personal capacity, or by the director on behalf of the company (ie, the company will be the client, not the director personally). As noted below, a solicitor owes many duties to his client, and he can ensure that these duties are met only if he knows the identity of his client.

A solicitor is also under a separate duty to obtain 'satisfactory evidence' of the identity of his clients (ie, are they who they say they are?). This obligation is imposed by the Money Laundering Regulations 2007 (SI 2007/2157) and is considered further at **15.2.3**.

10.2.3   Third party instructions

A solicitor may receive instructions from a third party on behalf of a client. For example, a client's daughter may seek to instruct a solicitor on behalf of her elderly mother, as the mother may have mobility problems in attending the solicitor's office.

Alternatively, a solicitor may receive instructions from one client purporting to instruct the solicitor on behalf of a number of clients. For example, a solicitor may be instructed by Mr Smith to purchase a property on behalf of Mr Smith and Mr Brown.

Where a solicitor receives such third party instructions, it may tend to show that the relevant Outcomes have not been achieved if he acts without satisfying himself that the person providing the instructions has the authority to do so on behalf of all of the clients (the mother in the first example; Mr Smith and Mr Brown in the second example) (Indicative Behaviour 1.25).

When considering whether to accept instructions from or on behalf of a number of clients, the solicitor must take into account any actual or potential conflicts of interests (see **Chapter 13**).

10.3   REFUSAL OF INSTRUCTIONS TO ACT

10.3.1   Introduction

Solicitors firms spend thousands of pounds in attempting to attract new clients to their business. They will also try to ensure that they retain their existing clients. However, there will be some clients for whom a solicitor will decline to act. For example, a solicitor may decline to act for a client who is known for not paying his legal fees.

Generally, like any other business, a solicitor is free to decide whether to accept or decline instructions to act for a particular client. However, this discretion is limited by the requirements of professional conduct set out in the Code, and also by the general law (see Outcome 1.3). A solicitor may not decline to act in certain circumstances.

10.3.2   Restrictions placed on the refusal of instructions

A solicitor must not unlawfully discriminate against anyone in his professional dealings (Outcome 2.1). Therefore, if a solicitor discriminates unlawfully when accepting or refusing instructions to act for a client, it may tend to show that he has not achieved this Outcome (Indicative Behaviour 2.5).

10.3.3   Situations where a solicitor may or has to decline to act

10.3.3.1   Duress or undue influence and vulnerable clients

A solicitor must provide services to his clients in a manner which protects their interests in their matter, subject to the proper administration of justice (Outcome 1.2). It follows, therefore, that it may tend to show that the relevant Outcomes have not been achieved if a solicitor acts for a client when there are reasonable grounds for believing that the instructions are affected by duress or undue influence, without satisfying himself that they represent the client's wishes (Indicative Behaviour 1.28).

The elderly, or those with language or learning difficulties, or mental health issues, are particularly susceptible to undue pressure from others. It may tend to show that the Outcomes have been achieved in taking instructions and during the course of the retainer where the solicitor has proper regard to the client's mental capacity or other vulnerability, such as incapacity or duress (Indicative Behaviour 1.6). Where a solicitor suspects that a client's instructions are tainted by duress or undue influence, it would be prudent for him therefore to take steps to ensure that the client's instructions are genuine, eg by arranging to interview the client alone, away from any third party such as a relative.

A solicitor should also bear in mind his duties under the Equality Act 2010, in particular the need to make reasonable adjustments in relation to clients with disabilities (Outcome 2.3 and see **8.11**). In its guidance 'Outcomes-focused regulation at a glance', the SRA provides the following as examples of evidence of good client care:

(a) In a case where a solicitor is concerned about the client's mental capacity, the file should clearly document the steps taken to establish that the client had the necessary capacity to instruct him on the matter.

(b) In a case where a solicitor was concerned about the client's ability to speak and/or understand English, the file should indicate whether an independent interpreter was used.

10.3.3.2 Where a solicitor cannot act in the client's best interests

A solicitor must treat his clients fairly (Outcome 1.1), and it may tend to show that the Outcomes have been achieved and that the solicitor has therefore complied with the Principles where the solicitor considers whether he should decline to act because he cannot act in the client's best interests (Indicative Behaviour 1.7). There is an overlap here with Principle 4 and other Outcomes and Indicative Behaviours in the Code, eg a solicitor should not act where there is an own-interest conflict or a client conflict (see **Chapter 13**), or where the solicitor holds 'material' confidential information for an existing or former client which would be relevant to a new instruction (see **Chapter 12**).

A solicitor must have the resources, skills and procedures to carry out his client's instructions (Outcome 1.4). Accordingly, the solicitor must consider the level and quality of service he will be able to provide to the client. Every solicitors' firm will have a maximum capacity of work with which the firm can deal effectively at any one time. If the solicitor or firm does not have the time or resources to deal with the client's matter then it would not be in that client's best interests to accept the instruction.

Equally, if a solicitor is approached by a prospective client about an area of law about which the solicitor knows very little, it would be in the client's best interests to be referred to another solicitor or firm which possesses the requisite knowledge.

10.3.3.3 Gifts of significant value

The Code also provides that it may tend to show that the Outcomes have been achieved and the Principles complied with if a solicitor refuses to act where his client proposes to make a gift of significant value to him or to a member of his family, or to a member of his firm or that person's family, unless the client takes independent legal advice (Indicative Behaviour 1.9).

The Code provides no further guidance on what would amount to 'significant value' in this context. However, the Law Society has issued a practice note, which indicates that an amount may be significant in itself, or as a proportion of the client's estate. It advises that a solicitor should carefully consider any gift worth more than £500 to determine whether it may be considered significant in the particular circumstances, and that it can be assumed that it would be significant if:

(a)   it is worth more than 1% of the client's current estimated net estate;

(b)   it might become valuable at some point, especially after the death of the client;

(c)   it provides a benefit to an individual which is more valuable than his relationship to the deceased reasonably justifies.

The note advises solicitors, before preparing a will in such circumstances, to consult the firm's compliance officer for legal practice (COLP) or a senior practice member, who will then consider the potential conflict of interests (see **Chapter 13**) and the best interests of the client, and to place a written summary of the decision with the file. The SRA Guidance on the Drafting and Preparation of Wills provides an example of a situation where it may be still appropriate to draft the will even if the client has not received independent legal advice. This is where the solicitor is drafting wills for his own parents and the survivor of them wishes to leave the residuary estate to the solicitor and his siblings in equal shares.

10.3.3.4   Compliance with the law and the Code

In deciding whether to act (or terminate his instructions) a solicitor must comply with the law and the Code (Outcome 1.3). For example, a solicitor instructed on the sale of a property might be instructed to draw up a false surveyor's report and send it to the purchaser in order to hide some defects to the structure of the property. If the solicitor agreed, he would be participating in a fraud against the purchaser. Clearly, instructions must be refused here.

Where a solicitor becomes aware that his client is involved in criminal conduct, the solicitor must consider very carefully the obligations placed on him by the Proceeds of Crime Act 2002 (see **Chapter 15**).

Examples of instructions which would not comply with the Code are where:

(a)   there is, or is likely to be, a conflict of interest between the solicitor and his client, or between two or more clients (see **Chapter 13**);

(b)   the solicitor holds material confidential information for an existing or former client which would be relevant to a new instruction (see **Chapter 12**);

(c)   the client instructs the solicitor to mislead or deceive the court (see **16.1.1**).

Also, entering into unlawful fee arrangements when accepting instructions from a client may tend to show that the Outcomes have not been achieved (Indicative Behaviour 1.27; see also Outcome 1.6). This would include an unlawful contingency fee (see **Chapter 11**).

10.4   DUTIES TO THE CLIENT DURING THE RETAINER

10.4.1   Introduction

A solicitor will owe the client a number of duties throughout the retainer. These duties are prescribed by the common law and the requirements of professional conduct. Some of these duties (such as the duty of confidentiality) will continue even after the retainer has been terminated. The following are examples of some of the duties that solicitors owe to their clients.

10.4.2   Duty of reasonable care and skill

In addition to the solicitor's duty of care in common law, s 13 of the Supply of Goods and Services Act 1982 provides that a supplier of services will carry out those services with reasonable care and skill. This term is implied into the retainer between a solicitor and his client, and therefore the solicitor may be sued for a breach of contract if the term is breached. However, this implied term does not apply to advocacy services provided before a court, tribunal, inquiry or arbitrator (Supply of Services (Exclusion of Implied Terms) Order 1982 (SI 1982/1771), art 2).

Nevertheless, the solicitor may be sued for negligence in both contentious and non-contentious proceedings. The House of Lords removed an advocate's protection from negligence claims in *Arthur JS Hall & Co v Simons* [2002] 1 AC 615. Accordingly, a solicitor who acts as an advocate may be sued in the tort of negligence if he breaches his duty of care to his client within court proceedings.

In certain circumstances, a solicitor may owe a duty of care to third parties, such as beneficiaries to an estate (see **16.5.6**).

10.4.3 Duty to act in the best interests of the client

As has been noted throughout this Part, a solicitor must act in the best interests of his client. This duty is taken from the Principles in the Code of Conduct, and also from common law.

The solicitor–client relationship is said to be a 'fiduciary relationship'. Under the common law, a fiduciary relationship is one where one party must act in the best interests of the other party. This means that the solicitor must put the interests of his client before his own. Another example of a fiduciary relationship is the doctor–patient relationship. Directors of a company also owe a fiduciary duty to the company itself.

Where such a relationship exists, one party may not make a secret profit at the expense of the other party. For example, a solicitor may be paid commission, say £50, when referring a client to a third party such as an accountant (see **Chapter 9**). As the solicitor owes a fiduciary duty to his client, this £50 must be accounted for to the client. This duty to account is also mirrored by the Code (see **11.14**).

Equally, there is a presumption of undue influence where a fiduciary duty exists. This means that in any dealings between a solicitor and his client, there will be a rebuttable presumption that the solicitor has exercised undue influence in persuading the client to enter into that dealing. In order to rebut this presumption, the solicitor would need to show that such influence had not been exercised, for example by making a full disclosure of all relevant facts, ensuring that the client took independent legal advice and understood the transaction, and ensuring that all dealings were fair and at arm's length.

10.4.4 Taking advantage of the client

As a result of the fiduciary relationship between the solicitor and client, the solicitor must not take advantage of the client. This is reflected in Principle 2 of the Code, which provides that a solicitor must act with integrity, and in certain of the Outcomes, eg that a solicitor must treat his clients fairly (Outcome 1.1).

10.4.5 Confidentiality

A solicitor and his firm have a duty to keep the affairs of their client confidential. This duty continues even after the retainer has been terminated. This topic is considered in detail in **Chapter 12**.

10.4.6 Disclosure

A solicitor owes the client a duty to disclose all relevant information to the client, regardless of the source of this information. This topic is considered in detail in **Chapter 12**.

10.4.7 Client care and costs

A solicitor is obliged to provide information on costs and other issues at the start of and throughout the matter, to enable the client to make informed decisions. A solicitor must also keep the client informed throughout the transaction and deal with the client's matter in a timely manner (see **Chapter 11**).

10.5 THE CLIENT'S AUTHORITY

A solicitor may derive authority from the retainer to bind the client in certain circumstances. This authority can be limited expressly by the client in the terms of the retainer. However, the solicitor should never seek to rely on this implied authority to bind the client. Express instructions should always be taken from the client prior to the solicitor taking any step in the proceedings or matter.

10.6 TERMINATION OF THE RETAINER

10.6.1 Introduction

As with any contractual relationship, the retainer may be terminated by either party, or by the general law.

10.6.2 Termination by the client

A client may terminate the retainer at any time for any reason. However, the client is likely to be liable to pay the solicitor's fees for work done up until the point of termination. A solicitor may require his costs to be paid prior to forwarding the file to the client (see **10.7**).

10.6.3 Termination by the solicitor

In contrast to the right of a client to terminate the retainer at will, the Code of Conduct restricts the right of a solicitor to terminate the retainer. Outcome 1.3 provides that when deciding whether to terminate his instructions, a solicitor must comply with the general law and the Code. Ceasing to act for a client without good reason and without providing reasonable notice may tend to show that a solicitor has not achieved this Outcome (Indicative Behaviour 1.26).

10.6.3.1 Good reason

In the Solicitors' Code of Conduct 2007 examples were given by the SRA of what constitutes 'a good reason' to terminate, and these continue to be helpful. They include where:

(a) the solicitor has to terminate the retainer because the instructions would involve the solicitor in a breach of the law or the requirements of professional conduct;

(b) the solicitor cannot obtain proper instructions from the client;

(c) there has been a breakdown in confidence within the relationship between the solicitor and client (eg, the client is not willing to accept the advice of the solicitor).

10.6.3.2 Reasonable notice

The SRA's previous guidance in the Code of Conduct 2007 provided that what amounts to 'reasonable notice' will depend on the circumstances. For example, the guidance stated that it would rarely be acceptable to stop acting for the client immediately before a court hearing, where it would be impossible for the client to find someone else to represent him at the hearing.

10.6.4 Termination by law

The retainer will be terminated automatically by law in certain circumstances. These include where the solicitor is declared bankrupt or either party loses mental capacity after the retainer has commenced.

Where the solicitor does not practise as a sole practitioner, his being declared bankrupt or losing mental capacity will have little practical effect, as one of his partners will take over the client's matter.

Where the client loses mental capacity, the solicitor should have regard to the Mental Capacity Act 2005 and its accompanying Code.

10.6.5 Responsibilities on termination

As a matter of good practice, a solicitor should confirm to the client in writing that the retainer has been terminated, and take steps to deal with any property of the client which may be held by the solicitor. For example, the solicitor may be holding client monies which, subject to the position on costs, should be returned to the client as soon as possible, together with any interest. The solicitor will also have to deal with the client's paperwork. It may tend to show that the Outcomes have been achieved as to client care if, when a solicitor has to cease acting for a client, he explains to the client his possible options for pursuing his matter (Indicative Behaviour 1.10).

Where the client's matter is ongoing and the client has instructed another firm of solicitors, it may be advisable to retain a copy of the file. The solicitor should also consider the client's rights and the solicitor's obligations under the Data Protection Act 1998. The Act requires that any personal data in those files are retained only for the purpose for which they were collected, although this will not prevent the solicitor from retaining a copy of the file in order to defend himself from any future claims of negligence.

10.7 LIENS

A lien is a legal right that allows a creditor to retain a debtor's property until payment. Accordingly, a solicitor may hold on to property already in his possession, such as client's papers, until his proper fees are paid. The SRA's previous guidance in the Code of Conduct 2007 suggested that where possible an undertaking to pay the costs should be accepted instead of the solicitor retaining the client's papers under a lien.

The court has the power under s 68 of the Solicitors Act 1974 to order the solicitor to deliver up any papers to the client. The SRA also has a similar power where it has intervened in a solicitor's practice (see **7.8.2**).

Alternatively, a solicitor may apply to court under s 73 of the Solicitors Act 1974 for a charging order over any personal property of the client recovered or preserved by the solicitor within litigation proceedings. The charging order may cover the solicitor's taxed costs for those proceedings.

10.8 EXAMPLES

EXAMPLE 1

Question You are instructed by Mr Evans on behalf of his elderly mother. He instructs you to transfer his mother's house into his name. He gives you a letter purportedly from his mother confirming these instructions. He explains that her age means that she is unable to visit your office to speak with you in person.

Should you accept these instructions?

Answer There are two issues here. First, as you have received these instructions from a third party, it may tend to show that you have not achieved the relevant Outcomes if you act for Mrs Evans, unless you are satisfied that Mr Evans has the authority to give those instructions (Indicative Behaviour 1.25).

Secondly, the circumstances (Mrs Evans' age, the facts that she is gifting away a valuable asset and her absence from your office) should give reasonable grounds to suspect duress or undue influence. It may tend to show that you have not achieved the Outcomes if you act for Mrs Evans without satisfying yourself that the instructions represent her wishes (Indicative Behaviour 1.28). To do so, you would need to interview Mrs Evans away from her son and assess whether you believe she genuinely wishes to transfer her house to her son.

Where there is no actual evidence of undue influence but the client wants to act against his or her best interests, it would be advisable to explain the consequences of the instructions and ask the client whether he or she wishes to proceed, and for this advice and consent to be documented.

EXAMPLE 2

Question You have acted for Ms Caldicott for a number of years, and consider her to be a good client. You are currently dealing with the sale of one of her businesses. She contacts you to express her disappointment that your firm has recently been acting in defence of a large corporation accused of polluting a local river. On this basis she demands that you transfer her files to Jones & Co Solicitors. You do not consider that you have done anything wrong, and wish to dispute Ms Caldicott's right to transfer solicitors. Can you do this?

Answer No. A client can terminate at any time and for any reason. Whilst you have a right to claim a lien over Ms Caldicott's files until any outstanding bills are paid, previous SRA guidance suggests that you should accept an undertaking from Jones & Co to pay your costs rather than exercising this right.

SUMMARY

Acceptance of instructions

(1)   The solicitor must ensure that the client understands the extent of the retainer between the solicitor and client.

(2)   Where the solicitor receives instructions from a third party, it may tend to show that the client care Outcomes have not been achieved if he acts for the client, unless he is satisfied that the third party has the authority to issue instructions on behalf of all the clients.

Refusal of instructions

(1)   A solicitor's ability to accept or decline instructions is limited by the general law and the requirements of professional conduct.

(2)   It may tend to show that the client care Outcomes have not been achieved where a solicitor discriminates unlawfully when refusing instructions to act for a client.

Duty to the client during the retainer

(1)   The solicitor has a duty to act with reasonable skill and care when providing services (such as legal advice).

(2)   The solicitor has a fiduciary duty to act in the best interests of the client. Accordingly, a solicitor must not take advantage of his client.

(3)   A solicitor owes various duties to the client throughout the retainer, including a duty of confidentiality and a duty of disclosure.

(4)   A solicitor should not seek to rely on any implied authority to bind his client.

Termination of the retainer

(1)   The retainer may be terminated by either party, or by law.

(2)   The solicitor's right to terminate the retainer is restricted by the law and the requirements of professional conduct.

(3)   As a matter of good practice, a solicitor should deal promptly with the papers and property of the client within his possession. In certain circumstances a solicitor may exercise a lien over this property until his fees are paid.

CHAPTER 11

CLIENT CARE AND COSTS

LEARNING OUTCOMES

After reading this chapter you will be able to understand:

- the obligation to give the client information
- the controls which exist over the charges solicitors may make to their clients
- how a client may challenge the charges made by a solicitor
- the need to account to clients for commissions received.

11.1 INTRODUCTION

The marketplace for legal services is a very competitive area. From high street firms to large city firms, the competition to work for the best clients in a particular matter is often fierce.

Firms often spend large amounts of money on marketing budgets to attract clients. It is therefore in the firms' best interests to try to keep their clients from instructing other firms by providing a high level of service.

Where a client becomes dissatisfied with his solicitors, it is often due to a lack of information concerning issues such as costs or how the matter is progressing. Accordingly, Chapter 1 of the Code of Conduct sets out the minimum standards of service that a client can expect to receive.

The Code is not prescriptive on exactly how a firm should comply with the Outcomes in Chapter 1, as different types of law firms will have in place differing client care systems. Also, the Notes to Chapter 1 make clear that the information a solicitor gives to clients will vary according to the needs and circumstances of the individual client and the type of work the solicitor is doing for him. For example, a client providing instructions on a conveyancing matter is unlikely to need the same information as a sophisticated commercial client who instructs the firm on a regular basis.

The aim of Chapter 1 links in with Principle 5 of the Code: the solicitor must provide a proper standard of service to his clients. This includes a proper standard of client care.

11.2 CLIENT CARE – CHAPTER 1

11.2.1 Clients able to make informed decisions

A solicitor must ensure that clients are in a position to make informed decisions about the services they need, how their matter will be handled and the options available to them (Outcome 1.12).

As part of this process, it may tend to show that the Outcomes have been achieved where a solicitor discusses whether the potential outcomes of the client's matter are likely to justify the expense or risk involved, including any risk of having to pay someone else's legal fees (Indicative Behaviour 1.13). For example, a complaint from clients is often that they were unaware that it would cost so much to achieve so little.

11.2.2 Level of service

In general terms, a solicitor must treat his clients fairly (Outcome 1.1). The services offered by a solicitor to his clients must be provided in a manner which protects their interests in their matter, subject to the proper administration of justice (Outcome 1.2). The service provided must also be competent, delivered in a timely manner, and take accounts of a client's needs and circumstances (Outcome 1.5).

It may tend to show that the Outcomes have been achieved where a solicitor agrees an appropriate level of service with his client, for example the type and frequency of communications (Indicative Behaviour 1.1). Some clients may want to be updated in writing on a regular basis. On the other hand, a client may want to hear nothing from a solicitor until a certain stage of a transaction has been reached.

11.2.3 Responsibilities

Both the solicitor and client will have their own responsibilities during a matter. For example, one of the responsibilities of the solicitor could be to keep the client informed of progress and seek the client's instructions where required. The solicitor will also expect the client to keep him updated as the matter progresses. It may tend to show that the Outcomes have been achieved where these responsibilities are explained to the client (Indicative Behaviour 1.2); and although not a requirement of the Code, it would be prudent to have a written record of this information from the outset.

11.2.4 Status and supervision

By ensuring that a client is told, in writing, the name and status of the person(s) dealing with the matter, and the name of the person responsible for its overall supervision, a solicitor may tend to show that he has achieved the Outcomes relating to client care (Indicative Behaviour 1.3). Again, it would seem prudent to do this at the start of the matter.

11.2.5 Restrictions on acting

Where a client has been referred to the solicitor by a third party and/or because of the way the client's matter is funded, there may be conditions placed on how the solicitor may act for the client. For example, a client may be referred to a solicitor by the client's insurer. Under the terms of acting, the solicitor may not be able to issue proceedings without the authority of the insurer (who will be funding any such action). Accordingly, it may tend to show that the Outcomes have been achieved by the solicitor explaining any limitations or conditions on what he can do for the client (Indicative Behaviour 1.5).

However, a solicitor must ensure that his independence and professional judgement are not prejudiced by virtue of any arrangement with a third party, and he should advise a client in circumstances where such an arrangement is not a client's best interests (see **9.4.2**).

11.2.6 Information on regulation

Clients must be informed whether and how the services being provided are regulated and how this affects the protections available to the client (Outcome 1.7). For solicitors, the regulator will be the SRA and, in some circumstances, the Financial Conduct Authority (see **Chapter 17**). Further requirements are set out in Chapter 8 of the Code (see **9.3.2.3**).

11.3 INFORMATION ABOUT COSTS

11.3.1 Introduction

One of the most important issues for a client is the overall cost of legal services. When an individual goes into a shop to buy something, it is easy for that person to work out how much the thing will cost and therefore whether he wants to spend that amount of money on buying the product.

The provision of legal services often does not work in the same way. Nevertheless, the client must be given the best possible information as to the overall costs of the matter if he is to be able to make an informed decision about whether he wants to go ahead with it.

11.3.2 Best possible information

A solicitor is obliged to provide the client with the best possible information about the likely overall cost of a matter, both at the time of engagement and when appropriate as his matter progresses (Outcome 1.13).

As for how a solicitor can show that he has provided the best possible information about costs, the Indicative Behaviours in Chapter 1 of the Code provide some guidance. The solicitor clearly explaining his fees and if and when they are likely to change may tend to show that the Outcomes have been achieved (Indicative Behaviour 1.14). For example, the client may be charged a fixed fee, or by reference to an hourly charge-out rate. Another Indicative Behaviour is warning the client about any other payments for which he may be responsible (Indicative Behaviour 1.15). For example, when dealing with a residential conveyancing matter, the solicitor will be obliged to obtain details concerning the property from local authority and Land Registry searches. It may also tend to show that the Outcomes have been achieved if a solicitor ensures that disbursements included in his bill reflect the actual amount spent or to be spent on behalf of the client (Indicative Behaviour 1.21).

It will often be impossible to provide an accurate estimate of the overall cost of a matter at the start. However, just providing the client with details of the solicitor's charge-out rate will rarely be sufficient. For example, if the only information the solicitor provides to a client is that his charge-out rate will be £200 per hour, the client will not know whether he will have to pay £200 for the matter to be finished (if the solicitor puts in one hour's work) or £20,000 (if the solicitor puts in 100 hours' work).

If a precise figure is not possible, the SRA's previous guidance in the Code of Conduct 2007 suggested that the solicitor should explain why the precise figure cannot be given and agree either:

(a) a ceiling figure, above which the solicitor's costs cannot go, without the client's permission; or

(b) a review date when the parties will revisit the costs position.

The solicitor must not forget expressly to include VAT in any hourly rate or quote. For example, a solicitor may quote his hourly rate as £200 plus VAT. If the solicitor fails to quote with VAT, the price the client pays will be deemed to include VAT. Accordingly, if a solicitor were to say that his charge-out rate was £200 per hour, that would be all the client was liable to pay. The solicitor would have to pay the VAT element to the authorities from this £200, and would therefore lose out.

11.3.3 Funding arrangements

It may tend to show that the Outcomes in Chapter 1 have been achieved if a solicitor discusses how the client will pay for the legal services, including whether public funding may be available, whether the client has insurance that might cover the fees and whether fees may be paid by someone else, such as a trade union (Indicative Behaviour 1.16).

11.3.3.1 Publicly-funded work

Where a solicitor is acting for a publicly-funded client, it may tend to show that the relevant Outcomes have been achieved if the solicitor explains how the client's publicly-funded status affects the costs (Indicative Behaviour 1.18). This might include the following:

(a)   the effect of the statutory charge (ie, that the client may have to repay money to the Legal Aid Agency should the client recover or preserve any assets in proceedings);

(b)   that the client may have to pay a fixed or periodic contribution to the Legal Aid Agency, and the consequences of not doing so;

(c)   the circumstances in which the client may have to pay his own legal costs or the costs of the other party; and

(d)   that even if the client is successful, the other party may not be ordered to pay (or be able to pay) his costs in full.

11.3.4 Costs issues in litigation

By discussing whether the potential outcomes of the client's matter are likely to justify the expense or risk involved, it may tend to show that a solicitor has achieved the Outcomes in Chapter 1 of the Code (Indicative Behaviour 1.13). This would include discussing any risk of having to pay someone else's legal fees. For example, in litigation the client may be ordered to pay the costs of the winning party. The solicitor should consider whether these costs might be covered by insurance.

Regardless of any costs order the court may make in favour of the client concerning litigation, it would be good practice for the client to be advised that he may still be liable to pay his own solicitor's costs. For example, the amount that the losing party in litigation is ordered to pay to the winning party will be assessed by the court, and it is unlikely to cover the entirety of the winning client's legal costs. Where the solicitor wishes to charge the client for any such excess, the solicitor must have entered into a written agreement with the client to that effect (see CPR, r 48.8(1A)).

The client will also remain liable to pay his solicitor's costs where the losing party is unable to meet the costs order. Again, it would be good practice for this to be made clear to the client prior to starting any litigious proceedings.

11.3.5 Conditional fee arrangements

The Outcomes in Chapter 1 also apply to conditional fee arrangements (see **11.7.3**). Where a solicitor is acting under a conditional fee arrangement, it may tend to show that the Outcomes have been achieved if the solicitor gives the client all relevant information relating to that arrangement (Indicative Behaviour 1.17). For example, this might include explaining the circumstances in which the client will be liable to pay the solicitor's costs.

11.3.6 Form of costs information

It may tend to show that the relevant Outcomes in Chapter 1 have been achieved where the solicitor provides the costs information in a clear and accessible form which is appropriate to the needs and circumstances of the client (Indicative Behaviour 1.19). Although not a requirement, it would be prudent for this to be done in writing.

11.4 CLIENT CARE LETTER

Under the Solicitors' Code of Conduct 2007, a solicitor was obliged to provide the necessary client care information to a client in writing, and this was routinely done in the form of a letter sent out to the client after the first interview, known as the 'client care letter'. Although only information about the complaints procedure is now required to be in writing by the Outcomes in Chapter 1 (see **7.4**), it is likely that solicitors will continue to provide the client care information and the terms of the firm's retainer in the form of a letter to the client for the avoidance of doubt, and to help show compliance with the Outcomes and the Principles. Additional, but in many respects overlapping, obligations on the provision of information to clients are contained in the Provision of Services Regulations 2009 (SI 2009/2999) (for example, stating the firm's VAT number). As with the information specified in the Code, this will usually be provided in the client care letter.

11.5 CONSUMER CONTRACTS REGULATIONS 2013

Solicitors need to ensure that they comply with the Consumer Contracts (Information, Cancellation and Additional Charges) Regulations 2013 (SI 2013/3134). These apply to a wide range of contracts made between solicitors and their clients and would include a contract to carry out legal work for a client. The Regulations distinguish between 'on-premises' and 'off-premises' contracts. Whilst most contracts will be concluded between a solicitor and his client at the solicitor's place of business ('on-premises'), there may be situations which will result in the contract falling within the definition of an 'off-premises' contract, for example where a solicitor visits a client at home and the client offers to engage him to carry out legal work. Even if the offer is accepted by the solicitor telephoning the client from his office the next day, this would be considered an 'off-premises' contract.

The Regulations specify that certain pieces of information must be provided to clients before they enter into the contract. Much of the information that solicitors are required to provide under the Regulations is likely to be included in their client care letter; however, the information required varies depending on what type of contract it is. For example, where a client has agreed to an 'off-premises' contract, he must additionally be informed that he has the right to cancel it without giving any reason or incurring any liability during the cancellation period (which in most cases is 14 days beginning on the date after the contract is entered into). Failure to do so is an offence under the Regulations. For this reason, solicitors need to ensure that if they are likely to enter into contracts in different types of circumstances, their standard letters contain any additional information required under the Regulations. Legal aid contracts do not fall within the Regulations.

11.6 FEES AND COSTS

11.6.1 Introduction

The retainer between the solicitor and client is a contract, and so the fees and charges the solicitor will levy for acting for the client will be agreed between the parties at the start of the retainer. However, restrictions are placed upon the fees a solicitor may charge, and also upon how the solicitor will be remunerated by the SRA and the general law. The rest of this chapter offers a summary of the main provisions; it is not intended to be a comprehensive guide.

These restrictions vary depending upon what type of work the solicitor has agreed to carry out for the client. A distinction is made between 'contentious' business and 'non-contentious' business. This distinction is particularly relevant when considering whether, and how, a client can challenge the bill of a solicitor.

11.6.2 Contentious business

Contentious business is defined as 'business done, whether as a solicitor or an advocate, in or for the purposes of proceedings begun before a court or an arbitrator, not being business which falls within the definition of non-contentious business or common form probate business' (Solicitors Act 1974, s 87). Accordingly, contentious business is work done in relation to proceedings. However, contentious business starts only once proceedings have been issued.

For example, a client may seek the advice of a solicitor with a view to suing his previous firm for negligence. The solicitor advises that the client should start proceedings, but suggests that a letter is sent to the previous firm beforehand, giving that firm seven days to offer appropriate compensation. The client is clearly contemplating litigious proceedings, but if the firm makes an acceptable offer before proceedings are issued, the solicitor's work will be classified as non-contentious.

11.6.3 Non-contentious business

Non-contentious business is defined as 'any business done as a solicitor which is not contentious business' (Solicitors Act 1974, s 87). This includes obvious examples such as conveyancing or commercial drafting work. The definition also includes all proceedings before tribunals, except the Lands Tribunal and the Employment Appeals Tribunal.

Non-contentious business is governed by the Solicitors' (Non-Contentious Business) Remuneration Order 2009 (SI 2009/1931).

11.7 OPTIONS AVAILABLE FOR SOLICITOR'S FEES

A solicitor may agree to charge a client for work done on a number of different bases. Some of these options are considered below. Whichever method of charging the client and solicitor agree, the overall amount of the charge will be regulated by statute and so the client may be able to challenge the bill at a later date (see **11.10**). It may tend to show that the Outcomes in Chapter 1 of the Code have been achieved if the solicitor clearly explains his fees (however charged) and if and when they are likely to change (Indicative Behaviour 1.14).

11.7.1 Hourly rate

Perhaps the most common method of charging clients is by use of an hourly rate, ie the client is charged for the time spent on the file. The client is informed at the start of the matter which fee earner will be working on the client's files, and the fee earner's respective charge-out rates. However, in order to achieve the Outcome that the client receive the best possible information about the overall cost of the matter (Outcome 1.13), it is unlikely that merely giving an hourly rate will be acceptable (see **11.3.2**).

11.7.2 Fixed fee

Alternatively a solicitor may agree to complete the work for a fixed fee, or a fixed fee plus VAT and disbursements. Fixed fees are often used for conveyancing transactions. If the solicitor agrees to act in return for a fixed fee, this fee cannot be altered at a later date (unless the client agrees) if the work turns out to be more expensive than the solicitor first expected.

11.7.3 Variable fees

A solicitor is permitted, in certain circumstances, to charge a fee which varies according to the outcome of the matter. One such example of a variable fee is a contingency fee. However, a solicitor must only enter fee agreements that are legal, and which he considers are suitable for the client's needs and take account of the client's best interests (Outcome 1.6; see also Indicative Behaviour 1.27).

Agreements which are permitted by law are conditional fee agreements (CFAs) and damages-based agreements (DBAs). An example of a conditional fee agreement is the 'no win, no fee' basis of charging that is popular in areas of work such as personal injury. Under such an agreement, the solicitor may agree to charge nothing if the client loses, but will charge his fees plus an agreed 'uplift' (or 'success fee', for example an extra 20%) in the event of success.

In respect of litigation or advocacy services, a solicitor may enter into (and enforce) a CFA if it complies with s 58 of the Courts and Legal Services Act 1990 (see also the Conditional Fee Agreements Order 2013 (SI 2013/689)). For example, the agreement must be in writing, signed by both the solicitor and the client, and, where a success fee is to be paid, specify the percentage of the success fee. The success fee cannot exceed a percentage specified by the Lord Chancellor (currently 100% uplift in the normal hourly charge rate, with the exception of personal injury cases where the cap is 25% of general damages recovered). The solicitor must carry out a proper risk assessment to calculate the amount of the success fee. A solicitor cannot enter into a CFA for any criminal work or family proceedings.

The CFA must also comply with any additional requirements specified by the SRA (see also **11.3.5**) and the Consumer Contracts (Information, Cancellation and Additional Charges) Regulations 2013 (see **11.5**). To aid compliance, The Law Society has published a model CFA for use by the profession.

If a client instructs a solicitor on a CFA (for example, on a 'no win, no fee' basis), this does not mean that the client will not have to pay any legal costs if he loses the case. Although he may not be liable to pay his solicitor's fees, he will usually have to pay disbursements such as court fees, barristers' fees and VAT. The client may also have to pay his opponent's costs. A solicitor should explore whether the client can obtain insurance to cover these costs in the event of losing the case (known as after-the-event insurance). He should also ask whether the client has before-the-event insurance which will cover the costs.

Following recommendations made by Lord Justice Jackson, significant changes have been introduced in respect of the costs of civil litigation, including CFAs. These changes have been effective since 1 April 2013, when the relevant provisions of the Legal Aid, Sentencing and Punishment of Offenders Act 2012 came into force. For example, with a few exceptions, the success fee and after-the-event insurance premiums will now be paid by the client, not the other side, if the client is successful.

A DBA (defined by s 58AA(3)(a) of the Courts and Legal Services Act 1990 and covered by the Damages-Based Agreements Regulations 2013 (SI 2013/609)) provides that, if the client recovers damages, the solicitor's fee is an agreed percentage of those damages. The DBA must not provide for a payment above an amount which, including VAT, is equal to 50% of the sums ultimately recovered by the client. Also, personal injury cases are subject to a cap of 25% of the general damages recovered. The points made above in respect of combining a CFA with after-the-event insurance cover (or before-the-event insurance cover) apply equally to a DBA.

A solicitor may enter into a contingency fee arrangement in respect of non-contentious work, but to be enforceable this must be in the form of a non-contentious business agreement (see **11.11**).

11.7.4 Other methods

A solicitor may agree to be remunerated by some other means. One such example would be a solicitor agreeing to accept shares in a new company in return for his work, rather than costs. However, in such circumstances the client should be advised to seek independent advice about such a costs agreement.

11.8 MONEY ON ACCOUNT

It is common for a solicitor to require a client to pay a sum of money to the solicitor at the start of the transaction on account of the costs and disbursements that will be incurred.

In contentious business, a solicitor may require a client to pay a reasonable sum to the solicitor on account of costs. If the client does not pay this money within a reasonable time, the solicitor may terminate the retainer (Solicitors Act 1974, s 65(2)).

There is no such statutory right in non-contentious business. Accordingly, where the solicitor requires money on account before starting a matter, the solicitor should make this a requirement of the retainer.

11.9 SOLICITOR'S BILL

11.9.1 Introduction

For a solicitor to be able to obtain payment from the client, certain formalities need to be complied with in respect of the solicitor's bill. These matters include (but are not limited to) the following:

(a) The bill must contain enough information for the client to be satisfied that the bill is reasonable, and also provide details of the period to which the bill relates.

(b) The bill must be signed by the solicitor or on his behalf by an employee authorised to do so. Alternatively, the solicitor/authorised employee may sign a covering letter which refers to the bill (Solicitors Act 1974, s 69(2A)).

(c) The bill must be delivered by hand to the client, by post to his home, business address or last known address, or by e-mail if the client has agreed to this method and provided an appropriate e-mail address (Solicitors Act 1974, s 69(2C)).

11.9.2 Interim bills

A solicitor may wish to bill his client for work done on the client's file before the matter has completed. This will particularly be the case where the client's matter is likely to go on for some months, such as protracted litigation. A solicitor may wish to issue interim bills throughout the matter.

There are two different types of interim bills. The first type are known as interim 'statute bills' because they comply with the provisions of the Solicitors Act 1974. Although they are interim bills, they are also self-contained final bills in respect of the work covered by them. Consequently, the solicitor may sue the client for non-payment of such bills and the client may apply to have them assessed by the court (see **11.10.1**). However, interim statute bills are rare and may arise during the retainer in only two ways:

(a) there is authority for issuing such bills in a 'natural break' in lengthy proceedings, but there is little authority as to what will actually amount to a natural break, and so this should perhaps be avoided as a basis for statute bills except in the clearest of cases;

(b) by agreement with the client, and The Law Society recommends that this right should be expressly reserved within the retainer. The Law Society's guidance provides that the solicitor must specify the time-limit within which the client must pay the interim bill, and must also expressly reserve the right to terminate the retainer in the event of non-payment.

The second, and more common, type of interim bill is the 'bill on account'. Such bills are effectively requests for payments on account of the final bill which will be delivered at the end of the matter/retainer. An advantage of this type of interim bill is that it does not need to represent the final figure for costs in respect of the work covered by it, so that when preparing his statute bill at the end of the matter the solicitor can assess a fair overall costs figure for all of the work done since the start of the retainer. However, unlike with an interim statute bill, a solicitor is unable to sue the client for non-payment of such a bill, and the client cannot apply to have the bill assessed. If the client does not pay the bill on account within a reasonable time then in contentious business the solicitor may terminate the receiver under s 65(2) of the Solicitors Act 1974 (see **11.8**). In the event that the client regards the amount of the bill as excessive, he can request that the solicitor issues a statute bill which he may then apply to have assessed by the court.

11.9.3 Interest on bills

In a non-contentious matter a solicitor may charge interest on the whole or the outstanding part of an unpaid bill with effect from one month after delivery of the bill, provided that notice of the client's right to challenge the bill has been given to him. The rate of interest chargeable must not exceed that which is payable on judgment debts. At the time of writing the rate is currently 8%.

In contentious business, The Law Society's guidance provides that a solicitor may charge interest on an unpaid bill where the solicitor expressly reserves this right in the retainer, or the client later agrees for a 'contractual consideration' to pay interest. Alternatively, where a solicitor sues the client for non-payment of fees, the court has the power to award the solicitor interest on the debt under s 35A of the Senior Courts Act 1981 or s 69 of the County Courts Act 1984.

The rate of interest will be the rate payable for judgment debts unless the solicitor and client expressly agree a different rate.

11.9.4 Enforcement

Subject to certain exceptions, a solicitor may not commence any claim to recover any costs due to the solicitor (such as suing the client) until one month has passed since the solicitor delivered his bill (Solicitors Act 1974, s 69). The bill must also be in the proper form (see **11.9.1**).

However, the High Court has the power under s 69 to allow the solicitor to commence such a claim against the client within this one-month period where the court is satisfied that the client is about to leave the country, be declared bankrupt (or enter into a composition with his creditors), or do anything else which would prevent or delay the solicitor obtaining his fees.

11.10 CLIENT'S RIGHT TO CHALLENGE THE BILL

The client may challenge the amount of a solicitor's bill, provided that he complies with certain requirements. These requirements depend upon how the client wishes to go about challenging the bill.

11.10.1 Assessment by the court

A client may apply to have his bill assessed by the court in both contentious and non-contentious proceedings. This is sometimes referred to as a bill being 'taxed'.

The client must apply to have the bill assessed within one month from the date of delivery. Where no application is made within this month, the client may still apply within 12 months of delivery, but will require the leave of the court for the bill to be assessed (Solicitors Act 1974, s 70).

The costs will be assessed by a judge or district judge sitting as a 'costs officer'. The costs officer has the power to assess the fees and disbursements of the solicitor.

The costs will (with certain exceptions) be assessed on an 'indemnity basis'. The court will allow only costs that have been reasonably incurred by the solicitor and which are reasonable in amount. Any doubt as to what is to be considered reasonable is resolved in the favour of the solicitor. However, the client may be ordered to pay the costs of the solicitor arising from the assessment process.

11.10.1.1 Non-contentious proceedings

Where a court is asked to assess a solicitor's bill in non-contentious proceedings, in deciding what is reasonable, the court must have regard to the following circumstances (Solicitors' (Non-Contentious Business) Remuneration Order 2009):

(a)   the complexity of the matter, or the difficulty or novelty of the questions raised;

(b)   the skill, labour, specialised knowledge and responsibility involved;

(c)   the time spent on the business;

(d)   the number and importance of the documents prepared or considered, without regard to length;

(e)   the place where and the circumstances in which the business or any part thereof is transacted;

(f)   the amount or value of any money or property involved;

(g)   whether any land involved is registered;

(h)   the importance of the matter to the client; and

(i)   the approval (express or implied) of the entitled person, or the express approval of the testator, to:

    (i)   the solicitor undertaking all or any part of the work giving rise to the costs, or

    (ii)   the amount of the costs.

11.10.1.2 Contentious proceedings

The factors the court must take into account when considering whether costs are reasonable are set out in CPR, r 44.5. These include (but are not limited to):

(a)   the conduct of the parties;

(b)   the amount or value of any money or property involved;

(c)   the importance of the matter to the parties;

(d)   the particular complexity of the matter, or the difficulty or novelty of the questions raised;

(e)   the skill, effort, specialised knowledge and responsibility involved;

(f)   the time spent on the case; and

(g)   the place where and the circumstances in which work, or any part of it, was done.

Subject to certain exceptions, a client cannot apply for an assessment of costs where the solicitor and client have entered into a contentious business agreement (see **11.12**).

11.10.2 Using the firm's complaints procedure

Solicitors must ensure that clients are informed of their right to challenge or complain about their bills (Outcome 1.14).

If the client is not satisfied with the firm's response, he may complain to the Legal Ombudsman. The Legal Ombudsman may then limit the solicitor's fees by, for example, directing the solicitor to refund all or part of any amount paid, or to remit all or part of his fees (see **Chapter 7** generally).

Further, the firm must also inform the client of the circumstances in which he may be liable to pay interest on an unpaid bill (Outcome 1.14)

11.11 NON-CONTENTIOUS BUSINESS AGREEMENTS

A solicitor and client may enter into a non-contentious business agreement in respect of the solicitor's remuneration for any non-contentious work. Under this agreement the solicitor may be remunerated by a gross sum, commission, a percentage, a salary, or otherwise.

To be enforceable, the agreement must comply with s 57 of the Solicitors Act 1974. For example, the agreement must:

(a)   be in writing;

(b)   be signed by the client;

(c)   contain all the terms of the agreement (including whether disbursements and VAT are included in the agreed remuneration).

Where the relevant provisions have been complied with, the client will be unable to apply to have his bill assessed by the court. However, the court may set the agreement aside if the amount charged by the solicitor is unfair or unreasonable.

11.12 CONTENTIOUS BUSINESS AGREEMENTS

A solicitor may enter into a contentious business agreement in respect of his remuneration for contentious work completed on behalf of the client (see Solicitors Act 1974, ss 59–63).

The agreement may provide for the solicitor to be remunerated by reference to a gross sum, an hourly rate, a salary or otherwise. However, the solicitor may not be remunerated by a contingency fee.

In order to be enforceable, the agreement must comply with certain requirements, including:

(a)   the agreement must state it is a contentious business agreement;

(b)   the agreement must be in writing;

(c)   the agreement must be signed by the client; and

(d)   the agreement must contain all the terms.

Where the contentious business agreement is enforceable, the client will be unable to apply to court for an assessment of costs (except where the agreement provides that the solicitor is to be remunerated by reference to an hourly rate.) However, the court may set aside the agreement if it is unfair or unreasonable.

11.13 OVERCHARGING

A solicitor must act in the best interests of the client and must treat his clients fairly. Therefore a solicitor must not overcharge for work done. Where a costs officer (when assessing a solicitor's bill in a non-contentious matter) reduces the amount of the costs by more than 50%, he must inform the SRA. Overcharging the client will be considered a breach of professional conduct.

11.14 COMMISSION

The solicitor–client relationship is a fiduciary relationship (see **10.4.3**), and so a solicitor must not make a secret profit whilst acting for the client. Outcome 1.15 of the Code obliges a solicitor to account to a client properly for any financial benefit he receives as a result of the client's instructions. The term 'financial benefit' includes any commission, discount or rebate (*Handbook* Glossary).

For example, a client may require specialist tax advice, and so may be referred by the solicitor to a tax consultant. The tax consultant may pay the solicitor commission in return for this referral.

Indicative Behaviour 1.20, which is relevant to a solicitor showing that he has achieved Outcome 1.15, states that where a solicitor receives a financial benefit as a result of acting for a client, it may tend to show that he has achieved the Outcomes if he either:

(a)   pays it to the client; or

(b)   offsets it against his fees; or

(c)   keeps it only where he can justify keeping it, and he has told the client the amount of the benefit (or an approximation of the amount) and the client has agreed that he can keep it.

Where the solicitor is carrying out an exempt regulated activity in respect of financial services (see **Chapter 17**), the solicitor must consider s 327 of the Financial Services and Markets Act 2000. Accordingly, to comply with s 327(3), the solicitor must likewise account to the client for all commission received.

11.15 EXAMPLE

Question	You have just submitted your final bill to Mr Waugh in respect of a partnership dispute. You managed to resolve the matter without having to issue proceedings. The next day you receive a call from Mr Waugh who claims your bill (£7,000 plus VAT) is too high.
	Assuming that your bill complies with the relevant formalities, what options are available to Mr Waugh to challenge your bill?
Answer	Mr Waugh has two options:

(a)   Assessment by the court

Mr Waugh has one month from receiving the bill to apply to have his bill assessed by the court (failing that, within 12 months from receiving the bill, but only with the court's leave). Both you and Mr Waugh will be bound by the results.

(b)   Using the firm's complaints procedure

Mr Waugh could make a formal complaint about the bill in accordance with the firm's complaint's procedure. If he is not satisfied with the firm's response he may complain to the Legal Ombudsman. In the event that the Legal Ombudsman makes a final determination about the bill (which can include a direction that you remit all or part of your fees) which is accepted by Mr Waugh, it will be binding on both of you.

SUMMARY

Client care

(1)   A solicitor must achieve the Outcomes on client care prescribed by the SRA in Chapter 1 of the Code.

(2)   The solicitor must ensure that clients are in a position to make informed decisions about the services they need, how their matter will be handled and the options available to them.

(3)   The solicitor must inform clients in writing of their right to complain to the Legal Ombudsman, both at the time of engagement and at the conclusion of the firm's complaint procedure.

(4)   Clients must be treated fairly.

Information about costs

(1)   A solicitor must give his client the best possible information as to the likely overall costs of a matter, both at the outset and when appropriate as the client's matter progresses.

(2)   It may tend to show that the relevant Outcomes have been achieved if a solicitor clearly explains his fees and if and when they are likely to change.

(3)   Providing information about costs in a clear and accessible form which is appropriate to the client's needs and circumstances may tend to show that the Outcomes in Chapter 1 have been achieved.

Fees and costs

(1)   A solicitor and client may agree the level of costs the solicitor may charge. However, this agreement is regulated by statute and the common law.

(2)   A distinction is made between costs in contentious matters and costs in non-contentious matters.

(3)   A solicitor's bill must contain prescribed information in order for the bill to be enforceable.

(4)   A client may challenge the costs of a solicitor both in contentious and non-contentious proceedings.

(5)   Generally, a solicitor may not sue to recover his costs from the client until one month has elapsed since the bill was delivered.

CHAPTER 12

CONFIDENTIALITY

LEARNING OUTCOMES

After reading this chapter you will be able to understand:

- the nature and extent of the duty of confidentiality
- the duty to disclose relevant information to the client
- legal professional privilege.

12.1 DUTY OF CONFIDENTIALITY

You [must] keep the affairs of clients confidential unless disclosure is required or permitted by law or the client consents. (Outcome 4.1 of the Code)

12.1.1 Introduction

Confidentiality is a fundamental principle of the solicitor–client relationship. For example, it is important that a solicitor receives all the relevant information from a client in order to give the best possible advice. A client would be dissuaded from informing his solicitor of all the relevant facts if he thought that this information would be released to the public. However, the obligation of confidentiality extends beyond obviously confidential information given to a solicitor by his client and includes all information about a client or matter, regardless of the source of that information. Solicitors must have in place effective systems and controls to enable risks to client confidentiality to be identified and to mitigate these risks (Outcome 4.5).

This duty will continue after the retainer has been terminated. Accordingly, a solicitor will owe a duty of confidentiality to former, as well as existing, clients. The duty also continues after the death of the client, whereupon the right to enforce or waive the duty of confidentiality is passed to the client's (or former client's) personal representatives. All members of a firm, including support staff, owe a duty of confidentiality to clients of the firm.

It may tend to show that the Outcomes have been achieved where the solicitor complies with the law in respect of his fiduciary duties in relation to both confidentiality and disclosure (Indicative Behaviour 4.2). Any breach of the duty of confidentiality will be a breach of professional conduct. The solicitor may be disciplined by the SRA, or by the Solicitors Disciplinary Tribunal (see **Chapter 7**). In addition, the client (or former client) may sue the solicitor for any breach of this duty.

The Outcomes and Indicative Behaviours concerning confidentiality are contained in Chapter 4 of the Code.

examples

Indicative Behaviours in Chapter 4 of the Code include specific examples which may tend to show that a solicitor has not achieved the Outcomes relating to the duty of confidentiality:

(a) disclosing the content of a will on the death of a client (including a former client), unless consent has been provided by the PRs for the content to be released (Indicative Behaviour 4.6);

(b) disclosing details of bills sent to clients (including former clients) to third parties, such as debt-factoring companies in relation to the collection of book debts, unless the client has consented (Indicative Behaviour 4.7).

A solicitor will have to take various practical steps to safeguard the identity of his clients. For example, he will have a file, or files, for particular clients and the client's name (and often address and type of matter, such as divorce) may be written on the file. If a solicitor routinely interviews clients at his desk, steps should be taken to ensure that the covers of these files are not left where they could be read by any other clients.

A number of solicitors' firms use the names of their clients in their marketing and publicity to illustrate the quality of clients that instruct their firm. Where solicitors wish to use the names of their clients in marketing materials, they must obtain the consent of these clients beforehand.

The Notes to Chapter 4 indicate that the protection of confidential information may be at particular risk where two or more firms merge and where an individual leaves one firm and joins another.

12.1.3 Where confidential information may be disclosed

Although no specific examples are contained in the Code as to when confidential information may be disclosed in the absence of the client's consent, there are circumstances in which disclosure is permitted by law. By way of example:

(a) pursuant to a statutory requirement, eg to HMRC in certain circumstances;

(b) pursuant to a statutory duty, such as in the Proceeds of Crime Act 2002 and the Money Laundering Regulations 2007 (see **Chapter 15**), and under the terrorism legislation;

(c) under a court order, or where a police warrant permits the seizure of confidential documentation.

If a solicitor is uncertain as to whether to disclose the confidential information, he should consider taking legal advice or contact the Professional Ethics Guidance Team. The solicitor must also bear in mind legal professional privilege (see **12.4**).

The SRA has also published ethics guidance which sets out examples of circumstances which, although still technically amount to a breach of the duty of confidentiality, may be taken into account as mitigation in the context of disciplinary action. It should be noted that none of them allows for disclosure after the event. The main examples set out in the guidance are as follows:

(a) *Where a client has indicated their intention to commit suicide or serious self-harm.* The SRA advises that, in the first instance, the solicitor should consider seeking consent from the client to disclose that information to a third party (for example, a ward nurse where the client is in hospital) but, where this is not possible or appropriate, the solicitor may decide to disclose the information to the relevant person or authority without consent in order to protect the client or another person.

(b) *Preventing harm to children or vulnerable adults.* This covers situations where the child or adult indicates that they are suffering sexual or other abuse, or where the client discloses abuse either by themselves or by another adult against a child or vulnerable adult. Whilst there is no requirement in law to disclose this information, the solicitor may consider that the threat to the person's life or health is sufficiently serious to justify a breach of the duty of confidentiality.

(c) *Preventing the commission of a criminal offence.* At common law there is no confidence in information of an iniquitous nature and so, if a solicitor is being used by a client to perpetrate a fraud or any other crime, the duty of confidentiality does not arise. In other circumstances, a breach may be mitigated where disclosure is made to the extent that the solicitor believes it necessary to prevent the client or a third party from committing a criminal act that the solicitor believes, on reasonable grounds, is likely to result in serious bodily harm.

12.1.4 Use of confidential material received by mistake

Due to the volume of information which passes between solicitors on a daily basis, occasionally mistakes may be made and information destined for a third party may be inadvertently disclosed to a solicitor. For example, a solicitor acting for one party in a matter may mis-address correspondence destined for his client to the solicitor acting for the other party. In this case, immediately on becoming aware of the error, the receiving solicitor must return the papers to the originating solicitor without reading them or otherwise making use of the information contained therein (*Ablitt v Mills & Reeve* (1995) *The Times*, 25 October).

12.2 DUTY OF DISCLOSURE

Any individual within a firm who is advising a client must make that client aware of all information material to that retainer of which the individual has personal knowledge (Outcome 4.2).

12.2.1 Limitations

In spite of the absolute terms of Outcome 4.2, Indicative Behaviour 4.4 sets out specific exceptions to the requirement to disclose all information material to the client's matter of which the solicitor is personally aware, and by observing these a solicitor may tend to show that he has achieved the relevant Outcomes:

(a) the client gives specific informed consent to non-disclosure or a different standard of disclosure arises. (It should be noted, however, that a solicitor should consider issues such as professional embarrassment (see **12.3.5**) prior to agreeing a different (ie lower) standard of disclosure);

(b) there is evidence that serious physical or mental injury will be caused to a person or persons if the information is disclosed to the client;

(c) legal restrictions effectively prohibit the solicitor from passing the information to the client, such as the provisions in the money laundering and anti-terrorism legislation;

(d) it is obvious that privileged documents have been mistakenly disclosed to the solicitor;

(e) the solicitor comes into possession of information relating to State security or intelligence matters to which the Official Secrets Act 1989 applies.

12.2.2 Duty of confidentiality overrides duty of disclosure

The duty of disclosure will often conflict with the duty of confidentiality. Consider the following situation:

> **EXAMPLE**
>
> Mr Smith instructs a solicitor to purchase a derelict plot of land from X Limited in order for him to build a new house. Another one of the solicitor's clients, Mrs Brown, sold the land to X Limited two years ago at a knock-down price as the land is contaminated. This information would be relevant to Mr Smith and so the solicitor would owe a duty to disclose the information to him. However, to do so would be to breach the solicitor's duty of confidentiality to Mrs Brown, even though the solicitor has completed the work for Mrs Brown and she no longer owns the land.

In situations such as this, your duty of confidentiality always takes precedence over your duty of disclosure (Outcome 4.3). The solicitor could tell Mr Smith only if Mrs Brown waived her confidentiality in respect of the information.

12.3   PLACING CONFIDENTIAL INFORMATION AT RISK

12.3.1   Introduction

In order to protect against any accidental disclosure, the Code provides that a solicitor (or firm) must not act in certain circumstances.

A solicitor must act in the best interests of the client and so must not place himself in a situation where any relevant information could be disclosed to another client, as any such disclosure would be against the best interests of the client to whom the solicitor owes a duty of confidentiality.

Accordingly, it may tend to show that the Outcomes have been achieved by a firm not acting for A where B is a client (including a former client) for whom it holds confidential information which is material to A, unless the confidential information can be protected (Indicative Behaviour 4.5). For examples of safeguards, see **12.3.4.1**.

In addition, a firm must not act for A in a matter where A has an interest which is adverse to B and B is a client (including a former client) for whom the firm holds confidential information which is material to A in that matter, unless the confidential information can be protected by the use of safeguards and certain other requirements are met (Outcome 4.4).

12.3.2   Is the information material?

For the purposes of Outcome 4.4 and Indicative Behaviour 4.5, the confidential information must be 'material'. The SRA's previous guidance in the Code of Conduct 2007 defined this as information which is:

(a)   relevant to your client's matter; and

(b)   of more than inconsequential interest to the client (ie, will the decision affect the client's decision-making?).

The question of whether the information is 'material' relates to the client to whom the duty of disclosure concerning the information is owed. In the example at **12.2.2**, the solicitor would need to consider whether the information that Mrs Brown provided to the firm is relevant to Mr Smith's land purchase (eg, Mr Smith will need to be advised to try to reduce the price). If so, this information would be 'material' to Mr Smith.

12.3.3   Do the clients have an 'adverse' interest?

For the purposes of Outcome 4.4, the interests of the clients must be 'adverse'. Adversity relates to the relationship between two respective clients. The previous SRA guidance in the Code of Conduct 2007 provided that this relationship will be said to be adverse where the client to whom the firm owes the duty of confidentiality is, or is likely to become, an opposing party in a matter to the client who is owed the duty of disclosure.

This would include a situation where the clients litigate against each other, are involved in mediation, or even if the clients are on opposing sides of a negotiation.

12.3.4 When it is possible to act under Outcome 4.4

Where the same individual within a firm holds confidential information for one party which is relevant to another client, that particular solicitor will be unable to act for both clients unless a client agrees to a lesser duty of disclosure. This will be regardless of whether the two clients have an interest adverse to each other. This is because that individual owes a personal duty of disclosure to his clients.

However, Outcome 4.4 provides that where a firm holds confidential information for one client (B), which is material to another client (A), and A has an interest adverse to B, the firm may still act for the client to whom the duty of disclosure is owed (ie A) if the confidential information can be protected by use of safeguards and the following requirements are met:

(a) the firm reasonably believes that A is aware of, and understands, the relevant issues and gives informed consent; and

(b) either B gives informed consent and the firm agrees with B the safeguards to protect B's information, or, where this is not possible, the firm puts in place effective safeguards, including information barriers which comply with common law; and

(c) it is reasonable in all the circumstances to act for A with such safeguards in place.

12.3.4.1 Information barriers

Safeguards include information barriers, which are practical steps taken to ensure that confidential information cannot pass from one client to another client. These steps were previously referred to within the profession as 'Chinese walls'. On a practical level they aim to prevent confidential information, given by a client to one part of a firm, from being made available to another part of the same firm.

The SRA, in its previous guidance in the Code of Conduct 2007, set out a number of measures which will normally be appropriate to protect confidential information by this method, and these will presumably remain pertinent to achieving the Outcomes in the current Code. These measures include the acknowledgement in writing by a client who might be interested in the confidential information that the information held by the firm will not be given to him. Also, that all members of the firm who hold the relevant confidential information are identified, have no involvement with the other client and must not discuss the information with anyone else in the firm.

Practical arrangements may also be appropriate. For example, in the case of current clients, that the groups acting for each of the clients affected are physically separated from each other (eg, in separate buildings or on separate floors), that confidential information on computer systems is protected by use of separate computer networks or password protection, and that the firm has systems in place for the opening of post, faxes and e-mails that ensure that the information is not disclosed to the other group.

It will be noted from the situation covered in (b) in **12.3.4** above, that where it is not possible to agree effective safeguards with the client to whom the duty of confidentiality is owed, it is still possible to act if the firm puts in place effective safeguards, including information barriers, which comply with the standards that are required by law at the time they are put in place. These standards will be established by case law.

Given the nature of the safeguards, information barriers will not be appropriate in every situation. Indeed the Notes to Chapter 4 of the Code make it clear that the following circumstances may make it difficult to implement effective safeguards and information barriers:

(a) the firm is small;

(b)   the physical structure or layout of the firm means that it will be difficult to preserve confidentiality; or

(c)   the clients are not sophisticated users of legal services.

12.3.4.2   Informed consent

In broad terms, the client(s) must consent after having understood and considered the risks and rewards involved in the situation. The SRA's previous guidance in the Code of Conduct 2007 indicated that one of the difficulties with seeking such consent is that it is often not possible to disclose sufficient information about the identity and business of the other client without breaching that other client's confidentiality. It would be for the firm to decide in each case whether it would be able to provide sufficient information for the client to be able to give 'informed consent'.

The SRA considered that 'informed consent' would generally be of use only to 'sophisticated clients', such as large companies with in-house legal advisers or other expertise, who would be able to assess the risks of giving their consent based on the information provided, and there is no reason to doubt that this will continue to be the case under the Code.

The exception allowing solicitors to act where they are holding confidential information will rarely be of use to, for example, matrimonial clients or personal injury clients.

12.3.4.3   Is it reasonable to act?

Lastly, the firm of solicitors must consider whether it would be reasonable to act for the new client (or to continue to act for two existing clients) in all the circumstances. The following example is based upon one given by the SRA's previous guidance notes in the Code of Conduct 2007:

> Shepherd Co Limited approaches your firm to act for it in the purchase of Derkin Co Limited. Derkin Co Limited is a former client of your firm and when acting for Derkin Co your firm obtained confidential information that the company has millions of pounds missing from its accounts. Even if the rules permitted your firm to act for Shepherd Co, your firm must consider whether it would be reasonable to act given the knowledge that the firm holds. You could not disclose the information to Shepherd Co due to your duty of confidentiality to Derkin Co.

12.3.5   Professional embarrassment

Even where Outcome 4.4 and Indicative Behaviour 4.5 would allow a firm to act for two clients, where the firm held confidential information for one client that was material to the other client's matter, a solicitor might still be obliged to refuse to act on the grounds of professional embarrassment.

A firm should decline to act where the information which it cannot disclose to the client would cause severe embarrassment to the firm if the fact that it had agreed to act in those circumstances ever came out.

The SRA's previous guidance in the Code of Conduct 2007 provided an example in which a firm agrees to act for a company to draft a contract of employment for a prospective employee, where the firm knows (but is unable to disclose to the client due to confidentiality) that the prospective employee is under investigation for fraud. The embarrassment here would stem from the fact that the firm would know that the client seeking to employ the prospective employee was wasting legal fees on an outcome that (if it knew all the facts) it would not wish to pursue.

The firm should also consider the Principles, such as whether it will be able to act in the best interests of the client in question, and public trust in the legal profession. Acting in the above situation would clearly not be in the best interests of the client, and arguably would also damage the reputation of the profession.

12.3.5.1 Example

Adapting the example at **12.2.2**, Mr Smith instructs a firm of solicitors to purchase a plot of derelict land. Mrs Brown, also a client of the firm, had previously sold the land and had informed another solicitor at the firm that the land was contaminated. The information is material to Mr Smith's matter – information concerning the state of the land is relevant to whether Mr Smith will want to buy it. However, the two clients' interests are not adverse to one another. There is no suggestion that Mr Smith and Mrs Brown are likely to be on opposing sides of a particular matter. Therefore, subject to any conflicts of interest, and providing the confidential information could be protected, the Code would not prevent the firm acting for both parties. However, the firm could not inform Mr Smith of the contamination – the firm's duty of confidentiality to Mrs Brown would remain. Nevertheless, the firm should decline instructions on the basis of professional embarrassment.

12.4 CONFIDENTIALITY AND PRIVILEGE

The obligation of confidentiality which a solicitor owes to his client is distinct from the issue of legal professional privilege. While confidentiality prevents a solicitor from disclosing any information relating to a client without that client's consent, legal professional privilege allows a solicitor to withhold specific information which he would otherwise be required to disclose, for example in court proceedings.

Legal professional privilege applies to information which is passed between a solicitor and a client, whether written or oral, directly or indirectly. The rationale behind this right to withhold information, even from the court, is similar to the rationale for the obligation of confidentiality – it exists to enable a client to speak to his solicitor without worrying that the information passed over might be disclosed at a later date.

However, there are limitations in place to prevent legal professional privilege being used as a cloak to hide information which a client does not wish a court to see. One type of legal professional privilege is legal advice privilege. It applies only to information passed between the client and a solicitor *acting in the capacity of a solicitor*. In other words, the communication must relate to the request for, or the provision of, advice to the client by the solicitor. If documents are sent to or from an independent third party, even if they are created for the purpose of obtaining legal advice, they will not be covered by this privilege, and therefore simply 'copying in' a solicitor will not mean the information can be withheld. If the communication is made for the purpose of committing a fraud or a crime, it will not attract privilege (*R v Cox and Railton* (1884) LR 14 QBD 153).

Clients and solicitors may also claim litigation privilege in respect of documents created for the sole or dominant purpose of litigation or other adversarial proceedings which have already commenced or are contemplated. This privilege also extends to communications between a solicitor and third parties. A related issue which also arises in the case of litigation is that anything said by a solicitor whilst speaking in court as an advocate is privileged. Therefore the solicitor cannot be sued for defamation in such circumstances.

A House of Lords case, *Three Rivers DC v Bank of England* [2004] UKHL 48, examines closely the limits of legal professional privilege. It was concerned with advice given in complex matters involving large corporate clients, but left unanswered important questions concerning which representatives of a large corporate client can be regarded as the client for the purpose of claiming privilege. A Court of Appeal case suggests that solicitors will have to take care to identify and restrict those within the client corporation from whom they take instructions and to whom they give advice.

Like the obligation of confidentiality, privilege continues beyond the death of a client (*Bullivant v A-G for Victoria* [1901] AC 196).

The court has power to decide whether or not a particular item is privileged.

12.5 EXAMPLES

EXAMPLE 1

Question   You acted for Mrs Evans for a number of years and drew up her will. Sadly Mrs Evans dies, and the following week you are contacted by her daughter, who is one of the beneficiaries in the will. She asks whether you can tell her who will receive her mother's house. Can you give her this information?

Answer   You must keep the affairs of all clients confidential (Outcome 4.1). Does this duty apply to former clients? Yes. In this case the duty of confidentiality will pass to Mrs Evans' PRs. Indicative Behaviour 4.6 indicates that if you disclosed the contents of the will to the daughter without the consent of the PRs, this may tend to show that you have not achieved the Outcome.

EXAMPLE 2

Question   You are an assistant solicitor acting for both X Co Ltd and Y Co Ltd in a patents dispute. They are both being sued by Z Co Ltd for breach of a patent. X Co Ltd manufactures widgets and Y Co Ltd distributes these products. Due to Y Co Ltd's lack of funds, X Co Ltd is paying your fees in respect of both clients.

You get a call from the managing director of X Co Ltd who tells you that he has concerns about the financial situation of Y Co Ltd. He states that it has fallen behind in paying X Co Ltd's invoices and he is likely to issue a winding-up petition within the next few days.

Can you tell Y Co Ltd this information? Can you continue to act for both parties?

Answer   You owe a duty of confidentiality to X Co Ltd under Outcome 4.1, but you also owe a personal duty to Y Co Ltd to disclose any 'material' information under Outcome 4.2. Is this information 'material' to Y Co Ltd, ie relevant to its matter and more than of inconsequential interest to it?

This information is clearly relevant to Y Co Ltd, particularly as X Co Ltd is currently funding the litigation. Therefore, can you inform Y Co Ltd of your conversation? No. Your duty of confidentiality takes precedence over your duty of disclosure (Outcome 4.3).

Can you continue to act for both parties? Unless X Co Ltd is willing to waive confidentiality to allow you to inform Y Co Ltd of your conversation, or Y gives specific informed consent to non-disclosure or a lower standard of disclosure arises, then no. You would have to cease acting for one (Y Co Ltd) or both clients.

SUMMARY

(1)   A solicitor (and his staff) must keep the affairs of his clients confidential.

(2)   The duty of confidentiality continues until the client permits disclosure or waives the confidentiality.

(3)   The duty of confidentiality may be overridden in exceptional circumstances.

(4)   The solicitor also has a personal duty to disclose to the client all information that is relevant to the client's matter.

(5)   The duty of confidentiality takes precedence over the duty of disclosure.

(6)   A firm must not risk breaching confidentiality by acting for a client, A, whose interests are adverse to another client, B, where the firm holds information for B that would be material to A's matter, unless appropriate safeguards can be put in place and certain other requirements are met.

(7)   In addition to the duty of confidentiality, a solicitor must also consider legal professional privilege. Where legal professional privilege applies, a solicitor can refuse to disclose communications between himself and a client.

CHAPTER 13

CONFLICT OF INTE

LEARNING OUTCOMES

After reading this chapter you will have learned about:

- the principles governing conflict of interests
- identifying and dealing with such conflicts.

13.1 INTRODUCTION

A solicitor must act in the best interests of his clients. There will be situations where the interests of two clients (or prospective clients) conflict. Where this happens it will be practically impossible for the solicitor to act in the best interests of the two clients simultaneously.

For example, a solicitor is asked to act for Mr Lacey and Mr Roberts, who are suing each other over a boundary dispute (an obvious situation where the interests of the two clients conflict). Both clients will ultimately want to win their case, and so the solicitor will have a duty to act in the best interests of each client and take steps to try to ensure that they are successful in their litigation. However, the solicitor would be placed in an impossible situation, as anything done to help Mr Lacey win his case will be detrimental to Mr Roberts' case (and therefore not in Mr Roberts' best interests).

For this reason, the SRA prohibits solicitors from acting where there is a conflict of interests between two or more clients, except in specified limited circumstances.

13.2 CHAPTER 3: CONFLICT OF INTERESTS

There are two situations where a conflict of interests may arise:

(a) a conflict between two or more clients (a 'client conflict'); or

(b) a conflict between the client's interests and the solicitor's interests (an 'own interest conflict').

A solicitor can never act where there is a conflict between himself and a current client, but there are limited circumstances in which a solicitor can act where there is a conflict between two or more current clients. The introduction to Chapter 3 of the Code of Conduct states that in deciding whether to act in these circumstances, the overriding consideration will be the

...of each of the clients concerned, and in particular whether the benefits to the ...he solicitor acting for all or both of the clients outweigh the risks.

...IENT CONFLICT

Introduction

For the purposes of Chapter 3 of the Code, a client conflict means any situation where:

(a)   the solicitor or firm owes separate duties to act in the best interests of two or more clients;

(b)   in relation to the same or related matters; and

(c)   those duties conflict, or there is a significant risk that those duties may conflict (*Handbook* Glossary).

Outcome 3.5 provides that a solicitor must not act if there is a client conflict, or a significant risk of a client conflict, unless the circumstances set out in Outcomes 3.6 or 3.7 apply (see **13.3.5**).

13.3.2 Former clients – confidential information.

A conflict of interests may arise only between two current clients of the firm. Where a client's retainer has been terminated the firm no longer owes a duty to act in that client's best interests, and so a conflict of interest cannot arise concerning the affairs of a former client.

However, even in the absence of a conflict of interests, a firm may be prevented from acting for a client where it holds confidential information for the former client which would be material to the work done for the new client. See **Chapter 12** for further details.

13.3.3 Same or related matters

It is easy to see how a conflict of interests might arise when advising two clients about the same matter. The first example in this chapter (at **13.1**) concerned two clients involved in the same matter – a court case. Indeed, declining to act for clients whose interests are in direct conflict, for example claimant and defendant in litigation, may tend to show that the Outcomes have been achieved (Indicative Behaviour 3.2). It may also tend to show that the Outcomes have been achieved by a solicitor declining to act for clients where he may need to negotiate on matters of substance on their behalf, for example negotiating on price between a buyer and a seller of property (Indicative Behaviour 3.3).

A conflict of interests can also arise concerning different but related matters. A matter will be related if it concerns the same asset or liability. For example, you could not act to sell a new house for one client whilst also acting for another client who is alleging that a part of the house has been built on his land. However, there would need to be some reasonable degree of relationship (such as in the above example) for a conflict to arise.

Where the only conflict between the parties is their wider business interests then this will not create any conflict of interest issues. For example, imagine that Isla Cola and Samet Cola are the two main cola distributors in England and Wales. A firm of solicitors could represent Isla Cola on a purchase of a new IT system for their factory, whilst also representing Samet Cola in the purchase of a fleet of cars for their management. Although the interests of Isla Cola and Samet Cola will conflict (as they will both want to sell more cola than the other firm), a solicitors' firm may act for both at the same time without breaching Outcome 3.5 as the purchases of the IT system and the cars are not related matters.

13.3.4 Significant risk of a conflict of interests

An actual conflict of interests is not required. A significant risk that your duties to act in the best interests of each client may conflict will be enough to satisfy Outcome 3.5.

For example, if Mr and Mrs Rowntree sought to instruct the same solicitor to act for them in their divorce from one another, the solicitor could not act for both of them. This would remain the case even if they explained that their divorce was an amicable one, and they had agreed the division of their assets and what should happen to the children. Even if there was no actual conflict between their interests (an unlikely event), the solicitor could not act, as there would be a significant risk that the duty to act in their best interests might conflict. For instance, Mrs Rowntree might want more of the matrimonial assets once the solicitor has advised her about her legal rights, and Mr Rowntree might not agree to this.

There is also a significant risk of a conflict arising where there is inequality of bargaining power between the clients. Accordingly, it may tend to show that the Outcomes have been achieved where a solicitor declines to act where there is unequal bargaining power between the clients (Indicative Behaviour 3.4); the example given is acting for a seller and buyer where a builder is selling to a non-commercial client. See also Outcome 3.3 at **13.6**.

13.3.5 Exceptions

13.3.5.1 Introduction

Where a conflict of interests exists, or where there is a significant risk that a conflict may exist, a firm of solicitors may still act for both parties in defined circumstances and with the consent of both parties.

The following exceptions were originally introduced by The Law Society and contained in the previous Code of Conduct following a period of lobbying by parts of the profession to liberalise the previous conflict of interest rules, which prohibited a firm acting where there was a conflict, or where the firm held confidential information for one client which was relevant to another client. The exceptions are now contained in Outcomes 3.6 and 3.7 of the Code.

The substantially common interest exception (Outcome 3.6)

Where there is a client conflict and the clients have a substantially common interest in relation to a matter or a particular aspect of it, a solicitor may act only if:

(a) the solicitor has explained the relevant issues and risks to the clients, and he has a reasonable belief that they understand those issues and risks;

(b) all the clients have given informed consent in writing to the solicitor acting;

(c) the solicitor is satisfied that it is reasonable for him to act for all the clients and that it is in their best interests; and

(d) the solicitor is satisfied that the benefits to the clients of him doing so outweigh the risks.

The *Handbook* Glossary defines 'a substantially common interest' as a situation in which there is a clear common purpose in relation to any matter or a particular aspect of it between the clients, and a strong consensus as to how it is to be achieved, and the client conflict is peripheral to this common purpose.

There are some Indicative Behaviours which apply specifically to this exception. It may tend to show that the Outcomes have been achieved if a solicitor declines to act under Outcome 3.6 where the clients cannot be represented even-handedly or will be prejudiced by lack of separate representation (Indicative Behaviour 3.5). Likewise, it may tend to show that the Outcomes have not been achieved if a solicitor acts for two or more clients in a conflict of interests under this exception where the clients' interests in the end result are not the same, for example one partner buying out the interest of another partner in their joint business or a seller transferring a property to a buyer (Indicative Behaviour 3.11), or where it is unreasonable to act because there is unequal bargaining power (Indicative Behaviour 3.12).

An example of when this exception might be used is where a solicitor is instructed by a group of people who want to set up a company. Having regard to the Indicative Behaviours, the solicitor should be careful to consider whether all of the clients can be represented even-handedly, or whether all or some will be prejudiced by lack of separate representation, and he must be alert to any unequal bargaining power amongst them.

The competing for the same objective (or 'commercial') exception (Outcome 3.7)

Where there is a client conflict and the clients are competing for the same objective, a solicitor may act only if:

(a)   the solicitor has explained the relevant issues and risks to the clients, and he has a reasonable belief that they understand those issues and risks;

(b)   the clients have confirmed in writing that they want the solicitor to act, in the knowledge that the solicitor acts, or may act, for one or more other clients who are competing for the same objective;

(c)   there is no other client conflict in relation to that matter;

(d)   unless the clients specifically agree, no individual acts for, or is responsible for the supervision of work done for, more than one of the clients in that matter; and

(e)   the solicitor is satisfied that it is reasonable for him to act for all the clients and that the benefits to the clients of his doing so outweigh the risks.

The *Handbook* Glossary sets out the meaning of some of the terminology used in this exception to aid in its interpretation. Clients will be 'competing for the same objective' in a situation in which two or more clients are competing for an 'objective' which, if attained by one client, will make that 'objective' unattainable to the other client or clients. The term 'objective' is further defined as

> an asset, contract or business opportunity which one or more clients are seeking to acquire or recover through liquidation (or some other form of insolvency process) or by means of an auction or tender process or a bid or offer which is not public.

Again, there are some Indicative Behaviours which apply specifically to this exception. It may tend that show that the Outcomes have been achieved where a solicitor acts for clients under Outcome 3.7 only where the clients are sophisticated users of legal services (Indicative Behaviour 3.6) and declines to act where the clients cannot be represented even-handedly or will be prejudiced by lack of separate representation (Indicative Behaviour 3.5). It may tend to show that the Outcomes have not been achieved if a solicitor acts for two buyers where there is a conflict of interest under this exception, for example where two buyers are competing for a residential property (Indicative Behaviour 3.5).

This exception is likely, therefore, to continue to be used for corporate clients only. For example, it would enable one firm to act for two companies bidding to take over a third company, despite the fact that the obligations to act in the best interests of the clients would conflict (both want to be successful in their bid to acquire the company, and any step taken by the firm to try to make this happen for one client would be detrimental to the interests of the other client).

13.3.5.2   Informed consent

One condition common to both exceptions is the concept of informed consent. A client providing consent will not be enough.

As noted in the previous chapter (see **12.3.4.2**), obtaining informed consent may apply mainly to sophisticated clients such as large companies, perhaps with in-house legal departments, which will have the expertise to appreciate the issues and risks involved, and make a decision based on those risks.

13.3.5.3 Is it reasonable to act?

When considering whether to use one of the above exceptions it also must be reasonable for the firm to act for all the clients.

The solicitor should consider – both at the outset and throughout the duration of the retainer – whether one client is at risk of prejudice if he is not represented separately (ie by another firm) from the other client(s). This will particularly be the case where one client is vulnerable, or where the parties do not have equal bargaining power.

13.3.5.4 Confidential information

Where a solicitor or firm does decide to act by taking advantage of one of the above exceptions, the firm may well put itself in a position where it holds material confidential information for one client which it has a duty to disclose to another client. Where this is the case, the firm will need to consider whether it should be acting where the confidential information would be placed at risk. See **Chapter 12** for more details.

13.4 CONFLICT OF INTERESTS BETWEEN TWO EXISTING CLIENTS

A solicitor may have agreed to act for two clients where, at the beginning of the transaction, there was no actual conflict or any significant risk of a conflict. However, a conflict may arise during the retainer.

Where such a conflict does arise between two existing clients, a solicitor must have regard not only to the conflict of interest, but also to the issues surrounding confidential information. The solicitor may continue to act for one of the clients but must ensure that his duty of confidentiality is not put at risk (see **Chapter 12** for more details).

13.5 OWN INTEREST CONFLICT

Outcome 3.4 provides that a solicitor must not act where there is an 'own interest' conflict, or a significant risk of an 'own interest' conflict. This refers to any situation in which a solicitor's duty to act in the best interests of any client in relation to a matter conflicts, or there is a significant risk that it may conflict, with his own interests in relation to that or a related matter (*Handbook* Glossary).

For example, a solicitor could not act for a client suing a company where the solicitor was a major shareholder in that company. The solicitor would be obliged to act in the best interests of the client and take steps to try to ensure that the client was successful in suing the company. In taking those steps the solicitor would be acting to the detriment of the company. If the client was successful, the company would have to pay the client damages and so its share price might drop. This would be detrimental to the company's shareholders – including the solicitor.

Further examples of situations in which a solicitor's interest might conflict with that of his client are provided in the Indicative Behaviours. Accordingly, it may tend to show that the Outcomes have not been achieved where a solicitor:

(a) in a personal capacity, sells to, buys from, lends to or borrows from a client, unless the client has obtained independent legal advice (Indicative Behaviour 3.8);

(b) advises a client to invest in a business in which the solicitor has an interest, which affects his ability to provide impartial advice (Indicative Behaviour 3.9);

(c) holding a power of attorney for a client, uses that power to gain a benefit for himself which in his professional capacity he would not have been prepared to allow to a third party (Indicative Behaviour 3.10).

See also Outcome 3.2 at **13.6**.

A solicitor must act in the best interests of his client. Thus a solicitor must not make a secret profit whilst acting for the client. Outcome 1.15 obliges a solicitor to account properly to clients for any financial benefit he receives as a result of his instructions (see **11.14**).

13.6   SYSTEMS AND CONTROLS FOR IDENTIFYING CONFLICTS

Given that the proper handling of conflicts of interests is important for public protection, there is an emphasis in the Code on firms having in place appropriate and effective systems and controls to identify and assess potential conflicts of interests (Outcome 3.1). The detail regarding what such systems and controls need to assess differs, however, depending on whether they relate to an 'own interest' conflict or a client conflict.

Outcome 3.2 provides that systems and controls for indentifying 'own interest' conflicts must be appropriate to the size and complexity of the firm, and to the nature of the work undertaken. They must enable the firm to assess all the relevant circumstances, including whether the solicitor's ability as an individual, or that of anyone within the firm, to act in the best interests of the client(s) is impaired by:

(a)   any financial interest;

(b)   a personal relationship;

(c)   the appointment of the solicitor, or a member of his family, to public office;

(d)   commercial relationships; or

(e)   his employment.

According to Outcome 3.3, the systems and controls for identifying client conflicts must also be appropriate to the size and complexity of the firm, and to the nature of the work undertaken. They must enable the firm to assess all relevant circumstances, including whether:

(a)   the clients' interests are different;

(b)   the ability to give independent advice to the clients may be fettered;

(c)   there is a need to negotiate between the clients;

(d)   there is an imbalance in bargaining power between the clients; or

(e)   any client is vulnerable.

Indicative Behaviour 3.1 provides that it may tend to show that the Outcomes have been achieved where a firm trains employees and managers to identify and assess potential conflicts of interests.

13.7   PROFESSIONAL EMBARRASSMENT

Even where there is no conflict of interests, nor any significant risk of a conflict, a solicitor may still decline to act for a client due to professional embarrassment. (See also **12.3.5** above.)

A solicitor should consider whether accepting instructions to act for a client would breach one of the Principles. One example might be acting against a former client. There would be no conflict of interest, as a conflict cannot arise between a current client and a former client. However, the solicitor must consider whether he would feel restricted in doing his best for the current client on the basis that he was acting against a former client (with whom the solicitor may have built up a good relationship). If so, the solicitor would not be acting in the best interests of the current client in accepting the instructions.

A solicitor may also take into account his own commercial considerations when deciding whether to accept instructions from a new client. For example, if your firm's major client is Isla Cola and you are asked to act for its major rival on a completely unrelated matter, you might decline to do so if you thought that Isla Cola would instruct another firm as a result.

13.8 LIMITED RETAINER

Where a conflict arises between two clients, either at the beginning of or during a transaction, an alternative to relying on one of the exceptions set out above (at **13.3.5**) may be to accept a limited retainer. The solicitor could be retained to act only in relation to those areas where no conflict exists, with each client seeking independent advice on the conflicting areas. It is necessary to make clear the terms of your retainer, and that there are defined areas where you cannot advise.

However, it is unlikely that the Outcomes of Chapter 3 will be achieved if a solicitor acts under a limited retainer where there is an unequal bargaining position between the two parties (Indicative Behaviour 3.4).

13.9 CONVEYANCING

The area of conveyancing is subject to additional requirements regarding acting for more than one party within a transaction. These are considered in more detail in **Property Law & Practice**.

13.10 EXAMPLES

EXAMPLE 1

Question You are approached by Mr Smith and Mr Jones. They are the sole partners of Smith, Jones & Co, a firm of solicitors. Mr Jones explains that he wishes to leave the partnership and that Mr Smith has agreed to buy his interest in the partnership. They suggest to you that they both have the same aim and do not wish to go to the expense of instructing different solicitors to act from them.

Can you or your firm act for both of them in agreeing the sale of Mr Jones' interest in the partnership?

Answer Is there a conflict of interests here? Yes. You would owe separate duties to act in the best interests of both clients in relation to the same matter. Do these interests conflict? Yes. Mr Jones will wish to receive as high a price as possible for his share in the partnership, whereas Mr Smith will want to pay as little as possible. Other issues of conflict will also arise in relation to liability for debts, etc.

Can the 'substantially common interest' exception be used here? Although it may appear initially that the two clients have a common interest – one wishes to sell and the other wishes to buy – their interest conflicts for the reasons stated above.

You must send at least one client to another firm of solicitors.

EXAMPLE 2

Question X Co Ltd is put up for sale as a result of continuing financial difficulties. A number of parties enter negotiations to buy the company as a going concern. Can your firm act for two of these parties (Party A and Party B)?

Answer Is there a conflict of interests here? Yes – clearly the interests of Party A and Party B conflict on the same matter as they both wish to buy X Co Ltd.

Therefore Outcome 3.5 would prevent your firm from acting for both parties. However, does an exception apply? It is possible that the 'commercial' exception under Outcome 3.7 could allow the firm to act for both parties on the basis that the clients are competing for the same objective (ie, to buy X Co Ltd as a going concern) which, if attained by one client, will make that objective unattainable to the other, and as long as the following conditions are met:

(a)   the firm has explained the relevant issues and risks to the clients, and it has a reasonable belief that they understand those issues and risks;

(b)   the clients have confirmed in writing that they want the firm to act, in the knowledge that the firm acts for another client who is competing for the same objective;

(c)   there is no other client conflict in relation to the matter;

(d)   unless the clients specifically agree, no individual acts for, or is responsible for the supervision of work done for, more than one of the clients in the matter; and

(e)   the firm is satisfied that it is reasonable for it to act for both of the clients and that the benefits to the clients of the firm doing so outweigh the risks.

The firm would also have to deal with protecting the confidential information of both clients. Outcome 4.4 would apply as the information obtained from either client would be 'material' to the other client, and both clients have an interest adverse to one another by virtue of competing for the same objective.

The firm would have to comply with the conditions imposed by Outcome 4.4, which include obtaining the informed consent of both clients and protecting the confidential information of both clients by the use of safeguards, including information barriers.

SUMMARY

(1)   A solicitor must not act where there is a conflict, or significant risk of a conflict, between the interests of two or more clients, or between the interests of the client and the solicitor.

(2)   Where there is a conflict between two or more clients, a solicitor may act if he can satisfy the requirements of the substantially common interest exception or the commercial exception.

(3)   Regardless of the requirements concerning conflicts of interests, the solicitor must also consider his duty of confidentiality.

(4)   A solicitor may decline to act if he is professionally embarrassed, or for commercial considerations.

CHAPTER 14

UNDERTAKINGS

LEARNING OUTCOMES

After reading this chapter you will be able to understand:

- what an undertaking is
- the operation and effect of giving an undertaking
- 'policing' and risk management of undertakings.

14.1 INTRODUCTION

In its Code of Conduct, the SRA defines an undertaking as 'a statement given orally or in writing, whether or not it includes the word "undertake" or "undertaking", made by or on behalf of you or your firm in the course of practice, or by you outside the course of practice but as a solicitor or REL to someone who reasonably relies upon it, that you or your firm will do something or cause something to be done, or refrain from doing something' (*Handbook Glossary*).

In other words, an undertaking could be said to be an enforceable promise. Any statement made by a solicitor to do or not do something, whether given to a client or to another third party (such as another solicitor), may be an undertaking. Indeed, even if such a promise is made on a solicitor's behalf by a member of his staff, it may constitute an undertaking.

A solicitor must perform all undertakings given by him within an agreed timescale or within a reasonable amount of time (Outcome 11.2)

As the definition makes clear, it is not necessary to use the word 'undertake' for the undertaking to be binding. Even a promise to give an undertaking will usually be interpreted as an undertaking, and therefore will be binding on the solicitor concerned.

Once the undertaking has been relied upon by the recipient, it can be withdrawn only by agreement.

Given the consequences for breaching an undertaking (see **14.3** below), the SRA makes it clear in the introduction to Chapter 11 of the Code that a solicitor is not obliged to give or accept an undertaking. Indeed, a solicitor should think carefully when considering whether to give an undertaking.

Undertakings are often given by solicitors in order to smooth the path of a transaction. They are a convenient method by which some otherwise problematic areas of practice can be avoided.

EXAMPLE

Imagine a solicitor is acting for Mr Taylor concerning the sale of his business. Mr Taylor has agreed that he will pay the legal costs of the purchaser if the purchaser buys the business. However, the purchaser of the business wants Mr Taylor to pay this money (an agreed £10,000) up front before the deal takes place, in order to fund the necessary due diligence process (eg, to examine the contracts and leases of the business to establish whether the business is worth the asking price).

The solicitor could give an undertaking to the purchaser's solicitors to pay £10,000 towards the purchaser's costs from the proceeds of sale of the business (assuming that the proceeds of sale would cover the £10,000). If accepted, the purchaser's solicitors might well be happy to complete the due diligence work without any money on account from their client. In the absence of such an undertaking the client would have to fund paying the £10,000 before receiving the proceeds of sale from the business.

14.3 BREACH OF AN UNDERTAKING

Where a solicitor gives an undertaking, the terms of that undertaking will be personally binding on the individual solicitor concerned.

For example, a solicitor is acting for a client who is in arrears with his mortgage payments. The client is taken to court by his mortgage company to repossess his house. To prevent the house being repossessed the client offers to pay the arrears (£10,000) within seven days. The mortgage company agrees to withdraw the repossession proceedings, but only on the basis that the solicitor gives an undertaking to pay the mortgage company £10,000 within seven days. If the solicitor agreed to give the undertaking in those terms and the client didn't come up with the money, the solicitor would be personally liable to pay the £10,000.

If a solicitor fails to comply with such an undertaking, the solicitor may be sued personally by the recipient. The solicitor will also breach the requirements of professional conduct and will be disciplined by the SRA or the Solicitors Disciplinary Tribunal (see **14.8**). The solicitor's firm may also be disciplined for a lack of supervision. It may tend to show that the firm has achieved the Outcomes, and therefore complied with the Principles, if it maintains an effective system that records when undertakings have been given and when they have been discharged (Indicative Behaviour 11.5).

14.4 ORAL AND WRITTEN UNDERTAKINGS

An undertaking will be binding regardless of whether it is given orally or in writing (*Handbook Glossary*). However, it is advisable to give undertakings in writing, so that there can be no dispute as to the terms of the undertaking. If, however, it is necessary in the circumstances to give an oral undertaking, the solicitor should ensure that an attendance note recording the undertaking is placed on the client's file and that it is confirmed in writing as soon as possible.

14.5 TERMS OF THE UNDERTAKING

14.5.1 Introduction

An undertaking is not a contract. For example, there is no obligation for consideration (whether in monetary or other forms) to be present for an undertaking to be enforceable against a solicitor. However, given the binding effect of undertakings, and the consequences for breach, a solicitor should take just as much care in drafting undertakings as he would do when drafting a contract for a client.

14.5.2 Wording of an undertaking

The SRA's previous guidance in the Code of Conduct 2007 provided that any ambiguity in the wording of the undertaking would be interpreted in favour of its recipient. As this is still likely to be the case, great care should be taken by the solicitor when drafting undertakings.

14.5.3 Acts outside the solicitor's control

From time to time, a solicitor may be called upon to undertake to perform an action which is outside of his control, such as to forward documents which are not in his possession. The simple fact that the solicitor is unable to perform the undertaking without the cooperation of his client or another third party does not discharge the solicitor's obligation to perform, and the undertaking remains enforceable.

In order to avoid this situation, a solicitor may seek to give an undertaking that, in respect of our example above, he will use his 'reasonable endeavours' to obtain and provide the documents requested. This will impose a lesser obligation upon the solicitor, just as such a 'reasonable endeavours' obligation in contract imposes a lesser obligation on the contracting party. However, it may not give the party who might seek to rely on it the same comfort as an absolute undertaking, and he may therefore choose not to accept it, which may cause delay to the transaction.

14.5.4 Undertakings 'on behalf' of a client

Whilst an undertaking is almost always made for the benefit of the solicitor's client (in order to smooth the transaction as explained above), it is made in the solicitor's name. However, an undertaking may be drafted as being made 'on behalf of' the solicitor's client. This will not prevent the undertaking from being enforceable as against the solicitor, who will remain personally liable.

It is possible for a solicitor to give an undertaking 'on behalf' of a client and exclude personal liability, but in order to do so the SRA's previous guidance in the Code of Conduct 2007 provided that the solicitor must clearly and expressly disclaim personal liability, or make it clear that he is simply informing the other side of his client's intentions. This is likely to remain the case under the current Code of Conduct.

Therefore an undertaking that seeks to exclude personal liability on behalf of the solicitor is legally possible. However, it is unlikely to be accepted by the proposed recipient, as his ability to enforce it (and therefore rely on it) will be greatly reduced.

14.5.5 Timescale

Outcome 11.2 expressly provides that undertakings must be performed 'within an agreed timescale', and therefore it is important that a timescale is expressed when the undertaking is given. Where no timescale has been agreed, however, the Outcome provides that the undertaking must be performed within a 'reasonable amount of time'.

14.5.6 Costs

Where an undertaking is given in respect of the payment of costs of another party, the term 'costs' will be implied to mean proper costs unless a specific amount is agreed. Therefore, a solicitor is able to request an assessment of the costs by the court if costs are not agreed.

14.6 CLIENT'S AUTHORITY

As has been made very clear in this chapter, an undertaking is a personal obligation on the solicitor who gave it, and therefore the solicitor will be held liable for it, even if performance would put the solicitor in breach of his duty to his client. A solicitor should therefore ensure that he has clear and express authority from his client before giving any undertakings. When such authority has been received, it may be withdrawn by the client at any time until the solicitor has acted upon it, even if it is expressed to be irrevocable.

14.7 CHANGE OF CIRCUMSTANCES

An undertaking will remain binding upon the solicitor if the circumstances change so that it is impossible to fulfil it, either wholly or partially. However, the recipient may agree to its variation or discharge.

It may tend to show that the outcomes in Chapter 11 of the Code have been achieved, and therefore the Principles complied with, if, where an undertaking is given which is dependent upon the happening of a future event and it becomes apparent the future event will not occur, the solicitor notifies the recipient of this (Indicative Behaviour 11.6).

14.8 ENFORCEMENT

14.8.1 The courts

The court is able to enforce an undertaking against a solicitor as an officer of the court. Accordingly, where an undertaking has been breached, an aggrieved party may seek compensation for any loss (for example, see *Udall v Capri Lighting Ltd* [1987] 3 All ER 262). Firms are obliged to carry indemnity insurance to cover such claims. However, the value of such claims may well fall within the excess of those policies, leading to personal liability for the solicitor concerned.

As outlined below, a breach of an undertaking is likely to be a breach of professional conduct. However, given the court's jurisdiction over solicitors concerning undertakings, the SRA's previous guidance provided that the SRA would not investigate a breach of an undertaking given to the court itself, unless the court reported the matter to the SRA, and this is likely to remain the case.

14.8.2 The SRA and the Solicitors Disciplinary Tribunal

If a solicitor fails to comply with the terms of an undertaking he has given, this will be a breach of professional conduct. The Legal Ombudsman, the SRA and the Solicitors Disciplinary Tribunal have no power to enforce the performance of an undertaking. Neither can these organisations direct that a solicitor pay compensation to an aggrieved third party. However, they may investigate the solicitor's conduct and impose disciplinary sanctions (up to and including, in the case of the Solicitors Disciplinary Tribunal, striking the solicitor off the roll of solicitors).

However, the SRA's previous guidance provided that where an undertaking has been obtained by fraud or deceit, it is unlikely that any action will be taken against the solicitor who has breached the undertaking.

14.9 LIABILITY OF OTHERS

The definition of 'undertaking' includes those made on behalf of the solicitor or his firm (see **14.1**). This includes undertakings given by non-admitted staff, and also undertakings give by anyone held out by the firm as representing the firm. For example, if an undertaking given by an assistant solicitor is not honoured, there will be a breach of professional conduct by the solicitor and also the partners of the firm. Accordingly, many firms have strict procedures in respect of recording undertakings given, and who within the firm is authorised to give undertakings (see also Indicative Behaviour 11.5).

14.10   STANDARD FORMS OF UNDERTAKING

Any written undertaking given by a solicitor should be tailored carefully to the circumstances. However, standard forms of wording exist for common undertakings, for example in conveyancing transactions.

14.11   EXAMPLES

EXAMPLE 1

A solicitor is instructed by a landlord regarding the renewal of a lease of a domestic property. The solicitor is told that the landlord is very keen to retain the existing tenant, rather than going to the expense of advertising the property and having it stand empty for possibly weeks whilst a new tenant is found.

The solicitor is told that the tenant will attend the solicitor's office tomorrow (the day the lease is due to expire), to 'tie up a few loose ends' and sign a new tenancy agreement.

The following day the tenant duly arrives at the solicitor's office. However, it soon becomes clear that there are problems to be resolved before the tenant will agree to the new tenancy. The tenant explains that the house is in a shabby state, and the only way that the tenant would be willing to agree to a new tenancy is if the landlord agrees to redecorate the entire house and fit new carpets.

The solicitor tries to negotiate with the tenant that the landlord will look at the matter after the new lease is signed. However, the tenant states that unless the issues are dealt with today, he will terminate the existing lease and rent some other property. The solicitor is unable to contact the landlord and so reluctantly gives an undertaking on behalf of the landlord that the property will be redecorated and the carpets replaced within one month. The tenant happily renews the lease.

The solicitor informs his client of the undertaking the next day. The landlord is outraged, and refuses to carry out the work.

The undertaking was given on behalf of a client, but as the solicitor did not expressly disclaim personal liability, the solicitor will be bound to comply with the undertaking. The tenant can enforce the undertaking by suing the solicitor. If the client maintains his stance and refuses to comply, the solicitor will personally have to pay for the redecoration and carpets. In addition to being sued by the tenant, the solicitor could also be reported to the Legal Ombudsman in the form of a complaint about the services provided by him.

The solicitor should not have given the undertaking without obtaining his client's authority and consent.

EXAMPLE 2

A solicitor is acting for a client concerning a large debt. The client owes Berkin Finance £100,000 and is being pressed to pay the debt. The client agrees to sell his holiday cottage by auction in order to pay the debt. The cottage is valued at £120,000 and the client is hopeful that he will receive at least this price at the auction.

Berkin Finance writes to the client stating that unless the debt is paid in full within seven days, it will commence court proceedings. As the auction is to be held in 10 days' time, the solicitor (acting on the instructions of the client) undertakes to Berkin Finance to pay £100,000 from the proceeds of sale of the cottage.

The cottage is sold at auction for £90,000. Berkin Finance demands the full £100,000 from the solicitor. Unfortunately for the solicitor, the SRA's previous guidance provided that where an undertaking is given to make a payment from the proceeds of sale of an asset, the solicitor must pay the full amount (ie, £100,000), regardless of whether the proceeds of sale are sufficient, and this is still likely to be the case under the current Code of Conduct.

The solicitor should have drafted the undertaking to state clearly that his liability would be limited to the money he received from the sale, or to make it clear that he was disclaiming all personal liability.

SUMMARY

(1)   An undertaking is any statement made by or on behalf of a solicitor or his firm (in the course of practice or outside of it but as a solicitor) to do or refrain from doing something, given to someone who reasonably places reliance upon it.

(2)   A solicitor will be personally bound to honour an undertaking, regardless of whether the undertaking was given orally or in writing.

(3)   Any ambiguity in the wording of an undertaking is likely to be construed against the party that gave it.

(4)   A solicitor should obtain his client's express authority before giving an undertaking.

(5)   An undertaking may be enforced by the court.

(6)   The SRA/Legal Ombudsman/Solicitors Disciplinary Tribunal do not have the power to enforce an undertaking. However, any breach of an undertaking may be considered a breach of professional conduct, or result in a complaint about services provided by a solicitor which may lead to sanctions against the solicitor concerned.

CHAPTER 15

MONEY LAUNDERING
PROCEEDS OF CRIME

LEARNING OUTCOMES

After reading this chapter you will be able to understand:

- solicitors' obligations under the Money Laundering Regulations 2007
- solicitors' obligations concerning money laundering under the Proceeds of Crime Act 2002.

15.1 INTRODUCTION

'Money laundering' is the process by which criminals seek to alter or 'launder' their proceeds of crime so that it appears that these funds come from a legitimate source.

Suppose a thief has stolen £1 million. The thief then instructs a number of intermediaries each to invest a relatively small proportion of the money. The investments can later be sold, and the thief then appears to be in possession of the proceeds of a legitimate transaction.

In this particular example the 'audit trail' by which investigators follow the proceeds of crime is not too difficult, but it does not take a great deal of imagination to see how a series of deals using different intermediaries and types of investment could throw the investigators off track.

Solicitors are targets for criminals in their efforts to launder their proceeds of crime. The purpose of regulation in this area is to disrupt serious crime (including terrorism) by inhibiting criminals' ability to reinvest or benefit from the proceeds of crime.

The purpose of this chapter is to introduce some of the issues relating to the Government's anti-money laundering legislation. Further guidance can be sought from The Law Society, which produces detailed advice on this subject.

15.2 THE MONEY LAUNDERING REGULATIONS 2007

15.2.1 Introduction

The Money Laundering Regulations 2007 (SI 2007/2157) came into force on 15 December 2007 and implemented the Third European Money Laundering Directive (2005/60/EC). The Regulations place obligations on 'relevant persons'. This is defined in reg 3, and includes 'independent legal professionals'. This is further defined in reg 3 as including (but not limited to):

> a firm or sole practitioner who by way of business provides legal or notarial services to other persons, when participating in financial or real property transactions . . .

fore the vast majority of solicitors firms will be subject to the Regulations. Failure to mply with the Money Laundering Regulations is a criminal offence.

In contrast to the previous regulations, the Money Laundering Regulations 2007 have sought to move away from a 'tick box' approach to a risk-based approach. Therefore obligations are placed on solicitors to know their clients and understand the transactions they have been instructed upon. On this basis, solicitors are expected to assess the risk that each transaction or client poses, and implement anti-money laundering measures as appropriate.

Firms which are subject to the Regulations must comply with, for example, the matters discussed in **15.2.2** to **15.2.5** below. What follows is simply an overview of the often complex requirements imposed upon solicitors. More guidance can be obtained from www.moneylaundering.lawsociety.org.uk.

15.2.2 Nominated officers and reporting procedures

A firm must have internal procedures in place for the identification and reporting of money laundering (reg 20). Most notably, reg 20(2)(d)(i) requires firms to appoint a person within the firm to act as a 'nominated officer', referred to in practice as a 'Money Laundering Reporting Officer' (MLRO).

The nominated officer (who will be a senior member of the firm) will receive reports from within the firm concerning any instances of suspected money laundering, and will then decide whether an external report (known as a suspicious activity report, or SAR) to the National Crime Agency (NCA) should be made.

15.2.3 Client due diligence (client identification)

15.2.3.1 Introduction

Subject to limited exceptions, firms carrying out relevant business are obliged to obtain verification of the identity of each of their clients (reg 7). The need to verify the client's identity includes the following circumstances:

(a) if the client and solicitor agree to form a business relationship; or

(b) occasional transactions, ie a single transaction or linked transactions, which amounts to 15,000 euros or more; or

(c) where the solicitor suspects money laundering or terrorist financing; or

(d) where the solicitor doubts the accuracy or adequacy of documents or information supplied to verify the client's identity.

The verification must take place before a business relationship is established and before an occasional transaction can be carried out (reg 9). However, a solicitor may verify the identity of the client during the establishment of a business relationship if:

(a) there is little risk of any money laundering or terrorist financing occurring;

(b) it is necessary not to interrupt the normal course of business; and

(c) the identity is verified as soon as possible.

However, the solicitor cannot:

(a) carry out a transaction with or for the client through a bank account; or

(b) allow funds or property to be transferred or final deals signed until verification is complete.

How the solicitor must verify the identity of the client varies according to the type of client involved and the risk of money laundering.

15.2.3.2 Simplified due diligence

Simplified due diligence will apply where the identity of the client means that the risk of money laundering or terrorist financing is low. The clients which qualify for simplified due diligence are specified in reg 13. These include companies listed on a regulated EEA market subject to specified disclosure obligations (such as a public limited company listed in the United Kingdom on the Stock Exchange), or a public authority within the United Kingdom.

The exact verification required depends on the identity of the client. For example, for a plc listed in the UK, the solicitor must obtain confirmation of the company's listing on the Stock Exchange.

15.2.3.3 Standard due diligence

Standard due diligence will apply to most clients. The solicitor is obliged to verify the identity of the client using 'documentation, data or information obtained from a reliable and independent source' (reg 5).

For natural persons, evidence of identity may be based on documents such as passports and photocard driving licences. The Law Society considers it good practice to have either:

(a) one government document which verifies either the person's name and address, or his name and date of birth; or

(b) a government document which verifies the client's full name, plus another supporting document which verifies his name and either his address or his date of birth.

For partnerships, it will be necessary to obtain information on the constituent individuals who make up the partnership. However, where partnerships are well-known, reputable organisations with long histories in their industries and with substantial public information about them, The Law Society's guidance advises that it should be sufficient to obtain their name, registered or trading address and nature of business.

For companies, it will be necessary to identify and verify the existence of the company. For private companies and those not listed on a regulated market (which is the London Stock Exchange for UK companies) the standard identifiers are the company's full name, business/registered address and nature of business, and the names of two directors or equivalent. Sources for verifying a company's identification may include the certificate of incorporation, details from Companies House obtained by way of a company search and filed audited accounts. The Law Society's guidance advises that it may also be appropriate to consider whether the person providing the instructions on behalf of the company has the authority to do so. In addition, where simplified due diligence does not apply (see **15.2.3.2**) it will be necessary to consider the identity of beneficial owners.

Beneficial owners

A solicitor must identify any 'beneficial owner' where the beneficial owner is not the client (reg 5). A beneficial owner is defined in reg 6, and the definition varies depending on the nature of the client.

In the case of companies, reg 6(1) defines a beneficial owner as any individual who:

(a) ultimately owns or controls (whether through direct or indirect control) more than 25% of the shares or voting rights in the body; or

(b) otherwise exercises control over the management of the company (eg members of the company board).

This regulation does not apply to a company listed on a regulated market. It does apply to UK limited liability partnerships.

> **EXAMPLE**
>
> A Co Ltd instructs a firm of solicitors. The solicitors will have to obtain documentary confirmation of the name, registered address and the directors of the company. This can be obtained by carrying out a company search at Companies House. However, the solicitors also need to identify any 'beneficial owner' of the company.
>
> If Mr Smith owns 50% of the shares, Mr Jones owns 30% of the shares and Mr McConnell owns the remaining 20%, Smith and Jones will be the beneficial owners.
>
> However, what happens if A Co Ltd is owned by B Co Ltd? The Law Society's guidance states that a risk-based decision should be taken as to whether to make further enquiries. However, it is common for law firms to seek to identify the beneficial owners of any parent company up to and including the ultimate parent entity.
>
> Therefore, if A Co Ltd is owned by B Co Ltd, the solicitor is likely to make enquiries to identify the beneficial owners of B Co Ltd and so on.

In the case of a partnership (other than a limited liability partnership), reg 6(2) defines a beneficial owner as any individual who:

(a)   ultimately is entitled to or controls (whether the entitlement or control is direct or indirect) more than a 25% share of the capital or profits of the partnership, or more than 25% of the voting rights in the partnership; or

(b)   otherwise exercises control over the management of the partnership (ie the ability to manage the use of funds or transactions outside of the normal management structure and control mechanisms).

In the case of a trust, reg 6(3) sets out three types of beneficial owners of a trust:

(a)   *Any individual entitled to a specified interest in at least 25% of the trust capital.* A person has a specified interest if, for example, he has an interest in possession in the capital of the fund (ie, a right to enjoy the use or possession of the fund) or an interest in remainder in the capital of the fund (ie, a right to the capital which is postponed to one or more prior interests in possession in the income of the fund).

(b)   *The class of persons in whose main interest the trust is set up or operates.* This covers any trust that includes those who do not fit within (a) above. It is necessary to identify the class of persons in whose main interest the trust operates. All discretionary trusts will fall within this category. The approach to identification for these purposes is to understand the nature of the class, eg 'the grandchildren of X', rather than having to identify each member of it.

(c)   *Individuals who control a trust.* The term 'control' in this context means certain powers which are exercisable alone, jointly with another person or with the consent of another person. Examples include the powers (under the trust instrument or by law) to add or remove a person as a beneficiary, or to appoint or remove trustees.

> **EXAMPLE**
>
> Mr James's will provides that after payment of legacies and testamentary expenses, his residuary estate passes to his children in equal shares. Mr James has died and is survived by four children, the youngest of whom is 16 years of age.
>
> On the death of Mr James, each of his children has a vested (ie a specified) interest in one quarter of the residuary estate, notwithstanding that the youngest child will not receive his share until he is 18 years old (he cannot yet give a valid receipt to the executors).

> After the estate of Mr James has been administered, all four children should be identified as beneficial owners of the trust as they are each entitled to a specified interest in at least 25% of the trust capital.

Whilst generally the beneficiaries of a trust will be individuals, they may at times be a company. If this is the case, it is necessary to apply reg 6(1) (above) to determine the beneficial owners of the company in question.

In the case of other arrangement or entities, for example unincorporated associations and foundations, beneficial ownership is dealt with by reg 6(6), but the detail is outside the scope of this book.

15.2.3.4 Enhanced due diligence

Enhanced due diligence applies where:

(a)   the solicitor has not met the client face to face;

(b)   there are higher risk factors in relation to money laundering or terrorist financing; or

(c)   the client is a Politically Exposed Person (PEP) (reg 14).

In these situations, a solicitor will have to apply enhanced due diligence measures. For example, where the client is not present on a face-to-face basis, reg 14(2) suggests that the client's identity is established by additional documents, or by ensuring that the first payment from the client to the solicitor is carried out through a bank account opened in the client's name.

A PEP is anyone who has held, within the last year, a 'prominent public function' for a State (other than within the UK), an EU institution or an international body (reg 14(5)). Prominent public functions include the following:

(a)   Heads of State, heads of government, ministers and deputy or assistant ministers;

(b)   members of parliament;

(c)   members of supreme courts, of constitutional courts or of other high-level judicial bodies whose decisions are not generally subject to further appeal, except in exceptional circumstances;

(d)   members of courts of auditors or of the boards of central banks;

(e)   ambassadors, chargés d'affaires and high-ranking officers in the armed forces;

(f)   members of the administrative, management or supervisory bodies of State-owned enterprises.

A PEP also includes the family members of the primary PEPs listed above (spouse, partner, children and their spouses or partners, and parents) and known close associates of the primary PEP, eg with whom there are close business relationships. Middle-ranking and junior officials, however, are not PEPs.

Where a solicitor is dealing with a PEP, additional obligations are placed on the solicitor, such as having approval from senior management to act for the client, and taking additional measures to identify the source of wealth and source of funds involved in the proposed transaction or business relationship (reg 14(4)).

15.2.3.5 Ongoing monitoring

A solicitor is obliged to undertake ongoing monitoring of business relationships, to ensure that the transactions are consistent with the solicitor's knowledge of the client (reg 8).

15.2.4 Training

Firms are obliged to provide training to their employees in respect of money laundering (reg 21). Employees should be made aware of the law relating to money laundering and terrorism financing (for example, the Proceeds of Crime Act 2002, the Terrorism Act 2000, and the Money Laundering Regulations 2007). The Regulations also specify that employees should be given regular training on how to recognise (and then deal with) transactions that potentially involve money laundering.

The Regulations do not specify how the training should take place. However, guidance provided by The Law Society suggests that appropriate methods of delivery may include face-to-face learning or e-learning. The Law Society's guidance also recommends the use of a staff manual on money laundering issues.

Where no such training is given, this may provide the employee with a defence to some of the offences under the Proceeds of Crime Act 2002 (see **15.3.3.7**).

15.2.5 Record keeping

A firm must keep various records in respect of money laundering. These include evidence supporting client due diligence (reg 19). This can be either a copy of the evidence provided to verify the client's identity (eg a copy of the client's passport, etc) or references to it. These records must be kept for at least five years from when the business relationship ends or the end of the occasional transaction.

The firm must also keep records of a business relationship or occasional transactions for a similar period. The Law Society also recommends that a detailed record is kept of suspicions and disclosures in respect of money laundering.

15.3 THE PROCEEDS OF CRIME ACT 2002

15.3.1 Introduction

The Proceeds of Crime Act 2002 makes it an offence to become involved in money laundering. For example, under s 327, it is an offence to conceal, disguise, convert or transfer criminal property, or remove criminal property from England and Wales, Scotland or Northern Ireland.

This chapter will focus on the three offences which most concern solicitors in their day-to-day practice.

15.3.2 Arrangements

15.3.2.1 Introduction

> A person commits an offence if he enters into or becomes concerned in an arrangement which he knows or suspects facilitates (by whatever means) the acquisition, retention, use or control of criminal property by or on behalf of another person. (Proceeds of Crime Act 2002, s 328(1))

15.3.2.2 Definitions

Section 328 is drafted very widely. For example, if a solicitor transferred a house to a relative of a client, where the solicitor knew or suspected that the house was purchased with the proceeds of crime, then the solicitor would '[become] concerned in an arrangement' and so would breach s 328(1).

There is no requirement that the funds pass through the hands of the person concerned with the arrangement, ie the solicitor.

'Criminal property' is defined by s 340 of the Act as a person's direct or indirect benefit from criminal conduct (if the offender knows or suspects that the property constitutes or represents such a benefit).

'Criminal conduct' is defined very widely, and includes any offence committed within the United Kingdom. This would include offences ranging from armed robbery to fraudulent receipt of welfare benefits. The definition also includes an international element. For example, if the offence occurred outside of the United Kingdom, it would still constitute criminal conduct if it would be classed as an offence if it had occurred within the United Kingdom. For example, a criminal robs a bank in France. This would still constitute 'criminal conduct' under the Act as robbery is an offence within the United Kingdom. It is irrelevant whether robbery is an offence in France. (However, there are exceptions to this international element – see **15.3.2.6.**)

15.3.2.3   Authorised disclosure

Disclosure prior to the act taking place

A solicitor does not commit an offence under s 328 if he makes an authorised disclosure to the firm's nominated officer as soon as is practically possible prior to the transaction taking place, and the authorisation of the nominated officer or the NCA is obtained to complete the transaction.

However, once the nominated officer has made a suspicious activity report to the NCA, the nominated officer is unable to give consent for the transaction to proceed until one of the following conditions is met:

(a) the nominated officer, having made a disclosure to the NCA, receives the consent of the NCA;

(b) the nominated officer, having made a disclosure to the NCA, hears nothing for seven working days (starting with the first working day after the disclosure is made);

(c) where consent is refused by the NCA, the nominated officer may not give consent for the transaction to proceed unless consent is subsequently granted within 31 days starting on the day refusal is given, or a period of 31 days has expired from the date of refusal. This 31-day period gives the authorities time to take action to seize assets or take other action with respect to the money laundering.

Disclosure during the prohibited act

A solicitor may seek to make an authorised disclosure whilst the prohibited act is ongoing. However, if the solicitor is to avoid breaching s 328 by making the disclosure, he must satisfy the provisions of s 338(2A):

(a) the disclosure is made whilst the prohibited act is ongoing; and

(b) when the alleged offender began to do the act, he did not know or suspect that the property constituted or represented a person's benefit from criminal conduct; and

(c) the disclosure is made as soon as is practicable after the alleged offender first knows or suspects that the property constitutes or represents a person's benefit from criminal conduct, and the disclosure is made on the alleged offender's own initiative.

Take the example of a solicitor conducting a conveyancing transaction on behalf of a client. Until the client exchanges contracts to sell the property, the solicitor has no knowledge or suspicion that the house was bought with the proceeds of crime. Accordingly, there is no breach of s 328, as the solicitor does not possess the requisite knowledge or suspicion. After contracts have been exchanged, the solicitor correctly begins to suspect that the house was bought with the proceeds of crime. Accordingly, he is now concerned in an arrangement which facilitates the acquisition, retention, use or control of criminal property and therefore is in breach of s 328.

In order to seek the protection of making an authorised disclosure, the solicitor must disclose his suspicions to his nominated officer on his own initiative, and must do so as soon as is practicable after his first suspicions arise.

Disclosure after the prohibited act

A solicitor may also seek to make an authorised disclosure after the prohibited act is been completed. However, the solicitor must have a good reason for his failure to disclose prior to his completing the act (s 338(3)). The disclosure must be made as soon as is practicable, and again the solicitor must make the disclosure on his own initiative.

15.3.2.4 Reasonable excuse for non-disclosure

A solicitor may have a defence to breaching s 328 where he intended to make an authorised disclosure but has a reasonable excuse for failing to do so. The Law Society's guidance states that a 'reasonable excuse' has not been defined by the courts. However, the guidance advises solicitors to document their reasons for non-disclosure.

15.3.2.5 Litigation proceedings

In *Bowman v Fels* [2005] EWCA Civ 226, the Court of Appeal considered whether taking steps in litigation could be construed as 'arranging' under s 328. The Court concluded that taking steps in litigation (including pre-action steps) and the resolution of issues in a litigious context were excluded from the scope of s 328. Therefore a solicitor would not be obliged to make an authorised disclosure.

> **EXAMPLE**
>
> A solicitor is acting for Mr Smith in divorce proceedings. Financial relief proceedings are issued by Mrs Smith, as she wishes to have the matrimonial home transferred into her sole name. The solicitor becomes aware that the house was purchased by Mr Smith with the proceeds of crime. The solicitor will not breach s 328 by merely conducting the litigation on behalf of Mr Smith.

It was originally thought that transferring the house from Mr Smith to Mrs Smith after the court proceedings would have fallen into the definition of an arrangement. However, the current Law Society guidance provides that dividing assets in accordance with a court judgment would not fall within this definition, therefore no consent would be required. However, the guidance goes on to state that careful consideration should be made of whether the client would be committing an offence by receiving stolen property.

The solicitor would not be able to take advantage of this exclusion if the litigation was a sham created for the purposes of money laundering.

15.3.2.6 'Overseas' defence

Despite the wide definition of 'criminal conduct' (see **15.3.2.2** above), a solicitor will not commit an offence under s 328 where the criminal conduct occurred outside of the United Kingdom and was not unlawful in the country where it happened. However, this defence is not available (subject to certain exceptions) where the offence would carry a sentence of imprisonment for 12 months or more were it to be carried out within the United Kingdom (see the Proceeds of Crime Act 2002 (Money Laundering: Exceptions to Overseas Conduct Defence) Order 2006 (SI 2006/1070)).

15.3.2.7 Penalties

An individual convicted under s 328 may receive a maximum sentence of 14 years' imprisonment.

15.3.3 Acquisition, use or possession

15.3.3.1 Introduction

A person commits an offence under s 329 of the Proceeds of Crime Act 2002 if he acquires, uses or has possession of criminal property.

15.3.3.2 Adequate consideration defence

An issue may arise in connection with s 329 where, for example, a solicitor receives money for his costs for work carried out for a client charged with a criminal offence and there is a possibility that the money in question is criminal property.

The adequate consideration defence applies if there was adequate consideration for acquiring, using and possessing the criminal property, unless the individual knew or suspected that those goods or services might help to carry out criminal conduct. The Crown Prosecution Service guidance for prosecutors says that this defence applies where professional advisers, such as solicitors, receive money for or on account of costs, including disbursements. However, the fees charged must be reasonable and the defence is not available if the value of the work is significantly less than the money received.

It must be borne in mind that returning the balance of money in an account to a client may be an offence under s 328 if the solicitor knows or suspects that the money is criminal property. In that case, an authorised disclosure must be made to avoid such an offence being committed (see **15.3.2.3**).

15.3.4 Failure to disclose

15.3.4.1 Introduction

A person commits an offence under s 330 of the Proceeds of Crime Act 2002 if:

(a) he knows or suspects, or has reasonable grounds to know or suspect, that a person is engaged in money laundering; and

(b) the information comes to him in the course of a business in the regulated sector; and

(c) the information may assist in identifying the money launderer or the location of any laundered property; and

(d) he does not make an authorised disclosure as soon as is practicable.

15.3.4.2 Objective test

A solicitor will commit this offence even where he genuinely did not know or suspect that a person was engaged in money laundering. The court will consider, based on the information available to the solicitor at the time, whether he *should* have known (or at least suspected) that money laundering was occurring. Accordingly, turning a blind eye to a transaction will not provide the solicitor with a defence.

15.3.4.3 Regulated sector

Firms will be within the 'regulated sector' if they undertake relevant business (see the Proceeds of Crime Act 2002, Sch 9). Most solicitors firms will fall within the regulated sector for at least some of the work with which they deal. The definition of 'regulated sector' is closely aligned to the definition given in the Money Laundering Regulations 2007 (see **15.2.1**).

15.3.4.4 The information

The information obtained by the solicitor must be of some use to the authorities. Accordingly, the solicitor must be able to identify, or believe the information may assist in identifying:

(a) the money launderer; or

(b)   the location of the laundered property.

If the solicitor is genuinely unable to provide this information, the solicitor will not breach s 330.

The solicitor cannot blindly assume that the information will be of no use to the authorities. When considering whether the solicitor has breached s 330, the court will consider whether it would have been reasonable to expect the solicitor to believe that the information would assist in identifying the offender, or locating the laundered property.

15.3.4.5 Authorised disclosure

A solicitor will be provided with a defence to s 330 if he makes an authorised disclosure to the firm's nominated officer as soon as practically possible. The disclosure on its own will be enough to grant an effective defence under s 330. However, the nominated officer will still consider whether the information should be forwarded to the NCA.

15.3.4.6 Reasonable excuse for non-disclosure

Once again, a solicitor will not commit this offence where he intended to make a disclosure and has a reasonable excuse for not doing so (see **15.3.2.4**).

15.3.4.7 Training

A further defence under s 330 concerns the training provided to an individual. Firms undertaking 'relevant business' are obliged to provide anti-money laundering training to their employees. If an employee does not know or suspect that a client is engaged in money laundering due to a lack of training then the employee may not commit the offence (see **15.2.2**).

15.3.4.8 Confidentiality and privilege

The position concerning a solicitor's duty of confidentiality in Chapter 4 of the Solicitors' Code of Conduct is considered below at **15.4**.

A solicitor is also under a duty at common law to keep confidential certain information given to him from a client. This is referred to as legal professional privilege (LPP). Communications will be protected from disclosure if they fall within 'advice privilege' or 'litigation privilege' (see **12.4**). However, LPP cannot be relied upon where the communication takes place with the purpose of carrying out an offence.

The Proceeds of Crime Act 2002 mirrors the common law position, in that a solicitor is not obliged under s 330 to disclose any information that comes to him as a professional legal adviser in privileged circumstances, eg in connection with giving or seeking legal advice, or in relation to legal proceedings, whether contemplated or actual. However, this exemption does not apply where the information is communicated with the intention of furthering a criminal purpose (eg, money laundering).

15.3.4.9 'Overseas' defence

A solicitor will not breach s 330 for failing to disclose where he believes that the money laundering is taking place outside of the United Kingdom, and money laundering is not unlawful in that country. The Secretary of State has the power to limit this defence, but at the time of writing has not taken any steps to do so.

15.3.4.10 Penalties

A person convicted of an offence under s 330 may receive a maximum sentence of five years' imprisonment.

15.3.5 Tipping off

15.3.5.1 The offences

There are two aspects of tipping off that must be avoided under s 333A.

Disclosing a suspicious activity report (s 333A(1))

It is an offence to disclose to any person that a suspicious activity report (on money laundering) has been made if that disclosure is likely to prejudice any investigation that follows such a report. For example, this offence would apply where a solicitor informs his client that an authorised disclosure has been made, with the intention of the client taking steps to frustrate any action taken by the law enforcement authorities. This would apply where a disclosure of suspicion is made to a MLRO, the NCA, the Police, or to HMRC.

> **EXAMPLE**
>
> Mr Wilkinson instructs his solicitor to sell his house. The solicitor suspects that the house was purchased with the proceeds of tax evasion and so makes an authorised disclosure under s 328. The transaction cannot be completed until the solicitor obtains the consent of his MLRO or the NCA (see **15.3.2.3**). Mr Wilkinson demands to know why his house sale has not been completed. The solicitor's trainee receives Mr Wilkinson's call and, having checked the file, informs Mr Wilkinson that an authorised disclosure has been made to the NCA. In these circumstances the trainee may breach s 333A unless he can rely on one of the defences (see **15.3.4.2**).

Disclosing an investigation (s 333A(3))

This is a more general offence, and applies regardless of whether or not a suspicious activity report has been made. The offence is committed where a disclosure is made to any person that an investigation into money laundering is being carried out, or is being contemplated, and that disclosure is likely to prejudice the money laundering investigation.

The idea behind both offences is to ensure that information is not leaked to the money launderer or another third party before the authorities have had the opportunity to investigate the matter and consider whether any enforcement action is necessary.

15.3.5.2 Defences

There are a number of defences to tipping off. These include that the person who made the disclosure did not know or suspect that the disclosure would prejudice an investigation into money laundering (s 333D (3) and (4)). Another defence is that the disclosure is made to the client for the purposes of dissuading the client from engaging in the alleged money laundering (s 333D(2)), although this exception should be treated with caution.

15.3.5.3 Penalties

Both the offences set out in **15.3.5.1** above carry a maximum penalty of an unlimited fine, and/or a maximum prison sentence of two years.

15.3.5.4 'Regulated sector'

These sections (ss 333A to 333D) only apply to the regulated sector. However, similar provisions apply to work completed outside of the regulated sector by virtue of s 342.

15.4 CONFIDENTIALITY

A solicitor is under a duty under Outcome 4.1 of the Code of Conduct to keep confidential the affairs of clients (including former clients). However, when making a disclosure under s 328 or s 330, the legislation expressly provides that such a disclosure will not breach this duty.

Nevertheless, the SRA's previous guidance advised that a solicitor should be mindful of the importance of the duty of confidentiality, and seek advice when uncertain as to whether to report confidential information.

15.5 EXAMPLES

EXAMPLE 1

Question   You are acting on a corporate transaction. Your client is buying X Co Ltd. During the course of your due diligence you discover that a number of X Co Ltd's lucrative contracts were obtained by paying bribes.

What obligations are you now under? Can you complete the transaction?

Answer   You need to consider whether anything of a criminal nature has occurred. Obtaining property using bribes is a criminal offence. These contracts will have generated cash which will be owned by X Co Ltd. Therefore when your client buys the company, it will be acquiring the proceeds of crime, which is an offence under s 329 of the Proceeds of Crime Act 2002. Simply by completing the transaction you will be concerned in an arrangement which facilitates the acquisition, retention, use or control of criminal property, which is an offence under s 328 of the Proceeds of Crime Act 2002. Therefore you need to report the matter to your Money Laundering Reporting Officer as soon as possible. He will then need to seek the consent of the NCA for the transaction to proceed.

EXAMPLE 2

Question   This is a continuation of the above question. The above information comes to you on the morning of the day for completion of the deal. You are unable to obtain the consent of the NCA in time to complete the deal. Therefore you must postpone completion of the deal to allow you to obtain this consent. Can you explain your reasons for the delay to the solicitors representing X Co Ltd?

Answer   No. This would constitute 'tipping off' – an offence under ss 333A–333D of the Proceeds of Crime Act 2002. This will place you in a very difficult position. Therefore it is vital that you disclose any suspicion to the Money Laundering Reporting Officer as soon as possible to attempt to avoid this situation.

SUMMARY

(1)   Money laundering is the process whereby the proceeds of crime are changed so that they appear to come from a legitimate source.

(2)   The Government has introduced legislation to disrupt this process.

(3)   Solicitors who undertake relevant business must comply with the Money Laundering Regulations 2007.

(4)   Under the Money Laundering Regulations 2007, firms must appoint a nominated officer, who will receive internal reports concerning money laundering and must consider whether to report the matter to the NCA.

(5)   A person commits an offence under s 328 of the Proceeds of Crime Act 2002 where he becomes concerned in an arrangement involving money laundering.

(6)   Section 328 does not apply to steps taken in litigation.

(7)   A person commits an offence under s 329 of the Proceeds of Crime Act 2002 if he acquires, uses or has possession of criminal property.

(8)   A solicitor within the regulated sector is obliged to disclose any suspected money laundering activity to his nominated officer under s 330 of the Proceeds of Crime Act 2002.

(9)   It is an offence to disclose to any person that a disclosure has been made where this may prejudice an investigation.

DUTIES OWED TO THE COURT AND THIRD PARTIES

LEARNING OUTCOMES

After reading this chapter you will be able to understand the duties owed by solicitors to:

- the court
- third parties generally
- other solicitors
- barristers.

16.1 INTRODUCTION

16.1.1 Duty to the court

The introduction to Chapter 5 of the Code explains that the chapter is about duties to clients and to the court if a solicitor is exercising a right to conduct litigation or acting as an advocate. The Outcomes apply to both litigation and advocacy, but there are some Indicative Behaviours which may be relevant only when a solicitor is acting as an advocate.

A solicitor must comply with his duties to the court (Outcome 5.6). A solicitor must also not attempt to deceive or knowingly or recklessly mislead the court, or be complicit in another person deceiving or misleading the court (Outcomes 5.1 and 5.2 respectively). The *Handbook* Glossary defines 'court' as any court, tribunal or enquiry of England and Wales, or a British court martial, or any court of another jurisdiction.

The Code provides examples of such behaviour in the form of the Indicative Behaviours in Chapter 5. Accordingly, it may tend to show that a solicitor has not achieved the Outcomes, and therefore not complied with the Principles, if he:

(a) constructs facts supporting the client's case, or drafts any documents relating to any proceedings containing any contention which the solicitor does not consider to be properly arguable or any allegation of fraud, unless the solicitor has been instructed to do so and he has material which he reasonably believes shows, on the face of it, a case of fraud (Indicative Behaviour 5.7);

(b) calls a witness whose evidence he knows is untrue (Indicative Behaviour 5.9);

(c) tampers with evidence or seeks to persuade a witness to change his evidence (Indicative Behaviour 5.11).

Where a solicitor becomes aware that he has inadvertently misled the court, it may tend to show that he has achieved the necessary Outcomes and complied with the Principles if he immediately informs the court, with the client's consent, or ceases to act if the client does not consent to this (Indicative Behaviour 5.4).

Similarly, it may tend to show that a solicitor has achieved the Outcomes if he refuses to continue acting for a client if he becomes aware that the client has committed perjury or misled (or attempted to mislead) the court, unless the client agrees to disclose the truth to the court (Indicative Behaviour 5.5). However, the SRA's previous guidance in the 2007 Code of Conduct stated that a solicitor is not obliged to stop acting where the client gives inconsistent evidence – there must be an intention on behalf of the client to submit false evidence, and this is likely to remain the case under the current Code.

A solicitor must comply with court orders which place obligations on him (Outcome 5.3), and it may tend to show that the Outcomes have been achieved if a solicitor advises his clients to comply with court orders made against them and advises them of the consequences of failing to comply (Indicative Behaviour 5.1).

Furthermore, a solicitor must not place himself in contempt of court (Outcome 5.4) and must ensure that evidence relating to sensitive issues is not misused (Outcome 5.7). Child witness evidence is dealt with by Indicative Behaviour 5.3. There is also an obligation on a solicitor to inform a client, where relevant, of the circumstances in which his duties to the court outweigh his obligations to the client (Outcome 5.5). There may be occasions when the obligation as a litigator or an advocate to act in the best interests of a client may conflict with his duty to the court. The Notes to Chapter 5 advise that in such situations a solicitor may need to consider whether the public interest is best served by the proper administration of justice and should take precedence over the client's interests.

Lastly, solicitors appearing before the court should exercise considerable caution when communicating with judges outside of the courtroom. It is advised by the SRA that advocates should communicate with judges in this fashion only when invited to do so and in the presence of the legal representative of the other client.

16.1.2 Witnesses

It may tend to show that the Outcomes in Chapter 5 of the Code have not been achieved if a solicitor, when acting as an advocate, names in open court a third party whose character would thereby be called into question, unless it is necessary for the proper conduct of the case (Indicative Behaviour 5.12). Likewise calling into question the character of a witness he has cross-examined unless that witness has been given the opportunity to answer the allegations during cross-examination (Indicative Behaviour 5.13), or suggesting that any person is guilty of a crime, fraud or misconduct, unless those allegations are material to the solicitor's own client's case and appear to him to be supported by reasonable grounds (Indicative Behaviour 5.8).

Should a solicitor wish, or require, in the best interests of his client, to take statements from a witness or potential witness, he may do so at any point in the proceedings. This remains the case whether or not that individual has already been interviewed by another party, or has been called as a witness by another party. However, the SRA's previous guidance suggested that the witness be interviewed in the presence of his legal representative. Attempting to influence a witness when taking a statement from him, with regard to the contents of that statement, may tend to show that a solicitor has not achieved the Outcomes in Chapter 5 (Indicative Behaviour 5.10).

A solicitor may not make (or offer to make) payments to a witness dependent upon their evidence or upon the outcome of the case (Outcome 5.8).

16.1.3 Duty to disclose law and facts

A solicitor who appears before the court for the defence in a criminal case, or for either party in a civil case, has no duty to inform the court of any evidence or witnesses which would prejudice the solicitor's own client.

In the Solicitors' Code of Conduct 2007, there was a duty on the part of a solicitor, when exercising a right to conduct litigation or act as an advocate, to draw to the court's attention relevant cases and statutory provisions and any material procedural irregularity. The accompanying Guidance Note indicated that if an advocate omitted, or made an incorrect reference to, a case or provision, it was the duty of the other advocate to draw attention to it even if it assisted the opponent's case (ie, whether or not it was in the best interests of his own client to do so).

The duties described above not do appear in the current Code as an Outcome. Instead, Indicative Behaviour 5.2 provides that it may tend to show that the solicitor has achieved the Outcomes of Chapter 5 if he draws the court's attention to relevant cases and statutory provisions, and to any material irregularity. Whilst no express mention is made of a situation in which to do this would not necessarily be in the interests of the solicitor's own client, the notes to the Principles in the Code state that where two or more Principles come into conflict, the Principle which takes precedent is the one which best serves the public interest, especially in the proper administration of justice (Principle 1). As a result, it is likely that the position reflects that in the Code of Conduct 2007 in that Principle 1 will take precedence over Principle 4 (acting in the best interests of the client) in such a situation.

16.2 REFUSING INSTRUCTIONS TO ACT

There are no longer any specific references in the Code to situations in which a solicitor must not refuse to act as an advocate. The introduction to Chapter 1 on 'Client care' states that a solicitor is generally free to decide whether or not to accept instructions in any matter, provided that he does not discriminate unlawfully (see also **10.3.2**).

If it is clear to a solicitor appearing as an advocate, or acting in litigation, that he or anyone else in his firm will be called as a witness in the matter, it may tend to show that the Outcomes have been achieved if the solicitor declines to appear/act unless he is satisfied that this will not prejudice his independence as an advocate or a litigator, or the interests of his clients or the interests of justice (Indicative Behaviour 5.6).

16.3 INSTRUCTING COUNSEL

A solicitor is obliged to act in the best interests of his client. Accordingly, where the client requires advocacy services, the solicitor must consider, based on the complexity of the case and the solicitor's own experience, whether it would be in the best interests of that client to instruct another solicitor within the firm or counsel to act as the advocate in the proceedings.

16.3.1 Duty to counsel

If it is in the client's best interests to instruct counsel, it remains the solicitor's duty to ensure that adequate instructions are provided to the chosen barrister. As an extension of the solicitor's duty to his client, he should ensure that these instructions, including any relevant supporting statements, information or documents, are provided in good time to allow adequate preparation of the case.

In order to provide such information, it may be necessary, if practicable, to arrange a conference with counsel, either with or without the client, to enable the barrister to discuss directly the nature of the case, obtain instructions or further information, and provide advice in a direct manner. It is a matter for the solicitor to ascertain whether such a conference would be appropriate and in the client's best interests, and if so, to arrange it.

16.3.2 Duty to the client when instructing an advocate

Notwithstanding the appointment of counsel and the duties the chosen barrister may owe to a solicitor's client, all the solicitor's duties to his client remain in full force and effect. Instructing counsel does not relieve the solicitor of those duties, particularly the overriding duty to act in the best interests of the client.

The solicitor must therefore exercise care in choosing the appropriate barrister for the case, taking into consideration the experience and seniority of counsel available. The solicitor should also ensure he is are happy with the quality of the advice given, to ensure that there are no obvious errors or inconsistencies. If such errors are apparent, clarification should be requested or a second opinion obtained (see, for example, *Regent Leisuretime v Skerrett* [2005] EWHC 2255).

16.3.3 Counsel's fees

A solicitor is responsible for appointing counsel and (subject to limited exceptions) is therefore responsible personally for the payment of counsel's fees. This applies regardless of whether the solicitor's client has provided the requisite monies. Many solicitors therefore request that their clients provide money on account to cover prospective barristers' fees.

16.3.4 Discrimination – choice of advocate

As noted at **16.3.2** above, a solicitor should select an advocate of sufficient seniority and experience to represent his client adequately in court. A solicitor may consult with his client when choosing a barrister. However, a solicitor must not unlawfully discriminate against anyone in his professional dealings (Outcome 2.1), and consequently must not discriminate when instructing a barrister on the grounds of, for example, age, race, sex or disability. If the client's request appears to be based on discriminatory grounds (eg, a male client defending himself in an Employment Tribunal against an allegation of sex discrimination may request to be represented by a female advocate), the SRA's previous guidance provided that the solicitor must discuss the issue with his client and ask the client to change his instructions. Where the client refuses, the solicitor must cease to act.

16.4   IMMUNITY FOR ADVOCACY WORK

In previous years, immunity was granted to advocates against claims of negligence or breach of contract in respect of advocacy work undertaken. However, this was abolished by the House of Lords in *Arthur JS Hall & Co (A Firm) v Simons* [2000] 3 All ER 673.

16.5   DUTY TO THIRD PARTIES

16.5.1 Not taking an unfair advantage

Outcome 11.1 provides that a solicitor must not use his position as a solicitor to take an unfair advantage of anyone. This applies to the solicitor acting in his personal capacity as well as within his practice, and relates to the protection of the integrity of the profession.

Particular care should be taken when dealing with unrepresented third parties. Usually a solicitor must act in the best interests of his client, but this duty is tempered by a solicitor being required not to take unfair advantage of another person. Accordingly, it may tend to show that the Outcomes in Chapter 11 have not been achieved if a solicitor takes unfair advantage of an opposing party's lack of legal knowledge where that party has not instructed a lawyer (Indicative Behaviour 11.7). The SRA's previous guidance in the 2007 Code of Conduct suggested that the solicitor should advise such an individual to seek independent legal advice.

In the event that a solicitor provides some form of help to an unrepresented third party, care should be taken that a retainer does not arise between the solicitor and the third party.

16.5.2 Public office and personal interests

Solicitors may sometimes be appointed to a public office, such as being a member of a planning committee or a district judge. The public office may provide the solicitor with confidential information or inside knowledge of, for example, policy, which may affect the solicitor's advice to the client or his approach to the matter.

The 'inside information' might also be available to the solicitor if another individual at the solicitor's practice (whether partner member or employee) held such an office, or indeed if it was held by a member of the solicitor's family.

If a solicitor takes unfair advantage of a public office held by him, a member of his family or his firm, it may tend to show that he has not achieved the Outcomes in the Code and therefore not complied with the Principles (Indicative Behaviour 11.10). The same would be the case if a solicitor were to use his professional status or qualification to take unfair advantage of another person to advance his personal interests (Indicative Behaviour 11.9).

16.5.3 Giving references

Under the general law of negligence, a solicitor will owe a duty of care to the subject of any reference given by that solicitor (see *Spring v Guardian Assurance plc* [1994] 3 All ER 129, HL). Accordingly, great care must be taken when giving any such reference to avoid incurring liability. Many firms have in place policies with regard to the giving of references, covering who may give them and the nature of the content.

Furthermore, giving a false reference would almost certainly breach the Code of Conduct, eg for damaging the public trust in solicitors and the provision of legal services (Principle 6).

16.5.4 Offensive letters

A solicitor is under a duty to act with integrity (Principle 2). Accordingly, a solicitor must not write to any third party in a manner that could be considered to be offensive.

16.5.5 Third parties and costs

It may tend to show that a solicitor has achieved the Outcomes in Chapter 11 of the Code if, when another person is paying the client's costs, the solicitor provides the third party with sufficient time and information to enable the costs to be agreed (Indicative Behaviour 11.1). In respect of claiming costs, however, it may tend to show that the Outcomes have not been achieved if the solicitor demands anything that is not legally recoverable. For example, when instructed to collect a simple debt, if a solicitor demands from the debtor the cost of the letter of claim, since such a cost is not legally recoverable at that stage (Indicative Behaviour 11.8).

16.5.6 Beneficiaries

Where a solicitor is instructed to administer a probate estate, the solicitor's client will be the PRs of the deceased's estate. However, in certain circumstances a solicitor will also owe a duty of care to the beneficiaries of that estate.

For example, in *Ross v Caunters* [1980] 1 Ch 297 a solicitor failed to warn a testator that the will should not be witnessed by a beneficiary. Accordingly, the beneficiary who witnessed the will was unable to claim her share of the estate. The solicitor was held liable in negligence to the beneficiary. See also *White v Jones* [1995] 1 All ER 891, where a solicitor was instructed to draw up a will. The client died approximately a month later, before the will had been drafted. The solicitor was successfully sued in negligence by the beneficiaries who missed out on their share of the estate as a result of the solicitor's failure to draft the will.

16.5.7 Contacting a represented third party

Where a client instructs a solicitor, it is often because the client lacks legal knowledge and skills, and therefore seeks the assistance of a legal expert. Accordingly, it may tend to show that the Outcomes have been achieved and the Principles complied with if a solicitor ensures that he does not communicate with another party when he is aware that the other party has retained a lawyer in a matter except:

(a)   to request the name and address of the other party's lawyer; or

(b)   where the other party's lawyer consents to him communicating with the client; or

(c)   where there are exceptional circumstances (Indicative Behaviour 11.4).

16.5.8 Dealing with unrepresented parties

The SRA's previous guidance provided that where a solicitor is dealing with an unrepresented third party, care should be taken that an implied retainer does not arise from the solicitor's dealings with that third party (see **16.5.1**).

Particular care should be taken when a solicitor discovers he is dealing with an unqualified person (see **18.2.1**) who is carrying out work reserved for solicitors, such as preparing papers for a grant of probate. The solicitor is advised to inform the SRA and seek immediate advice from the Professional Ethics Guideance Team.

16.5.9 Agents' costs

As with counsel's fees, a solicitor is personally responsible for meeting the fees of agents or others he appoints on behalf of his client. This extends only to costs properly incurred. Again, this applies whether or not the solicitor has been put in funds, and therefore the solicitor may ask for monies on account prior to incurring such expenditure. Alternatively, the solicitor and agent may agree that the agent's fee will become payable on receipt by the solicitor of the client's payment.

16.6 RELATIONS WITH OTHER SOLICITORS

A solicitor must act with integrity (Principle 2). Therefore a solicitor must treat other solicitors with due respect in all their communications, whether written or oral.

16.6.1 Agency

As noted at **16.5.9** above, solicitors are personally liable to pay the fees of any agent they instruct on behalf of their clients. This applies even when that agent is another solicitor. Solicitors frequently appoint other solicitors to attend court on their behalf, for example where it is not cost-efficient for the solicitor to travel some distance to attend court. The instructing solicitor therefore remains liable for meeting such costs, regardless of whether his client has put him in funds, unless he agrees otherwise with the solicitor-agent.

16.6.2 Other solicitors' clients

One of the Indicative Behaviours in Chapter 11 deals with communicating with another party who the solicitor knows has retained a lawyer in the matter (see **16.5.7**).

16.7 EXAMPLES

EXAMPLE 1

Question   You are representing your client in an employment tribunal. Your client is suing for unfair dismissal. He was sacked for allegedly stealing a laptop. During cross-examination he denies that he ever had the laptop in his possession. Later that day he confides in you that he took the laptop and sold it to a friend to fund a holiday. What should you do here?

Answer   You must not attempt to deceive or mislead the court, or be complicit in another person deceiving or misleading the court, which includes the tribunal (Outcomes 5.1 and 5.2). Following your conversation, you are aware that your client has committed perjury within court proceedings. It may tend to show that you have achieved the Outcomes of the Code and therefore complied with the Principles if you refuse to continue to act for the client unless the client agrees to disclose the truth to the tribunal (Indicative Behaviour 5.5). You cannot inform the tribunal of the truth (or your reasons for withdrawal) without the consent of the client as to do so would be a breach of confidentiality (Outcome 4.1).

EXAMPLE 2

Question   A solicitor instructs counsel on behalf of a client to provide advice on a particular piece of law. Counsel's fee is £1,000 plus VAT. Before the solicitor can bill the client, the client is declared bankrupt. Who is responsible for the counsel's fee?

Answer   The solicitor. This is why many solicitors request that their clients provide them with money on account before instructing counsel.

SUMMARY

The solicitor and the court

(1)   A solicitor must not mislead or deceive the court. A solicitor must also comply with any order of the court which places obligations on him.

(2)   A solicitor must not offer to make payments to witnesses dependent upon their evidence or the outcome of the case.

(3)   Calling a witness whose evidence the solicitor knows to be untrue, or attempting to influence a witness when taking a statement from him as to the contents of that statement, may tend to show that a solicitor has not achieved the Outcomes of the Code and therefore not complied with the Principles.

(4)   Drawing the court's attention to relevant cases and statutory provisions (even if they help the other side) may tend to show that a solicitor has achieved the necessary Outcomes and complied with the Principles.

(5)   A solicitor still owes his client a duty to act in the client's best interests even when the solicitor has instructed counsel to act for that client.

Duty to third parties

(1)   A solicitor must not take an unfair advantage of any person, either for the solicitor's own benefit or for another person's benefit.

(2)   It may tend to show that a solicitor has not achieved the Outcomes of the Code, and therefore not complied with the Principles, if he takes unfair advantage of a public office held by him.

(3)   In certain circumstances a solicitor owes a duty of care to third parties, such as beneficiaries.

(4)   A solicitor must act with integrity when dealing with other solicitors.

CHAPTER 17

FINANCIAL SERVICES

LEARNING OUTCOMES

After reading this chapter you will be able to understand:

- the structure of financial services regulation
- how solicitors are regulated in carrying out financial services work.

17.1 INTRODUCTION

From time to time, solicitors engage in financial services work. To do this, they must be sufficiently competent in that area of practice, and in some cases will need to comply with certain regulations imposed by the Financial Conduct Authority (FCA) and/or The Law Society and Solicitors Regulation Authority (SRA).

Such work could arise:

(a) in conveyancing, if a client needs help in finding a mortgage and a supporting package, which could include a life insurance policy;

(b) in probate, when the executors sell off the deceased's assets;

(c) in litigation, if helping a successful client to invest damages just won;

(d) in company work, in making arrangements for a client to buy or sell shares in a company, and also in arranging corporate finance;

(e) in family work, if arrangements have to be made on a divorce in respect of endowment life policies and/or a family business;

(f) in tax planning or portfolio management, for a private client including trustees.

Under Principle 4 of the Code of Conduct, a solicitor would be in breach of his duty to act in the client's best interests if he did not have sufficient expertise in the area concerned. Therefore, a trainee solicitor should not give investment advice to a client unless the trainee is an expert in that field.

However, many activities in connection with investments are subject to regulation under the Financial Services and Markets Act 2000 (FSMA 2000) and, for example, to give advice on these, or even to make arrangements for clients to acquire or dispose of them, may require the solicitor to be authorised to carry out that activity. To do this without authority could involve the commission of a criminal offence. Thus you will, when handling a matter in which investments are involved, even if only peripherally, need to be doubly careful before advising and assisting such clients. You will need to ask yourself two questions:

(a) Have I got the necessary skill and knowledge?

(b) What am I 'permitted' to do under the financial services regulations?

17.2 SOURCE MATERIAL

The FSMA 2000 gained Royal Assent on 14 June 2000. It contains 433 sections and 22 Schedules. The regulatory regime for financial services came into force at midnight on 30 November 2001. The Financial Services Act 2012, which received Royal Assent of 19 December 2012, extensively amends the FSMA 2000. The provisions of that Act will come into force, or in some cases have already come into force, on such dates as the Treasury specifies in commencement orders. The substance of the provisions of the FSMA 2000 discussed below, however, has remained unchanged.

The FSMA 2000 provides only a general framework, and the detail is in secondary legislation (eg, Orders in Council made by the Treasury). In order to understand the whole of the regulation, it is necessary to study the FSMA 2000 and the various Orders made by the Treasury, for example:

(a) Financial Services and Markets Act 2000 (Regulated Activities) Order 2001, SI 2001/544 (RAO 2001);

(b) Financial Services and Markets Act 2000 (Professions) (Non-Exempt Activities) Order 2001, SI 2001/1227;

(c) Financial Services and Markets Act 2000 (Financial Promotion) Order 2005, SI 2005/1529 (FPO 2005);

(d) Financial Services and Markets Act 2000 (PRA-regulated Activities) Order 2013, SI 2013/556.

The regulation of financial services is a complex and detailed area. This chapter will serve only as an introduction to the regulatory framework. Further guidance may be sought from The Law Society.

Materials on financial services work include:

(a) the SRA Financial Services (Scope) Rules 2001 (Scope Rules 2001);

(b) the SRA Financial Services (Conduct of Business) Rules 2001 (COB Rules 2001).

These may be found on the SRA's website at <www.sra.org.uk> and form part of the SRA *Handbook*.

17.3 FINANCIAL SERVICES REGULATORY STRUCTURE

The FSMA 2000 in effect established the Financial Services Authority (FSA) whose authority was vast and included the regulation of financial services. Following the financial crisis of 2007/08 and criticisms of the regulatory system at the time, the Government announced major reforms in the regulatory structure, including the abolition of the FSA in its current form. Three new regulatory bodies were established under the Financial Services Act 2012: the Financial Conduct Authority (FCA), the Prudential Regulation Authority (PRA) and the Financial Policy Committee (FPC). The FCA and PRA have taken over the majority of the FSA's functions, whilst the FPC (a committee of the Bank of England) is responsible for monitoring the stability of the whole UK financial system and so will not of itself directly supervise firms. The new regulatory structure came into effect on 1 April 2013.

17.3.1   The Financial Conduct Authority (FCA)

The FCA inherited most of the FSA's market regulatory functions, including responsibility for the conduct of business regulation of all firms (such as solicitors' firms), including dual-regulated firms (see **17.3.2**), and for the prudential regulation of firms (ie their safety and soundness) not regulated by the PRA (known as FCA-authorised or FCA-only firms).

The FCA is set the following objectives in the FSMA 2000 (as amended):

(a)   securing an appropriate degree of protection for consumers (the consumer protection objective);

(b)   protecting and enhancing the integrity of the UK financial system (the integrity objective);

(c)   promoting effective competition in the interests of consumers in the market, including for regulated financial services (the competition objective).

It also shares a set of 'regulatory principles' with the PRA and these are set out in s 3B of the FSMA 2000.

The FCA has been given powers not previously granted to the FSA, including being able to require firms to withdraw or amend misleading financial promotions (see **17.11**) with immediate effect and to block the launch of, or stop, a service or product. On 1 April 2014 the FCA took over responsibility for the regulation of consumer credit and second charge mortgages secured over property, both formerly regulated by the Office of Fair Trading (see **17.9**).

From 1 April 2013, the FCA took over the FSA's role relating to the regulation and supervision of the London Interbank Offered Rate (LIBOR), an internationally recognised interest rate benchmark used to set a range of financial transactions. This was against a background of widespread concerns about the operation of LIBOR among regulators and users of LIBOR, including attempts to manipulate it. LIBOR is now a 'specified benchmark' for the purposes of two new regulated activities in the RAO 2001 (see **17.6**), namely providing information in relation to, and administering, a specified benchmark. The manipulation of a specified benchmark is also now a criminal offence under the Financial Services Act 2012.

17.3.2   The Prudential Regulation Authority (PRA)

The PRA is a subsidiary of the Bank of England and is responsible for the authorisation, prudential regulation and general supervision of those firms which manage significant financial risks, namely banks, building societies, insurers, credit unions, certain investment firms and Lloyd's of London. These firms are known as PRA-authorised firms or dual-regulated firms, as they will also be regulated by the FCA for conduct purposes (see **17.3.1**).

The Financial Services and Markets Act 2000 (PRA-regulated Activities) Order 2013 sets out which regulated activities in the RAO 2001 (see **17.6**) are PRA-regulated activities, and any firm with permission to carry out such activities will be designated a PRA-authorised firm. The activities include accepting deposits and effecting a contract of insurance and dealing with investments as principal.

17.4   THE GENERAL FRAMEWORK

Businesses carrying on certain activities, known as 'regulated activities', will need to be authorised by the appropriate regulator, which in the case of a solicitors' firm will be the FCA. The FSMA 2000 contains a special provision for professional firms which do not carry out 'mainstream' investment business but may carry out a regulated activity in the course of carrying out their professional work, such as corporate work. If certain conditions are satisfied, such a firm will be exempt from having to obtain authority from the FCA, provided it is regulated and supervised by a professional body designated by the Treasury (a designated professional body or 'DPB'). The SRA is a DPB for these purposes.

17.5   THE NEED FOR AUTHORITY

There are two main restrictions of most relevance to solicitors:

(a)   carrying out a regulated activity;

(b)   making a financial promotion.

Section 19 of the FSMA 2000 provides that: 'No person may carry on a regulated activity in the UK unless authorised or exempt' (the 'General Prohibition'). Authorised persons are persons with permission granted by the appropriate regulator (the FCA) under the FSMA 2000. A further offence is that of making an unauthorised financial promotion under s 21. Breach of either of these provisions could result in the commission of a criminal offence. Breach of s 19 could also render unenforceable any resulting agreement which has as a party to it the person who contravened s 19, or made with an authorised person carrying on a regulated activity.

17.6   REGULATED ACTIVITY

17.6.1   The four tests

The definition of a 'regulated activity' is set out in s 22 of the FSMA 2000 and has been substantially amended by the Financial Services Act 2012.

In order to determine if an activity is regulated there are four tests:

(a)   Are you in business?

(b)   Is there a specified activity (see **17.6.3** below)?

(c)   Is there a specified investment (see **17.6.2** below), or does the specified activity relate to information about a person's financial standing or the setting of a specified benchmark?

(d)   Is there an exclusion?

The particular activities and investments are specified by the Treasury in the RAO 2001 (as amended) under the FSMA 2000, s 22. Information about a person's financial standing includes providing, or advising upon, credit reference and credit information services (FSMA 2000, Sch 2). The term 'benchmark' is defined in s 22(6) of the FSMA 2000. Originally the only 'specified' benchmark set out in the RAO 2001 was LIBOR (see **17.3.1**), but as from 1 April 2015 a further seven benchmarks were added.

17.6.2   Specified investments

These include:

(a)   company stocks and shares (but not shares in the share capital of open-ended investment companies or building societies incorporated in the UK);

(b)   debentures, loan stock and bonds;

(c)   government securities, such as gilts;

(d)   unit trusts and open-ended investment companies (OEICs), which are similar to unit trusts, but use the structure of a company rather than a trust;

(e)   insurance contracts (including life policies and pension policies) (see **17.10**);

(f)   mortgages;

(g)   home reversion/home purchase plans (the former enables a homeowner to sell the whole or a proportion of his property to a finance provider in order to raise funds, and he then becomes a tenant of the property, whilst the latter serves the same purpose as a mortgage but is structured in a way that is compliant with Islamic law);

(h)   deposits. (These would include cash ISAs and sums of money held in bank or building society accounts. However, the only specified activity relating to these investments is 'accepting deposits', which is mainly carried out by banks and building societies. The main specified investment activities set out in **17.6.3** do not apply to deposits. Sums received by solicitors acting in the course of their business are exempt under the RAO 2001.)

Investments that will not be relevant include:

(a) interests in land;

(b) certain National Savings products.

17.6.3 Specified investment activities

In relation to specified investments, these include (but are not limited to):

(a) dealing as agent;

(b) arranging;

(c) managing;

(d) safeguarding;

(e) advising;

(f) lending money on/administering a regulated mortgage contract.

There are also specified activities that are very particular in their scope, such as establishing, operating or winding up a collective investment scheme or personal pension scheme.

17.6.3.1 Dealing as agent

This involves buying, selling, subscribing for or underwriting the investments where you deal on behalf of a client (ie, rather than on your own account) and commit that client to transactions. For example, selling shares on behalf of a client pursuant to a financial order made on divorce.

17.6.3.2 Arranging

Solicitors will have many clients whose transactions involve investments (eg, endowment policies in conveyancing, unit trusts and shares in probate, etc). The solicitor will very often be involved as the contact between the client and the life company, or the client and the stockbroker. It is in this context that the solicitor may be 'arranging'. Arrangements are excluded where the solicitor merely introduces clients to a person authorised by the FCA (an authorised third person – ATP) and the introduction is made with a view to the provision of independent advice to the client. However, this exclusion does not apply where the transaction relates to an insurance contract. If you do something more than just introduce the client in respect of the investment (eg, you help the client to complete an application form), you will be 'arranging'.

17.6.3.3 Managing

Managing requires active participation beyond the mere holding of investments and applies only to 'discretionary management' (ie, involving the exercise of discretion). This investment activity will be most common in firms that undertake probate and trust work, where the solicitor is acting as trustee or personal representative.

17.6.3.4 Safeguarding

This involves safeguarding and administering investments belonging to a client. This is also particularly relevant for firms which undertake probate and trust work.

17.6.3.5 Advising

This involves giving advice to a person in his capacity as an investor on the merits of his buying, selling, subscribing for, or underwriting an investment. Advice must be about a specific investment; generic advice is outside the scope of the FSMA 2000. Thus you can, if you have the knowledge, advise a client to invest in shares rather than gilts, but if you advise the client to buy shares in a particular company, say Tesco, this will be a regulated activity.

If you do not have the requisite knowledge to provide generic advice, or if the client requires advice on a specified investment, you could refer him to a person authorised by the FCA (an ATP) with a view to the ATP providing that advice. Thus if a client wants advice on what shares to buy, you could refer him to an authorised stockbroker. It will be the stockbroker who 'advises' the client under the FSMA 2000. The referral to the ATP would not amount to a specified activity.

17.6.3.6   Example

> **EXAMPLE**
>
> You have recently managed to secure a large settlement in respect of your client's recent litigation matter. The client tells you that he wishes to invest this money in buying shares in a local company, and asks you which company he should invest in.
>
> Referring to the four-stage test described at **17.6.1**, the client is seeking your advice in your capacity as a solicitor, so you are 'in business'. Shares are a specified investment, and you have been asked to advise on the purchase of these shares – advising is a specified investment activity. Therefore if you are to give this advice you need to take advantage of an exclusion or exemption (see below). If you provide this advice without relying on an exclusion or exemption, you will breach the 'general prohibition' under s 19 of the FSMA 2000, which is a criminal offence.

17.6.4   Exclusions

There are various exclusions set out in the RAO 2001. If an exclusion applies to a particular activity you are carrying out, you do not need to be authorised for that particular transaction. Those exclusions likely to be relevant to solicitors include:

(a)   introducing (see **17.6.3.2**);

(b)   using an ATP;

(c)   acting for an execution-only client;

(d)   acting as trustee or personal representative;

(e)   the 'professional/necessary' exclusion;

(f)   the 'takeover' exclusion.

17.6.4.1   Authorised third persons – the ATP exclusion

If you do something more than merely 'introduce' the client to an ATP (see **17.6.3.5**), you could be 'arranging' or even ' dealing as the client's agent'. However, these will be excluded under RAO 2001, arts 22 and 29 if the transaction is entered into with or through an ATP on the advice given to the client by the ATP.

You cannot rely on this exclusion if you receive from any person other than the client any pecuniary reward (eg, commission) or other advantage, for which you do not account to your client, arising out of his entering into the transaction.

This exclusion will not apply if the transaction relates to an insurance contract.

17.6.4.2   The execution-only client exclusion

There is an exclusion similar to the ATP exclusion where the client, in his capacity as an investor, is not seeking and has not sought advice from the solicitor as to the merits of the client's entering into the transaction (or, if the client has sought such advice, the solicitor has declined to give it but has recommended that the client seek such advice from an authorised person). There is the same restriction in respect of commissions and contracts of insurance.

17.6.4.3 Trustees or personal representatives

The exclusion applies to arranging, managing, safeguarding and advising fellow trustees and/ or beneficiaries. It also applies to lending money on, or administering a regulated mortgage contract.

This exclusion has limitations. It is available to a solicitor acting as a trustee or PR, and not to a solicitor acting *for* a trustee or PR. However, the exclusion does apply if a member of the firm is a trustee or PR but the activity is actually carried out by other members of the firm. Note that the exclusion does not apply if the solicitor is remunerated for what he does 'in addition to any remuneration he receives as trustee or personal representative, and for these purposes a person is not to be regarded as receiving additional remuneration merely because his remuneration is calculated by reference to time spent'. For managing and safeguarding, the exclusion is also not available if the solicitor holds himself out as providing a service comprising managing or safeguarding.

The Law Society's guidance provides that this exclusion will not apply to contracts of insurance.

17.6.4.4 Activities carried on in the course of a profession or non-investment business – the 'professional/necessary' exclusion

This applies to advising, arranging, safeguarding and dealing as agent. There is an exclusion if the activity is performed in the course of carrying on any profession or business and may reasonably be regarded as a necessary part of other services provided in the course of that profession or business. However, the exclusion does not apply if the activity is remunerated separately from the other services. Examples of where this exclusion may apply include: in matrimonial work, arranging the sale or transfer of a joint endowment insurance; or in probate work, arranging for the sale of *all* the assets to pay IHT.

17.6.4.5 Activities carried on in connection with the sale of a body corporate – the takeover exclusion

This exclusion applies to arranging, advising and dealing as agent. It will apply to a transaction to acquire or dispose of shares in a body corporate (other than an OEIC), or for a transaction entered into for the purposes of such an acquisition or disposal, if:

(a)   the shares consist of or include 50% or more of the voting shares in the body corporate; and

(b)   the acquisition or disposal is between parties each of whom is a body corporate, a partnership, a single individual or a group of connected individuals.

It is possible to add the number of shares being acquired by a person to those already held by him in order to determine whether the 50% limit has been achieved.

Even if the above criteria are not met, eg the number of shares acquired is less than 50%, but the object of the transaction may nevertheless reasonably be regarded as being the acquisition of day-to-day control of the affairs of the body corporate, the exclusion still applies.

This is an extremely valuable exclusion for the corporate department where a client is seeking to take over, or sell its interest in, a company, whether public or private.

This exclusion does not apply to advising on, arranging, or dealing as an agent in respect of buying or selling contracts of insurance.

17.6.4.6 Summary table

The table below summarises the specified investment activities to which the exclusions apply.

Specified activity	Applicable exclusions
Dealing as agent	• ATP • Execution-only • Professional/necessary • Takeover
Arranging	• Introducing • ATP • Execution-only • Professional/necessary • Acting as trustee/PR • Takeover
Advising	• Professional/necessary • Acting as trustee/PR • Takeover
Managing	• Acting as trustee/PR
Safeguarding	• Professional/necessary • Acting as trustee/PR

17.6.4.7 Example

> **EXAMPLE**
>
> You are approached by Mrs Patel, who owns 100% of the share capital in X Co Ltd. Mrs Patel wishes to sell 75% of these shares to her son.
>
> Referring to the four tests described at **17.6.1**, the client is seeking your advice and assistance in your capacity as a solicitor, so you are 'in business'. Shares are a specified investment, and in dealing with the matter you will be carrying out specified investment activities (eg advising and arranging). Therefore you need to rely on an exclusion or exemption to avoid breaching s 19 of the FSMA 2000 and committing a criminal offence.
>
> Here you are transferring more than 50% of X Co Ltd, and so can rely on the takeover exclusion described above. Therefore you may complete this work without breaching the general prohibition.

17.7 EXEMPTION FOR PROFESSIONAL FIRMS – s 327 EXEMPTION

17.7.1 Introduction

Under s 326 of the FSMA 2000, the Treasury can designate a professional body (a DPB), and has so designated The Law Society (this role will now be undertaken by the SRA).

Under s 327, the general prohibition in s 19 of the FSMA 2000 will not apply to a regulated activity carried on by a firm of solicitors if the following conditions are met:

(a)   the firm must not receive from a person other than its client any pecuniary or other advantage arising out of the activity for which it does not account to its client;

(b)   the manner of providing 'any service in the course of carrying on the activities must be incidental to the provision' by the firm of professional services, ie services regulated by the SRA.

(c)   the firm must carry out only regulated activities permitted by the DPB, ie the SRA.

(d)   the activities must not be prohibited by an order made by the Treasury, or any direction made by the FCA under s 328 or s 329;

(e)   the firm must not carry on any other regulated activities.

Each of these criteria is discussed further below.

17.7.2   The firm must not receive from a person other than its client any pecuniary or other advantage

If the firm wishes to take advantage of the s 327 exemption then it must account for any such pecuniary advantage to its client. This is mirrored by Outcome 1.15 of the Code. Indicative Behaviour 1.20 provides guidance as to the ways in which this may be achieved (see **11.14**).

17.7.3   Incidental

There are two 'incidental' tests: a specific test and a general test.

The 'specific' test relates to the particular client concerned. Under the Scope Rules 2001, the relevant regulated activity must arise out of, or be complementary to, the provision of a particular professional service to a particular client. The firm could not, therefore, carry out a regulated activity in isolation for a client; the relevant regulated activity must 'arise out of' or be 'complementary to' some other service being provided by it. This other service must not be a regulated activity but must be a 'professional', ie legal, service (eg, in corporate work, giving legal advice, drafting documents or dealing with a regulatory matter; or in probate work, winding up the estate or giving tax advice). It follows that the professional service being provided to the client should be the primary service, and the regulated activity should be 'incidental' or 'subordinate' to the provision of the professional service. Note also that both the professional service and the regulated activity must be supplied to the same person. Thus, in a probate matter, where the probate client is the executor, advice to a beneficiary under the will would not satisfy this test.

To satisfy the 'general' test of being incidental, the activities carried out by the firm which would otherwise be regulated cannot be a major part of the firm's activities. For example, a firm will be ineligible if its income from investment business is half or more of its total income. Further factors are:

(a)   the scale of regulated activity in proportion to other professional services provided;

(b)   whether and to what extent the exempt regulated activities are held out as separate services; and

(c)   the impression given of how the firm provides those activities, for example through advertising its services.

17.7.4   The firm must carry out only regulated activities permitted by the DPB

The role of setting out rules concerning the s 327 exemption, once occupied by The Law Society, now falls to the SRA. Accordingly, the SRA has published the SRA Financial Services (Scope) Rules 2001 (see below) and the SRA Conduct of Business (COB) Rules 2001 for this purpose (see **17.8**). Firms must comply with the requirements prescribed by these rules at all times when seeking to use this exemption.

For example, under the SRA Financial Services (Scope) Rules 2001:

(a)   a solicitor may not recommend, or arrange, for a client to buy or subscribe for a packaged retail investment product (ie, financial products which the Government perceives as ones in respect of which ordinary investors require the most protection, such as certain life policies, unit trusts, and shares in open-ended investment companies). However, a solicitor may advise the client to dispose of a packaged retail investment product, or give negative advice (ie, advise the client not to purchase a packaged retail investment product). There are also restrictions, for example, on advising an individual to acquire certain specified investments (eg, to buy quoted shares), recommend that a client enter into regulated mortgage contracts, or recommend/make arrangements for the client to buy/dispose of rights or interests in a personal pension scheme;

(b) discretionary management is allowed only in prescribed circumstances, for example where the firm, partner or employee is a trustee/PR and an ATP is used when buying an investment. This means that if a solicitor is the trustee of a trust and wishes to acquire some shares, the solicitor will need to be advised by an ATP;

(c) if a firm wishes to undertake insurance mediation (see **17.10**), it must appoint a compliance officer and be registered on the FCA Register;

(d) firms that carry on a credit-related activity (as defined in the *Handbook* Glossary) or a connected activity (see **17.9**) are required to comply with the relevant provisions and guidance set out in the FCA's Consumer Credit Sourcebook (CONC).

For more detail on the above, please consult the Scope Rules 2001, which may be found on the SRA's website at <www.sra.org.uk> and in the SRA *Handbook*.

17.7.5 The activities must not be prohibited by Treasury order or the FCA

The Treasury has set out, in the FSMA 2000 (Professions) (Non-Exempt Activities) Order 2001, a list of activities that cannot be provided by professional firms under the s 327 exemption. The activities that are most relevant to solicitors are incorporated into the SRA Financial Services (Scope) Rules 2001.

The FCA also has power, under s 328, to issue directions (in writing) limiting the application of the exemption in respect of different classes of persons or different descriptions of regulated activities.

17.7.6 The firm must not carry on any other regulated activities

The s 327 exemption cannot be used by firms which are authorised by the FCA. For example, a firm could be authorised by the FCA concerning defined regulated activities. Such a firm could not use s 327 for any other 'non-mainstream' regulated activities.

17.8 THE SRA FINANCIAL SERVICES (CONDUCT OF BUSINESS) RULES 2001

17.8.1 When do the Rules apply?

The SRA Financial Services (Conduct of Business) Rules 2001 (COB Rules 2001) apply only when the firm is carrying out an exempt regulated activity; they do not apply if the firm is not carrying out a regulated activity at all.

17.8.2 Status disclosure (COB Rules 2001, r 3)

A firm must provide clients with certain information concerning the status of the firm. For example, the firm must confirm to the client that it is not authorised by the FCA, and explain that complaints and redress mechanisms are provided through the SRA and the Legal Ombudsman. Any information that is provided under r 3 must be given in a manner that is clear, fair and not misleading.

17.8.3 Best execution (COB Rules 2001, r 4)

A solicitor must act in the best interests of his clients (Principle 4 of the Code of Conduct). Therefore, the firm must carry out transactions for clients as soon as possible and on the best terms available.

17.8.4 Transactions (COB Rules 2001, r 5)

The firm must keep records of:

(a) instructions from clients to carry out transactions; and

(b) instructions to third parties to carry them out.

17.8.5 Commissions (COB Rules 2001, r 6)

Under the COB Rules 2001, r 6, the firm must keep records of commissions received in respect of regulated activities and how those commissions were dealt with.

17.8.6 Execution-only clients (COB Rules 2001, r 8)

Where a firm acts for an execution-only client (see **17.6.4.2**) and the investment concerned is a packaged retail investment product, it must send a letter to the client confirming that he or she is not relying on the advice of the solicitor, and the firm must keep a copy of this letter.

This rule would apply, for example, when the packaged retail investment product is a contract of insurance. Here the 'execution only' exclusion would not apply, and therefore the solicitor would have to rely on the exemption for professional firms (see **17.7**) (and thus comply with the COB Rules).

17.9 CONSUMER CREDIT ACTIVITY

With effect from 1 April 2014, consumer credit activity (for example, credit brokerage, debt collecting under a consumer credit or hire agreement, debt advice and debt management or administration) became a regulated activity for the purposes of s 22 of the FSMA 2000, following the transfer of responsibility for the regulation of such activities from the Office of Fair Trading to the FCA. The activities (known as credit-related activities) are set out in Pt 2 and Pt 3A of the RAO 2001. Accordingly, solicitors carrying out such activities will need to be authorised by the FCA to carry out this business, or ensure that the activities fall within the s 327 exemption (see **17.7**). Representing a client in a litigation matter which has arisen from a consumer credit or hire agreement is not a credit-related activity for these purposes.

A solicitor could be carrying out a credit-related activity by virtue of the way in which he accepts the payment of his fees, including allowing a client time to pay. However, such an arrangement will be regarded as an exempt agreement under the RAO 2001 if all of the following conditions apply:

(a) the number of repayments does not exceed 12;

(b) the payment term does not exceed 12 months; and

(c) the credit is provided without interest or other charges.

In most other cases, such arrangements are likely to be covered by the s 327 exemption.

17.10 INSURANCE MEDIATION

The Government decided to extend regulation to all general insurance selling and administration in order to comply with the Insurance Mediation Directive (2002/92/EC) approved by the European Parliament on 30 September 2003.

A firm will be carrying out 'insurance mediation' where it carries out (or agrees to carry out) the following activities in relation to contracts of insurance:

(a) advising;

(b) arranging;

(c) acting as agent;

(d) assisting in the administration and performance of such contracts, in particular in the event of a claim.

'Contracts of insurance' are defined widely, and include life policies (eg endowment policies), buildings insurance, after-the-event legal insurance, and pension policies.

Thus, whatever the type of insurance policy involved, if a solicitor assists a client to obtain one, even if all he does is to introduce the client to an insurance broker, the solicitor will be carrying out a specified activity. Similarly, if a solicitor is involved in an insurance claim against an insurance company, this will also be caught. All of these activities involve 'insurance mediation'.

Given that the main exclusions will almost certainly not apply to insurance mediation, the firm will have to rely on the s 327 exemption (see **17.7**), seek authorisation from the FCA, or rely on the limited exceptions available for insurance mediation activities (which are beyond the scope of this book).

EXAMPLE

You are acting for Mr George on purchasing a commercial property. Your client needs to obtain defective title insurance. You offer to arrange this for your client.

Using the four tests described at **17.6.1**, you are providing this service to your client and so are 'in business'. Contracts of insurance are a specified investment and arranging is a specified investment activity. Therefore you need to rely on an exclusion or exemption to avoid breaching s 19 of the FSMA 2000 and committing a criminal offence.

However, none of the exclusions applies to contracts of insurance. Therefore, in order to arrange the insurance, you must use the s 327 exemption. Here, arranging the insurance is incidental to your dealing with the property transaction. If your firm can comply with the other conditions outlined above (eg the COB and Scope Rules) then you will be able to arrange the defective title insurance without breaching the general prohibition.

17.11   FINANCIAL PROMOTIONS

17.11.1   Financial Services and Markets Act 2000, s 21

As a result of the FSMA 2000, s 21, a solicitor who is not authorised by the FCA will be unable to make a financial promotion (ie 'communicate an invitation or inducement to engage in investment activity') unless its contents are approved by an authorised person. The structure of the definitions is similar to that for regulated activities, with the Treasury having power by order to specify which investments and activities are 'controlled'. Broadly, the definitions are much the same, although not quite identical.

The result is that you can use almost the same tests as for regulated activities, namely:

(a)   Are you in business?

(b)   Are you making an invitation or inducement?

(c)   In connection with an investment?

(d)   In connection with an investment activity?

Notice, however, that the 'exclusion' test is not applicable. Thus, although you may be carrying out an activity which is not regulated, it may be 'controlled' and subject to the restrictions on financial promotions. The result is that almost anything you may say or write in connection with many transactions could be construed as a financial promotion. Thus if a solicitor advises PRs to sell the deceased's assets, this could be an invitation to deal in investments if, for example, the estate included shares or gilts.

All communications are caught, both real-time and non-real-time. A real-time communication is any communication made in the course of a personal visit, telephone conversation or other interactive dialogue. A non-real-time communication is any other communication, eg, letters e-mails, or brochures. Therefore communications to the other side (eg, letters) and communications to advisers (eg, a fax to a broker) are included just as much as communications to clients.

A real-time communication is 'solicited' where it is made in the course of a personal visit, telephone call or other interactive dialogue, if that call, visit or dialogue:

(a)   was initiated by the recipient (eg, the client) of the communication; or

(b)   takes place in response to an express request from the recipient of the communication (see FPO 2005, art 8).

17.11.2   Exemptions

There are then some exemptions set out in the FPO 2005. Many of these are in terms similar to the exclusions for regulated activities. These include:

(a)   trustees, PRs (FPO 2005, arts 53/54);

(b)   takeover of body corporate (FPO 2005, art 62).

17.11.3   Exemption for exempt professional firms

There are two exemptions designed specifically for firms claiming the special exemption under the FSMA 2000 for exempt regulated activities (see **17.7**). These deal with real-time and non-real-time promotions.

17.11.3.1   Real-time promotions (FPO 2005, art 55)

A solicitor who carries on exempt regulated activities may make a real-time promotion, for example during a meeting or a telephone conversation:

(a)   if made to a client who has, prior to the communication being made, engaged the solicitor to provide professional services; and

(b)   where the controlled activity to which the communication relates is exempt because of the exemption for professional firms, or is excluded from being a regulated activity by the 'necessary' exclusion; and

(c)   where the controlled activity to which the communication relates would be undertaken for the purposes of, and be incidental to, the provision of professional services to or at the request of the client.

The effect is that if the activity is excluded from being a regulated activity by an exclusion other than the 'necessary' exclusion, art 55 does not apply.

17.11.3.2   Non-real time promotions (FPO 2005, art 55A)

This applies to letters, e-mails, brochures, websites, etc, where the solicitor carries on exempt regulated activities, provided the promotion contains certain specific statements.

17.11.4   One-off promotions (FPO 2005, arts 28/28A)

One-off, non-real-time communications and solicited real-time communications are exempt under the FPO 2005, art 28 if certain conditions are satisfied. Basically the communication must be one that is personal to the client.

One-off, unsolicited real-time communications are exempt under art 28A, provided the solicitor believes on reasonable grounds:

(a)   that the client understands the risks associated with engaging in the investment activity to which the financial promotion relates; and

(b)   that, at the time of the communication, the client would expect to be contacted by the solicitor in relation to that investment activity.

17.11.5   Introducers (FPO 2005, art 15)

You may make any real-time communication in order to introduce a client to an ATP, provided:

(a)   you are not connected to (eg, a close relative of) the ATP;

(b) you do not receive other than from the client any pecuniary reward or other advantage arising out of making the introduction; and

(c) the client is not seeking and has not sought advice from you as to the merits of his engaging in investment activity (or, if the client has sought such advice, you have declined to give it, but have recommended that the client seeks such advice from an authorised person).

17.12 EXAMPLES

EXAMPLE 1

Question   You are approached Mr McParlane and Mr Ferguson. Between them and Mr Smith they own 100% of the share capital in Y Co Ltd, the company they founded. Mr McParlane owns 40% of the share capital, Mr Ferguson owns 40% and Mr Smith owns the remaining 20%. The shares carry equal voting rights.

They inform you that Mr McParlane wishes to retire from the business, and Mr Ferguson wishes to buy out his interest in the company. They want you to act for both of them in negotiating and arranging this transfer.

You decline to act for both of them due to the conflict of interest between them (see Chapter 13), but agree to act for Mr McParlane in the sale of his shares to Mr Ferguson. Your firm is not authorised by the FCA. Can you act for Mr McParlane without breaching s 19 of FSMA 2000?

Answer   You are advising Mr McParlane as a solicitor, so you are 'in business'. Shares are a specified investment, and in dealing with the sale you would be taking part in a specified investment activity (arranging or advising). Therefore you need to take advantage of an exclusion or exemption.

Can you use the takeover exclusion? This applies to a transaction to acquire or dispose of shares in a body corporate. Although the transfer of shares does not include 50% or more of the voting shares in the company, the transfer will give Mr Ferguson more than 50% of the voting shares; therefore the exclusion will apply. You can act for Mr McParlane without breaching the general prohibition and committing a criminal offence.

EXAMPLE 2

Question   Review the example given at **17.10**. Would it have made any difference if the client was dealing with the property purchase himself, and just came to you to arrange the defective title insurance?

Answer   Yes.

You are still in business, and carrying out a specified investment activity (arranging) in relation to a specified investment (a contract of insurance). None of the exclusions apply to contracts of insurance.

However, here the s 327 exemption is not available as the work you have been instructed to do is not incidental to your provision of legal work.

SUMMARY

Regulated activity

In order to determine if an activity is regulated there are four tests:

(1)   Are you in business?

(2)   Is there a specified investment?

(3)   Is there a specified investment activity (or an activity related to information about a person's financial standing or the setting of a specified benchmark)?

(4)   Is there an exclusion?

Specified investments

(1)   These include:

    (a)   shares (but not shares in the share capital of an open-ended investment company or building society incorporated in the UK);

    (b)   debentures;

    (c)   gilts;

    (d)   unit trusts and OEICs;

    (e)   contract of insurance;

    (f)   mortgages;

    (g)   home reversion/home purchase plans;

    (h)   deposits.

(2)   Investments that will not be relevant include:

    (a)   interests in land;

    (b)   National Savings products.

Specified investment activities

These include:

(1)   dealing as agent;

(2)   arranging;

(3)   managing;

(4)   safeguarding;

(5)   advising.

Exclusions

These include:

(1)   introducing;

(2)   ATP;

(3)   execution-only;

(4)   trustee/PR;

(5)   professional/necessary;

(6)   takeover.

Exempt regulated activities

(1)   A firm not authorised by the FCA should pay attention to:

    (a)   FSMA 2000;

    (b)   RAO 2001;

    (c)   any rules made by the FCA;

    (d)   SRA Scope Rules 2001.

(2)   Conditions set out in the FSMA 2000, the RAO 2001 and the Scope Rules 2001 overlap.

(3)   The main conditions for claiming the s 327 exemption are:

(a)   the activity must arise out of, or be complementary to, the provision of a particular professional service to a particular client;

(b)   the manner of provision by the firm of any service in the course of carrying out the activities is incidental to the provision by the firm of professional services;

(c)   the firm must account to the client for any reward or other advantage which the firm receives from a third party;

(d)   the Scope Rules do not prohibit the firm using the exemption.

(4)   Packaged retail investment products. Generally, you are not allowed to recommend or arrange for a client to buy or subscribe for a packaged retail investment product, for example:

(a)   certain life policies;

(b)   unit trusts;

(c)   OEICs.

(5)   There are also restrictions on advising an individual to acquire certain specified investments (eg, shares in publicly quoted companies).

Conduct of Business Rules

(1)   The SRA COB Rules 2001 apply only when the firm is carrying out an exempt regulated activity; they do not apply if the firm is not carrying out a regulated activity at all.

(2)   The SRA COB Rules 2001 cover:

(a)   best execution;

(b)   records of transactions;

(c)   records of commissions;

(d)   letters to execution-only clients.

Financial promotions

(1)   There are four questions:

(a)   Are you in business?

(b)   Do you make an invitation or inducement?

(c)   Is there a specified investment?

(d)   Is there a specified investment activity?

(2)   There are two special exemptions for professional firms:

(a)   real-time promotions;

(b)   non-real-time promotions.

(3)   Other exemptions include:

(a)   one-off promotions;

(b)   introducers;

(c)   trustees, PRs;

(d)   takeover of body corporate.

REQUIREMENTS OF PRACTICE

LEARNING OUTCOMES

After reading this chapter you will be able to understand:

- the need to satisfy the SRA Suitability Test 2011
- the need to hold a practising certificate and comply with other practising requirements
- the need to submit accountants' reports
- the requirement for indemnity insurance
- the need for effective supervision.

18.1 THE SRA SUITABILITY TEST 2011

18.1.1 Applicability

This test came into force on 6 October 2011 and applies to:

(a) students and trainee solicitors;

(b) qualified lawyers from other jurisdictions seeking qualification via a formal transfer;

(c) those seeking admission as solicitors;

(d) compliance officers, owners and/or managers at the point of and throughout their period of authorisation; and

(e) former solicitors seeking restoration to the roll of solicitors.

The aim is for the test to apply the same standards to all those working within the profession, whether to not they are solicitors.

18.1.2 Outcomes of the test

The Outcomes which apply to the test are that:

(a) solicitors are of the required standard of character and suitability (Outcome SB1);

(b) authorised role holders are fit and proper to hold those roles (Outcome SB2); and

(c) clients, and the wider public, will have confidence that Outcome SB1 has been demonstrated (Outcome SB3).

Those subject to the test must also comply with the Principles set out in the Code of Conduct (see **Chapter 8**).

18.1.3 Requirements

Those applying for eligibility to commence or continue a period of recognised training, admission or restoration to the roll must comply with the basic requirements set out in Part 1 of the test, as discussed below.

18.1.3.1 Criminal offences

If an applicant has been convicted of a criminal offence, the action taken by the SRA will depend upon the type of offence involved. These are dealt with in the following categories:

(a) *Convictions for criminal offences which will result in the application being refused unless there are exceptional circumstances.* These include offences resulting in a custodial or suspended sentence, involving dishonesty, perjury, fraud and/or bribery, or which demonstrated behaviour showing signs of discrimination towards others.

(b) *Those in respect of which the SRA will more likely than not refuse the application.* These include convictions for criminal offences not falling within the category described in (a) above, but which have an impact upon the applicant's 'character and suitability' (defined as satisfying the requirement of s 3 of the Solicitors Act 1974 in order that an individual shall be admitted as a solicitor). These also include an offence involving dishonesty for which a caution has been accepted.

(c) *Those in respect of which the SRA may refuse the application.* This includes where an applicant has received a local warning from the police or accepted a caution from the police for an offence not involving dishonesty.

18.1.3.2 Disclosure

Failing to disclose any material information relating to the application will amount to prima facie evidence of dishonest behaviour. Criminal convictions or cautions which are 'protected' by virtue of the amended Rehabilitation of Offenders Act 1974 (Exceptions) Order 1975 (SI 1975/1023) are not, however, required to be disclosed.

18.1.3.3 Behaviour not compatible with that expected of a prospective solicitor

Being responsible for certain behaviour will result in the application being refused unless there are exceptional circumstances. This includes behaviour which is dishonest or violent, or where there is evidence of discrimination towards others.

18.1.3.4 Assessment offences

Unless there are exceptional circumstances, an application will be refused if the applicant has committed and/or been adjudged by an education establishment to have committed a deliberate assessment offence which amounts to plagiarism or cheating to gain an advantage for himself or for others.

18.1.3.5 Financial behaviour

Unless there are exceptional circumstances, an application will be refused if there is evidence:

(a) that the applicant cannot manage his finances properly and carefully;

(b) that the applicant has deliberately sought to avoid responsibility for his debts; and/or

(c) of dishonesty in relation to the management of the applicant's finances.

If an applicant has been declared bankrupt, entered into any individual voluntary arrangements or has had a county court judgment issued against him, it will raise a presumption that there has been evidence that he cannot manage his finances properly and carefully.

18.1.3.6   Regulatory history

Examples of when an application will be refused on this basis (unless there are exceptional circumstances) are where an applicant has been made the subject of a serious disciplinary finding, sanction or action by a regulatory body, has failed to disclose information to a regulatory body when required to do so or has significantly breached the requirements of a regulatory body. A rebuke, reprimand or warning about an applicant's conduct by a regulatory body may result in the application being refused, unless there are exceptional circumstances.

Those seeking to become authorised role holders must comply with both the basic requirements in Part 1 and the additional requirements set out in Part 2 (which are beyond the scope of this book).

18.2   PRACTISING CERTIFICATES

18.2.1   Requirement to hold a certificate

Section 1 of the Solicitors Act 1974 states:

> No person shall be qualified to act as a solicitor unless—
>
> (a)   he has been admitted as a solicitor, and
>
> (b)   his name is on the roll, and
>
> (c)   he has in force a certificate issued by the Society . . . authorising him to practise as a solicitor (in this Act referred to as a 'practising certificate').

Any person who does not comply with this section will fall within the definition of an 'unqualified person' (Solicitors Act 1974, s 87) and so cannot practise as a solicitor.

Any person who practises as a solicitor without having a practising certificate will commit a criminal offence.

18.2.2   Persons who need a certificate

The following persons are amongst those who must hold a current practising certificate:

(a)   a solicitor who administers an oath;

(b)   all solicitors in private practice;

(c)   any person held out, or employed, explicitly or implicitly as a practising solicitor;

(d)   any person undertaking work reserved for solicitors in England and Wales (subject to limited exceptions);

(e)   any person, who is admitted as a solicitor and has his name on the roll (see **18.2.3**), who is employed by a solicitor (or recognised body) in connection with the provision of any legal service (for example as a paralegal);

(f)   any person involved in legal practise whose work depends upon him being a solicitor.

18.2.3   The roll

The SRA keeps a list of all solicitors, called 'the roll', containing details such as their date of birth, date of admission, and principal place of business in the case of a practising solicitor. Entries on the roll are available for inspection by the public. A solicitor does not have to hold a practising certificate to remain on the roll of solicitors.

18.2.4   Issue of certificates

Those who are required to hold a practising certificate must apply to the SRA each year to have their certificates renewed. All practising certificates become due for renewal on 31 October each year. A fee is payable on renewal of the certificate. A new fee policy was put in place in 2010 which splits the fee between the individual solicitor (flat fee) and the firm (a fee based on its turnover), although in reality the firm may be willing to pay the fee in its entirety.

Solicitors and firms also have to make a fixed yearly contribution to the SRA's Compensation Fund (see **7.11**).

A solicitor is obliged to inform the SRA promptly of any material changes to relevant information about himself, including serious financial difficulty, action taken against him by another regulator, and serious failure to comply with or achieve the Principles, rules and Outcomes in the SRA *Handbook* (Outcome 10.3).

18.2.5   The SRA Practising Regulations 2011

As the issuer of practising certificates, the SRA, pursuant to the SRA Practising Regulations 2011, has a certain level of discretion regarding their issue. Where reg 3 applies, the SRA may grant or decline to grant the certificate, or may impose conditions on the certificate. Regulation 3 applies in specific circumstances, including:

(a)   where the solicitor has been reprimanded by the Solicitors Disciplinary Tribunal, struck off or suspended by the court, or where the applicant has been refused approval to be a manager, owner or compliance officer of an authorised body or whose authority has been suspended or revoked by the SRA/another approved regulator;

(b)   where the SRA has requested an explanation from the solicitor in respect of his conduct, and the SRA has notified the solicitor that it does not regard the solicitor's response (or lack of response) as satisfactory;

(c)   where the solicitor has failed to obtain or deliver an accountant's report (see **18.4**);

(d)   where the solicitor has been suspended from practice and that suspension has come to an end;

(e)   where the solicitor's practising certificate is currently subject to a condition;

(f)   where the solicitor is an undischarged bankrupt.

In any of these circumstances, the SRA has the discretion to impose conditions on the issue of, or refuse to issue, a practising certificate. However, the SRA may impose a condition on a certificate only where one of the requirements of reg 7 is met. For example, where the SRA considers that the solicitor is likely to put at risk the interests of clients, third parties or the public by taking certain steps in relation to legal practice, and that imposing conditions would, in the public interest, restrict, limit or halt the taking of such steps. This may, for example, include additional requirements for filing accountants' reports more frequently than normal if the solicitor in question was found to have been in breach of the SRA Accounts Rules.

18.2.6   Refusal of certificate

Whilst the SRA is granted a discretion with regard to the issue of practising certificates in certain circumstances, measures are in place to ensure that it cannot unreasonably withhold, or impose conditions on, a practising certificate. For example, reg 8 provides that where the SRA refuses to issue or replace a practising certificate, the applicant may appeal to the SRA and thereafter to the High Court.

18.2.7   Suspension of certificate

Where a bankruptcy order is made against a solicitor, his practising certificate is automatically suspended (Solicitors Act 1974, s 15(1)). The SRA may also suspend a current practising certificate if the solicitor is convicted of a crime involving dishonesty or deception, or an indictable offence (Solicitors Act 1974, s 13B).

18.2.8   Post-admission training requirements

The SRA has introduced a new approach to ensure that solicitors remain competent post admission. In place of solicitors undertaking a set number of hours of training each year, the regime involves:

(a) reflection on the quality of their practice by reference to a Competence Statement (consisting of a statement of solicitor competence, the threshold standard and a statement of legal knowledge) and addressing learning and development needs; and

(b) making an annual declaration that they have considered their training needs and taken measures to maintain their competence.

This has been mandatory for all solicitors from 1 November 2016.

18.3 ADDITIONAL PRACTISING REQUIREMENTS

18.3.1 Higher rights of audience

Solicitors are granted rights of audience in all courts upon qualification, but cannot exercise those rights in the higher courts, namely the Crown Court, High Court, Court of Appeal and Supreme Court, until they have complied with additional requirements set out in the SRA Higher Rights of Audience Regulations 2011.

18.3.2 Criminal advocacy

With effect from 30 September 2013, solicitors who carry out criminal advocacy (as defined in the *Handbook* Glossary) can do so only where accredited by the SRA under the SRA Quality Assurance Scheme for Advocates (Crime) Regulations 2013 (known as the QASA Regulations).

18.4 ACCOUNTANTS' REPORTS

Under s 34 of the Solicitors Act 1974 and the SRA Accounts Rules, unless exempt, solicitors who have held or received client money must obtain an accountant's report within six months of their accounting period.

The purpose of the report is to certify compliance with the SRA Accounts Rules. Any breach of the Rules should be identified by the accountant, and, if the accountant finds it necessary to qualify the report, such a report must be delivered to the SRA within six months of the end of the accounting period.

To be independent, the accountant should not be employed by the solicitor's firm or any connected business, and the report must include the name of the individual accountant who has prepared the report.

A recognised or licensed body may obtain one report for the firm.

As outlined in **18.2.5**, the SRA may require a solicitor to deliver an accountant's report in all circumstances, or more frequent delivery of reports, as a condition on his practising certificate following disciplinary proceedings.

18.5 INDEMNITY INSURANCE

18.5.1 Requirement for insurance

Under Outcome 7.13 of the Code of Conduct, firms are required to assess and purchase the level of professional indemnity insurance that is appropriate for its current and past practice, taking into account potential levels of claim by its clients and others and any alternative arrangements the firm or its clients may make. The insurance must meet certain minimum requirements set out in the SRA Indemnity Insurance Rules 2013.

The requirement does not apply to assistant solicitors, trainees, or other individuals employed by a solicitors practice, who will be covered by any insurance taken out by the firm or their principal.

This insurance protects the solicitor against civil claims made against him in the course of his practice; it also protects an injured client by ensuring that solicitors in practice have sufficient monies in place to meet claims made against them.

In previous years, The Law Society ran its own insurance scheme and firms were obliged to obtain their insurance through this scheme. However, firms must now take out insurance with one or more participating insurers in accordance with the SRA Indemnity Insurance Rules 2013, and ensure that they have qualifying insurance in place at all times. The participating insurer has to comply with certain minimum terms and conditions (for example, see **18.5.2**).

Claims against uninsured firms are dealt with by way of grants from the SRA Compensation Fund (see **7.11**).

18.5.2   Amount of cover

The sum insured for any one claim (exclusive of defence costs) must be at least £3,000,000 for relevant recognised and licensed bodies, and at least £2,000,000 in all other cases. The term 'relevant recognised bodies' excludes sole practitioners and non-LLP partnerships. However, this may not be the minimum level of cover they need in order to provide adequate insurance protection for their practice. Firms may therefore take out 'top-up' cover to increase the amount covered under their insurance.

The Code of Conduct provides that solicitors must ensure that clients have the benefit of compulsory professional indemnity insurance, and that they do not exclude or attempt to exclude liability below the minimum required level (Outcome 1.8). If a solicitor seeks to limit his liability to a client to a level above the minimum required by the SRA Indemnity Insurance Rules 2013, ensuring that this limitation is in writing and is brought to the client's attention may tend to show that he has achieved the relevant Outcomes of the Code (Indicative Behaviour 1.8). In addition, under the Provision of Services Regulations 2009 (SI 2009/2999), it is necessary to make available to clients information about the firm's compulsory layer of professional indemnity insurance, including details of the insurer and the territorial coverage of its insurance.

18.6   RESPONSIBILITY OF MANAGERS OF RECOGNISED AND LICENSED BODIES

Managers of recognised and licensed bodies must ensure that their practice complies with the requirements of professional conduct. In certain cases, they will be held to be liable for any breach. For example, where one partner breaches the SRA Accounts Rules, every other partner of the firm will be jointly responsible for this breach and liable to be disciplined. This will be the case even if the other partners had no knowledge of what the 'rogue' partner was doing.

For breaches other than breaches of the SRA Accounts Rules, the SRA has a discretion as to whether to pursue disciplinary action against the other principals (eg partners, members of an LLP, etc).

18.7   SUPERVISION

18.7.1   Qualified to supervise

Under the SRA Practice Framework Rules 2011 (which came into effect from 6 October 2011), at least one of the lawyer managers of an authorised body (eg, a partner or member of an LLP) must be 'qualified to supervise'.

'Qualified to supervise' is defined in Rule 12 as being someone who has:

(a)   completed the training specified from time to time by the SRA for this purpose (currently at least 12 hours of training on management skills); and

(b)   been entitled to practise as a lawyer for at least 36 months within the last 10 years; and

(c)   must be able to demonstrate this if asked by the SRA.

These requirements replicate those set out in the Solicitors' Code of Conduct 2007.

18.7.2   Responsibilities of supervision and management

Chapter 7 of the Code of Conduct sets out requirements concerning the management and supervision of the firm. The SRA recognises that the overarching responsibility for the management of the business in the broadest sense rests with the managers. Accordingly, the managers must, for example:

(a)   identify, monitor and manage risks to achieve compliance with all the Principles, rules and Outcomes, and other requirements of the SRA *Handbook*, and take steps to address issues identified (Outcome 7.3);

(b)   comply with legislation applicable to their business, including anti-money laundering and data protection legislation (Outcome 7.5);

(c)   train individuals working in the firm to maintain a level of competence appropriate to their work and level of responsibility (Outcome 7.6);

(d)   have a system for supervising clients' matters, to include the regular checking of the quality of work by suitably competent and experienced people (Outcome 7.8).

The Code does not go on to specify the precise arrangements that should be put in place to meet these Outcomes. The introduction to the Chapter makes it clear that the managers of the firm should determine what arrangements are appropriate. Factors to be taken into account include the size and complexity of the firm, the number, experience and qualifications of the employees, the number of offices and the nature of work undertaken.

18.8   SEPARATE BUSINESSES

A solicitor's ability to set up and run a business which provides legal services of a type normally supplied by solicitors is limited by the Outcomes in Chapter 12 of the Code.

The object of Chapter 12 is very clear. It is important that clients or members of the public are protected when they obtain mainstream legal services from a firm regulated by the SRA. It is vital that the public is not confused or misled by a solicitor incorporating non-regulated services into his solicitors' practice.

A separate business essentially means a business which is not authorised by the SRA or another approved regulator.

Solicitors should ensure, and have safeguards in place to ensure, that clients are clear about the extent to which the services that they and the separate business offer are regulated (Outcome 12.1) and that the separate business or any of its services is not represented, directly or indirectly, as being regulated by the SRA (Outcome 12.2).

The separate business cannot carry on 'reserved legal activities' (which include the exercise of a right of audience, the conduct of litigation and probate activities) or immigration work unless that work is regulated by the Office of the Immigration Services Commissioner (Outcome 12.3). These are 'mainstream' legal services which the SRA considers members of the public would expect a lawyer to offer. Historically, examples of the kind of services that a separate business offered are alternative dispute resolution, financial services and an estate agency. However, the SRA Practice Framework Rules 2011 have been amended to permit recognised bodies and sole practices to offer a wider range of services than before, including the kind of services mentioned above (see Rule 13.2), and so a separate business would no longer be required in order to offer these.

A solicitor should only refer, recommend or introduce a client to the separate business or divide a client's matter between his regulated business and the separate business where the client has given informed consent (Outcome 12.4).

18.9   DUTY TO THE SOLICITORS REGULATION AUTHORITY

18.9.1   Duty to cooperate

A solicitor must cooperate fully with the SRA and the Legal Ombudsman at all times, including in relation to any investigation about a claim for redress against him (Outcome 10.6).

A solicitor must also comply promptly with any written notice from the SRA (Outcome 10.8). Such a notice may be served where the SRA is investigating whether the solicitor or firm is complying with the requirements of professional conduct. All documents held and all information and explanations requested are to be produced for inspection by the SRA (Outcome 10.9).

Lastly, a solicitor must not attempt to prevent anyone from providing information to the SRA or the Legal Ombudsman (Outcome 10.7).

18.9.2   Investigating claims for redress

Solicitors and recognised/licensed bodies must, if required to do so by the SRA on a particular matter, act promptly to investigate whether a person may have a claim for redress resulting from an act or omission of the firm. The firm must provide the SRA with a report into the matter, notify the individual of the details of the potential claim, and provide details of the firm's complaints procedure and of the Legal Ombudsman (Outcome 10.11).

18.9.3   Reporting serious misconduct

A solicitor is obliged, pursuant to Outcome 10.4, to report to the SRA promptly serious misconduct by any person or firm authorised by the SRA, or any employee, manager or owner of such a firm (taking into account, where necessary, the duty of confidentiality to the client).

18.10   EXAMPLES

EXAMPLE 1

Question   You are a manager in a recognised body. You learn that one of your clients has complained to the Legal Ombudsman that one of the assistant solicitors under your supervision has been acting on a matter where his interests conflict with those of the client? Who may be disciplined by the SRA in these circumstances?

Answer   The SRA may discipline the solicitor concerned. However, instead of or in addition to this action, the SRA will look at whether this solicitor was adequately supervised. Therefore the SRA could pursue you as the manager responsible and/or the recognised body in this regard.

EXAMPLE 2

Question   You are a manager in a recognised body. Whilst completing a file review of an assistant solicitor, you discover that he has persuaded an elderly client to transfer his house (worth £300,000) to him for £50,000. It appears that the assistant solicitor convinced the client that the house was worth only £40,000. What are you obliged to do?

Answer   You are obliged to report any serious misconduct by a solicitor to the SRA (Outcome 10.4). Whether misconduct can be considered 'serious' will depend on the circumstances, but conduct involving deception, dishonesty or a serious criminal offence will amount to serious misconduct. Given the circumstances, the solicitor's conduct is clearly serious misconduct. You must report the matter to the SRA.

SUMMARY

SRA Suitability Test

(1) Those intending to become solicitors, those seeking to become authorised role holders within authorised bodies and former solicitors seeking restoration to the roll of solicitors must satisfy the SRA Suitability Test 2011.

(2) Certain behaviour, including the committing of certain criminal or assessment offences, will result in the application to become a solicitor/authorised role holder being refused by the SRA unless there are exceptional circumstances.

Practising certificates and related matters

(1) The Solicitors Act 1974, s 1 states:

No person shall be qualified to act as a solicitor unless—

(a) he has been admitted as a solicitor, and

(b) his name is on the roll, and

(c) he has in force a certificate issued by the Society ... authorising him to practise as a solicitor (in this Act referred to as a 'practising certificate').

(2) Practising certificates are issued annually by the SRA.

(3) The SRA may grant or refuse an application for a certificate. The SRA may also grant a certificate subject to specified conditions.

(4) Solicitors wishing to exercise higher rights of audience and carrying out criminal advocacy must comply with additional SRA requirements.

(5) Solicitors' firms are obliged to obtain an annual accountant's report.

Indemnity Insurance

(1) The SRA Indemnity Insurance Rules 2013 require solicitors to take out compulsory insurance cover against the risks of professional negligence or other civil liability claims.

(2) Firms can insure with any approved commercial insurer.

(3) Relevant recognised and licensed bodies must obtain cover to a minimum £3 million per individual claim (a minimum of £2 million in all other cases). Voluntary top-up cover may be required.

Supervision

(1) At least one lawyer manager of an authorised body must be 'qualified to supervise'.

(2) Regardless of whether they are 'qualified to supervise', managers should determine what arrangements are appropriate for the management and supervision of their firms, to meet the Outcomes of the Code.

SRA CODE OF CONDUCT

CHAPTER 1 – CLIENT CARE

Outcomes

You must achieve these outcomes:

O(1.1)   you treat your *clients* fairly;

O(1.2)   you provide services to your *clients* in a manner which protects their interests in their matter, subject to the proper administration of justice;

O(1.3)   when deciding whether to act, or terminate your instructions, you comply with the law and the Code;

O(1.4)   you have the resources, skills and procedures to carry out your *clients'* instructions;

O(1.5)   the service you provide to *clients* is competent, delivered in a timely manner and takes account of your *clients'* needs and circumstances;

O(1.6)   you only enter into fee agreements with your *clients* that are legal, and which you consider are suitable for the *client's* needs and take account of the *client's* best interests;

O(1.7)   you inform *clients* whether and how the services you provide are regulated and how this affects the protections available to the *client*;

O(1.8)   *clients* have the benefit of your *compulsory professional indemnity insurance* and you do not exclude or attempt to exclude liability below the minimum level of cover required by the *SRA Indemnity Insurance Rules*;

O(1.9)   *clients* are informed in writing at the outset of their matter of their right to complain and how *complaints* can be made;

O(1.10) *clients* are informed in writing, both at the time of engagement and at the conclusion of your *complaints* procedure, of their right to complain to the *Legal Ombudsman*, the time frame for doing so and full details of how to contact the *Legal Ombudsman*;

O(1.11) *clients' complaints* are dealt with promptly, fairly, openly and effectively;

O(1.12) *clients* are in a position to make informed decisions about the services they need, how their matter will be handled and the options available to them;

O(1.13) *clients* receive the best possible information, both at the time of engagement and when appropriate as their matter progresses, about the likely overall cost of their matter;

O(1.14) *clients* are informed of their right to challenge or complain about your bill and the circumstances in which they may be liable to pay interest on an unpaid bill;

O(1.15) you properly account to *clients* for any *financial benefit* you receive as a result of your instructions;

O(1.16) you inform *clients* if you discover any act or omission which could give rise to a claim by them against you.

Indicative behaviours

Acting in the following way(s) may tend to show that you have achieved these outcomes and therefore complied with the *Principles*:

Dealing with the client's matter

IB(1.1)   agreeing an appropriate level of service with your *client*, for example the type and frequency of communications;

IB(1.2)   explaining your responsibilities and those of the *client*;

IB(1.3)   ensuring that the *client* is told, in writing, the name and status of the person(s) dealing with the matter and the name and status of the person responsible for its overall supervision;

IB(1.4)   explaining any arrangements, such as fee sharing or *referral arrangements*, which are relevant to the *client's* instructions;

IB(1.5)   explaining any limitations or conditions on what you can do for the *client*, for example, because of the way the *client's* matter is funded;

IB(1.6)   in taking instructions and during the course of the retainer, having proper regard to your *client's* mental capacity or other vulnerability, such as incapacity or duress;

IB(1.7)   considering whether you should decline to act or cease to act because you cannot act in the *client's* best interests;

IB(1.8)   if you seek to limit your liability to your *client* to a level above the minimum required by the *SRA Indemnity Insurance Rules*, ensuring that this limitation is in writing and is brought to the *client's* attention;

IB(1.9)   refusing to act where your *client* proposes to make a gift of significant value to you or a member of your family, or a member of your *firm* or their family, unless the *client* takes independent legal advice;

IB(1.10)   if you have to cease acting for a *client*, explaining to the *client* their possible options for pursuing their matter;

IB(1.11)   you inform *clients* if they are not entitled to the protections of the *SRA* Compensation Fund;

IB(1.12)   considering whether a *conflict of interests* has arisen or whether the *client* should be advised to obtain independent advice where the *client* notifies you of their intention to make a claim or if you discover an act or omission which might give rise to a claim;

Fee arrangements with your client

IB(1.13)   discussing whether the potential outcomes of the *client's* matter are likely to justify the expense or risk involved, including any risk of having to pay someone else's legal fees;

IB(1.14)   clearly explaining your fees and if and when they are likely to change;

IB(1.15)   warning about any other payments for which the *client* may be responsible;

IB(1.16)   discussing how the *client* will pay, including whether public funding may be available, whether the *client* has insurance that might cover the fees, and whether the fees may be paid by someone else such as a trade union;

IB(1.17)   where you are acting for a *client* under a fee arrangement governed by statute, such as a conditional fee agreement, giving the *client* all relevant information relating to that arrangement;

IB(1.18)   where you are acting for a publicly funded *client*, explaining how their publicly funded status affects the costs;

IB(1.19) providing the information in a clear and accessible form which is appropriate to the needs and circumstances of the client;

IB(1.20) where you receive a *financial benefit* as a result of acting for a client, either:

(a) paying it to the client;

(b) offsetting it against your fees; or

(c) keeping it only where you can justify keeping it, you have told the client the amount of the benefit (or an approximation if you do not know the exact amount) and the client has agreed that you can keep it;

IB(1.21) ensuring that *disbursements* included in your bill reflect the actual amount spent or to be spent on behalf of the client;

Complaints handling

IB(1.22) having a written *complaints* procedure which:

(a) is brought to clients' attention at the outset of the matter;

(b) is easy for clients to use and understand, allowing for *complaints* to be made by any reasonable means;

(c) is responsive to the needs of individual clients, especially those who are vulnerable;

(d) enables *complaints* to be dealt with promptly and fairly, with decisions based on a sufficient investigation of the circumstances;

(e) provides for appropriate remedies; and

(f) does not involve any charges to clients for handling their *complaints*;

IB(1.23) providing the client with a copy of the *firm's complaints* procedure on request;

IB(1.24) in the event that a client makes a *complaint*, providing them with all necessary information concerning the handling of the *complaint*.

Acting in the following way(s) may tend to show that you have not achieved these outcomes and therefore not complied with the *Principles*:

Accepting and refusing instructions

IB(1.25) acting for a client when instructions are given by someone else, or by only one client when you act jointly for others unless you are satisfied that the *person* providing the instructions has the authority to do so on behalf of all of the clients;

IB(1.26) ceasing to act for a client without good reason and without providing reasonable notice;

IB(1.27) entering into unlawful fee arrangements such as an unlawful contingency fee;

IB(1.28) acting for a client when there are reasonable grounds for believing that the instructions are affected by duress or undue influence without satisfying yourself that they represent the client's wishes.

CHAPTER 3 – CONFLICTS OF INTERESTS

Outcomes

You must achieve these outcomes:

Systems

O(3.1) you have effective systems and controls in place to enable you to identify and assess potential *conflicts of interests*;

O(3.2) your systems and controls for identifying *own interest conflicts* are appropriate to the size and complexity of the *firm* and the nature of the work undertaken, and enable you to assess all the relevant circumstances, including whether your ability as an individual, or that of anyone within your *firm*, to act in the best interests of the *client(s)*, is impaired by:

(a)   any financial interest;

(b)   a personal relationship;

(c)   the appointment of you, or a member of your *firm* or family, to public office;

(d)   commercial relationships; or

(e)   your employment;

O(3.3) your systems and controls for identifying *client conflicts* are appropriate to the size and complexity of the *firm* and the nature of the work undertaken, and enable you to assess all relevant circumstances, including whether:

(a)   the *clients'* interests are different;

(b)   your ability to give independent advice to the *clients* may be fettered;

(c)   there is a need to negotiate between the *clients*;

(d)   there is an imbalance in bargaining power between the *clients*; or

(e)   any *client* is vulnerable;

Prohibition on acting in conflict situations

O(3.4) you do not act if there is an *own interest conflict* or a significant risk of an *own interest conflict*;

O(3.5) you do not act if there is a *client conflict*, or a significant risk of a *client conflict*, unless the circumstances set out in Outcomes 3.6 or 3.7 apply;

Exceptions where you may act, with appropriate safeguards, where there is a client conflict

O(3.6) where there is a *client conflict* and the *clients* have a *substantially common interest* in relation to a matter or a particular aspect of it, you only act if:

(a)   you have explained the relevant issues and risks to the *clients* and you have a reasonable belief that they understand those issues and risks;

(b)   all the *clients* have given informed consent in writing to you acting;

(c)   you are satisfied that it is reasonable for you to act for all the *clients* and that it is in their best interests; and

(d)   you are satisfied that the benefits to the *clients* of you doing so outweigh the risks;

O(3.7) where there is a *client conflict* and the *clients* are *competing for the same objective*, you only act if:

(a)   you have explained the relevant issues and risks to the *clients* and you have a reasonable belief that they understand those issues and risks;

(b)   the *clients* have confirmed in writing that they want you to act, in the knowledge that you act, or may act, for one or more other *clients* who are *competing for the same objective*;

(c)   there is no other *client conflict* in relation to that matter;

(d)   unless the *clients* specifically agree, no individual acts for, or is responsible for the supervision of work done for, more than one of the *clients* in that matter; and

(e)   you are satisfied that it is reasonable for you to act for all the *clients* and that the benefits to the *clients* of you doing so outweigh the risks.

Indicative behaviours

Acting in the following way(s) may tend to show that you have achieved these outcomes and therefore complied with the *Principles*:

IB(3.1)   training *employees* and *managers* to identify and assess potential *conflicts of interests*;

IB(3.2)   declining to act for *clients* whose interests are in direct conflict, for example claimant and defendant in litigation;

IB(3.3)   declining to act for *clients* where you may need to negotiate on matters of substance on their behalf, for example negotiating on price between a buyer and seller of a property;

IB(3.4)   declining to act where there is unequal bargaining power between the *clients*, for example acting for a seller and buyer where a builder is selling to a non-commercial *client*;

IB(3.5)   declining to act for *clients* under Outcome 3.6 *(substantially common interest)* or Outcome 3.7 *(competing for the same objective)* where the *clients* cannot be represented even-handedly, or will be prejudiced by lack of separate representation;

IB(3.6)   acting for *clients* under Outcome 3.7 *(competing for the same objective)* only where the *clients* are sophisticated users of legal services;

IB(3.7)   acting for *clients* who are the lender and borrower on the grant of a mortgage of land only where:

    (a)   the mortgage is a standard mortgage (i.e. one provided in the normal course of the lender's activities, where a significant part of the lender's activities consists of lending and the mortgage is on standard terms) of property to be used as the borrower's private residence;

    (b)   you are satisfied that it is reasonable and in the *clients'* best interests for you to act; and

    (c)   the certificate of title required by the lender is in the form approved by the *Society* and the Council of Mortgage Lenders.

Acting in the following way(s) may tend to show that you have not achieved these outcomes and therefore not complied with the *Principles*:

IB(3.8)   in a personal capacity, selling to or buying from, lending to or borrowing from a *client*, unless the *client* has obtained independent legal advice;

IB(3.9)   advising a *client* to invest in a business, in which you have an interest which affects your ability to provide impartial advice;

IB(3.10)   where you hold a power of attorney for a *client*, using that power to gain a benefit for yourself which in your professional capacity you would not have been prepared to allow to a third party;

IB(3.11)   acting for two or more *clients* in a *conflict of interests* under Outcome 3.6 *(substantially common interest)* where the *clients'* interests in the end result are not the same, for example one partner buying out the interest of the other partner in their joint business or a seller transferring a property to a buyer;

IB(3.12)   acting for two or more *clients* in a *conflict of interests* under Outcome 3.6 *(substantially common interest)* where it is unreasonable to act because there is unequal bargaining power;

IB(3.13)   acting for two buyers where there is a *conflict of interests* under Outcome 3.7 *(competing for the same objective)*, for example where two buyers are competing for a residential property;

IB(3.14)   acting for a buyer (including a lessee) and seller (including a lessor) in a transaction relating to the transfer of land for value, the grant or assignment of a lease or some other interest in land for value.

CHAPTER 4 – CONFIDENTIALITY AND DISCLOSURE

Outcomes

You must achieve these outcomes:

O(4.1)   you keep the affairs of *clients* confidential unless disclosure is required or permitted by law or the *client* consents;

O(4.2)   any individual who is advising a *client* makes that *client* aware of all information material to that retainer of which the individual has personal knowledge;

O(4.3)   you ensure that where your duty of confidentiality to one *client* comes into conflict with your duty of disclosure to another *client*, your duty of confidentiality takes precedence;

O(4.4)   you do not act for A in a matter where A has an interest adverse to B, and B is a *client* for whom you hold confidential information which is material to A in that matter, unless the confidential information can be protected by the use of safeguards, and:

    (a)   you reasonably believe that A is aware of, and understands, the relevant issues and gives informed consent;

    (b)   either:

        (i)   B gives informed consent and you agree with B the safeguards to protect B's information; or

        (ii)   where this is not possible, you put in place effective safeguards including information barriers which comply with the common law; and

    (c)   it is reasonable in all the circumstances to act for A with such safeguards in place;

O(4.5)   you have effective systems and controls in place to enable you to identify risks to *client* confidentiality and to mitigate those risks.

Indicative behaviours

Acting in the following way(s) may tend to show that you have achieved these outcomes and therefore complied with the *Principles*:

IB(4.1)   your systems and controls for identifying risks to *client* confidentiality are appropriate to the size and complexity of the *firm* or *in-house practice* and the nature of the work undertaken, and enable you to assess all the relevant circumstances;

IB(4.2)   you comply with the law in respect of your fiduciary duties in relation to confidentiality and disclosure;

IB(4.3)   you only outsource services when you are satisfied that the provider has taken all appropriate steps to ensure that your *clients'* confidential information will be protected;

IB(4.4)   where you are an individual who has responsibility for acting for a *client* or supervising a *client's* matter, you disclose to the *client* all information material to the *client's* matter of which you are personally aware, except when:

    (a)   the *client* gives specific informed consent to non-disclosure or a different standard of disclosure arises;

    (b)   there is evidence that serious physical or mental injury will be caused to a person(s) if the information is disclosed to the *client*;

    (c)   legal restrictions effectively prohibit you from passing the information to the *client*, such as the provisions in the money-laundering and anti-terrorism legislation;

    (d)   it is obvious that privileged documents have been mistakenly disclosed to you;

(e)   you come into possession of information relating to state security or intelligence matters to which the Official Secrets Act 1989 applies;

IB(4.5)   not acting for A where B is a *client* for whom you hold confidential information which is material to A unless the confidential information can be protected.

Acting in the following way(s) may tend to show that you have not achieved these outcomes and therefore not complied with the *Principles*:

IB(4.6)   disclosing the content of a will on the death of a *client* unless consent has been provided by the personal representatives for the content to be released;

IB(4.7)   disclosing details of bills sent to *clients* to third parties, such as debt factoring companies in relation to the collection of book debts, unless the *client* has consented.

Proceeds of Crime Act 2002

PART 7
MONEY LAUNDERING

OFFENCES

327.   Concealing etc

(1)   A person commits an offence if he—

    (a)   conceals criminal property;

    (b)   disguises criminal property;

    (c)   converts criminal property;

    (d)   transfers criminal property;

    (e)   removes criminal property from England and Wales or from Scotland or from Northern Ireland.

(2)   But a person does not commit such an offence if—

    (a)   he makes an authorised disclosure under section 338 and (if the disclosure is made before he does the act mentioned in subsection (1)) he has the appropriate consent;

    (b)   he intended to make such a disclosure but had a reasonable excuse for not doing so;

    (c)   the act he does is done in carrying out a function he has relating to the enforcement of any provision of this Act or of any other enactment relating to criminal conduct or benefit from criminal conduct.

(2A)   Nor does a person commit an offence under subsection (1) if—

    (a)   he knows, or believes on reasonable grounds, that the relevant criminal conduct occurred in a particular country or territory outside the United Kingdom, and

    (b)   the relevant criminal conduct—

        (i)   was not, at the time it occurred, unlawful under the criminal law then applying in that country or territory, and

        (ii)   is not of a description prescribed by an order made by the Secretary of State.

(2B)   In subsection (2A) 'the relevant criminal conduct' is the criminal conduct by reference to which the property concerned is criminal property.

(2C)   A deposit-taking body that does an act mentioned in paragraph (c) or (d) of subsection (1) does not commit an offence under that subsection if—

    (a)   it does the act in operating an account maintained with it; and

    (b)   the value of the criminal property concerned is less than the threshold amount determined under section 339A for the act.

(3)   Concealing or disguising criminal property includes concealing or disguising its nature, source, location, disposition, movement or ownership or any rights with respect to it.

328.   Arrangements

(1)   A person commits an offence if he enters into or becomes concerned in an arrangement which he knows or suspects facilitates (by whatever means) the acquisition, retention, use or control of criminal property by or on behalf of another person.

(2)   But a person does not commit such an offence if:

   (a)   he makes an authorised disclosure under section 338 and (if the disclosure is made before he does the act mentioned in subsection (1)) he has the appropriate consent;

   (b)   he intended to make such a disclosure but had a reasonable excuse for not doing so;

   (c)   the act he does is done in carrying out a function he has relating to the enforcement of any provision of this Act or of any other enactment relating to criminal conduct or benefit from criminal conduct.

(3)   Nor does a person commit an offence under subsection (1) if—

   (a)   he knows, or believes on reasonable grounds, that the relevant criminal conduct occurred in a particular country or territory outside the United Kingdom, and

   (b)   the relevant criminal conduct—

      (i)   was not, at the time it occurred, unlawful under the criminal law then applying in that country or territory, and

      (ii)   is not of a description prescribed by an order made by the Secretary of State.

(4)   In subsection (3) 'the relevant criminal conduct' is the criminal conduct by reference to which the property concerned is criminal property.

(5)   A deposit-taking body that does an act mentioned in subsection (1) does not commit an offence under that subsection if—

   (a)   it does the act in operating an account maintained with it; and

   (b)   the arrangement facilitates the acquisition, retention, use or control of criminal property of a value that is less than the threshold amount determined under section 339A for the act.

329. Acquisition, use and possession

(1)   A person commits an offence if he—

   (a)   acquires criminal property;

   (b)   uses criminal property;

   (c)   has possession of criminal property.

(2)   But a person does not commit such an offence if:

   (a)   he makes an authorised disclosure under section 338 and (if the disclosure is made before he does the act mentioned in subsection (1)) he has the appropriate consent;

   (b)   he intended to make such a disclosure but had a reasonable excuse for not doing so;

   (c)   he acquired or used or had possession of the property for adequate consideration;

   (d)   the act he does is done in carrying out a function he has relating to the enforcement of any provision of this Act or of any other enactment relating to criminal conduct or benefit from criminal conduct.

(2A)   Nor does a person commit an offence under subsection (1) if—

   (a)   he knows, or believes on reasonable grounds, that the relevant criminal conduct occurred in a particular country or territory outside the United Kingdom, and

   (b)   the relevant criminal conduct—

      (i)   was not, at the time it occurred, unlawful under the criminal law then applying in that country or territory, and

      (ii)   is not of a description prescribed by an order made by the Secretary of State.

(2B)   In subsection (2A) 'the relevant criminal conduct' is the criminal conduct by reference to which the property concerned is criminal property.

(2C) A deposit-taking body that does an act mentioned in subsection (1) does not commit an offence under that subsection if—

    (a)   it does the act in operating an account maintained with it; and

    (b)   the value of the criminal property concerned is less than the threshold amount determined under section 339A for the act.

(3)   For the purposes of this section—

    (a)   a person acquires property for inadequate consideration if the value of the consideration is significantly less than the value of the property;

    (b)   a person uses or has possession of property for inadequate consideration if the value of the consideration is significantly less than the value of the use or possession;

    (c)   the provision by a person of goods or services which he knows or suspects may help another to carry out criminal conduct is not consideration.

330.   Failure to disclose: regulated sector

(1)   A person commits an offence if the conditions in subsections (2) to (4) are satisfied:

(2)   The first condition is that he—

    (a)   knows or suspects; or

    (b)   has reasonable grounds for knowing or suspecting,

that another person is engaged in money laundering.

(3)   The second condition is that the information or other matter—

    (a)   on which his knowledge or suspicion is based; or

    (b)   which gives reasonable grounds for such knowledge or suspicion,

came to him in the course of a business in the regulated sector.

(3A)   The third condition is—

    (a)   that he can identify the other person mentioned in subsection (2) or the whereabouts of any of the laundered property; or

    (b)   that he believes, or it is reasonable to expect him to believe, that the information or other matter mentioned in subsection (3) will or may assist in identifying the other person or the whereabouts of any of the laundered property.

(4)   The fourth condition is that he does not make the required disclosure to—

    (a)   a nominated officer; or

    (b)   a person authorised for the purposes of this Part by the Director General of the National Crime Agency,

as soon as is practicable after the information or other matter mentioned in subsection (3) comes to him.

(5)   The required disclosure is a disclosure of—

    (a)   the identity of the other person mentioned in subsection (2), if he knows it;

    (b)   the whereabouts of the laundered property, so far as he knows it; and

    (c)   the information or other matter mentioned in subsection (3).

(5A)   The laundered property is the property forming the subject-matter of the money laundering that he knows or suspects, or has reasonable grounds for knowing or suspecting, that other person to be engaged in.

(6)   But he does not commit an offence under this section if—

    (a)   he has a reasonable excuse for not making the required disclosure;

    (b)   he is a professional legal adviser or ... relevant professional adviser, and

        (i)   if he knows either of the things mentioned in subsection (5)(a) and (b), he knows the thing because of information or other matter that came to him in privileged circumstances, or

(ii)   the information or other matter mentioned in subsection (3) came to him in privileged circumstances, or

(c)   subsection (7) or (7B) applies to him.

(7)   This subsection applies to a person if:

(a)   he does not know or suspect that another person is engaged in money laundering; and

(b)   he has not been provided by his employer with such training as is specified by the Secretary of State by order for the purposes of this section.

(7A)   Nor does a person commit an offence under this section if—

(a)   he knows, or believes on reasonable grounds, that the money laundering is occurring in a particular country or territory outside the United Kingdom, and

(b)   the money laundering—

(i)   is not unlawful under the criminal law applying in that country or territory, and

(ii)   is not of a description prescribed in an order made by the Secretary of State.

(7B)   This subsection applies to a person if—

(a)   he is employed by, or is in partnership with, a professional legal adviser or a relevant professional adviser to provide the adviser with assistance or support,

(b)   the information or other matter mentioned in subsection (3) comes to the person in connection with the provision of such assistance or support, and

(c)   the information or other matter came to the adviser in privileged circumstances.

(8)   In deciding whether a person committed an offence under this section the court must consider whether he followed any relevant guidance which was at the time concerned:

(a)   issued by a supervisory authority or an appropriate body;

(b)   approved by the Treasury; and

(c)   published in a manner it approved as appropriate in its opinion to bring the guidance to the attention of persons likely to be affected by it.

(9)   Disclosure to a nominated officer is a disclosure which—

(a)   is made to a person nominated by the alleged offender's employer to receive disclosures under this section; and

(b)   is made in the course of the alleged offender's employment.

(9A)   But a disclosure which satisfies paragraphs (a) and (b) of subsection (9) is not to be taken as a disclosure to a nominated officer if the person making the disclosure—

(a)   is a professional legal adviser or ... relevant professional adviser,

(b)   makes it for the purpose of obtaining advice about making a disclosure under this section, and

(c)   does not intend it to be a disclosure under this section.

(10)   Information or other matter comes to a professional legal adviser or ... relevant professional adviser in privileged circumstances if it is communicated or given to him:

(a)   by (or by a representative of) a client of his in connection with the giving by the adviser of legal advice to the client;

(b)   by (or by a representative of) a person seeking legal advice from the adviser; or

(c)   by a person in connection with legal proceedings or contemplated legal proceedings.

(11)   But subsection (10) does not apply to information or other matter which is communicated or given with the intention of furthering a criminal purpose.

(12)   Schedule 9 has effect for the purpose of determining what is—

(a)   a business in the regulated sector;

(b)   a supervisory authority.

(13)   An appropriate body is any body which regulates or is representative of any trade, profession, business or employment carried on by the alleged offender.

(14)   A relevant professional adviser is an accountant, auditor or tax adviser who is a member of a professional body which is established for accountants, auditors or tax advisers (as the case may be) and which makes provision for—

(a)   testing the competence of those seeking admission to membership of such a body as a condition for such admission; and

(b)   imposing and maintaining professional and ethical standards for its members, as well as imposing sanctions for non-compliance with those standards

331.   Failure to disclose: nominated officers in the regulated sector

(1)   A person nominated to receive disclosures under section 330 commits an offence if the conditions in subsections (2) to (4) are satisfied—

(2)   The first condition is that he—

(a)   knows or suspects; or

(b)   has reasonable grounds for knowing or suspecting,

that another person is engaged in money laundering.

(3)   The second condition is that the information or other matter—

(a)   on which his knowledge or suspicion is based; or

(b)   which gives reasonable grounds for such knowledge or suspicion,

came to him in consequence of a disclosure made under section 330.

(3A)   The third condition is—

(a)   that he knows the identity of the other person mentioned in subsection (2), or the whereabouts of any of the laundered property, in consequence of a disclosure made under section 330,

(b)   that that other person, or the whereabouts of any of the laundered property, can be identified from the information or other matter mentioned in subsection (3), or

(c)   that he believes, or it is reasonable to expect him to believe, that the information or other matter will or may assist in identifying that other person or the whereabouts of any of the laundered property.

(4)   The fourth condition is that he does not make the required disclosure to a person authorised for the purposes of this Part by the Director General of SOCA as soon as is practicable after the information or other matter mentioned in subsection (3) comes to him.

(5)   The required disclosure is a disclosure of—

(a)   the identity of the other person mentioned in subsection (2), if disclosed to him under section 330,

(b)   the whereabouts of the laundered property, so far as disclosed to him under section 330, and

(c)   the information or other matter mentioned in subsection (3).

(5A)   The laundered property is the property forming the subject-matter of the money laundering that he knows or suspects, or has reasonable grounds for knowing or suspecting, that other person to be engaged in.

(6)   But he does not commit an offence under this section if he has a reasonable excuse for not making the required disclosure.

(6A)   Nor does a person commit an offence under this section if—

(a)   he knows, or believes on reasonable grounds, that the money laundering is occurring in a particular country or territory outside the United Kingdom, and

(b)   the money laundering—

(i)   is not unlawful under the criminal law applying in that country or territory, and

(ii)   is not of a description prescribed in an order made by the Secretary of State.

(7)   In deciding whether a person committed an offence under this section the court must consider whether he followed any relevant guidance which was at the time concerned:

(a)   issued by a supervisory authority or any other appropriate body;

(b)   approved by the Treasury; and

(c)   published in a manner it approved as appropriate in its opinion to bring the guidance to the attention of the persons likely to be affected by it.

(8)   Schedule 9 has effect for the purpose of determining what is a supervisory authority.

(9)   An appropriate body is a body which regulates or is representative of a trade, profession, business or employment.

332.   Failure to disclose: other nominated officers

(1)   A person nominated to receive disclosures under section 337 or 338 commits an offence if the conditions in subsections (2) to (4) are satisfied.

(2)   The first condition is that he knows or suspects that another person is engaged in money laundering.

(3)   The second condition is that the information or other matter on which his knowledge or suspicion is based came to him in consequence of a disclosure made under the applicable section.

(3A)   The third condition is—

(a)   that he knows the identity of the other person mentioned in subsection (2), or the whereabouts of any of the laundered property, in consequence of a disclosure made under the applicable section,

(b)   that that other person, or the whereabouts of any of the laundered property, can be identified from the information or other matter mentioned in subsection (3), or

(c)   that he believes, or it is reasonable to expect him to believe, that the information or other matter will or may assist in identifying that other person or the whereabouts of any of the laundered property.

(4)   The fourth condition is that he does not make the required disclosure to a person authorised for the purposes of this Part by the Director General of the National Crime Agency as soon as is practicable after the information or other mater mentioned in subsection (3) comes to him.

(5)   The required disclosure is a disclosure of—

(a)   the identity of the other person mentioned in subsection (2), if disclosed to him under the applicable section;

(b)   the whereabouts of the laundered property, so far as disclosed to him under the applicable section; and

(c)   the information or other matter mentioned in subsection (3).

(5A)   The laundered property is the property forming the subject-matter of the money laundering that he knows or suspects that other person to be engaged in.

(5B)   The applicable section in section 337 or, as the case may be, section 338.

(6)   But he does not commit an offence under this section if he has a reasonable excuse for not making the required disclosure.

(7)   Nor does a person commit an offence under this section if—

   (a)   he knows, or believes on reasonable grounds, that the money laundering is occurring in a particular country or territory outside the United Kingdom, and

   (b)   the money laundering—

      (i)   is not unlawful under the criminal law applying in that country or territory, and

      (ii)   is not of a description prescribed in an order made by the Secretary of State.

333A.   Tipping off: regulated sector

(1)   A person commits an offence if—

   (a)   the person discloses any matter within subsection (2);

   (b)   the disclosure is likely to prejudice any investigation that might be conducted following the disclosure referred to in that subsection; and

   (c)   the information on which the disclosure is based came to the person in the course of a business in the regulated sector.

(2)   The matters are that the person or another person has made a disclosure under this Part—

   (a)   to a constable,

   (b)   to an officer of Revenue and Customs,

   (c)   to a nominated officer, or

   (d)   to a National Crime Agency officer authorised for the purposes of this Part by the Director General of that Agency,

of information that came to that person in the course of a business in the regulated sector.

(3)   A person commits an offence if—

   (a)   the person discloses that an investigation into allegations that an offence under this Part has been committed is being contemplated or is being carried out;

   (b)   the disclosure is likely to prejudice that investigation; and

   (c)   the information on which the disclosure is based came to the person in the course of a business in the regulated sector.

(4)   A person guilty of an offence under this section is liable—

   (a)   on summary conviction to imprisonment for a term not exceeding three months, or to a fine not exceeding level 5 on the standard scale, or to both;

   (b)   on conviction on indictment to imprisonment for a term not exceeding two years, or to a fine, or to both.

(5)   This section is subject to—

   (a)   section 333B (disclosures within an undertaking or group etc),

   (b)   section 333C (other permitted disclosures between institutions etc), and

   (c)   section 333D (other permitted disclosures etc).

333B.   Disclosures within an undertaking or group etc

(1)   An employee, officer or partner of an undertaking does not commit an offence under section 333A if the disclosure is to an employee, officer or partner of the same undertaking.

(2)   A person does not commit an offence under section 333A in respect of a disclosure by a credit institution or a financial institution if—

   (a)   the disclosure is to a credit institution or a financial institution,

   (b)   the institution to whom the disclosure is made is situated in an EEA State or in a country or territory imposing equivalent money laundering requirements, and

(c) both the institution making the disclosure and the institution to whom it is made belong to the same group.

(3) In subsection (2) 'group' has the same meaning as in Directive 2002/87/EC of the European Parliament and of the Council of 16th December 2002 on the supplementary supervision of credit institutions, insurance undertakings and investment firms in a financial conglomerate.

(4) A professional legal adviser or a relevant professional adviser does not commit an offence under section 333A if—

(a) the disclosure is to professional legal adviser or a relevant professional adviser,

(b) both the person making the disclosure and the person to whom it is made carry on business in an EEA State or in a country or territory imposing equivalent money laundering requirements, and

(c) those persons perform their professional activities within different undertakings that share common ownership, management or control.

333C. **Other permitted disclosures between institutions etc**

(1) This section applies to a disclosure—

(a) by a credit institution to another credit institution,

(b) by a financial institution to another financial institution,

(c) by a professional legal adviser to another professional legal adviser, or

(d) by a relevant professional adviser of a particular kind to another relevant professional adviser of the same kind.

(2) A person does not commit an offence under section 333A in respect of a disclosure to which this section applies if—

(a) the disclosure relates to—

(i) a client or former client of the institution or adviser making the disclosure and the institution or adviser to whom it is made,

(ii) a transaction involving them both, or

(iii) the provision of a service involving them both;

(b) the disclosure is for the purpose only of preventing an offence under this Part of this Act;

(c) the institution or adviser to whom the disclosure is made is situated in an EEA State or in a country or territory imposing equivalent money laundering requirements; and

(d) the institution or adviser making the disclosure and the institution or adviser to whom it is made are subject to equivalent duties of professional confidentiality and the protection of personal data (within the meaning of section 1 of the Data Protection Act 1998).

333D. **Other permitted disclosures etc**

(1) A person does not commit an offence under section 333A if the disclosure is—

(a) to the authority that is the supervisory authority for that person by virtue of the Money Laundering Regulations 2007; or

(b) for the purpose of—

(i) the detection, investigation or prosecution of a criminal offence (whether in the United Kingdom or elsewhere),

(ii) an investigation under this Act, or

(iii) the enforcement of any order of a court under this Act.

(2) A professional legal adviser or a relevant professional adviser does not commit an offence under section 333A if the disclosure—

(a) is to the adviser's client, and

(b) is made for the purpose of dissuading the client from engaging in conduct amounting to an offence.

(3) A person does not commit an offence under section 333A(1) if the person does not know or suspect that the disclosure is likely to have the effect mentioned in section 333A(1)(b).

(4) A person does not commit an offence under section 333A(3) if the person does not know or suspect that the disclosure is likely to have the effect mentioned in section 333A(3)(b).

333E. Interpretation of sections 333A to 333D

(1) For the purposes of sections 333A to 333D, Schedule 9 has effect for determining—

(a) what is a business in the regulated sector, and

(b) what is a supervisory authority.

(2) In those sections—

'credit institution' has the same meaning as in Schedule 9;

'financial institution' means an undertaking that carries on a business in the regulated sector by virtue of any of paragraphs (b) to (i) of paragraph 1(1) of that Schedule.

(3) References in those sections to a disclosure by or to a credit institution or a financial institution include disclosure by or to an employee, officer or partner of the institution acting on its behalf.

(4) For the purposes of those sections a country or territory imposes 'equivalent money laundering requirements' if it imposes requirements equivalent to those laid down in Directive 2005/60/EC of the European Parliament and of the Council of 26th October 2005 on the prevention of the use of the financial system for the purpose of money laundering and terrorist financing.

(5) In those sections 'relevant professional adviser' means an accountant, auditor or tax adviser who is a member of a professional body which is established for accountants, auditors or tax advisers (as the case may be) and which makes provision for—

(a) testing the competence of those seeking admission to membership of such a body as a condition for such admission; and

(b) imposing and maintaining professional and ethical standards for its members, as well as imposing sanctions for non-compliance with those standards.

334. Penalties

(1) A person guilty of an offence under section 327, 328 or 329 is liable—

(a) on summary conviction, to imprisonment for a term not exceeding six months or to a fine not exceeding the statutory maximum or to both; or

(b) on conviction on indictment, to imprisonment for a term not exceeding 14 years or to a fine or to both.

(2) A person guilty of an offence under section 330, 331 or 332 is liable:

(a) on summary conviction, to imprisonment for a term not exceeding six months or to a fine not exceeding the statutory maximum or to both; or

(b) on conviction on indictment, to imprisonment for a term not exceeding five years or to a fine or to both.

(3) A person guilty of an offence under section 339(1A) is liable on summary conviction to a fine not exceeding level 5 on the standard scale.

CONSENT

335. Appropriate consent

(1) The appropriate consent is—

    (a) the consent of a nominated officer to do a prohibited act if an authorised disclosure is made to the nominated officer;

    (b) the consent of a constable to do a prohibited act if an authorised disclosure is made to a constable;

    (c) the consent of a customs officer to do a prohibited act if an authorised disclosure is made to a customs officer.

(2) A person must be treated as having the appropriate consent if—

    (a) he makes an authorised disclosure to a constable or a customs officer, and

    (b) the condition in subsection (3) or the condition in subsection (4) is satisfied.

(3) The condition is that before the end of the notice period he does not receive notice from a constable or customs officer that consent to the doing of the act is refused.

(4) The condition is that—

    (a) before the end of the notice period he receives notice from a constable or customs officer that consent to the doing of the act is refused; and

    (b) the moratorium period has expired.

(5) The notice period is the period of seven working days starting with the first working day after the person makes the disclosure.

(6) The moratorium period is the period of 31 days starting with the day on which the person receives notice that consent to the doing of the act is refused.

(7) A working day is a day other than a Saturday, a Sunday, Christmas Day, Good Friday or a day which is a bank holiday under the Banking and Financial Dealings Act 1971 in the part of the United Kingdom in which the person is when he makes the disclosure.

(8) References to a prohibited act are to an act mentioned in section 327(1), 328(1) or 329(1) (as the case may be).

(9) A nominated officer is a person nominated to receive disclosures under section 338.

(10) Subsections (1) to (4) apply for the purposes of this Part.

336. Nominated officer: consent

(1) A nominated officer must not give the appropriate consent to the doing of a prohibited act unless the condition in subsection (2), the condition in subsection (3) or the condition in subsection (4) is satisfied.

(2) The condition is that—

    (a) he makes a disclosure that property is criminal property to a person authorised for the purposes of this Part by the Director General of the National Crime Agency, and

    (b) such a person gives consent to the doing of the act.

(3) The condition is that—

    (a) he makes a disclosure that property is criminal property to a person authorised for the purposes of this Part by the Director General of the National Crime Agency, and

    (b) before the end of the notice period he does not receive notice from such a person that consent to the doing of the act is refused.

(4) The condition is that—

    (a) he makes a disclosure that property is criminal property to a person authorised for the purposes of this Part by the Director General of the National Crime Agency,

    (b) before the end of the notice period he receives notice from such a person that consent to the doing of the act is refused, and

(c)   the moratorium period has expired.

(5)   A person who is a nominated officer commits an offence if—

    (a)   he gives consent to a prohibited act in circumstances where none of the conditions in subsections (2), (3) and (4) is satisfied, and

    (b)   he knows or suspects that the act is a prohibited act.

(6)   A person guilty of such an offence is liable—

    (a)   on summary conviction, to imprisonment for a term not exceeding six months or to a fine not exceeding the statutory maximum or to both, or

    (b)   on conviction on indictment, to imprisonment for a term not exceeding five years or to a fine or to both.

(7)   The notice period is the period of seven working days starting with the first working day after the nominated officer makes the disclosure.

(8)   The moratorium period is the period of 31 days starting with the day on which the nominated officer is given notice that consent to the doing of the act is refused.

(9)   A working day is a day other than a Saturday, a Sunday, Christmas Day, Good Friday or a day which is a bank holiday under the Banking and Financial Dealings Act 1971 in the part of the United Kingdom in which the nominated officer is when he gives the appropriate consent.

(10)   References to a prohibited act are to an act mentioned in section 327(1), 328(1) or 329(1) (as the case may be).

(11)   A nominated officer is a person nominated to receive disclosures under section 338.

DISCLOSURES

337.   Protected disclosures

(1)   A disclosure which satisfies the following three conditions is not to be taken to breach any restriction on the disclosure of information (however imposed).

(2)   The first condition is that the information or other matter disclosed came to the person making the disclosure (the discloser) in the course of his trade, profession, business or employment.

(3)   The second condition is that the information or other matter—

    (a)   causes the discloser to know or suspect, or

    (b)   gives him reasonable grounds for knowing or suspecting,

that another person is engaged in money laundering.

(4)   The third condition is that the disclosure is made to a constable, a customs officer or a nominated officer as soon as is practicable after the information or other matter comes to the discloser.

(4A)   Where a disclosure consists of a disclosure protected under subsection (1) and a disclosure of either or both of—

    (a)   the identity of the other person mentioned in subsection (3), and

    (b)   the whereabouts of property forming the subject-matter of the money laundering that the discloser knows or suspects, or has reasonable grounds for knowing or suspecting, that other person to be engaged in,

the disclosure of the thing mentioned in paragraph (a) or (b) (as well as the disclosure protected under subsection (1)) is not to be taken to breach any restriction on the disclosure of information (however imposed).

(5)   A disclosure to a nominated officer is a disclosure which—

    (a)   is made to a person nominated by the discloser's employer to receive disclosures under section 330 or this section, and

       (b)   is made in the course of the discloser's employment.

338. Authorised disclosures

(1)   For the purposes of this Part a disclosure is authorised if—

     (a)   it is a disclosure to a constable, a customs officer or a nominated officer by the alleged offender that property is criminal property, . . . and

     (c)   the first, second or third condition set out below is satisfied.

(2)   The first condition is that the disclosure is made before the alleged offender does the prohibited act.

(2A) The second condition is that—

     (a)   the disclosure is made while the alleged offender is doing the prohibited act,

     (b)   he began to do the act at a time when, because he did not then know or suspect that the property constituted or represented a person's benefit from criminal conduct, the act was not a prohibited act, and

     (c)   the disclosure is made on his own initiative and as soon as is practicable after he first knows or suspects that the property constitutes or represents a person's benefit from criminal conduct.

(3)   The third condition is that—

     (a)   the disclosure is made after the alleged offender does the prohibited act,

     (b)   he has a reasonable excuse for his failure to make the disclosure before he did the act, and

     (c)   the disclosure is made on his own initiative and as soon as it is practicable for him to make it.

(4)   An authorised disclosure is not to be taken to breach any restriction on the disclosure of information (however imposed).

(4A) Where an authorised disclosure is made in good faith, no civil liability arises in respect of the disclosure on the part of the person by or on whose behalf it is made.

(5)   A disclosure to a nominated officer is a disclosure which—

     (a)   is made to a person nominated by the alleged offender's employer to receive authorised disclosures, and

     (b)   is made in the course of the alleged offender's employment.

(6)   References to the prohibited act are to an act mentioned in section 327(1), 328(1) or 329(1) (as the case may be).

339. Form and manner of disclosures

(1)   The Secretary of State may by order prescribe the form and manner in which a disclosure under section 330, 331, 332 or 338 must be made.

(1A) A person commits an offence if he makes a disclosure under section 330, 331, 332 or 338 otherwise that in the form prescribed under subsection (1) or otherwise than in the manner so prescribed.

(1B) But a person does not commit an offence under subsection (1A) if he has a reasonable excuse for making the disclosure otherwise than in the form prescribed under subsection (1) or (as the case may be) otherwise than in the manner so prescribed.

(2)   The power under subsection (1) to prescribe the form in which a disclosure must be made includes power to provide for the form to include a request to a person making a disclosure that the person provide information specified or described in the form if he has not provided it in making the disclosure.

(3)   Where under subsection (2) a request is included in a form prescribed under subsection (1), the form must—

     (a)   state that there is no obligation to comply with the request, and

(b) explain the protection conferred by subsection (4) on a person who complies with the request.

(4) A disclosure made in pursuance of a request under subsection (2) is not to be taken to breach any restriction on the disclosure of information (however imposed).

(5) . . .

(6) . . .

(7) Subsection (2) does not apply to a disclosure made to a nominated officer.

339ZA. Disclosures to the NCA

Where a disclosure is made under this Part to a constable or an officer of Revenue and Customs, the constable or officer of Revenue and Customs must disclose it in full to a person authorised for the purposes of this Part by the Director General of the National Crime Agency a soon as practicable after it has been made.

339A. Threshold amounts

(1) This section applies for the purposes of sections 327(2C), 328(5) and 329(2C).

(2) The threshold amount for acts done by a deposit-taking body in operating an account is £250 unless a higher amount is specified under the following provisions of this section (in which event it is that higher amount).

(3) An officer of Revenue and Customs, or a constable, may specify the threshold amount for acts done by a deposit-taking body in operating an account—

(a) when he gives consent, or gives notice refusing consent, to the deposit-taking body's doing of an act mentioned in section 327(1), 328(1) or 329(1) in opening, or operating, the account or a related account; or

(b) on a request from the deposit-taking body.

(4) Where the threshold amount for acts done in operating an account is specified under subsection (3) or this subsection, an officer of Revenue and Customs, or a constable, may vary the amount (whether on a request from the deposit-taking body or otherwise) by specifying a different amount.

(5) Different threshold amounts may be specified under subsections (3) and (4) for different acts done in operating the same account.

(6) The amount specified under subsection (3) and (4) as the threshold amount for acts done in operating an account must, when specified, not be less than the amount specified in subsection (2).

(7) The Secretary of State may by order vary the amount for the time being specified in subsection (2).

(8) For the purposes of this section, an account is related to another if each is maintained with the same deposit-taking body and there is a person who, in relation to each account, is the person or one of the persons entitled to instruct the body as respects the operation of the account.

INTERPRETATION

340. Interpretation

(1) This section applies for the purposes of this Part.

(2) Criminal conduct is conduct which—

(a) constitutes an offence in any part of the United Kingdom, or

(b) would constitute an offence in any part of the United Kingdom if it occurred there.

(3) Property is criminal property if—

(a)   it constitutes a person's benefit from criminal conduct or it represents such a benefit (in whole or part and whether directly or indirectly), and

(b)   the alleged offender knows or suspects that it constitutes or represents such a benefit.

(4)   It is immaterial—

(a)   who carried out the conduct;

(b)   who benefited from it;

(c)   whether the conduct occurred before or after the passing of this Act.

(5)   A person benefits from conduct if he obtains property as a result of or in connection with the conduct.

(6)   If a person obtains a pecuniary advantage as a result of or in connection with conduct, he is to be taken to obtain as a result of or in connection with the conduct a sum of money equal to the value of the pecuniary advantage.

(7)   References to property or a pecuniary advantage obtained in connection with conduct include references to property or a pecuniary advantage obtained in both that connection and some other.

(8)   If a person benefits from conduct his benefit is the property obtained as a result of or in connection with the conduct.

(9)   Property is all property wherever situated and includes—

(a)   money;

(b)   all forms of property, real or personal, heritable or moveable;

(c)   things in action and other intangible or incorporeal property.

(10)   The following rules apply in relation to property—

(a)   property is obtained by a person if he obtains an interest in it;

(b)   references to an interest, in relation to land in England and Wales or Northern Ireland, are to any legal estate or equitable interest or power;

(c)   references to an interest, in relation to land in Scotland, are to any estate, interest, servitude or other heritable right in or over land, including a heritable security;

(d)   references to an interest, in relation to property other than land, include references to a right (including a right to possession).

(11)   Money laundering is an act which—

(a)   constitutes an offence under section 327, 328 or 329,

(b)   constitutes an attempt, conspiracy or incitement to commit an offence specified in paragraph (a),

(c)   constitutes aiding, abetting, counselling or procuring the commission of an offence specified in paragraph (a), or

(d)   would constitute an offence specified in paragraph (a), (b) or (c) if done in the United Kingdom.

(12)   For the purposes of a disclosure to a nominated officer—

(a)   references to a person's employer include any body, association or organisation (including a voluntary organisation) in connection with whose activities the person exercises a function (whether or not for gain or reward), and

(b)   references to employment must be construed accordingly.

(13)   References to a constable include references to a person authorised for the purposes of this Part by the Director General of the National Crime Agency.

(14)   'Deposit-taking body' means—

(a)   a business which engages in the activity of accepting deposits; or

(b)   The National Savings Bank.

PROFESSIONAL CONDUCT

Chapter 6: The Legal Profession

Topic	Summary
Professional conduct	Professional conduct is the term that is used to describe the rules, regulations and requirements with which a solicitor must comply. Solicitors are in a position of trust, and so a higher standard of behaviour is expected of them than of members of the public.
Solicitors Regulation Authority (SRA)	The SRA regulates solicitors in England and Wales. It also controls such matters as training and entry into the profession.
The Law Society	The Law Society is the representative body for solicitors in England and Wales. Membership is voluntary, but all solicitors (and those who are employed by them) are bound by the requirements of professional conduct whether or not they are members of The Law Society.
Different aspects of practice	The legal profession is made up of a number of different types of organisation. Within these organisations, there are a number of roles that a solicitor may fill. However, most solicitors in private practice are employed by recognised bodies.

Chapter 7: Regulating the Profession

Topic	Summary
Solicitors Regulation Authority (SRA)	The SRA publishes and enforces rules and requirements concerning how solicitors, authorised bodies and their employees behave and conduct their business. The subject matter of this Part is the SRA Code of Conduct 2011.
Complaints against solicitors	Every firm must have a complaints handling procedure, and must ensure that complaints are dealt with promptly, fairly, openly and effectively (Outcome 1.11). If a complaint cannot be resolved by the firm, the client must be given details of the Legal Ombudsman.
Legal Ombudsman	The Legal Ombudsman is the sole point of receipt for complaints concerning services provided by solicitors and other types of legal practitioner, and refers any allegations of breaches of the requirements of professional conduct concerning solicitors to the SRA.

Topic	Summary
Powers of the Legal Ombudsman	Where the Legal Ombudsman makes a determination following a complaint, it has the power to order the firm of solicitors to limit its fees, or to direct that the firm must compensate the client up to the sum of £50,000 (plus interest) amongst other sanctions. The Legal Ombudsman cannot pay compensation to a client itself.
Powers of the SRA – professional misconduct	Where a finding of professional misconduct is made, the SRA may discipline the firm or regulated individual by imposing disciplinary sanctions, or referring the matter to the Solicitors Disciplinary Tribunal. The SRA may also revoke or suspend authorisation of the firm.
Solicitors Disciplinary Tribunal	The Solicitors Disciplinary Tribunal hears and determines applications relating to allegations of professional misconduct. It is independent of the SRA and The Law Society. It has the power to suspend a solicitor, to fine a solicitor an unlimited amount and, in the most extreme cases, to strike a solicitor off the roll – which will effectively end his career.
Negligence	In addition to or instead of the actions that the SRA may take against a solicitor, a solicitor may be sued by his client in the tort of negligence. A solicitor owes his client a duty of care. Where this duty is breached, and the client suffers a foreseeable loss as a result of that breach, the solicitor may be sued for negligence. Firms must carry compulsory indemnity insurance against such actions.
The SRA Compensation Fund	The SRA Compensation Fund is maintained by the SRA. Payment may be made from the Fund when a client has suffered loss as a result of a defaulting practitioner's act or omission.

Chapter 8: The Principles

Topic	Summary
The SRA Code of Conduct	The profession is regulated by the Government and by requirements of conduct set out by the SRA.
The Principles	The Principles are contained within the SRA *Handbook*. They underpin all of the *Handbook* requirements, including the Code of Conduct. They define the fundamental ethical and professional standards expected of all firms and individuals when providing legal services.
Integrity	The Principles provide that a solicitor must act with integrity, for example towards clients, the courts, lawyers and the public. A solicitor is in a position of trust, and so must behave in an appropriate manner to reflect that position.

Topic	Summary
Best interests of clients	The Principles include the solicitor's duty to act in the best interests of each client. This places an obligation on the solicitor always to act in good faith, and always to do his best for his clients.
Public confidence	A solicitor must also behave in a way that maintains the trust the public places in him and in the provision of legal services. Therefore a solicitor must not do anything that would be likely to damage this trust. This obligation extends to both the solicitor's behaviour within practice, and outside of it in his daily life.
Breach of the Principles	Where a solicitor breaches the Principles, he may well be guilty of professional misconduct. In serious cases, this could also lead to him being 'struck off' the roll of solicitors, which would effectively end his career.

Chapter 9: Obtaining Instructions

Topic	Summary
General principles	A solicitors' firm must take steps to try to maintain and increase its market share in order to prosper. However, a solicitor must at all times comply with the general law and the Code of Conduct. In particular, no matter what financial pressure he is under, a solicitor should always be independent and impartial when giving advice to a client.
Advertising	Solicitors are free to publicise their practices, provided that they comply with the general law on advertising in force at the time and with the Outcomes in Chapter 8 of the Code of Conduct.
Chapter 8	Chapter 8 of the Code applies to all forms of publicity. It provides that all publicity issued by, or on behalf of, law firms must not be misleading or inaccurate.
Cold calling	Outcome 8.3 provides that a solicitor may not cold call the general public. However, this restriction does not apply to contacting clients or former clients.
Referrals of business	A solicitor may enter into an arrangement with a third party to refer clients from that third party. However, such arrangements must comply with the Outcomes in Chapter 9 of the Code.
Protection of the clients' interests	The clients' interests must be protected, regardless of the interests of an introducer or the solicitor's interest in receiving referrals (Outcome 9.2)
Solicitors' independence (Outcome 9.1)	A solicitor must not place himself in a position whereby his advice to a client is affected due to an attempt not to offend a referrer of work.

Topic	Summary
Referral fees	A solicitor may pay to or receive referral fees from a third party, but must comply with the Outcomes in Chapter 9. For example, clients must be informed of any financial or other interest which an introducer has in referring the client to the solicitor.
Fee sharing	Clients must be informed of any fee-sharing arrangement that is relevant to their matter.
Introductions to third parties	A solicitor may wish to refer clients to third parties, such as another lawyer or a financial services provider. Such introductions must comply with the Outcomes in Chapter 6 of the Code.

Chapter 10: The Retainer

Topic	Summary
The retainer	The contract between a solicitor and his client is often referred to as a retainer. The contract is governed by the general law, and also the requirements of professional conduct.
Acceptance and refusal of instructions	When deciding whether to act or to terminate instructions, the solicitor must comply with the law and the Code (Outcome 1.3)
Unlawful discrimination	A solicitor must not unlawfully discriminate against anyone in the course of his professional dealings. Therefore, discriminating unlawfully when accepting or refusing instructions to act for a client may tend to show that the relevant Outcomes have not been achieved (Indicative Behaviour 2.5).
Acceptance of third party instructions	It may tend to show that the solicitor has not achieved the relevant Outcomes if he acts for a client when instructions are given by someone else, unless he is satisfied that the person providing the instructions has the authority to do so on behalf of all the clients (Indicative Behaviour 1.25).
Duty to the client during the retainer	A solicitor owes the client a number of duties throughout the retainer. For example, s 13 of the Supply of Goods and Services Act 1982 provides that a supplier of services (such as a solicitor) will carry out those services with reasonable care and skill.
Termination of the retainer	A client may terminate the retainer at any time and for any reason. Ceasing to act for a client without good reason and without providing reasonable notice, may tend to show that the relevant Outcomes have not been achieved (Indicative Behaviour 1.26).

Topic	Summary
Responsibilities on termination	It is good practice for a solicitor to confirm to the client in writing that the retainer has been terminated, and to take steps to deal with any property of the client that may be held by the solicitor. In certain circumstances a solicitor may exercise a lien over the property until his fees are paid.

Chapter 11: Client Care and Costs

Topic	Summary
Client care	A solicitor must achieve the Outcomes on client care as prescribed by the SRA, including treating clients fairly.
Client's ability to make informed decisions	The solicitor must ensure that clients are in a position to make informed decisions about the services they need, how their matter will be handled and the options available to them (Outcome 1.12).
Protection of clients' interests	The solicitor must provide services in a manner that protects clients' interests in their matter, subject to the proper administration of justice (Outcome 1.2).
Level of service	The service provided to clients must be competent, delivered in a timely manner and take account of the client's needs and circumstances (Outcome 1.5).
Costs information	A solicitor is obliged to provide his client with the best possible information as to the likely overall costs of a matter, both at the time of engagement and when appropriate as the matter progresses (Outcome 1.13).
Fee agreements	A solicitor must only enter into fee agreements with clients that are legal, and which he considers are suitable for the client's needs and take account of the client's best interests (Outcome 1.6).
Solicitor's fees	A solicitor and client may agree the level of costs that the solicitor may charge. However, this agreement is regulated by statute and the common law. A distinction is made between costs in contentious matters and costs in non-contentious matters.
Solicitor's bill	A solicitor's bill must contain prescribed information in order for the bill to be enforceable.
Client's right to challenge the bill	A client may challenge the costs of a solicitor in both contentious and non-contentious matters. Generally speaking, in both types of matters the client may apply to have the costs assessed by the court. The client may also complain to the firm about the level of charges under the firm's complaints procedure, and subsequently to the Legal Ombudsman.
Suing on a bill	Generally, a solicitor may not sue to recover his costs from the client until one month has elapsed since the bill was delivered.

Topic	Summary
Overcharging	A solicitor must act in the best interests of the client and must not take advantage of his client. Therefore a solicitor must not overcharge for work done. Overcharging may well be considered by the SRA as a breach of professional conduct.

Chapter 12: Confidentiality

Topic	Summary
Duty of confidentiality	A solicitor (and his staff) must keep the affairs of his clients and former clients confidential except where disclosure is required or permitted by law or the client consents (Outcome 4.1).
Overriding the duty of confidentiality	Information which is the subject of the duty of confidentiality may be disclosed as prescribed by law.
Duty of disclosure	The solicitor also has a duty to disclose to the client all information that is material to the client's matter of which he has personal knowledge (Outcome 4.2). The duty of confidentiality takes precedence over the duty of disclosure (Outcome 4.3).
Placing confidential information at risk	Where a solicitors' firm holds confidential information for one client, it must not risk breaching confidentiality by acting for (or continuing to act for) another client on a matter where the information might reasonably be expected to be material, and where the clients have an adverse interest to one another, unless proper arrangements can be made to protect the confidential information. These proper arrangements include issues such as obtaining informed consent and erecting information barriers.
Professional embarrassment	Even when a solicitor would be permitted to act for two clients on a matter pursuant to the Code, he may still have to refuse instructions on the basis of professional embarrassment.
Privilege	In addition to the duty of confidentiality, a solicitor must also consider legal professional privilege. Where legal professional privilege applies, a solicitor can refuse to disclose communications between himself and a client.

Chapter 13: Conflict of Interests

Topic	Summary
General principles	A solicitor must not act where there is a conflict, or a significant risk of a conflict between the interests of two or more clients (a 'client conflict') (Outcome 3.5).

Topic	Summary
Same or related matters	The conflict of interest must arise in relation to the same matter, or related matters. A matter will be related if it concerns the same asset or liability. However, there would need to be some reasonable degree of relationship for a conflict to arise.
Former clients	Due to the definition of a conflict of interest, a conflict cannot arise with a former client. However, the solicitor may still be prevented from acting if he holds confidential information concerning the former client.
Exceptions	Where there is a conflict between two clients, a solicitor may act if he can satisfy the requirements of the substantially common interest exception (Outcome 3.6) or the commercial exception (Outcome 3.7).
Conflict between the solicitor's and client's interests	A solicitor must not act where there is a conflict or significant risk of a conflict between the client's interests and the solicitor's interests (an 'own interest conflict'). There are no exceptions to this rule (Outcome 3.4).
Systems and controls for identifying conflicts	A solicitor must have in place controls to enable him to identify and assess potential conflicts of interests, and which are appropriate to the size and complexity of the firm and to the nature of the work undertaken (Outcomes 3.1, 3.2 and 3.3).

Chapter 14: Undertakings

Topic	Summary
Definition	An undertaking is a statement, given orally or in writing, whether or not it includes the word 'undertake' or 'undertaking', made by or on behalf of a solicitor or his firm, in the course of practice, or by him outside the course of practice but as a solicitor or REL, to someone who reasonably places reliance on it, that the solicitor or his firm will do something or cause something to be done, or refrain from doing something (*Handbook* Glossary). Essentially an undertaking is an enforceable promise.
Effect and time for performance	An undertaking is personally binding on the giver of the undertaking. All undertakings must be performed within an agreed timescale, or within a reasonable time (Outcome 11.2).
Ambiguity	Any ambiguity in the wording of the undertaking is likely to be construed against the party that gave the undertaking.

Topic	Summary
Undertakings 'on behalf of a client'	It is possible for a solicitor to give an undertaking on behalf of a client and exclude personal liability. However, the solicitor must clearly and expressly disclaim personal liability or make it clear that he is simply informing the other side of his client's intentions.
Change of circumstances	An undertaking will remain binding upon a solicitor even if the circumstances change so that it is impossible to fulfil the undertaking. It may tend to show that the relevant Outcomes have been achieved in circumstances where an undertaking is given which is dependent upon the happening of a future event and it becomes apparent that the future event will not occur, if the solicitor notifies the recipient of this (Indicative Behaviour 11.6).
Effective systems to record undertakings	It may tend to show that the relevant Outcomes have been achieved if the solicitor maintains an effective system for the recording of undertakings given and discharged (Indicative Behaviour 11.5).
Breach	Breach of an undertaking is prima facie professional misconduct. The SRA/Legal Ombudsman/Solicitors Disciplinary Tribunal do not have the power to enforce an undertaking. However, any breach may lead to sanctions against the solicitor concerned.
The courts	The court is able to enforce an undertaking against a solicitor as an officer of the court. Accordingly, where an undertaking has been breached, the aggrieved party may sue the solicitor for compensation for any loss.

Chapter 15: Money Laundering and the Proceeds of Crime Act 2002

Topic	Summary
Money laundering	'Money laundering' is the process by which criminals seek to alter or 'launder' their proceeds of crime so that it appears that these funds come from a legitimate source. Solicitors are often targets for criminals in their efforts to launder the proceeds of their crimes. The Government has introduced legislation to disrupt this process.
Money Laundering Regulations 2007	Solicitors who undertake 'relevant business' must comply with the Money Laundering Regulations 2007. 'Relevant business' includes the provision of legal services which involves participation in a 'financial or real property transaction', and so the vast majority of solicitors' firms will be subject to the Regulations.
Nominated officer	Under the Money Laundering Regulations 2007, firms must appoint a nominated officer, who will receive internal reports concerning money laundering and must consider whether to report the matter to the National Crime Agency.

Topic	Summary
Arrangements	A person commits an offence under s 328 of the Proceeds of Crime Act 2002 where he becomes concerned with an arrangement involving money laundering. However, s 328 does not apply to steps taken in litigation. An individual convicted under s 328 may receive a maximum sentence of 14 years' imprisonment.
Acquisition, use or possession	A person commits an offence under s 329 of the Proceeds of Crime Act 2002 if he acquires, uses or has possession of criminal property. The adequate consideration defence may be available to a solicitor in relation to money received for or on account of costs from a client.
Failure to disclose	A solicitor within the regulated sector is obliged to disclose any suspected money laundering activity to his nominated officer (s 330). Failure to do so may result in a maximum sentence of five years' imprisonment.
Tipping off	It is an offence to disclose to any person that a disclosure has been made to a nominated officer or the National Crime Agency where this disclosure may prejudice an investigation (ss 333A–333D), or that an investigation into money laundering is being carried out or contemplated. An individual convicted under ss 333A–333D may receive a maximum penalty of two years' imprisonment.

Chapter 16: Duties Owed to the Court and Third Parties

Topic	Summary	References
Misleading or deceiving the court and contempt	A solicitor is under a duty never to mislead or deceive the court or be complicit in another person's misleading or deceiving the court.	Outcomes 5.1 and 5.2
	A solicitor must also comply with any orders of the court, and must not become in contempt of court.	Outcomes 5.3 and 5.4
Witnesses	A solicitor must not make (or offer to make) payments to witnesses dependent upon the nature of the evidence given, or on the outcome of the case.	Outcome 5.8
Duty to the court	Where relevant, clients must be informed of the circumstances in which a solicitor's duties to the court outweigh his obligations to the client. A solicitor must comply with his duties to the court.	Outcomes 5.5 and 5.6
Instructing counsel	A solicitor must act in the best interests of his client. Accordingly, if it is in the client's best interests to instruct counsel, the solicitor must ensure that adequate instructions are provided to the chosen barrister. Instructing counsel does not relieve the solicitor of his duties towards his client, particularly the duty to act in the client's best interests.	

Topic	Summary	References
Duty to third parties	A solicitor must not take an unfair advantage of any person, either for the solicitor's own benefit or for another person's benefit (such as the client). Particular care should be taken when dealing with unrepresented third parties.	Outcome 11.1
Recovering costs	A solicitor must not demand anything from a third party which is not legally recoverable.	
Represented third parties	Subject to limited exceptions, it may tend to show that the Outcomes have been achieved by a solicitor ensuring that he does not communicate directly with third parties where the solicitor knows that the third party has instructed a legal representative.	Indicative Behaviour 11.4
Beneficiaries	In certain circumstances, a solicitor owes a duty of care to third parties, such as beneficiaries. If this duty is breached, the solicitor may be sued by the third party.	
Dealings with other solicitors	A solicitor must act with integrity. Therefore a solicitor must treat other solicitors with due respect in all their communications.	Principle 2

Chapter 17: Financial Services

Topic	Summary
General prohibition	Section 19 of the Financial Services and Markets Act (FSMA) 2000 provides that 'no person may carry on a regulated activity in the UK unless authorised or exempt'.
Regulated activity	A person carries out a regulated activity when, while in business, he carries out a specified investment activity in relation to a specified investment or a specified activity related to information about a person's financial standing or the setting of a specified benchmark, and cannot take advantage of an exclusion.
Specified investment	Specified investments include company stocks and shares, debentures, unit trusts, insurance contracts and mortgages.
Specified investment activities	Specified investment activities include advising, arranging, dealing as agent, managing and safeguarding.
Exclusions	Numerous exclusions exist, such as the authorised third party exclusion. Each exclusion has different conditions and restrictions. If a solicitor can take advantage of an exclusion, he will not be carrying out a regulated activity.

Topic	Summary
Exempt regulated activities	As an alternative to using an exclusion, a firm may seek to use the s 327 exemption to avoid breaching the general prohibition. Once again, a number of conditions must be satisfied. These include that the activity the firm carries out must be incidental to the provision of legal services by the firm. The firm must also comply with the Scope and COB Rules.
Financial promotions	A solicitor who is not authorised by the Financial Conduct Authority is unable to make a financial promotion unless its contents are approved by an authorised or exempt person (FSMA 2000, s 21). Once again, this prohibition is subject to exclusions.

Chapter 18: Requirements of Practice

Topic	Summary	References
SRA Suitability Test 2011	Those intending to become solicitors, authorised role holders and former solicitors seeking restoration to the roll of solicitors must satisfy the SRA Suitability Test 2011. Certain behaviour will result in an application being refused by the SRA, unless there are exceptional circumstances.	
Requirement to hold a practising certificate	No person may act as a solicitor unless he has been admitted as a solicitor, his name is on the roll of solicitors, and he holds a current practising certificate.	Solicitors Act 1974, s 1
Practising certificates	Practising certificates are issued annually by the SRA, which has a certain level of discretion as to whether to issue a certificate to a particular person. In certain circumstances the SRA may decline to issue a certificate or may impose conditions on the certificate.	
Suspension of practising certificate	A practising certificate is automatically suspended where a bankruptcy order is made against the solicitor concerned. The SRA may also suspend a practising certificate if the solicitor is convicted of a crime involving dishonesty or deception.	
Additional practising requirements	Solicitors who wish to exercise higher rights of audience and carry out criminal advocacy must comply with additional SRA requirements.	
Accountants' reports	All solicitors who hold a practising certificate and also hold client monies must obtain an independent accountant's report each year. The purpose of the report is to certify compliance with the SRA Accounts Rules. One report may be obtained for a firm as a whole.	

Topic	Summary	References
Indemnity insurance	The Solicitors Indemnity Insurance Rules 2013 require solicitors to take out compulsory insurance cover against the risks of professional negligence or other civil liability claims. Firms can insure with any approved commercial insurer. Relevant recognised and licensed bodies must obtain cover to a minimum of £3 million per individual claim (a minimum of £2 million in all other cases). Voluntary top-up cover may be required.	
Responsibility of managers	Managers must ensure that their firm complies with the requirements of professional conduct. In certain cases, managers will be held liable for any breach.	
Supervision	At least one lawyer manager of every authorised body must be 'qualified to supervise'. This means that he must have been entitled to practise as a lawyer for at least 36 months within the last 10 years, and must have completed at least 12 hours of training on management skills. Regardless of whether they are 'qualified to supervise', managers are obliged to make arrangements for the effective management of the firm.	SRA Practice Framework Rules 2011
Duty to the SRA and the Legal Ombudsman	A solicitor is under a duty to cooperate with the SRA and the Legal Ombudsman at all times.	Outcome 10.6
Reporting serious misconduct	A solicitor is obliged to report to the SRA any incident of serious misconduct by any person or firm authorised by the SRA, or any employee, manager or owner of any such firm.	Outcome 10.4

EU LAW

PART III

EU LAW

SOURCES OF EU LAW

LEARNING OUTCOMES

After reading this chapter you will be able to understand:

- what types of EU legislation there are
- the various treaties which have developed EU law
- the status of the decisions of the Court of Justice
- the key elements of the latest EU Treaty.

19.1 INTRODUCTION

The UK in 2016 voted to leave the EU. As the mechanics of leaving will take many months, EU law will remain binding on the UK in the meantime. It is unclear at the time of writing to what extent the UK and EU will make agreement for the free movement of persons, capital and trade once the UK leaves, but it is possible that some of the Treaty Articles discussed in the following chapters will remain enforceable in UK courts.

Even if no such agreement is made, EU law will in any event continue to be important for many UK lawyers, as their clients will often be multinational and/or operate within Europe. Even if advising clients which operate solely within the UK, lawyers will often deal with UK laws which have been influenced by EU principles in their drafting. It is important therefore that you gain a sound understanding of principles of EU law despite the UK's decision to leave the EU.

19.2 BACKGROUND

The Treaty on European Union (the 'Maastricht Treaty') took Europe into a new stage of development, with more ambitious objectives, in order, in the words of the preamble to the Treaty, 'to continue the process of creating an ever closer union among the peoples of Europe'. This drive towards a closer union continued with the Treaty of Amsterdam, the Treaty of Nice and the Treaty of Lisbon, all of which made amendments to (rather than replaced) the original EC Treaty (the Treaty of Rome 1957) and the Treaty on European Union. The Treaty on European Union retains its original name, but the EC Treaty, post-Lisbon, is now called the Treaty on the Functioning of the European Union (TFEU). It should be noted that Articles of the EC Treaty which survived Lisbon are numbered differently in the TFEU – see **19.10**.

Post-Lisbon, the European Court of Justice was renamed the Court of Justice, and the court below it (the Court of First Instance) was renamed the General Court. Perhaps confusingly, the two courts together form an institution called the Court of Justice of the European Union (CJEU). Most decisions that you will look at as a lawyer will be of the (higher) Court of Justice, although commentators are likely to continue calling it the European Court of Justice (or ECJ) for some time.

The sources of EU law are:

(a)   the Treaties;

(b)   Regulations;

(c)   Directives;

(d)   the jurisprudence of the CJEU (and its predecessors).

Regulations and Directives are secondary legislation made under Article 288 TFEU. How these sources of law become part of English law will be discussed in **Chapter 21**.

Article 288 TFEU also provides for the making of Decisions, Recommendations and Opinions. Of these, only Decisions are legally binding, and they bind only the person (Member State, company or individual) to whom they are addressed.

The Court of Justice has been highly influential in developing both substantive areas of EU law (eg, the free movement of goods) and general principles of EU law, such as proportionality.

19.3   THE TREATIES

19.3.1   The Treaty of Rome 1957

The primary aim of the Treaty of Rome ('the EEC Treaty') was to create a European Economic Community, a common market, for the original six signatories: France, West Germany, Italy, The Netherlands, Belgium and Luxembourg. This common market required not only the abolition of customs duties and quotas for goods passing between the six, but also a recognition on the part of the Member States that their populations had a right to share directly in the benefits of the new system. In particular, the Member States had to recognise the right of workers to move freely throughout the Community, and the right of individuals and companies to set up in business or to provide services throughout the Community.

From its very beginning, it was apparent that the Community was more than a mere free trade zone. One of the stated objectives in the preamble to the Treaty was 'to lay the foundations of an ever closer union among the peoples of Europe'. It is also central to an understanding of the Treaty to remember that it created supra-national institutions, not least the Court of Justice (see **Chapter 20**). The result was, in the words of the Court itself in *Van Gend en Loos v Nederlandse Belastingadministratie* [1963] ECR 1, a 'new legal order of international law for the benefit of which the States have limited their sovereign rights, albeit within limited fields, and the subjects of which comprise not only Member States but also their nationals' (see **Chapter 21**).

The most important provisions, as far as the achievement of a common market is concerned, are those dealing with free movement, in particular of goods, persons and services, and competition law. These will be considered at **Chapters 23–26**.

19.3.2   The Merger Treaty 1965

Since the Treaty of Paris 1951, there had existed a European Coal and Steel Community (ECSC), created by the original six signatories of the Treaty of Rome. That Treaty had also established supra-national institutions, including a High Authority, the equivalent of the EC Commission.

In 1957, at the same time as the European Economic Community was established, the same signatories created the European Atomic Energy Community (EurAtom). The European Economic Community and EurAtom shared with the ECSC only the Court and the Assembly set up under the Treaty of Paris. In 1965, the institutions of the three Communities were merged. The Merger Treaty is therefore concerned with their integration within a single organisational structure.

19.3.3 The Accession Treaties

In 1973, the UK, the Republic of Ireland and Denmark joined the Community, followed in 1981 by Greece and in 1986 by Spain and Portugal. Sweden, Finland and Austria joined on 1 January 1995. The European Union welcomed 10 new countries in 2004: Cyprus, the Czech Republic, Estonia, Hungary, Latvia, Lithuania, Malta, Poland, Slovakia and Slovenia. Bulgaria and Romania joined on 1 January 2007, and Croatia joined on 1 July 2013, bringing the total number of Member States to 28. Current candidate countries at the time of writing are: Albania, Iceland, Montenegro, Serbia, the former Yugoslav Republic of Macedonia and Turkey; and potential candidates are Bosnia and Herzegovina, and Kosovo. No date has yet been set for their accession.

19.3.4 The Single European Act 1986

The Single European Act 1986 saw further significant developments in the Community. It formalised as an objective the completion of the single European market envisaged in the EC Treaty, and set a date for its achievement: 31 December 1992. This required enormous legislative activity by the Community in an attempt to overcome remaining barriers to trade, not least the problem of varying trading standards. In order to make this a manageable task, the Single European Act introduced a streamlined legislative process. When single market measures came to the Council for approval, unanimity was not to be required. Instead, only a qualified majority would be needed (see **Chapter 20**). The Single European Act also extended the areas which would be expressly within the Community's competence, including areas such as the environment and the health and safety of workers.

19.3.5 The European Economic Area Treaty 1992

The effect of the European Economic Area Treaty was to create a 'European Economic Area' (EEA) consisting of the Member States of the EC and the European Free Trade Agreement (EFTA) countries (Sweden, Norway, Finland, Austria and Iceland, but not Switzerland which decided in referendum not to ratify the Treaty). Within this area, EC law relating to free movement and to competition law applies, together with all the related Regulations and Directives. The EEA came into effect on 1 January 1994. However, on 1 January 1995, Sweden, Finland and Austria all joined the European Union, leaving just Norway, Iceland and Liechtenstein as members of the EEA but not of the EU. Switzerland remains in EFTA.

19.3.6 The Treaty on European Union 1992 ('the Maastricht Treaty')

The Treaty on European Union (TEU), signed at Maastricht, came into force on 1 November 1993. It officially renamed the 'EEC' the 'EC' and founded, on the base of the European Community, a European Union. It also renamed the Treaty of Rome the EC Treaty. It made a number of important amendments to the Treaty, in particular:

(a)   the EC undertook to act in any given area only if Community action was a better means of achieving the desired end than action by the individual Member States (the principle of subsidiarity);

(b)   every EC national became a citizen of the European Union;

(c)   the EC specifically assumed responsibility for developing policies in areas such as public health, consumer protection and education. These had previously been dealt with primarily as issues affecting free movement;

(d)   the European Parliament was given greater powers (co-decision));

(e)   the Council was to take decisions on a qualified majority basis on a wider range of matters, such as consumer protection, using the co-decision procedure.

The Maastricht Treaty did not just amend the Treaty of Rome. It also set out Union objectives, the most important being the promotion of economic and social progress to be achieved by economic and monetary union. The Union also agreed to develop a common foreign and security policy, and to cooperate in the fields of justice and home affairs. Importantly, the Union also undertook expressly to respect fundamental rights, as guaranteed by the European Convention for the Protection of Human Rights and Fundamental Freedoms 1950. Previous European Court case law had already shown, however, that Member States must respect human rights law when acting on a Community matter.

19.3.7   The Amsterdam Treaty

The Amsterdam Treaty entered into force at the beginning of May 1999. The Treaty paved the way for EU enlargement. It also provided for greater cooperation in employment matters and for incentive measures to help boost employment. It incorporated into the EC the TEU Social Chapter, which means that all Member States are bound by its provisions. The Treaty also established a new section on freedom, security and justice, which brings some areas into the framework of the EC Treaty from the 'third pillar' (Justice and Home Affairs) of the Maastricht Treaty. It also strengthened provisions relating to environmental protection. There was a strengthening of public health and consumer protection, and the principle of subsidiarity was clarified. Lastly, there was an increase in the number of matters to be decided under qualified majority rules and a substantial increase in the use of the co-decision procedure (see **20.4.2**). In the TEU, there is a revised section on common foreign and security policy.

19.3.8   The Treaty of Nice

The Treaty of Nice came into force on 1 February 2003 and made changes to the Institutions of the Community with a view to accommodating enlargement. In particular it reduced the number of decisions where a power of veto may be used in the Council. This was felt necessary due to its being less likely that unanimous agreement might be reached with an increased number of countries. In addition, a change was made in the weighting of the votes which each country has in Council meetings. The Treaty also made numerical changes to the Parliament and the Commission, with each Member State having only one Commissioner each.

19.3.9   The Treaty of Lisbon

The Treaty of Lisbon brought to an end several years of negotiation about institutional issues. Its main highlights include:

(a)   the European Council (a body composed of the leaders of the Member States) became a formal EU institution, with an independent President;

(b)   the European Parliament became an equal co-legislator with the Council of Ministers in the vast majority of cases;

(c)   national vetoes were removed in a number of areas, including fighting climate change, energy security and emergency aid;

(d)   EU competencies widened to cover areas which were previously the realm of Member States, eg international trade, energy policies, judicial and police cooperation;

(e)   the European Union became a single organisation; there is no longer a European Community. This means that it is no longer correct to speak of EC law; rather, it should be referred to as EU law;

(f)   voting weights between the Member States in the Council of Ministers will be adjusted between 2014 and 2017: qualified majority voting will be based on a 'double majority' of 55% of Member States' votes, accounting for 65% of the EU's population.

19.4 REGULATIONS

Article 288 TFEU envisages that secondary legislation is needed to put its broad objectives into effect. It provides that the Council and the Commission 'shall, in accordance with the provisions of this Treaty make Regulations ... '. It goes on to state that a Regulation shall have general application (ie, it will apply throughout the EU in exactly the terms in which it is made). Further, Article 288 TFEU states that a Regulation shall be directly applicable in all Member States, ie no Member State need pass any implementing measure to make the contents of the Regulation form part of its own national law, except in the unusual situation when the Regulation itself expressly requires the Member State to do so. In fact, according to the European Court in *Variola sPA v Amministrazione Italiana della Finanze* [1973] ECR 981, it would ordinarily be wrong for a Member State to disguise the EU origin of the measure by introducing national legislation to enact it.

Many important EU legal measures have taken the form of Regulations, for example, Regulation 1612/68, which sought to make a reality of the free movement of workers provisions in the Treaty, and the Merger Regulation, Regulation 4064/89, under which big multi-national mergers are vetted by the Commission for their effect on competition.

19.5 DIRECTIVES

Article 288 TFEU also gives the Council and the Commission power to issue Directives. It is clear from that Article, however, that their legal effect is quite different from that of Regulations. A Directive is stated to be 'binding, as to the result to be achieved, upon each Member State to which it is addressed, but shall leave to the national authorities the choice of form and methods'. Unlike Regulations, Directives therefore do need a response from each Member State. Unless the national law of the Member State already achieves the objective of the Directive, the Member State must implement it within the specified time-limit. The form of implementing measure may vary from State to State, as may the precise words used to give effect to the Directive. This means that, unlike Regulations, Directives are not of general application throughout the EU in the terms in which they are drafted. Typical UK implementing measures are statutes and statutory instruments.

Directives have been issued across a wide range of areas, for example, Directive 2006/54, known as the Equal Treatment Directive, the several Company Law Directives, the Environmental Protection Directive (85/337) and the Product Liability Directive (85/374). In order to bring the Single Market into being, the Commission drafted over 200 separate Directives.

19.6 THE JURISPRUDENCE OF THE COURT OF JUSTICE

The fundamental principles of EU law found in the TFEU and earlier versions of it are set out in outline only, so the Court has inevitably played a leading role in developing EU law. The Court has not been reluctant to assume this role and has made a major contribution to the evolution of the EU. By interpreting the Treaty and secondary legislation according to the overall purposes of the EU, the Court has often pushed governments further than they might have initially intended to go.

Judgments of the Court are now vital to an understanding of the freedoms upon which the EU is based and to the principles of competition law (another major field of EU activity). In addition, the Court has developed certain general principles of EU law, of which the most important are proportionality (see **Chapter 25**), legal certainty and respect for fundamental rights (see **Chapter 27**). As far as the last of these is concerned, the Court's approach can be seen in *Nold (J) KG v EC Commission* [1974] ECR 491, where it stated that fundamental rights, derived from the constitutional traditions common to the Member States and from the international treaties to which they are signatories (in particular, the European Convention on Human Rights), form an integral part of the general principles of EU law.

In applying 'legal certainty' the Court has sometimes ruled that its more surprising interpretations of the Treaty should be non-retrospective, for example in *Defrenne (Gabrielle) v SABENA* [1976] ECR 455 and *Barber v Guardian Royal Exchange Assurance Group* [1991] 1 QB 344 (see **21.3.1**) where direct claims for equal pay and equal pensions were allowed under what is now Article 157 TFEU. To have held otherwise would have had serious financial consequences in the Member States. Ordinarily, Court judgments are retrospective, ie they go back to the date of the original legislation that the Court is interpreting.

19.7 OTHER EU MEASURES

Apart from the measures already indicated, there exist two other EU measures which have only limited legal effect under Article 288 TFEU.

Decisions are binding only on the parties to whom the Decisions are addressed (Article 288 TFEU). The best examples are Commission Decisions under the competition rules in Articles 101 and 102 TFEU. Their Decisions that an agreement or conduct infringes Article 101 or 102 TFEU, that an exemption should be given under Article 101(3) TFEU, or that fines be imposed are all subject to review by the General Court. Subject to this, they bind the parties and must be given effect by national courts. Thus, a Decision that an agreement is exempt will (subject to review) validate the agreement before a national court.

The least effective measure of all is a Council Recommendation. This is certainly not legally binding and cannot create any Community rights, but is still worth referring to as 'persuasive opinion' on a particular issue. A good example is the Code of Practice on Sexual Harassment set out at [1992] OJ L49/1. This can be referred to for guidance to determine whether employers who have allowed such conduct are guilty of sex discrimination under the Sex Discrimination Act 1975 (see *Wadman v Carpenter Farrer Partnership* [1993] 3 CMLR 93 (EAT)).

19.8 CONCLUSION

If a client has a problem which has an EU dimension, this could be because it clearly raises questions of substantive EU law, perhaps in relation to one of the freedoms such as free movement of goods or workers. In this case, a solicitor must, of course, pay careful attention to the TFEU itself. It will often be necessary to look at the secondary legislation which supplements that particular area of the Treaty, as well as at decided cases on the subject.

On the other hand, a client's problem may have an EU aspect because of the ever-increasing pervasiveness of EU law: for example, a business client may be concerned about the significance of the recent Directives on workplace safety. In this case, a detailed consideration of the relevant legislation will be vital, including an appreciation of how it can interact with relevant domestic law (see further **Chapter 21**).

For information as to how to research a problem of EU law and how to use the possible sources, see Chapter 7 of **Skills for Lawyers**.

19.9 OVERVIEW OF THE TREATY ON THE FUNCTIONING OF THE EUROPEAN UNION

(1) To create the internal market, the TFEU guarantees four freedoms:
    (a) free movement of goods (Articles 34–36 TFEU);
    (b) free movement of services (Article 56 TFEU);
    (c) free movement of persons, ie workers (Article 45 TFEU) and firms (Article 49 TFEU right of establishment);
    (d) free movement of capital (Articles 63–66 TFEU).
(2) To create the customs union, it imposes a common external tariff and prohibits internal custom duties (Article 30 TFEU).

(3) To prevent distortion in the market, it:

    (a) prohibits anti-competitive practices by undertakings (Articles 101, 102 TFEU);

    (b) prohibits discrimination against EU nationals, both generally (Article 18 TFEU) and under particular Articles (eg, on free movement), or through indirect taxes (Article 110 TFEU);

    (c) guarantees equal pay between men and women (Article 157 TFEU).

19.10 CONVERSION TABLE – NOTABLE ARTICLE NUMBERS

Pre-Amsterdam	Post-Amsterdam	Post-Lisbon
Article 5 (State obligations)	Article 10	Article 4(3) TEU
Article 30 (goods)	Article 28	Article 34 TFEU
Article 36 (goods – excl)	Article 30	Article 36 TFEU
Article 48 (workers)	Article 39	Article 45 TFEU
Article 52 (establishment)	Article 43	Article 49 TFEU
Article 59 (services)	Article 49	Article 56 TFEU
Article 85 (competition)	Article 81	Article 101 TFEU
Article 86 (competition)	Article 82	Article 102 TFEU
Article 119 (sex discrimination)	Article 141	Article 157 TFEU
Article 177 (references)	Article 234	Article 267 TFEU

THE INSTITUTIONS

LEARNING OUTCOMES

After reading this chapter you will be able to understand:

- the identity of the various institutions which make up the EU
- their composition
- their roles
- how they work together to create EU legislation.

20.1 INTRODUCTION

The Treaty of Rome established the following institutions of the Community (now 'Union'):

(a) the Council;

(b) the Commission;

(c) the Parliament;

(d) the Court.

The Single European Act created the Court of First Instance. This was renamed 'the General Court' by the Treaty of Lisbon. The Treaty on European Union made the already existing Court of Auditors into a fifth institution. Although they do not have the status of institutions, mention will be made below of the Committee of Permanent Representatives (COREPER), the Economic and Social Council and the Committee of the Regions (see **20.9–20.11**). There will also be a brief explanation of how EU law is made.

The Treaty of Lisbon made the European Council a formal institution for the first time.

20.2 THE COUNCIL

20.2.1 What is its membership?

The Council consists of one government representative from each Member State. The representative need not be the same person at every Council meeting: it depends on the matters on the agenda at that particular meeting. If, for example, the Council were discussing the environment, the representatives would be the ministers responsible for the environment. The Heads of State meet as a separate body – the European Council.

Each Member State takes it in turn to be the President of the Council; the Presidency rotates every six months.

20.2.2 What is its role?

The Treaty of Rome gave the Council responsibility for ensuring that the Treaty's objectives were attained. The Council ensures the coordination of policies and, above all, takes decisions within the Union. This means that it is the Council, acting with the Parliament, rather than the Commission which is responsible for the final decision as to whether a Regulation should be made or a Directive should be issued, although the Commission does have some decision-making powers (see **20.4**).

20.2.3 How does it take decisions?

After the Treaty of Lisbon, almost all policy areas are decided by qualified majority vote. A qualified majority is obtained when at least 55% of Member States, comprising at least 65% of EU citizens, vote in favour of a proposal. This does not apply, however, when the Council votes on a matter not proposed by the Commission, where 72% of Member States must vote in favour (while the population requirement remains the same).

Clearly, the population threshold has an element of weighted voting in it, with the larger nations being able to contribute bigger populations to the calculation. For example, Germany has 16.5% of the EU's population within her borders, giving Germany a greater say under this new system.

20.3 THE EUROPEAN COUNCIL

20.3.1 What is its membership?

The European Council consists of the Heads of State or Government of the Member States, together with its President and the President of the Commission.

20.3.2 What is its role?

The European Council defines the general political direction and priorities of the European Union. However, it does not exercise legislative functions. It meets twice every six months and, except where the Treaties provide otherwise, its decisions are by consensus. In some cases, however, the Treaties provide for the European Council to adopt decisions by unanimity or by qualified majority.

Article 15 TEU requires the President of the European Council to:

(a)   chair it and drive forward its work;

(b)   ensure the preparation and continuity of its work;

(c)   endeavour to facilitate cohesion and consensus within it; and

(d)   present a report to the European Parliament after every European Council meeting.

20.4 THE EUROPEAN COMMISSION

20.4.1 What is its membership?

There are 28 EU Commissioners, one from each Member State, each of whom is responsible for a particular area of Union competence. The Commission is divided into 23 Directorates-General which are responsible for such matters as the environment (Directorate-General XI) and competition law (Directorate-General IV). The Commissioners are appointed by the Council (ie effectively by the Member States), but once appointed they must be independent of national loyalties. They cannot be recalled by their appointing State. They hold office for a fixed term of five years, although this is subject to renewal. Each Commissioner's appointment must be approved by all Member States and, since Amsterdam, by the President and by the European Parliament. The President of the Commission is appointed by the Council and the European Parliament. The appointment is for a fixed term of two years, although this also is renewable. The Commission is based in Brussels.

20.4.2 What is its role?

The Treaty of Rome required the Commission to pursue infringements of EU law. It can, for example, take action before the European Court against Member States who breach EU law. It is also responsible for enforcing EU competition policy and has the power to exact fines for any breach. Above all, however, the Commission is responsible for initiating EU policy and legislation. It has some delegated powers of law making, particularly in the field of competition law, where (under the authority of an enabling Council Regulation 19/65) it has issued Block Exemption Regulations (see **Chapter 26**).

20.4.3 How does it reach its decisions?

Within the Commission, decisions are taken on a simple majority basis.

20.5 THE PARLIAMENT

20.5.1 What is its membership?

There are 751 members of the European Parliament (MEPs) (750 plus a President). All MEPs are directly elected, although the voting systems throughout the Union are not uniform. The number of MEPs which each State has is set by the Council and the Parliament itself. A draft decision fixing the numbers was annexed to the TFEU. Numbers per State are roughly in line with the size of the State, eg Germany was allocated 96 seats, France 74, the UK 73 and so on, down to Malta with 6 seats.

The MEPs sit in the Parliament according to their political sympathies (political groups) rather than according to national origin. MEPs are elected for a five-year term. The Parliament holds plenary sessions in Strasbourg for one week per month. Much of its work is, however, done in committees (and plenary sessions) in Brussels. It is organised by an Executive (including a President, ie Speaker) based in Luxembourg.

20.5.2 What is its role?

The Parliament's role was traditionally a consultative one. In a number of areas, the Treaty of Rome provided that once the Commission had initiated a proposal for legislation and the Council had given its preliminary approval to it, the Parliament had to be given an opportunity to comment. It had to respond to the proposal within a reasonable time and the Council had to take its responses into account, although it was not bound by them.

The Single European Act developed the role of the Parliament by introducing a co-operation procedure in certain areas, for example single market legislation. This meant that if the Council did not wish to accept the Parliament's comments, the Parliament had to be given a second opportunity to respond. If it continued to object to the Council's version of the measure, the Council could adopt it in its original form only if it did so unanimously within three months. The Single European Act also increased the number of matters on which the Parliament had to be consulted so as to include most matters relating to the single market.

The Treaty on European Union further increased the role of the Parliament. In certain limited areas it introduced a 'co-decision' procedure which involved the Parliament further in the legislative process. If the Parliament proposed amendments to draft legislation and these amendments were not accepted by the Council, the Parliament could veto the legislation. This procedure applied to measures intended to develop the single market.

The Amsterdam and Nice Treaties greatly extended the areas in which the co-decision procedure was used. They also streamlined this procedure.

The Treaty of Lisbon made further changes, so that virtually all decisions are now made under the co-decision procedure. It also renamed this procedure the 'ordinary legislative procedure'.

Consequently, the Parliament's role has increased greatly over the years, from a simple consultative role to being a major part of the decision-making process. Today, almost all Regulations and Directive require Parliament's approval or they do not become law.

The Parliament has the right to ask questions of the Commission and, in the last resort, it has the power to remove the whole Commission, though not individual Commissioners. (This almost happened at the beginning of 1999. The Commission actually resigned around four weeks after the threat of censure.) The Council, too, must report to the Parliament.

20.6   THE COURT OF JUSTICE

20.6.1   What is its membership?

There are currently 28 judges of the Court of Justice (one from each Member State), each of whom must be eligible for appointment to the highest judicial office in the country from which he or she comes. There must be at least one judge from each Member State. Each judge is appointed for six years at a time. Their appointments are staggered, so they do not all retire at once. There is no retirement age for a judge, nor can one be recalled by the Member State which made the appointment. He or she can be removed only by the unanimous resolution of the other judges and Advocates-General. The judges elect one of their number to be President of the Court for a three-year term.

In addition to the judges, there are also nine Advocates-General. Their task is to assist the judges in reaching their decisions. One Advocate-General will be assigned to each case, and will hear the evidence and read the papers available to the Court. He will then prepare a reasoned opinion indicating the conclusion to which he would come in that case. The Court is not bound to follow that opinion. When the case is reported, the Advocate-General's opinion is reported, together with the decision of the Court. The Court sits in Luxembourg.

20.6.2   What is its role?

The Treaty of Rome required the Court to ensure that EC law (now EU law) is observed throughout the EU. The three usual ways in which a case may come before it are:

(a)   as a result of a reference by a national court under the Article 267 TFEU preliminary rulings procedure (see **21.7**);

(b)   as a result of an action brought by the Commission against a Member State pursuant to its powers under Article 258 TFEU;

(c)   as a result of an action brought by one Member State against another under Article 259 TFEU.

If a Member State fails to comply with a judgment of the Court of Justice, the Treaty on European Union allows the Court to impose a fine on that Member State.

20.6.3   How are such cases heard?

The Court of Justice usually sits in chambers and consists of three, five or seven judges. In particularly important cases, 13 judges will hear the case. In very rare situations, they can sit as a full court. The procedure is largely by means of written submissions, following a typical civil law (as distinct from common law) pattern. There is very limited scope for oral argument. Barristers and solicitors have a right of audience before the Court, although if a solicitor wishes to appear in the Court following an Article 267 TFEU reference (see **21.7**) he may do so only if he had a right of audience before the court or tribunal which made the reference.

The working language of the court during deliberations is French, although, at hearings, the parties present their arguments in their own language (with simultaneous translation). Each case will have its own official language. One judge (*le juge rapporteur*) puts together a draft judgment synthesising judicial opinions on which the judges then vote.

When the Court has reached a decision, it delivers a single, succinct judgment. No dissenting judgments are delivered.

20.6.4 The nature of EU legal reasoning

The Treaty of Rome was drafted by States which shared a civil law heritage. The original judges of the Court of Justice had been trained in civil law systems which, although they might diverge significantly in their substantive provisions, shared a similar approach to legal reasoning. In particular, such judges were familiar with legislation which provided a framework of principles and which was not intended to be interpreted in an exclusively literal way. They were therefore accustomed to drawing inspiration from the spirit behind legislation. This approach was particularly necessary when interpreting the Treaty of Rome, which is very much a framework treaty. In addition, the early judges of the Court were conscious of the role entrusted to them by the Treaty and the accompanying responsibility to ensure that EC law (now EU law) was a uniform body of legal principles which took effect in the same way throughout the entire Community.

Thus, from a very early stage, it is possible to recognise the purposive (or 'teleological') approach adopted by the Court of Justice. This entailed the Court interpreting the Treaty of Rome, and later subordinate legislation, in accordance with the ethos of the Treaty of Rome. In doing so it had to bear in mind the fundamental freedoms upon which the Community was expressly stated to be based and, in particular, Article 12 EC (now Article 18 TFEU), which prohibits discrimination on the grounds of nationality.

20.6.5 Precedent

In accordance with the civil law tradition, there is no use of precedent as such in the Court of Justice. However, although the Court is not bound by its own previous decisions, it has tended to develop a body of consistent case law. The Court may cite earlier cases in its judgment, and the Advocate-General is likely to discuss earlier decisions in his opinion.

Decisions of the Court are reported in an official set of reports, the *European Court Reports* (ECR). There is also a commercial series of reports called the *Common Market Law Reports* (CMLR).

20.7 THE GENERAL COURT

The Court of First Instance (CFI) was established by the Single European Act because of the heavy work-load faced by the Court of Justice. Many of the cases before the Court of Justice concerned disputes between Community institutions and their employees. These staff cases were assigned to the CFI, as were competition law cases (ie, appeals from Commission decisions banning agreements, imposing fines, etc). As a result of provisions in the Treaty on European Union, the Council transferred to the CFI all of the Court of Justice's jurisdiction apart from most preliminary references and cases involving infringement proceedings against Member States. Appeals on points of law lay to the Court of Justice itself. The Treaty of Nice contained provisions for the CFI to share more of the Court of Justice's workload.

The Treaty of Lisbon renamed the CFI 'the General Court', but otherwise made few changes to its role and the way it operates.

20.8 THE COURT OF AUDITORS

The Court of Auditors is responsible for auditing the accounts of the EU and its institutions. It has 28 members appointed by the Council.

20.9 THE COMMITTEE OF PERMANENT REPRESENTATIVES (COREPER)

The Committee of Permanent Representatives (COREPER) was created by the Merger Treaty. It comprises ambassadors of the Member States. They undertake much of the detailed analysis of Commission proposals on behalf of the Council. If COREPER can agree a response to such a proposal, that response will be automatically approved by the Council. Only if there is disagreement at COREPER level will a matter be actively discussed in the Council.

20.10 THE ECONOMIC AND SOCIAL COMMITTEE (ESC)

The Economic and Social Committee (ESC) is a body which comprises representatives of different sectional interests throughout the EU. There are 353 representatives, for example, of business, of the trade unions and of consumers. The ESC's role is purely consultative.

20.11 THE COMMITTEE OF THE REGIONS

The role of this Committee is purely advisory. It consists of 353 members appointed by the Council.

SUMMARY

The four main institutions have the following primary responsibilities:

(1)   the Commission develops policy and proposes legislation;

(2)   the Council and the Parliament are the decision-making bodies;

(3)   the Court ensures that the law which emerges from these three institutions is interpreted correctly and consistently.

THE RELATIONSHIP BETWEEN EU LAW AND NATIONAL LAW

LEARNING OUTCOMES

After reading this chapter you will be able to understand:

- what it means to be an EU citizen
- how EU laws can be applied directly in court
- how national courts can take EU law into account in making decisions
- which law has priority where there is a conflict between EU law and national law
- how courts resolve doubts about the meaning of EU law.

21.1 INTRODUCTION

The primary source of EU law is the Treaty on the Functioning of the European Union (TFEU). Under English law, international treaties are not automatically part of national law, so when the UK joined the (then) EC, the Treaty of Rome (as it was then known) had to be incorporated into English law. This was done by the European Communities Act 1972.

However, the interrelationship between the EU and the national legal system is not entirely the product of national statute. If it were, there might be a diversity of approach to EU law in the various Member States. The Court of Justice has instead developed two key concepts:

(a) that EU law can, in certain circumstances, be relied on directly in national proceedings; and

(b) that, when it is utilised, it takes priority over any conflicting national law.

Taken together, these two concepts can give a client a right of action and a remedy which otherwise might not be available under national law.

21.2 EU LAW AND THE EU CITIZEN

European Union law, as incorporated into English law by the European Communities Act 1972 (ECA 1972), may have two possible effects on the citizen. First, it may have 'direct effect' (see **21.3**), ie it can create rights which may be relied on in national courts directly against the State or another legal person. Secondly, EU law (in particular, Directives) may have 'indirect effect' (see **21.5**) in that courts should comply with EU law when interpreting national legislation.

21.3   THE CONCEPT OF DIRECT EFFECT

In *Van Gend en Loos v Nederlandse Belastingadministratie* [1963] ECR 1 (see **22.2.1**), the Court of Justice recognised the existence of the Community as a 'new legal order'. In that case, an importer of goods from Germany into The Netherlands argued that Article 12 of the EC Treaty (now Article 30 TFEU), which prohibited any increase in customs tariffs for goods passing from one Member State to another, meant that a reclassification of his products into a higher tariff was unlawful. Consequently, he sought to rely on Article 12 of the EC Treaty to claim back from the Dutch customs authorities, which had extracted the increased tariff, the money he had paid. The question for the Court was whether the Treaty could be used in that way by an individual citizen rather than a Member State or the Commission. The Court of Justice held that it could if the provision in question met certain conditions: it would have to be clear, precise and unconditional; and it would have to leave the Member State with no discretion as to how it should be implemented. In other words, if the provision in question is sufficiently clear, precise and unconditional to create an 'enforceable right' for the client, as did Article 12 of the EC Treaty, that right can be enforced through the national courts in preference to national law. In *Van Gend en Loos* itself, the Court found that an individual could rely on Article 12 of the EC Treaty directly to recover the extra tax from the government.

21.3.1   Direct effect and the provisions of the Treaty

It has now been established that, applying the criteria set out in *Van Gend en Loos*, all the fundamental Treaty provisions have direct effect, in particular:

(a)   Article 34 TFEU (ex Article 30 EC) on free movement of goods (*Ianelli and Volpi sPA v Meroni* [1977] ECR 557);

(b)   Article 45 TFEU (ex Article 48 EC) on free movement of workers (*Van Duyn v Home Office* [1974] ECR 1337);

(c)   Article 49 TFEU (ex Article 52 EC) on freedom of establishment (*Reyners v The Belgian State* [1974] ECR 631);

(d)   Article 56 TFEU (ex Article 59 EC) on freedom to provide services (*Van Binsbergen (JHM) v Bestuur van de Bedrijfsvereniging voor de Metaalnijverheid* [1974] ECR 1299);

(e)   Article 101 TFEU (ex Article 85 EC) on anti-competitive agreements (*Belgische Radio en Televisie v SV SABAM* [1974] ECR 313);

(f)   Article 102 TFEU (ex Article 86 EC) on abuse of a dominant position (*Garden Cottage Foods v Milk Marketing Board* [1984] AC 130); and

(g)   Article 157 TFEU (ex Article 119 EC) on equal pay (*Defrenne (Gabrielle) v SABENA* [1976] ECR 455).

In addition, Article 18 TFEU (ex Article 6 EC) (discrimination), Articles 63–66 TFEU (ex Articles 73b–73g EC) (capital), Article 107 TFEU (ex Article 92 EC) (State aids) and Article 111 TFEU (ex Article 95 EC) (discriminatory indirect taxes on goods) are considered to have direct effect.

21.3.2   Direct effect and Regulations

Regulations are said by Article 288 TFEU to be 'directly applicable', ie they are part of national law and do not need implementing legislation. They are binding in the form in which they are made. However, they still have to be sufficiently 'clear, precise and unconditional' to create directly effective rights.

21.3.3   Direct effect and Directives

Directives are not of general application throughout the Community but require implementing measures, which are likely to vary from one Member State to another. Despite this, the Court of Justice has held, for example in *Van Duyn v Home Office* (see **21.3.1**), that in appropriate circumstances even Directives may be directly effective. The reason for this is that

Article 288 TFEU expressly states that a Directive is to be legally binding on the State to which it is addressed; this would be meaningless unless there was some possibility that Directives themselves could be relied on where the Member State failed to implement them. However, in the case of Directives, any rights they contain can have direct effect only after the time-limit for implementing the Directive has elapsed (see, eg, *Pubblico Ministero v Ratti* [1979] ECR 1629). Thereafter, again provided that the rights in the Directive are sufficiently clear, precise and unconditional, they can be relied on *against the State*, even though not implemented in national law.

21.3.4 'Horizontal' direct effect

In the early cases on direct effect, the defending party was always the State or some State agency, such as the customs authorities in *Van Gend en Loos* ('vertical' direct effect). Subsequent cases have shown that a party may rely on a Treaty provision, or even a Regulation (but not a Directive), where the other party is not a State body ('horizontal' direct effect). So, for example, in *Defrenne v SABENA* (see **21.4.1**) the plaintiff relied on Article 119 of the EC Treaty (now Article 157 TFEU) against a private employer.

Again, Directives are different. A Directive can be used only against a Member State or an 'emanation of the State'. This is clear from *Marshall v Southampton and South West Hampshire Area Health Authority (Teaching)* [1986] ECR 723. The rationale here is that allowing the use of a Directive against a Member State that is in delay encourages it to implement that Directive. A non-State body, on the other hand, has no power to influence the implementation of a Directive. If it is clear that the defendant is the State or a State body, it is also apparent from *Marshall* that it makes no difference whether or not the State is fulfilling a public function in the circumstances which gave rise to the case. In *Marshall*, the defendant health authority had dismissed the female plaintiff because she had reached the age of 62, although a male employee would not have been dismissed until the age of 65. The plaintiff argued that this breached the Equal Treatment Directive. The defendant conceded that it was a State body but argued that, as it was acting purely as an employer of the plaintiff, the Directive could not be relied upon against it. This argument failed before the Court of Justice.

From cases following *Marshall*, it appears that other emanations of the State for this purpose include a police force (*Johnston v Chief Constable of the RUC* [1986] ECR 1651) and a local authority (*Re London Boroughs* [1990] 3 CMLR 495 and *East Riding of Yorkshire County Council v Gibson* [2000] 3 CMLR 329).

The Court of Justice has subsequently given guidance on the meaning of the term 'emanation of the State'. According to *Foster v British Gas* [1990] ECR I-3133, it must be some body (whatever its legal form) which is carrying out a public service under the control of the State, or which has for that purpose special powers. In *Foster*, the English court applied that definition to find that British Gas prior to privatisation was an emanation of the State. On the other hand, it has since been held by the Court of Appeal in *Doughty v Rolls Royce plc* [1992] IRLR 126 that Rolls Royce was not an emanation of the State when it was in public ownership because it was not providing a public service. By contrast, the High Court has ruled that even the privatised water boards are sufficiently controlled by State regulators to satisfy the criteria in *Foster* (see *Griffin v South West Water Services Ltd* [1995] IRLR 15). Clearly even the privatised British Gas or British Telecom could be regarded as State bodies if this case is correct.

This distinction between public and non-public bodies inevitably means that some individuals will be protected by the provisions of a Directive while others will not. This is especially evident in the employment field, where employees of the State or State bodies will have an advantage over employees of a private employer. The Court of Justice in *Marshall* pointed out that such unfairness is easily countered by the Member State: it can implement the Directive.

Lastly, it should be remembered that even though enforceable only against the State, a Directive may still have indirect consequences for private persons. In *R v Durham, ex p Huddleston* [2000] 1 WLR 1484, a developer obtained from a planning authority permission to develop a site. An objector argued that the development had not been subjected to an environmental impact assessment as required by Directive 85/337. This had direct effect against the local planning authority (an emanation of the State) which was compelled to reconsider the permission. The effect was financially disastrous for the developer.

21.4   THE SUPREMACY OF EU LAW

The Court of Justice, in the seminal case of *Amministrazione delle Finanze dello Stato v Simmenthal* [1978] ECR 629, held that it was fundamental to EU law that EU law should be supreme over the domestic law of the Member States. In this way, EU law would apply uniformly throughout the EU. According to *Simmenthal*, 'every national court must ... accordingly set aside any provision of national law which may conflict with' EU law. The Court of Justice has reinforced that message on numerous occasions.

The courts of individual Member States have, from time to time, found the concept of supremacy difficult to accept. After the European Communities Act 1972, the English courts tended to rely upon interpreting English law to comply with EU law as far as possible. In recent years, however, the courts have been increasingly prepared to give effect to the *Simmenthal* doctrine. This can be seen in the case of *R v Secretary of State for Transport, ex p Factortame (No 2)* [1990] 3 WLR 818, in which some Spanish fishermen challenged the Merchant Shipping Act 1988 as being incompatible with EU law. The House of Lords referred the matter to the Court of Justice under the procedure in Article 177 of the EC Treaty (now Article 267 TFEU) (see **21.7**). In the meantime, the fishermen sought interim relief to suspend the operation of the Act until the Court of Justice replied to the reference. They argued that if the Act continued to operate, their livelihoods would be so seriously affected that the ruling of the Court of Justice might prove to be academic. The House of Lords refused relief, partly because it had no power to suspend the effect of an Act of Parliament, and partly because under English law an interim injunction could not be granted against the Crown. The House of Lords did, however, refer to the Court of Justice a second question: Was it right to refuse relief? The Court responded that where an individual seeks to rely on EU law, a rule of national procedure cannot be invoked in the national courts which would effectively deny the individual that right. The English court then granted the interim relief (see further **22.4**).

21.5   THE CONCEPT OF INDIRECT EFFECT

It would therefore seem clear that when a national court is confronted by national legislation and directly-effective EU legislation which conflict, the court should, under the principle of the supremacy of EU law, apply EU law to the dispute. However, there may be situations in which EU legislation does not have direct effect and a staightforward preference for it cannot be made. This might be the case where a Directive lacks the qualities necessary to give direct effect, as where it is being used against a non-State body.

In such cases, it may be possible to argue that the Directive has indirect effect. The national court is not asked to apply the Directive instead of the national legislation, but is asked to *interpret* the national legislation in the light of the EU Directive.

Accordingly, in *Litster v Forth Dry Dock & Engineering Co Ltd* [1990] 1 AC 546, the House of Lords interpreted the Transfer of Undertakings (Protection of Employment) Regulations 1981 (SI 1981/1794) in the light of Directive 77/187, which the Regulations purported to implement, even though that interpretation was contrary to the meaning on the face of the Regulations. In *Marleasing SA v La Comercial Internacional de Alimentacion SA* [1990] ECR I-4135, the Court of Justice took the concept of 'indirect effect' a stage further by ruling that national law should be interpreted, as far as possible, to give effect to an EU Directive, whether or not the Directive pre-dates the national law. The Court of Justice expressly based the latter decision on Article 5 of the EC Treaty (now Article 4(3) TEU), which requires Member States to take all necessary steps to ensure the fulfilment of their obligations. Contrary to its earlier ruling in *Duke v GEC Reliance Ltd (formerly Reliance Systems)* [1988] AC 618, the House of Lords later conceded that, in interpreting the Sex Discrimination Act 1975, it must take account of the Equal Treatment Directive 76/207 and Court rulings on its interpretation. See *Webb v EMO Air Cargo (UK)* [1994] IRLR 482, where the House of Lords accepted that (from 1978 onwards) it was obliged to interpret the Act in line with the later Directive, even though, in their Lordships' view, the result was not what Parliament had intended when passing the Act.

21.6 ACTION AGAINST A STATE FOR FAILURE TO IMPLEMENT A DIRECTIVE

The European Commission has the responsibility of monitoring the implementation rates of Member States, and it has the power to bring a State in default before the Court of Justice. An individual cannot take this action. However, following *Francovich and Bonifacti v Italy* [1992] IRLR 84, an individual may, in appropriate circumstances, sue a State for damages for failure to implement a particular Directive. In that case, Italy had failed to implement Directive 80/987 which would have established a fund available to employees dismissed by insolvent businesses which could not pay them their arrears of salary. Although the Directive was sufficiently precise in the rights it set out to create, these rights were conditional on there being a relevant fund. They were thus not directly effective. However, the Court of Justice gave a right of action against the State itself for non-implementation, relying on Article 5 of the EC Treaty (now Article 4(3) TEU), which requires Member States to take all appropriate measures to ensure the fulfilment of their obligations. The Court of Justice said that a right of action arises where three conditions are met:

(a)   the Directive confers rights on individuals;

(b)   the content of the rights is identifiable from the Directive;

(c)   there is a causal link between the failure to implement and the damage.

This is clearly what we would call in English law a claim in tort.

The action itself would be brought before the relevant national court in accordance with the appropriate national procedure (in England, this would be a High Court action against the Attorney-General). That procedure would have to ensure an effective remedy for the plaintiff.

In R v *Secretary of State for Transport, ex p Factortame (No 4)* [1996] 2 WLR 506, the Court ruled on whether the Spanish fishermen could recover damages for breach of Article 52 of the EC Treaty (now Article 49 TFEU) for being denied the right to form UK fishing companies (see **22.4–22.5**). The Court introduced a further condition for State liability in this type of case, ie damages are recoverable only where the breach of the Treaty is sufficiently serious, that is where the State manifestly and gravely disregards the limits on its own powers. This extra condition has also been applied in a case of an incorrectly implemented Directive. In R v HM *Treasury, ex p British Telecommunications plc* [1996] All ER (EC) 411, it was held that no damages are recoverable against the State if it has made a reasonable mistake in interpreting the Directive when drafting its implementing legislation. This is a very important case for governments, because the broad principles of EU law do provide plenty of scope for innocent, non-negligent interpretation. This will not, however, excuse governments which rely on negligent advice from their lawyers, as happened in the *Factortame* case. The British Government was eventually required to pay damages; the House of Lords accepting that the law on establishment and discrimination being clear, there was a sufficiently serious breach (R v *Secretary of State for Transport, ex p Factortame (No 5)* [1999] 4 All ER 906, HL).

However, note that the non-implementation of a Directive will still be assessed under the original *Francovich* test, since non-implementation is a sufficiently serious breach in itself (see *Dillenkofer and Others v Germany* [1996] 3 CMLR 469).

21.7   ARTICLE 267 TFEU REFERENCE PROCEDURE

21.7.1   What is the purpose of this procedure?

The Article 267 TFEU reference procedure enables the Court of Justice to give a preliminary ruling to a national court principally on the interpretation of the Treaty, although it can also rule on the validity of acts of Union institutions. This means that the Court of Justice will not, as such, rule on the compatibility of national law with EU law, or on the application of EU law to particular facts. This is the national court's responsibility. Thus, in *Foster v British Gas* [1990] ECR I-3133 (see **21.3.4**) the Court of Justice explained how an emanation of the State could be recognised, and the English court then applied the definition to British Gas. It may be, however, that in stating the principle, the Court of Justice, in effect, indicates how it must apply to the facts before the national court. The advantage of Article 267 TFEU is that it provides a mechanism which enables the Court of Justice to ensure that EU law develops along parallel lines throughout the Union.

21.7.2   How does the procedure work?

Article 267 TFEU distinguishes two situations.

21.7.2.1   Where the case is being heard before a court from which there is no judicial remedy

In this case, the national court must make a reference if it believes that a clarification of the EU point is necessary in order to decide the case. It may not be necessary where the point of EU law is irrelevant to the case, where there is an existing Court of Justice judgment on the matter, or where the court believes the correct interpretation to be obvious (see *CILFIT Srl v Ministro della Sanitro* [1982] ECR 3415).

A particularly striking example of this is the case involving part-timers (*Equal Opportunities Commission v Secretary of State for Employment* [1994] 1 All ER 910 (HL)). This is another illustration of the point that discrimination, here in relation to pay between men and women (Article 157 TFEU), always includes unjustifiable indirect discrimination. In this context, paying part-timers less than full-timers means indirectly paying women less than men because most part-timers are women. Thus, the House of Lords ruled that legislation requiring part-timers to work for five years before qualifying for redundancy payments/unfair dismissal compensation (whereas full-timers qualified after two years) was unlawful because it was a breach of equal pay under Article 157 TFEU. There was no objective reason for the discrimination. The House emphatically rejected Government arguments that it would create new jobs by reducing the burdens on business, saying that there was no evidence that this was the case. No reference was made to the Court of Justice because the position in EU law was clear. The provisions of the Employment Protection (Consolidation) Act 1978, which had stood for 13 years, were declared unlawful without the need for a reference. The Act has since been amended. In the light of subsequent cases (notably *R v Secretary of State for Employment, ex p Seymour-Smith* [1999] 3 WLR 460), it is suggested that the House of Lords should have made a reference.

21.7.2.2   Where the case is being heard before any other court or a tribunal that is exercising a judicial function

In this case, the court or tribunal has a discretion whether to make a reference. Again, the Court of Justice's opinion must be necessary in order for a decision to be reached. Throughout the Union, a wide range of lower courts and tribunals have made references under Article 267 TFEU (or its predecessors, Article 177 and Article 234 EC), including UK magistrates' courts and social security appeal tribunals.

In either case, the question whether a reference should be made is one for the court rather than the parties to the case. Once the court has decided that a reference should be made, it should then draft the questions to which it requires a reply. In certain cases, the Court of

Justice has reformulated these questions so that they more accurately reflect the issue that needs to be addressed. Although the Court has no discretion, as such, as to whether it replies to a reference, it has refused to respond where there is no genuine dispute between the parties and where the reference was made in order to raise wider political issues (*Foglia v Novello* [1980] ECR 745).

SUMMARY

If a client seeks advice on a problem where there could be an EU dimension, remember:

(1)   EU law can also be used in its own right if it meets the criteria for direct effect (see **21.3**);

(2)   if there is EU legislation which has direct effect, an English court or tribunal must prefer it to conflicting domestic law (see **21.4**);

(3)   EU legislation can affect the interpretation of domestic law (see *Marleasing SA v La Comercial Internacional de Alimentacion SA* [1990] ECR I-4135 at **21.5**);

(4)   in case of doubt as to the meaning of EU law, consider a reference to the Court of Justice under Article 267 TFEU (see **21.7**).

SEEKING A REMEDY IN NATIONAL COURTS

LEARNING OUTCOMES

After reading this chapter you will be able to understand:

- how to use EU law to defend yourself in a legal action
- how to use EU law offensively in court and what remedies you may be entitled to
- the limits on the use of EU law, both in terms of the amount of compensation and the time limits for use.

22.1 INTRODUCTION

This chapter is an attempt to consolidate the rules and think more practically about how they can be applied in English courts when acting for a client. It serves as a warning to English solicitors who believe that they can advise their clients on English law alone. Ignoring relevant EU law is undoubtedly solicitor's negligence. Although there have been no reported cases in England, lawyers have been successfully sued in other States for ignoring, say, the competition rules (and thus putting their client at risk of a fine or void agreements), or for ignoring EU Regulation 1215/2012 on jurisdiction (and thus losing their client's case by suing in the wrong jurisdiction). A lawyer who advises on English law alone will thus often give wrong advice on English law, because English law by definition includes EU law – lock, stock and barrel.

22.2 EU LAW AS A DEFENCE

As EU law overrides conflicting national law, directly-effective EU law can always be used as a defence to any civil claim, prosecution or tax claim that is based on that national law. Thus, for example, since Article 101 TFEU makes restrictive agreements void, a defendant can plead Article 101 TFEU when sued in a civil claim for breach of the agreement. Likewise, if Articles 34, 45, 49 and 56 TFEU make measures restricting free movement of goods, services and working persons unlawful, a client prosecuted under such national measures can plead the Articles of the Treaty as a defence. In tax claims, a client can plead the VAT Directive (77/388) or the Treaty provisions on non-discrimination (Article 110 TFEU). Thus, where an exemption from VAT exists in the Directive but not in the UK tax legislation, a taxpayer can plead the Directive as defence to a demand for tax; VAT is very much an EU tax and cannot be collected in circumstances not allowed for under the Directive.

22.3 EFFECTIVE REMEDIES

In relation to more active remedies, the Court of Justice has made it plain in cases like R v *Secretary of State for Transport, ex p Factortame (No 2)* [1990] 3 WLR 818, that national courts must provide a sufficient remedy to protect EU rights. In general, this would be the nearest equivalent national remedy. Where no adequate remedy is available under national law, the court must provide one to protect the EU right in question (as it did in *Factortame*). Thus, a client may be better protected by asserting an EU right than he is under national law (examples being *Marshall v Southampton Area Health Authority (No 2)* [1993] 3 CMLR 293, discussed below at **22.9**, and R v *Secretary of State for Transport, ex p Factortame (No 4)* [1996] 2 WLR 506).

It should also be noted that administrative decisions affecting EU law must be reasoned, 'proportional' and subject to review by a higher tribunal. Neither the duty to give reasons nor 'proportionality' are well established under English administrative law, so that once again the client asserting an EU right may be better protected when dealing with administrative institutions.

22.4 INJUNCTIONS/INTERIM INJUNCTIONS

If one thinks of actual remedies available to protect EU rights, probably the first thing one would think of would be an injunction. This is certainly available to be used against a private person to restrain a breach of Articles 101 or 102 TFEU (see *Garden Cottage Foods v Milk Marketing Board* [1984] AC 130). Thus, a client who feels he is being excluded from a particular market because of a restrictive agreement breaching Article 101 TFEU, or an abuse of a dominant position breaching Article 102 TFEU, can get an injunction to restrain such unlawful behaviour, and get back into the market.

However, the remedy of injunction or interim injunction is also available against the Government to restrain a breach of EU rules, despite the fact that under English law interim injunctive relief is not normally available to suspend statutes or statutory instruments (see R v *Secretary of State for Transport, ex p Factortame (No 2)* [1990] 3 WLR 818).

In *Factortame*, some Spanish fishermen had set up a UK company to operate UK trawlers with the intention of exploiting the UK fishing quota in the North Sea. The Merchant Shipping Act 1988 provided that, in order to qualify as a UK company for this purpose, the company must itself be owned at least 75% by UK nationals who were UK residents. Not surprisingly, the Spanish fishermen who found themselves excluded by this rule complained that the Act was contrary to the Treaty in that it denied their right of establishment as a UK company (Article 52 of the EC Treaty (now Article 49 TFEU)) and discriminated against them as EC (now EU) nationals (Article 6 of the EC Treaty (now Article 18 TFEU)). Faced with this issue, the House of Lords felt obliged to make a reference to the Court of Justice, but the question then arose as to whether the House of Lords would be bound to grant interim relief protecting the fishermen's rights until the Court could rule on the main issue. This issue, too, was referred to the Court of Justice, which replied, somewhat more promptly than normal, that the national court must grant an interim injunction to suspend the Act of Parliament where this was necessary to protect the EC (now EU) rights pending the ruling from the Court. Eventually, the ruling came back (R v *Secretary of State for Transport, ex p Factortame (No 3)* [1991] 3 All ER 769) that the 1988 Act did contravene the Treaty and therefore, in relation to EC (now EU) nationals, the provisions concerned had to be suspended indefinitely.

It should be noted that *Factortame* involved an urgent case where the fishermen's livelihood was being threatened in circumstances where damages (at the time uncertain) would not have been an adequate remedy. The ruling does not mean that in EU cases the court need not follow the normal balance of convenience test when deciding when to grant an interim injunction, nor that the court need not take into account other factors, for example public policy, when exercising its discretion. In two other cases, a reference was made but an interim injunction was refused in the meantime. These cases are *R v HM Treasury, ex p British Telecommunications plc* [1994] 1 CMLR 621 and *R v Heritage Secretary, ex p Continental TV (Red Hot TV)* [1993] 2 CMLR 333. Both cases rested on the 'balance of convenience', with the adequacy of damages being a particular fact in the first case and public policy (protecting sensitive viewers from pornographic television) being a factor in the second.

22.5 DAMAGES FOR BREACH OF EU RIGHTS

Again, there seems little doubt that damages are available against private persons for breach of their statutory duty, for example for anti-competitive behaviour under Articles 101 or 102 TFEU. Although there have been no reported court decisions of damages being awarded, the House of Lords in *Garden Cottage Foods v Milk Marketing Board* [1984] AC 130 was certainly of the opinion that damages could be recovered. A large number of cases have been settled on the basis that this is the case. It would seem, however, in the light of *Factortame (No 4)*, that a purely innocent, non-negligent infringement of the competition rules would attract no damages from the national courts just as it would attract no fine from the Commission (see below). Ignorance of the law, however, is no excuse!

Where the defendant concerned is the Government, the claim for tort damages under English public law is a little more complicated. According to the Court of Appeal in *Bourgoin SA v Ministry of Agriculture, Fisheries and Food* [1985] 3 WLR 1027, the Government cannot be liable for damages for exercising its powers unlawfully unless it is guilty of deliberate abuse of power ('misfeasance in public office'). This may be a true reflection of English public law, but the decision in *Bourgoin* itself (where the court refused to award damages for what was a flagrant breach of Article 30 of the EC Treaty (now Article 34 TFEU), a ban on importing French turkeys) is now clearly contrary to the Court of Justice rulings in *Factortame* and *Francovich*. The House of Lords suggested as much (obiter) in *Kirklees MBC v Wickes Building Supplies Ltd* [1992] 3 All ER 717, where their Lordships suggested that the Government would have had to compensate Sunday traders if the Shops Act 1950 was found to be in breach of Article 30 of the EC Treaty (now Article 34 TFEU), ie the traders would have been entitled to issue writs against the Attorney-General for damages for all the loss sustained through breach of the statutory duty under Article 30 of the EC Treaty (now Article 34 TFEU). Clarification of the position in regard to damages was given finally by the Court of Justice in *Factortame (No 4)* [1996] 2 WLR 506, where the question was whether the Spanish fishermen were entitled to damages against the Government for the period in which they were prevented from operating their trawlers before they got their interim injunction. The Court having given its ruling on EU law that damages can be awarded where the breach is sufficiently serious (see **21.4**), the English courts then had to determine whether this was such a case. The House of Lords finally awarded damages to the fishermen, thus bringing the long saga to an end (*Factortame (No 5)* [1999] 4 All ER 906).

See also **21.6**.

22.6 REPAYMENT OF DISCRIMINATORY TAX/VAT

Again, if the tax has been unlawfully collected in breach of Article 110 TFEU or in breach of the VAT Directives, the requirement that an adequate remedy be given means that this tax must be repaid in full with interest (see the Court's ruling in *Amministrazione delle Finanze dello Stato v Spa San Giorgio* [1983] ECR 359). For reasons which will be explained at **22.8**, it may be that the normal time-limit for reclaiming tax under national tax law cannot run to protect the Government until such time as the Government brings its own tax law into line with EU law. This case does recognise a principle of 'unjust enrichment'. Thus, tax should not be repaid where it has been passed on to a customer who cannot himself be traced.

22.7 STATUTORY REMEDIES

Initially when asserting an EU right, one starts by looking at the nearest equivalent national remedy. Thus, the client who asserts EU rights in the context of employment law, for example equal pay under Article 157 TFEU, or sex discrimination under the Equal Treatment Directive (2006/54), is effectively asserting statutory employment rights and therefore must take his claim to an employment tribunal where the remedies and procedures he will be seeking will be equivalent to those under the Equal Pay Act 1970 and the Sex Discrimination Act 1975. In two respects, however, time-limits and limits on compensation, the remedies provided for breach of these EU rights may be better than those for the equivalent rights under national law.

22.8 TIME-LIMITS

Although initially the national time-limits will apply to the claim, the Court of Justice has made it clear that these cannot be used to protect the Government where the claim is based on a Directive which the Government has failed to implement. In other words, the claimant cannot be deprived of a right by the Government delaying implementation for so long that he is out of time. In such circumstances the Government is estopped from relying on its own wrong, and therefore the time-limit begins to run only when it has righted that wrong by introducing national legislation that complies with the Directive (see *Emmott v Minister for Social Welfare and Attorney-General* [1991] IRLR 387). The Court seems to have reduced the effectiveness of this ruling in *Johnson v Chief Adjudication Officer (No 2)* [1995] IRLR 187, where it indicates that a time-limit which limits back-payments of social security may be enforceable even where the Government is in breach of a Directive. The same rule applies to tax (see now *Edilizia Industriale v Ministero delle Finanze* [1999] 2 CMLR 995. The normal national time-limits will of course be available to protect a private person, for example an employer faced with a claim for equal pay under Article 157 TFEU. But even these may not start to run until the employee is aware of his rights under Article 157 TFEU (see *Cannon v Barnsley Metropolitan Borough Council* [1992] IRLR 474). The Court has made it clear in the case of *Fischer* [1994] IRLR 662, that the time-limit must not make it impossible to exercise the EU rights which national courts and governments are obliged to protect. There are thus two basic rules that national time-limits must satisfy (see *Comet BV v Produktschap voor Siergewassen* [1997] ECR 2043). First, they must still leave the applicant with an effective remedy and not make recovery virtually impossible. Secondly, they must be equivalent to time-limits in similar national claims. This second principle of non-discrimination is well-illustrated by the case of *Levez v TH Jennings (Harlow Pools) Ltd* [1999] IRLR 764, where the two-year time-limit on back pay in equal pay cases was held to be unlawful as in other similar claims for race and disability discrimination there was no such limit. The EAT's ruling followed guidance from the Court of Justice in *Levez v TH Jennings (Harlow Pools) Ltd* [1999] All ER (EC) 1. The time-limits for making these claims are not, however, discriminatory. In *Biggs v Somerset County Council* [1996] ICR 364, the Court of Appeal refused to allow a claim brought by a part-time employee for unfair dismissal compensation as equal pay under Article 119 of the EC Treaty (now Article 157 TFEU), when it was brought 18 years after the dismissal but within three months of the House of Lords ruling in *Equal Opportunities Commission v Secretary of State for Employment* [1994] 1 All ER 910 (see **21.7.2**).

22.9 LIMITS ON COMPENSATION

As indicated above, EU rules like those protecting against sex discrimination under the Equal Treatment Directive do require an adequate remedy. Thus, the Court of Justice has ruled that the national limits on compensation under the Sex Discrimination Act 1975 (now the Equality Act 2010) (the maximum until November 1993 was £11,000) cannot be used to protect a State employer in a claim based on an EU Directive. This is the now famous case of *Marshall v Southampton Area Health Authority (No 2)* [1993] 3 CMLR 293. Mrs Marshall, who established her right to compensation for breach of the EU Directive in *Marshall v Southampton and West Hampshire Area Health Authority (Teaching)*, then went back to an industrial tribunal where her compensation was assessed at over £20,000. This figure included an assessment of interest. However, both the EAT and the Court of Appeal ruled that the compensation had to be restricted to the limit set by the Sex Discrimination Act 1975, which not only restricted compensation (at the time to £6,000) but also denied the award of interest. On a reference from the House of Lords, the Court ruled that compensation must be awarded without limit and that in assessing compensation the tribunal must, to give an adequate remedy, award interest. The Government reacted promptly and commendably to this ruling by removing both the upper limit and the restriction on interest for all discrimination and equal pay claims with effect from November 1993 (see Sex Discrimination and Equal Pay (Remedies) Regulations 1993, SI 1993/2798). It should be noted that in relation to rights under English law which do not implement EU rights, it is perfectly lawful for the law to provide an inadequate remedy. Thus, 'unfair dismissal' compensation is still limited by statute.

CHAPTER 23

FREE MOVEMENT OF WORKERS

LEARNING OUTCOMES

After reading this chapter you will be able to understand:

- what EU nationality means
- what EU nationality grants in terms of rights for the workforce
- the extent to which a worker can take his family to another Member State whilst working there
- the circumstances in which a worker and/or his family can be denied entry into a Member State.

23.1 INTRODUCTION

The EC Treaty gave (and the TFEU now gives) the right of free movement within the Union to people who wished to take up offers of employment made from outside their home State. This fundamental Treaty right has been buttressed by a considerable amount of secondary legislation. Further, EU law has developed to the stage where the rights of individuals to move within the EU are not necessarily dependent on the desire to take up employment. Indeed, as a consequence of the Single European Act, from 1 January 1993, internal barriers to movement within the EU should have been removed. Further, Article 20 TFEU now states that every EU national shall be a citizen of the European Union. Under Article 21 TFEU, the Union citizen has the right to move and reside freely within the territory of the Member States, subject to the limitations and conditions in the Treaty and in other legislation.

23.2 WHAT DOES THE TREATY PROVIDE?

Free movement of workers is guaranteed by Article 45 TFEU, which gives the EU worker the right of entry and residence for the purpose of taking up employment. According to Article 45(2) TFEU, Member States must abolish

> any discrimination based on nationality between workers of the Member States as regards employment, remuneration and other conditions of work and employment.

'Work and employment' has been interpreted very widely to include sportspeople. Hence, in *Union Royale Belge des Sociétés de Football Association ASBL v Bosman* [1996] All ER (EC) 97, the Court of Justice made it plain that restrictions on the number of EU nationals in football teams imposed by UEFA and requirements for large transfer fees in cross-border transfers were both illegal.

23.2.1   How is nationality interpreted?

Nationality is entirely a matter for the domestic law of each Member State, which means that, inevitably, rules vary. In particular, not all Member States permit their nationals to hold dual nationality. One result of this was seen in *Micheletti v Delegacion del Gobierno en Cantabria* [1992] ECR I-4238. The case concerned a dual national of Argentina and Italy who sought entry into Spain. Entry was refused because under Spanish law only the nationality of the State in which the person had last been habitually resident was recognised, and in this case that was Argentina. The Court of Justice found, however, that, as he was an Italian national under Italian law, he was an EC (now EU) migrant worker protected by Article 48 of the EC Treaty (now Article 45 TFEU), so that entry into Spain could not be denied.

23.2.2   What rights of residence does the EU national obtain under Article 45 TFEU?

The EU national has an absolute right of residence so long as he remains in work. If the worker becomes involuntarily unemployed, Directive 2004/38 will continue to guarantee him a right to reside in the host State. However, if he becomes voluntarily unemployed his position is changed as (in accordance with most social security systems) he would be disqualified from social security benefits. Under Directive 2004/38, he has a right of residence simply by being a citizen of another Member State as long as he has sufficient resources not to be a burden on the host State. If a worker becomes permanently disabled or reaches retirement age, his right of permanent residence continues under this Directive as well.

An individual can claim the rights of a worker as long as he is genuinely employed, even if his work is part time and obtained so that EU rights can be asserted, and even if the salary paid is below a minimum wage limit (*Levin v Secretary of State for Justice* [1982] 1 ECR 1035).

A period of five years' residence gives the worker and/or his family (see **23.4**) a right of permanent residence.

23.2.3   What terms of employment is an EU national entitled to expect?

An EU national can claim the same terms as those offered to a national of the host State. Article 45(2) TFEU expressly refers to the right not to be discriminated against as regards conditions of work. So, in the case of *Allué (Pilar) and Coonan (Mary Carmel) v Università degli Studi di Venezia* [1991] 1 CMLR 283, an Italian law which provided that non-Italians who accepted jobs in Italy to teach a language could only enter into fixed-term contracts for one year was contrary to Article 48(2) of the EC Treaty (now Article 45(2) TFEU). In addition, Regulation 1612/68, Article 7, and Directive 2004/38, Article 24 prohibit discrimination in relation to conditions of employment, dismissal, social and tax advantages, training and union membership.

23.2.4   What about his social security rights?

Social security rights are governed by Regulation 1408/71, which basically guarantees to EU nationals the social security benefits of the host State. However, where the benefits are dependent on contributions, a worker's entitlement will take into account contributions to the equivalent benefit in his home State or other Member States in which he has worked. The Regulation does not provide for harmonisation of benefits or of levels of benefits throughout the Union.

23.2.5   Does an EU national have a right of entry to look for work?

Article 45 TFEU (or its predecessors) has been interpreted to mean that an EU national has a right of entry to look for work and a reasonable period of residence to find it. This is confirmed in Directive 2004/38, which grants a three-month right of residence without qualifying as a worker. In the UK, the immigration rules used to allow such a person to be deported if he did not succeed in finding work after six months. The Court of Justice held this rule to be consistent with EU law in *R v Immigration Appeals Tribunal, ex p Antonissen* [1991] 2

CMLR 373, although it stressed that the job seeker might still have a right of residence if he had reasonable prospects of finding work. (There is no longer a fixed time-limit for finding work in the UK.) An EU national has a right to remain in the host State as an ordinary citizen if his resources are adequate and he is covered by health insurance by virtue of Directive 2004/38 on the right to residence for EU citizens.

23.3 WHEN DOES THE TREATY ALLOW MEMBER STATES TO DENY ENTRY?

Article 45(3) TFEU permits derogations on grounds of public policy, public security and public health. Because these are derogations from one of the fundamental freedoms of the EU, the Court of Justice has interpreted them strictly. Further, Directive 2004/38 has made it clear that only personal conduct can be taken into account. Even prior criminal convictions will not necessarily entitle the Member State to deny entry. They will do so only where they indicate that the individual represents a current threat to public security. For example, in *Astrid Proll v Entry Clearance Officer* [1988] 2 CMLR 387, the former Baader Meinhoff terrorist was allowed entry into the UK because she did not represent a present threat.

Article 45(4) TFEU provides that the rights granted earlier in the Article do not apply to employment in the public service. This has been interpreted strictly by the Court of Justice in *Commission of European Communities v Belgium; Re Public Employees (No 1)* [1980] ECR 3881 to mean only 'posts involving the exercise of official authority and functions related to safeguarding the general interests of the State'.

23.4 CAN THE WORKER BRING HIS FAMILY WITH HIM?

Because a worker might be deterred from moving to another Member State if he could not take his family with him, Directive 2004/38 enables him to do so. It does, however, limit the family members who are entitled to entry to the spouse, registered partner, children under 21 and dependent relatives of the worker or spouse/partner. Member States do, however, have an obligation to 'facilitate entry and residence' of any other family members who are dependants or members of the household. It is not necessary for family members to be EU nationals. The host State can refuse entry to family members only in those circumstances which allow it to refuse entry to the worker himself (see **23.3** above). The rights of a spouse are not dependent on his or her residing with the worker, and thus can terminate only if the worker leaves the host State permanently (*Diatta v Land Berlin* [1985] ECR 567). Prior to Directive 2004/38 there was no clear European authority as to whether deportation could follow divorce, but in *Baumbast v Secretary of State for the Home Department* [2002] ECR I-7091 the mother of children was entitled to remain having been awarded custody. Directive 2004/38 provides for the spouse (or unmarried cohabitee) to remain in the country if he or she has resided for three years, or if they have been awarded custody or access to children, or alternatively if the court feels that allowing them to remain is warranted in the circumstances.

Directive 2004/38 lays down formal requirements for entry (including visa) and for obtaining residence documents. Thereafter, the family have the same rights as the worker himself to jobs, social security and education.

SUMMARY

If an EU national or a family member is refused entry or residence rights by UK immigration authorities, he will be allowed to invoke his EU rights before the appropriate immigration authority or Appeal Tribunal, or as a defence in criminal proceedings where deportation is being considered.

If an EU national believes that he has been discriminated against in relation to employment, he should, as usual, follow the appropriate national procedure in the host State to obtain a suitable remedy. In England, this would mean commencing proceedings before an employment tribunal under the Equality Act 2010. It is important to remember that, to comply with EU law, such national procedure must not discriminate, even indirectly, against the EU national and must give an effective remedy for breach of EU law (see **22.9**).

FREEDOM OF ESTABLISHMENT AND PROVISION OF SERVICES

LEARNING OUTCOMES

After reading this chapter you will be able to understand:

- the rights which a self-employed individual or business has to ply his or its trade in another Member State temporarily
- the rights which a self-employed individual or business has to establish himself or itself permanently in another Member State
- the possibility of persons relying on the above rights to bring their family with them
- what exceptions exist which may stop someone relying on his rights
- the right of the recipient of services to travel to another Member State to receive services.

24.1 INTRODUCTION

The freedom of establishment is the right to base one's business in another Member State permanently. This right is guaranteed by the TFEU, with the important qualification that it cannot give the establishing business greater rights than those enjoyed by businesses operated by nationals of the host Member State. Thus a French business wishing to establish itself in England would have to comply with laws affecting an English business relating, for example, to employment, health and safety, and taxes and social security (except to the extent that these might discriminate directly or indirectly against the foreign firm). The governing Article in the TFEU is Article 49.

The freedom to provide services guarantees that a business can provide a service across an EU frontier even if that business does not want to be permanently based outside its home State. As with the right of establishment, the right to provide services is granted on the basis that the services will be provided subject to the same conditions as apply to nationals of the State in which the service is supplied (again subject to these rules constituting indirect discrimination). The governing Article in the TFEU is Article 56.

Although under both Articles the firm concerned must comply with the same conditions which apply to local nationals, those conditions are likely to be tighter for establishment. In

Gebhard v Consiglio dell'Ordine degli Avvocati e Procuratori di Milano [1996] All ER (EC) 139, it was held that a German lawyer giving advice on German law in Italy was prima facie 'established' there by virtue of his permanent office and his adoption of the title Avvocato. Had he merely been providing services, he could have relied on his home title as a German lawyer and the earlier Directive on free movement of legal services. However, by establishing himself in Italy, he had to requalify as an Italian lawyer.

In the cases taken to the Court of Justice under Articles 49 and 56 TFEU, emphasis has often successfully been placed on Article 18 TFEU which prohibits discrimination on the ground of nationality, wherever the matter is covered by the Treaty.

Article 18 TFEU has direct effect, so that provisions of UK statutes can be disapplied by UK courts in so far as they directly or indirectly discriminate against other EU nationals. Residence requirements are a good example of indirect discrimination.

24.2   THE RIGHT OF ESTABLISHMENT: ARTICLE 49 TFEU

Article 49 TFEU provides that restrictions on the freedom of establishment by nationals of a Member State in the territory of another Member State must be abolished. This freedom is stated to include the right to take up and pursue activities as self-employed persons and to set up and manage undertakings, in particular companies or firms, under the conditions laid down for its own nationals by the law of the country where the establishment is effected.

24.2.1   What is the implication of this Article?

Article 49 TFEU means that no Member State can, through its legislation or administrative practices, impose a nationality barrier to businesses which wish to be based permanently in another Member State. In *R v Secretary of State for Transport, ex p Factortame (No 3)* [1991] 3 All ER 769, Article 52 of the EC Treaty (now Article 49 TFEU) was invoked by Spanish fishermen who operated British-registered fishing boats but who were prevented from fishing the British quota because the Merchant Shipping Act 1988 laid down nationality and residence requirements for the owners of shares in companies operating such boats. The Court of Justice held that such legislation was contrary to Article 52 of the EC Treaty (see **22.4**).

24.2.2   Are there any limitations on the kind of undertaking which can benefit from Article 49 TFEU?

Article 49 TFEU refers in particular to companies and firms. This phrase is defined in Article 54 TFEU to mean 'companies or firms constituted under civil or commercial law including co-operative societies'. The meaning of company or firm is really a matter for the law of the home State. A French company wishing to set up a branch or subsidiary in England can do so provided it meets the requirements under French law for being a company. It must not hold itself out as having been incorporated under English law. The only qualification here is that EU law requires that an undertaking wishing to rely on Article 49 TFEU must be a profit-making body.

It is particularly important to realise, however, that an entrepreneur wishing to set up a company can choose the State with the least regulatory company regime and then establish a branch back in the State he wishes to trade in. In *Centros Ltd v Erhvervsog Selskabsstyrelsen* [1999] 2 CMLR 551, the Court of Justice recognised that it was legitimate to set up a company in the UK and trade through a branch in Denmark, even though the purpose was to avoid the Danish requirements for a minimum paid-up share capital.

24.3   THE RIGHT TO PROVIDE SERVICES: ARTICLE 56 TFEU

According to Article 56 TFEU, restrictions on the freedom to provide services within the EU must be abolished in respect of nationals of Member States who are established in a State of the Community other than that of the person for whom the services are intended. Services for this purpose, according to Article 57 TFEU, are services normally provided for remuneration. In *Commission of European Communities v France* [1991] ECR I-659, for example, it was held that a French law which required tourist guides to hold a licence dependent on the passing of an examination in France was contrary to Article 59 of the EC Treaty (now Article 56 TFEU) as being unnecessary and discriminatory. There are many similar cases. This Article also means that a business providing services in another Member State had the right to bring its own employees into the host State to enable it to perform those services, even where they would not have been entitled to claim rights under Article 48 of the EC Treaty (now Article 45 TFEU) (eg, because of transitional rules for nationals of new EU Member States or because the workforce includes immigrants from outside the EU) (*Rush Portuguesa v Office National d'Immigration* [1990] ECR I-1417, *Van der Elst* [1994] ECR I-3803). The workers would, of course, need to be lawfully employed in the State where the employer is established and might need visas to enter the host country; they would not need fresh work permits. The Court of Justice, however, stresses that the host State can impose its own mandatory rules for workers' protection. Since statutory protection for workers in some countries (eg, the UK) is less than in other countries (eg, Germany), this might enable British firms to provide services to Germany using their British workforce at cheaper rates than German firms which have to pay their employees a higher minimum wage. A Directive on Posted Workers (96/71) was adopted in September 1996 and implemented in the UK by the Equal Opportunities (Employment Legislation) (Territorial Limits) Regulations 1999 (SI 1999/3163). Under the Regulations, a UK company posting its workers in another EU State (eg, whilst working on a building contract) will have to comply with local employment laws where the posting is longer (usually) than one month. The employees can enforce these rights in their UK employment tribunal (as well as in local courts).

24.4 SECONDARY LEGISLATION

In 2006 the EU passed Directive 2006/123, the 'Services Directive', which was designed to help service providers and recipients benefit from freedom of establishment and freedom to provide services across borders by simplifying administrative procedures and removing obstacles for service activities.

The Directive also applies to freedom of establishment, and so is relevant to Articles 49 and 56 TFEU.

The provisions of the Directive are complex, and beyond the scope of this book; however, the key highlights are:

- Industries are included within it unless expressly excluded (but there is a long list of excluded industries within the Directive).
- The Directive includes an obligation on Member States to set up single points of contact for those wishing to establish or provide services, to make it easier to obtain information.
- Making applications and following procedures must be straightforward, including the possibility of procedures to be completed at a distance and/or by electronic means.
- The Directive sets out restrictions on 'authorisation schemes', ie schemes by which applicants must seek permission from the State before carrying out certain activities. The aim is again to simplify, and to prevent unfair denial of business opportunities.

24.5 CONSTRAINTS UNDER ARTICLES 49 AND 56 TFEU

The in-coming business is subject to the laws that would apply to a business operated by nationals of that State. This can create barriers to the business wishing to operate across a frontier. The host State may require, perhaps, that all such businesses obtain the authority of the State before they can start to operate. Professional people may be required to conform to rules of professional conduct, professional qualifications or to the rules of a professional body within the host State.

Article 57 of the EC Treaty (now Article 53 TFEU) envisaged that a series of Directives would be issued dealing with mutual recognition and harmonisation of professional regulations. In the light of this, the European Commission, recognising the public interest in maintaining standards while wishing to minimise unnecessary barriers to cross-border enterprise, tried to develop uniform codes in certain sectors which would apply throughout the Community. These 'sectoral' Directives apply to medical professions such as doctors, nurses, dentists and vets, but the development of harmonised professional training and qualifications in all professions would have taken many years. So after the Court of Justice held that Articles 52 and 59 of the EC Treaty (now Articles 49 and 56 TFEU) were directly effective (see *Reyners v The Belgian State* [1974] ECR 631 and *Van Binsbergen (JHM) v Bestuur van de Bedrijfsvereniging voor de Metaalnijverheid* [1974] ECR 1299 at **21.3.1**), the Commission changed its approach to one of encouraging mutual recognition of standards. Thus a professional qualified in one State must, in principle, be recognised in another State to the extent that his qualification is equivalent.

A particularly important Directive in this respect is Directive 89/48 on recognition of higher education qualifications. The effect of the Directive is that where entry into a particular profession depends upon the candidate having obtained a 'diploma' which proves that he has completed at least three years' professional education and training, a non-national cannot be denied entry to that profession if he holds the equivalent 'diploma' which would entitle him to enter the profession in his home State. However, if there are substantial differences in the content of the course leading to the diploma in the home State, the Directive allows the host State to require the candidate to follow an adaptation period of no more than three years. As an alternative, the candidate could choose to take an aptitude test. The Directive makes special provision regarding entry to the legal profession. It allows a State to specify whether a candidate must take an aptitude test or follow a period of adaptation. Thus, in England and Wales, qualified lawyers from other EU States must pass The Law Society's Qualified Lawyers Transfer Test (QLTT) before they can be admitted as solicitors. Solicitors from Ireland are, however, admitted without a test, as their qualification is equivalent. The more recent establishment Directive of 1998 (98/5) provides for automatic requalification after a period of practise as a foreign lawyer.

The principle behind Directive 89/48 has been extended to cover diplomas awarded after one year's post-secondary education by Directive 92/51.

In *Van Binsbergen (JHM) v Bestuur van de Bedrijfsvereniging voor de Metaalnijverheid* [1974] ECR 1299, the Court of Justice held that professional rules of conduct regulating the legal profession would not be in breach of Community (now EU) law provided they did not discriminate against the non-national, they were objectively justifiable and they were not disproportionate to the aim to be achieved. Hence, a lawyer established in France had the right to provide services by representing clients before Belgian tribunals. He could not be forced to establish himself in Belgium. Simply having an address for service in Belgium would be proportional to any need for supervision of his activities. (A Directive has now adopted the *Van Binsbergen* line and allows qualified EU lawyers to represent their clients before foreign tribunals within the EU (see Directive 77/249).) A similar approach can be seen in the case of *Commission of European Communities v Germany* [1988] ECR 5427, which was concerned with the regulation of the German insurance sector. In that case, the Court held that restrictions on the right of an insurance company to provide services in Germany would be acceptable only if they were objectively justified, in the general public good and if they applied to all undertakings so far as they were not regulated in their home State.

Lastly, it would seem that if there is only a tenuous link between the services being provided and a particular restrictive provision, the latter will not be in breach of EU law (see *Society for the Protection of the Unborn Child (Ireland) v Grogan (Stephen)* [1991] 3 CMLR 849). That case concerned Irish legislation prohibiting the supply of information on abortion facilities provided outside Ireland. The Court of Justice acknowledged that the overseas clinics provided services within the meaning of Article 59 of the EC Treaty (now Article 56 TFEU), but went on to hold that since the information in question was being made available by student unions rather than by the clinics themselves, there was an insufficient link between the restriction and the provision of the services. Had the clinics been advertising directly themselves (or through an advertising agency), the position would have been different. (The ban on these leaflets may raise questions of freedom of speech under Article 10 of the European Convention on Human Rights – see **Chapter 27**.)

24.6 CAN THE SELF-EMPLOYED PERSON BRING HIS FAMILY WITH HIM TO THE HOST STATE?

Directive 2004/38 (as mentioned in **Chapter 23**) applies to freedom of establishment as it does to workers (see **23.4**).

24.7 DEROGATIONS FROM ARTICLES 49 AND 56 TFEU

It is possible to derogate from Articles 49 and 56 TFEU on grounds of public health, public security and public policy (Articles 52 and 62 TFEU). The interpretation of these terms is the same as that under Article 45(3) TFEU and Directive 2004/38 (see **23.3**). Moreover, the right of establishment does not apply to activities involving, even occasionally, 'the exercise of official authority' (Article 51 TFEU). Thus a number of 'legal professions', for example judges, magistrates, court registrars and notaries (but not lawyers), can be reserved to home nationals.

24.8 RIGHTS OF POTENTIAL RECIPIENTS OF SERVICES UNDER EU LAW

In *Luisi and Carbone v Ministero del Tesoro* [1984] ECR 377, the Court of Justice interpreted Article 59 of the EC Treaty (now Article 56 TFEU) to mean that potential recipients of services had the right to go to another Member State to receive those services and that tourists qualified as potential recipients of services. This approach was further developed in *Cowan v Le Trésor Public (The Treasury)* [1989] ECR 195, which concerned a British tourist who was the victim of a criminal assault while in France. His claim for compensation from the French Criminal Injuries Compensation Board was denied because he was not a French national. On an Article 267 TFEU reference, the Court of Justice held that compensation could not be denied to a recipient of compensation services on grounds of nationality.

In a number of cases, the Court of Justice has considered whether this approach entitles a national of a Member State to take advantage of education services elsewhere in the EU. Strictly speaking, State education cannot constitute 'services' because, under Article 57 TFEU, services must normally be paid for. In cases such as *Gravier v City of Liège* [1985] ECR 593, however, it was held that students cannot be asked to pay an additional fee for educational courses because they are non-nationals, provided the course represents vocational training, ie it facilitates access to a particular trade or profession. Even if the courses are normally free (ie not 'services') they still relate to a Treaty matter (training), and therefore any discrimination is unlawful under Article 18 TFEU (see **24.1**).

24.9 SUMMARY AND CONCLUSION

24.9.1 Distinguish between establishment and services

Establishment (Article 49 TFEU) implies permanence; services (Article 56 TFEU) are more temporary. Hence, the presence of a permanent office implies establishment under Article 49 TFEU (see *Gebhard v Consiglio dell'Ordine degli Avvocati e Procuratori di Milano* [1996] All ER (EC) 139 at **24.1**).

24.9.2   Restriction on free movement

Where services are involved, for Article 56 TFEU to apply there must be a restriction on free movement. However, services may move in four different ways.

(a)   The provider of services moves to another Member State to provide services on a temporary basis (the normal case).

(b)   The recipient of services moves to receive services (eg, as a tourist – see *Cowan v Le Trésor Public* [1989] ECR 195 at **24.8**).

(c)   The provider moves to another Member State to provide services to nationals of his own State (eg, a British interpreter/guide/ski instructor who accompanies a party of British tourists abroad).

(d)   Neither provider nor recipient moves, but services are provided by post, fax, telephone, broadcast, etc.

This last situation arose in the instructive case of *Alpine Investments BV v Minister Van Financien* [1995] All ER (EC) 543, which concerned Dutch financial services laws banning the cold-calling of customers at home or abroad. The Dutch company prosecuted in this case argued that the law banning the cold-calling of foreign clients infringed Article 59 of the EC Treaty (now Article 56 TFEU). Clearly, the law in question did not discriminate against foreign service providers, but it still restricted the export of services because it directly affected access to the market in other States. Nevertheless, the restriction could be objectively justified in the general interest on grounds of consumer protection or the good reputation of the industry. Moreover, the restriction was proportional (the fact that other countries had no (or less strict) controls on cold-calling was considered irrelevant). It should be noted that, as in the *Cassis de Dijon* case (see **25.2.2**), restrictions like this, which apply without distinction to all service providers, could be justified on a wider range of grounds than those which appear in Article 52 TFEU (public policy, public security and public health).

24.9.3   Need to satisfy local conditions

Whether seeking establishment or providing services, the foreign national who tries to work abroad must satisfy local conditions for pursuit of the activity in question. However (according to *Gebhard*; see **24.9.1**), these conditions:

(a)   must be non-discriminatory;

(b)   must be justified by imperative requirements in the general interest;

(c)   must be suitable for securing the attainment of the objective which they pursue; and

(d)   must not go beyond what is necessary to achieve it.

24.9.4   General approach to free movement under EU law

The approach of the Court of Justice in *Gebhard* is very similar to that already established by the Court in relation to goods (see the key case of *Cassis de Dijon* at **25.2.2**). It has been stressed that the approach is common to all cases of free movement. It thus applies in relation to workers under Article 45 TFEU (see *Bosman* at **23.2**), to establishment under Article 49 TFEU (*Gebhard*), and to services under Article 56 TFEU (*Alpine Investments* at **24.9.2**).

FREE MOVEMENT OF GOODS

LEARNING OUTCOMES

After reading this chapter you will be able to understand:

- what rights a producer of goods has to take his goods to another Member State in order to sell them
- what rights a Member State's government has to ban or restrict the importation of undesirable goods
- the extent to which a producer is allowed to advertise his goods in another Member State, and the extent to which the government can restrict this
- what a producer can do if he believes his rights to import, advertise and sell his goods are illegally restricted.

25.1 INTRODUCTION

The free movement of goods is one of the fundamental freedoms on which the EU is based. One of the most important aims of the original Treaty of Rome was to create a single market in goods throughout all the Member States of the Community. Following amendments to the Treaty by the Single European Act 1986, this aim was intended to be achieved by 31 December 1992. Because of the importance of this freedom, the Court of Justice has consistently interpreted the relevant Treaty provisions in such a way as to give maximum effect to this basic objective.

25.2 WHAT DOES THE TREATY PROVIDE?

The principal Treaty provision is Article 34 TFEU, which states that:

> Quantitative restrictions on imports and all measures having equivalent effect shall be prohibited between Member States.

Article 35 TFEU makes similar provision in relation to exports, ie the requirement for or refusal of an export licence.

25.2.1 What is meant by 'quantitative restrictions'?

Quantitative restrictions are limitations on the import of goods fixed by reference to quantitative criteria, ie amount or value ('quotas'). A complete ban on the import of a particular type of goods is also such a restriction (see *Commission of European Communities v Italy* [1961] ECR 317).

25.2.2 What is meant by a 'measure having equivalent effect to a quantitative restriction'?

The phrase 'a measure having equivalent effect to a quantitative restriction' (MEQR) is not defined in the Treaty itself but was defined by the Court of Justice in *Dassonville* [1974] ECR 837. In that case, the phrase was said to extend to 'all trading rules enacted by Member States that are capable of hindering, directly or indirectly, actually or potentially, intra-Community trade'.

It is important to note the following about this definition.

(a)   A measure having equivalent effect does not have to have an immediate or substantial effect on intra-Community (now Union) trade. In particular, it is clear from *Re Prantl (Karl)* [1984] ECR 1299 that the Court of Justice will not apply a de minimis principle here. This means that any legislation which is capable of affecting trade between Member States, even indirectly, because it is not the primary aim of the legislation, can infringe Article 34 TFEU. However, the case of *Criminal Proceedings Against Keck and Mithouard* [1995] 1 CMLR 101 shows that for 'selling arrangements' the measure must have the effect of putting the imported goods at a disadvantage before it can be said to restrict imports. Contrary to the view expressed earlier in cases involving Sunday trading laws (*Torfaen Borough Council v B&Q plc* [1989] ECR 765), a restriction on volume of imports (ie, the argument that with shops shut there will be fewer sales and therefore fewer imports) is not enough if domestic goods are at the same disadvantage.

(b)   A measure having equivalent effect must be taken by an 'organ of the State'. Actions by private individuals, companies or other undertakings cannot fall within this definition. However, this requirement will be satisfied even if the Member State acts through another undertaking. In *Commission of European Communities v Ireland; Re 'Buy Irish' Campaign* [1982] ECR 4005, the Irish Government initiated a campaign to encourage Irish consumers to buy home-produced goods. The campaign was launched by an Irish Government Minister and was funded by the Government, but was actually managed by a guarantee company set up for the purpose. The fact that it was not the Irish Government which was directly running the campaign did not prevent it being a measure having effect equivalent to a quantitative restriction. Likewise, other State bodies, for example local authorities, licensing authorities or courts, may see their 'measures' (eg, injunctions) controlled in the same way.

(c)   A measure having equivalent effect need not affect imported products alone, that is, be 'distinctly applicable' to imports. It could be a measure applying to all goods, domestic and imported, without distinction ('indistinctly applicable'), for example national technical standards. The difference is that whereas the latter can be justified under the 'rule of reason' and so do not infringe Article 34 TFEU at all (see *Cassis de Dijon* below), the former are justifiable only under Article 36 TFEU. The following cases involved distinctly applicable measures. In *International Fruit Co NV v Produktschap voor Groenten en Fruit (No 3)* [1971] ECR 1107, a requirement that a licence be obtained before apples could be imported into France was struck down by the Court of Justice as an infringement of Article 30 of the EC Treaty (now Article 34 TFEU). Similarly, in *Rewe-Zentralfinanz e GmbH v Landwirtschaftskammer* [1975] ECR 843, a requirement that apples had to be inspected before they could be imported into Germany was also held to breach Article 30 of the EC Treaty. Although these types of measure do not completely prevent the marketing of the product, they do result in delay and inconvenience for the importer, which may lead to fewer such products being imported. In both these cases, the measures could not be justified under Article 36 of the EC Treaty (now Article 36 TFEU) which is restrictively interpreted.

Increasingly, the Court of Justice has found measures to be within the *Dassonville* definition, and therefore caught by Article 34 TFEU, where the domestic product is also affected by the measure in question. The leading case is *Rewe Zentral v Bundesmonopolverwaltung fur Branntwein (Cassis de Dijon)* [1979] ECR 649. A German law required that spirits such as Cassis de Dijon should be of a stipulated alcoholic strength. Cassis was significantly less strong and therefore could not be sold on the German market. The Court held that the German law fell within the *Dassonville* definition and was in breach of Article 30 of the EC Treaty (now Article 34 TFEU). The case is considered vital to the development of a single market in that it shows that imported products do not have to be changed to meet national technical standards unless the need to do so is justified. The case is considered further in **25.3.1**.

25.3 ARE THERE CIRCUMSTANCES IN WHICH ARTICLE 34 TFEU WILL NOT APPLY?

25.3.1 The 'rule of reason'

Although it is no answer to an Article 34 TFEU complaint to say that the measure in question affects the equivalent domestic product as well as the imported one, it is important to know whether or not this is the case. This is because only such a measure can benefit from the 'rule of reason' approach of the Court of Justice in *Cassis de Dijon* referred to above. The Court recognised in that case that if goods were lawfully manufactured in a particular way in a given Member State, they should ordinarily be entitled to move throughout the rest of the Union. However, where the EU itself had not imposed Union-wide standards, disparities between Member States' legislation could be acceptable. In the words of the Court:

> [O]bstacles to movement within the Community [now Union] resulting from disparities between the national laws relating to the marketing of products must be accepted in so far as those provisions are necessary in order to satisfy mandatory requirements relating in particular to the effectiveness of fiscal supervision, the protection of public health, the fairness of commercial transactions and the defence of the consumer.

The list of mandatory requirements is not closed. The Court has since added to them the protection of the environment (see *Commission of European Communities v Denmark; sub nom Re Disposable Beer Cans* [1989] 1 CMLR 619), the protection of culture (eg, the cinema from the threat of video cassettes in *Cinethèque v Fédération Nationale des Cinemas Français* [1986] 1 CMLR B65) and employment in the Sunday trading cases. The list inevitably includes (but is much wider than) the list of justifications in Article 36 TFEU.

In order for a measure to be 'necessary' to satisfy a mandatory requirement, the aim of the measure in question must be justifiable in EU law and the measure taken must be *proportionate* to that aim. Therefore, if the aim could be achieved by a measure which was less restrictive of the free movement of goods, the measure taken will be held to be disproportionate. In *Cassis de Dijon*, the German Government successfully argued that the law in question was for the defence of the consumer, but the Court found that it was nevertheless disproportionate to its objective: the same aim could have been achieved by a law requiring that such spirits should be clearly labelled with their alcoholic strength.

25.3.2 The Treaty on the Functioning of the European Union

Where a government measure is distinctly applicable (ie, provides different conditions for imported goods), it can only be justified under the terms of the Treaty, ie Article 36 TFEU.

Article 36 TFEU provides a number of important exceptions to Article 34 TFEU. It states that:

> The provisions of Articles 34 to 35 shall not preclude prohibitions or restrictions on imports, exports or goods in transit justified on grounds of public morality, public policy or public security; the protection of health and life of humans, animals or plants; the protection of national treasures possessing artistic, historical or archaeological value; or the protection of industrial or commercial property. Such prohibitions or restrictions shall not, however, constitute a means of arbitrary discrimination or a disguised restriction on trade between Member States.

As this Article derogates from a fundamental principle of the EU, the Court construes it strictly; in particular, no further justifiable restrictions can be read into the list given above.

Further, the burden of establishing that a measure does come within Article 36 TFEU will fall on the relevant Member State.

The following points should be borne in mind when considering the exceptions in Article 36 TFEU.

25.3.2.1 Public morality

The Court of Justice will not seek to impose its own standards of morality; what is required in this area will be a matter for each Member State (see *DPP v Darby; DPP v Henn* [1979] ECR 3795). It is important to appreciate the significance of the final sentence of Article 36 TFEU, ie the measure taken by the Member State must not amount to arbitrary discrimination against the imported product, or to a disguised restriction on trade. In *Darby and Henn*, the seizure of imported pornography by UK customs was not in breach of Article 30 of the EC Treaty (now Article 34 TFEU) as that type of pornography could not be lawfully sold in the UK. On the other hand, in *Conegate v Customs and Excise Commissioners* [1986] ECR 1007, the import of rubber dolls into the UK could not be prevented because if they had been produced in this country they could lawfully have been sold here.

25.3.2.2 Public policy

A Member State cannot invoke public policy whenever it is convenient to do so to avoid falling foul of Article 34 TFEU. The Court of Justice has made it clear that this exception can be used only where there is a serious threat to a fundamental interest of society. See, for example, *R v Thompson (Brian Ernest)* [1978] ECR 2247, where it was applied to the right to mint coinage. Economic reasons, for example protection of industry from competition, are never, however, acceptable.

25.3.2.3 Public security

Similarly, public security cannot be readily called upon in defence of a breach of Article 34 TFEU. It seems clear only that it extends to the need to safeguard essential public services. Note *Campus Oil Ltd v The Minister for Industry and Energy* [1984] ECR 2727, where the Irish Government required importers of petrol to buy a percentage of their needs from an Irish refinery to ensure that the refinery remained viable. It seems that it can relate to the State's internal as well as external security (*Minister of Finance v Richardt* [1992] 1 CMLR 61).

25.3.2.4 Public health

In the absence of EU standards, Member States are entitled to decide what is appropriate for their own citizens in the field of public health. In the case of *Aragonesa de Publicidad v Departmamento de Sanidad y Seguridad Social de la Generalitat de Cataluna* [1991] OJ C220/8, the Court of Justice upheld on public health grounds Spanish legislation which prohibited roadside advertisements for strong spirits. Despite the later case of *Keck and Mithouard* (see **25.4.1**), this case may still involve a measure equivalent to quantitative restriction (MEQR) as it may be indirectly discriminatory against imported spirits not known to the Spanish public. It is, however, clearly justified.

Again, it is essential to pay close attention to the last sentence of Article 36 TFEU. For example, in *Commission of European Communities v United Kingdom; sub nom Re Imports of Poultry Meat* [1982] ECR 2793, where the UK Government prohibited the import of French poultry into the UK, ostensibly in order to avoid the spread of Newcastle Disease, the evidence indicated that the prohibition was unnecessarily restrictive and in reality was intended to protect the English poultry industry. It should be noted that in most areas there are now Directives laying down the minimum requirements for health or animal welfare. For example, EU Directives lay down minimum rules for the carriage of live animals and their stunning before slaughter. It is not a sufficient justification for the refusal of an export licence for live animals that these rules may be ignored in the importing State (see *R v Ministry of Agriculture,*

Fisheries and Food, ex p Hedley Lomas (Ireland) Ltd [1996] All ER (EC) 493). The refusal will breach Article 35 TFEU.

25.3.2.5 The protection of national treasures and intellectual property rights

The exception for the protection of national treasures, although not yet used, is likely to be of value where a Member State wishes to impose an export ban on items representing part of its national heritage, ie in breach of Article 35 TFEU.

Intellectual property rights have posed difficulties for the Court of Justice. In the absence of Union-wide regimes, such rights are granted by individual Member States and relate only to the territory of the State in question. This offers enterprises an opportunity to divide up the market on national lines. This is clearly contrary to the spirit of the Union. Because of this the Court of Justice has been careful not to over-extend the protection given to intellectual property rights in Article 36 TFEU. Accordingly, the Court has distinguished between the existence and the exercise of intellectual property rights. Thus, measures (eg, court injunctions keeping out imports of goods infringing a patent) are not caught by Article 34 TFEU even if their effect is to restrict imports (because of Article 36 TFEU).

In order to protect the existence of intellectual property rights, however, the Court has had to decide what the existence of each right amounts to. It has done this by developing the concept of the 'specific subject matter' of a right. Thus, for example, the specific subject matter of a patent is the exclusive right to use an invention for the manufacture of products and to be the first to market them (*Centrafarm BV and De Peijper v Sterling Drug Inc* [1974] ECR 1147). This means that once a company has marketed (or consented to the marketing of) a drug in, say, France, it cannot thereafter purport to use its patent rights in, say, the UK to prevent the import of the patented product. The products marketed in France could therefore be re-imported into the UK and the patent holder or UK court could not interfere with their free movement. The company's rights over that particular product were 'exhausted' when it consented to its marketing in France. The Court of Justice has adopted a similar approach to trade mark rights and copyright. This protection of 'parallel imports' through exhaustion of rights applies only where the goods are marketed within the EU. The Court has ruled in *Silhouette International Schmied GmbH & Co KG v Hartlauer Handelsgesellschaft mbH* [1998] 3 WLR 1218 that following the harmonisation of trade mark rights through the 1989 Directive, Member States' laws can no longer recognise a wider principle of world-wide exhaustion (ie, through marketing outside the EU). Thus manufacturers can use their national trade marks to keep out goods which they authorised for sale only in countries outside the EU.

25.4 SUMMARY OF THE POSITION REGARDING TRADING MEASURES

The problem may be tackled by asking a series of questions.

25.4.1 Is the measure an MEQR (*Dassonville* test)?

To be an MEQR, the rule in question must affect the product itself, ie require some change, before it can be sold in the territory. In general, rules about *selling arrangements* (ie, the arrangements for selling the product once it is imported), for example Sunday trading, licensing hours, and prohibitions on selling at a loss (*Keck and Mithouard*), do not come within the *Dassonville* formula and thus (in the absence of discrimination) need no justification. Although they may restrict the volume of imports (if you sell less, you import less), these measures do not put imports at a disadvantage and thus cannot count as MEQRs.

Advertising restrictions, for example bans on leaflets (*GB-INNO-BM v Confédération du Commerce Luxembourgeoise Asbl* [1991] 2 CMLR 801) or comparative advertising (*Unwesen in den Wirtschaft eV v Yves Rocher GmbH* (1994) *Financial Times*, 9 June), may well put the imported product at a disadvantage because advertising is the most effective way for new imported products to penetrate a market. The rival domestic products may well be better known. It would, however, seem that restrictions on retailers advertising their sales (eg, *Hünermund v Landespothekerkammer*

Baden-Württemberg [1993] ECR I-6787, where German pharmacists were prohibited from advertising off the premises, or *Leclerc v TFI Publicité* [1995] ECR I-179, where French retailers could not advertise at all on French television and thus were restricted in advertising their cheap foreign fuel) are to be treated as selling arrangements under *Keck and Mithouard*. By contrast, a blanket ban on advertising a particular product, for example alcoholic products or toys, would be seen, it is felt, as either a restriction to be justified under the 'rule of reason' in *Cassis de Dijon* or a case of indirect discrimination against imports which would have to be justified on similar objective criteria (see *Konsumentombudsmannen (KO) v De Agostini (Svenska) Forlag AB; Konsumentom-budsmannen (KO) v TV-Shop I Sverige AB (De Agostini)* [1997] All ER (EC) 687).

25.4.2 If it is an MEQR, does it apply only to imports (ie distinctly applicable measures) or directly discriminate (as selling arrangements)?

The best example of this is the French ban on British beef. This could only be justified under Article 30 EC (now Article 36 TFEU) (eg, protection of public health) but the French failed to prove a sufficient health risk. It therefore was a distinctly applicable breach which the French had failed to justify.

Likewise, an injunction prohibiting the imports of goods said to infringe a national patent could only be justified under Article 36 TFEU (protection of intellectual property rights).

25.4.3 Does the measure apply to all products (ie indistinctly applicable measures) or (if a selling arrangement) indirectly discriminate?

Measures which apply to all goods (domestic and imported) without distinction will be caught by Article 34 TFEU only if they put the imported goods at a disadvantage compared with domestic goods. Thus, where the imported product has to be adapted before it can be sold on the domestic market it is prima facie at a disadvantage compared with domestic products which are made to domestic specifications. Here, because we are dealing with indirect discrimination, the measure infringes Article 34 TFEU unless it can be shown to be justified by a public interest objective (eg, consumer protection, health, environment, etc – the list given in *Cassis de Dijon* is not exhaustive) which is proportional and takes precedence over the free movement of goods. If so justified, there is no Article 34 TFEU infringement. Measures falling into this category would be German measures on purity of spirits (*Cassis de Dijon*), sausages, beer, etc; packaging rules (eg, Danish or German rules on recyclable bottles or containers – these may be justified on environmental protection grounds (see *Commission of European Communities v Kingdom of Denmark; sub nom Re Disposable Beer Cans* [1989] 1 CMLR 619)), rules on labelling, weight, trade marks, etc. In *Verband Sozialer Wettbewerb eV v Clinique Laboratories SNC and Estée Lauder Cosmetics* (Case C-315/92) [1994] ECR I-317, the cosmetic 'Clinique' could not be marketed under that mark in Germany because it was considered to suggest therapeutic properties which it did not have. Since the cosmetic had to be repackaged for sale in Germany, there was clearly an indirect restriction on imports which could not be justified on the basis of protecting consumers from confusion.

Since the effect of *Cassis de Dijon* is that Member States must mutually recognise different product standards which give equivalent protective effect, modern product standard Directives under the '1992' campaign (and after) have merely set a minimum level of protection ('the essential requirements') which different national products can satisfy. The obligatory Euro standard is a thing of the past, except for hazardous products like drugs and motor cars where full harmonisation of the specification requirements may be needed. In other areas, Euro standards are considered optional.

25.5 HOW TO USE ARTICLE 34 TFEU

Article 34 TFEU is directly effective; this means it can be relied upon before national courts and tribunals. It can therefore be used defensively, for example in response to a criminal prosecution for breach of trading standards in another Member State, or offensively, for example to challenge a 'buy national' campaign. In the latter case, the challenger must follow the most appropriate national procedure and claim the most effective national remedy. The Court of Justice has made it clear that a Member State is under an obligation to provide an effective remedy for infringement of EU rights. Thus, a challenge to a Government-sponsored 'buy national' campaign in the UK would be made by judicial review proceedings for a declaration that the Government was acting ultra vires, accompanied by a claim for an injunction (see R *v Secretary of State for Transport, ex p Factortame (No 2)* (Case C-213/89) [1990] 3 WLR 818) or possibly damages (see R *v Secretary of State for Transport, ex p Factortame (No 4)* [1996] 2 WLR 506). The case of *Brasserie du Pêcheur*, decided with *Factortame (No 4)*, concerned a damages claim under Article 30 of the EC Treaty (now Article 34 TFEU) by beer importers who fell foul of Germany's purity laws. Since the particular restrictions (relating to a ban on additives) were not manifestly unlawful at the time, no damages were payable.

It should be noted that all new national rules on product standards have to be notified to Brussels under Directive 83/189. The failure to do so will invalidate the national law because Directive 83/189 has direct effect. (See *CIA Security International SA v Signalson SA* [1996] 2 CMLR 781.) This, too, may be used as a defence.

COMPETITION LAW

LEARNING OUTCOMES

After reading this chapter you will be able to understand:

- what restrictions there may be on a business's ability to make arrangements with other businesses which relate to how they ply their trade
- what restrictions there may on a business's ability to make decisions which impact on other businesses
- what consequences there may be for breach of legislation is this area
- what exceptions may be relied upon to escape liability.

26.1 INTRODUCTION

The regulation of competition between businesses is as important to the Union as the attainment of the freedoms discussed in the previous chapters. It is of little use to provide that goods can move freely throughout the Union unless at the same time businesses are able to trade across frontiers without facing improper competition. Improper competition, particularly where it has the effect of dividing up markets along national lines, must be controlled. Thus, Article 3(1)(b) TFEU states that one of the activities of the Union is the institution of a system ensuring that competition in the internal market is not distorted. This system is principally established in two Articles of the Treaty: Articles 101 and 102 TFEU. Article 101 TFEU controls anti-competitive agreements, while Article 102 TFEU regulates an abuse of a dominant position. It should be remembered that the object of any competition law is greater customer choice, either of manufacturers (different brands) or of dealers supplying the same brand. More competition equals more choice; this in turn compels competing manufacturers (or dealers) to cut costs and improve quality of goods or services.

26.2 ANTI-COMPETITIVE AGREEMENTS: ARTICLE 101 TFEU

26.2.1 What does Article 101 TFEU provide?

Article 101 TFEU provides that:

> The following shall be prohibited as incompatible with the internal market: all agreements between undertakings, decisions by associations of undertakings and concerted practices which may affect trade between Member States and which have as their object or effect the prevention, restriction or distortion of competition within the internal market ...

It then gives examples of the types of conduct which would be caught by this definition, such as fixing prices, controlling production and sharing markets. To discover what other practices may be within Article 101 TFEU, it is necessary to look at the Article in detail.

26.2.1.1   Agreements between undertakings

The term 'undertaking' is not defined in the Treaty but is taken to include any business enterprise, whatever legal form it may take. In particular, under English law it will include a company or a partnership, a sole trader or a trade association. A parent and a subsidiary company are usually taken to amount to a single undertaking for this purpose. Likewise, agreements between a company and its employees or agents are unlikely to be agreements 'between undertakings' as they lack the necessary independence.

Not only written agreements between two or more such undertakings but also less formal arrangements, such as a mere understanding or 'gentlemen's agreement', may breach Article 101 TFEU (see the *Quinine Cartel* case, *Boehringer Mannheim GmbH v Commission of the European Communities* [1970] ECR 661). It was originally thought that Article 85 of the EC Treaty (now Article 101 TFEU) applied only to agreements between potential competitors, ie 'horizontal agreements' between undertakings at the same level of the production process, for example the traditional cartel where manufacturers meet in secret to carve up markets or fix prices. The agreement may, however, be a 'vertical' one, that is between undertakings involved at different stages of the manufacturing or trading process, for example an agreement between a wholesaler and a retailer. Even if the manufacturer is not involved in distribution itself, restrictions, eg on prices or exports, can affect competition between distributors (see, for example, *Consten SA and Grundig-Verkaufs-GmbH (Etablissements) v EEC Commission* [1996] CMLR 418).

26.2.1.2   Decisions by associations of undertakings

The phrase 'decisions by associations of undertakings' would include, for example, decisions taken by a trade association, whether or not they were legally binding.

26.2.1.3   Concerted practices

An enterprise may breach Article 101 TFEU if it deliberately co-ordinates its behaviour with another business in the same market, for example if they agree to raise prices at the same time and by the same amount. It is not necessary to be able to prove an agreement that they should do so; the fact of synchronised activity may be enough, so that, in the words of the European Court in *Dyestuffs* [1972] ECR 619, 'the parties have substituted practical co-operation for the risks of competition'. It is important to appreciate that a business is entitled to respond to market conditions, including the behaviour of its competitors. This may well mean that enterprises operating within the same market do show similar behaviour without there being a 'concerted practice'.

26.2.1.4   How much of an effect does there have to be on trade between Member States?

Article 101 TFEU states that it is necessary that the agreement, etc 'may' have an effect on trade. According to the Court of Justice in *STM v Maschinenbau Ulm* [1966] ECR 235:

> it must be possible to foresee with a sufficient degree of probability on the basis of a set of objective factors of law or fact that the agreement in question may have an influence, direct or indirect, actual or potential, on the pattern of trade between Member States.

Such an effect may result even where the parties to the agreement or concerted practice are based within one Member State if the effect is to distort competition elsewhere in the EU, for example because a company based in another Member State is unable to break into that market (see *Vereeniging van Cementhandelaren v Commission of the European Communities (No 2)* (Case 8/72) [1972] ECR 977 (the *Dutch Cement* case)).

It can even occur where the parties are based outside the EU, provided the agreement or practice is implemented within it (*Re Wood Pulp Cartel* [1988] ECR 5193).

It has been held by the Court of Justice that Article 101 TFEU can apply to exclusive distribution agreements in countries outside the EU (here Russia, the Ukraine and Slovenia), which contain restrictions on exporting into the EU. Here, the distribution agreements for Yves St Laurent Perfumes were subject to French law and jurisdiction. The French courts therefore would be entitled to rule that the agreements were invalid under Article 81(2) EC (now Article 101(2) TFEU) (see *Javico v Yves St Laurent* (1998) *Financial Times*, 13 May).

This part of Article 101 TFEU therefore determines the jurisdiction of the EU competition authorities. But it also sets out clearly the policy of EU competition law, which is partly to create a single market. Agreements which have the effect of partitioning the single market (eg, exclusive territories for dealers) are prima facie likely to infringe Article 101 TFEU.

26.2.1.5 '. . . which have as their object or effect'

If, objectively, the parties intend the agreement or the practice to prevent, restrict or distort competition, there is no need to consider further what the effect of the agreement might be. On the other hand, if that is not the object, but it would be its effect, then Article 101 TFEU will still be breached.

26.2.1.6 'the prevention, restriction or distortion of competition'

The words 'the prevention, restriction or distortion of competition' are given their ordinary meaning. However, if the effect is likely to be minimal, Article 101(1) TFEU will not be breached (*Volk v Verwaecke* [1969] ECR 295). See further the Commission's Notice on Agreements of Minor Importance in **26.2.4**.

It should be remembered that even if the agreement has no effect on competition between the parties, it may still be prohibited by Article 101 TFEU if its effect is to restrict competition with third parties. This is the case with vertical agreements such as the exclusive distribution agreement which may restrict intra-brand competition between the different dealers.

26.2.2 Can an undertaking apply for clearance that its arrangements are outside Article 101 TFEU?

This possibility was removed as from 1 May 2004, except that the Commission does have the power 'to adopt a decision of a declaratory nature finding that the prohibition in Article [101] or Article [102] of the Treaty does not apply'. Indications are that this power will be used sparingly. Parties must generally now 'self-assess', ie decide for themselves whether their arrangement is permitted by Article 101(3) TFEU. Their decision may be challenged by national competition authorities, the Commission, or by national courts, should it be relevant in court proceedings.

26.2.3 What is the result if there is a breach of Article 101 TFEU?

According to Article 101(2) TFEU, any agreement or decision prohibited by Article 101(1) TFEU is automatically void. This means that any agreement is unenforceable. It may be possible to sever offending clauses from the agreement and leave the rest of it standing. Whether this is possible depends on the domestic law to which the agreement is subject. Thus, under English law, such clauses can be severed if the remaining agreement still reflects accurately the agreement reached by the parties (*Chemidus Wavin v Société pour la Transformation et l'Exploitation des Resines Industrielles SA* [1978] 3 CMLR 514). Because Article 101(1) TFEU has been held to be directly effective, it seems that a party whose business interests are being or have been harmed by the anti-competitive agreement may seek an injunction to restrain operation of the agreement and may be able to claim damages (*Garden Cottage Foods v Milk Marketing Board* [1983] 3 WLR 143). In addition, the Commission and national competition authorities have the power to levy fines upon the parties to an anti-competitive agreement, the size of the fine (up to a maximum of 10% of turnover) being dependent on the degree of fault. A recent fine for Microsoft was in the sum of £335 million.

26.2.4   Are there any ways out for a business which seems to be at risk of breaching this Article?

There are primarily three ways in which a business may avoid breaching Article 101 TFEU.

26.2.4.1   The Notice on Agreements of Minor Importance

The Commission, which is responsible for implementing the EU's competition policy, has issued a Notice on Agreements of Minor Importance. According to this Notice, only agreements which have an appreciable effect on trade between Member States should be taken as breaching Article 101 TFEU. The questions parties must ask themselves to decide whether they fit within the Notice are:

- Does the parties' combined market share exceed 10% in the case of a *horizontal* arrangement (ie between those at the same level of the supply chain, such as competitors) or 15% in the case of a *vertical* arrangement (such as between supplier and distributor, or distributor and wholesaler)? If it does, the Notice does not apply.

- Is competition in the market restricted by the cumulative effect of similar agreements entered into by a number of suppliers or distributors? If so, the Notice will not apply if the parties' market share is not less than 5%.

- If the arrangement is horizontal, does it have provisions which have as their object the prevention, restriction or distortion of competition, such as those fixing prices, limiting exports or sales, or allocating markets or customers? If so, the Notice will not apply.

- If the arrangement is vertical, does it contain any 'hardcore' restrictions prohibited by the vertical restraints block exemption (see **26.2.5**)? If not, the Notice will not apply.

If the parties meet the requisite criteria, the Notice will apply and the arrangement will be assumed not to have an appreciable effect on trade and so will be taken as not breaching Article 101.

The Notice does not give complete legal protection because the market may be a very specialised one where even small companies (especially with patent protection) may have more than the relevant percentage.

26.2.4.2   Article 101(3) TFEU

It may be possible to avoid the effects of Article 101(2) TFEU for a particular agreement because of the operation of Article 101(3) TFEU. This provides for exemption for any agreement which:

(a)   contributes to improving the production or distribution of goods, or to promoting technical or economic progress; and

(b)   allows consumers a fair share of the resulting benefit; and

(c)   does not impose on the undertakings concerned restrictions which are not indispensable to the attainment of these objectives; and

(d)   does not afford such undertakings the possibility of eliminating competition in respect of a substantial part of the products in question.

Thus, to satisfy Article 101(3) TFEU, the agreement must bring with it certain benefits while at the same time not including excessive restriction of competition.

As mentioned at **26.2.2** above, parties must decide for themselves whether they fit within Article 101(3) TFEU.

26.2.4.3   Using a block exemption

The Commission in the early years of the Community was inundated with individual notifications, and it was not unusual for years to go by without a reply being received from the

Commission. To try to deal with this volume of agreements, the Commission began to introduce block exemptions (as Article 101(3) TFEU and its predecessors allow them) for particular categories of agreement which fulfil the conditions for an exemption.

Note that since the Commission alone can give an exemption, severance by national courts is not possible as the parties must stick to the terms of the block exemption before it can apply (see *Delimitis v Henninger Braü* [1991] ECR 1-935). Thus, firms which wish to have the certainty of a valid agreement must take particular care to draft their agreements to fit the relevant block exemption. If they include restrictions which are not allowed by the block exemption, the block exemption cannot apply and the national court generally cannot sever restrictions before applying the block exemption.

26.2.5 Using a typical block exemption: vertical restraints

In May 2010, a block exemption was passed which covered all types of vertical arrangements, such as exclusive distribution, exclusive purchasing (eg, beer ties) and franchising. This is Regulation 330/2010. It exempts in Article 2(1) all vertical agreements (ie, between two or more parties at different levels of the production or distribution chain). There are basically four things to check.

26.2.5.1 Is it vertical?

Under the exemption in Article 2(1), the parties to the agreement must be at different levels, but this would take in a number of different agreements involving goods or services, such as exclusive distribution, selective distribution, franchises and exclusive purchasing. Exemptions would also cover exclusive supply agreements (eg, where a large retailer persuades a supplier of parts to supply only him). Unlike previous block exemptions, it is no longer necessary to identify which type of vertical agreement one is dealing with.

The exemption can apply to multi-party agreements provided they are still vertical. Thus Article 2(2) specifically refers to agreements between a supplier and a trade association of small retailers. There is no reason why a British manufacturer wishing to distribute his product in France should not agree to supply the various retailers in such a trade association and achieve national retail coverage that way rather than supply an individual distributor.

It can also apply even though the chosen distributor is another manufacturer and thus a potential competitor. There is a danger here of the arrangements operating as a horizontal cartel, but provided the arrangements are not reciprocal the exemption can still apply (Article 2(4)).

The exemption does not apply to agreements which are primarily concerned with licensing intellectual property (IP) rights, for example patent, trade mark, copyright or software licences (Article 2(3)). Licensing of 'technology' (patents, software copyright, know-how) is covered by a Technology Transfer Block Exemption (Regulation 316/2014).

26.2.5.2 Prohibited list

Assuming that the agreement is vertical then the exemption under Article 2(1) applies to all vertical restraints otherwise prohibited by Article 101 TFEU, unless the agreement contains prohibited clauses. So, the second stage is to check the prohibited list in Article 4. Some of the prohibited clauses are directed to particular types of agreement, so it may be helpful to see how this applies to exclusive distribution and selective distribution.

If it is *exclusive distribution* the clauses to avoid are as follows:

(a) Article 4(a) – price fixing. This includes minimum prices (which effectively prevent discounts) as well as fixed prices. It does not include maximum or recommended prices unless the price has become in practice fixed through pressure from the supplier. It may be worth considering why prices would be recommended – this may be more justified in selective distribution or franchising than in exclusive distribution.

(b)   Article 4(b) – Restrictions on the buyer's resales to customers or into other territories. It should be noticed that only restrictions on the buyer (the distributor) are prohibited; the block exemption would certainly cover restrictions on the supplier selling into the buyer's territory (the essence, of course, of exclusive distribution).

As far as restrictions on the buyer are concerned, it is permissible to prohibit the distributor from *actively* marketing the goods in territories reserved to the supplier or allocated to other distributors. Passive sales (where the customer approaches the dealer unsolicited) can never be restricted. The enterprising customer must always be allowed to shop around the network to get the cheapest deal. With new methods of marketing over the Internet, which knows no frontiers, the distinction between active and passive sales into other territories becomes a fine one. Fortunately, the Commission's guidelines make it clear that having a website is not actively selling outside the territory. A UK customer can thus check the websites of the dealers in, say, France, Germany and Italy, and order from the cheapest. That is a passive sale and the agreement cannot prohibit the dealer from meeting that order without imperiling the validity of the agreement itself.

Although the agreement can stop the distributor from actively selling to a reserved territory or customer group, it cannot stop him from selling to a customer who would resell to such customers (see Article 4(b), first indent). This is the parallel importer (or exporter), the enterprising dealer who buys from the distributor with the cheapest prices with a view to reselling in those territories where prices are highest. Any restrictions on such sales would lose the block exemption.

If it is *selective distribution* the supplier must again avoid price fixing, but he is even more restricted in the limitations he can put on dealers' customers. The definition of 'selective distribution' appears in Article 1(c). The dealers must be selected on the basis of specified criteria. These might be their qualifications to handle the product (eg, computers or other hi-tech products), or to give the right ambience to accord with the image of the brand (eg, perfumes). The dealers in the network undertake, therefore, not to sell to unauthorised dealers, but other restrictions on sales are all black-listed. Thus dealers must be permitted to supply other selected dealers (Article 4(d)) and selected retailers cannot be prevented from supplying end-users, whether actively or passively (Article 4(c)). Thus, it is not possible to give selected dealers any territorial protection at all from other dealers, who will all compete, whether actively or passively, for the customers of each other.

26.2.5.3   Market share

Once it is clear there are no prohibited clauses, the agreement (and all its restrictions) is covered by the exemption, but it is still necessary to check whether either party has more than 30% of the relevant market. If either has, the block exemption cannot apply (Article 3). The rationale for this is that the Commission needs to be satisfied that the agreement does not substantially eliminate competition. Equally, the bigger the market share, the closer the firm comes to being dominant on that market, at which point many of the restrictions permitted under the block exemption would be seen as abuses under Article 102 TFEU. Thirty per cent has always been taken as the bottom line for dominance. So, even though most cases would be well over 40%, the Commission would still want to vet these agreements individually to be sure.

26.2.5.4   Severable restrictions

This leaves one final step, which is to check through Article 5 to see whether there are any severable restrictions in the agreement. These restrictions, which all concern non-compete obligations, do not destroy the exemption given to other vertical restraints. The national court is permitted to sever them from the agreement (assuming this is possible under its own national rules). The restrictions are:

(a) *Non-compete obligations (including exclusive purchase)*. These must be for a fixed term under five years, although, for beer ties with tenanted pubs, the duration could be the length of the lease. Any indefinite exclusive purchase obligation will thus be void but severable. Article 1(b) defines such clauses to include those where the buyer has to take more than 80% of his purchases from the supplier. Thus, in beer ties, the pub may well be taking a guest beer. If guest beers make up less than 20% of the beer supply, the supplier needs to be wary of Article 5.

(b) *Post-term restrictive covenants*. As under English law, these are void if unjustified. But, under Article 5(b), they benefit from the exemption only if they are confined to the same premises, the same goods and a maximum duration of one year. Moreover, and most importantly, they can be justified only if they are there to protect trade secrets ('know-how'). It is unlikely that such covenants could ever be justified in exclusive distribution. There will, however, be trade secrets to protect in franchises, and possibly in selective distribution.

(c) Lastly, selective distribution dealers can never be prevented from selling competing goods, but such clauses are severable.

26.2.6 Agency agreements

The Commission has stated in its Guidance Note to the Vertical Restraints Regulation that such agreements will be outside Article 101 TFEU provided the agent accepts no financial risks and the principal is responsible for setting prices and terms. The point here is that such an agent is integrated into the principal's business and thus is not an independent undertaking. The Commission has now put the Notice in its new guidelines on vertical agreements.

26.2.7 Mergers

In principle, when two companies merge (eg, one takes over the other) they cease to be independent undertakings and thus the agreement between them cannot be caught by Article 101 TFEU.

26.3 ABUSE OF A DOMINANT POSITION: ARTICLE 102 TFEU

26.3.1 What is the general effect of Article 102 TFEU?

Article 102 TFEU renders unlawful any behaviour which amounts to an abuse of its position by an undertaking which is dominant in its particular market. It will therefore be crucially important, when faced with a potential breach of Article 102 TFEU, to identify the relevant market; it will be seen that undertakings with quite small shares of one market can be dominant in a section of that market and so be at risk from Article 102 TFEU. It will also be seen that a distinction has to be drawn between an undertaking legitimately taking advantage of what may be a hard-won dominant position and an undertaking which illegitimately abuses that position.

26.3.2 What does Article 102 TFEU provide?

According to Article 102 TFEU:

> Any abuse by one or more undertakings of a dominant position within the internal market or in a substantial part of it shall be prohibited as incompatible with the internal market in so far as it may affect trade between Member States.

The Article then goes on to give a non-exclusive list of the types of behaviour which might amount to such an abuse, for example an undertaking imposing unfair trading conditions, such as unfair prices.

26.3.2.1 What is a dominant position within the internal market?

It is by no means essential for an undertaking to be in a monopoly position throughout the EU. The guiding principle here is that an undertaking is likely to be dominant where its economic strength allows it to behave independently of other operators within the market (*United Brands Co (New Jersey, USA) and United Brands Continentaal B (Rotterdam, The Netherlands) v EC Commission* [1978] ECR 207). An example of the principle is where a manufacturing company can set prices or conditions of supply to retailers of its product without regard to the prices or conditions imposed by its competitors. This is more likely to be the case where the undertaking has a larger market share. (In *Hilti v Commission of the European Communities* [1992] 4 CMLR 16, for example, an undertaking was held to be dominant with a 70–80% share of its market.) However, a relatively low market share does not necessarily mean that the undertaking is not dominant. In *United Brands*, dominance was established although the company had a market share of only 40–45%. A particularly important factor to take into account here is whether there are barriers to entry for other undertakings who might wish to enter the market. Does the allegedly dominant undertaking, for example, possess intellectual property rights which would create such a barrier? Whether or not an undertaking is dominant can be considered only in relation to a particular market. In order to identify the relevant market it is important to look at two things: the product market and the geographic market.

How is the product market recognised?

The key question in recognising the product market is 'what other product, if any, can be substituted for the product in question, given the nature of it, its price and its intended use?'. If a number of products are interchangeable, from the point of view of the user, it is arguable that they are all part of one market. On the other hand, if there is no acceptable alternative to the product in question then it can form a market on its own. In *United Brands*, the Court of Justice found that bananas represented a single market because, in certain respects, bananas could not easily be replaced by another fruit. In particular, children and the elderly or the infirm might find it easier to digest bananas than any other fruit.

Similarly, in *Hugin Kassareregister AB and Hugin Cash Registers v EC Commission* [1979] ECR 1869, the Court of Justice found that spare parts for Hugin cash registers represented a separate market in their own right because, once a customer had bought a Hugin machine, no other spare parts could be used. Clearly, if the product market is drawn so narrowly, an undertaking may find itself dominant even if its share of, say, the fruit market or the market for spare parts for cash registers generally is very small.

How is the geographic market recognised?

It is important to look at the geographic area within which the undertaking markets the product where the conditions of competition are the same. Here, too, the definition of the geographical scope of the market is based on substitutability; how far will customers look for their substitute product if the firm's product is unobtainable or too pricey. In many cases, this will be the whole of the single market, but factors such as cultural preferences, the personal nature of services contracts and the costs of transporting heavier goods may restrict the market to a particular region or country.

Article 102 TFEU applies where an undertaking is dominant in the common market or a substantial part of it. Dominance within a single Member State is likely to be within a substantial part of the common market.

26.3.2.2 What amounts to an abuse of a dominant position?

There are broadly two types of abusive behaviour: one affects competitors or potential competitors in the field; the other affects consumers. Abuse affecting competitors would include pricing the undertaking's products so low that those competitors are forced out of the market, or requiring purchasers of one type of product to buy other products produced by the same undertaking in order to tie them in to a single supplier. Examples of abuses affecting consumers would be setting prices extortionately high, or requiring the product to be sold in certain outlets only.

26.3.3 Are there any exceptions to Article 102 TFEU?

There is no equivalent in Article 102 TFEU of Article 101(3) TFEU (see **26.2.4.2**); the Commission cannot grant an individual exemption from Article 102 TFEU, nor are there block exemptions. Even if an undertaking is entitled to claim the benefit of a block exemption under Article 101(3) TFEU for its activities, that does not necessarily mean that such activities do not amount to an abuse of a dominant position (*Tetra Pak Rausing SA v Commission of the European Communities* [1991] FSR 654). The Commission will, in theory, give guidance letters on whether an action represents a breach, but it is thought that such guidance letters will be few and far between.

26.3.4 What are the sanctions for breach of Article 102 TFEU?

The Commission and national competition authorities have the power to fine undertakings for breaches of Article 102 TFEU. As there is no possibility of exemption, there is no equivalent of Article 101(3) TFEU. Behaviour in breach of Article 102 TFEU may also give rise to civil liability. It seems that under English law, an injunction can be granted to restrain breaches of Article 102 TFEU, and it is arguable that damages could also be sought (see *Garden Cottage Foods* at **26.2.3**).

26.4 CHAPTER SUMMARY

Article 102 TFEU cases are likely to be rare for most solicitors. Article 101 TFEU, however, is likely to be of much greater relevance.

In drafting commercial agreements, such as licensing agreements for intellectual property rights, distribution agreements, joint ventures (or other arrangements with potential competitors), franchise agreements and exclusive purchasing arrangements (eg, beer ties with public houses or solus agreements for petrol stations), the practitioner has to take Article 101 TFEU into account. He should consider in turn:

(1) whether the restrictive agreement might affect trade between Member States, but remember that many agreements between UK parties have such potential;

(2) whether it is covered by the Notice on Agreements of Minor Importance (but this is only limited security as market share may change). The determination of the relevant market is as critical here as under Article 102 TFEU;

(3) for full certainty that the agreement is valid; however, the parties must draft their agreement to fit the relevant block exemption Regulation (eg Regulation 330/2010);

(4) if the parties wish to include clauses which are not permitted by a block exemption, the agreement is likely to be void under Article 101(2) TFEU and thus (subject to severance) unenforceable in the national courts, unless the parties show that the agreement fits within the exemption contained in Article 101(3) TFEU.

The following is an illustration of how Article 101 TFEU might apply to an exclusive distribution agreement (based on *Consten SA and Grundig-Verkaufs-GmbH v EEC Commission* [1996] CMLR 418).

EXAMPLE

Widgets Ltd, a UK manufacturer with 15% of the EU widgets market, has a network of exclusive distributors at the wholesale level in France, UK and Germany (see diagram below). It sells to its distributors at £5 per widget and they then mark the price up when selling on to retailers. The UK distributor (a wholly-owned subsidiary) charges £10, whereas the German distributor charges only £6. To protect its position in the UK, therefore, Widgets Ltd imposes clauses on the German wholesaler which prevent it selling to customers outside its territory (export bars) and from selling to dealers in Germany who could resell outside (ie sales to parallel importers). It is hoped that it would thus have absolute territorial protection from competition on prices with its other EU distributors.

Such protection is, however, contrary to Article 101 TFEU and will attract fines, potential tort claims and void agreements. The block exemption on vertical agreements (Regulation 330/2010) allows territorial exclusivity and a ban on active sales (advertising, etc) outside the territory, but not a ban on passive sales (ie to unsolicited customers who place orders on their own initiative), nor a ban on sales to parallel exporters (see Article 4(b), first indent). Retailers across the EU are perfectly entitled to buy from the cheapest wholesaler in the network.

A DISTRIBUTION SYSTEM

HUMAN RIGHTS

THE EUROPEAN CONVENTION ON HUMAN RIGHTS

LEARNING OUTCOMES

After reading this chapter you will be able to understand:

- the background to the Convention
- how the Convention relates to English and EU law
- how to interpret the Convention
- the main rights that are protected by the Convention
- when a right has been interfered with
- how to petition the European Court of Human Rights.

27.1 INTRODUCTION TO HUMAN RIGHTS

Since the Human Rights Act 1998 (HRA 1998) came into force, the subject of human rights has been treated as a pervasive topic on the Legal Practice Course. Perhaps more than any other pervasive topic, its reach is long, and it has begun to make its presence felt in almost every area of law and practice. A copy of the HRA 1998 may be found at **Appendix 1 to Part IV**.

Before starting a Legal Practice Course students are expected to have a 'basic knowledge and understanding of the relevant human rights conventions and legislation' (see Appendix to the Solicitors Regulation Authority, Legal Practice Course Outcomes, 2007). This part of this book is intended to act as a reminder of the key points and put them in a practical context. This chapter re-introduces you to the European Convention on Human Rights and some of the most important Convention rights. **Chapter 28** deals with the mechanism by which the HRA 1998 makes those rights enforceable in the UK.

27.2 INTRODUCTION TO THE CONVENTION

The UK was instrumental in drafting the European Convention for the Protection of Human Rights and Fundamental Freedoms 1950 (European Convention on Human Rights) (ECHR). The Convention was drafted by members of the Council of Europe (a body unrelated to the European Union) in the aftermath of the Second World War and the human rights abuses which took place during it. The UK was one of the original signatories on 4 November 1950. The Convention came into force on 3 September 1953. However, unlike many of the other signatories, the UK did not incorporate the Convention into its own legal system. The

Government believed that incorporation was unnecessary because the rights contained in the Convention already existed in British common law.

The original ECHR contained the civil and political rights to be found in classical liberal thought, such as freedom of expression, freedom of religion and freedom from interference with privacy. A series of protocols, some of which have been ratified by the UK, deal with certain other matters including the right to education and the right to peaceful enjoyment of private property (First Protocol) and the prohibition of the death penalty (Sixth Protocol).

The most imaginative feature of the ECHR was that it imposed an international judicial system for the protection of human rights on Europe. It is the most developed of regional systems for the protection of human rights.

27.3   THE RELATIONSHIP BETWEEN THE ECHR AND ENGLISH LAW

The HRA 1998 (which came into force in October 2000) has bridged the gap between domestic and international law so far as the Convention is concerned. Domestic English courts are now empowered to enforce Convention rights. Exactly how they may do so will be discussed in **Chapter 28**.

27.4   THE RELATIONSHIP BETWEEN THE ECHR AND THE EU

While there is a close relationship between the EU and the ECHR, the two are distinct and should not be confused. In particular, bear in mind the following differences.

(a)   Far more countries are signatories to the ECHR than are members of the EU.

(b)   The EU's concern with human rights has traditionally been limited. Some rights are protected. Article 157 TFEU, for example, deals with sex discrimination.

(c)   The ECHR confers rights on everyone within the jurisdiction of a State which is party to the Convention, and not just those who are nationals of the State in question. This is important for asylum seekers, for example: EU law is usually concerned only with the rights of nationals of Member States.

(d)   The ECHR has its own institutions and procedures, in particular the European Court of Human Rights (ECtHR) which sits in Strasbourg, not Luxembourg or Brussels.

There have been suggestions since 1977 that the EU might become a party to the ECHR. So far this has not happened, and indeed the Court of Justice ruled that the Council has no power to accede to the ECHR under the Treaty as currently drafted (see *Opinion No 2/94* [1996] ECR I-1759, 28 March 1996). But the Court of Justice has said that EU law will draw upon the jurisprudence of the ECHR because it represents the common traditions of the EU Member States in the field of human rights. Note that the Maastricht Treaty makes an express reference to human rights and in particular to the ECHR: see the Recitals and TEU, Article 6.

27.5   THE SUBSTANTIVE LAW OF THE ECHR

27.5.1   The Convention rights

These are the main rights protected by the Convention:

(a)   right to life (Article 2);

(b)   prohibition of torture (Article 3);

(c)   prohibition of slavery and forced labour (Article 4);

(d)   right to liberty and security (Article 5);

(e)   right to a fair trial (Article 6);

(f)   no punishment without lawful authority (Article 7);

(g)   right to respect for family and private life (Article 8);

(h)   right to freedom of thought, conscience and religion (Article 9);

(i)   right to freedom of expression (Article 10);

(j)   right to freedom of assembly and association (Article 11);

(k)   right to marry (Article 12);

(l)   prohibition of discrimination (Article 14);

(m)   right to peaceful enjoyment of possessions (First Protocol, Article 1);

(n)   right to education and right of parents to educate children in accordance with religious and philosophical convictions (First Protocol, Article 2).

The most important of these rights are described below (**27.5.3–27.5.9**).

27.5.2   Some general considerations when dealing with Convention rights

27.5.2.1   Drafting

The Convention is drafted in quite a different way from a United Kingdom statute. In the UK, legislative drafting tends to be very tight and exhaustive. The rights in the Convention are deliberately left open-ended, and the Strasbourg organs do not interpret the Convention in the same way as English judges interpret domestic legislation. Lawyers in the UK must appreciate this different way of working.

27.5.2.2   Absolute and limited rights

Some of the Convention rights are absolute. For example, the right to freedom from torture: the Convention allows no circumstances in which torture could be legitimate. But most of the rights are subject to limitations and qualifications. For example, the right to freedom of expression may be interfered with where the matters being expressed are defamatory or harmful to national security. Much of the argument in Convention cases turns not on whether there has been an interference with Convention rights, but on whether that interference is justifiable. In considering the interference, the ECtHR has invented a number of tools with which UK lawyers need to be familiar.

27.5.2.3   Judicial method

Once it has been established that a Convention right has been interfered with, the court must consider whether the interference is justified (unless the right is one which is absolute, in which case no interference is allowed).

There are four key concepts which the ECtHR uses.

The rule of law

No matter how desirable the end to be achieved, any interference with a Convention right must be based on some ascertainable law, and not on an arbitrary executive decision. Without detailed authorisation by law, any interference, however justified, will violate the Convention. For example, telephone tapping by the police in the 1970s was regulated by nothing more than an internal police guidance note which was not available to the public. The interference with the right to respect for correspondence (Article 8) was not therefore justified by law and was contrary to the Convention (*Malone v United Kingdom* (1984) 7 EHRR 14).

Legitimate aims

The defendant must say why the right is being interfered with, and the reason must be a legitimate one. Many of the Articles (eg, Articles 8, 9, 10 and 11) set out what sorts of aims are legitimate, for example the interests of public safety, national security or the protection of the rights and freedoms of others. For example, if a prisoner's correspondence is being read by the prison authorities then the prevention of disorder or crime within the prison would be a legitimate reason for the interference with Article 8 if there was a genuine belief that there was a risk. But the routine reading of mail would not be legitimate (*Campbell v United Kingdom* (1992) 15 EHRR 137).

Proportionality

The cliché usually used to describe the doctrine of proportionality is that the State cannot use a sledgehammer to crack a nut. In the more formal language of the court, any restriction on a right must be 'necessary in a democratic society' or based on some 'pressing social need'. For example, in the domestic UK case of *Lindsay v Customs & Excise Commissioners* [2002] EWCA Civ 267, [2002] STC 588, the defendant had been caught by customs officers driving his Ford Focus car into the UK containing 18,400 cigarettes, 10 kilos of handrolling tobacco, 31 litres of beer and 3 litres of spirits. The goods were for members of his family, for which he had received payment. This was unlawful. As well as seizing the goods, the customs officers seized his car and refused to return it to him. The Court of Appeal held that the interference with the defendant's right to peaceful enjoyment of his possessions by the forfeiture of his car, although within the legal powers of the customs officers, was disproportionate for small-scale smuggling of this nature.

Note that the principle of proportionality in EU law is neither expressed nor applied in the same way as the principle of proportionality under the ECHR. Although there is some common ground, the so-called four-stage analysis of proportionality which was explained in *Bank Mellat v Her Majesty's Treasury (No 2)* [2014] AC 700 at [20] and [72]–[76], in relation to the justification under domestic law (in particular, under the Human Rights Act 1998) of interferences with fundamental rights, is not applicable to proportionality in EU law (see *R (on the application of Lumsdon) v Legal Services Board* [2015] UKSC 41 at [26]).

Margin of appreciation

This is the Strasbourg equivalent of what in Brussels is called subsidiarity. It means that the States which are party to the Convention are allowed a degree of leeway out of sensitivity to their own political and cultural traditions. For example, the case of *Handyside v United Kingdom* (1976) 1 EHRR 737 concerned the publication in England in 1971 of *The Little Red School Book*, a children's book including a section on sex. The publisher had been convicted under the Obscene Publications Act 1959. The ECtHR had to consider the UK Government's argument that the interference with the publisher's right to freedom of expression was necessary for the purpose of the 'protection of morals'. The Court accepted that such a matter was within the competence of national authorities and a standard could not be imposed by an international body:

> By reason of their direct and continuous contact with the vital forces of their countries, state authorities are in principle in a better position than the international judge to give an opinion. (para 48)

The majority of commentators agree that, by its nature, the doctrine of the margin of appreciation will not be relevant to cases decided under the HRA 1998 by UK courts. The doctrine exists to take account of the geographical and cultural gaps between an international court and the various countries it supervises. Within a unitary domestic legal system it will serve no purpose.

27.5.3   Article 5: The right to liberty and security

1.   Everyone has the right to liberty and security of person. No one shall be deprived of his liberty save in the following cases and in accordance with a procedure prescribed by law:

 (a)   the lawful detention of a person after conviction by a competent court;

 (b)   the lawful arrest or detention of a person for non-compliance with the lawful order of a court or in order to secure the fulfilment of any obligation prescribed by law;

 (c)   the lawful arrest or detention of a person effected for the purpose of bringing him before the competent legal authority on reasonable suspicion of having committed an offence or when it is reasonably considered necessary to prevent his committing an offence or fleeing after having done so;

(d) the detention of a minor by lawful order for the purpose of educational supervision or his lawful detention for the purpose of bringing him before the competent legal authority;

(e) the lawful detention of persons for the prevention of the spreading of infectious diseases, of persons of unsound mind, alcoholics or drug addicts or vagrants;

(f) the lawful arrest or detention of a person to prevent his effecting an unauthorised entry into the country or of a person against whom action is being taken with a view to deportation or extradition.

2. Everyone who is arrested shall be informed promptly, in a language which he understands, of the reasons for his arrest and of any charge against him.

3. Everyone arrested or detained in accordance with the provisions of paragraph 1(c) of this Article shall be brought promptly before a judge or other officer authorised by law to exercise judicial power and shall be entitled to trial within a reasonable time or to release pending trial. Release may be conditioned by guarantees to appear for trial.

4. Everyone who is deprived of his liberty by arrest or detention shall be entitled to take proceedings by which the lawfulness of his detention shall be decided speedily by a court and his release ordered if the detention is not lawful.

5. Everyone who has been the victim of arrest or detention in contravention of the provisions of this Article shall have an enforceable right to compensation.

Article 5 is the most lengthy of the Convention rights. To determine whether there is a deprivation of liberty within the meaning of and engaging the protection of Article 5(1), three conditions must be satisfied:

(a) an objective element of 'a person's confinement to a certain limited place for a not negligible length of time';

(b) a subjective element, namely that the person has not 'validly consented to the confinement in question'; and

(c) the deprivation of liberty must be one for which the State is responsible. See generally *A Local Authority v A, B, C, D and E* [2010] EWHC 978 (Fam), *P (by his litigation friend The Official Solicitor) v Cheshire West & Chester Council* [2014] UKSC 19 and *Secretary of State for Justice v Staffordshire County Council* [2016] EWCA Civ 1317.

Can a control order amount to a deprivation of liberty? In *AH v Secretary of State for the Home Department* [2011] EWCA Civ 787, the control order included the following obligations: a 14-hour curfew between 6pm and 8am in a flat in Norwich; a prohibition on communications equipment other than a landline telephone; and a geographical boundary comprising the centre and inner suburbs of Norwich. At first instance the judge concluded that a curfew of 14 hours was not, by itself, tantamount to a deprivation of liberty. He then addressed 10 individual features of the control order relied upon by the appellant in order to see whether their cumulative effect, when taken with the length of the curfew, was such as to amount to a deprivation of liberty. He concluded that this was not a case of deprivation of liberty but that it 'falls just on the restriction on liberty side of the line and so does not engage Article 5'. The decision was upheld on appeal. Also see *AP v Secretary of State for the Home Department* [2010] 3 WLR 51, where Lord Brown said at (para 4): 'I nevertheless remain of the view that for a control order with a 16 hour curfew to be struck down as involving a deprivation of liberty, the other conditions imposed would have to be unusually destructive of the life the controlee might otherwise have been living.'

Can an adult, in the exercise of parental responsibility, impose, or authorise others to impose, restrictions on the liberty of his or her child? Yes, but the restrictions so imposed must not in their totality amount to deprivation of liberty that engages the Article 5 rights of the child: see *Neilson v Denmark* (1988) 11 EHRR 175, *Re K* [2002] 2 WLR 1141 and *RK (by her litigation friend the Official Solicitor) v BCC* [2011] EWCA Civ 1305. As to the actions of the police in restraining an autistic, epileptic young man when such restraint was in the circumstances hasty, ill-informed and damaging to him, see ZH (*a protected party by his litigation friend, GH*) *v Commissioner of Police of the Metropolis* [2013] EWCA Civ 69.

Does the opportunity for a prisoner, who is subject to an indeterminate sentence, to rehabilitate himself and demonstrate that he no longer presents a danger to the public fall within Article 5? Yes, held the ECtHR in *James v UK* (2013) 56 EHRR 12. However, the Supreme Court refused to follow that judgment in R (*on the application of Hanley*) *v Secretary of State for Justice* [2014] UKSC 66. The Court held that it was only implicit in the scheme of the Article that the State had a duty to provide a reasonable opportunity for a prisoner subject to an indeterminate sentence to rehabilitate himself and demonstrate that he no longer presented a danger to the public. However, that is an ancillary duty, which cannot be brought within the express language of the Article and does not therefore affect the lawfulness of detention.

Article 5 is of particular importance to criminal litigation practitioners, especially in challenging arrests and detentions. Its overall purpose is to ensure that no one is deprived of his or her liberty in an arbitrary fashion (*Engel v Netherlands* (1979–80) 1 EHRR 647, para 58 and *Austin v Commissioner of Police of the Metropolis* [2009] UKHL 5).

The Article has two distinct limbs. Paragraph 1 prohibits interference with liberty or security of person except in certain, well-defined circumstances. No distinction tends to be made in Strasbourg jurisprudence between the two concepts of liberty and security of person. Paragraphs 2–5 provide a set of procedural rights for detainees.

27.5.3.1 Lawful detention

Paragraph 1 insists in particular that any detention must be 'lawful' (the word is used in each of subparas (a)–(f)). This requires that the domestic law upon which a detention is based must be accessible and precise. The paragraph also requires that the detention be 'in accordance with a procedure prescribed by law'. This calls for a consideration of how the detainer has gone about detaining the individual rather than why. Where there is no procedure prescribed by domestic law, or where the detainer has failed to follow it, Article 5 will have been breached (see *Secretary of State for Justice v RB* [2011] EWCA Civ 1608).

The attempt made in Article 5(1)(a) to (f) to codify the exceptions more precisely makes it unusually inflexible if applied according to its literal meaning in a situation of armed conflict. In some circumstances, some of the six grounds may adventitiously accommodate military detention. But as the Strasbourg Court recognised in *Hassan v UK* (2014) 38 BHRC 358, they are not designed for such a situation and are not well adapted to it. Moreover, *Hassan* does not add a notional seventh ground of permitted military detention in the course of armed conflict.

> Its effect is rather to recognise that sub-paragraphs (a) to (f) cannot necessarily be regarded as exhaustive when the Convention is being applied to such a conflict, because their exhaustive character reflects peacetime conditions. This means that where the armed forces of a Convention state are acting under a mandate from the Security Council to use all necessary measures, article 5(1) cannot be taken to prevent them from detaining persons for imperative reasons of security. (per Lord Sumption in *Abd Ali Hameed Al-Waheed v Ministry of Defence* [2017] UKSC 2 at para 68)

As a result, in an international armed conflict, a system of judicial control over detention may not always be required.

Is there a breach if the person is detained in the 'wrong' place, for example in prison rather than in a detention centre for deportees? This happened in R (*on the application of Dritan Krasniqi*) *v Secretary of State for the Home Department* [2011] EWCA Civ 1549. The Court held that a claim cannot be based solely on an irregularity in the selection of the place of detention. It might be different if it was shown that the conditions of detention were unduly harsh, as in *Mayeka v Belgium* [2007] 1 FLR 1726. There, a 5-year-old child was detained for two months, alone among strangers, in an adult detention centre. This caused her such distress and potential psychological damage that it amounted both to inhuman treatment contrary to Article 3 and to a violation under Article 5 of the principle that the place and conditions of detention must be related to the permitted ground of deprivation of liberty. See also R (on the application of Idira) v Secretary of State for the Home Department [2015] EWCA Civ 1187.

Can Article 5(1)(c) apply in a case of detention for preventive purposes followed by early release, that is, before the person could practically be brought before a court? Yes – see R (on the application of Hicks) v Commissioner of Police for the Metropolis [2017] UKSC 9.

27.5.3.2 Reasons

Paragraph 2 provides a right for those placed under arrest to be given reasons. These do not need to be in writing, and formal notification is not necessary if the reasons are made clear during the arrest (X v Netherlands 5 YB 224, at 228).

27.5.3.3 Judicial supervision

Paragraph 3 requires that the person under arrest be brought promptly before a judge (usually a magistrate in the UK). The paragraph also provides for trial within a reasonable time, or for release pending trial (ie bail). There is a presumption that bail will be granted unless there are good reasons not to grant it (for example, because there is a risk that the accused will fail to appear at the trial: Stögmüller v Austria (1969) 1 EHRR 155).

27.5.3.4 Challenge and review

Paragraph 4 requires that a speedy procedure must be available by which detention can be challenged. The habeas corpus procedure in the UK fulfils this requirement, so long as it concludes swiftly. The ECtHR has also held that where the circumstances of detention vary over time a regular reviewing procedure must exist.

Many cases turn on the question of whether or not a period of detention is reasonable. In O'Dowd v UK [2010] ECHR 1324, the ECtHR stressed that this cannot be assessed in the abstract. Whether it is reasonable for an accused to remain in detention must be considered in each case according to its special features. Continued detention may be justified in a given case only if there are specific indications of a genuine requirement of public interest which, notwithstanding the presumption of innocence, outweighs the rule of respect for individual liberty laid down in Article 5. The persistence of reasonable suspicion that the person arrested has committed an offence is a condition sine qua non for the lawfulness of the continued detention, but after a certain lapse of time it no longer suffices. The Court must then establish whether the other grounds given by the judicial authorities continued to justify the deprivation of liberty. Where such grounds were relevant and sufficient, the Court must also be satisfied that the national authorities displayed special diligence in the conduct of the proceedings. In judging whether the special diligence requirement has been met, the Court will have regard to periods of unjustified delay, to the overall complexity of the proceedings and to any steps taken by the authorities to speed up proceedings to ensure that the overall length of detention remains reasonable.

In R (on the application of Whiston) v Secretary of State for Justice [2014] UKSC 39, a prisoner was released before he became automatically entitled to release. He was recalled, still within the custodial period of his sentence, because his whereabouts could no longer be monitored in the community. The Secretary of State's recall decision was not subject to judicial control. The issue was whether the recall constituted a fresh deprivation of liberty so as to engage Article 5(4) and provide a right of review, or whether the renewed detention remained justified by the original sentence of imprisonment. The Supreme Court held the latter. In doing so the Court refused to follow its previous decision in R (on the application of Smith) v Parole Board [2005] UKHL 1.

27.5.3.5 Compensation

Paragraph 5 provides a right to compensation for any interference with Article 5 rights. In practice, this is unlikely to add anything to the availability of damages (and possibly exemplary damages) in tort for wrongful arrest or unlawful detention.

The enforceable right to compensation is not intended to provide compensation for claimants whose convictions were reached by a lawfully constituted court but which were quashed on appeal: *W v Ministry of Justice* [2015] EWCA Civ 742.

The right to compensation will be important where there is no entitlement to damages at common law, eg the applicant is ordered to remain in custody by a civil court. This happened in *Stellato v Ministry of Defence* [2010] EWCA Civ 1435 where the applicant was unlawfully detained under an order of the Court of Appeal for 14 days until released by the Supreme Court. That he was subsequently unlawfully detained by the defendant for a further 59 days also entitled him to damages at common law.

27.5.4 Article 6: The right to a fair trial

1. In the determination of his civil rights and obligations or of any criminal charge against him, everyone is entitled to a fair and public hearing within a reasonable time by an independent and impartial tribunal established by law. Judgment shall be pronounced publicly but the press and public may be excluded from all or part of the trial in the interest of morals, public order or national security in a democratic society, where the interests of juveniles or the protection of the private life of the parties so require, or to the extent strictly necessary in the opinion of the court in special circumstances where publicity would prejudice the interests of justice.

2. Everyone charged with a criminal offence shall be presumed innocent until proved guilty according to law.

3. Everyone charged with a criminal offence has the following minimum rights:
   (a) to be informed promptly, in a language which he understands and in detail, of the nature and cause of the accusation against him;
   (b) to have adequate time and facilities for the preparation of his defence;
   (c) to defend himself in person or through legal assistance of his own choosing or, if he has not sufficient means to pay for legal assistance, to be given it free when the interests of justice so require;
   (d) to examine or have examined witnesses against him and to obtain the attendance and examination of witnesses on his behalf under the same conditions as witnesses against him;
   (e) to have the free assistance of an interpreter if he cannot understand or speak the language used in court.

Article 6 is arguably the most important, and certainly the most utilised, of all the Convention rights. It provides for a right to fair criminal and civil trials, and lays down certain procedural standards. It is of direct importance to all litigators, and therefore indirectly to all lawyers.

27.5.4.1 Determination of civil rights or a criminal charge

Paragraph 1 lays down the basic 'due process' standards for the determination of civil and criminal matters. The phrase 'in the determination of his civil rights' needs some explanation. It does not simply cover every issue which might be the subject of a trial in civil law as an English lawyer would understand that expression. The Strasbourg case law on this is complex. All proceedings between private individuals and private bodies are included. Not all proceedings involving public authorities are, and here further research may be necessary. Broadly, a distinction is made between those decisions of public bodies which affect private law rights (which are within the scope of the Article) and those affecting public law rights (which are not). For example, disciplinary proceedings that might result in the removal of professional status (*Le Compte v Belgium* [1982] ECC 240) are included. Likewise, planning decisions affect property rights and are included. Actions to sue public authorities for compensation will be included, because private law rights in tort or contract are involved. The fact that a claim depends on a failure to comply with the terms of a government policy, rather than of legislation, is not in itself a reason why it cannot involve the determination of a civil right (R (on the application of K) v Secretary of State for Defence [2016] EWCA Civ 1149).

Decisions of public authorities affecting education involve public law, not private law rights, and are not subject to Article 6 requirements (*Simpson v United Kingdom* (1989) 64 DR 188). For the same reason, decisions on the categorisation of prisoners for security purposes are not covered (*Brady v United Kingdom* (1979) 3 EHRR 297), neither are government decisions on asylum (*R (K)(Iran) v Secretary of State for the Home Department* [2010] EWCA Civ 115), or decisions by a local housing authority under s 193(5) of the Housing Act 1996 that it has discharged its duty to secure accommodation available for occupation by a homeless applicant (*Ali v Birmingham CC* [2010] UKSC 8), or decisions of an independent appeal panel as to whether a pupil should be permanently excluded from school (*R (on the application of V) v Independent Appeal Panel for Tom Hood School* [2010] EWCA Civ 142).

What is a criminal charge for the purposes of Article 6? To determine this, three questions must be answered. How is the offence classified in domestic law? What is the nature of the offence? What is the nature and purpose of the penalty; how severe is it? See *Engel v Netherlands* (1979–80) 1 EHRR 647. However, the minor nature of a penalty does not prevent it from being 'criminal' under the Convention and classification under national law is not decisive (*Glantz v Finland* [2014] STC 2263).

Is there a right to legal representation in civil proceedings? The more the proceedings are akin to criminal proceedings, the more positive the answer is yes. For the purposes of Article 6, there is no clear-cut dividing line between civil and criminal proceedings, so the courts approach the issue on the basis of a sliding scale, at the bottom of which are civil wrongs of a relatively trivial nature, and at the top of which are serious crimes meriting substantial punishment. So civil disciplinary proceedings that might lead to a person being barred from practising his profession are likely to attract this right: see *R (on the application of G) v Y City Council* [2010] EWCA Civ 1 and *R (on the application of G) v X School Governors* [2011] UKSC 30.

27.5.4.2   A fair trial

Paragraph 1 sets out the minimum requirements for a fair trial. These are:

(a)   a fair and public hearing;

(b)   an independent and impartial tribunal;

(c)   trial within a reasonable period;

(d)   public judgment (with some exceptions); and

(e)   a reasoned decision.

As the most litigated Article, a great deal of case law has grown up around these requirements. The approach of the ECtHR in interpreting and applying Article 6(1) is generous to applicants, and the Court reaches its decisions 'bearing in mind the prominent place which the right to a fair trial holds in a democratic society' (*Delcourt v Belgium* (1979–80) 1 EHRR 355). Not only have these decisions built on the requirements expressly contained in the paragraph set out above, they have read other rights into the paragraph. These include:

(a)   the right of access to a court (eg, *Osman v United Kingdom* (2000) 29 EHRR 245: police immunity a denial of the right of access to a court);

(b)   equality of arms (*Dombo Beheer BV v Netherlands* (1994) 18 EHRR 213); and

(c)   the right to participate effectively in proceedings (*Stanford v United Kingdom* (Case A/282) (1994) *The Times*, 8 March: poor court room acoustics; *Re L (a child)* (2013) LTL 4 February, CA: refusal to adjourn hearing for legal representation to be obtained; *R v JP* [2014] EWCA Crim 2064: refusal to allow cross-examination of child witness).

Should a fugitive from justice be denied these Convention rights? In *Conde Nast Publications Ltd v UK* (2008) Application No 00029746/05, LTL 29 February, the applicant publishers had been sued successfully for defamation. The claimant had left America and moved to France before being sentenced for an offence in respect of which he had pleaded guilty. The High Court had allowed the claimant to give his evidence by video link from a Paris hotel. The House of Lords had upheld that decision. The applicants argued that the principle of equality of arms was broken and so the proceedings were unfair. The ECtHR held that the UK Government could not be condemned under Article 6 for providing the claimant with facilities that were available to other litigants simply because of his status as a fugitive from justice. Why? Because the deprivation of such facilities would run counter to the Convention guarantee of equal treatment that is inherent in the principle of equality of arms.

Until 2010 there had been a presumption against requiring a child to attend court to give evidence in family proceedings. However, in *Re W (Children)* [2010] UKSC 12, the Supreme Court held that this could not be reconciled with the need to strike a fair balance between the rights protected by Articles 6 and 8 (see **27.5.5**). So a court considering whether to call a child as a witness has to weigh the advantages this will bring to the determination of the truth against the damage it might do to the welfare of that or any other child. Striking that balance in care proceedings might mean that a child is not called in the great majority of cases, but that must be the result of the court's considered judgment and not a presumption.

Furthermore, in civil litigation, paragraph 1 has been held to require a right to legal aid should the circumstances of the case demand it, especially 'by reason of the complexity of the procedure of the case' (*Airey v Ireland* (Case A/32) (1979) 2 EHRR 305; see also *Steel and Morris v United Kingdom* [2005] ECHR 68416/01 (the so-called 'McDonald's libel case'). Article 6(3)(c) expressly requires legal aid in criminal litigation.

27.5.4.3 Presumption of innocence

Paragraph 2 provides for the presumption of innocence in criminal trials. 'Reverse onus' provisions, which place the burden of proof upon a defendant to demonstrate his innocence, do not necessarily violate Article 6(2) (*Lingens v Austria* (1981) 26 DR 171; also *R v Director of Public Prosecutions, ex p Kebilene* [2000] 2 AC 326, the first HRA 1998 case to reach the House of Lords (now the Supreme Court)). In *Murray v United Kingdom (Right to Silence)* (1996) 22 EHRR 29, the ECtHR ruled that the drawing of adverse inferences from the exercise by the accused of his right to silence did not violate the Article either. However, in *Saunders v United Kingdom* (1996) 23 EHRR 313, the use of statements obtained by compulsion by inspectors exercising statutory powers under the Companies Act 1985 was held to be a violation of Article 6(2).

Since the HRA 1998 came into force the issue of reverse onus provisions has been raised in domestic UK litigation in several motoring cases. For example, in *R v Drummond* [2002] EWCA Crim 527, [2002] 2 Cr App R 25, the defendant was accused of causing death by dangerous driving and driving with excess alcohol. He tried to rely on the 'hip flask' defence, that he had drunk alcohol after the accident and before the arrival of the police to steady his nerves. The legislation placed the burden upon him to prove that this was the case rather than requiring the prosecution to show that he had drunk the alcohol before the accident. The Court of Appeal held that the imposition of this burden on the defendant was justified and he lost his appeal against conviction.

In *R v Keogh* [2007] EWCA Civ 528, the Court of Appeal held that the reverse burdens of proof contained in s 2(3) and s 3(4) of the Official Secrets Act 1989 were incompatible with Article 6. Why? Because the Act can operate effectively without the imposition of those reverse burdens. The Court held that it was not necessary to impose them and to do so would be disproportionate and unjustifiable.

27.5.4.4 Procedural safeguards in criminal trials

Because of the serious nature of criminal litigation, paragraph 3 provides specific procedural rights in this context. These are rights for the defendant:

(a)   to be informed promptly of the accusation against him;

(b)   to have adequate time and facilities to prepare his defence;

(c)   to choose his legal representative and to receive legal aid if necessary;

(d)   to call witnesses and to cross-examine witnesses against him; and

(e)   to have free access to an interpreter if necessary (see R v Foronda [2014] NICA 17).

CASE EXAMPLE

In a criminal trial, if hearsay evidence is admitted against the accused, there is no opportunity to cross-examine that witness. So is the trial still fair? Yes, provided there is a good reason for the non-attendance of the witness. But what if his statement is the only or decisive evidence against the accused? Then there must be sufficient counterbalancing factors, including strong procedural safeguards, to ensure a fair trial.

The Grand Chamber of the ECtHR applied these tests in *Al-Khawaja and Tahery v UK* (Application Nos 26766/05 and 22228/06) (2011) The Times, 22 December.

Mr Al-Khawaja was a consultant physician. He was charged with indecently assaulting two female patients. Both made statements to the police. However, one complainant committed suicide before the trial. Her statement was admitted as hearsay evidence and read to the jury. The Grand Chamber held that had been necessary as there was no other way the evidence could be given. Moreover, the trial was fair as: (a) the judge directed the jury that her hearsay evidence should carry less weight because she had not been seen, heard or cross-examined; and (b) the jury also heard evidence from the other complainant and two of deceased woman's friends in whom she had confided soon after the incident.

Mr Tahery was charged with stabbing another man in the back during a gang fight. Only one witness claimed to have seen him do this. The witness gave a statement to the police. This was admitted as hearsay evidence and read to the jury because the judge found the witness was afraid of giving evidence. Whilst that may have been a good reason, the Grand Chamber found the trial to have been unfair. The hearsay evidence amounted to an uncorroborated eyewitness statement. The fact that Mr Tahery could challenge the statement himself and the trial judge's clear and forceful warning to the jury in his summing up did not sufficiently counterbalance the difficulties caused to the defence by the admission of the untested evidence.

These rights have caused a great deal of litigation. Reference to the case law or to a specialist work is needed to understand them fully.

27.5.5   Article 8: The right to respect for private and family life

1.   Everyone has the right to respect for his private and family life, his home and his correspondence.

2.   There shall be no interference by a public authority with the exercise of this right except such as is in accordance with the law and is necessary in a democratic society in the interests of national security, public safety or the economic wellbeing of the country, for the prevention of disorder or crime, for the protection of health or morals, or for the protection of the rights and freedoms of others.

Article 8 has been used creatively by lawyers and judges. Its essential object is to protect the individual against arbitrary action by public authorities (*Kroon v Netherlands* (1994) 19 EHRR 263). It has been used in cases where it might seem quite at home, such as those involving phone tapping or interference with prisoners' mail. But it has also been used in contexts which might come as a surprise to those who drafted it, such as the rights of transsexuals to have official records amended to recognise their status, the right to an environment unpolluted by noise and chemicals, and the right to practise one's sexuality freely.

Paragraph 1 protects four distinct rights.

27.5.5.1   Private life

This encompasses:

(a)   noise pollution issues (*Rayner v United Kingdom* (1986) 47 DR 5);

(b)   pollution by waste (*López Ostra v Spain* (1994) 20 EHRR 277);

(c)   sexual orientation (*Smith and Grady v United Kingdom* (2000) 29 EHRR 548 and *Bull v Hall* [2013] UKSC 73);

(d)   the unauthorised disclosure of confidential data to third parties (*MS v Sweden* (1999) 28 EHRR 313);

(e)   covert police surveillance (*Wood v United Kingdom* [2004] ECHR 23414/02);

(f)   the monitoring by an employer of office telephone calls without warning (*Halford v United Kingdom* (1997) 24 EHRR 523);

(g)   the opening and censoring of prisoner's confidential correspondence with a court (*Klyakhin v Russia* [2004] ECHR 46082/99);

(h)   administration of medication against wishes (*Glass v United Kingdom* [2004] ECHR 61827/00);

(i)   a State's obligation to make adequate and effective efforts to assist a person in his attempt to have his child returned to him with a view to exercising his parental rights (*Monory v Romania* [2005] ECHR 71099/01);

(j)   unauthorised publication of photographs (*Douglas v Hello!* [2003] 3 All ER 996; *RocknRoll v News Group Newspapers Ltd* [2013] EWHC 24 (Ch) and *Weller v Associated Newspapers Limited* [2015] EWCA Civ 1176);

(k)   the retention of fingerprint and DNA data after a person is acquitted of a criminal offence (*Marper v UK* [2007] ECHR 110);

(l)   the taking and retention of photographs by the police of a member of the public in the street (*Wood v Commissioner of Police of the Metropolis* [2009] EWCA Civ 414);

(m)   legal professional privilege relating to the seeking and giving of legal advice by a qualified lawyer but not by an accountant (*R (on the application of Prudential Plc) v Special Commissioner of Income Tax* [2013] UKSC 1);

(n)   the reputation of an individual (*In the Matter of Guardian News & Media Ltd v HM Treasury* [2010] UKSC 1);

(o)   the prohibition or restriction on the ability to work (*Sidabras v Lithuania* (2006) 42 EHRR 6 and *R (on the application of MA) v National Probation Service* [2011] EWHC 1332);

(p)   the dignity and privacy of prisoners in their cells (*Grant v Ministry of Justice* [2011] EWHC 3379) and their ability to exercise (*Malcolm v Secretary of State for Justice* [2011] EWCA Civ 1538), and the same-sex relationship between two prisoners (*Bright v Secretary of State for Justice* [2014] EWCA Civ 1628);

(q)   the administration of a police caution and the requirement to disclose it (*R (on the application of T) v Chief Constable of Greater Manchester* [2014] UKSC 35);

(r)   in limited circumstances, the decision to prosecute an individual (*SXH v CPS* [2014] EWCA Civ 90);

(s)   the potential humiliation and embarrassment of being searched by a police officer (*R (on the application of Roberts) v Commissioner of Police of the Metropolis* [2014] EWCA Civ 69);

(t)   an exclusion zone imposed by a prison governor as a condition of a prisoner's release on licence (*R (on the application of Bentham) v Governor of Usk & Prescoed Prison* [2014] EWHC 2469 (Admin));

(u)   the systematic collection and retention by police authorities of electronic data about individuals (*R (on the application of Catt) v Commissioner of Police of the Metropolis* [2015] UKSC 9);

(v)   the retention and use of gender data by the State (*R (on the application of C) v Secretary of State for Work & Pensions* [2016] EWCA Civ 47);

(w) the denial of a right to a free abortion, thereby putting stress and pressure on women who cannot afford to pay (R (*on the application of A*) (*A Child By Her Mother and Litigation Friend*) *v Secretary of State for Health* [2015] EWCA Civ 771); and

(x) the denial of citizenship (R (*on the application of Johnson*) *v Secretary of State for the Home Department* [2016] UKSC 56).

The touchstone for Article 8(1)'s engagement is whether the claimant enjoys on the facts a 'reasonable expectation of privacy'. So is it engaged by a teenage boy, involved in an incident of public disorder and rioting, when the police release CCTV still images of some of those involved that include the boy to local newspapers for publication appealing to the public for help in identifying the suspects? The question split the Supreme Court in *In the matter of an application by JR38 For Judicial Review (Northern Ireland)* [2015] UKSC 42. By 3:2 the Court answered the question in the negative.

27.5.5.2 Family life

It is disruption of the family unit which is most likely to offend against this aspect of Article 8. This might include, for example, a situation in which the State wishes to take a child into care or make an adoption order against the wishes of a parent (see *Re Q (a child)* [2011] EWCA Civ 1610). It is also an extremely important issue for immigration lawyers, as deportation, extradition and immigration controls may often result in families being broken up.

In *Schalk and Kopf v Austria* (Application No 30141/04, 24 June 2010) and *Oliari and Others v Italy* (Application Nos 18766/11 and 36030/11, 21 July 2015), the ECtHR recognised that, even absent a legal status, stable and committed same-sex relationships amount to family life. In *Schalk's* case (at para 94) it was held that 'the relationship of the applicants, a co-habiting same-sex couple living in a stable de facto partnership, falls within the notion of "family life", just as the relationship of a different-sex couple in the same situation would'. In *Vallianatos and Others v Greece* (Application Nos 29381/09 and 32684/09, 7 November 2013) (at para 81), the Court stated that civil partnerships 'as an officially recognised alternative to marriage have an intrinsic value for applicants irrespective of the legal effects, however narrow or extensive, that they would produce'. Earlier in its judgment the court found that the measures, in that case making provision for civil partnerships for different-sex couples only, fell squarely within the ambit of Article 8, and stated at para 73 that 'in view of the rapid evolution in a considerable number of member States regarding the granting of legal recognition to same-sex couples, "it [would be] artificial to maintain the view that, in contrast to a different-sex couple, a same-sex couple [could not] enjoy 'family life' for the purposes of Article 8"'.

'Family' clearly includes those with blood and marital links, but has also been extended by the ECtHR to include other emotional ties. In *K v United Kingdom* (1986) 50 DR 199, the ECtHR said 'the question of the existence or non-existence of "family life" is essentially a question of fact depending upon the real existence in practice of close personal ties'.

Does a private or family life include such interests as an individual's social life; a person's life being centred, or work being dependent on, a particular activity; family involvement in a particular activity; the social and economic impact on a local community of the loss of a particular activity; cultural heritage; loss of job or loss of business? In R (*on the application of the Countryside Alliance and Others*) *v AG* [2007] UKHL 52, the claimants put forward these interests as part of their case that the ban on hunting wild mammals with dogs under the Hunting Act 2004 engaged Article 8. However, the House of Lords (now the Supreme Court) observed that these arguments stretched the ambit of Article 8 far wider than had ever been recognised in Strasbourg jurisprudence and the House held that Article 8 was not engaged.

27.5.5.3 Home

Clearly, there is some overlap between private life, family life and home life. This element of Article 8(1) specifically protects the right to occupy one's home without harassment or interference. Noise nuisance can violate this right (*Arrondelle v United Kingdom* (1982) 26 DR 5). So can entry by the police to search or for other purposes. In *McLeod v United Kingdom* (1999) 27 EHRR 493, the police accompanied an estranged husband into the former matrimonial home. As there was little risk of disorder, the ECtHR held that this was a disproportionate interference with the applicant's right to home life.

In the context of housing law, the Article does not extend to the right to have a home (*Buckley v United Kingdom* (1996) 23 EHRR 101). But might it constitute a defence to possession proceedings? Yes, any public sector occupier at risk of losing his home must have the opportunity to have the proportionality of that step considered by the county court, and that consideration can include factors such as his personal circumstances: see *Kay v UK* [2010] ECHR 1322 and *Manchester City Council v Pinnock* [2010] UKSC 45. There is no clear and constant jurisprudence of the ECtHR that the proportionality test implied into Article 8(2) applies where there is a private landlord. In *McDonald (by her litigation friend) v McDonald* [2014] EWCA Civ 1049, a private landlord obtained a possession order of a property held on an assured shorthold tenancy after serving a statutory notice to quit. The Court held that Article 8(2) did not apply.

27.5.5.4   Correspondence

It was under this provision that *Malone v United Kingdom* (1984) 7 EHRR 14 was brought, successfully challenging telephone tapping by the police without statutory authority. This resulted in the enactment of the Interception of Communications Act 1985 to grant the police statutory powers. Similar issues were raised in the *Halford* case (see **27.5.5.1**). The Regulation of Investigatory Powers Act 2000 is an important piece of legislation in this area which now, amongst other things, governs interference with communications by employers. As for interference with written correspondence, most of the case law concerns prisoners' rights. Broadly they may correspond freely with their lawyers, but prison authorities may interfere with other correspondence so long as this is justified (*Golder v United Kingdom* (1975) 1 EHRR 524; *Silver v United Kingdom* (1983) 5 EHRR 347).

27.5.5.5   Justification for interference

Article 8 is not absolute. Paragraph 2 sets out reasons which may justify interference with para 1 rights. The principle of proportionality requires that the interference must be the minimum necessary to achieve the legitimate aim (for example, see *R (on the application of M) v Chief Constable of Hampshire* [2014] EWCA Civ 1651 and the *McLeod* case at **27.5.5.3** above).

27.5.6   Article 10: The right to freedom of expression

1.   Everyone has the right to freedom of expression. This right shall include freedom to hold opinions and to receive and impart information and ideas without interference by public authority and regardless of frontiers. This Article shall not prevent States from requiring the licensing of broadcasting, television or cinema enterprises.

2.   The exercise of these freedoms, since it carries with it duties and responsibilities, may be subject to such formalities, conditions, restrictions or penalties as are prescribed by law and are necessary in a democratic society, in the interests of national security, territorial integrity or public safety, for the prevention of disorder or crime, for the protection of health or morals, for the protection of the reputation or rights of others, for preventing the disclosure of information received in confidence, or for maintaining the authority and impartiality of the judiciary.

The ECtHR has described this right as 'one of the essential foundations of a democratic society and one of the conditions of its progress' (*Handyside v United Kingdom* (1976) 1 EHRR 737). It is particularly useful to the press and broadcast media, as well as other publishers and political organisations. The right extends to receiving as well as imparting information. However, this does not oblige public authorities to disclose information against their will (*The Gaskin Case* [1990] 1 FLR 167, no right of access to fostering records held by a local authority).

It merely prohibits restrictions on the receipt of information, for example information about abortion in Ireland (*Open Door Dublin Well Women v Ireland* (1992) 15 EHRR 244).

Justice should be open to public scrutiny, and the media are the conduit through which most members of the public receive information about court proceedings (*R v Cornick* [2014] EWHC 3623 (QB)). So it follows that the principle of open justice is inextricably linked to the freedom of the media to report court proceedings (see *A v BBC* [2014] UKSC 25). It is therefore a general principle that, in the vast majority of cases, a defendant in a criminal case can be expected to be named, unless there is an absolute necessity for anonymity. Similar considerations apply in civil proceedings (*PNM v Times Newspapers Ltd* [2014] EWCA Civ 1132).

Where there is an interference with Article 10 rights, it will be incompatible with the Convention unless:

(a)   it is prescribed by law;

(b)   it pursues a legitimate aim (see para 2);

(c)   it is necessary in a democratic society; and

(d)   it is proportionate.

EXAMPLE

The Video Recordings Act 2010 requires the British Board of Film Classification (BBFC) to classify all video works, subject to exemptions in respect of educational, sporting or musical works which are not supplied for profit. The purpose of the legislation is to provide information for the public so as to enable choices in viewing material unsuitable for children, or extreme violence or pornography. The classifications of U, PG, 12, 15 and 18 are familiar to all. In R v Dryzner [2014] EWCA Crim 2438, the Court held that the classification requirements that the Act imposed are lawful, necessary and proportionate for the protection of public health and morals.

For a more contentious case that split the Supreme Court, *see R (on the application of Lord Carlile of Berriew QC) v Secretary of State for the Home Department* [2014] UKSC 60.

27.5.6.1   Defamation

The ECtHR recognises that individuals have a right to have their reputations protected. But defamation claims are an interference with Article 10 rights and so must be justified using the criteria listed above on a case-by-case basis. In *Tolstoy Miloslavsky v United Kingdom; Lord Aldington v Watts* (1995) 20 EHRR 442, for example, the ECtHR found that a damages award of £1.5 million was disproportionate.

The ECtHR has also recognised, however, that criticism of public figures, especially politicians, is more easily justifed under Article 10. In *Lingens v Austria* (1986) 8 EHRR 407 it said:

> The limits of acceptable criticism are ... wider as regards a politician as such than as regards a private individual. Unlike the latter, the former inevitably and knowingly lays himself open to close scrutiny of every word and deed by both journalists and the public at large, and he must consequently display a greater degree of tolerance. (para 42)

What about pressure groups? In *Steel and Morris v United Kingdom* [2005] ECHR 68416/01 (the so-called 'McDonald's libel case') the ECtHR stated that

> [t]he Court considers, however, that in a democratic society even small and informal campaign groups ... must be able to carry on their activities effectively and that there exists a strong public interest in enabling such groups and individuals outside the mainstream to contribute to the public debate by disseminating information and ideas on matters of general public interest such as health and the environment ... If, however, a State decides to provide such a remedy [defamation] to a corporate body,

it is essential, in order to safeguard the countervailing interests in free expression and open debate, that a measure of procedural fairness and equality of arms is provided for. ... (paras 89 and 95)

27.5.6.2 Prior restraint

The use of injunctions to prevent publication of material in advance is viewed with suspicion by the ECtHR. In the *Spycatcher* case (*Guardian Newspapers v United Kingdom* (1992) 14 EHRR 153) it said:

[T]he dangers inherent in prior restraint are such that they call for the most careful scrutiny ... News is a perishable commodity and to delay its publication, even for a short period, may well deprive it of all its value and interest. (para 60)

For example, a journalist was denied an injunction restraining the BBC from broadcasting his image as part of a documentary exposing alleged wrongdoing in investigative journalism, because the evidence had not demonstrated that the risk of harm to him would be materially increased (*Mahmood v BBC* [2014] EWHC 4207 (QB)). However, in *OPO v MLA* [2014] EWCA Civ 1277, an injunction was granted restraining the defendant, a talented performing artist, from publishing a book describing his traumatic upbringing, which included the suffering of sexual abuse. The claimant was the defendant's autistic young son, and the Court held that he had sufficiently favourable prospects of establishing at trial his claim that publication would constitute intentional conduct causing him psychiatric harm.

The concern which the Strasbourg Court has is reflected in s 12 of the HRA 1998 (see the **Appendix to Part IV**).

In *Cream Holdings Ltd and Others v Banerjee and Others* [2004] UKHL 44, the House of Lords stated:

Section 12(3) makes the likelihood of success at trial an essential element in the court's consideration of whether to make an interim order. ... There can be no single, rigid standard governing all applications for interim restraint orders. Rather, on its proper construction the effect of section 12(3) is that the court is not to make an interim restraint order unless satisfied the applicant's prospects of success at the trial are sufficiently favourable to justify such an order being made in the particular circumstances of the case. As to what degree of likelihood makes the prospects of success 'sufficiently favourable', the general approach should be that courts will be exceedingly slow to make interim restraint orders where the applicant has not satisfied the court he will probably ('more likely than not') succeed at the trial. In general, that should be the threshold an applicant must cross before the court embarks on exercising its discretion, duly taking into account the relevant jurisprudence on article 10 and any countervailing Convention rights. But there will be cases where it is necessary for a court to depart from this general approach and a lesser degree of likelihood will suffice as a prerequisite. Circumstances where this may be so include those mentioned above: where the potential adverse consequences of disclosure are particularly grave, or where a short-lived injunction is needed to enable the court to hear and give proper consideration to an application for interim relief pending the trial or any relevant appeal.

The Supreme Court in *PJS v News Group Newspapers Ltd* [2016] UKSC 26 held that: (i) neither Article 8 nor Article 10 has preference over the other; (ii) where their values are in conflict, what is necessary is an intense focus on the comparative importance of the rights being claimed in the individual case; (iii) the justifications for interfering with or restricting each right must be taken into account; and (iv) the proportionality test must be applied.

27.5.7 Article 11: The right to freedom of assembly and association

1. Everyone has the right to freedom of peaceful assembly and to freedom of association with others, including the right to form and to join trade unions for the protection of his interests.

2. No restrictions shall be placed on the exercise of these rights other than such as are prescribed by law and are necessary in a democratic society in the interests of national security or public safety, for the prevention of disorder or crime, for the protection of health or morals or for the protection of the rights and freedoms of others. This Article shall not prevent the imposition of

lawful restrictions on the exercise of these rights by members of the armed forces, of the police or of the administration of the State.

This Article contains two distinct rights: freedom of peaceful assembly and freedom of association.

27.5.7.1 Freedom of peaceful assembly

This extends to anyone who intends to organise a peaceful march or static assembly. The possibility of violence arising because of the intentions of counter-demonstrators or extremist infiltrators does not affect the right (*Christians Against Racism and Fascism v United Kingdom* (1980) 21 DR 138). By exercising the right on a public highway, the protesters' activities must not become a nuisance nor unreasonably impede the right of others to pass (see *Secretary of State for the Environment, Food and Rural Affairs v Meier* [2009] UKSC 11). So whilst protesters might assemble peacefully in a public place such as St Paul's Cathedral in London, they are not entitled to establish a substantial encampment of tents on the highway there (see *City of London v Tammy Samede* (*representative of those persons taking part in a protest camp at St Paul's Churchyard, London EC4*) [2012] EWHC 34).

The sorts of restrictions which para 2 envisages include limitations on the location of a demonstration or the route of a march.

Does the right to peaceful assembly under Article 11 mean that the police force has a responsibility to facilitate peaceful protests even if they are technically unlawful? No, held the Supreme Court in *DB v Chief Constable of Police Service of Northern Ireland* [2017] UKSC 7. At para 60 the Court quoted with approval the decision in *Eva Molnar v Hungary* (Application No 10346/05), where the ECtHR considered a complaint that the applicant's rights under Article 11 had been infringed by police dispersing a peaceful demonstration in which she had participated, merely because prior notification of the protest had not been given. At paras 34–38 the ECtHR said this:

> 34. The Court observes that paragraph 2 of article 11 entitles States to impose 'lawful restrictions' on the exercise of the right to freedom of assembly. The Court notes that restrictions on freedom of peaceful assembly in public places may serve the protection of the rights of others with a view to preventing disorder and maintaining the orderly circulation of traffic.
>
> 35. The Court reiterates that a prior notification requirement would not normally encroach upon the essence of that right. It is not contrary to the spirit of article 11 if, for reasons of public order and national security, *a priori*, a High Contracting Party requires that the holding of meetings be subject to authorisation (see *Nurettin Aldemir v Turkey*, nos 32124/02, 32126/02, 32129/02, 32132/02, 32133/02, 32137/02 and 32138/02 (joined) [2007] ECHR 1121, para 42, 18 December 2007).
>
> 36. However, in special circumstances when an immediate response might be justified, for example in relation to a political event, in the form of a spontaneous demonstration, to disperse the ensuing demonstration solely because of the absence of the requisite prior notice, without any illegal conduct by the participants, may amount to a disproportionate restriction on freedom of peaceful assembly (see *Bukta*, cited above, paras 35 and 36). It is important for the public authorities to show a certain degree of tolerance towards peaceful gatherings if the freedom of assembly guaranteed by article 11 of the Convention is not to be deprived of all substance (see *Nurettin Aldemir*, cited above, para 46).
>
> 37. Nevertheless, in the Court's view, the principle established in the case of *Bukta* cannot be extended to the point that the absence of prior notification can never be a legitimate basis for crowd dispersal. Prior notification serves not only the aim of reconciling, on the one hand, the right to assembly and, on the other hand, the rights and lawful interests (including the right of movement) of others, but also the prevention of disorder or crime. In order to balance these conflicting interests, the institution of preliminary administrative procedures is common practice in member states when a public demonstration is to be organised. In the Court's view, such requirements do not, as such, run counter to the principles embodied in article 11 of the Convention, as long as they do not represent a hidden obstacle to the freedom of peaceful

assembly protected by the Convention (see *Balcik v Turkey*, no 25/02, para 49, 29 November 2007).

38. The Court therefore considers that the right to hold spontaneous demonstrations may override the obligation to give prior notification to public assemblies only in special circumstances, namely if an immediate response to a current event is warranted in the form of a demonstration. In particular, such derogation from the general rule may be justified if a delay would have rendered that response obsolete.

27.5.7.2 Freedom of association

This covers the right of individuals to join together, especially in organisations like political parties and trade unions. It also extends to the right not to join such organisations. For example, compulsory membership of a union (a 'closed shop') will usually be contrary to the Convention (*Young, James and Webster v United Kingdom* (1982) 4 EHRR 38).

The right does not extend to a right to negotiate with employers via collective bargaining (*Swedish Engine Drivers' Union v Sweden* (1976) 1 EHRR 617). Neither does it include a right to strike (*Schmidt and Dahlstrom v Sweden* (1979–80) 1 EHRR 632). But it does include the right to claim for unfair dismissal from employment based on political affiliation or opinion (*Redfearn v UK* [2012] ECHR 1878).

27.5.8 Article 14: The prohibition on discrimination

The enjoyment of the rights and freedoms set forth in this Convention shall be secured without discrimination on any ground such as sex, race, colour, language, religion, political or other opinion, national or social origin, association with a national minority, property, birth or other status.

Article 14 is not as important as it may at first appear. It is vital to realise that the right not to be discriminated against cannot be relied upon on its own. It may only be invoked in conjunction with another Convention right.

As the Court has consistently held, Article 14 of the Convention complements the other substantive provisions of the Convention and the Protocols. It has no independent existence since it has effect solely in relation to 'the enjoyment of the rights and freedoms' safeguarded by those provisions. Although the application of Article 14 does not presuppose a breach of those provisions – and to this extent it is autonomous – there can be no room for its application unless the facts at issue fall within the ambit of one or more of the latter. (*Van Raalte v Netherlands* (1997) 24 EHRR 503 at para 33)

A claimant relying on Article 14 must first establish that a substantive Convention right is in issue. There need not necessarily have been a breach of that right. It must only be shown that the facts fall within the ambit of that provision. What Article 14 prohibits is discrimination. What this means is that if there is a prejudicial difference in treatment of persons in relevantly similar situations on the facts of the particular case, the difference in treatment must have an objective and reasonable justification (see, for example, R (*Chester*) *v Secretary of State for Justice* [2013] UKSC 63). In deciding whether there has been discrimination in this sense, the position of the claimant must be compared with that of those in 'relevantly similar or analogous' situations (*Larkos v Cyprus* (1990) 30 EHRR 597). If there is a prejudicial difference in treatment, that difference in treatment must pursue a legitimate aim and bear a reasonable relationship to the aim sought to be realised (*Belgian Linguistic Case (No 2)* (1979–80) 1 EHRR 252). There are, therefore, two distinct questions: (i) has there been disadvantageous treatment of persons in relevantly similar situations; and (ii) if so, does it have reasonable and objective justification?

CASE EXAMPLES

(1) *Abdulaziz v United Kingdom; Cabales v United Kingdom; Balkandali v United Kingdom* (1985) 7 EHRR 471, an immigration case. The exclusion from the UK of spouses of new entrants in certain circumstances was held not to breach Article 8. However, the admission of the spouses of male entrants but the exclusion of spouses of female entrants breached Article 14.

(2) *R (on the application of Chapti) v Secretary of State for the Home Department* [2011] EWHC 3370, an immigration case. The requirement that a foreign spouse applying to settle in the UK with his or her partner had to produce a test certificate of knowledge of the English language engaged Article 8. However, the aims of the rule, namely to promote integration and to protect public services, were legitimate aims and did not amount to a disproportionate interference with family life. Was Article 14 breached because nationals of English-speaking countries and those with educational qualifications that were taught in English or obtained from institutions in English-speaking countries were exempt from the requirement? No, held the court, this was rational in the light of the aims of the rule. Further, there was no evidence that the rule indirectly discriminated on the grounds of nationality, ethnic origins or disability.

(3) *Humphreys v Revenue & Customs Commissioners* [2010] EWCA Civ 56, a social security case. The claimant was the father of a child for whom he claimed child tax credits. The refusal of that claim engaged Article 1 of the First Protocol (see **27.5.9**). The refusal was based on the fact that he was the child's minority carer. His mother was awarded the child tax credit as she cared for the child more nights each week. Whilst this was discrimination for the purposes of Article 14, the Court of Appeal held that it was justified. See also *R (on the application of SG) v Secretary of State for Work and Pensions* [2014] EWCA Civ 156.

You will have noted that Article 14 ends with the words 'other status'. Who might fall within that category? The ECtHR has interpreted this as meaning a personal characteristic (see *Kjeldsen, Busk Madsen and Pedersen v Denmark* (1976) 1 EHRR 711, para 56). It is therefore necessary to examine whether the ground for different treatment in a case amounts to a status in the sense of a personal characteristic (see *R (on the application of S) v Chief Constable of South Yorkshire* [2004] UKHL 39). This led the Court of Appeal, for example, in *R (on the application of RJM) v Secretary of State for Work and Pensions* [2007] EWCA Civ 614, to hold that a person who chooses to be homeless or to sleep rough does not fall within this provision. 'Impecuniosity', at any rate if defined by reference to an inability to pay a particular government fee, is not a relevant status for the purposes of Article 14: *R (on the application of Williams (by his litigation friend)) v Secretary of State for the Home Department* [2017] EWCA Civ 98.

27.5.9 Protocol 1, Article 1: The right to peaceful enjoyment of possessions

Every natural or legal person is entitled to the peaceful enjoyment of his possessions.

No one shall be deprived of his possessions except in the public interest and subject to the conditions provided for by law and by the general principles of international law.

The preceding provisions shall not, however, in any way impair the right of a State to enforce such laws as it deems necessary to control the use of property in accordance with the general interest or to secure the payment of taxes or other contributions or penalties.

'Possessions' in this Article has a wide meaning. It includes, amongst other things, land, money, shares and goodwill.

The Article contains two distinct rights:

(a) the right not to be deprived of possessions, subject to certain conditions; and

(b)   the right not to have the State control possessions, subject to certain conditions.

Deprivation covers situations in which title is transferred or extinguished, for example the creation of a presumption of title in land in favour of the State (*Holy Monasteries v Greece* (1994) 20 EHRR 1). Control covers situations falling short of this, for example limiting the amount of rent which a landlord may charge, placing restrictions upon developing property and rules restricting rights of inheritance.

In both cases interference with the right is permissible in the public interest or the general interest (a distinction which is of little importance). The guiding principle is one of fair balance between individual and community interests. In striking this balance regard must always be had to the principle of proportionality (see **27.5.2**) and the split Court of Appeal decision upholding the legislation banning the sale of tobacco from automatic vending machines: *R (on the application of Sinclair Collis Ltd) v Secretary of State for Health* [2011] EWCA Civ 437.

In *Hammersmith and Fulham LBC v Monk* [1992] 1 AC 478, it was held that at common law a periodic joint residential tenancy is terminated automatically if one joint tenant unilaterally serves a notice to quit on the landlord. Is that incompatible with the other joint tenant's rights under Protocol 1, Article 1? No, held the Supreme Court in *Sims v Dacorum BC* [2014] UKSC 63. A husband had no right to remain in a local authority property as a sole tenant after his wife had left and given notice to the local authority landlord quitting the joint tenancy.

27.5.10   Identifying and addressing Convention rights

27.5.10.1   Has there been an interference with a Convention right?

Do the facts complained of disclose an interference with the enjoyment of any particular right or rights?

CASE EXAMPLE 1

Assume that you are a solicitor and a court has made a wasted costs order against you. What rights might be relevant? Is the order a determination of your civil rights such that Article 6 is engaged? Or is it a criminal charge for the purposes of that Article? Otherwise, is it an interference with your possessions for the purposes of the First Protocol, Article 1? In fact the ECtHR has already answered all these questions in the negative (see, eg, *Tormala v Finland* (2004) Application No 41528/98).

CASE EXAMPLE 2

Assume that you are protesting peacefully against an arms fair being held in London. You are stopped by two police officers and searched. You are handed a copy of Stop/Search Form 5090 which records that you were stopped and searched under s 44 of the Terrorism Act 2000. The search was said to be for 'articles concerned in terrorism'. The whole incident lasts about 20 minutes. What rights might be engaged? Have you been deprived of your liberty under Article 5? Has there been a lack of respect for your private life such that Article 8 is engaged? Have your rights to free expression and free assembly protected by Articles 10 and 11 been infringed? The House of Lords (now the Supreme Court) answered all of these questions in the negative (or otherwise felt that the measures were justified): see *R (on the application of Gillan and Another) v Commissioner of Police for the Metropolis and Another* [2006] UKHL 12. However, for a similar case where the House of Lords held that Articles 10 and 11 were infringed, see *R (on the application of Laporte) v Chief Constable of Gloucestershire* [2006] UKHL 55. Moreover, when the *Gillian* case was heard by the Grand Chamber of the ECtHR, it held that Article 8 was engaged and infringed (see [2010] ECHR 28 (Application No 4158/05)).

> **CASE EXAMPLE 3**
>
> In R *(on the application of Naik) v Secretary of State for the Home Department* [2011] EWCA Civ 1546, the applicant was a leading Muslim writer and public speaker. In 2010, two days before he was due to arrive in the UK on a lecture tour, the Secretary of State excluded him and revoked his existing visa on the basis that he had made a number of statements supporting terrorism. As a foreign national outside the UK, could he rely on Article 10? The Court of Appeal held that Article 10 was engaged in respect of the applicant's supporters in the UK and (without deciding the issue) possibly also in respect of the applicant personally.

How are you going to be able to identify relevant rights in the future? You need to have in mind the structure of the Articles. A breakdown of the key Articles by way of a checklist appears in the **Appendix to Part IV.**

Once any particular qualified right has been identified, the following questions need to be answered. The detail may be found at **27.5.2.3** above:

(a)   Is the interference prescribed by law?

(b)   Does the interference have a legitimate aim under the relevant Article?

(c)   Is the interference proportionate?

(d)   Is the interference within any appropriate margin of appreciation?

> **CASE EXAMPLE**
>
> In *Connors v UK* (2004) Application No 66746/01, the applicant, a gypsy, complained that he and his family had been evicted by a local authority from its gypsy caravan site in breach of Article 8.
>
> The parties were agreed that Article 8 was engaged as the eviction of the applicant from the site on which he had lived with his family in his caravan disclosed an interference with his right to respect for his private life, family life and home. The parties were also agreed, in the context of the second paragraph of Article 8, that the interference was in accordance with the law and pursued a legitimate aim, namely, the protection of the rights of other occupiers of the site by the local authority which owned and managed the site. The question for the Court was whether the interference was 'necessary in a democratic society' in pursuit of that aim, ie if there was a 'pressing social need' and, in particular, if it was proportionate to the legitimate aim pursued. As to the scope of the margin of appreciation, the Court indicated that this depends on the context of the case, with particular significance attaching to the extent of the intrusion into the personal sphere of the applicant. The procedural safeguards available to the individual are especially material in determining whether the respondent State has, when fixing the regulatory framework, remained within its margin of appreciation. In particular, the court must examine whether the decision-making process leading to measures of interference was fair and such as to afford due respect to the interests safeguarded to the individual by Article 8.
>
> The Court found that the eviction of the applicant and his family from the local authority site was not attended by the requisite procedural safeguards, namely the requirement to establish proper justification for the serious interference with his rights. Consequently it could not be regarded as justified by a 'pressing social need' or proportionate to the legitimate aim being pursued. There had, accordingly, been a violation of Article 8 of the Convention.

27.5.10.2   Everyday situations in which the HRA 1998 might apply

In June 2009 the Commission for Equality and Human Rights (CEHR – see **28.5**) published a report entitled, *Human Rights Inquiry*. At Chapter 1, section 3, it produced a list of everyday situations in which the HRA 1998 might apply. This is reproduced in the **Appendix to Part IV**.

27.5.10.3   Business and human rights

The publication entitled 'Guiding Principles on Business and Human Rights: Implementing the United Nations "Protect, Respect and Remedy" Framework' recognises the important role that business plays in society and the need for business to respect human rights. In particular, it identifies that business enterprises should:

(a)   avoid infringing on the human rights of others and should address adverse human rights impacts with which they are involved;

(b)   avoid causing or contributing to adverse human rights impacts through their own activities, and address such impacts when they occur;

(c)   prevent or mitigate adverse human rights impacts that are directly linked to their operations, products or services by their business relationships, even if they have not contributed to those impacts;

(d)   put in place policies and processes that include a policy commitment to meet their responsibility to respect human rights; a human rights due diligence process to identify, prevent, mitigate and account for how they address their impacts on human rights; and processes to enable the remediation of any adverse human rights impacts they cause or to which they contribute.

A copy of the document is available at <http://www.ohchr.org/Documents/Publications/GuidingPrinciplesBusinessHR_EN.pdf>.

Legislation is starting to push this agenda forward. For example, the Modern Slavery Act 2015 requires certain businesses to prepare and publish a slavery and trafficking statement for each financial year from the year ending 31 March 2016. Further examples of how businesses can impact certain human rights can be found in the 'Reference Annex to the IBA Practical Guide on Business and Human Rights for Business Lawyers'. This is reproduced in the **Appendix to Part IV**. A copy of the entire document is available at <http://www.ibanet.org/LPRU/Reference-Annex-to-the-IBA-Practical-Guide.aspx>.

See also the Equality and Human Rights Commission's publication, 'Business and human rights: a seven-step guide for managers'. A copy of the document is available at <https://www.equalityhumanrights.com/en/human-rights/business-and-human-rights-seven-step-guide-managers>.

27.6   PETITIONING THE COURT IN STRASBOURG

27.6.1   Introduction

Despite the HRA 1998, there will be situations where an individual is denied a remedy under UK law, for example because primary legislation is clearly incompatible with the Convention, or because there is some gap in the legislation which cannot be filled by the common law and in either case the Government will not make amends. In such cases, the individual can petition the ECtHR in Strasbourg. This will be the last resort, however, as the Convention requires the applicant to exhaust domestic remedies (including the HRA 1998) before going to Strasbourg.

27.6.2   Procedural law of the ECHR

A complaint will be addressed to the Secretary of the Court of Human Rights. The initial complaint does not need to be on a special form, although one would have to be completed eventually. Under the rules made under the Eleventh Protocol, a chamber of the court will determine admissibility. Around 90% of complaints are ruled inadmissible, usually because of failure to exhaust domestic remedies, or because they are 'manifestly ill-founded' or because they fail to meet the time-limit of six months from the exhaustion of the final domestic remedy. The initial decision on admissibility will be taken by a committee of three.

Once the committee has judged a complaint admissible, the ECtHR will try to reach a friendly settlement with the government concerned, which must include the reform of any offending rules. Failing a settlement, there will be further submissions, including an oral hearing at which, as well as the parties, relevant organisations like Liberty or Justice may be represented. The ECtHR (usually a chamber of seven, but exceptionally a Grand Chamber of 17) may award compensation as part of its judgment, but the judgment itself does not change the law in the UK. That is a matter for the UK Government. There is also a right of appeal to the Grand Chamber on issues of general importance (subject to the permission of the first chamber). The Rules of Court were published in January 2014 and can be found on the ECtHR website. A flowchart summarising the procedure follows.

THE HUMAN RIGHTS ACT 1998

LEARNING OUTCOMES

After reading this chapter you will have learned:

- how the Convention affects statutory interpretation
- when a declaration of incompatibly may be made
- what public authorities fall within the HRA 1998
- what is meant by the doctrine of direct effect
- the procedure for using the HRA 1998
- when damages might be awarded under the HRA 1998
- the role of the Equality and Human Rights Commission.

28.1 INTRODUCTION

> It is clear that the 1998 Act must be given its full import and that long or well entrenched ideas may have to be put aside, sacred cows culled. (per Lord Slynn in R v Lambert [2001] UKHL 37 at para 6)

In brief, the effect of the HRA 1998 is to make it possible for litigants in the UK to rely on Convention rights in our own domestic courts without the delay and expense incurred by taking the case to the ECtHR in Strasbourg. The constitutional issues which are raised by this are potentially momentous. Giving the judiciary a yardstick against which they can measure UK legislation and find it to be wanting has obvious impacts on the traditional conception of parliamentary supremacy. The HRA 1998 attempts to defuse this by the device of the declaration of incompatibility (see **28.3.3**). It also shifts power towards the judiciary, giving them greater scope to determine difficult, perhaps emotive and politically charged questions. This raises questions about the accountability of our judges.

28.1.1 Five central planks

There are five central planks of the HRA 1998. First, all legislation, whether primary or subordinate, must, if possible, be interpreted so as to be compatible with the ECHR. Secondly, where it is not possible to interpret primary legislation so as to be compatible with the ECHR, certain courts can make a declaration of incompatibility. Thirdly, where it is not possible to interpret subordinate legislation so as to be compatible with the Convention, the courts have power to disapply it. Fourthly, all public authorities, including courts and tribunals, must, if possible, act in a way that is compatible with the ECHR. Lastly, individuals who believe that their ECHR rights have been infringed by a public authority can rely on the ECHR to take proceedings in English courts rather than having to apply to Strasbourg.

28.1.2 Practice areas

All lawyers in the UK must bear Convention rights in mind. These rights have much more impact in some areas of law than others. For example, criminal law and immigration practitioners need to have regard to the HRA 1998 on a day-to-day basis. However, the HRA 1998 requires that all legislation be read in accordance with Convention rights and that all public authorities make their decisions in accordance with them: any lawyer who makes use of legislation or who has dealings with organs of the State does so against the backdrop of the HRA 1998.

28.2 CONVENTION RIGHTS

The concept of Convention rights is central to the HRA 1998. There are certain rights from the ECHR which are listed in Sch 1 to the 1998 Act. The most important are those discussed in **Chapter 27**.

Section 2 requires that any court or tribunal determining a Convention right must take into account any decision of the Strasbourg institutions, in particular judgments of the ECtHR. Notice that these decisions are not binding in the same way that decisions of higher courts within the UK are, or even decisions of the Court of Justice in the context of EU law. Decisions of the Strasbourg Court need only be taken into account. Clearly, they will be highly persuasive, but should a UK court feel the need to decide the matter differently then it is free to do so. See, for example, R *v Horncastle* [2009] UKSC 14.

Decisions on the meaning to be given to Convention rights may involve UK courts and lawyers looking further afield than Strasbourg. The House of Lords (now the Supreme Court) accepted that it is appropriate to look to case law from other jurisdictions in determining such matters (R *v Khan* [1997] AC 558). Most other countries have an established constitutional human rights document with a well-developed jurisprudence, especially those from common law jurisdictions such as New Zealand and Canada.

28.3 THE MECHANISMS OF THE ACT

28.3.1 Introduction

The HRA 1998 seeks to give Convention rights effect in UK law through two pathways. Whenever legislation is relevant, lawyers are able to rely on a rule of statutory interpretation that legislation should be read in line with Convention rights. Even where there is no legislation in issue, all public authorities have an obligation to act in accordance with Convention rights.

28.3.2 The interpretative obligation

Section 3(1) reads:

> So far as it is possible to do so, primary legislation and subordinate legislation must be read and given effect in a way which is compatible with the Convention rights.

This interpretative obligation applies whether the legislation in question was passed before or after the HRA 1998. All legislation must be read in such a way as to be compatible with Convention rights, even if it is unambiguous, so long as the wording will bear such an interpretation.

> **CASE EXAMPLES**
>
> (1)   In *Re* S [2002] 2 AC 313, Lord Nicholls described s 3 as 'a powerful tool whose use is obligatory' (para 38). He acknowledged, however, the difficulty of 'identifying the limits of interpretation in a particular case', adding (at para 40): 'For present purposes it is sufficient to say that a meaning which departs substantially from a fundamental feature of an Act of Parliament is likely to have crossed the boundary between interpretation and amendment. This is especially so where the departure has important practical repercussions which the court is not equipped to evaluate ...'. In that case it was held that the proposed re-interpretation (favoured by a majority of the Court of Appeal) would have departed fundamentally from the legislative scheme. Where Parliament had entrusted to local authorities, not the courts, the responsibility for looking after children subject to care orders, the proposed interpretation (involving a so-called 'starring system') would have enabled the court to exercise a 'newly created supervisory function' (para 42).
>
> (2)   The case of R *v* A (No 2) [2002] 1 AC 45 concerned the provisions of the Youth and Criminal Evidence Act 1999 that protected complainants in proceedings for sexual offences. Section 41 placed strict limits on the scope for evidence or cross-examination of complainants about their own sexual behaviour. As Lord Steyn said, the practically 'blanket exclusion' of prior sexual history between the complainant and the accused posed 'an acute problem of proportionality' (para 30). Notwithstanding the apparently clear language of the section, it was held that it could be re-interpreted under s 3 to the extent that justice required the admission of such evidence or cross-examination. Lord Steyn said: 'In my view section 3 requires the court to subordinate the niceties of language of section 41(3)(c), and in particular the touchstone of coincidence, to broader considerations of relevance judged by logical and common sense criteria of time and circumstance. After all, it is realistic to proceed on the basis that the legislature would not, if alerted to the problem, have wished to deny the right to an accused to put forward a full and complete defence by advancing truly probative material.' It was held that the section should be read as subject to an implied provision that 'evidence or questioning required to ensure a fair trial under Article 6 of the Convention should not be treated as inadmissible' (para 45).

28.3.2.1   Nature of opponent irrelevant

This principle applies whether the other party is public or private. So long as a litigant can find a piece of legislation to which the Convention right can be pinned, the nature of his opponent does not matter. For example, R (*on the application of Sacker*) *v HM Coroner for the County of West Yorkshire* [2004] UKHL 11 involved an inquest into a prisoner's death. The House of Lords (now the Supreme Court) had to rule on the interpretation of the word 'how' in s 11(5) of the Coroners Act 1988, in the context of 'how' the prisoner had died. In order to protect Article 2 rights, the House of Lords held that it was not simply to be interpreted as meaning 'by what means', but rather 'by what means in and in what circumstances'.

28.3.2.2   Ministerial statements

Section 19 gives judges an extra spur to find a construction which is compatible with Convention rights. It provides that all Bills introduced into Parliament must be accompanied by a statement from the sponsoring Minister on the compatibility or otherwise of the Bill with Convention rights. Clearly, Ministers will almost invariably make statements of compatibility: were a Minister to stand up and state that a Bill did not comply with Convention rights, some very good reasons why it should be enacted in spite of this would have to be provided. The doctrine in *Pepper v Hart* [1993] AC 59 allows the courts to look to such ministerial statements in *Hansard* as background evidence of parliamentary intention (see *Wilson v Secretary for Trade and Industry* [2003] UKHL 40). Equipped with such evidence, courts may feel especially justified in straining legislative wording where necessary to give it a meaning compatible with Convention rights. Indeed, in *R v A (No 2)* [2002] 1 AC 45, Lord Hope observed (at para 69):

> These statements may serve a useful purpose in Parliament. They may also be seen as part of the parliamentary history, indicating that it was not Parliament's intention to cut across a Convention right ... No doubt they are based on the best advice that is available. But they are no more than expressions of opinion by the minister. They are not binding on the court, nor do they have any persuasive authority.

28.3.3   Declarations of incompatibility

Section 4 applies to higher courts (the High Court, Crown Courts, the Employment Appeals Tribunal and above). It empowers them to make declarations of incompatibility. This provides a fallback for situations in which a court recognises that legislation does not comply with Convention rights but, because of the clear words used by the legislator, does not feel that it is possible to give it a purposive interpretation. For example, the Divisional Court, the Court of Appeal and the Supreme Court all agreed to make a declaration of incompatibility in respect of s 82 of the Sexual Offences Act 2003 (see *R (on the application of F) v Secretary of State for the Home Department* [2010] UKSC 17). Why? The section imposes on all who are sentenced to 30 months' imprisonment or more for a sexual offence a duty to keep the police notified of where they are living and if they travel abroad. As there is no provision in the Act for any individual review of these requirements, the duty was a disproportionate interference with the Article 8 rights of those individuals.

What approach should the court take? In *R (Chester) v Secretary of State for Justice* [2013] UKSC 63, the Supreme Court strongly urged any court that was considering remedies under the HRA 1998 to adopt the practice of asking in what way the particular claimant's Convention rights had been violated. As Baroness Hales observed at [102]:

> That leaves the possibility of a declaration of incompatibility under section 4(2) of the Human Rights Act 1998. This applies 'in any proceedings in which a court determines whether a provision of primary legislation is compatible with a Convention right': section 4(1). This does appear to leave open the possibility of a declaration in abstracto, irrespective of whether the provision in question is incompatible with the rights of the individual litigant. There may be occasions when that would be appropriate. But in my view the court should be extremely slow to make a declaration of incompatibility at the instance of an individual litigant with whose own rights the provision in question is not incompatible. Any other approach is to invite a multitude of unmeritorious claims.

See also *R (T) v Chief Constable of Greater Manchester Police* [2014] UKSC 35.

28.3.3.1   Declaration must be necessary

Any declaration must be 'necessary'. In *R v HM Attorney General, ex p Rusbridger* [2003] UKHL 38, [2003] 3 All ER 784, a newspaper sought a declaration as to the proper construction of s 3 of the Treason Felony Act 1848 (which made it an offence punishable by imprisonment for life or any shorter period to 'compass by publication to deprive or depose the Queen from the Crown'). No prosecution had been brought under the section since 1883. The newspaper wished to publish a series of articles urging abolition of the monarchy and asked the Attorney-General to clarify the legal position under s 3. He refused. The House of Lords (now the Supreme Court) held that it was not appropriate to bring proceedings against the part of s 3 of the 1848 Act that appeared to criminalise the advocacy of republicanism since it was a relic of a bygone age. The idea that it could survive scrutiny under the HRA 1998 was unreal. It was clear that no one who advocated the abolition of the monarchy by peaceful and constitutional means was at any risk of prosecution or conviction. The litigation was therefore unnecessary and the application was dismissed.

28.3.3.2 Applicant must benefit from declaration

In *Lancashire County Council v Taylor* [2005] EWCA Civ 284, the Court of Appeal had to determine if a litigant can obtain a declaration of incompatibility on a ground from which he cannot benefit. The Court stated that the primary objective of the ECHR is to secure for individuals the rights and freedoms set out in the Convention. The HRA 1998 and the Convention also play an educative role by promoting the observance of human rights and thus the Convention. One way in which this objective is achieved is by requiring a Minister to make a statement of compatibility with regard to any new legislation in accordance with s 9 of the HRA 1998. But it is not the intention of the HRA 1998 or the Convention that members of the public should use these provisions if they are not adversely affected by them to change legislation because they consider that the legislation is incompatible with the Convention.

28.3.3.3 Effect

These declarations are a compromise between the need to provide a remedy in such cases and the attachment of the UK to the doctrine of parliamentary supremacy which prevents courts from striking down Acts of Parliament. They flag up the incompatibility but provide no further redress. They do not affect the continuing operation of the offending legislation (s 4(6)).

Clearing up the aftermath of such a declaration is left to the politically accountable organs of State: the Government and Parliament. Section 10 and Sch 2 allow Ministers to amend an incompatible Act by a 'fast track' procedure rather than having to put amending legislation through the full process in both Houses of Parliament. Broadly speaking, this allows Ministers to lay before Parliament a 'remedial order' amending the offending legislation. The order will take effect after 120 days, so long as no objections are made by either House. In emergencies the remedial order can take effect immediately, but will automatically cease to have effect if not given positive approval by both Houses within 120 days. See, for example, the Terrorism Act 2000 (Remedial) Order 2011 (SI 2011/631) which followed the ECtHR's decision in the case of *Gillian*, detailed in Case Example 2 at **27.5.10.1**.

However, remedial action is optional. The HRA 1998 places no obligation on Ministers to do anything after a declaration of incompatibility is made. Even if they decide to take action, they do not have to do so via the fast track. Remember, though, that the road to Strasbourg is not closed. If a UK court declares legislation to be incompatible with Convention rights and the UK Government does not take adequate steps to put matters right, then a judgment could be sought in the ECtHR. The Government would then have an obligation in international law to act.

28.3.3.4 Subordinate legislation as *ultra vires*

Declarations of incompatibility are reserved in the main for primary legislation, that is Acts of Parliament. Delegated or subordinate legislation (usually made by Ministers under an enabling power in an Act of Parliament) is more easily attacked. Striking out such subordinate legislation does not offend against the principle of parliamentary supremacy. In fact by ensuring that Ministers only use enabling powers in an appropriate way it reinforces the will of Parliament. Because of this, courts have never shied away from ruling subordinate legislation to be ultra vires and therefore inoperative. They will continue to do so in circumstances in which subordinate legislation is incompatible with Convention rights and it is not possible to place a purposive interpretation upon it in accordance with s 3.

28.3.3.5 Worked example

In *Westminster City Council and The First Secretary of State v Morris; R (on the application of Badu) v London Borough of Lambeth and The First Secretary of State* [2005] EWCA Civ 1184, the Court of Appeal declared s 185 of the Housing Act 1996 incompatible. The Court arrived at its decision by taking the following steps.

(a)   The provision made by s 185(4) of the Housing Act 1996 precluding a British parent from establishing a priority need for housing assistance where the claim is based on a resident dependent child who is ineligible for UK citizenship and, therefore, subject to immigration control, was within the ambit of Article 8 of the ECHR.

(b)   The effect of s 185(4), when read with Article 8, was plainly discriminatory within the meaning of Article 14 of the Convention because the differential treatment for which it provides turns on national origin, or on a combination of one or more of the following forms or aspects of status: nationality, immigration control, settled residence and social welfare.

(c)   Regardless of the precise basis of the differential treatment, it could only be justified, particularly under Article 8, if there were 'very weighty' or 'solid' grounds for it, or if it could be shown that it is a proportionate and reasonable response to a perceived need to discourage 'benefit tourism' by British citizens or the 'overstaying' of any of their dependent children subject to immigration control.

(d)   The justification advanced in the proceedings on behalf of the Secretary of State was neither 'very weighty' nor 'solid', nor did it amount to a proportionate and reasonable response by him to his concerns.

(e)   It was not apparent that the Executive in proposing, or Parliament in enacting, s 185(4) gave consideration to its potential discriminatory impact in any of the respects proscribed by Article 14 or to the justification, if any, for it; but even if they did, the enactment of such a provision, with such effect, could not have fallen within even the very wide ambit of discretion allowed to the Government and Parliament in such matters.

(f)   On the issue of compatibility and whether a court should, in the exercise of its discretion under s 4(2) of the HRA 1998, make a declaration of incompatibility, it is immaterial that there may be other forms of statutory protection, and the Court should grant a declaration.

28.3.3.6   Declarations made

In September 2011 the Ministry of Justice published a report detailing the 27 declarations that had been made since the HRA 1998 came into force. The details are reproduced in the **Appendix to Part IV**.

28.3.3.7   'Wait and see'

Increasingly, courts appear reluctant to address the issue of formal remedies. In two high profile cases in 2017, the Supreme Court and Court of Appeal side-stepped human rights issues respectively as follows:

> So far as concerns the [Home Office Immigration] instructions, we have indicated those aspects which require revision. However, given the passage of time, including new legislation, it would be wrong for this court to attempt to indicate how those defects should now be corrected. It is preferable to adjourn the question of remedies to allow time for the Secretary of State to consider her position, and to indicate to the appellants and to the court how she proposes to amend the instructions or other guidance to accord with the law as indicated in this judgment. The court will receive written submissions on such proposals, and consider whether a further hearing is necessary. (R *(on the application of MM (Lebanon)) v Secretary of State for the Home Department* [2017] UKSC 10 at para 110)

> It is not the role of the court to set a deadline for compliance and the function of the court is certainly not to micro-manage areas of social and economic policy, particularly in sensitive areas such as this where changes will affect society as a whole. It is the court's role to say whether or not the discriminatory measure and the Government's decision to undertake a proper assessment of the optimum way forward in the light of the demand by couples (whether same-sex or different-sex) for civil partnerships as well as marriage is objectively justified now. I therefore do not think it is appropriate to set a deadline for the Government or to give any concrete indication as to when the discriminatory measure will no longer be justified. I do, however, note that as time passes it will

become increasingly difficult to persuade the court that there is still a need to 'wait and see' or that an approach to civil partnership primarily based on the demand for that status by same-sex couples alone is justifiable. The Government will have to decide whether to abolish the status of civil partnership or extend it to different-sex couples and it is for the Government and for Parliament to decide how to keep the matter under active review. (per Beatson LJ at para 162 in *Keidan v Secretary of State for Education* [2017] EWCA Civ 81)

28.3.4 Public authorities

Public authorities may find themselves challenged because the statutory framework within which they operate gives rise to the indirect application of Convention rights via the interpretative obligation as described in **28.3.2**. However, in addition, the Convention can be applied directly to their activities: it is not necessary for a litigant first to find a legislative provision to interpret purposively. Section 6(1) provides simply:

> It is unlawful for a public authority to act in a way which is incompatible with a Convention right.

28.3.4.1 What is a public authority?

Section 6 does not fully define public authority but does say that it includes 'any person certain of whose functions are functions of a public nature'. The dividing line between public and private bodies is a difficult one to draw. The question has exercised the minds of judicial review lawyers for some time because only public bodies are susceptible to judicial review (eg, *R v Panel on Takeovers and Mergers, ex p Datafin plc* [1987] QB 815). It has also been an issue for EU lawyers because of the important distinction between the horizontal and vertical effect in EU law (eg, *Foster v British Gas Case* (C-188/89) [1990] ECR I-3133). For the purposes of the HRA 1998 there is no doubt that the departments of central government are public authorities, nor that local government is a public authority. Large companies which exercise quasi-public regulatory authorities are likely to be regarded as public authorities when exercising their public functions. But there are many grey areas which will doubtless be a fertile ground for litigation.

There are two decisions of the House of Lords (now the Supreme Court) which inform the approach courts should take when determining whether a body is a public body within the meaning of the HRA 1998. These are *Aston Cantlow and Wilmcote with Billisley Parochial Church Council v Wallbank* [2003] UKHL 37 and *YL v Birmingham City Council* [2007] UKHL 27. In *R (on the application of Weaver) v London & Quadrant Housing Trust* [2009] EWCA Civ 587, Elias LJ summarised the following principles from these cases:

(1)   The purpose of section 6 is to identify those bodies which are carrying out functions which will engage the responsibility of the UK before the ECtHR.

(2)   In conformity with that purpose, a public body is one whose nature is, in a broad sense, governmental. However, it does not follow that all bodies exercising such functions are necessarily public bodies; many functions of a kind historically performed by government are also exercised by private bodies, and increasingly so with the growth of privatisation. Moreover, this is only a guide since the phrase used in the Act is public function and not governmental function.

(3)   In determining whether a body is a public authority, the courts should adopt what Lord Mance in *YL* described as a 'factor-based approach' (para 91). This requires the court to have regard to all the features or factors which may cast light on whether the particular function under consideration is a public function or not, and weigh them in the round.

(4)   In applying this test, a broad or generous application of section 6(3)(b) should be adopted.

(5)   In *Aston Cantlow* Lord Nicholls said (para 12) that the factors to be taken into account 'include the extent to which in carrying out the relevant function the body is publicly funded, or is exercising statutory powers, or is taking the place of central government or local authorities, or is providing a public service.'

(6)   As to public funding, it was pointed out that it is misleading to say that a body is publicly subsidised merely because it enters into a commercial contract with a public body (Lord Scott,

para 27; Lord Neuberger para 141). As Lord Mance observed (para 105): 'Public funding takes various forms. The injection of capital or subsidy into an organisation in return for undertaking a non-commercial role or activity of general public interest may be one thing; payment for services under a contractual arrangement with a company aiming to profit commercially thereby is potentially quite another.'

(7)   As to the second matter, the exercise of statutory powers, or the conferment of special powers, may be a factor supporting the conclusion that the body is exercising public functions, but it depends why they have been conferred. If it is for private, religious or purely commercial purposes, it will not support the conclusion that the functions are of a public nature: see Lord Mance in YL at paragraph 101. However, Lord Neuberger thought that the 'existence of wide ranging and intrusive set of statutory powers ... is a very powerful factor in favour of the function falling within section 6(3)(b)' and he added that it will often be determinative (para 167).

(8)   The third factor, where a body is to some extent taking the place of central government or local authorities, chimes with Lord Nicholls' observation that generally a public function will be governmental in nature. This was a theme running through the *Aston Cantlow* speeches, as Lord Neuberger pointed out in YL, para 159. That principle will be easy to apply where their powers are formally delegated to the body concerned.

(9)   The fourth factor is whether the body is providing a public service. This should not be confused with performing functions which are in the public interest or for the public benefit. As Lord Mance pointed out in YL (para 105), the self-interested endeavour of individuals generally works to the benefit of society, but that is plainly not enough to constitute such activities public functions. Furthermore, as Lord Neuberger observed (para 135), many private bodies, such as private schools, private hospitals, private landlords, and food retailers, provide goods or services which it is in the public interest to provide. This does not render them public bodies, nor their functions public functions. Usually the public service will be of a governmental nature.

28.3.4.2   Examples

So, for example, the BBC is to be regarded as a public authority under the HRA 1998. When it takes a decision not to broadcast certain matter it must have regard to Article 10, the right to freedom of expression (R *(on the application of ProLife Alliance) v British Broadcasting Corporation* [2002] EWCA Civ 297, [2002] 2 All ER 756). Similarly, the police, when they exercise their powers at common law to arrest to prevent a breach of the peace, must have regard to Article 5, the right to liberty and security of the person. However, a large and flourishing private-sector provider of residential care homes was not a public authority, and did not have to act in accordance with Convention rights when deciding to close a care home, despite the applicant having lived there for 17 years (R *(on the application of Heather and Others) v Leonard Cheshire Foundation* [2002] EWCA Civ 366). See also YL *(by her litigation friend) v Birmingham City Council* [2007] UKHL 27.

28.3.4.3   Defences

Sometimes a public authority will attempt to argue that it had no choice but to act in the way it did because it was merely obeying obligations imposed by an Act of Parliament. In such cases there are two possibilities. The court may use the interpretative obligation in s 3 to read the offending legislation in such a way that the public authority was not restricted as it thought; in such a case, the public authority will be regarded as having made an error of law and an appropriate remedy will be awarded against it. Alternatively, the court may agree with the public authority's reading of the legislation, which may be so clear that it cannot be purposively interpreted in line with Convention rights. In this case, the public authority will have the defence that as a result of the legislation in question it could not have acted differently (s 6(2)) and the other party will have to content themselves with a declaration of incompatibility against the legislation.

28.3.4.4 Acts of a public authority outside the UK

What is the territorial scope of s 6? Does it apply to a public authority that acts both within and outside the UK? In R *(on the application of Al-Skeini) v Secretary of State for Defence* [2007] UKHL 26, the claimants were relatives of Iraqi citizens who, it was claimed, had been unlawfully killed by members of British armed forces in southern Iraq in 2003. The Secretary of State argued that the 1998 Act did not apply outside the territory of the UK and that the deceased had not been within the jurisdiction of the UK for the purposes of Article 1 of the Convention when they were killed. The House of Lords (now the Supreme Court) rejected these arguments. It held that s 6 should be interpreted as applying not only when a public authority acted within the UK, but also when it acted within the jurisdiction of the UK for the purposes of Article 1 of the Convention but outside the territory of the UK. Why? The House of Lords stated that the purpose of the 1998 Act was to provide remedies in domestic law to those whose human rights had been violated by a UK public authority. Making such remedies available for acts of a UK authority in the territory of another State is not offensive to the sovereignty of the other State.

> The exception to the territoriality principle acknowledged in *Al-Skeini* in the case of physical power and control over a person depends on the fact of such physical power and control. Its significance is that it enables the contracting state to act to secure certain Convention rights depending on the circumstances and the degree of physical power and control it possesses. (per Lloyd Jones LJ in *Al-Saadoon v Secretary of State for Defence* [2016] EWCA Civ 811 at para 105)

Do British troops operating on foreign soil fall within the jurisdiction of the UK? In R *(on the application of Smith) v Secretary of State for Defence* [2010] UKSC 29, the Supreme Court held that the answer is yes, but only when a soldier is on a British base. Note, however, that when the ECtHR heard the *Al-Skeini* case referred to above (see [2011] ECHR 1093, Application No 55721/07), the Grand Chamber held (at paras 149 and 150):

> It can be seen, therefore, that following the removal from power of the Ba'ath regime and until the accession of the Interim Government, the United Kingdom (together with the United States) assumed in Iraq the exercise of some of the public powers normally to be exercised by a sovereign government. In particular, the United Kingdom assumed authority and responsibility for the maintenance of security in South East Iraq. In these exceptional circumstances, the Court considers that the United Kingdom, through its soldiers engaged in security operations in Basrah during the period in question, exercised authority and control over individuals killed in the course of such security operations, so as to establish a jurisdictional link between the deceased and the United Kingdom for the purposes of Article 1 of the Convention.

> Against this background, the Court recalls that the deaths at issue in the present case occurred during the relevant period: the fifth applicant's son died on 8 May 2003; the first and fourth applicants' brothers died in August 2003; the sixth applicant's son died in September 2003; and the spouses of the second and third applicants died in November 2003. It is not disputed that the deaths of the first, second, fourth, fifth and sixth applicants' relatives were caused by the acts of British soldiers during the course of or contiguous to security operations carried out by British forces in various parts of Basrah City. It follows that in all these cases there was a jurisdictional link for the purposes of Article 1 of the Convention between the United Kingdom and the deceased. The third applicant's wife was killed during an exchange of fire between a patrol of British soldiers and unidentified gunmen and it is not known which side fired the fatal bullet. The Court considers that, since the death occurred in the course of a United Kingdom security operation, when British soldiers carried out a patrol in the vicinity of the applicant's home and joined in the fatal exchange of fire, there was a jurisdictional link between the United Kingdom and this deceased also.

28.3.5 Direct effect in cases not involving public authorities

There is a significant gap in the way in which the HRA 1998 allows Convention rights to be enforced. It would appear from s 6 that Convention rights can only be applied directly against public authorities. Experience from the domain of EU law has shown that this can lead to unfairness. For example, employees of public authorities may enjoy more rights than employees of private authorities. Such an interpretation of s 6 would not prevent claimants against private defendants from relying on the interpretative obligation in s 3. But, to take advantage of the interpretative obligation, they would have to be litigating a point which was dealt with by UK legislation which itself was capable of a Convention-compatible interpretation. Claimants against public authorities would have a simpler solution by applying Convention rights directly under s 6.

However, it would seem that a doctrine of direct effect in cases involving private bodies is being developed by the courts. For example, *Venables and Thompson v News Group Newspapers Ltd and Others* [2001] 2 WLR 1038 involved an application to the court by the two boys convicted of murdering Jamie Bulger. After their release from prison, they wanted an injunction preventing the press from revealing their new identities. Their application was based partly on Article 2 because they feared for their lives should their identities become public. It was argued on their behalf that, because the court is a public authority (the HRA 1998 says so in s 6(3)), the court has a duty under s 6(1) to ensure that Convention rights are protected even when it decides cases involving private litigants. This was accepted by Dame Elizabeth Butler-Sloss. She said (para 24):

> It is clear that, although operating in the public domain and fulfilling a public service, the defendant newspapers cannot sensibly be said to come within the definition of public authority in s 6(1) of the 1998 Act. Consequently, Convention rights are not directly enforceable against the defendants ... That is not, however, the end of the matter, since the court is a public authority, see s 6(3), and must itself act in a way compatible with the Convention, see s 6(1), and have regard to European jurisprudence ...

The injunction was granted.

28.4 PROCEDURE FOR USING THE ACT

> One principal achievement of the Act is to enable the Convention rights to be directly invoked in the domestic courts. In that respect the Act is important as a procedural measure which has opened a further means of access to justice for the citizen, more immediate and more familiar than a recourse to the Court in Strasbourg. (per Lord Clyde in *R v Lambert* [2001] UKHL 37 at para 135)

The s 3 interpretative obligation (see **28.3.2**) may be raised in any court or tribunal hearing in which the meaning of a legislative provision needs to be construed.

Many HRA points are raised in criminal proceedings by defendants. This may be on the basis that an Act upon which the prosecution seeks to rely does not bear the meaning which the prosecution attributes to it when s 3 is applied. Alternatively, it may be that the defence wish to raise a 'freestanding' HRA point, not linked to any legislation, that the police or the Crown Prosecution Service have acted contrary to Convention rights and therefore have broken s 6.

The other procedure which is commonly used to raise Convention rights against public authorities is judicial review under CPR, Part 54. Under this procedure, the Divisional Court is well accustomed to scrutinising the decisions of public authorities and measuring them against a variety of standards of legality and procedural fairness. The HRA 1998 adds another string to the bow of judicial review lawyers.

28.4.1 Locus standi test

The HRA 1998 introduces some special procedural rules for s 6 challenges to public authorities. Section 7(1) introduces a *locus standi* test for such challenges. The claimant must be a 'victim' of the unlawful act. Existing Strasbourg case law on this expression says that to qualify a person must be actually and directly affected by the act or omission which is the subject of the complaint. This is a narrower gateway than the usual judicial review test of 'sufficient interest'.

28.4.2 Limitation

Section 6 challenges are also subject to a one-year limitation period from the date on which the offending act took place (s 7(5)).

> As a matter of ordinary language, the wording of section 7(5)(a) contemplates that an 'act' is a single event which occurred on a single date. No express provision is made for an act which extends over a period of time. There is no difficulty in applying this approach in the paradigm case of a single act which takes place at a clearly identifiable point of time. The act should not be confused with its consequences. If it takes place more than one year before proceedings are brought, the claim is barred by section 7(5)(a) even if its consequences do not appear until later. (per the Master of the Rolls in *O'Connor v Bar Standards Board* [2016] EWCA Civ 775 at para 19)

The period may be extended if the court considers it equitable having regard to all the circumstances. As for the approach to the exercise of discretion, see *Williams v London Borough of Hackney* [2017] EWCA Civ 26. At para 85 the Court of Appeal referred to the decision of the Supreme Court in *Rabone v Pennine NHS Trust* [2012] UKSC 1 where Lord Dyson at para 75 identifies the principles that should guide the court in these terms:

> The relevant principles are not in dispute. The court has a wide discretion in determining whether it is equitable to extend time in the particular circumstances of the case. It will often be appropriate to take into account factors of the type listed in section 33(3) of the Limitation Act 1980 as being relevant when deciding whether to extend time for a domestic law action in respect of personal injury or death. These may include the length of and reasons for the delay in issuing the proceedings; the extent to which, having regard to the delay, the evidence in the case is or is likely to be less cogent than it would have been if the proceedings had been issued within the one-year period; and the conduct of the public authority after the right of claim arose, including the extent (if any) to which it responded to requests reasonably made by the claimant for information for the purpose of ascertaining facts which are or might be relevant. However, I agree with what the Court of Appeal said in *Dunn v Parole Board* [2009] 1 WLR 728, paras 31, 43 and 48 that the words of section 7(5)(b) of the HRA mean what they say and the court should not attempt to rewrite them. There can be no question of interpreting section 7(5)(b) as if it contained the language of section 33(3) of the Limitation Act 1980.

The time limit is also subject to any stricter time-limit imposed by the particular procedure being used. If judicial review is used, an application must usually be made 'promptly and in any event within three months' (CPR, Part 54).

The s 3 interpretative obligation is not subject to these special provisions for locus standi or limitation period. The usual rules will apply for whatever procedure is chosen.

28.4.3 Remedies

Section 8 provides for remedies in s 6 challenges to public authorities. It empowers a court to award such remedies within its powers as it considers just and appropriate. This will include injunctions to restrain breaches of Convention rights and damages.

28.4.4 Damages

28.4.4.1 General principles

The role of damages in human rights litigation has significant features which distinguish it from the approach to the award of damages in a private law contract or tort action. As Lord Woolf CJ stated in *Anufrijeva v Southwark London Borough Council* [2004] QB 1124:

> The following points need to be noted.
> (a) The award of damages under the HRA is confined to the class of unlawful acts of public authorities identified by section 6(1): see section 8(1) and (6).
> (b) The court has a discretion as to whether to make an award (it must be 'just and appropriate' to do so) by contrast to the position in relation to common law claims where there is a right to damages: section 8(1).

(c)   The award must be necessary to achieve 'just satisfaction'; language that is distinct from the approach at common law where the claimant is invariably entitled, so far as money can achieve this, to be restored to the position he would have been in if he had not suffered the injury of which complaint is made. The concept of damages being 'necessary to afford just satisfaction' provides a link with the approach to compensation of the Court of Human Rights under article 41.

(d)   The court is required to take into account in determining whether damages are payable and the amount of damages payable the different principles applied by the Court of Human Rights in awarding compensation ... (para 55)

In the following paragraph Lord Woolf said that in considering whether to award compensation and, if so, how much, 'there is a balance to be drawn between the interests of the victim and those of the public as a whole' and that the court has 'a wide discretion in respect of the award of damages for breach of human rights'. He described damages as 'not an automatic entitlement but ... a remedy of last resort'. Later, at para 66, in discussing the principles applied by the Strasbourg Court, he said that the approach is an equitable one and that 'the "equitable basis" has been cited by the Court of Human Rights both as a reason for awarding damages and as a basis upon which to calculate them'.

Lord Woolf's analysis was approved by the House of Lords (now the Supreme Court) in *R (Greenfield) v Secretary of State for the Home Department* [2005] 1 WLR 673 and the Court of Appeal in *Dobson v Thames Water Utilities Ltd* [2009] EWCA Civ 28. To summarise, the Convention serves principally public law aims; the principal objective is to declare any infringement and to put a stop to it. Compensation is ancillary and discretionary. The interests of the individual are part of the equation, but so are those of the wider public.

Note that when the *Dobson* case was tried (see [2011] EWHC 3253), the court held that the defendant was liable to the claimants for its negligent failure to control odour from its sewerage facility. However, the award of damages at common law was made only to the claimants who were property owners, and this was said to constitute just satisfaction for the purposes of s 8(3) of the HRA 1998. As a result, no additional compensation was payable to those claimants who did not have a proprietary interest, such as children living in an affected property. See also *R (on the application of Infinis Plc) v Gas and Electricity Markets Authority* [2011] EWHC 1873 (Admin).

Section 9 of the HRA 1998 prevents damages being awarded in respect of a judicial act done in good faith. In order to show that a judicial act was not done in good faith, a claimant has to show that there was an ulterior purpose (*Webster v Ministry of Justice* [2014] EWHC 3995 (QB)).

28.4.4.2   ECtHR principles

The fundamental principle underlying the award of compensation by the ECtHR is that the Court should achieve what it describes as *restitutio in integrum*. The applicant should, insofar as this is possible, be placed in the same position as if his Convention rights had not been infringed.

Where the breach of a Convention right has clearly caused significant pecuniary loss, this will usually be assessed and awarded. For example, awards of compensation were made to homosexuals, discharged from the armed forces, in breach of Article 8, for loss of earnings and pension rights in *Lustig-Prean and Beckett v UK* (2001) 31 EHRR 601 and *Smith and Grady v UK* (2001) 31 EHRR 620. But a problem arises in relation to the consequences of the breach of a Convention right which are not capable of being computed in terms of financial loss.

None of the rights in Part 1 of the Convention are of such a nature that their infringement will automatically give rise to damage that can be quantified in financial terms. Infringements may involve a variety of treatment of an individual which is objectionable in itself. The treatment may give rise to distress, anxiety and, in extreme cases, psychiatric trauma. The primary object of the proceedings will often be to bring the adverse treatment to an end. If this is achieved, it may constitute 'just satisfaction', or it may be necessary to award damages to compensate for the adverse treatment that has occurred.

More particularly, damages may be awarded for anxiety and distress that has been occasioned by the breach. However, an admission of the breach and an apology may be a sufficient remedy where no damage measurable in financial terms has occurred: see R *(on the application of Degainis) v Secretary of State for Justice* [2010] EWHC 137, where the defendant failed promptly to secure a review of the applicant's release from prison, thereby breaching his Article 5(4) rights, but the judge found that that did not cause him to spend longer in custody nor suffer the sort of frustration or anxiety that might otherwise have merited an award of damages under Article 5(5). Contrast that with R *(on the application of Hester) v Secretary of State for Justice* (2011) LTL, 20 December. Here, the breach of Article 5(4) was admitted and the court found that the applicant had been unlawfully detained for 12 weeks. However, the court was not satisfied that the applicant had suffered any distress or medical problems, and assessed the appropriate award of damages at £500 per week. That amounted in total to £6,000, but as the Secretary of State had already offered precisely that sum to the applicant, the court ordered that he should pay the defendant's costs from the date of that offer. See also ZH (*a protected party by his litigation friend, GH) v Commissioner of Police of the Metropolis* [2013] EWCA Civ 69.

28.4.4.3 Domestic comparators

Where a court decides that it is appropriate to award damages, the level might be assessed by reference to any existing domestic comparators. These might include guidelines issued by the Judicial College, as well as the levels of awards made by the Criminal Injuries Compensation Board, the Parliamentary Ombudsman and the Local Government Ombudsman. These may all provide some rough guidance where the consequences of the infringement of human rights are similar to that being considered in the comparator selected.

28.4.4.4 Modest awards

In cases where there is no ready domestic comparator to assist in the assessment of damages (see **28.4.4.3**), the general principle is that the scale of damages should be modest and not aim to be significantly more or less generous than the ECtHR would award (see R *(Greenfield) v Secretary of State for the Home Department* [2005] 1 WLR 673).

See further, for example, *Northamptonshire CC v AS, KS and DS (by his children's guardian)* [2015] EWFC 7 (where the local authority agreed to pay what appear to be modest damages to a child and his mother for breaches of Articles 6 and 8 of the ECHR, arising from its failures in the conduct of care proceedings) and *Re H (a child: breach of Convention rights: damages)* [2014] EWFC 38 (where the amount of damages is discussed at [84] to [91]).

28.4.5 Other claims

Claims which introduce Convention rights indirectly via the interpretative obligation are not subject to s 8. If they are civil claims, they will have available whatever remedies are available for the cause of action being used (eg, tort).

28.5 THE COMMISSION FOR EQUALITY AND HUMAN RIGHTS

The CEHR is a non-departmental public body that is intended to act as a central point of advice and guidance on all equality and human rights issues in Great Britain. Its remit is to promote awareness and understanding of human rights, and to encourage good practice by public authorities in meeting their obligations under the HRA 1998. The CEHR has powers to take human rights cases on behalf of minorities who suffer discrimination (see Equality Act 2006, s 30(3)). The Commission's web address is <www.equalityhumanrights.com>.

Since February 2009 the CEHR has intervened in several cases before the ECtHR involving issues about housing, immigration, family law, employment law, the right to a fair trial and other matters, including whether the concept of family life under the ECHR includes same-sex couples; whether the ban on the use of intercept evidence in court should be lifted; whether persons subject to immigration control who wish to marry outside the Church of England (whether in a civil or religious ceremony) should be subject to requirements that do not apply to those who have a Church of England wedding; and whether the protections of the HRA 1998 extend to the actions of UK troops abroad.

HUMAN RIGHTS ACT 1998

Introduction

1. The Convention Rights

(1) In this Act 'the Convention rights' means the rights and fundamental freedoms set out in—

    (a)   Articles 2 to 12 and 14 of the Convention,

    (b)   Articles 1 to 3 of the First Protocol, and

    (c)   Article 1 of the Thirteenth Protocol,

as read with Articles 16 to 18 of the Convention.

(2) Those Articles are to have effect for the purposes of this Act subject to any designated derogation or reservation (as to which see sections 14 and 15).

(3) The Articles are set out in Schedule 1.

(4) The Secretary of State may by order make such amendments to this Act as he considers appropriate to reflect the effect, in relation to the United Kingdom, of a protocol.

(5) In subsection (4) 'protocol' means a protocol to the Convention—

    (a)   which the United Kingdom has ratified; or

    (b)   which the United Kingdom has signed with a view to ratification.

(6) No amendment may be made by an order under subsection (4) so as to come into force before the protocol concerned is in force in relation to the United Kingdom.

2. Interpretation of Convention rights

(1) A court or tribunal determining a question which has arisen in connection with a Convention right must take into account any—

    (a)   judgment, decision, declaration or advisory opinion of the European Court of Human Rights,

    (b)   opinion of the Commission given in a report adopted under Article 31 of the Convention,

    (c)   decision of the Commission in connection with Article 26 or 27(2) of the Convention, or

    (d)   decision of the Committee of Ministers taken under Article 46 of the Convention,

whenever made or given, so far as, in the opinion of the court or tribunal, it is relevant to the proceedings in which that question has arisen.

(2) Evidence of any judgment, decision, declaration or opinion of which account may have to be taken under this section is to be given in proceedings before any court or tribunal in such manner as may be provided by rules.

(3) In this section 'rules' means rules of court or, in the case of proceedings before a tribunal, rules made for the purposes of this section—

    (a)   by the Lord Chancellor or the Secretary of State, in relation to any proceedings outside Scotland;

    (b)   by the Secretary of State, in relation to proceedings in Scotland; or

    (c)   by a Northern Ireland department, in relation to proceedings before a tribunal in Northern Ireland—

(i)   which deals with transferred matters; and

(ii)   for which no rules made under paragraph (a) are in force.

Legislation

3.   Interpretation of legislation

(1)   So far as it is possible to do so, primary legislation and subordinate legislation must be read and given effect in a way which is compatible with the Convention rights.

(2)   This section—

(a)   applies to primary legislation and subordinate legislation whenever enacted;

(b)   does not affect the validity, continuing operation or enforcement of any incompatible primary legislation; and

(c)   does not affect the validity, continuing operation or enforcement of any incompatible subordinate legislation if (disregarding any possibility of revocation) primary legislation prevents removal of the incompatibility.

4.   Declaration of incompatibility

(1)   Subsection (2) applies in any proceedings in which a court determines whether a provision of primary legislation is compatible with a Convention right.

(2)   If the court is satisfied that the provision is incompatible with a Convention right, it may make a declaration of that incompatibility.

(3)   Subsection (4) applies in any proceedings in which a court determines whether a provision of subordinate legislation, made in the exercise of a power conferred by primary legislation, is compatible with a Convention right.

(4)   If the court is satisfied—

(a)   that the provision is incompatible with a Convention right, and

(b)   that (disregarding any possibility of revocation) the primary legislation concerned prevents removal of the incompatibility,

it may make a declaration of that incompatibility.

(5)   In this section 'court' means—

(a)   the Supreme Court;

(b)   the Judicial Committee of the Privy Council;

(c)   the Court Martial Appeal Court;

(d)   in Scotland, the High Court of Justiciary sitting otherwise than as a trial court or the Court of Session;

(e)   in England and Wales or Northern Ireland, the High Court or the Court of Appeal;

(f)   the Court of Protection, in any matter dealt with by the President of the Family Division, the Chancellor of the High Court or a puisne judge of the High Court.

(6)   A declaration under this section ('a declaration of incompatibility')—

(a)   does not affect the validity, continuing operation or enforcement of the provision in respect of which it is given; and

(b)   is not binding on the parties to the proceedings in which it is made.

5.   Right of Crown to intervene

(1)   Where a court is considering whether to make a declaration of incompatibility, the Crown is entitled to notice in accordance with rules of court.

(2)   In any case to which subsection (1) applies—

(a)   a Minister of the Crown (or a person nominated by him),

(b)   a member of the Scottish Executive,

(c)   a Northern Ireland Minister,

(d)   a Northern Ireland department,

is entitled, on giving notice in accordance with rules of court, to be joined as a party to the proceedings.

(3) Notice under subsection (2) may be given at any time during the proceedings.

(4) A person who has been made a party to criminal proceedings (other than in Scotland) as the result of a notice under subsection (2) may, with leave, appeal to the House of Lords against any declaration of incompatibility made in the proceedings.

(5) In subsection (4)—

'criminal proceedings' includes all proceedings before the Court Martial Appeal Court; and

'leave' means leave granted by the court making the declaration of incompatibility or by the Supreme Court.

Public Authorities

6. Acts of public authorities

(1) It is unlawful for a public authority to act in a way which is incompatible with a Convention right.

(2) Subsection (1) does not apply to an act if—

  (a) as the result of one or more provisions of primary legislation, the authority could not have acted differently; or

  (b) in the case of one or more provisions of, or made under, primary legislation which cannot be read or given effect in a way which is compatible with the Convention rights, the authority was acting so as to give effect to or enforce those provisions.

(3) In this section 'public authority' includes—

  (a) a court or tribunal, and

  (b) any person certain of whose functions are functions of a public nature,

but does not include either House of Parliament or a person exercising functions in connection with proceedings in Parliament.

(4) . . .

(5) In relation to a particular act, a person is not a public authority by virtue only of subsection (3)(b) if the nature of the act is private.

(6) 'An act' includes a failure to act but does not include a failure to—

  (a) introduce in, or lay before, Parliament a proposal for legislation; or

  (b) make any primary legislation or remedial order.

7. Proceedings

(1) A person who claims that a public authority has acted (or proposes to act) in a way which is made unlawful by section 6(1) may—

  (a) bring proceedings against the authority under this Act in the appropriate court or tribunal, or

  (b) rely on the Convention right or rights concerned in any legal proceedings, but only if he is (or would be) a victim of the unlawful act.

(2) In subsection (1)(a) 'appropriate court or tribunal' means such court or tribunal as may be determined in accordance with rules; and proceedings against an authority include a counterclaim or similar proceeding.

(3) If the proceedings are brought on an application for judicial review, the applicant is to be taken to have a sufficient interest in relation to the unlawful act only if he is, or would be, a victim of that act.

(4) If the proceedings are made by way of a petition for judicial review in Scotland, the applicant shall be taken to have title and interest to sue in relation to the unlawful act only if he is, or would be, a victim of that act.

(5)   Proceedings under subsection (1)(a) must be brought before the end of—

   (a)   the period of one year beginning with the date on which the act complained of took place; or

   (b)   such longer period as the court or tribunal considers equitable having regard to all the circumstances,

   but that is subject to any rule imposing a stricter time limit in relation to the procedure in question.

(6)   In subsection (1)(b) 'legal proceedings' includes—

   (a)   proceedings brought by or at the instigation of a public authority; and

   (b)   an appeal against the decision of a court or tribunal.

(7)   For the purposes of this section, a person is a victim of an unlawful act only if he would be a victim for the purposes of Article 34 of the Convention if proceedings were brought in the European Court of Human Rights in respect of that act.

(8)   Nothing in this Act creates a criminal offence.

(9)   In this section 'rules' means—

   (a)   in relation to proceedings before a court or tribunal outside Scotland, rules made by the Lord Chancellor or Secretary of State for the purposes of this section or rules of court,

   (b)   in relation to proceedings before a court or tribunal in Scotland, rules made by the Secretary of State for those purposes,

   (c)   in relation to proceedings before a tribunal in Northern Ireland—

      (i)   which deals with transferred matters; and

      (ii)   for which no rules made under paragraph (a) are in force,

      rules made by a Northern Ireland department for those purposes,

   and includes provision made by order under section 1 of the Courts and Legal Services Act 1990.

(10)   In making rules, regard must be had to section 9.

(11)   The Minister who has power to make rules in relation to a particular tribunal may, to the extent he considers it necessary to ensure that the tribunal can provide an appropriate remedy in relation to an act (or proposed act) of a public authority which is (or would be) unlawful as a result of section 6(1), by order add to—

   (a)   the relief or remedies which the tribunal may grant; or

   (b)   the grounds on which it may grant any of them.

(12)   An order made under subsection (11) may contain such incidental, supplemental, consequential or transitional provision as the Minister making it considers appropriate.

(13)   'The Minister' includes the Northern Ireland department concerned.

8.   Judicial remedies

(1)   In relation to any act (or proposed act) of a public authority which the court finds is (or would be) unlawful, it may grant such relief or remedy, or make such order, within its powers as it considers just and appropriate.

(2)   But damages may be awarded only by a court which has power to award damages, or to order the payment of compensation, in civil proceedings.

(3)   No award of damages is to be made unless, taking account of all the circumstances of the case, including—

   (a)   any other relief or remedy granted, or order made, in relation to the act in question (by that or any other court), and

   (b)   the consequences of any decision (of that or any other court) in respect of that act, the court is satisfied that the award is necessary to afford just satisfaction to the person in whose favour it is made.

(4) In determining—

    (a)   whether to award damages, or

    (b)   the amount of an award,

the court must take into account the principles applied by the European Court of Human Rights in relation to the award of compensation under Article 41 of the Convention.

(5) A public authority against which damages are awarded is to be treated—

    (a)   in Scotland, for the purposes of section 3 of the Law Reform (Miscellaneous Provisions) (Scotland) Act 1940 as if the award were made in an action of damages in which the authority has been found liable in respect of loss or damage to the person to whom the award is made;

    (b)   for the purposes of the Civil Liability (Contribution) Act 1978 as liable in respect of damage suffered by the person to whom the award is made.

(6) In this section—

'court' includes a tribunal;

'damages' means damages for an unlawful act of a public authority; and

'unlawful' means unlawful under section 6(1).

9.   Judicial acts

(1) Proceedings under section 7(1)(a) in respect of a judicial act may be brought only—

    (a)   by exercising a right of appeal;

    (b)   on an application (in Scotland a petition) for judicial review; or

    (c)   in such other forum as may be prescribed by rules.

(2) That does not affect any rule of law which prevents a court from being the subject of judicial review.

(3) In proceedings under this Act in respect of a judicial act done in good faith, damages may not be awarded otherwise than to compensate a person to the extent required by Article 5(5) of the Convention.

(4) An award of damages permitted by subsection (3) is to be made against the Crown; but no award may be made unless the appropriate person, if not a party to the proceedings, is joined.

(5) In this section—

'appropriate person' means the Minister responsible for the court concerned, or a person or government department nominated by him;

'court' includes a tribunal;

'judge' includes a member of a tribunal, a justice of the peace (or, in Northern Ireland, a lay magistrate) and a clerk or other officer entitled to exercise the jurisdiction of a court;

'judicial act' means a judicial act of a court and includes an act done on the instructions, or on behalf, of a judge; and

'rules' has the same meaning as in section 7(9).

Remedial Action

10.   Power to take remedial action

(1) This section applies if—

    (a)   a provision of legislation has been declared under section 4 to be incompatible with a Convention right and, if an appeal lies—

       (i)   all persons who may appeal have stated in writing that they do not intend to do so;

(ii)   the time for bringing an appeal has expired and no appeal has been brought within that time; or

(iii) an appeal brought within that time has been determined or abandoned; or

(b)   it appears to a Minister of the Crown or Her Majesty in Council that, having regard to a finding of the European Court of Human Rights made after the coming into force of this section in proceedings against the United Kingdom, a provision of legislation is incompatible with an obligation of the United Kingdom arising from the Convention.

(2)   If a Minister of the Crown considers that there are compelling reasons for proceeding under this section, he may by order make such amendments to the legislation as he considers necessary to remove the incompatibility.

(3)   If, in the case of subordinate legislation, a Minister of the Crown considers—

(a)   that it is necessary to amend the primary legislation under which the subordinate legislation in question was made, in order to enable the incompatibility to be removed, and

(b)   that there are compelling reasons for proceeding under this section,

he may by order make such amendments to the primary legislation as he considers necessary.

(4)   This section also applies where the provision in question is in subordinate legislation and has been quashed, or declared invalid, by reason of incompatibility with a Convention right and the Minister proposes to proceed under paragraph 2(b) of Schedule 2.

(5)   If the legislation is an Order in Council, the power conferred by subsection (2) or (3) is exercisable by Her Majesty in Council.

(6)   In this section 'legislation' does not include a Measure of the Church Assembly or of the General Synod of the Church of England.

(7)   Schedule 2 makes further provision about remedial orders.

Other Rights and Proceedings

11.   Safeguard for existing human rights

A person's reliance on a Convention right does not restrict—

(a)   any other right or freedom conferred on him by or under any law having effect in any part of the United Kingdom; or

(b)   his right to make any claim or bring any proceedings which he could make or bring apart from sections 7 to 9.

12.   Freedom of expression

(1)   This section applies if a court is considering whether to grant any relief which, if granted, might affect the exercise of the Convention right to freedom of expression.

(2)   If the person against whom the application for relief is made ('the respondent') is neither present nor represented, no such relief is to be granted unless the court is satisfied—

(a)   that the applicant has taken all practicable steps to notify the respondent; or

(b)   that there are compelling reasons why the respondent should not be notified.

(3)   No such relief is to be granted so as to restrain publication before trial unless the court is satisfied that the applicant is likely to establish that publication should not be allowed.

(4)   The court must have particular regard to the importance of the Convention right to freedom of expression and, where the proceedings relate to material which the respondent claims, or which appears to the court, to be journalistic, literary or artistic material (or to conduct connected with such material), to—

(a) the extent to which—

    (i)   the material has, or is about to, become available to the public; or

    (ii) it is, or would be, in the public interest for the material to be published;

(b) any relevant privacy code.

(5) In this section—

'court' includes a tribunal; and

'relief' includes any remedy or order (other than in criminal proceedings).

13. Freedom of thought, conscience and religion

(1) If a court's determination of any question arising under this Act might affect the exercise by a religious organisation (itself or its members collectively) of the Convention right to freedom of thought, conscience and religion, it must have particular regard to the importance of that right.

(2) In this section 'court' includes a tribunal.

...

21. Interpretation, etc

(1) In this Act—

'amend' includes repeal and apply (with or without modifications);

'the appropriate Minister' means the Minister of the Crown having charge of the appropriate authorised government department (within the meaning of the Crown Proceedings Act 1947);

'the Commission' means the European Commission of Human Rights;

'the Convention' means the Convention for the Protection of Human Rights and Fundamental Freedoms, agreed by the Council of Europe at Rome on 4th November 1950 as it has effect for the time being in relation to the United Kingdom;

'declaration of incompatibility' means a declaration under section 4;

'Minister of the Crown' has the same meaning as in the Ministers of the Crown Act 1975;

'Northern Ireland Minister' includes the First Minister and the deputy First Minister in Northern Ireland;

'primary legislation' means any—

(a) public general Act;

(b) local and personal Act;

(c) private Act;

(d) Measure of the Church Assembly;

(e) Measure of the General Synod of the Church of England;

(f) Order in Council—

    (i)   made in exercise of Her Majesty's Royal Prerogative;

    (ii) made under section 38(1)(a) of the Northern Ireland Constitution Act 1973 or the corresponding provision of the Northern Ireland Act 1998; or

    (iii) amending an Act of a kind mentioned in paragraph (a), (b) or (c);

and includes an order or other instrument made under primary legislation (otherwise than by the Welsh Ministers, the First Minister for Wales, the Counsel General to the Welsh Assembly Government, a member of the Scottish Executive, a Northern Ireland Minister or a Northern Ireland department) to the extent to which it operates to bring one or more provisions of that legislation into force or amends any primary legislation;

'the First Protocol' means the protocol to the Convention agreed at Paris on 20th March 1952;

'the Eleventh Protocol' means the protocol to the Convention (restructuring the control machinery established by the Convention) agreed at Strasbourg on 11th May 1994;

'the Thirteenth Protocol' means the protocol to the Convention (concerning the abolition of the death penalty in all circumstances) agreed at Vilnius on 3rd May 2002;

'remedial order' means an order under section 10;

'subordinate legislation' means any—

(a)   Order in Council other than one—

    (i)   made in exercise of Her Majesty's Royal Prerogative;

    (ii)   made under section 38(1)(a) of the Northern Ireland Constitution Act 1973 or the corresponding provision of the Northern Ireland Act 1998;

    (iii) or amending an Act of a kind mentioned in the definition of primary legislation;

(b)   Act of the Scottish Parliament;

(ba)   Measure of the National Assembly for Wales;

(bb)   Act of the National Assembly for Wales;

(c)   Act of the Parliament of Northern Ireland;

(d)   Measure of the Assembly established under section 1 of the Northern Ireland Assembly Act 1973;

(e)   Act of the Northern Ireland Assembly;

(f)   order, rules, regulations, scheme, warrant, byelaw or other instrument made under primary legislation (except to the extent to which it operates to bring one or more provisions of that legislation into force or amends any primary legislation);

(g)   order, rules, regulations, scheme, warrant, byelaw or other instrument made under legislation mentioned in paragraph (b), (c), (d) or (e) or made under an Order in Council applying only to Northern Ireland;

(h)   order, rules, regulations, scheme, warrant, byelaw or other instrument made by a member of the Scottish Executive, Welsh Ministers, the First Minister for Wales, the Counsel General to the Welsh Assembly Government, a Northern Ireland Minister or a Northern Ireland department in exercise of prerogative or other executive functions of Her Majesty which are exercisable by such a person on behalf of Her Majesty;

'transferred matters' has the same meaning as in the Northern Ireland Act 1998; and

'tribunal' means any tribunal in which legal proceedings may be brought.

(2)   The references in paragraphs (b) and (c) of section 2(1) to Articles are to Articles of the Convention as they had effect immediately before the coming into force of the Eleventh Protocol.

(3)   The reference in paragraph (d) of section 2(1) to Article 46 includes a reference to Articles 32 and 54 of the Convention as they had effect immediately before the coming into force of the Eleventh Protocol.

(4)   The references in section 2(1) to a report or decision of the Commission or a decision of the Committee of Ministers include references to a report or decision made as provided by paragraphs 3, 4 and 6 of Article 5 of the Eleventh Protocol (transitional provisions).

(5)   ...

22.   Short title, commencement, application and extent

(1)   This Act may be cited as the Human Rights Act 1998.

(2)   Sections 18, 20 and 21(5) and this section come into force on the passing of this Act.

(3)   The other provisions of this Act come into force on such day as the Secretary of State may by order appoint; and different days may be appointed for different purposes.

(4)   Paragraph (b) of subsection (1) of section 7 applies to proceedings brought by or at the instigation of a public authority whenever the act in question took place; but otherwise that subsection does not apply to an act taking place before the coming into force of that section.

(5)   This Act binds the Crown.

(6)   This Act extends to Northern Ireland.

(7)   ...

SCHEDULE 1

The Convention Rights

Article 2
Right to life

1.   Everyone's right to life shall be protected by law. No one shall be deprived of his life intentionally save in the execution of a sentence of a court following his conviction of a crime for which this penalty is provided by law.

2.   Deprivation of life shall not be regarded as inflicted in contravention of this Article when it results from the use of force which is no more than absolutely necessary:

  (a)   in defence of any person from unlawful violence;

  (b)   in order to effect a lawful arrest or to prevent the escape of a person lawfully detained;

  (c)   in action lawfully taken for the purpose of quelling a riot or insurrection.

Article 3
Prohibition of Torture

No one shall be subjected to torture or to inhuman or degrading treatment or punishment.

Article 4
Prohibition of Slavery and Forced Labour

1.   No one shall be held in slavery or servitude.

2.   No one shall be required to perform forced or compulsory labour.

3.   For the purpose of this Article the term 'forced or compulsory labour' shall not include:

  (a)   any work required to be done in the ordinary course of detention imposed according to the provisions of Article 5 of this Convention or during conditional release from such detention;

  (b)   any service of a military character or, in case of conscientious objectors in countries where they are recognised, service exacted instead of compulsory military service;

  (c)   any service exacted in case of an emergency or calamity threatening the life or well-being of the community;

  (d)   any work or service which forms part of normal civic obligations.

Article 5
Right to Liberty and Security

1.   Everyone has the right to liberty and security of person. No one shall be deprived of his liberty save in the following cases and in accordance with a procedure prescribed by law:

  (a)   the lawful detention of a person after conviction by a competent court;

  (b)   the lawful arrest or detention of a person for non-compliance with the lawful order of a court or in order to secure the fulfilment of any obligation prescribed by law;

(c)   the lawful arrest or detention of a person effected for the purpose of bringing him before the competent legal authority on reasonable suspicion of having committed an offence or when it is reasonably considered necessary to prevent his committing an offence or fleeing after having done so;

(d)   the detention of a minor by lawful order for the purpose of educational supervision or his lawful detention for the purpose of bringing him before the competent legal authority;

(e)   the lawful detention of persons for the prevention of the spreading of infectious diseases, of persons of unsound mind, alcoholics or drug addicts or vagrants;

(f)   the lawful arrest or detention of a person to prevent his effecting an unauthorised entry into the country or of a person against whom action is being taken with a view to deportation or extradition.

2.   Everyone who is arrested shall be informed promptly, in a language which he understands, of the reasons for his arrest and of any charge against him.

3.   Everyone arrested or detained in accordance with the provisions of paragraph 1(c) of this Article shall be brought promptly before a judge or other officer authorised by law to exercise judicial power and shall be entitled to trial within a reasonable time or to release pending trial. Release may be conditioned by guarantees to appear for trial.

4.   Everyone who is deprived of his liberty by arrest or detention shall be entitled to take proceedings by which the lawfulness of his detention shall be decided speedily by a court and his release ordered if the detention is not lawful.

5.   Everyone who has been the victim of arrest or detention in contravention of the provisions of this Article shall have an enforceable right to compensation.

Article 6
Right to a Fair Trial

1.   In the determination of his civil rights and obligations or of any criminal charge against him, everyone is entitled to a fair and public hearing within a reasonable time by an independent and impartial tribunal established by law. Judgment shall be pronounced publicly but the press and public may be excluded from all or part of the trial in the interest of morals, public order or national security in a democratic society, where the interests of juveniles or the protection of the private life of the parties so require, or to the extent strictly necessary in the opinion of the court in special circumstances where publicity would prejudice the interests of justice.

2.   Everyone charged with a criminal offence shall be presumed innocent until proved guilty according to law.

3.   Everyone charged with a criminal offence has the following minimum rights:

(a)   to be informed promptly, in a language which he understands and in detail, of the nature and cause of the accusation against him;

(b)   to have adequate time and facilities for the preparation of his defence;

(c)   to defend himself in person or through legal assistance of his own choosing or, if he has not sufficient means to pay for legal assistance, to be given it free when the interests of justice so require;

(d)   to examine or have examined witnesses against him and to obtain the attendance and examination of witnesses on his behalf under the same conditions as witnesses against him;

(e)   to have the free assistance of an interpreter if he cannot understand or speak the language used in court.

Article 7
No Punishment Without Law

1. No one shall be held guilty of any criminal offence on account of any act or omission which did not constitute a criminal offence under national or international law at the time when it was committed. Nor shall a heavier penalty be imposed than the one that was applicable at the time the criminal offence was committed.

2. This Article shall not prejudice the trial and punishment of any person for any act or omission which, at the time when it was committed, was criminal according to the general principles of law recognised by civilised nations.

Article 8
Right to Respect for Private and Family Life

1. Everyone has the right to respect for his private and family life, his home and his correspondence.

2. There shall be no interference by a public authority with the exercise of this right except such as is in accordance with the law and is necessary in a democratic society in the interests of national security, public safety or the economic well-being of the country, for the prevention of disorder or crime, for the protection of health or morals, or for the protection of the rights and freedoms of others.

Article 9
Freedom of Thought, Conscience and Religion

1. Everyone has the right to freedom of thought, conscience and religion; this right includes freedom to change his religion or belief and freedom, either alone or in community with others and in public or private, to manifest his religion or belief, in worship, teaching, practice and observance.

2. Freedom to manifest one's religion or beliefs shall be subject only to such limitations as are prescribed by law and are necessary in a democratic society in the interests of public safety, for the protection of public order, health or morals, or for the protection of the rights and freedoms of others.

Article 10
Freedom of Expression

1. Everyone has the right to freedom of expression. This right shall include freedom to hold opinions and to receive and impart information and ideas without interference by public authority and regardless of frontiers. This Article shall not prevent States from requiring the licensing of broadcasting, television or cinema enterprises.

2. The exercise of these freedoms, since it carries with it duties and responsibilities, may be subject to such formalities, conditions, restrictions or penalties as are prescribed by law and are necessary in a democratic society, in the interests of national security, territorial integrity or public safety, for the prevention of disorder or crime, for the protection of health or morals, for the protection of the reputation or rights of others, for preventing the disclosure of information received in confidence, or for maintaining the authority and impartiality of the judiciary.

Article 11
Freedom of Assembly and Association

1. Everyone has the right to freedom of peaceful assembly and to freedom of association with others, including the right to form and to join trade unions for the protection of his interests.

2. No restrictions shall be placed on the exercise of these rights other than such as are prescribed by law and are necessary in a democratic society in the interests of national

security or public safety, for the prevention of disorder or crime, for the protection of health or morals or for the protection of the rights and freedoms of others. This Article shall not prevent the imposition of lawful restrictions on the exercise of these rights by members of the armed forces, of the police or of the administration of the State.

Article 12
Right to Marry

Men and women of marriageable age have the right to marry and to found a family, according to the national laws governing the exercise of this right.

Article 14
Prohibition of Discrimination

The enjoyment of the rights and freedoms set forth in this Convention shall be secured without discrimination on any ground such as sex, race, colour, language, religion, political or other opinion, national or social origin, association with a national minority, property, birth or other status.

Article 16
Restrictions on Political Activity of Aliens

Nothing in Articles 10, 11 and 14 shall be regarded as preventing the High Contracting Parties from imposing restrictions on the political activity of aliens.

Article 17
Prohibition of Abuse of Rights

Nothing in this Convention may be interpreted as implying for any State, group or person any right to engage in any activity or perform any act aimed at the destruction of any of the rights and freedoms set forth herein or at their limitation to a greater extent than is provided for in the Convention.

Article 18
Limitation on Use of Restrictions on Rights

The restrictions permitted under this Convention to the said rights and freedoms shall not be applied for any purpose other than those for which they have been prescribed.

The First Protocol

Article 1
Protection of Property

Every natural or legal person is entitled to the peaceful enjoyment of his possessions. No one shall be deprived of his possessions except in the public interest and subject to the conditions provided for by law and by the general principles of international law.

The preceding provisions shall not, however, in any way impair the right of a State to enforce such laws as it deems necessary to control the use of property in accordance with the general interest or to secure the payment of taxes or other contributions or penalties.

Article 2
Right to Education

No person shall be denied the right to education. In the exercise of any functions which it assumes in relation to education and to teaching, the State shall respect the right of parents to ensure such education and teaching in conformity with their own religious and philosophical convictions.

Identifying and Addressing Convention Rights: a Checklist

Article 2

- Was there an intentional deprivation of life?
- Was it in execution of a court sentence following conviction of a crime for which the sentence is the death penalty?
- Was it for a ground permitted under para 2?
- Did it comply with the conditions set out in para 2?

Article 3

- Was there torture or inhuman or degrading treatment or punishment?

Article 4

- Was there slavery or servitude (para 1)?
- Was there forced or compulsory labour (para 2) save as excluded by para 3?

Article 5 (para 1)

- Was there a deprivation of liberty?
- Was it in accordance with a procedure prescribed by law?
- Was it for any of the grounds permitted by paras (a) to (f)?

Article 6, civil matters

- Was a civil right or obligation determined?
- Were the rights under para 1 met?

Article 6, criminal matters

- Did the proceedings concern a criminal charge?
- Were the rights under para 1 met?

Article 7

- Did the act or omission constitute a criminal offence at the time it was committed?

Article 8

- Was there an interference with a person's private or family life, home or correspondence?
- Was any interference lawful (para 2)?
- Was any interference necessary pursuant to the reasons set out in para 2?
- Article 9
- Was there an interference with a person's freedom of thought or conscience?
- Was there an interference with a person's religion? If so, was it lawful and necessary (para 2)?

Article 10

- Was there an interference with a person's right to freedom of expression?
- Was any interference lawful (para 2)?
- Was any interference necessary pursuant to the reasons set out in para 2?

Article 11

- Was there an interference with a person's freedom of peaceful assembly or association?
- Was any interference lawful (para 2)?
- Was any interference necessary pursuant to the reasons set out in para 2?

Article 12

- Was the person of marriageable age?
- Did the person comply with national laws?
- Was there an interference with a person's right to marry or found a family?

First Protocol, Article 1

- Was there an interference with a person's peaceful enjoyment of his possessions?
- Was any interference lawful?
- Was any interference necessary pursuant to any of the specified grounds?

First Protocol, Article 2

- Was there a denial of the right to education?
- Was there a lack of respect of parents' religious or philosophical views?

Article 14

- Is another ECHR right or freedom in issue?
- Has there been discrimination on any of the specified grounds?

EVERYDAY SITUATIONS IN WHICH THE HRA 1998 MIGHT APPLY

Not being able to eat properly while in hospital or a care home (Articles 2 and 8).

Provision of facilities or food which do not meet religious or cultural needs (Article 9).

Abuse or neglect of older people, those who are learning disabled or other vulnerable people (Articles 2 and 3).

Lack of respect for privacy on a hospital ward (Article 8).

Disproportionate use of stop-and-search powers against young black males and other ethnic minorities (Article 14).

Not respecting gay and lesbian partners as next-of-kin and inheritors of tenancies (Articles 8 and 14).

Excessive surveillance of law-abiding people (Article 8).

Loss of personal data by public officials (Article 8).

Curfews preventing law-abiding young people from going out at night (Article 8).

Failures by the authorities to protect people from being stalked and harassed (Articles 2, 3 and 8).

Not being sufficiently protected from domestic violence (Articles 2, 3 and 8).

Not being allocated suitable housing for special needs that have been identified (Article 8).

Bullying of all kinds in schools (Articles 3 and 8).

Disregard of gay and lesbian couples in adoption policies (Article 14).

Unexplained death in prisons, police stations and psychiatric hospitals (Article 2).

Wearing religious symbols or dress at work or in schools (Article 9 and Protocol 1, Article 2).

Inadequate provision for children with special educational needs (Protocol 1, Article 2 and Article 14).

Refusal to permit the staging or broadcasting of artistic works (Article 10).

Refusal to allow people to attend a demonstration (Articles 10 and 11).

RESPONDING TO HUMAN RIGHTS JUDGMENTS

Cm 8162

Annex A: Declarations of incompatibility

Since the Human Rights Act 1998 came into force on 2 October 2000, 27 declarations of incompatibility have been made. Of these:

- 19 have become final (in whole or in part) and are not subject to further appeal;
- 8 have been overturned on appeal; and

Of the 19 declarations of incompatibility that have become final:

- 12 will have been remedied by later primary legislation;
- 2 will have been remedied by a remedial order under section 10 of the Human Rights Act;
- 4 related to provisions that had already been remedied by primary legislation at the time of the declaration;
- 1 is under consideration as to how to remedy the incompatibility.

Information about each of the 27 declarations of incompatibility is set out below in chronological order. All references to Articles are to the Convention rights, as defined in the Human Rights Act 1998, unless stated otherwise.

This information was last updated on 8 August 2011, and will not reflect any changes after that date.

Contents

R (on the application of Uttley) v Secretary of State for the Home Department (Administrative Court; [2003] EWHC 950 (Admin); 8 April 2003)

Bellinger v Bellinger (House of Lords; [2003] UKHL 21; 10 April 2003)

R (on the application of M) v Secretary of State for Health (Administrative Court; [2003] EWHC 1094 (Admin); 16 April 2003)

R (on the application of Wilkinson) v Inland Revenue Commissioners (Court of Appeal; [2003] EWCA Civ 814; 18 June 2003)

R (on the application of Hooper and others) v Secretary of State for Work and Pensions (Court of Appeal; [2003] EWCA Civ 875; 18 June 2003)

R (on the application of MH) v Secretary of State for Health (Court of Appeal; [2004] EWCA Civ 1609; 3 December 2004)

A and others v Secretary of State for the Home Department (House of Lords; [2004] UKHL 56; 16 December 2004)

R (on the application of Sylviane Pierrette Morris) v Westminster City Council & First Secretary of State (No 3) (Court of Appeal; [2005] EWCA Civ 1184; 14 October 2005)

R (Gabaj) v First Secretary of State (Administrative Court; unreported; 28 March 2006)

R (on the application of Baiai and others) v Secretary of State for the Home Department and another (Administrative Court; [2006] EWHC 823 (Admin); 10 April 2006)

Re MB (Administrative Court; [2006] EWHC 1000 (Admin); 12 April 2006)

R (on the application of (1) June Wright (2) Khemraj Jummun (3) Mary Quinn (4) Barbara Gambier) v (1) Secretary of State for Health (2) Secretary of State for Education & Skills (Administrative Court; [2006] EWHC 2886 (Admin); 16 November 2006)

R (Clift) v Secretary of State for the Home Department; Secretary of State for the Home Department v Hindawi and another (House of Lords; [2006] UKHL 54; 13 December 2006)

Smith v Scott (Registration Appeal Court (Scotland); [2007] CSIH 9; 24 January 2007)

Nasseri v Secretary of State for the Home Department (Administrative Court; [2007] EWHC 1548 (Admin); 2 July 2007)

R (Wayne Thomas Black) v Secretary of State for Justice (Court of Appeal; [2008] EWCA Civ 359; 15 April 2008)

R (on the application of (1) F (2) Angus Aubrey Thompson) v Secretary of State for the Home Department (Administrative Court; [2008] EWHC 3170 (Admin); 19 December 2008)

R (on the application of Royal College of Nursing and others) v Secretary of State for Home Department (Administrative Court; [2010] EWHC 2761; 10 November 2010)

EXAMPLES OF HOW BUSINESS CAN IMPACT CERTAIN HUMAN RIGHTS

Relevant human right	The right explained	How business might impact that right
Right to life	• Right not to be deprived of life arbitrarily or unlawfully; • right to have one's life protected, for example from physical attacks or health and safety risks.	• Lethal use of force by security forces (State or private) to protect company resources, facilities or personnel; • operations that pose life-threatening safety risks to workers or neighbouring communities through accident/exposure to toxic chemicals; • manufacture and sale of products with lethal flaws or dual-use products.
Right to be free from slavery, servitude and forced labour	• Slavery occurs when one human effectively owns another; • freedom from servitude covers other forms of egregious economic exploitation, like trafficking of workers or debt bondage; • rights to freedom from slavery and servitude are absolute rights; • forced or compulsory labour is defined by the ILO as all work or service that is extracted under menace of any penalty and for which the person has not voluntarily offered themselves; • providing wages does not necessarily mean that work is not forced labour if the other aspects of the definition are met.	• Business operations that take place in certain countries or cultural contexts may, knowingly or unknowingly, benefit from forced labour, either directly or through supply chains; • business practices that put workers in a position of debt bondage through company loans, payment of fees or other means; • transportation of people/goods that facilitates the trafficking of forced or bonded labour.

Relevant human right	The right explained	How business might impact that right
Right to privacy	• Individuals have a right to be protected from arbitrary, unlawful or unreasonable interference with their privacy, family, home or correspondence and from attacks on their reputation.	• Failing to protect the confidentiality of personal data on employees, customers or other stakeholders; • providing information to government authorities without the individual's permission, in response to government requests that do not follow required national procedures and/or that are not in line with international human rights law.
Right to health	• Individuals have a right to the highest attainable standard of physical and mental health; • this includes the right to control over one's health and body and freedom from interference.	• Pollution from business operations creates negative health impacts on workers and surrounding communities; • sale of products that are hazardous to the health of end users/customers; • failure to implement effective OH&S standards.
Rights of protection for the child	• Children are in need of special protection because of their potentially vulnerable status as minors; • a child has the right to a name, to be registered and to acquire a nationality; • children must be protected from sexual and economic exploitation; • ILO standards set minimum employment ages for hazardous work (18 years) and regular work (15 years, unless the country exercises the exception for developing States, which is 14 years), though there are some carefully prescribed exceptions.	• Business activities might be relying on child labour, either directly or through their supply chains; • where child labour is discovered, businesses can impact other rights (such as the right to an adequate standard of living) if they fail to take account of the best interests of the child in determining the appropriate response.

Relevant human right	The right explained	How business might impact that right
Right of self-determination	• Right of peoples, rather than individuals; • Peoples are entitled to determine their political status, pursue economic, social and cultural development, dispose of their land's natural resources and not be deprived of their own means of subsistence; • The right of indigenous peoples to self-determination has been specifically recognised by the international community.	• Any activity that might have impacts on indigenous peoples or their lands whether through acquisition, construction or operation.

PROBATE AND ADMINISTRATION

SUCCESSION TO PROPERTY ON DEATH: THE BACKGROUND LAW

LEARNING OUTCOMES

After reading this chapter you will be able to:

- identify what property is capable of passing by will
- identify whether a will is valid
- decide the effect of a will
- explain the intestacy rules and decide who is entitled to property under the rules
- identify the circumstances in which a person can make a claim under the Inheritance (Provision for Family and Dependants) Act 1975 and the factors the court will take into account when considering a claim.

29.1 INTRODUCTION

When a person dies, one of the most important questions is who will inherit that person's property. This chapter explains the matters that are relevant when answering that question.

The first thing people usually ask is whether or not there is a will. However, many valuable assets pass independently of the terms of the will; and even if there is a will, the court may override its terms under the Inheritance (Provision for Family and Dependants) Act 1975 if it concludes that reasonable financial provision was not made for a close relative or dependant.

This chapter therefore looks at all the ways in which property can pass on death and the circumstances in which the court can alter the disposition of property under the Inheritance (Provision for Family and Dependants) Act 1975. It also looks at how to make a valid will and at the way in which wills take effect.

29.2 WHAT PROPERTY CAN PASS UNDER A WILL AND THE INTESTACY RULES?

When an individual dies, he may have provided for the disposition of his property on death by leaving a valid will. A will can operate to dispose of most types of property which an individual may own on death. A gift in a valid will of 'all my estate to my son, John' would include property held in the sole name of the testator at the time of his death in a variety of different forms, such as cash, money in bank and building society accounts, stocks and shares and other investments, land and chattels.

If an individual does not dispose of such property by will, it passes on his death according to the intestacy rules.

However, there are some important types of property which pass on death independently of the terms of the will and the intestacy rules. For many people the bulk of their property will pass in this way.

29.3 WHAT PROPERTY PASSES INDEPENDENTLY OF THE WILL AND INTESTACY RULES?

A number of different kinds of property pass independently of the terms of any will or the intestacy rules, some much more significant than others.

29.3.1 Joint property

Where property is held by more than one person as joint tenants in equity, on the death of one joint tenant his interest passes by survivorship to the surviving joint tenant(s).

> **EXAMPLE**
>
> George makes a will leaving all his estate to a charity. He and his brother Harry have a joint bank account and own a house as joint tenants in equity. On George's death his interests in the house and the bank account pass automatically to Harry, not to the charity under the terms of George's will.

The doctrine of survivorship does not apply to land held on a tenancy in common. The share of each tenant in common passes on his death under his will (or under the intestacy rules).

29.3.2 Nominated property

There are statutory provisions allowing individuals to 'nominate' what is to happen to certain types of funds after the nominator's death. The statutory provisions apply to deposits not exceeding £5,000 in certain trustee savings banks, friendly societies, and industrial and provident societies.

A nomination is a direction to the institution to pay the money in the account, on the death of the investor, to a chosen ('nominated') third party.

If an individual has an account to which these provisions apply and has made a nomination, on his death the property passes to the chosen nominee regardless of the terms of the will (if any) or intestacy rules. If no nomination has been made, the money in the account will pass under the will or intestacy in the usual way.

There are very few statutes which allow new nominations to be made, although those already made will continue to be valid unless and until revoked.

29.3.3 Insurance policies

Where a person takes out a simple policy of life assurance, the benefit of that policy belongs to him. On his death, the policy matures and the insurance company will pay the proceeds to his representatives who will distribute the money according to the terms of his will or the intestacy rules.

However, a person may take out a life assurance policy expressed to be for the benefit of specified individuals. This is effectively a gift on trust for those individuals. It may be done in two ways:

(a)   Under the terms of the Married Women's Property Act 1882, s 11. Under this section, a person taking out a life assurance policy on his own life may express the policy to be for the benefit of his spouse and/or children. This creates a trust in favour of the named beneficiaries.

(b)   Alternatively, a policy may be expressly written in trust for or assigned to named beneficiaries.

In either case, once given away, the benefit of the policy does not belong to the policy holder. On the policy holder's death, the policy matures and the insurance company will pay the proceeds to the named beneficiaries (or to trustees for them) regardless of the terms of the deceased's will. The policy holder makes a transfer of value of the policy at the date of the gift, but usually this is very low.

29.3.4 Pension benefits

Many pension schemes provide for the payment of benefits if an employee dies 'in service'. Commonly, a lump sum calculated on the basis of the employee's salary at the time of his death is paid by the trustees of the pension fund to members of the family or dependants chosen at their discretion. Such discretionary schemes usually allow the employee to leave a letter of wishes for the trustees indicating which people he would like to benefit. The employee's choice is not binding on the pension fund trustees, but they will normally abide by his wishes.

Such pension benefits do not belong to the employee during his lifetime and pass on death independently of the terms of any will and of the intestacy rules.

A few pension schemes provide that the lump sum must be paid to the employee's personal representatives (PRs). The PRs must then distribute the money according to the terms of the employee's will or the intestacy rules.

PRACTICAL POINT

When trying to decide who is entitled to take assets following a death, always deal with assets in the following order:

(a)   property passing independently of the will and intestacy rules;

(b)   property passing by will;

(c)   property undisposed of by will and therefore passing under the intestacy rules.

29.4 THE REQUIREMENTS FOR A VALID WILL

In order to create a valid will, a testator must have the necessary capacity and intention, and must observe the formalities for execution of wills laid down in the Wills Act 1837. Once the will is made, it may be revoked by subsequent marriage or the formation of a civil partnership, by destruction or by a later will.

29.4.1 Capacity

In order to make a valid will, an individual must be aged 18 or over (with certain limited exceptions) and must have the requisite mental capacity. This testamentary capacity was defined in *Banks v Goodfellow* (1870) LR 5 QB 549 as 'soundness of mind, memory and understanding'. The testator must understand:

(a)   the nature of his act and its broad effects;

(b)   the extent of his property (although not necessarily recollecting every individual item); and

(c)   the moral claims he ought to consider (even if he decides to reject such claims and dispose of his property to other beneficiaries).

In addition, the testator must not be suffering from any insane delusion which affects the disposition of property.

29.4.1.1 Proof and presumptions

At common law, the person who puts forward a will has to prove that all necessary elements, including mental capacity, are present. This is normally not particularly burdensome as, where a person generally showed no sign of mental confusion, it will be presumed that he retained that capacity when he made his will. If, however, there is anything to put his capacity in doubt, the presumption will not apply and the PRs will have to prove capacity on the basis of the *Banks v Goodfellow* test.

The Mental Capacity Act (MCA) 2005 came into force on 1 April 2007. It introduced a statutory test to determine whether a person had capacity to take a decision. Section 1(2) provides that 'for the purposes of this Act a person must be assumed to have capacity unless it is established that he lacks capacity'. There was some uncertainty as to whether the Act applied to capacity to make a will.

In *Scammell v Farmer* [2008] EWHC 1100 (Ch), which was the first case to consider the effect of the Act, the judge concluded that the Act applies only to decisions taken under the Act by the Court of Protection on behalf of another, so it ought not to apply to the assessment of a person's capacity to make his own will. Some later cases doubted this. However, in *Kicks v Leigh* [2014] EWHC 3926 (Ch), Judge Stephen Morris QC reviewed all the cases and said that he preferred the analysis in *Scammell*. In *Walker v Badmin* [2014] All ER (D) 258 (Nov), Judge Nicholas Strauss QC also reviewed the case law and concluded that the *Banks v Goodfellow* test for testamentary capacity applied rather than the MCA 2005 test. Although the Court of Appeal might take a different view, it seems likely that this is the correct answer and the MCA 2005 has not affected the common law test.

29.4.2 Intention

When the will is signed, the testator must have both general and specific intention. This means that the testator must intend to make a will (as opposed to any other sort of document), and must also intend to make the particular will now being executed (ie the testator must know and approve its contents).

29.4.2.1 Proof and presumptions

The burden of proving the testator's knowledge and approval falls on the person putting forward the will, but there is one presumption which will usually assist.

A testator who has capacity and has executed his will, having read it, is presumed to have the requisite knowledge and approval. However, this presumption does not apply in the situations listed below.

Testator blind/illiterate/not signing personally

The presumption that the testator knew and approved the contents of his will does not apply if the testator was blind or illiterate, or another person signed the will on the testator's behalf (eg, because he had an injured hand).

In these cases, the probate registrar will require evidence to prove knowledge and approval. It is usual in such cases to include a statement at the end of the will stating that the will was read over to the testator, or read by the testator who knew and approved the contents.

Suspicious circumstances

Similarly, the presumption of knowledge and approval does not apply if there are suspicious circumstances surrounding the drafting and/or execution of the will (eg, the will has been prepared by someone who is to be a major beneficiary under its terms or who is a close relative of a major beneficiary).

In such cases, because the presumption does not apply, the person putting forward the will must remove the suspicion by proving that the testator did actually know and approve the will's contents.

In *Gill v Woodall* [2010] EWCA Civ 1430, the Court of Appeal found that the presumption did not apply where Mrs Gill, a Yorkshire farmer, who was on excellent terms with her daughter and grandson, left everything to the RSPCA after leading her daughter to believe that she would inherit everything. Mrs Gill suffered from a severe anxiety disorder. The Court of Appeal held that the circumstances of the case were so unusual that the presumption did not apply, and that the RSPCA had not proved that Mrs Gill had known and approved the contents of her will.

Note: Conduct issues for those regulated by the SRA

Those regulated by the SRA are required to act with integrity and in the best interests of clients (Principles 2 and 4). They must not act if there is a significant risk that the duty to act in the best interests of the client conflicts with their own interests. There is such a risk where someone prepares a will which benefits himself or someone close to him.

The SRA's Code of Conduct 2011 in Chapter 1 (Client Care) includes as an Indicative Behaviour:

> refusing to act where your client proposes to make a gift of significant value to you or a member of your family, or a member of your firm or their family, unless the client takes independent legal advice

29.4.2.2 Undue influence and mistake

Where a testator with capacity appears to have known and approved the contents of the will, any person who wishes to challenge the will (or any part of it) must prove one or more of the following to prevent some or all of the will from being admitted to probate. (There are no presumptions, so the person claiming invalidity on one of these grounds must prove it.)

Force, fear, fraud or undue influence

A will is invalid if it is shown that the testator made the will (or part of it) as a result of force or fear (through actual or threatened injury), or fraud (eg, after being misled by some pretence) or undue influence (where the testator's freedom of choice was overcome by intolerable pressure, even though his judgement remained unconvinced).

Notice that it is necessary to *prove* undue influence in relation to a will. This is different from the position in relation to a lifetime gift. If a donor makes a lifetime gift which requires explanation (for example, because it is large in relation to the donor's other assets) to a person who is in a position of trust and confidence, there is a presumption of undue influence. The donee will be able to keep the gift only if he can provide the court with a satisfactory explanation. The need for proof of undue influence in relation to wills makes it very difficult for someone challenging the will to succeed. The person alleging undue influence will need to collect evidence from family, friends and carers.

Mistake

All or part of the will may be included by mistake. Any words included without the knowledge and approval of the testator will be omitted from probate. In this respect, it is important to distinguish between actual mistake (ie absence of knowledge and approval) and misunderstanding as to the true legal meaning of words used in the will. In the latter case mistaken words will not be omitted.

29.4.3 Formalities for execution

Section 9 of the Wills Act 1837 (as substituted by Administration of Justice Act 1982, s 17) provides:

No will shall be valid unless—

(a)   it is in writing, and signed by the testator, or by some other person in his presence and by his direction; and

(b)   it appears that the testator intended by his signature to give effect to the will; and

(c)   the signature is made or acknowledged by the testator in the presence of two or more witnesses present at the same time; and

(d)   each witness either—

   (i)   attests and signs the will; or

   (ii)   acknowledges his signature,

in the presence of the testator (but not necessarily in the presence of any other witness),

but no form of attestation shall be necessary.

There is one exception to the rule that wills must comply with the requirements of s 9. A will made on actual military service or by a mariner or seaman at sea is valid and may be in any form, including a mere oral statement: Wills Act 1837, s 11. The only requirement is that the 'testator' intends to dispose of his property after his death. It is the circumstances in which the will is made that are important, not the circumstances of death. In *Ayling v Summers* [2010] 1 All ER 410 the testator made an oral statement of wishes in 1990 while he was under orders to join his ship, and died, retired, in 2005; his statement was held to be a valid privileged will.

29.4.3.1   Proof and presumptions

If the will includes a clause which recites that the s 9 formalities were observed, a presumption of due execution is raised. The will is valid unless there is proof that the formalities were not observed. Such a clause is called an attestation clause.

An example of an attestation clause is:

Signed by the testator in our joint presence and then by us in his/hers.

If the will does not contain an attestation clause, the district judge (or registrar) must require an affidavit of due execution from a witness or any other person who was present during the execution, or, failing that, an affidavit of handwriting evidence to identify the testator's signature, or refer the case to a judge (all of which involve time and expense).

29.4.3.2   Witnesses

There are no formal requirements relating to the capacity of witnesses, although they must be capable of understanding the significance of being the witness to a signature.

If either of the witnesses is a beneficiary under the will or is the spouse or a civil partner of a beneficiary, the will remains valid but the gift to the witness or to the witness's spouse fails (Wills Act 1837, s 15; see **29.5.3**).

It is important for solicitors preparing wills to give clear instructions to their clients explaining how to sign and witness the will, and warning that beneficiaries and those married to beneficiaries should not be witnesses.

If the will is returned to the solicitor for storage, the solicitor is under a duty to check the signatures to see whether ss 9 and 15 appear to have been complied with.

Failure to carry out these duties may lead to liability in negligence.

29.4.4   Revocation

Testators can always revoke a will during their lifetime, provided they have testamentary capacity. There are three ways of revoking a will.

29.4.4.1   By a later will or codicil

Under the Wills Act 1837, s 20, a will may be revoked in whole or in part by a later will or codicil. Normally, a will contains an express clause revoking all earlier wills and codicils.

If a will does not contain an express revocation clause, it operates to revoke any earlier will or codicil by implication to the extent that the two are inconsistent.

Exceptionally, the court may decide that a testator's intention to revoke an earlier will by an express revocation clause was conditional upon a particular event (eg, the effectiveness of a gift in the new will). If that condition is not satisfied, the revocation may be held to be invalid so that the earlier will remains effective (this is sometimes called the doctrine of 'dependent relative revocation').

29.4.4.2 By marriage or formation of a civil partnership

If the testator marries or forms a civil partnership after executing a will, the will is automatically revoked (Wills Act 1837, s 18, as substituted by the Administration of Justice Act 1982). The rule does not apply where a testator makes a will prior to a forthcoming marriage or civil partnership if it appears from the will that the testator was expecting to marry or form a civil partnership with a particular person and does not intend the will to be revoked (s 18(3)). Unless the will states that it is conditional on the marriage or civil partnership taking place, it will take effect unless expressly revoked, even if the expected marriage/civil partnership does not happen.

For example, Fred and Frances are engaged. They make wills in expectation of marriage and then have a row and break off the engagement. Fred dies 10 years later without changing his will. Frances will take his estate.

Note that as a result of the Marriage (Same Sex Couples) Act 2013 a marriage may, since 29 March 2014, be between a same sex couple as well as an opposite sex couple.

It is possible for civil partners to convert a civil partnership into a same sex marriage. A new subsection (5) was inserted into s 18 of the Wills Act 1837 to provide that, where a civil partnership is converted to a marriage, the conversion will not revoke an existing will of either party nor affect any dispositions in the wills.

If the testator makes a will and is later divorced, or if the civil partnership is dissolved (or the marriage or civil partnership is annulled or declared void), then under the Wills Act 1837, s 18A (amended by the Law Reform (Succession) Act 1995 with effect from 1 January 1996) the will remains valid but:

(a)   provisions of the will appointing the former spouse or civil partner as executor or trustee take effect as if the former spouse or civil partner had died on the date on which the marriage or civil partnership is dissolved or annulled; and

(b)   any property, or interest in property, which is devised or bequeathed to the former spouse or civil partner passes as if the former spouse or civil partner had died on that date. See **29.5.3.1** below.

This means that substitutional provisions in the will which are expressed to take effect if the testator's spouse/civil partner predeceases him will also take effect if the marriage/civil partnership is dissolved or annulled.

29.4.4.3 By destruction

A will may be revoked by 'burning, tearing or otherwise destroying the same by the testator or by some person in his presence and by his direction with the intention of revoking the same' (Wills Act 1837, s 20). Physical destruction without the intention to revoke is insufficient; a will destroyed accidentally or by mistake is not revoked. If its contents can be reconstructed (eg, from a copy), an order may be obtained allowing its admission to probate as a valid will.

Physical destruction is required: symbolic destruction (eg, simply crossing out wording or writing 'revoked' across the will) is not sufficient, although if a vital part (eg, the signature) is destroyed, this partial destruction may be held to revoke the entire will. If the part destroyed is less substantial or important, then the partial destruction may revoke only that part which was actually destroyed.

Note that the destruction must be in the testator's presence and by his direction. Destruction in another room is ineffective to revoke the will. Where a will is destroyed without the intention to revoke, it is possible to obtain probate of a copy, draft or reconstruction. See **30.5.2.4**.

Occasionally, the court may apply the doctrine of dependent relative revocation to save a will, on the basis that the testator's intention to revoke his will by destruction was conditional upon some future event (eg, upon the later execution of a new will). If that event did not in fact take place, the original will may be valid even though it was destroyed. The contents of the original will may be reconstructed from a copy or draft.

29.4.5 Alterations

If a will has been altered, the basic rule is that the alterations are invalid unless it can be proved that they were made before the will was executed, or unless the alterations are executed like a will (the initials of the testator and witnesses in the margin beside the alteration are sufficient for this purpose).

If a will includes invalid alterations, the original wording will stand if the original words are 'apparent', ie can still be read. If the original words have been obliterated in such a way that they can no longer be read, those words have effectively been revoked by destruction. The rest of the will remains valid, and takes effect with the omission of the obliterated words.

Again, the court may decide that the testator's intention to revoke the obliterated words was conditional only. This inference is most likely to be drawn where the testator attempted to replace the obliterated words with a substitution. The implied condition is that the testator intended to revoke the original words only if the substitution was effective. As it is not, the original words remain valid and, if they can be reconstructed (eg, from a copy or draft), they will take effect.

EXAMPLE

Tamal makes a professionally drawn will which leaves '£10,000 to my nephew, Nalin'. After executing the will, Tamal decides he wants to change the legacy to Nalin:

(1)   He draws a thin line through '£10,000' and writes above it '£20,000'.

   This is an unexecuted alteration and will have no effect. The gift remains a gift of £10,000.

(2)   He does exactly the same thing but writes his name next to the alteration and gets two people to witness his signature.

   This is an executed alteration and takes effect to alter the gift to £20,000.

(3)   He draws a thick line through '£10,000' in such a way that the original wording is wholly unreadable.

   This is an obliteration and will be treated as revoking the original gift. The gift is treated as a gift of nothing.

(4)   He does exactly the same thing but writes '£20,000' above the obliteration.

   This is an obliteration and would be treated as revoking the original gift were it not for the fact that Tamal has substituted words. A court is likely to conclude that Tamal's intention to revoke the original gift was conditional on the substitution being able to take effect. As the substitution is not effective, the original gift will take effect (provided it is possible to discover what the original gift was).

29.5 HOW A WILL TAKES EFFECT

When a testator dies, the people dealing with the estate must decide (usually with the help of a solicitor) the effect of the will in the light of the circumstances at the date of the testator's death. They will need to consider what property the testator owned when he died and which of the people named in the will have survived the testator in order to decide the effect of the gifts.

If the will refers to beneficiaries by description, it will be necessary to identify the people fulfilling the description.

The people dealing with the estate will be called executors, if they were appointed by the will, and administrators, if there was no appointment in the will. There are statutory rules as to who is able to act as an administrator (see **Chapter 30**). Both executors and administrators may be referred to generically as 'personal representatives'.

29.5.1 What property passes under the gifts in the will?

As seen in **29.2** above, certain types of property pass independently of the will either because they have their own rules of succession (eg, joint property), or because the testator did not own them beneficially at death (eg, life assurance policies written in trust).

When the PRs have decided what property is capable of passing under the will, they must apply the terms of the will to the property.

29.5.1.1 Basic rule

The basic rule is stated in the Wills Act 1837, s 24, which provides:

> every will shall be construed, with reference to the real estate and personal estate comprised in it, to speak and take effect as if it had been executed immediately before the death of the testator, unless a contrary intention shall appear by the will.

This means that a gift of 'all my estate' or 'all the rest of my estate' takes effect to dispose of all property the testator owned when he died, whether or not the testator owned it at the time the will was made.

29.5.1.2 Ademption

A specific legacy, ie a gift of a particular item or group of items of property, will fail if the testator no longer owns that property at death. The gift is said to be 'adeemed'. Ademption usually occurs because the property has been sold, given away or destroyed during the testator's lifetime.

> **EXAMPLE**
>
> In her will Ellen gives 'my engraved gold bracelet' to her sister Grace and the rest of her estate to her husband Harry. Ellen no longer owns the bracelet when she dies. Grace receives nothing: her legacy is adeemed. All Ellen's estate passes to Harry under the residuary gift.

Problems may arise where the asset has been retained but has changed its nature since the will was made. For example, where the will includes a specific gift of company shares, the company may have been taken over since the will was made so that the testator's shareholding has been changed into a holding in the new company. In such a case, the question is whether the asset is substantially the same, having changed merely in name or form, or whether it has changed in substance. Only if there has been a change in substance will the gift be adeemed.

Another area of potential difficulty occurs where the testator disposes of the property described in a specific gift but before his death acquires a different item of property which answers the same description; for example a gift of 'my car' or 'my piano' where the original car or piano has been replaced since the will was made. It has been held that the presumption in such a case is that the testator meant only to dispose of the particular asset he owned at the date of the will so that the gift is adeemed. By referring to 'my' car or piano, the testator is taken to have shown a contrary intention as specified in s 24. It has been suggested that this construction may vary according to the circumstances and that the respective values of the original and substituted assets may be taken into account.

If the property given is capable of increase or decrease (eg, 'my shares', 'my jewellery'), the testator will normally be taken to have made a gift of any items satisfying the description at death.

EXAMPLE

Thea makes a will leaving 'all my jewellery' to her niece, Nepota. After the date of the will, all her jewellery is stolen. Six months later she receives money from her insurance company and buys new jewellery. Then she dies.

(1)   Because Thea has used a phrase which is capable of increase and decrease, she is treated as intending to pass whatever jewellery she has at the date of her death. Nepota will, therefore, take the replacement items.

(2)   Had the gift been of 'my pearl necklace', Thea would probably be treated as intending to pass only the necklace she owned at the date of the will. Nepota would not have taken any replacement necklace.

(3)   Had Thea died after receiving the insurance money but before buying replacement assets, Nepota would have taken nothing. She has no right to the insurance money under the terms of the gift.

A testator may wish to add to or change a will in a minor way and so may execute a supplementary codicil. A codicil is a supplement to a will which, to be valid, must be executed in the same way as a will. The significance of a codicil in the context of a gift of property is that it republishes the will as at the date of the codicil. Thus, if the testator makes a will in 1990 leaving 'my gold watch' to a legatee, loses the watch in 2000 and replaces it, the gift of the watch in the will is adeemed. If, however, the testator executes a codicil to the will in 2003, the will is read as if it had been executed in 2003 and so the legatee will take the replacement watch.

29.5.2 Has the beneficiary survived the testator?

29.5.2.1 Basic rule

A gift in a will fails or 'lapses' if the beneficiary dies before the testator. If a legacy lapses, the property falls into residue, unless the testator has provided for the possibility of lapse by including a substitutional gift. If a gift of residue lapses, the property passes under the intestacy rules, unless the testator has included a substitutional gift in the will. Where no conditions to the contrary are imposed in the will, a gift vests on the testator's death. This means that provided the beneficiary survives the testator, for however short a time, the gift takes effect. If the beneficiary dies soon after the testator the property passes into the beneficiary's estate.

It is possible to show a contrary intention, for example by wording a gift to make it clear that the property is to pass to whoever is the holder of a position or office at the date of the testator's death.

There is a presumption that, as regards people, a will is construed at the date it is made. A gift made to 'the eldest son of X' is construed as a gift to the person fulfilling that description at the date the will is made. If that person dies, the gift does not pass to the eldest surviving son. However, if the testator makes a codicil to the will, it republishes the will and the will is treated as made at the date of the republication. Hence, if the eldest son dies between the date of the will and the codicil, the will is construed as referring to the person who is the eldest son at the date of the codicil.

29.5.2.2 Law of Property Act 1925, s 184

The principle outlined above means that if the deaths of the testator and beneficiary occur very close together, it is vital to establish who died first. The law of succession does not accept the possibility that two people might die at the same instant. If the order of their deaths cannot be proved, s 184 provides that the elder of the two is deemed to have died first. If the testator was older than the beneficiary, the gift takes effect and the property passes as part of the beneficiary's estate.

29.5.2.3 Survivorship clauses

Commonly, gifts in wills are made conditional upon the survival of the beneficiaries for a specific period of time, such as 28 days. These survivorship provisions prevent a gift from taking effect where the beneficiary survives the testator for only a relatively short time or is deemed to have survived by s 184. As with any other contingent gift, if the beneficiary fails to satisfy the contingency, the gift fails.

29.5.2.4 Lapse of gifts to more than one person

A gift by will to two or more people as joint tenants will not lapse unless all the donees die before the testator. If a gift is made 'to A and B jointly' and A dies before the testator, the whole gift passes to B.

If the gift contains words of severance, for example 'everything to A and B in equal shares', this principle does not apply. If A dies before the testator, A's share lapses and B takes only one share. The lapsed share will pass under the intestacy rules unless the testator included a substitutional gift to take effect if one of the original beneficiaries predeceased.

If the gift is a class gift (eg, 'to my children equally if more than one'), there is no lapse unless all the members of the class predecease the testator.

29.5.2.5 Wills Act 1837, s 33: gifts to children and remoter issue

This section applies to all gifts by will to the testator's children or remoter issue (for the meaning of 'issue', see **29.6.2.1**) unless a contrary intention is shown in the will and its effect is to incorporate an implied substitution provision into such gifts. It provides that where a will contains a gift to the testator's child or remoter descendant and that beneficiary dies before the testator, leaving issue of his own who survive the testator, the gift shall not lapse but shall pass instead to the beneficiary's issue. The issue of a deceased beneficiary take the gift their parent would have taken in equal shares.

EXAMPLE

Tom's will includes a gift of £40,000 to his daughter, Caroline. Caroline and her daughter Sarah both die before Tom, but Caroline's son, James, and Sarah's children, Emma and Daniel, all survive him. Under s 33, the legacy is saved from lapse. James takes half the gift (£20,000). Sarah would have taken the other half but, as she has predeceased Tom, her half passes to her own children equally. Thus, Emma and Daniel take £10,000 each.

Section 33 does not apply if the will shows a contrary intention. This is usually shown by including an express substitution clause.

The Estates of Deceased Persons (Forfeiture Rule and Law of Succession) Act 2011 inserted a new s 33A into the Wills Act 1837, with the result that in certain circumstances for the purposes of the Wills Act a person may be deemed to have predeceased the testator. See **29.5.3.5** below.

29.5.3 Does the gift fail for any other reason?

29.5.3.1 Divorce or dissolution of a civil partnership

Under the Wills Act 1837, s 18A (as substituted by the Law Reform (Succession) Act 1995), where after the date of the will the testator's marriage or civil partnership is dissolved or annulled or declared void, 'any property which, or an interest in which, is devised or bequeathed to the former spouse or civil partner shall pass as if the former spouse or civil partner had died' on the date of the dissolution or annulment of the marriage or civil partnership.

> **EXAMPLE**
>
> Fauzia makes a will in which she leaves all her estate to her husband, Sabiq, with a substitutional provision that, if Sabiq dies before her, the property should pass to her children equally. Fauzia and Sabiq are later divorced but Fauzia does not change her will. She dies, survived by Sabiq and the children. Under s 18A, the gift to Sabiq fails. Even though Sabiq in fact survived Fauzia, the substitutional gift takes effect and Fauzia's estate passes to the children.

29.5.3.2 Beneficiary witnesses will

Under the Wills Act 1837, s 15, a gift by will fails if the beneficiary, his spouse or civil partner witnesses the will.

29.5.3.3 Disclaimer

A beneficiary need not accept a gift given to him by will. He can disclaim the gift, which will then fall into residue or, in the case of disclaimer of a gift of residue, pass on intestacy.

However, a beneficiary who has received a benefit from a gift (eg, a payment of income) is taken to have accepted the gift and may no longer disclaim.

29.5.3.4 Forfeiture

The forfeiture rule provides that, as a matter of public policy, a person should not be able to inherit from a person he has been convicted of killing. The rule applies in cases both of murder and manslaughter, but not in cases where the killer was insane within the meaning of the *McNaghten* rules.

In cases of manslaughter (but not murder) the killer may apply within three months of conviction for relief from forfeiture under the Forfeiture Act 1982. The time-limit is strict and the court has no discretion to extend the period.

29.5.3.5 The Estates of Deceased Persons (Forfeiture Rule and Law of Succession) Act 2011

This Act came into effect on 1 February 2011. Section 2 inserts a new s 33A into the Wills Act 1837 which provides, subject to contrary intention in the will, that a person who disclaims or forfeits an entitlement under a will is to be treated for the purposes of the Wills Act as having predeceased the testator.

> **EXAMPLE**
>
> Terry is murdered by his daughter, Denise. His will leaves everything to Denise who has a son, Sean.
>
> Denise forfeits her entitlement under the will but she will be treated as if she had predeceased Terry, with the result that s 33 of the Wills Act 1837 will apply and Terry's property will pass to Sean.

29.5.4 Identifying the beneficiaries

Where the beneficiaries are referred to by name, identification is usually just a matter of locating them.

Where the will refers to a class of beneficiaries, for example 'my children', 'my nieces', there may be some doubt as to who fulfils that description. Unless the will provides otherwise, such a gift will be a gift only to the testator's own children or nieces and not to the children or relatives of the testator's spouse or civil partner (so-called step-children), or to those of a cohabitee.

In *Reading v Reading* [2015] EWHC 946 (Ch) the court found that there was sufficient evidence to demonstrate that the testator had intended his step-children to share a pecuniary legacy with his own children: the will included a substitutional gift of residue to both his own children and his step-children in the event that his second wife predeceased him, the general wording suggested step-children were intended to share in both cases, and the solicitor who prepared the will had recorded in his attendance note that the step-children were to share but had failed to word the will correctly.

The normal meaning of issue is direct descendants of any generation so, as well as the testator's children, it will include grandchildren, great-grandchildren and so on.

Adopted children are normally treated as children of the adoptive parents, although the will may provide otherwise. In the case of succession to property under modern wills, it is irrelevant whether or not a child's parents are married to each other.

There are special rules which apply to determine the parentage of children born as a result of assisted reproduction (see Human Fertilisation and Embryology Act 2008). These are beyond the scope of this book.

The Gender Recognition Act 2004 came into force on 4 April 2005. Transsexuals who have obtained a full gender recognition certificate from the Gender Recognition Panel are legally recognised in their acquired gender. Hence a gift to 'my nieces' would include a nephew who had changed gender and obtained a certificate.

29.6 THE EFFECT OF THE INTESTACY RULES

The intestacy rules contained in the Administration of Estates Act 1925 (AEA 1925) apply to decide who is entitled to an individual's property when he dies without disposing of it by will.

This may occur because the deceased has died intestate (ie, without a valid will), or because his will failed to dispose of all his estate (partial intestacy).

The intestacy rules apply only to property which is capable of being left by will (see **29.2**).

EXAMPLE

Laura dies intestate, survived by her husband, Michael, and their two children. Laura and Michael owned their house as beneficial joint tenants. Laura had taken out a life assurance policy for £100,000 which is written in trust for the children, and she owned investments worth £150,000. The intestacy rules do not affect Laura's share of the house (which passes to Michael by survivorship) or the life policy (which passes to the children under the terms of the trust). Only the investments pass under the intestacy rules.

Note that the Inheritance and Trustees' Powers Act 2014 made significant changes to the entitlement of surviving spouses and civil partners on intestacy in the case of deaths occurring on or after 1 October 2014. The previous rules made more limited provision for spouses and civil partners. These earlier rules are not considered here.

29.6.1   Statutory trust for payment of debts, etc

The intestacy rules impose a trust over all the property (real and personal) in respect of which a person dies intestate (AEA 1925, s 33). This trust is similar to the usual express trust found in a will and includes a power of sale: it provides that the PRs must pay the funeral, testamentary and administration expenses, and any debts of the deceased. The balance remaining (after setting aside a fund to meet any pecuniary legacies left by the deceased in the will) is the 'residuary estate' to be shared among the family under the rules of distribution set out in s 46 of the AEA 1925. The PRs have power under s 41 to appropriate assets in or towards satisfaction of a beneficiary's share (with the beneficiary's consent).

29.6.2   Spouse or civil partner and issue

29.6.2.1   Definitions

Under the intestacy rules, a spouse is the person to whom the deceased was married at his death, whether or not they were living together. A same sex spouse has exactly the same rights as an opposite sex spouse.

A divorced spouse is excluded. A cohabitee has no rights under the intestacy rules.

Civil partners are treated in the same way as spouses.

The term 'issue' includes all direct descendants of the deceased: ie, children, grandchildren, great grandchildren, etc. Adopted children (and remoter descendants) are included, as are those whose parents were not married at the time of their birth. Descendants of the deceased's spouse or civil partner ('step' children) are not issue of the deceased unless adopted.

29.6.2.2   Entitlements

Where the intestate is survived by both spouse or civil partner and issue, the 'residuary estate' (as defined in **29.6.1**) is distributed as follows:

(a)   The spouse or civil partner receives the personal chattels absolutely. 'Personal chattels' are defined in s 55(1)(x) of the AEA 1925 as tangible movable property, other than any such property which—

    (i)   consists of money or securities for money, or

    (ii)   was used at the death of the intestate solely or mainly for business purposes, or

    (iii)   was held at the death of the intestate solely as an investment.

(b)   In addition, the spouse or civil partner receives a 'statutory legacy' of £250,000 free of tax and costs plus interest from death until payment. The rate of interest payable is the Bank of England rate that had effect at the end of the day on which the intestate died.

(c)   The rest of the residuary estate (if any) is divided in half. One half is held on trust for the spouse or civil partner absolutely. The other half is held for the issue on the statutory trusts.

The intestate's spouse or civil partner must survive the intestate for 28 days in order to inherit. The Law Reform (Succession) Act 1995 provides that, where the intestate's spouse or civil partner dies within 28 days of the intestate, the estate is distributed as if the spouse or civil partner has not survived the intestate.

29.6.2.3   Applying the statutory trusts

The statutory trusts determine membership of the class of beneficiaries, and the terms on which they take, as follows.

(a)   The primary beneficiaries are the children of the intestate who are living at the intestate's death. Remoter issue are not included, unless a child has died before the intestate.

(b)   The interests of the children are contingent upon attaining the age of 18 or marrying or forming a civil partnership under that age. Any child who fulfils the contingency at the intestate's death takes a vested interest.

(c)   If any child of the intestate predeceased the intestate, any children of the deceased child (grandchildren of the deceased) who are living at the intestate's death take their deceased parent's share equally between them, contingently upon attaining 18 or earlier marriage or formation of a civil partnership. Great grandchildren would be included only if their parent had also predeceased the intestate. This form of substitution and division is known as a '*per stirpes*' distribution.

(d)   If children or issue survive the intestate but die without attaining a vested interest, their interest normally fails and the estate is distributed as if they had never existed. However, s 3 of the Estates of Deceased Persons (Forfeiture Rule and Law of Succession) Act 2011 provides that if they die without attaining a vested interest but leaving issue, they will be treated as having predeceased the intestate so that they can be replaced by their own issue (see **29.6.5.1**).

EXAMPLE

Joanne dies intestate survived by her husband, Kenneth, and their children, Mark (who has a son, Quentin) and Nina. Their daughter, Lisa, died last year. Lisa's two children, Oliver and Paul, are living at Joanne's death.

Joanne's estate consists of her share in the house, held as joint tenants with Kenneth, and other property worth £570,000 after payment of debts, funeral and testamentary expenses. This figure includes personal chattels worth £20,000.

DISTRIBUTION

Joanne's share in the house passes to Kenneth by survivorship. The rest of her estate passes on intestacy.

£
  20,000   personal chattels to Kenneth
250,000   statutory legacy to Kenneth

The remaining £300,000 is divided in half.

150,000   for Kenneth absolutely
150,000   for the issue on the statutory trusts
570,000

The statutory trusts apply to determine the distribution between Joanne's issue as follows.

Mark and Nina, Joanne's children, are living at her death and take one share each. The share Lisa would have taken had she survived is held for her children, Oliver and Paul, in equal shares. The interests of Nina, Oliver and Paul are contingent upon attaining 18 or earlier marriage or formation of a civil partnership.

> Thus, Mark has a vested interest in one-third of the issues' half. He is entitled to £50,000 on Joanne's death. If Mark should die shortly after Joanne, his share would form part of his estate on death. Quentin has no entitlement under Joanne's intestacy.
>
> Nina has a contingent interest in one-third of the issues' half, which will vest when she is 18 or if she marries or forms a civil partnership before 18. If Nina should die under the age of 18 and without marrying or forming a civil partnership, her interest would fail. One half of Nina's share would pass to Mark and the other half would be held for Oliver and Paul equally. However, if Nina has a child who survived her, the child would take Nina's place as a result of s 3 of the Estates of Deceased Persons (Forfeiture Rule and Law of Succession) Act 2011.
>
> Oliver and Paul have contingent interests in one-sixth of the issues' half, which will vest at 18 or earlier marriage or formation of a civil partnership. If Oliver should die under the age of 18 and without marrying or forming a civil partnership (or having an illegitimate child), his share would pass to Paul (and vice versa). If both Oliver and Paul were to die under the age of 18 and without marrying or forming a civil partnership (or having an illegitimate child), their shares would be divided equally between Mark and Nina (provided she reaches 18, marries or forms a civil partnership).

29.6.2.4   Right of spouse or civil partner to require appropriation of the matrimonial home

If the matrimonial home forms part of the estate passing on intestacy, the surviving spouse or civil partner can require the PRs to appropriate the matrimonial home in full or partial satisfaction of any absolute interest in the estate (Intestates' Estates Act 1952, s 5).

If the property is worth more than the entitlement of the spouse or civil partner, the spouse or civil partner may still require appropriation provided he or she pays the difference, 'equality money', to the estate.

The election must be made in writing to the PRs within 12 months of the grant of representation.

29.6.3   Spouse or civil partner and no issue

Where the intestate leaves a surviving spouse or civil partner but no issue, the whole estate, however large, passes to the spouse or civil partner absolutely. Other relatives, such as parents, brothers and sisters, grandparents and cousins, are not entitled.

The spouse or civil partner must survive the intestate for 28 days in order to take. If the spouse or civil partner dies within that period, the estate is distributed as if the spouse or civil partner had not survived the intestate.

29.6.4   Distribution where there is no surviving spouse or civil partner

Where there is no surviving spouse or civil partner (or, for deaths after 1 January 1996, where the spouse or civil partner dies within 28 days of the intestate), the 'residuary estate' is divided between the relatives in the highest category in the list below:

(a)   issue on the 'statutory trusts' (see **29.6.2**), but if none,

(b)   parents, equally if both alive, but if none,

(c)   brothers and sisters of the whole blood on the 'statutory trusts', but if none,

(d)   brothers and sisters of the half blood on the 'statutory trusts', but if none,

(e)   grandparents, equally if more than one, but if none,

(f)   uncles and aunts of the whole blood on the 'statutory trusts', but if none,

(g)   uncles and aunts of the half blood on the 'statutory trusts', but if none,

(h)   the Crown, Duchy of Lancaster, or Duke of Cornwall (*bona vacantia*).

29.6.4.1   The statutory trusts

Each category other than parents and grandparents takes 'on the statutory trusts'. This means that members of the specified class share the estate equally (children under 18 take their interest contingently upon attaining 18 or marrying earlier), and that issue of a deceased relative may take that relative's share. This means that relatives not mentioned in s 46 (eg, nephews, nieces and cousins) may inherit on intestacy if their parents died before the intestate.

> **EXAMPLE 1**
>
> Tom dies intestate. He was not married to his partner, Penny, although the couple have a son, Simon, aged 13, Tom's only child. Tom's parents predeceased him but he is survived by his only sibling, his brother, Bob, aged 40.
>
> Tom's estate is held on trust for Simon, contingently upon attaining 18 or marrying earlier. If Simon dies before the contingency is fulfilled, Tom's estate passes to Bob absolutely.

> **EXAMPLE 2**
>
> Vera, a widow aged 80, is cared for by her step-daughter, Carol (the child of her deceased husband's first marriage). Her only living blood relatives are cousins, the children of her mother's brothers and sisters. Vera dies intestate. Her estate is divided 'per stirpes' between her cousins (and the children of any cousins who predeceased her). Carol receives nothing from Vera's estate.

Section 3 of the Estates of Deceased Persons (Forfeiture Rule and Law of Succession) Act 2011 provides that a person with an interest on the statutory trusts who dies before reaching the age of 18 or marrying or forming a civil partnership will be treated as having predeceased. The effect is that if such a person has an illegitimate child, the child can take the share his or her parent would have taken provided the child fulfils the statutory trusts.

29.6.4.2   Adopted and illegitimate children

Adopted children are treated for intestacy purposes as the children of their adoptive parents and not of their natural parents. If a person who was adopted dies intestate without spouse or issue, his estate will be distributed between the closest relatives in the adoptive family. An adopted child may also inherit on the intestacy of any member of his adoptive family.

Similarly, the intestacy rules are applied regardless of whether or not a particular individual's parents were married to each other. However, on the intestacy of an individual whose parents were not married to each other, it is presumed that the individual has not been survived by his father or by any person related to him through his father unless the contrary is shown (Family Law Reform Act 1987, s 18(2)). This presumption avoids any necessity for the PRs to make enquiries where the identity or whereabouts of the father is unknown. The presumption does not apply where the father is named on the intestate child's birth certificate (Family Law Reform Act 1987, s 18(2ZA)).

> **EXAMPLE**
>
> Jessica, whose parents did not marry, dies intestate. Her only known relative is a half brother, the child of her mother's later marriage. Nothing is known of Jessica's father or any other children he may have had. Jessica's PRs may distribute her estate to her half brother, relying on the presumption in s 18(2).

The Human Fertilisation and Embryology Act 2008 makes it possible for a child to have a second female parent (where a child is conceived using donated sperm and/or eggs and the mother is in a civil partnership or where the parties have agreed that this is to be the case).

The Family Law Reform Act 1987, s 18(2) and s 18(2ZA) apply in the same way to a second female parent as they apply to a father.

If a child with a contingent interest in the estate of an intestate relative is adopted before fulfilling the statutory trusts, he loses his entitlement. The Inheritance and Trustees' Powers Act 2014 introduced a limited saving. Section 4 provides that any contingent interest (other than a contingent interest in remainder) which the adopted person had immediately before the adoption in the estate of a deceased parent is preserved. The change applies also to gifts in a will of a deceased parent as well as on intestacy, for example '£100,000 to be divided amongst such of my children as reach 18'. The change is limited to parents, so an adopted child will still lose a contingent entitlement to the estate of other relatives.

The Adoption and Children Act 2002 already preserved vested interests of children who are adopted before their interest falls into possession.

There are provisions in the Human Fertilisation and Embryology Act 2008 which apply to children born as a result of surrogacy arrangements and techniques of assisted reproduction. The details are beyond the scope of this book.

29.6.4.3 *Bona vacantia*

Where an estate passes *bona vacantia*, the Crown, Duchy of Lancaster or Duke of Cornwall has a discretion to provide for dependants of the intestate, or for other persons for whom the intestate might reasonably have been expected to make provision.

Genealogists say that it is rare for an estate to be truly *bona vacantia*. They can usually trace some relatives (provided the estate is large enough to meet their fees).

29.7 THE INHERITANCE (PROVISION FOR FAMILY AND DEPENDANTS) ACT 1975

The Inheritance (Provision for Family and Dependants) Act 1975 (I(PFD)A 1975) allows certain categories of people who may be aggrieved because they have been left out of a will, or are not inheriting on an intestacy, to apply for a benefit from the estate following the testator's or intestate's death. The I(PFD)A 1975 may also be used by a person who has received some benefit under the will or intestacy but is dissatisfied with the amount of the inheritance.

Note that the Inheritance and Trustees' Powers Act 2014 made some limited changes to the I(PFD)A 1975 in the case of deaths occurring on or after 1 October 2014. The previous legislation is not considered here.

The I(PFD)A 1975 applies only where the deceased died domiciled in England and Wales. It does not apply where a person originally domiciled in England and Wales has acquired a domicile of choice elsewhere.

Section numbers below refer to the I(PFD)A 1975 unless otherwise stated.

29.7.1 When should a claim be made?

An application must be brought within six months of the date of issue of the grant of representation to the deceased's estate (s 4). However, the court has a discretion to extend this time-limit. In the case of deaths on or after 1 October 2014 (the date on which the Inheritance and Trustees' Powers Act 2014 came into force) it is possible to make an application before the grant is issued.

29.7.2 Who can make a claim?

The following persons can make a claim (s 1(1)):

(a)   the spouse or civil partner of the deceased;

(b)   a former spouse or civil partner of the deceased who has not remarried (except where, on the granting of the decree of dissolution or nullity, the court made an order barring the former spouse or civil partner from making a claim);

(c)   a child of the deceased (whatever the child's age);

(d)   any person treated by the deceased as a child of the family in relation to any marriage or civil partnership of the deceased, or otherwise in relation to any family in which the deceased at any time stood in the role of a parent (eg, a step-child or child of a cohabitee);

(e)   any person who, immediately before the death of the deceased, was being maintained by him either wholly or in part. A person is 'maintained' if 'the deceased was making a substantial contribution in money or money's worth towards the reasonable needs of that person, other than a contribution made for full valuable consideration pursuant to an arrangement of a commercial nature' (s 1(3));

(f)   any person who, during the whole of the period of two years ending immediately before the date when the deceased died, was living:

(i)   in the same household as the deceased, and

(ii)   as the husband or wife of the deceased;

(g)   any person who, during the whole of the period of two years ending immediately before the date when the deceased died, was living:

(i)   in the same household as the deceased, and

(ii)   as the civil partner of the deceased.

29.7.3   What must the applicant prove?

The only ground for a claim is that 'the disposition of the deceased's estate effected by his will or the law relating to intestacy, or a combination of his will and that law, is not such as to make reasonable financial provision for the applicant'. Section 1(2) sets out two standards for judging 'reasonable financial provision':

(a)   'the surviving spouse standard', which allows a surviving spouse or civil partner such financial provision as is reasonable in all the circumstances 'whether or not that provision is required for his or her maintenance' (s 1(2)(a)); and

(b)   'the ordinary standard', which applies to all other categories of applicant and allows 'such financial provision as it would be reasonable in all the circumstances ... for the applicant to receive for his maintenance' (s 1(2)(b)).

29.7.4   What factors does the court take into account?

Section 3 contains guidelines to assist the court in determining whether the will and/or intestacy does make reasonable financial provision for the applicant. Some matters should be considered for every claimant (ie, the common guidelines). There are also special guidelines for each category of applicant.

The common guidelines in s 3(1) are:

(a)   the financial resources and needs of the applicant, other applicants and beneficiaries of the estate now and in the foreseeable future;

(b)   the deceased's moral obligations towards any applicant or beneficiary;

(c)   the size and nature of the estate;

(d)   the physical or mental disability of any applicant or beneficiary;

(e)   anything else which may be relevant, such as the conduct of the applicant.

The special guidelines vary with the category of applicant. For example, where the applicant is the surviving spouse or civil partner, the court takes into account the applicant's age and contribution to the welfare of the family, the duration of the marriage or civil partnership and the likely financial settlement if the marriage or civil partnership had ended in divorce or dissolution rather than death. On an application by a child of the deceased the applicant's education or training requirements are considered. (The courts have shown a reluctance to award financial provision to adult, able-bodied children unless there is a particular need.)

When considering the common and special guidelines, the court takes into account:

(a) the facts at the date of the hearing (s 3(5)); and

(b) with regard to the financial resources and needs of the applicant:

    (i)   his earning capacity; and

    (ii) his financial obligations and responsibilities (s 3(6)).

29.7.5 What orders can the court make?

The court has wide powers to make orders against the 'net estate' of the deceased, including orders for periodical payments, lump sum payments or the transfer of specific property to the applicant.

The 'net estate' against which an order can be made includes not only property which the deceased has, or could have, disposed of by will or nomination, but also the deceased's share of joint property passing by survivorship if the court so orders.

In making an order, the court will declare how the burden of the order is to be borne, ie which beneficiary is to lose part or all of the property he would otherwise have taken.

For inheritance tax (IHT) purposes, the altered disposition of the estate is treated as taking effect from death.

If the order alters the amount passing to the deceased's spouse, the amount of any inheritance tax payable on the estate will be affected.

29.7.6 Protecting the PRs

Personal representatives should be advised not to distribute the estate until six months have elapsed from the issue of the grant. In any event, they must not distribute once they have notice of a possible claim. If PRs do distribute within the six-month period and an applicant subsequently brings a successful claim, the PRs will be personally liable to satisfy the claim if insufficient assets remain in the estate. Where a court permits an application out of time, the PRs will not be liable personally if they have distributed the estate, but the claimant may be able to recover property from the beneficiaries.

SUMMARY

(1) Important types of property pass independently of a will or the intestacy rules.

(2) To be valid a will must:

    (a) be made by a testator with capacity who knows and approves the contents and is not subject to undue influence;

    (b) be properly executed in accordance with Wills Act 1837, s 9;

    (c) remain unrevoked.

(3) Gifts in wills may fail as a result of:

    (a) ademption;

    (b) lapse;

    (c) divorce or dissolution of a civil partnership;

    (d) beneficiary witnesses will disclaimer;

    (e) forfeiture.

---

(4)   The intestacy rules apply to property which is undisposed of by will. The rules are contained in the Administration of Estates Act 1925.

(5)   Family members and dependants can ask the court to alter the disposition of the deceased's estate if they feel that reasonable financial provision has not been made for them. The relevant legislation is contained in the Inheritance (Provision for Family and Dependants) Act 1975.

PROBATE PRACTICE AND PROCEDURE

LEARNING OUTCOMES

After reading this chapter you will be able to:

- decide whether a grant of representation is required and, if so, who has the best right to take it
- decide what probate papers are required to obtain the grant
- explain the effect of a grant of representation
- recognise situations in which a limited grant is required
- recognise situations in which the chain of representation is required
- identify situations in which it is appropriate to use caveats and citations.

30.1 INTRODUCTION

When someone dies, it is necessary for assets in his name to be transferred into the names of his beneficiaries. To do this, it is normally necessary to obtain a court document authorising the deceased's personal representatives (PRs) to transfer his assets. This document is called a grant of representation.

This chapter deals with the process of obtaining a grant of representation and, in particular, with the various documents that the PRs must produce to the Probate Registry and with whether inheritance tax is payable.

The final paragraphs look at how to deal with problems that arise where PRs die before completing the administration and at disputes.

At the time of writing, the process of applying for a grant is governed by the Non-contentious Probate Rules 1987 (NCPR 1987) (SI 1987/2024). However, they will be replaced by new Probate Rules which are currently available in draft form. The new Rules do not make substantive changes but modernise and simplify the process of obtaining a grant: for example, all Latin names are dropped, so caveats become objections, and oaths are replaced by Statements of Truth. As yet we do not have a date for the introduction of the new Rules.

30.2   WHO ARE THE PRS?

The PRs will be either the deceased's executors, or intended administrators. 'Personal representative' is a generic term which covers both.

30.2.1   The executors

If the will is valid and contains an effective appointment of executors of whom one or more is willing and able to prove the deceased's will, a grant of probate will be issued to the executor(s) willing to act (see **30.9**).

30.2.2   Administrators with the will annexed

If there is a valid will but there are no persons willing or able to act as executors, then the next persons entitled to act are administrators with the will annexed, who should be appointed in accordance with the NCPR 1987, r 20 (see **30.10**).

30.2.3   Administrators (simple administration)

If a deceased left no will, or no valid will, the estate will be administered in accordance with the law of intestacy by administrators appointed by the application of NCPR 1987, r 22 (see **30.11**).

30.2.4   Number of PRs required

One executor may obtain a grant and act alone. This is so, even if the estate contains land which may be sold during the administration, because a receipt for the proceeds of sale from one executor is sufficient for the purchaser. This is in contrast to the position of trustees where, if a good receipt for the proceeds of sale of land is to be given to a purchaser, it must be given by at least two trustees (or a trust corporation).

In the case of administrators (with or without the will), it is normally sufficient for one to act in the administration of the estate. However, where the will or intestacy creates a life or minority interest, two administrators are normally required.

30.2.5   Authority of PRs before the grant

An executor derives authority to act in the administration of an estate from the will. The grant of probate confirms that authority. Although the executor has full power to act from the time of the deceased's death, the executor will be unable to undertake certain transactions (eg, sale of land) without producing the grant as proof of authority.

An administrator (with or without the will) has very limited powers before a grant is made. His authority stems from the grant which is not retrospective to the date of death.

30.3   FIRST STEPS AFTER RECEIVING INSTRUCTIONS

Following a person's death, the PRs and their professional advisers will have to deal with a number of matters quickly.

30.3.1   The deceased's will

Ascertain whether the deceased made a will. If so, ensure all executors named in the will receive copies of it.

30.3.2 Directions as to cremation, etc

Give immediate consideration to the terms of the will to ascertain any special directions by the deceased as to cremation, or the use of his body for medical research or other purposes. It is desirable for testators to make their relatives aware of any such wishes before death.

30.3.3 Details of assets and liabilities

Obtain details of the deceased's property and of any debts outstanding at the date of death, by obtaining building society passbooks, share certificates and details of bank accounts, etc. Ask the deceased's bank manager whether the bank holds in safe custody any share certificates or other property owned by the deceased (the bank manager will require sight of the death certificate before giving such information).

From these details, it is possible to begin to evaluate the size of the deceased's estate, and the amount of any liability to inheritance tax.

30.3.4 Details of the beneficiaries

If there is a will, the adviser must establish the identity of the beneficiaries and the nature and extent of their entitlements (eg, whether as legatee or as residuary beneficiary). If specific legacies have been given, it is important to ascertain whether the property given by those specific gifts is part of the estate (if not the gift(s) will have adeemed) (see **29.5.1.2**). If the deceased has died intestate, it is necessary to establish which members of the family have survived so that the basis of distribution of the estate may be established in accordance with the rules discussed at **29.6**.

30.3.5 Missing and/or unknown creditors and beneficiaries

Personal representatives are responsible for administering the estate correctly. This means that they have to collect in all the assets, pay all the debts and transfer the remaining funds and assets to those entitled under the will or intestacy.

If the PRs fail to pay someone who is entitled either as a creditor or as a beneficiary, they will be personally liable to that person.

They may have two problems:

(a) There may be creditors of whom they are unaware or unknown relatives (eg, children born outside marriage whose existence has been kept secret).

(b) They may not know the whereabouts of some beneficiaries who may have lost contact with the deceased's family.

They can protect themselves against *unknown* claims by advertising for claimants under the Trustee Act 1925, s 27. Provided they wait for the time period specified in the section (at least two months), the PRs will be protected from liability if an unknown claimant later appears. However, the claimant will have the right to claim back assets from the beneficiaries who received them.

In relation to unknown claims, the following procedure should be adopted.

30.3.5.1 Early advertisement

In view of the minimum notice period of two months, PRs should advertise as early as possible in the administration. If they are executors, they may advertise at any time after the death; if they are administrators, they have power to advertise at any time after obtaining their grant.

30.3.5.2 Placing the advertisement

The PRs should give notice of the intended distribution of the estate, requiring any person interested to send in particulars of his claim, whether as a creditor or as a beneficiary, by:

(a)   advertisement in the *London Gazette*;

(b)   advertisement in a newspaper circulating in the district in which land owned by the deceased is situated; and

(c)   'such other like notices, including notices elsewhere than in England and Wales, as would, in any special case, have been directed by a court of competent jurisdiction in an action for administration'.

If the personal representatives are in any doubt as to what notices should be given, they should apply to the court for directions. Printed forms for the advertisements may be obtained from law stationers.

30.3.5.3 Time for claims

Each notice must require any person interested to send in particulars of his claim within the time specified in the notice, which must not be less than two months from the date of the notice.

30.3.5.4 Searches in case of land

The PRs should also make searches which the prudent purchaser of land would make in the Land Registry, the Land Charges Register and the Local Land Charges Registry, as appropriate. The purpose of these searches is to reveal the existence of any liability in relation to the deceased's ownership of an interest in land, for example a second mortgage.

30.3.5.5 Distribution after notices

When the time-limit in the notice has expired, the PRs may distribute the deceased's estate, taking into account only those claims of which they have actual knowledge, or which they discover as a result of the advertisements. The PRs are not personally liable for any other claim, but a claimant may pursue the claim by following the assets into the hands of the beneficiaries who have received them from the PRs.

The Trustee Act 1925, s 27 will not give any protection to PRs who knows that there is a person with a claim but cannot find him. It protects only against *unknown* claims.

30.3.5.6 Missing known creditors and beneficiaries

Where PRs cannot trace a known beneficiary, they must consider one of the following:

(a)   Keeping back assets in case the claimant appears. This is unpopular with the other beneficiaries.

(b)   Taking an indemnity from the beneficiaries that they will meet any claims if the claimant reappears. This is dangerous for the PR as the beneficiaries may have no assets when the claimant appears.

(c)   Taking out insurance to provide funds. This can be expensive and, as the claimant may be entitled to interest, it is difficult to know what sum to insure.

(d)   Applying to the court for an order authorising the PRs to distribute the estate on the basis that the claimant is dead. This is referred to as a *Benjamin* order after the case in which it was first ordered (*Re Benjamin* [1902] 1 Ch 723). This protects the PRs from liability, although the claimant retains the right to recover the assets from the beneficiaries. Applying to court is an expensive process, but it is the only solution that offers the PR full protection.

30.4 DECIDING WHETHER A GRANT OF REPRESENTATION IS NECESSARY

A grant enables the PRs to prove their authority to deal with the deceased's assets which passes under the will or the intestacy rules. However, it is not always necessary to obtain a grant of representation to deal with assets. The ability to access assets without a grant is particularly useful where the deceased's family needs funds immediately for paying inheritance tax or other purposes.

A fee must be paid to the Probate Registry. The current fee is a flat fee charged irrespective of the size of the estate. However, in March 2016 the Government issued a Consultation Paper which proposed introducing a banded system linked to the size of the estate. The intention is to increase the 'take' from probate fees and use the surplus to contribute to the general cost of running the courts.

A grant may not be required in the three situations which follow.

30.4.1 Assets which may pass to the PRs without a grant

30.4.1.1 Administration of Estates (Small Payments) Act 1965

Orders made under this Act permit payments to be made under various statutes and statutory instruments to persons appearing to be beneficially entitled to the assets without formal proof of title. This facility is restricted, in that it is not available if the value of the asset exceeds £5,000; in addition, as the payments are made at the discretion of the institutions concerned, it is not possible for PRs to insist that payments should be made. If payment is refused, the PRs will have to obtain a grant before the asset can be collected. This can present practical problems where inheritance tax is payable, as the tax normally has to be paid before obtaining the grant and there may be no funds accessible to the personal representatives. Subject to these points, payments can be made in respect of, for example:

(a)   money in the National Savings Bank and Trustee Savings Bank (but not in other bank accounts);

(b)   National Savings Certificates and Premium Bonds; and

(c)   money in building societies and friendly societies.

30.4.1.2 Chattels

Movable personal property such as furniture, clothing, jewellery and cars can normally be sold without the PRs having to prove formally to the buyer that they are entitled to sell such items.

30.4.1.3 Cash

Normally, the PRs do not require a grant when taking custody of any cash found in the deceased's possession (ie found in the home of the deceased as opposed to deposited in a bank or other account).

30.4.2 Assets not passing through the PRs' hands

30.4.2.1 Joint property

On death, any interest in property held by the deceased as beneficial joint tenant with another (whether it is an interest in land or personalty, eg a bank account) passes by survivorship to the surviving joint tenant. As it does not pass via the PRs, any grant is irrelevant. The survivor has access to the property and can prove title to the whole of it merely by producing the deceased's death certificate. Since it is common for married couples and civil partners to own property jointly, there are many occasions where a grant is not required for this reason.

(Conversely, if the property is held by persons as beneficial tenants in common, the share of each tenant in common passes on his death to his PRs for distribution, and a grant will be required.)

30.4.3   Property not forming part of the deceased person's estate

The deceased may have insured his/her own life, but in such a way that the policy and its proceeds are held in trust for others. This trust may be established by writing the policy under the Married Women's Property Act 1882, s 11 ('a Married Women's Property Act policy') for the spouse or children of the deceased, or by making a separate declaration of trust for those or other beneficiaries. On death, the policy money is payable to the trustees of the policy on production of the death certificate. A grant is not required since the money does not form part of the estate. As the deceased had no beneficial interest in the policy or its proceeds (because of the trust), no inheritance tax will be payable on the proceeds. Such a policy is particularly advantageous, as the proceeds make tax-free provision for dependants of the deceased and can be collected in immediately following the death.

30.4.3.1   Pension benefits

Death in service benefits under a pension scheme are often payable to persons to be selected at the discretion of the pension fund trustees. Payments are made to the beneficiaries on production of the death certificate. A grant is not required, since the pension benefits do not form part of the deceased's estate. This is another method of making tax-free provision for dependants, and such provision can also be collected in immediately following the death.

30.5   APPLYING FOR GRANT

Where a grant is required, it is necessary to apply to the Principal Registry of the Family Division or to a district probate registry. The application is made by lodging such of the following documents as are appropriate to the particular case:

(a)   receipted HM Revenue & Customs (HMRC) Form IHT421 confirming payment of any inheritance tax or Form IHT205 if the estate is 'excepted' (see **30.7**);

(b)   the deceased's will and codicil, if any, plus two A4 photocopies. The original will and codicil(s), if any, must be marked (ie, signed for identification purposes) by the executors (or administrators if there are no proving executors) and the solicitor before whom the supporting oath is sworn or affirmed;

(c)   the oath, sworn or affirmed by the executors or administrators;

(d)   any affidavit evidence which may be required (see **30.5.2**);

(e)   probate court fees. At the time of writing this is a flat fee of £155 but may be increased (see below).

On 24 February 2017 the Ministry of Justice announced that to help reduce the funding shortfall on the cost of the general court system, probate fees would be increased significantly from May 2017 and payable on a sliding scale.

The proposed new fees

Value of probate estate (before inheritance tax)	Proposed fee
Up to £50,000	£0
Exceeds £50,000 but does not exceed £300,000	£300
Exceeds £300,000 but does not exceed £500,000	£1,000
Exceeds £500,000 but does not exceed £1m	£4,000
Exceeds £1m but does not exceed £1.6m	£8,000
Exceeds £1.6m but does not exceed £2m	£12,000
Above £2m	£20,000

The Joint Select Committee on Statutory Instruments rejected the draft regulation implementing the increase on the basis that increases of this order amounted to taxation and, as such, required the consent of Parliament. The General Election was called before this could happen so at the time of writing the future is uncertain.

30.5.1 Admissibility of will to probate

It is important to check the will carefully to make sure that it is valid and admissible to probate. If it is not, application will be made instead for a grant of simple administration.

To ensure that the will is admissible, check the following:

(a)   the will is the last will of the testator;

(b)   that it has not been validly revoked;

(c)   that it is executed in accordance with the Wills Act 1837, s 9; and

(d)   that it contains an attestation clause which indicates that the will was executed in accordance with the requirements of the Wills Act 1837 and raises a presumption of 'due execution'.

30.5.2 The registrar's additional requirements

If the application is in order, the registrar will issue the original grant, sealed with the court seal and signed by him. In some cases, before issuing the grant, the registrar may require further evidence. At present evidence to the probate registry is presented in the form of oaths and affidavits, which are sworn statements. These will be replaced by Statements of Truth when the new Probate Rules come into effect, but at the time of writing there is no date for the change.

30.5.2.1 Affidavit of due execution

If there is no attestation clause, if the clause is in some respect defective, or if there are circumstances raising doubt about the execution of the will, the registrar will require affidavit evidence, usually from an attesting witness, to establish that the will has been properly executed. The evidence is provided by means of an affidavit of due execution.

If there is doubt about the mental capacity of the testator to make the will, the affidavit of a doctor may be necessary. In such cases, it is helpful if a doctor examined the testator to ascertain whether he had sufficient capacity at the time the will was made.

30.5.2.2 Affidavit as to knowledge and approval

It may appear to the registrar that there is doubt as to whether the testator was aware of the contents of the will when he executed it. This may arise through blindness, illiteracy or frailty of the testator, or because of suspicious circumstances, for example where the person who prepared the will for the testator benefits substantially by its terms.

In any of these circumstances, the attestation clause should have been suitably adapted, ideally by indicating that the will was read over to the testator or was independently explained to him. In the absence of this, the registrar will require to be satisfied that the testator had knowledge and approval of the contents of the will. The evidence is provided by means of an affidavit of knowledge and approval of contents made by someone who can speak as to the facts. Normally, this will be one of the attesting witnesses, but it could be an independent person who explained the provisions of the will to the testator.

30.5.2.3 Affidavit of plight and condition

If the state of the will suggests that it has been interfered with in some way since execution, the registrar will require further evidence by way of explanation. This may arise:

(a)   where the will has been altered since its execution;

(b)   where there is some obvious mark on it indicating a document may have been attached to it (eg, the marks of a paper clip, raising a suggestion that some other testamentary document may have been attached); or

(c)   where it gives the appearance of attempted revocation.

Generally, the explanation required will take the form of an affidavit of plight and condition made by some person having knowledge of the facts.

30.5.2.4   Lost will

A will which was known to have been in the testator's possession but which cannot be found following the death is presumed to have been destroyed by the testator with the intention of revoking it.

However, if the will has been lost or accidentally destroyed, probate may be obtained of a copy of the will, such as a copy kept in the solicitor's file, or a reconstruction. In such a case, application should be made to the registrar, supported by appropriate affidavit evidence from the applicant for the grant of probate.

30.6   COMPLETING THE IHT ACCOUNT

30.6.1   Purpose of an IHT account

One of the first steps towards obtaining the grant of representation is the preparation of the appropriate IHT account and the calculation of any inheritance tax payable.

If the estate is not an 'excepted estate' (see **30.7**), the PRs will prepare an IHT400 and whichever of the supporting schedules are relevant to the estate. For example, if the deceased made lifetime gifts, the PRs must complete schedule 403 which deals with lifetime gifts.

The IHT400 is an inventory of the assets to which the deceased was beneficially entitled and of his liabilities, and is the form for claiming reliefs and exemptions and calculating the inheritance tax payable. It should be delivered within 12 months of the end of the month in which the death occurred. Usually PRs aim to deliver the account within six months to comply with inheritance tax time-limits for the payment of interest. Until the account is submitted no grant of representation can be issued.

Where inheritance tax is payable, it is necessary to apply for a reference number before submitting the IHT400. Application may be made online or by post using schedule IHT422.

Inheritance tax is payable on all property to which the deceased was beneficially entitled immediately before his death, whether or not such property vests in his PRs. Certain types of property qualify for tax relief, for example business or agricultural property, or an exemption may apply because of the identity of the beneficiary (ie the surviving spouse or a charity) (see **4.4.3**).

The rate of inheritance tax is 0% on transfers within the nil rate band (£325,000 for tax year 2017/18) and 40% on the balance, unless at least 10% of the chargeable estate is passing to charity in which case the reduced rate of 36% is charged.

Where surviving spouses or civil partners die on or after 9 October 2007, they can inherit any unused proportion of the nil rate band of the first spouse or civil partner to die. The PRs of the survivor must make a claim using schedule 402.

> **EXAMPLE**
>
> Paul died in January 2008 (when the nil rate band was £300,000). He left £60,000 to his sister and everything else to his civil partner, Leo.
>
> Paul therefore had four-fifths of his nil rate band unused.

> Leo dies in August 2020 when the nil rate band is £500,000, leaving everything to his nephews and nieces. Leo's PRs can claim an additional four-fifths of the 2020/21 nil rate band. As a result the nil rate band available on Leo's death will be £500,000 + ($\frac{4}{5}$ x £500,000) = £900,000.

For deaths on or after 6 April 2017, there is an additional nil rate band (the 'RNRB') available to those who leave a residence or interest in a residence to lineal descendants. The value of the new RNRB is £100,000 in tax year 2017/18, rising by £25,000 a year until 2020/21, after which it will rise in line with the Consumer Prices Index. A surviving spouse or civil partner can inherit unused RNRB from a predeceased spouse or civil partner.

30.6.1.1 Paying the inheritance tax

Inheritance tax on property without the right to pay by instalments (see **4.8.1.2**) must be paid within six months of the end of the month in which the death occurred. Failure to do so causes interest to become payable. For example, if a person dies on 10 January, inheritance tax is due on 31 July, or on delivery of the IHT400 if this is earlier. Until this tax has been paid, no grant can issue to the deceased's estate.

Where there is property which qualifies for the right to pay the tax by instalments, none of the tax on that property is due until the expiry of the six-month period. If the option is exercised, only the first instalment of one-tenth must then be paid. In an estate where it is not possible to deliver the IHT400 within that period, all tax on non-instalment option property plus the appropriate number of instalments on property with the option and interest must be paid on delivery of the account. Interest runs on all tax not paid on the due date.

The tax payable on the estate is apportioned between the instalment and non-instalment option property using the method described in **4.7.2**.

30.6.2 Valuations

30.6.2.1 General principles

Assets in the estate are valued at 'the price which the property might reasonably be expected to fetch if sold in the open market' immediately before the death (IHTA 1984, s 160).

30.6.2.2 Jointly-owned assets

There is a special valuation rule where the deceased was the co-owner (as tenant in common or as beneficial joint tenant) of land at his death. The market value of the land at the date of death will normally be discounted to reflect the difficulty of selling a part interest in land. The probate value of the deceased's interest is the discounted market value at the date of death divided proportionately between the co-owners. A discount of 15% is normally considered reasonable for residential property and a discount of 10% for investment property. A share in a residential property is relatively unattractive because of the rights of the other co-owner to occupy the property. Buying a share in an investment property is less unattractive as it is relatively unimportant whether the capital sum spent buys the whole or part of an income stream.

> **EXAMPLE**
>
> Mary and her sister, Nellie, owned a house as joint tenants, in which they live together. The value of the house at Mary's death was £400,000. Apply a 15% discount.
>
> The discount is £400,000 × 15% = £60,000
>
> and her half share £400,000 – £60,000 = £340,000 ÷ 2 = £170,000.
>
> The probate value of Mary's share is £170,000.

The discount is not available where the co-ownership is of an asset other than land. For such assets, for example bank and building society accounts, the probate value is the account balance as at the date of death (plus interest) divided proportionately between the joint owners.

Where the co-owners of land are spouses or civil partners, the related property rules (see **4.4.2.1**) apply. HMRC has always refused to allow any discount in value on the basis of these rules. This normally means that each spouse or civil partner will be treated as owning a proportionate part of the value of the whole. *Arkwright v IRC* [2004] WLTR 181 suggested that if one spouse or civil partner is terminally ill, the value of his or her share might be reduced. So far there is no reported case in which such a discount has been obtained.

30.6.3 Funding the inheritance tax

Where there is tax to pay on delivery of an IHT400, the PRs must arrange for the appropriate amount of money to be sent to HMRC with the account. When this tax is paid, the receipted Probate Summary (IHT421) is sent with the other documents (see **30.5**) to the appropriate Probate Registry so that the grant can issue. Funding the tax bill may be problematic as all the deceased's assets vesting in the PRs are 'frozen', and therefore may be untouchable, until the grant issues giving the proof of title to the PRs.

The options which may be available to raise funds to pay the inheritance tax are set out below.

30.6.3.1 Direct payment scheme

HMRC has reached an agreement with the British Banker's Association and the Building Societies Association on a procedure allowing PRs to arrange payment of inheritance tax to HMRC directly from the deceased's accounts.

The scheme is voluntary on the part of the institutions, so PRs must check whether the relevant banks and building societies are part of the scheme.

The procedure is as follows:

(a)   The PRs must provide whatever identification the relevant banks and building societies require. They should do this well in advance of applying for a grant so as to avoid any unnecessary delay in the application.

(b)   The PRs complete a separate IHT423 for each bank and building society from which money is to be transferred.

(c)   The PRs send each IHT423 to the relevant bank or building society at the same time that they send the IHT400 and supporting schedules to HMRC. The IHT423 includes an IHT reference number provided by HMRC to allow HMRC to match up the payment with the correct estate.

(d)   The bank or building society will send the money direct to HMRC. Once HMRC has received the money and is satisfied that the amount is correct, it will return the receipted Probate Summary (IHT421) to the solicitor.

The process is not quick, so where there is an urgent need for a grant PRs will want to find an alternative source of funding.

Solicitors have for many years had private arrangements with banks and building societies under which the bank or building society transfers funds directly to HMRC from the deceased's accounts. These arrangements can continue.

30.6.3.2 Life assurance

Where the proceeds of a policy of insurance on the deceased's life are payable to the estate, the life assurance company, like a bank, may be willing to release funds to pay the inheritance tax directly to HMRC and not to the PRs or their solicitors.

30.6.3.3   Assets realisable without production of the grant

By applying the Administration of Estates (Small Payments) Act 1965 (see **30.4.1**), assets may, in some cases, be realised without production of a grant. The maximum value of any one asset that may be realised is £5,000. The Act gives discretion to the institution to allow assets to be realised in this way. Where an estate is large or complex, this discretion will often not be exercised. In such cases, a grant must first be obtained and produced to release the asset concerned.

30.6.3.4   Loans from beneficiaries

Wealthy beneficiaries may be prepared to fund the tax from their own resources, on condition that they will be repaid from the deceased's estate once the grant issues. Alternatively, beneficiaries may already have received assets as a result of the death which they are prepared to use to pay the tax, such as money from a jointly held bank account, or the proceeds of a life policy vested in them under the Married Women's Property Act 1882. However, many beneficiaries may not be able to afford to make a loan.

30.6.3.5   Bank borrowing

Banks which do not participate in the voluntary scheme will still usually lend against an undertaking to repay the loan given by the PRs. A bank may also require an undertaking from the solicitor to repay the loan from the proceeds of the estate. Whether or not the solicitor is a PR, any undertaking should be limited to 'such proceeds as come into the solicitor's control'. Undertakings to pay money should be carefully worded so as to ensure payment is not due from the solicitor personally.

Bank borrowing is expensive, because the bank will charge an arrangement fee and interest on the amount borrowed. Money borrowed should be repaid at the earliest opportunity so as to honour any undertaking and to stop interest running. Income tax relief is available to the PRs for interest paid on a separate loan account in respect of inheritance tax payable on personalty vesting in them.

30.6.3.6   National Savings and Government stock

Payment of tax may also be made from National Savings Bank accounts or from the proceeds of National Savings Certificates, any Government stock held on the National Savings register or any other National Savings investment.

30.6.3.7   Heritage property in lieu of tax

Taxpayers can offer HMRC an asset in lieu of tax (IHTA 1984, s 230(1)). The Secretary of State must agree to accept such assets and the standard required of such objects is very high. The item must be 'pre-eminent for its national, scientific, historic or artistic interest'.

30.6.3.8   Obtaining a grant on credit

In exceptional cases where the PRs can demonstrate that it is impossible to pay the inheritance tax in advance, HMRC will allow the grant to be obtained on credit.

30.7   THE REQUIREMENT FOR AN IHT ACCOUNT

30.7.1   Inheritance Tax (Delivery of Accounts) (Excepted Estates) Regulations 2004

If the estate is an excepted estate, there is no need for an IHT400 to be submitted, although HMRC can demand one within 35 days of the date of issue of the grant of representation. If an estate which initially appears to be excepted is subsequently found not to be so, the PRs must submit the IHT400 within six months of the discovery.

The precise requirements for qualifying as an excepted estate change each year and are becoming extremely complex. You will find it easier to focus on the broad description of the requirements rather than on the detail.

For deaths on or after 1 September 2006 there are three categories of excepted estate, and the requirements are as follows:

- Category 1 – 'small' estates

   Broadly, estates falling into this category are those where the gross value of the estate for inheritance tax purposes, plus the chargeable value of any 'specified transfers' (defined below) in the seven years prior to death, does not exceed the current nil rate threshold.

   For deaths before 6 April 2010 the nil rate threshold for this purpose included only the deceased's own nil rate band and ignored any nil rate band transferred from a predeceased spouse or civil partner. For deaths on or after that date the nil rate threshold is increased to take account of transferred nil rate band, but only if the whole of the nil rate band of the first spouse or civil partner was transferred. If the first spouse or civil partner had used any part of their nil rate band, nothing is added for this purpose.

   (For applications between 6 April and 1 August each year the threshold will be the threshold for the previous tax year.)

   In full, the Regulations for this category require the following:

   (a)   the deceased died, domiciled in the United Kingdom;

   (b)   the value of the estate is attributable wholly to property passing:

       (i)   under his will or intestacy,

       (ii)   under a nomination of an asset taking effect on death,

       (iii)   under a single settlement in which he was entitled to an interest in possession in settled property, or

       (iv)   by survivorship in a beneficial joint tenancy or, in Scotland, by survivorship in a special destination;

   (c)   of that property:

       (i)   not more than £150,000 represents property which, immediately before that person's death, was settled property; and

       (ii)   not more than £100,000 represents property situated outside the United Kingdom;

   (d)   the deceased made no chargeable transfers in the seven years before death other than specified transfers (defined below) where the aggregate value transferred (ignoring business or agricultural relief) did not exceed £150,000; and

   (e)   the aggregate of:

       (i)   the gross value of the deceased's estate, plus

       (ii)   the value transferred by any specified transfers (defined below), plus

       (iii)   the value transferred by any specified exempt transfers (defined below),

       did not exceed the nil rate threshold for the deceased (increased to take account of a full nil rate band transferred from a deceased spouse or civil partner in the case of deaths on or after 6 April 2010).

- Category 2 – 'exempt' estates

   These are estates where the bulk of the estate attracts the spouse (or civil partner) or charity exemption. The gross value of the estate plus specified transfers (defined below) must not exceed £1 million and the net chargeable estate after deduction of liabilities and spouse and/or charity exemption must not exceed the nil rate threshold.

As with Category 1 estates, transferred nil rate band can increase the nil rate threshold for this purpose, but only if the death is on or after 6 April 2010 and on the first death the whole nil rate band was transferred to the surviving spouse.

In full, the Regulations for this category require the following:

(a) the deceased, domiciled in the United Kingdom;

(b) the value of the estate is attributable wholly to property passing:

    (i) under his will or intestacy,

    (ii) under a nomination of an asset taking effect on death,

    (iii) under a single settlement in which he was entitled to an interest in possession in settled property, or

    (iv) by survivorship in a beneficial joint tenancy or, in Scotland, by survivorship in a special destination;

(c) of that property:

    (i) not more than £150,000 represents property which, immediately before that person's death, was settled property (settled property passing on death to a spouse or charity is ignored for this purpose); and

    (ii) not more than £100,000 represents property situated outside the United Kingdom;

(d) the deceased made no chargeable transfers during the period of seven years ending with his death other than specified transfers (defined below) where the aggregate value transferred (ignoring business or agricultural relief) did not exceed £150,000;

(e) the aggregate of:

    (i) the gross value of that person's estate, plus

    (ii) the value transferred by any specified transfers (defined below) made by that person, plus

    (iii) the value transferred by any specified exempt transfers (defined below),

    did not exceed £1,000,000;

(ea) there is property left after deduction of liabilities to pass to spouse or charity; and

(f) the aggregate of:

    (i) the value of the estate after deducting allowable liabilities, spouse and charity exemptions, plus

    (ii) specified transfers (defined below), plus

    (iii) specified exempt transfers (defined below),

    did not exceed the nil rate threshold.

'Specified transfers' for Categories 1 and 2

These are chargeable transfers of cash, personal chattels or tangible moveable property, quoted shares or securities, or an interest in or over land (unless the land becomes settled or is subject to a reservation of benefit) made in the seven years before death. This means that if someone makes a gift which does not fall within this category in the seven years before death (for example, a transfer of unquoted shares), the estate cannot be excepted under Categories 1 or 2.

When valuing the specified transfers, business and agricultural property relief is ignored so the unrelieved value has to be taken into account.

'Specified exempt transfers' for Categories 1 and 2

These are transfers of value made during the seven years before death which are exempt under one of the following exemptions:

(a) s 18 (transfers between spouses (or civil partners));

(b)   s 23 (gifts to charities);

(c)   s 24 (gifts to political parties);

(d)   s 24A (gifts to housing associations);

(e)   s 27 (maintenance funds for historic buildings, etc); or

(f)   s 28 (employee trusts).

In the case of deaths occurring on or after 1 March 2011, gifts which are exempt under the normal expenditure out of income exemption are treated for this purpose as chargeable if they exceed £3,000 in any one tax year.

- *Category 3 – 'non-domiciled' estates*

    The third category is where the deceased was never domiciled or treated as domiciled in the United Kingdom, with only limited assets in the United Kingdom.

    In full, the Regulations for this category require the following:

    (a)   he was never domiciled in the United Kingdom or treated as domiciled in the United Kingdom by s 267 of the IHTA 1984; and

    (b)   the value of the estate situated in the United Kingdom is wholly attributable to cash or quoted shares or securities passing under his will or intestacy or by survivorship in a beneficial joint tenancy or, in Scotland, by survivorship in a special destination, the gross value of which does not exceed £150,000.

EXAMPLE 1

Adam has just died. His will leaves his estate to his wife Brenda and daughter Clare in equal shares. He is UK domiciled and has made no lifetime transfers.

His estate consists of:	£
House owned jointly with Brenda (half share)	80,000
Building society a/c (sole name)	100,000
Personal chattels	2,000
Life interest in a trust fund set up in his father's will (value of capital assets)	30,000
Debts (funeral bill and credit cards)	(2,000)

This is a Category 1 ('small') excepted estate. This fact will also be noted on the oath. Adam's estate satisfies the criteria and it has an inheritance tax value of £212,000 gross (note that inheritance tax exemptions and reliefs are ignored when ascertaining the gross inheritance tax estate).

EXAMPLE 2

Davina has just died. Her will leaves £50,000 to her son, Ernst, and the residue to her husband, Ferdinand. She is UK domiciled. Her only specified transfer was made two years ago when she gave £100,000 to Ernst.

Her estate consists of:	£
House owned jointly with Fernando (half share)	400,000
Quoted Investments	100,000
Bank and building society accounts	50,000
Personal chattels	15,000
Specified transfer	100,000
Debts (funeral bill and credit cards)	(5,000)

This is a Category 2 ('exempt') excepted estate. The aggregate of the gross value of the estate, plus the chargeable value of specified transfers in the seven years prior to death does not exceed £1 million; the net chargeable estate after deduction of liabilities and the spouse exemption does not exceed the current nil rate threshold of £325,000

> **EXAMPLE 3**
>
> Fred has just died leaving his estate to his two children. His wife Freda died last year and left everything to Fred.
>
> Fred's gross estate is £600,000, and consists of a house and money in the bank. He has made no lifetime gifts.
>
> This is a Category 1 ('small') excepted estate because Fred's nil rate threshold is increased to £650,000 as a result of inheriting Freda's nil rate band.

> **EXAMPLE 4**
>
> Assume the facts were the same as in Example 3, except for the fact that Freda had left a legacy of £5,000 to her grandson. Because Fred did not inherit the whole of Freda's nil rate band, his nil rate threshold is not increased for the purposes of the excepted estates regulations.
>
> His estate is therefore not excepted.

> **EXAMPLE 5**
>
> Eduardo is an Italian who has never been domiciled in the UK. He dies with £100,000 in a UK bank account. Under his will, his entire estate passes to his nephew.
>
> The estate is excepted as a 'non-domiciled' estate because it fulfils the requirements:
>
> • Eduardo was never domiciled in the UK.
> • The value of his UK estate is wholly attributable to cash.
> • His whole UK estate passes by will and does not exceed £150,000.

Note that an estate cannot be excepted if one of the alternatively secured pension provisions applies to it. However, alternatively secured pensions are beyond the scope of this book and are not considered further.

30.7.1.1 Procedure

In England and Wales and Northern Ireland all applications for probate in relation to excepted estates must be accompanied by Form IHT205 (or Form IHT207 for those domiciled abroad).

The IHT205 is a short form based on the document completed by applicants in person. The Probate Service will forward the forms to HMRC on a weekly basis.

HMRC will select a random sample to review. In addition, it 'will use other information sources to identify those estates nearer to the IHT threshold' where it feels that there is a risk that inheritance tax may be payable.

30.7.2 Form IHT400

Form IHT400 must be used whenever the deceased dies domiciled in the UK and the estate is not an 'excepted' estate.

The PRs must complete Form IHT400 and relevant supporting schedules, and sign a declaration that the contents are true. They must calculate the amount of any inheritance tax payable and ensure that any inheritance tax due on delivery of the account is paid. HMRC will receipt and return the accompanying IHT421.

When the PRs apply to the Probate Registry they must file the receipted IHT421 with the probate papers as proof that the relevant inheritance tax has been paid.

30.8 OATHS: GENERAL BACKGROUND

30.8.1 Types and purpose of oaths

Every application for a grant of representation must be supported by the appropriate form of oath. The three most common types of oath are as follows:

(a)   oath for executors;

(b)   oath for administrators with will annexed;

(c)   oath for administrators.

The oaths differ from each other in detail but they have a common purpose, namely:

(a)   to give details of the deceased;

(b)   to set out the basis of the applicant's claim to take the grant;

(c)   to require the applicant to swear that he will administer the estate correctly;

(d)   in the case of oaths for executors and oaths for administrators with the will annexed, to identify and exhibit the will and any codicils;

(e)   to swear to the value of the estate passing under the grant.

Unless the appropriate oath is accurately completed and submitted to the Probate Registry by, or on behalf of, those PRs who may properly make an application, no grant of representation will be issued.

30.8.2 Swearing or affirming the oath

Before the oath is submitted to the Probate Registry, the PRs must swear or affirm the truth of its contents. This must be done before a commissioner for oaths or a solicitor holding a current practising certificate, neither of whom is connected with the firm of solicitors acting for the PRs. The PRs may prefer to affirm, in which case they say 'I do solemnly sincerely and truly declare and affirm that ...'. A PR who swears the oath will be required to hold the New Testament or Bible whilst saying 'I swear by Almighty God that ...'.

Once the oath has been sworn or affirmed it should be sent to the Probate Registry with any will, the IHT account and the appropriate probate court fees.

When the new Probate Rules are in force, a statement of truth will replace an oath or affirmation.

30.8.3 The value of the estate passing under the grant

The oath must include the gross value of the property passing under the grant and the net value (ie after deduction of debts of the estate). The net figure is the probate estate on which probate fees are payable. The figures given will be repeated on the grant of representation issued by the Probate Registry.

The Probate Registry is not concerned with property passing otherwise than under the grant, so the value of joint property passing by survivorship or property passing under a trust is not included. The full value of property passing under the grant must be included. Inheritance tax exemptions and reliefs are irrelevant for this purpose.

If the estate is a Category 1 ('small') excepted estate, the PRs must swear that it is not necessary to deliver an IHT account. They do not need to give the exact value of the property passing under the grant.

In relation to the gross value, they need only state that it does not exceed the nil rate band threshold.

In relation to the net value, they must round it up to the nearest whole thousand and state on the oath that it does not exceed that figure. This assists government departments, such as the

DWP, that may need to check the deceased's eligibility for benefits received, and charities, who may want an indication of their likely entitlement where they are residuary beneficiaries.

If the estate is a Category 2 ('exempt') excepted estate, the PRs again swear that it is not necessary to deliver an IHT account, but this time they must give the exact figures for the gross and net property passing under the grant.

30.9 OATH FOR EXECUTORS

30.9.1 Entitlement to act

Executors are appointed by a valid will. They take a grant of probate. One executor may obtain a grant and act alone.

> **EXAMPLE 1**
>
> Alex by his will appoints Brian and Colin to be his executors and leaves his entire estate to a named charity.
>
> Brian and/or Colin can apply for a grant of probate by lodging an oath for executors, and the will, with the Probate Registry.

The appointment of executors is not affected by the fact that the will may fail to dispose of some or all of the deceased's estate.

> **EXAMPLE 2**
>
> Diana has just died. Her will appoints Eric as her executor and leaves her entire estate to Freda. Freda died before Diana whose estate will therefore be distributed according to the intestacy rules. Eric is alive and prepared to act as executor. Eric will apply for a grant of probate by swearing an oath for executors.

30.9.2 Capacity to act

Capacity to act as executor is judged at the time of the application for the grant.

30.9.2.1 Executor lacking capacity to act

A person appointed as an executor by the will but who, at the testator's death, does not have the mental capacity to act, cannot apply for the grant.

30.9.2.2 Minors

There is no prohibition on a testator naming a minor as his executor. However, if the executor is still a minor at the testator's death he cannot act as an executor nor obtain a grant of probate until he attains majority.

Where one of several executors is a minor, the other(s) being adults, probate can be granted to the adult executor(s) with power reserved to the minor to take a grant at a later date (for an explanation of 'power reserved', see **30.9.4**). If the administration of the estate has not been completed by the time the minor attains 18 years, he can then apply for a grant of double probate to enable him to act as executor alongside the other proving executor(s).

EXAMPLE

George dies appointing his wife, Ingrid and his son Harry (aged 16) as his executors.

Where the minor is the only executor appointed by the will (or the adult executors are not able or willing to act), someone must take the grant on behalf of the minor as it would be impracticable to leave the testator's estate unadministered until the executor reaches 18 years. A grant of letters of administration with will annexed for the use and benefit of the minor will be made, usually to the parent(s) or guardian(s) of the minor, until the minor attains 18 years. On obtaining majority the executor may apply for a cessate grant of probate.

30.9.2.3 The former spouse or civil partner

If the testator appointed his spouse or civil partner as his executor and the marriage or civil partnership subsequently ends, that appointment will fail unless the testator has shown a contrary intention in the will (Wills Act 1837, s 18A: see **29.4.4.2**).

If the spouse or civil partner was one of several executors, the others may apply for the grant of probate without him or her. If the spouse was appointed as a sole executor, application should be made for a grant of letters of administration with will annexed. In either case, the oath to lead to the appropriate grant should cite the fact and date of the divorce.

30.9.3 Renunciation

Persons appointed as executors may renounce their right to take the grant, provided that they have not intermeddled in the estate. Intermeddling consists of doing tasks a PR might do, for example notifying the deceased's bank of the death. By intermeddling, executors accept their appointment. Once executors have intermeddled, they must take the grant.

Provided there has been no intermeddling, executors who do not wish to act can renounce their rights. Rights as executor then cease and the administration of the estate proceeds as if the executor had never been appointed.

The renunciation must be made in writing, signed by the person renouncing (the signature must be witnessed), and the renunciation must be filed at the Probate Registry. This is normally done by the PRs who are applying for a grant when they lodge their application at the Probate Registry.

Executors who are also appointed as trustees will remain trustees despite renouncing the executorship. They will have to disclaim the trusteeship as well if they want to act in neither capacity.

30.9.4 Power reserved

There is no limit on how many executors can be appointed by the will, but probate will be granted to a maximum of four executors. Power may be reserved to the other(s) to take out a grant in the future if a vacancy arises.

> **EXAMPLE 1**
>
> Alan's will appoints B, C, D, E and F to be his executors. All are willing and able to act. C, D, E and F apply for a grant of probate. 'Power is reserved' to B. If F dies before the administration is complete, B can then apply for a grant. B must apply if he wishes to act; there is no automatic substitution.
>
> If there is a dispute between the executors as to which of them should apply for a grant, this may be resolved by summons before a registrar (NCPR 1987, r 27(6)).

There is no need for every executor to act. A person appointed as one of several executors may not wish to act initially, but he may not want to take the irrevocable step of renouncing his right to a grant of probate.

> **EXAMPLE 2**
>
> Alan appoints Ben and Charles as his executors. When Alan dies, Ben is working in Germany but is due to return to England in 12 months' time. Ben does not feel that he should act as executor whilst abroad and is happy to let Charles act alone initially, but he does want to help in the administration if it has not been completed by the time he returns to England.
>
> Charles should apply for the grant 'with power reserved' to Ben to prove at a later stage.

One executor is always sufficient. As we shall see later, this is not the case for administrators.

30.10 OATH FOR ADMINISTRATORS WITH WILL ANNEXED

30.10.1 Entitlement to act

As the title of this oath suggests, it is used in an estate where there is a valid will but no executor willing and able to apply for a grant of probate.

There may be no executor because:

(a) the will fails to appoint executors; or

(b) the appointment was of the testator's spouse or civil partner and has failed as a result of the testator's divorce (Wills Act 1837, s 18A; see **29.4.4**);

(c) the executor has predeceased the testator;

(d) the executor has died after the testator but before taking the grant; or

(e) the executor has renounced.

If there is a valid will but no executor and the will does not dispose of all the estate, the appropriate grant is still letters of administration with will annexed. The property undisposed of by the will is distributed according to the intestacy rules (see **29.6**).

30.10.2 NCPR 1987, r 20

The order of priority of the person(s) entitled to a grant of letters of administration with will annexed is governed by NCPR 1987, r 20. The rule states as follows:

> Where the deceased died on or after 1 January 1926 the person or persons entitled to a grant in respect of a will shall be determined in accordance with the following order of priority, namely—
>
> (a) the executor ... ;
>
> (b) any residuary legatee or devisee holding in trust for any other person;
>
> (c) any other residuary legatee or devisee (including one for life) or where the residue is not wholly disposed of by the will, any person entitled to share in the undisposed of residue (including the Treasury Solicitor when claiming bona vacantia on behalf of the Crown), provided that—

(i)   unless a registrar otherwise directs, a residuary legatee or devisee whose legacy or devise is vested in interest shall be preferred to one entitled on the happening of a contingency, and

(ii)   where the residue is not in terms wholly disposed of, the registrar may, if he is satisfied that the testator has nevertheless disposed of the whole or substantially the whole of the known estate, allow a grant to be made to any legatee or devisee entitled to, or to share in, the estate so disposed of, without regard to the persons entitled to share in any residue not disposed of by the will;

(d)   the personal representative of any residuary legatee or devisee (but not one for life, or one holding in trust for any other person), or of any person entitled to share in any residue not disposed of by the will;

(e)   any other legatee or devisee (including one for life or one holding in trust for any other person) or any creditor of the deceased, provided that, unless a registrar otherwise directs, a legatee or devisee whose legacy or devise is vested in interest shall be preferred to one entitled on the happening of a contingency;

(f)   the personal representative of any other legatee or devisee (but not one for life or one holding in trust for any other person) or of any creditor of the deceased.

30.10.2.1   Clearing off

Each applicant is listed in priority in r 20. When applying for the grant, any person falling into categories (b) and below must explain on the oath why there is no applicant from a higher-ranked category. This is called 'clearing off'. A person in a lower-ranked category may apply only if there is nobody in a higher category willing and able to take the grant. The applicant must explain the basis of his own claim to the grant.

The categories will now be considered in detail with examples of clearing off.

'(a)   the executor ...'

The NCPR 1987, r 20 in fact provides the 'order of priority for grant where deceased left a will'. This covers both grants of probate and letters of administration with the will annexed. An executor who has been appointed in the will and is able and willing to act has first right to a grant.

The remaining categories assume that, for whatever reason, no executor is available.

'(b)   any residuary legatee or devisee holding in trust ...'

> **EXAMPLE**
>
> Arthur has died leaving a will. Although he failed to appoint executors, he left his residue to Brian and Claire on trust for Debbie. Brian and Claire are the residuary legatees (or devisees, depending on the type of trust property) holding on trust and so they have first right to a grant. Clearly, Arthur was happy for them to deal with his property otherwise he would not have appointed them as trustees. They will have to state that 'no executor was appointed in the will and we are the residuary legatees holding on trust named in the will'.

'(c)   any other residuary legatee or devisee ...'

> **EXAMPLE 1**
>
> Amanda has died leaving a will appointing Boris as her executor and giving the residuary estate to Carol, ie Carol is the residuary legatee and devisee.
>
> Carol can apply for a grant only if Boris is unable or unwilling to act. She must 'clear off' Boris by saying, 'the executor named in the will has [renounced probate] or [predeceased the deceased] and I am the residuary legatee and devisee named in the will' or as the case may be.

Note: strictly it is also necessary to clear off trustees of residue by stating that there is 'no residuary legatee or devisee holding on trust for any other person'. However, as the lack of appointment is apparent from the face of the will, this is often not done. Such practice is acceptable to the probate registrars.

EXAMPLE 2

The facts are the same as in Example 1, but Boris was appointed 'executor and trustee' and the residue was given to Carol for life.

Carol must clear off Boris in both capacities by saying, 'the executor and trustee named in the will has [renounced probate] etc ...'.

'... or ... any person entitled to share in the undisposed of residue'

If a partial intestacy arises because the will fails to dispose of all or part of the residuary estate, those people entitled to the residue by virtue of the intestacy rules (see **29.6**) may apply for a grant under NCPR 1987, r 20, but they must show why they are entitled to the grant by clearing off all persons in higher-ranked categories.

EXAMPLE

Damien's will appoints Errol to be his sole executor and residuary beneficiary. Errol died last month and Damien has just died. Damien's closest living relative is his mother, Florence.

As the sole residuary beneficiary has predeceased the deceased (and the gift is not saved by any substitutional gift), the residue is undisposed of and will be distributed according to the intestacy rules. Damien has left no spouse or civil partner and no issue but is survived by his mother, Florence, who is next entitled to the property.

Florence will apply for a grant of letters of administration with will annexed by clearing off the executor. She must also establish her entitlement to the undisposed of property and, therefore, to the grant. She will say 'the executor and residuary legatee and devisee has predeceased the deceased [and the deceased died a bachelor without issue] and I am the mother of the deceased'.

'(d)   the personal representative of a deceased residuary legatee or devisee ...'

Where there is no proving executor and, for example, the residuary beneficiary survives the testator to take a vested interest in the estate but then dies without having taken the grant, that beneficiary's PR may apply for the grant. This is because the gift under the will forms part of the beneficiary's estate and needs to be collected by his PR.

EXAMPLE

Gazala died last week leaving a will appointing Hafsa as executrix and giving the residuary estate to Imran absolutely. Hafsa has predeceased Gazala; Imran died yesterday. Imran's will appoints Jamila as his sole executrix and beneficiary.

Jamila may apply for a grant of letters of administration with will annexed to Gazala's estate. To do so the oath must clear off Hafsa and Imran by saying, 'the sole executrix predeceased the deceased and the sole residuary legatee and devisee named in the said will survived the deceased and has since died without having proved the said will and I am the executrix of the deceased residuary legatee and devisee'.

'(e)   any other legatee or devisee ... or any creditor of the deceased ...'

This category covers any other beneficiary under the will, for example, a specific devisee who has been left the deceased's house, or a pecuniary legatee who has been left money by the deceased. It also covers creditors of the deceased.

'(f)   the personal representative of any other legatee or devisee ... or of any creditor ...'

This category works on the same principles as category (d) above.

30.10.2.2   Beneficiary with vested interest preferred

Where there is more than one person of equal rank but one has a vested and one a contingent interest in the estate, the court generally prefers an application by the beneficiary with the vested interest.

> **EXAMPLE**
>
> Kalima's will leaves her residuary estate to her two children, Laila and Masoud, contingent on their attaining 25 years of age. There is no executor appointed in the will and at Kalima's death Laila is 30 years old and Masoud 23 years old.
>
> Laila and Masoud can make a joint application, but if they were to apply separately the court would prefer Laila because Masoud's interest is still contingent.

30.10.3   Minors

A minor cannot act as administrator with will annexed, nor can he apply for a grant. His parent(s) or guardian(s) may apply for a grant 'for his use and benefit' on his behalf. The grant is limited until he attains the age of 18.

If there is a person not under a disability who is entitled in the same degree as the minor then that person will be preferred to the guardian of the minor (NCPR 1987, r 27(5)).

30.10.4   The number of administrators

30.10.4.1   Maximum number

If there are several people entitled to act as administrators, the grant will not issue to more than four of them (Senior Courts Act 1981, s 114). It is not possible for an administrator to have power reserved to him.

If a person is entitled to act as administrator but does not obtain a grant (eg, because there are four other applicants), this does not affect that person's beneficial entitlement to the estate.

30.10.4.2   Number in the same category

Subject to the provisions of s 114 of the Senior Courts Act 1981 (see **30.14.1** below), where two or more people are entitled in the same degree, a grant can be made on the application of any one of them without notice to the other or others (NCPR 1987, r 27(4)).

> **EXAMPLE**
>
> Jane dies leaving her residuary estate by will to her two adult brothers, Ken and Larry. Jane's will does not appoint an executor. Larry does not wish to act.
>
> Ken can apply for a grant alone. This does not affect Larry's beneficial entitlement to half the estate.

30.10.4.3   Need for two administrators

Where there is a life interest, or property passes to a minor (whether the interest is vested or contingent), the court normally requires a minimum of two administrators to apply for the grant (Senior Courts Act 1981, s 114).

EXAMPLE 1

Abhijeet has just died leaving a valid will which:

(a)   appoints Balinder his executor;

(b)   gives £1,000 to Fraz (aged 6) contingent on reaching 21;

(c)   gives the residue of his estate to Pardeep and Parminder.

As executor, Balinder has the best right to take a grant. If Balinder renounces probate, at least two people must apply for a grant of letters of administration because there is a minority interest, ie the legacy to Fraz. Pardeep and Parminder have the best right to take a grant.

EXAMPLE 2

Quentin's will fails to appoint an executor. He leaves his estate to his wife Rose for life, remainder to his adult son, Sam.

Two administrators are required because of Rose's life interest. Rose and Sam should both apply.

EXAMPLE 3

Tahir's will leaves his residuary estate to his friend Una, whom he has also appointed executrix. Una has predeceased Tahir. Tahir is divorced and has three children, Varisha (21), Wahid (19), and Zafir (15).

Tahir therefore dies partially intestate. By virtue of the intestacy rules his children take the residuary estate on the statutory trusts.

Two administrators are required because part of the estate goes to Zafir who is a minor. Varisha and Wahid should both apply.

Section 114(2) of the Senior Courts Act 1981 gives the court power, where it appears to the court to be expedient in all the circumstances, to appoint an individual as sole administrator despite the existence of a minority or life interest.

30.10.5   Renunciation

Any person entitled to apply for a grant of letters of administration with will annexed can renounce in the same way as an executor, except that an administrator does not lose the right to renounce by intermeddling. Renunciation does not affect any beneficial entitlement of the administrator or any appointment as a trustee.

30.11   OATH FOR ADMINISTRATORS

30.11.1   Entitlement to act

This oath is required if the deceased has died totally intestate.

The person or persons entitled to the grant are listed in NCPR 1987, r 22 as set out below. The order is the same as the order or entitlement on intestacy:

(1) Where the deceased died on or after 1 January 1926, wholly intestate, the person or persons having a beneficial interest in the estate shall be entitled to a grant of administration in the following classes in order of priority, namely—

    (a) the surviving spouse or civil partner;

    (b) the children of the deceased and the issue of any deceased child who died before the deceased;

    (c) the father and mother of the deceased;

    (d) brothers and sisters of the whole blood and the issue of any deceased brother or sister of the whole blood who died before the deceased;

    (e) brothers and sisters of the half blood and the issue of any deceased brother or sister of the half blood who died before the deceased;

    (f) grandparents;

    (g) uncles and aunts of the whole blood and the issue of any deceased uncle or aunt of the whole blood who died before the deceased;

    (h) uncles and aunts of the half blood and the issue of any deceased uncle or aunt of the half blood who died before the deceased.

(2) In default of any person having a beneficial interest in the estate, the Treasury Solicitor shall be entitled to a grant if he claims bona vacantia on behalf of the Crown.

(3) If all persons entitled to a grant under the foregoing provisions of this rule have been cleared off, a grant may be made to a creditor of the deceased or to any person who, notwithstanding that he has no immediate beneficial interest in the estate, may have a beneficial interest in the event of an accretion thereto.

Some of the descriptions of relations require further explanation, as follows.

30.11.1.1 'Children'

On an intestacy, no distinction is drawn between those who have been born legitimate or have been adopted, or those whose parents were not married (subject to the qualification in the Family Law Reform Act 1987, s 18(2) – see **29.6.5.2**).

Equally entitled with the deceased's children are the children or grandchildren of any child who predeceased the deceased. Step-children (ie, children of the deceased's spouse or civil partner) are not children for this purpose unless the deceased adopted them.

30.11.1.2 'Brothers and sisters'

Brothers and sisters of the deceased are also known as 'siblings'. A sibling is of the 'whole blood' where they share both parents in common with the deceased, and of the 'half blood' where they have only one common parent.

EXAMPLE

Susan has been married twice. By Tom she had two children, Una and Victoria, and by Arshad she had a son, Wisan.

Una and Victoria are sisters of the whole blood.

Wisan is their brother of the half blood.

30.11.1.3 'Uncles and aunts'

Uncles and aunts of 'the whole blood' are the children of both grandparents of the intestate. Aunts and uncles of the 'half blood' are the children of only one of the deceased's grandparents.

EXAMPLE

David has died recently and his closest living relations are his uncles, Ben and Charles. David's mother, Ann, and his uncle, Ben, were children of the same parents; Charles was the son of David's grandfather, Fred, and Fred's mistress, Joan.

Ben is David's uncle of the whole blood.

Charles is David's uncle of the half blood.

30.11.2 Clearing off

Each category is listed in priority in NCPR 1987, r 22. Like the applicant under NCPR 1987, r 20 (see **30.10.2**), an applicant under r 22 must explain on the oath why nobody in a higher category is able to apply for the grant (again, this is called 'clearing off') and describe his own relationship to the deceased.

Where there is a surviving spouse or civil partner and he or she is applying for the grant either alone or with others, there is nobody with a higher priority to clear off and therefore there is no need to add any clearing off words to the oath.

Where there is no surviving spouse or civil partner, this fact must be stated by saying that the deceased died intestate, 'a bachelor', or 'a spinster', or 'a widower', or 'a widow', or a surviving civil partner, as the case may be. There is no need to indicate whether a marriage was between same sex or opposite sex partners. It is sufficient to refer to a widow or widower.

Where the applicant needs to clear off categories of relation in addition to the spouse or civil partner, he will do so by stating that the deceased died intestate 'without issue' or 'parents' or 'brothers and sisters of the whole blood' or 'their issue' etc.

EXAMPLE 1

Alice, a widow, has died intestate, survived by her son who will take the grant.

The oath will read:

died INTESTATE a widow.

EXAMPLE 2

Barraq, who is unmarried, has just died intestate aged 92 years. He is survived by his two brothers who will take the grant.

The oath will read:

died INTESTATE a bachelor without issue or parents.

Later in the oath the applicant will explain his own relationship to the deceased.

30.11.3 The need for a beneficial interest in the estate

Unless the applicant is the Treasury Solicitor or a creditor, he must have a beneficial interest in the estate (or would have such an in interest if there was an accretion to the estate) by virtue of the intestacy rules; hence there is a similarity of entitlement under NCPR 1987, r 22 and under AEA 1925, s 46 (see **29.6**).

EXAMPLE 1

Chandra, who is unmarried, dies intestate survived by her mother and one brother.

Only the mother can apply for the grant because she is solely and absolutely entitled to Chandra's estate under the intestacy rules.

EXAMPLE 2

David dies intestate survived by his wife, Eve, and adult son, Fred. Excluding personal assets, David's estate is valued at £500,000.

As Eve and Fred share the estate by virtue of the intestacy rules, Fred can apply for the grant if Eve does not, although Eve ranks in priority and must be cleared off if Fred applies for the grant.

EXAMPLE 3

The facts are the same as in Example 2 but David's estate is £190,000. Prima facie, Fred would seem to have no interest and would therefore be unable to apply for a grant if Eve failed to do so. But Fred can apply in these circumstances on the basis that if additional assets were found in David's estate, Fred would then share the estate with Eve. It is irrelevant that David's estate never actually increases above £190,000. Again, Eve ranks in priority.

30.11.4 Minors

A minor cannot act as administrator, neither can he apply for a grant. The same procedure as that discussed at **30.10.3** above should be followed.

30.11.5 Renunciation

A person entitled to a grant under NCPR 1987, r 22 can renounce his right to the grant in the same way as an administrator with the will annexed. If he is the only relative of the deceased with a beneficial entitlement, the grant will be made to a creditor of the deceased. Renunciation does not affect any beneficial entitlement of the administrator.

EXAMPLE

Graeme dies intestate survived by one brother, Henry, and an uncle, Jack. Graeme owes Kalya £100.

Henry has the best right to a grant under r 22. As Jack has no beneficial interest in the estate under the intestacy rules, he cannot apply for the grant if Henry fails to do so. In that event Kalya should apply for the grant of letters of administration.

It is common for a creditor to take the grant if the estate is insolvent.

30.11.6 The number of administrators

The rules applying to the number of administrators with will annexed apply equally to administrators of a totally intestate estate.

30.11.6.1 Maximum number

The grant will issue to a maximum of four administrators. If there are more than four people with an equal entitlement, it is not possible to have 'power reserved' to a non-proving administrator.

30.11.6.2 Number in the same category

Where two or more people are entitled in the same degree, a grant can be made on the application of any one of them without notice to the other(s).

30.11.6.3 Need for two administrators

A minimum of two administrators is generally required where the intestacy creates minority interests through property being held for minors on the 'statutory trusts'. The court may dispense with the need for two administrators in special circumstances.

EXAMPLE 1

John dies intestate in March 2015 with a net estate for probate purposes of £300,000, and is survived by his wife, Kala, and children, Laksha (20) and Madesh (16).

Kala and Laksha must take the grant. Two administrators are needed because the intestacy creates a minority interest. Madesh cannot be an administrator because he is a minor.

EXAMPLE 2

Nigel dies intestate, a bachelor without issue. Both his parents are dead.

His sister and the issue of his deceased brother are equally entitled to apply for the grant as they share the estate under the intestacy rules. Both Olive and Quentin must apply because Rachel is a minor.

PRACTICAL POINT

What documents may have to be filed with the Probate Registry to get a grant? For a deceased domiciled in England and Wales, the following:

- an oath sworn or affirmed by the PRs explaining their right to take a grant

- any will and codicils

- affidavits explaining any unusual features

- an IHT400 or IHT205

> - if inheritance tax is due, a receipted IHT421 as proof that inheritance tax due has been paid
>
> - probate fee
>
> - any renunciations of the right to act.
>
> Note: If the direct payment scheme is being used, the PRs must send an IHT423 to each bank or building society from which funds are to be transferred.

30.12 EFFECT OF GRANT

30.12.1 Grant of probate

A grant of probate confirms the authority of the executor(s) which stems from the will and arises from the time of the testate's death (see **30.2**).

The grant provides conclusive evidence of the title of the executor(s) and of the validity and contents of the will.

30.12.2 Grant of administration (with or without will)

A grant of administration (with or without will annexed) confers authority on the administrator and vests the deceased's property in the administrator. Until the grant is issued, the administrator has no authority to act and the deceased's property is vested in the President of the Family Division.

The grant provides conclusive evidence of the administrator's title and of the validity and contents of any will (or intestacy). Normally, the grant is not retrospective to the date of the deceased's death.

30.13 LIMITED GRANTS

A grant of representation is normally general, ie it is expressed to relate to 'all the estate which by law devolves to and vests in the personal representatives of the deceased'.

When necessary, a grant may be limited; for example, it may be:

(a)   limited as to a specified part of the deceased's property. For example, a novelist might appoint literary executors to administer his literary estate; general executors would be responsible for his general estate;

(b)   limited to settled land. Any settled land vested in the deceased is usually excepted from a general grant if the land remains settled after his death. The trustees of the settlement will submit an oath limited to the settled land;

(c)   limited to a special purpose. For example, if the person entitled to apply for a grant is a minor then application should be made by his parent(s) or guardian(s) for a grant for his use and benefits. The practice in making such grants is governed by NCPR 1987, r 2.

30.14 THE CHAIN OF REPRESENTATION AND GRANT DE BONIS NON ADMINISTRATIS

30.14.1 Introduction

If there are several proving PRs administering an estate and one dies after taking the grant but before the administration has been completed, the surviving PRs continue to act. The continuing PRs' powers remain unaffected. Where the death leaves a sole surviving PR, the court may exercise its powers to appoint an additional PR. This might happen, for example, where there is a life or minority interest and the court wishes there to continue to be two PRs (Senior Courts Act 1981, s 114).

If a person entitled to be the PR (either as the executor under a will, or by virtue of NCPR 1987, r 20 or r 22) survives the deceased but then dies himself without taking out a grant of representation, the AEA 1925, s 5 provides that his rights concerning the grant die with him (unless it is an exceptional case where his PR may apply for a grant under NCPR 1987, r 20).

EXAMPLE 1

Abdul dies, appointing Eman as his executrix and leaving his estate to Rafi. Eman dies a few days after Abdul and without having proved his will. Rafi should apply for a grant of letters of administration with will annexed to Abdul's estate.

The position is more complicated on the death of a sole or sole surviving PR if the administration is incomplete.

EXAMPLE 2

Anthony died six months ago, appointing Edward as his sole executor.

Edward obtained a grant of probate to Anthony's estate and had begun to deal with the assets when he died. The house is on the market but unsold and the final inheritance tax assessment cannot be agreed because tax is being paid on the house by instalments. The administration is therefore incomplete. What happens? That depends on whether or not the chain of representation applies. See **30.14.2**.

30.14.2 Chain of representation

The office of executor is personal to the executor appointed by the testator in his will. Because it is an office of personal trust an executor cannot assign that office (although he can appoint an attorney). However, the AEA 1925, s 7 provides that in one case the office of executor will pass automatically to someone else. This is called the 'chain of representation'. This happens only where an executor who has taken out a grant of probate dies without completing the administration and appoints someone as his own executor. If that person takes out a grant of probate he will automatically become the executor of both estates.

30.14.2.1 Unbroken chain

The chain of representation is applicable only where there is an unbroken sequence of proving executors.

EXAMPLE

Colin died, leaving a will appointing Diane as his executrix.

Diane proved the will and obtained a grant of probate.

Diane died before she had completed the administration of Colin's estate.

Diane's will appointed Eric to be her executor. If Eric applies for probate of Diane's will, he automatically becomes executor of Colin's estate.

It is not possible to accept the office of executor to Diane's estate and refuse to be executor by representation of Colin's estate.

30.14.2.2 AEA 1925, s 7

Section 7 provides that an executor by representation:

(a)   has the same rights in respect of the testator's estate as if he was the original executor; and

(b)   is, to the extent to which the testator's estate has come into his hands, answerable as if he was the original executor.

30.14.2.3   Broken chain

If for any reason there are no successive executors, the chain of representation will be broken.

EXAMPLE 1

Fiona appointed Graham to be her executor. Graham obtained probate to Fiona's estate. Graham then died intestate. Graham's PR under NCPR 1987, r 22 is Ian, who obtains a grant of letters of administration to Graham's estate. Ian will not become the executor of Fiona's estate.

EXAMPLE 2

Jaan died intestate and Kaleema obtained a grant of letters of administration to his estate. Kaleema died leaving a will appointing Laila to be her executrix. Laila proved Kaleema's will and obtained probate. Laila does not become the executrix of Jaan's estate.

30.14.3   Grant *de bonis non administratis*

In situations where the chain of representation does not apply because there are no successive proving executors, a grant *de bonis non administratis* must be obtained to the original estate (usually known as a 'grant *de bonis non*'). The grant *de bonis non* may be one of administration with the will or one of simple administration, depending on the circumstances.

It is issued in estates where the sole, or sole surviving, PR has died after obtaining the grant but without having completed the administration, and it relates only to the unadministered part of the estate. Two requirements apply:

(a)   there must have been a prior grant of probate or letters of administration to a PR who has now died; and

(b)   the chain of representation must not apply.

The grant *de bonis non* will issue to the person who would have been entitled had the original PR never taken the grant. The order of priority will depend on NCPR 1987, r 20 or r 22, as appropriate.

30.15   CAVEATS AND CITATIONS

Caveats and citations are available under the NCPR 1987 to assist in the event of a dispute over the right to take out a grant of representation to an estate.

30.15.1   Caveats (NCPR 1987, r 44)

The effect of a caveat is to prevent the issue of a grant of representation. The person lodging or entering a caveat is called a 'caveator'. A caveat might be used, for example, where a beneficiary believes the executor named in the will lacks the mental capacity to act, or where the validity of the will is questioned.

EXAMPLE 1

The will appoints Eric as executor, gives a legacy to Ann and the residue to Ben.

Eric wants to act as executor but Ann challenges his capability. Ann should enter a caveat before a grant of representation is issued so that the court can decide who should act as PR.

> **EXAMPLE 2**
>
> On Dinar's death a homemade will is found appointing Eisaz as executor and sole beneficiary. Fahima would be entitled to Dinar's estate under the intestacy rules and Fahima believes the will is invalid. She should enter a caveat to prevent any grant of representation issuing until the court has decided the validity or otherwise of the will.

30.15.2   Citations (NCPR 1987, r 46)

Only executors or persons specified under NCPR 1987, r 20 or r 22 can take a grant of representation. If the person initially entitled to take the grant refuses to do so and also refuses to renounce, the estate would remain unadministered and the beneficiaries would be left waiting indefinitely for their inheritance. In such circumstances, a citation provides a remedy.

There are several types of citation which may be issued by the Probate Registry at the request of a beneficiary ('the citor').

30.15.2.1   Citation to take probate

A citation to take probate may be used where an executor has lost his right to renounce probate by intermeddling in the estate (eg, by informing the deceased's bank of his death, see **30.9.3**) but has not applied for a grant of probate and shows no signs of so doing. Once cited, the executor must proceed with an application for a grant of probate. If he does not (without good reason) the citor can apply to the court for an order allowing the executor to be passed over and a grant of letters of administration with will annexed to issue to the person(s) entitled under NCPR 1987, r 20.

30.15.2.2   Citation to accept or refuse a grant

A citation to accept or refuse a grant is the standard method of clearing off a person with a prior right to any type of grant who has not applied, and shows no intention of applying, for a grant. If the person cited does not take steps to take out the grant, a grant may be issued to the citor.

> **EXAMPLE**
>
> Adam's will appoints Bert his executor and Clare the residuary beneficiary. Bert takes no steps towards administering the estate or proving the will. Clare may cite Bert to act and, if Bert does nothing, Clare may apply by virtue of NCPR 1987, r 20 for a grant of letters of administration with will annexed.

30.15.3   The new Probate Rules

When the new Probate Rules are in force, caveats will become known as 'objections'. The person entering an objection to the issuing of a grant is called an 'objector'.

Citations will be replaced by notifications. The old citation to an intermeddling executor to take a grant of probate is subsumed into a notification to accept or refuse to take a grant, or to give reasons why a person should not be ordered to take a grant in accordance.

30.16   AN ALTERNATIVE TO CITATION

To compel an unwilling person to take a grant is likely to produce more problems than it solves. If a person is unwilling to act as executor in the administration of an estate, it is often preferable to apply to the Probate Registry under the Senior Courts Act 1981, s 116 for an order passing over that person in favour of someone else. For example, in *Re Biggs* [1966] 1 All ER 358, an executor had intermeddled but then refused to have anything to do with the estate. The Probate Registry ordered that he be passed over.

SUMMARY

(1)   When a person dies, someone must deal with the administration of the estate. Those who take on this task are referred to generically as 'personal representatives' (PRs). They may be executors or administrators.

(2)   Executors are appointed by the will and take a grant of probate.

(3)   If there is no executor able and willing to act, those entitled to property take a grant of administration (with the will annexed if there is one). Priority is governed by the Non-Contentious Probate Rules 1987.

(4)   Some assets (eg joint property, life policies assigned or written in trust during the deceased's lifetime) do not pass through the hands of the PRs.

(5)   The process for obtaining a grant involves completing an IHT400 or, if the estate is excepted, an IHT205, and sending it to HMRC with any tax due.

(6)   The following should be sent to the Probate Registry:

- an oath sworn or affirmed by the PRs explaining their right to take a grant

- any will and codicils

- affidavits explaining any unusual features

- if inheritance tax is due, a receipted IHT421 as proof that inheritance tax due has been paid

- probate fee

- any renunciations of the right to act.

(7)   One executor is always sufficient. Two administrators are required if there is a minority or life interest.

CHAPTER 31

ADMINISTRATION OF AN ESTATE

LEARNING OUTCOMES

After reading this chapter you will be able to:

- explain the meaning of the 'administration period'
- explain the duties of a PR during the administration period
- protect the PRs from personal liability
- identify the powers of PRs when dealing with the administration
- identify the steps necessary to administer the estate and complete the administration.

31.1 INTRODUCTION

Once the PRs have obtained the grant, they are able to start the administration of the estate. The work involved in administering an estate is basically the same whether the deceased left a will or died intestate. However, in the latter case, the beneficiaries will be ascertained by application of the law of intestacy rather than from construction of the will.

Broadly speaking, the PRs have to:

- collect the deceased's assets;
- pay the deceased's funeral and testamentary expenses and debts;
- distribute the legacies; and
- complete the administration and distribute the residuary estate.

This chapter looks at the different aspects of the PRs' duties and at how they can protect themselves from personal liability.

31.2 THE ADMINISTRATION PERIOD

The 'administration period' commences at the moment immediately following the death and ends when the PRs are in a position to vest the residue of the estate in the beneficiaries, or the trustees if a trust arises under the will or the intestacy law.

Note, however, that a PR holds office for life. If further assets or liabilities are discovered after the residue has all been transferred, the PRs will still have to deal with them.

31.3   DUTIES OF THE PRS

The Administration of Estates Act 1925 (AEA 1925), s 25 (as substituted by AEA 1971, s 9) states that the PRs of a deceased person shall be under a duty to 'collect and get in the real and personal estate of the deceased and administer it according to law'.

The duties to be undertaken by a PR are onerous. A PR who has accepted liability is personally liable for loss to the estate resulting from any breach of duty he commits as PR (although he is not generally liable for breaches committed by a co-PR). There are several types of breach of duty, including:

(a)   failing to protect the value of assets;

(b)   failing to pay the people entitled to assets.

The Trustee Act 1925 (TA 1925), s 61 gives the court power at its discretion to relieve a PR from liability for breach of duty if satisfied that the PR 'has acted honestly and reasonably and ought fairly to be excused for the breach'. Alternatively, an executor may be able to rely on a clause in the deceased's will providing protection from liability for mistakes made in good faith.

31.4   PROTECTION AGAINST LIABILITY

As we saw at **30.3.5**, PRs can protect themselves against personal liability to unknown beneficiaries by complying with the requirements of the TA 1925, s 27.

31.4.1   Missing beneficiaries

As we saw at **30.3.5**, the TA 1925, s 27 will not protect PRs against claims from beneficiaries whose existence is known but who cannot be traced. The only way they can fully protect themselves in such a case is to apply to court for a *Benjamin* order.

Before making an order, the court will require evidence that the fullest possible enquiries were made to trace the missing person. If the court considers the advertisements made in addition to the TA 1925, s 27 are insufficient, it will direct that further enquiry be made.

An application to court is expensive so, as an alternative, PRs may take out insurance to cover the risk.

31.4.2   Inheritance (Provision for Family and Dependants) Act 1975

The PRs will be personally liable where an applicant under the I(PFD)A 1975 successfully obtains an order for 'reasonable financial provision' from the estate. They can protect themselves against such liability by waiting more than six months following the date of the grant of representation before distributing the assets. If earlier distribution is required, PRs should ensure they retain sufficient assets to satisfy an order should an applicant be successful within six months of the grant.

31.5   ADMINISTRATIVE POWERS OF PRS

31.5.1   Statutory powers of PRs and trustees

The PRs have a wide range of powers which they may exercise in carrying out the administration of an estate. These powers are largely conferred on them by statute. The AEA 1925 gives some powers specifically to PRs. The TA 1925 and the Trustee Act 2000 (TA 2000) confer powers on trustees for use in administering a trust. Since 'trustee' in the TA 1925 and TA 2000 includes a 'personal representative', PRs (executors and administrators) have these powers as well.

The TA 2000 modifies in various ways powers previously available to PRs and trustees. The main purpose of the Act is to remedy certain deficiencies by bringing the law into line with what has been regarded as good drafting practice for some years.

The TA 2000 deals with powers to invest trust property, appoint agents and nominees, remuneration of trustees (and PRs) and to insure trust property. A duty of care requires trustees (and PRs) when exercising many of their powers under the Act to exercise the skill and care reasonable in the circumstances, having regard to any special knowledge or expertise of the trustee.

31.5.2   Powers granted by a will

31.5.2.1   Modification of statutory powers

Many of the statutory powers may be modified by express provision contained within a will. If there are no executors who prove the will but the will is proved by administrators with the will annexed, they also have these modified powers available to them.

31.5.2.2   Additional powers

In addition to modification of statutory powers, a will often grants powers which are not available at law, for example power to advance capital to a person to whom a life interest has been given, or to lend capital to such a person; in the absence of any such express power, the executors have no implied power to advance or lend capital to a life tenant.

31.5.2.3   Will drafting

It is good drafting practice for a will to set out in full all the powers of the executors so that the position is clear on the face of the will, thus avoiding the possibility of a particular power available at law being overlooked. Whether the following powers are available to the PRs at all, or in modified form, will depend on the terms of the particular will and the circumstances of the estate.

31.5.3   Provisions concerning the administration of the estate

The provisions which follow may be included in the will to simplify the administration of the estate. However, in a homemade will or a very simple professionally-drafted will, the draftsman may decide not to extend the executors' statutory powers.

31.5.3.1   Power to appropriate assets without consent of beneficiary

The statutory provisions

The AEA 1925, s 41 gives PRs the power to appropriate any part of the estate in or towards satisfaction of a pecuniary legacy or share in the residuary estate provided that the appropriation does not prejudice any specific beneficiary. Thus, if the will gives a pecuniary legacy to a beneficiary, the PRs may allow that beneficiary to take chattels or other assets in the estate up to the value of his legacy, provided that these assets have not been specifically bequeathed by the will. The section provides that the beneficiary (or his parent or guardian if he is a minor) must consent to the appropriation.

Specimen clause

> Power to exercise the power of appropriation conferred by section 41 of the Administration of Estates Act 1925 without obtaining any of the consents required by that section.

This provision is commonly included in order to relieve the PRs of the duty to obtain formal consent. Nevertheless, the PRs would informally consult the beneficiaries concerned.

There is no statutory power for trustees to appropriate assets so, if they are to have power to appropriate, an express clause must be included.

31.5.3.2 Power to insure

The statutory provision

The TA 1925, s 19 (as substituted by TA 2000, s 34) gives PRs and trustees power to insure trust property against any risks, to the full value of the property, and to pay premiums out of either capital or income.

Before the TA 2000, the statutory power of insurance was inadequate, and so it was normal to extend it by including an express power. However, this is no longer necessary.

The TA 2000 only provides trustees with a power to insure trust *property*. If trustees wish to be able to insure the *life* of a beneficiary or of the settlor (eg, where there is a risk of a charge to inheritance tax if death occurs within seven years), they will require an express power.

31.5.3.3 Power to accept receipts from or on behalf of minors

The statutory provision

Under the general law, an unmarried minor could not give a good receipt for capital or income. A married minor can give a good receipt for income only (LPA 1925, s 21). Parents and guardians used not to be able to give a good receipt on behalf of minors unless specifically authorised to do so in the will.

The Children Act 1989 provides that parents with parental responsibility have the same rights as guardians appointed under the Act. These rights are set out at s 3 and include the right to receive or recover money for the benefit of the child. Therefore, since the Children Act, parents and guardians have been able to give a good receipt to PRs.

Extended statutory power

There are often tensions within families, and a client may not be happy for a parent or guardian to give a good receipt for a legacy. In such a case, it may be preferable to leave the legacy to another adult to hold on trust for the minor.

Other alternatives are:

(a)   leaving a legacy to trustees to hold for the benefit of the minor rather than to the child directly;

(b)   including a clause allowing the PRs to accept the receipt of the child himself if over 16 years old – the provision may be incorporated into the legacy itself, or may be included in a list of powers in the will.

31.5.4 Provisions concerning the administration of a trust

At the end of the administration of an estate, the PRs may be able to distribute the residue to the beneficiaries, thus completing their task. However, in some cases distribution will be delayed and the PRs will hold the residue (or part of it) as trustees. This may happen:

(a)   where the beneficiary has a contingent interest, and so cannot be given the property until the interest vests; or

(b)   where the interests in the property are divided, for example between income and capital.

In either of these cases, the statutory powers of the trustees may also be extended.

31.5.4.1 Power to invest trust funds

The statutory provision

Under the general law, trustees have a duty to invest trust money. The TA 2000, s 3 gives trustees a 'general power of investment' enabling them to invest as if they were absolutely entitled to the trust property themselves. This wide power excludes investment in land, other than by mortgage, but further powers in relation to land are contained in s 8 (see **31.5.4.2**). In exercising the investment power, trustees are required to take proper advice and to review investments of the trust from time to time. They must have regard to the standard investment criteria, namely the suitability to the trust of any particular investment and to the need for diversification of investments of the trust.

An express investment clause can be included but is no longer necessary.

31.5.4.2   Power to purchase land

The statutory provisions

The TA 2000, s 8 gives trustees power to acquire freehold or leasehold land in the UK for 'investment, for occupation by a beneficiary or for any other reason'. When exercising their power, the trustees are given 'all the powers of an absolute owner in relation to the land'.

The statutory power does not authorise the purchase of land abroad, nor does it allow trustees to purchase an interest in land with someone else (eg, a beneficiary). An express power will be needed if the trustees are to have such powers.

Specimen clause

> My trustees may apply trust money in
> — the purchase of land or an interest in land anywhere in the world, and
> — the improvement of such land.

31.5.4.3   Power to sell personalty

Trustees holding land in their trust have the power to sell it under their powers of an absolute owner. However, there is some doubt whether trustees who do not hold land have an implied power of sale. For this reason, some wills may continue to impose an express trust for sale over residue. The alternative solution is to include power in the will (among the administrative provisions) giving the trustees express power to sell personalty.

Specimen clause

> Power to sell mortgage or charge any asset of my estate as it they were an absolute beneficial owner.

31.5.4.4   Power of maintenance

The statutory powers of maintenance and advancement (see **31.5.4.5**) are extremely important to PRs and trustees.

The statutory provisions

Where trustees are holding a fund for a minor beneficiary, the TA 1925, s 31 gives them power to use income they receive for the minor's maintenance, education or benefit. The section provides that if the trustees continue to hold the trust funds after the beneficiary reaches 18 (for example, where the interest is contingent on reaching 21 or 25), they must pay the income to the beneficiary from 18 onwards.

The TA 1925, s 31 (as amended by the TA 2000 and the Inheritance and Trustees' Powers Act 2014) states (inter alia):

> (1)   Where any property is held by trustees in trust for any person for any interest whatsoever, whether vested or contingent, then, subject to any prior interests or charges affecting that property—
>
>   (i)   during the infancy of any such person, if his interest so long continues, the trustees may, at their sole discretion, pay to his parent or guardian, if any, or otherwise apply for or

towards his maintenance, education, or benefit, the whole or such part, if any, of the income of that property as the trustees may think fit, whether or not there is—

(a)   any other fund applicable to the same purpose; or

(b)   any person bound by law to provide for his maintenance or education; and

(ii)   if such person on attaining the age of eighteen years has not a vested interest in such income, the trustees shall thenceforth pay the income of that property and of any accretion thereto under subsection (2) of this section to him, until he either attains a vested interest therein or dies, or until failure of his interest:

(2)   During the infancy of any such person, if his interest so long continues, the trustees shall accumulate all the residue of that income by investing it, and any profits from so investing it, from time to time in authorised investments, and shall hold those accumulations ...

(3)   This section applies in the case of a contingent interest only if the limitation or trust carries the intermediate income of the property ...

As originally drafted, s 31 allowed the trustees to apply only so much of the income as was 'reasonable'. This was an objective test and it was common to vary the statutory provision to allow the trustees an unfettered discretion. For trusts *'created or arising'* on or after 1 October 2014, this amendment is no longer required. If a trust is created by will, it is the date of death not execution that is significant.

Application of section 31

EXAMPLE – TRUST 1

The trustees are holding £100,000 for Mary (16) who has a vested interest in the capital. Under s 31(1), the trustees have the power to pay all or part of the income to Mary's parent or guardian, or 'otherwise apply' it for Mary's maintenance, education or benefit. This could include paying bills (eg, school fees) directly.

Section 31(2) directs the trustees to accumulate any income not used for maintenance and invest it.

EXAMPLE – TRUST 2

The trustees are holding £100,000 for Dora (14) who has an interest in the capital contingent on reaching 21. They may pay or apply the income for Dora's maintenance, education or benefit in the same way as the trustees of Trust 1.

The trustees are holding £100,000 for Charles (19) who also has an interest in the capital contingent on reaching 21. Section 31(1)(ii) directs them to pay all the income to Charles until his interest vests (ie until he is 21), when he will receive the capital, or fails (ie if he dies before he is 21). The same will apply to the income from Dora's share from her 18th birthday onwards.

EXAMPLE – TRUST 3

The trustees are holding £200,000 for Henry for life with remainder to Stephen (10). They have no power to use the income for Stephen's benefit as Henry is entitled to it. If Henry dies while Stephen is still a minor, s 31 will apply to allow the trustees to apply income for Stephen's maintenance, etc during the period from Henry's death until Stephen is 18 (when they will transfer the capital to Stephen).

PRACTICAL POINT

Summary of the effect of the Trustee Act 1925, s 31:

(1) *Beneficiaries under 18 with vested or contingent interests.* These beneficiaries cannot insist on receiving income as the trustees have a discretion to apply income or accumulate it, ie add it to the capital of the trust fund.

(2) *Beneficiaries reaching 18 who become entitled to capital at that age.* These beneficiaries are entitled to receive capital and any accumulated income.

(3) *Beneficiaries reaching 18 who have a right to income but not capital, eg a life tenant.* These beneficiaries are entitled to receive the available income each year, plus any income from previous years which was accumulated instead of being paid to them.

(4) *Beneficiaries reaching 18 who become entitled to capital at a later age.* From age 18 these beneficiaries have a right to the available income. When they reach the age at which they are entitled to receive the capital, they will get the capital plus any income accumulated before they reached 18.

Extending section 31 – specimen clause

> Section 31 of the Trustee Act 1925 shall apply as if the age of 21 years were substituted for all references to the age of 18 wherever they occur in s 31 (references to 'infancy' being construed accordingly).

The clause removes the right for a contingent beneficiary to receive all the income from the age of 18. The trustees' discretion under s 31 to pay or apply income for maintenance, or to accumulate any surplus will continue until the beneficiary is 21. Thus in Trust 2 the trustees would have a discretion over the payment of income to Charles even though he is over 18.

31.5.4.5 Power to advance capital

The statutory provisions

The TA 1925, s 32 (as amended by the Inheritance and Trustees' Powers Act 2014) allows trustees in certain circumstances to permit a beneficiary with an interest in capital to have the benefit of his capital entitlement sooner than he would receive it under the basic provisions of the trust.

Section 32 states:

(1) Trustees may at any time or times pay or apply any capital money subject to a trust, or transfer or apply any other property forming part of the capital of the trust property, for the advancement or benefit, in such manner as they may, in their absolute discretion, think fit, of any person entitled to the capital of the trust property or of any share thereof, whether absolutely or contingently on his attaining any specified age ... and whether in possession or in remainder or reversion ...

Provided that—

(a) property (including any money) so paid, transferred or applied for the advancement or benefit of any person must not, altogether, represent more than the presumptive or vested share or interest of that person in the trust property; and

(b) if that person is or becomes absolutely and indefeasibly entitled to a share in the trust property the money or other property so paid, transferred or applied shall be brought into account as part of such share; and

(c) no such payment transfer or application shall be made so as to prejudice any person entitled to any prior life or other interest, whether vested or contingent, in the money or other property paid, transferred or applied unless such person is in existence and of full age and consents in writing to such payment or application.

As originally drafted, s 32 only allowed the trustees to advance up to one half of a beneficiary's vested or presumptive share. It was common to vary the statutory provision to allow the trustees an unfettered discretion. For trusts *'created or arising'* on or after 1 October 2014, this amendment is no longer required. If a trust is created by will, it is the date of death not execution that is significant.

Where more than one beneficiary has an interest in a trust fund, any advance made must be brought into account on final distribution (s 32(1)(b)). Advances are brought into account at their cash value at the date of the advance, unless the trustees make the advance on the basis that it is be treated as a proportionate part of the capital (s 32(1A)).

Application of section 32

EXAMPLE – TRUST 1

Madhu has a vested interest in £100,000 capital. Section 32 allows the trustees to release some of the capital for Madhu's benefit. 'Benefit' is widely construed: money could be used to pay educational or living expenses. The trustees may advance the whole of Madhu's entitlement, ie £100,000.

EXAMPLE – TRUST 2

Charles and Dora have contingent interests in capital, their presumptive shares being £100,000 each. Section 32 applies to allow the trustees to release up to £100,000 for the benefit of either beneficiary. The trustees could transfer money or assets directly to Charles as he is old enough to give a valid receipt. The power applies even though the interests of Charles and Dora are contingent. If either beneficiary dies before the age of 21 there is no right to recover any advance even though that beneficiary's interest in capital has failed.

If the trustees give £50,000 to Charles now, he will receive £50,000 less than Dora when the fund is finally distributed to them, unless the trustees make the advance on the basis that he is to be treated as having received 25% of the value of the fund, in which case he will receive 25% less.

EXAMPLE – TRUST 3

Henry has only an interest in income and s 32 does not permit the release of capital to him. The section does apply to Stephen's vested interest in remainder, and permits the trustees to apply up to £100,000 (half his interest) for Stephen's benefit.

Such an advance would prejudice Henry since his income would be substantially reduced. Section 32(1)(c) provides that no advance may be made without Henry's written consent.

Extending section 32 – specimen clause 1

> I leave it within the discretion of my trustees whether and to what extent the beneficiary shall bring into account any payments received under this clause.

This clause supersedes s 32(1)(b) and means that if, in Trust 2, £50,000 was advanced to Charles, the trustees could on distribution still divide the remaining fund equally between Charles and Dora.

Extending section 32 – specimen clause 2

> Power to pay or apply capital money from my residuary estate to any extent to or for the benefit of my husband.

> Power to advance capital money from my residuary estate to my husband by way of loan to any extent upon such terms and conditions as my trustees may in their absolute discretion think fit.

These provisions would permit the trustees in Trust 3 to give or lend capital from the fund to Henry even though he has only an interest in income, not capital. Such a clause may be included to give more flexibility in case the income proves insufficient for Henry's needs. Henry still remains dependent on the discretion of the trustees.

31.5.4.6 Power to accept receipts from and on behalf of minors

The statutory provisions

Where a trust arises in favour of a beneficiary who is a minor, the trustees have statutory powers of maintenance and advancement under ss 31 and 32 of the TA 1925. Section 31 specifically allows the trustees to pay income to the child's parent or guardian or 'otherwise apply' it for the child's maintenance, education or benefit. Similarly, s 32 empowers the trustees to pay 'or apply' capital for the beneficiary's advancement or benefit. Thus, even before the Children Act 1989, the trustees had no difficulty in obtaining a good receipt when exercising these powers.

31.5.4.7 Control of trustees by beneficiaries

The Trusts of Land and Appointment of Trustees Act 1996 (TLATA 1996), s 19 provides that where beneficiaries are of full age and capacity and together entitled to the whole fund, they may direct the trustees to retire and appoint new trustees of the beneficiaries' choice. This means that in a case where the beneficiaries could by agreement end the trust under the rule in *Saunders v Vautier* (1841) 4 Beav 115, they now have the option of allowing the trust to continue with trustees of their own choice. The provision may be expressly excluded by the testator. If, under the terms of the trust, the position could arise where all the beneficiaries are in existence and aged over 18 but the trust has not ended, the testator may wish to prevent the beneficiaries from choosing their own trustees.

Specimen clause

> The provisions of section 19 of the Trusts of Land and Appointment of Trustees Act 1996 shall not apply to any trust created by this will so that no beneficiary shall have the right to require the appointment or retirement of any trustee or trustees.

31.5.4.8 Trusts of land

The TLATA 1996 gives special powers (see below) to a beneficiary under a trust of land who has an interest in possession. If, under the terms of the will, a trust with an interest in possession could arise the will may amend those powers. The Act does not define 'interest in possession', so it presumably has its usual meaning; a beneficiary has an interest in possession if he is entitled to claim the income of the fund as it arises (normally either because he has a life interest, or because he is over 18 and entitled to claim income under the TA 1925, s 31).

Duty to consult beneficiaries

Trustees exercising any function relating to the land must consult any beneficiary who is of full age and beneficially entitled to an interest in possession in the land and, so far as consistent with the 'general interest of the trust', give effect to the wishes of any such beneficiary (TLATA 1996, s 11). The duty to consult may be excluded by the will and often is.

Specimen clause

> The provisions of section 11 of the Trusts of Land and Appointment of Trustees Act 1996 shall not apply so that it shall not be necessary for my trustees to consult any beneficiaries before carrying out any function relating to land.

Beneficiary's rights of occupation

A beneficiary with a beneficial interest in possession, even if not of full age, has the right to occupy land subject to the trust if the purposes of the trust include making the land available for occupation by him, or if the trustees acquired the land in order to make it so available (TLATA 1996, s 12). There is no power to exclude s 12, but a declaration that the purpose of the trust is not for the occupation of land may be included in the will.

Specimen clause

> The purposes of any trust created by this will do not include making land available for occupation of any beneficiary [although my trustees have power to do so if they wish].

31.5.4.9 Holding the balance between beneficiaries

One of the duties of trustees is to ensure that a fair balance is kept between the interests of the beneficiaries. This is particularly important where different beneficiaries are entitled to income and capital, for example where property is left on trust for X for life with remainder to Y, as in Trust 3 at **31.5.4.5** above. The trustees must ensure that the investments they choose produce a reasonable income for X, the life tenant, and preserve the capital reasonably safely for Y, the remainderman.

The trust instrument may authorise trustees to treat the interests of one beneficiary as of paramount importance and relieve them of the duty to treat beneficiaries impartially. This is particularly common where a trust is created for the benefit of a surviving spouse and others.

Specimen clause

> In exercising the powers conferred by clause [   ] my Trustees shall be entitled to have regard solely to the interests of my surviving spouse and to disregard all other interests or potential interests under my Will.

31.5.4.10 Trusts (Capital and Income) Act 2013

The requirement to preserve a fair balance between income and capital beneficiaries led to the development of various rules, equitable and statutory, requiring apportionment of income and capital.

For example, the Apportionment Act 1870, s 2 provides that income such as rent and dividends is to be treated as accruing from day to day and apportioned accordingly. Thus, where interest is received after death but part relates to the pre-death period, the income would have to be apportioned. The part accruing before death would be capital, while that accruing after death is income.

While designed to achieve fairness between different classes of beneficiaries, the various apportionment rules led to lengthy and expensive calculations, and it was generally accepted that they were more trouble than they were worth. They were routinely excluded in professionally drawn wills.

The Trusts (Capital and Income) Act 2013, s 1 disapplies these apportionment rules for trusts created or arising on or after 1 October 2013, so it is unnecessary to include an express clause in wills prepared after that date.

It will still be necessary to look at earlier trusts to check whether an exclusion is included.

31.5.5 Miscellaneous additional powers

31.5.5.1 Charging clause

Background law

The rule of equity that a trustee may not profit from his trust applies both to trustees and executors. Its effect is that an executor or trustee may claim only out-of-pocket expenses and may not charge for time spent in performing his office unless expressly authorised.

The TA 2000, ss 28–31 have made various changes to the general rule of law governing the remuneration of 'professional' trustees.

Professional trustees are defined as those whose business includes the provision of services in connection with the management or administration of trusts.

A professional trustee charging for services is now entitled to charge for all services, even if they are services which are capable of being provided by a lay person (TA 2000, s 28(2)). Previously, express authority was required.

Where a will or trust instrument does not contain a charging clause, a professional trustee acting in a non-charitable trust can charge reasonable remuneration *if authorised to do so in writing by each of the co-trustees* (s 29(2)). This means that it is still desirable to include a charging clause as a sole trustee will be unable to charge and a co-trustee will be able to do so only with the permission of co-trustees.

A charging clause used to be regarded as a legacy, but this is no longer the case (s 28(4)). This means that a partner in a firm authorised by the will to charge can witness the will without losing the entitlement to charge. If there are insufficient funds to pay the pecuniary legacies in full, the legacies will abate proportionally unless the will provides otherwise. As a charging clause is no longer a legacy, it is not necessary to provide that the charges be paid in priority to other legacies.

Note that, if a person engaged in a profession or business not connected with the administration of trusts is to have power to charge for time spent dealing with the trust, there must be express authority in the trust instrument.

In any case where a professional executor or trustee is appointed such as a bank, a firm of solicitors, an individual solicitor or an accountant, a power to charge should be included in the will so that the testator is aware of the position.

Power to charge – specimen clause

> Any of my trustees being a solicitor or other person engaged in any profession or business may charge and be paid his usual professional charges for work done by him or his firm in the administration of my estate and the trusts arising under my will including acts which a trustee not engaged in any profession or business could have done personally.

Power to appoint a trust corporation – specimen clause

> Power to appoint a trust corporation to be the sole trustee or one of the trustees of my will upon such terms and conditions in all respects as may be acceptable to the corporation so appointed.

Provision of this latter kind is not commonly included in practice. Its purpose is to ensure that, if individual trustees wish to retire and no substitutes can readily be found, a bank (or other trust corporation) may be appointed even though there may be minor beneficiaries who are unable to give the required consent to the bank's usual terms and conditions, particularly in relation to charging.

31.5.5.2 Power to carry on business

Where an estate includes a business which was run by the deceased as a sole (unincorporated) trader, the powers of the PRs to run the business are limited. For example, they may only run the business with a view to selling it as a going concern and may use only those assets employed in the business at the date of death. These powers may be extended by will, although in practice PRs are unlikely to wish to involve themselves in the detailed running of a business. It may be preferable to bequeath the business by specific legacy and to appoint the legatee as a special PR of the business.

31.6 COLLECTING THE DECEASED'S ASSETS

31.6.1 Duty of the PRs

As you saw at **29.2**, some assets pass independently of the will and intestacy rules. The PRs have no obligation, or indeed power, to deal with these assets.

Assets which pass under the will or intestacy rules devolve on the PRs, who are under an obligation to collect and administer it for the benefit of those entitled.

In order to collect the property, the PRs generally produce their grant of representation to whoever is holding the various assets, for example to the deceased's bank or building society. If the bank is holding share certificates or documents of title to land, these also will be handed over to the PRs once the grant has been produced. In most cases, an office copy grant will be accepted as evidence of title.

In some cases, a grant is not required to collect certain assets. As explained at **30.4.1**, it may be possible to realise assets without production of a grant under the Administration of Estates (Small Payments) Act 1965.

31.6.2 Property not devolving on the PRs

The following examples illustrate types of property which do not devolve on the PRs and which therefore will not pass under any will or under the intestacy law.

31.6.2.1 Life interest

> **EXAMPLE**
>
> Terry died some years ago having by his will left property to Henry and Ian on trust for sale 'for Andrew for life, remainder for Ben'. Andrew has recently died. Assuming Ben is of full age and capacity, Henry and Ian will transfer the property to him in accordance with the terms of Terry's will.

31.6.2.2 Joint tenancy

> **EXAMPLE**
>
> Aamir and Barack own property as beneficial joint tenants at law and in equity. On Aamir's death his interest passes by operation of the right of survivorship to Barack the surviving joint tenant.

31.6.2.3 Policy held in trust for others

As explained at **29.2.3**, any proceeds of an insurance policy written in trust for third parties, or written under the Married Women's Property Act 1882, s 11 for the benefit of the deceased's spouse and/or children, will be paid to the trustees of the policy on proof of death, usually by production of the death certificate. The trustees will then distribute the proceeds among the beneficiaries in accordance with the trusts of the policy.

31.6.2.4 Pension schemes

As you saw at **29.3.4** and **30.4.3**, death in service benefits payable under an occupational pension scheme established by the deceased's former employers, where the trustees have a discretion as to whom to pay the benefits, do not devolve on the deceased's PRs and do not form part of his estate for succession purposes. In exercising their discretion as to payment, the trustees will have regard to any 'letter of wishes' given to them by the deceased person during his lifetime; however, they are not bound to give effect to these wishes.

31.7 PAYING THE DECEASED'S FUNERAL AND TESTAMENTARY EXPENSES AND DEBTS

31.7.1 Preliminary considerations

31.7.1.1 Immediate sources of money

As soon as monies can be collected from the deceased's bank or building society, or realised through insurance policies etc, the PRs should begin to pay the deceased's outstanding debts and the funeral account. Administration expenses, for example estate agents' and valuers' fees, will arise during the course of administration of the estate and will have to be settled from time to time while the administration is proceeding.

31.7.1.2 Repayment of loan to pay inheritance tax

It may be necessary to raise money to repay a loan from the deceased's bank to pay inheritance tax to obtain the grant. If an undertaking has been given to the bank in connection with the loan, it will probably be a 'first proceeds' undertaking. This means that the PRs must use money first realised by them during the administration to repay the bank. Failure to do so will be a breach of the terms of the undertaking.

31.7.1.3 Which assets to sell?

The PRs must take considerable care when deciding which assets they will sell to raise money for payment of the various outgoings from the deceased's estate. They should consider the following points.

Provisions of the deceased's will

The will may direct from which part of the deceased's estate the debts, funeral account, testamentary and administration expenses should be paid; usually they will be paid from the residue. In the absence of such direction, the PRs must follow the statutory rules for the incidence of liabilities as outlined below. In any event, it will be generally incorrect for PRs to sell property given specifically by will (eg, a gift of the testator's valuable stamp collection to his nephew) unless all other assets in the estate have been exhausted in payment of the debts, etc.

The beneficiaries' wishes

Where possible, the wishes of the beneficiaries of the residuary estate should be respected by the PRs. Although the PRs have power to sell any assets in the residuary estate, it is clearly appropriate that the residuary beneficiaries should be consulted before any sale takes place. Generally, beneficiaries have clear views as to which assets they desire to be retained for transfer to them; other assets may be sold by the PRs to raise the necessary money, possibly following receipt of professional advice as to particular sales.

Tax consequences

Before selling assets, the PRs should consider the amount of any capital gains (or losses) likely to arise as a result of the sale, and the availability of any exemptions, etc. Full use should be made of the annual exemption for CGT. If assets are to be sold at a loss (compared to their value at the date of death) CGT loss relief may be available for the PRs, as may 'loss relief' for inheritance tax purposes. An explanation of these reliefs is contained at **31.9.6**.

31.7.2 Funeral and testamentary expenses and debts

31.7.2.1 Funeral expenses

Reasonable funeral expenses are payable from the deceased's estate. In all cases, it is a question of fact what funeral expenses are reasonable.

31.7.2.2 Testamentary expenses

The phrase 'testamentary and administration expenses' is not defined in the AEA 1925, but it is generally considered to mean expenses incident to the proper performance of the duties of a PR. The phrase will include:

(a)   the costs of obtaining the grant;

(b)   the costs of collecting in and preserving the deceased's assets;

(c)   the costs of administering the deceased's estate, for example solicitors' fees for acting for the PRs, valuers' fees incurred by PRs in valuing the deceased's stocks and shares or other property; and

(d)   any inheritance tax payable on death on the deceased's property in the UK which vests in the PRs (IHTA 1984, s 211).

31.7.3 Administration of assets: solvent estate

The rules applying to the payment of funeral and testamentary expenses and debts depend on whether the estate is solvent or insolvent. The insolvent estate is considered at **31.7.4**.

31.7.3.1 The statutory order for payment of debts

Section 34(3) of the AEA 1925 states:

> Where the estate of a deceased person is solvent his real and personal estate shall, subject to rules of court and the provisions hereinafter contained as to charges on property of the deceased, and to the provisions, if any, contained in his will, be applicable towards the discharge of the funeral, testamentary and administration expenses, debts and liabilities payable thereout in the order mentioned in Part II of the First Schedule to this Act.

Part II of the First Schedule lays out an order which the PRs must follow when deciding which part of the deceased's estate should be used for the purposes of payment of the funeral and testamentary expenses and debts. Under the order generally, assets forming part of the residue are to be used before using property given to specific legatees.

'Subject ... to'

However, the effect of the proviso 'subject to' is that the operation of s 34(3) is expressly subject to two important rules or provisions, as follows:

(a)   The AEA 1925, s 35, which deals with secured debts, ie debts owing by the deceased which are charged on particular items of property. A common example is a loan secured by legal mortgage on the deceased's house. The effect of this rule is that a beneficiary taking the asset takes it subject to the debt and will be responsible for paying the debt.

(b)   The deceased's will can vary the provisions implied by the AEA 1925, ss 34(3) and/or 35. To vary s 35 it is necessary to have an express reference to the mortgage.

A suitable clause would be:

I GIVE my country cottage to my daughter free of mortgage.

A direction to pay 'debts' from residue is not sufficient to vary s 35. It will be construed as a direction to pay from residue debts *other than* those charged on particular assets.

31.7.4 The insolvent estate

31.7.4.1 Meaning of insolvency

An estate is insolvent if the assets are insufficient to discharge in full the funeral, testamentary and administration expenses, debts and liabilities. In such cases, the creditors will not be paid in full (or at all) and the beneficiaries under the will or the intestacy provisions may receive nothing from the estate. In doubtful cases, the PRs should administer the estate as if it is insolvent. Failure to administer an insolvent estate in accordance with the statutory order is a breach of duty by the PRs.

In the case of an insolvent estate which is being administered by the deceased's PRs out of court (this being the most common method of administration), the order of distribution in the Administration of Insolvent Estates of Deceased Persons Order 1986 (SI 1986/1999) should be followed.

Secured creditors, for example those holding a mortgage or charge over the deceased's property, are in a better position than unsecured creditors in that they may (inter alia) realise the security, ie sell the property by exercising a power of sale as mortgagee or chargee.

31.8 PAYING THE LEGACIES

31.8.1 Introduction

Once the funeral, testamentary and administration expenses and debts have been paid, or at least adequately provided for by setting aside sufficient assets for the purpose, the PRs should consider discharging the gifts arising on the death, other than the gifts of the residuary estate. They may also consider making interim distributions to the residuary beneficiaries on account of their entitlement.

31.8.2 Specific legacies

It is unusual for property given by specific bequest or devise to be needed for payment of the deceased's funeral and testamentary expenses and debts. Once the PRs are satisfied that the property will not be so required, they should consider transferring it to the beneficiary, or to trustees if a trust arises, for example if the property is given to a beneficiary contingently on attaining a stated age and the beneficiary has not yet reached that age.

The method of transferring the property to the beneficiary or trustee will depend on its particular nature. For example, the legal estate in a house or flat should be vested in a beneficiary by a document known as an assent. If the specific legacy is of company shares, a stock transfer form should be used.

In the case of specific gifts only, the vesting of the asset in the beneficiary is retrospective to the date of death, so that any income produced by the property, for example dividends on a specific gift of company shares, belongs to the beneficiary. He is not entitled to the income as it arises but must wait until the PRs vest the property in him. As the beneficiary is entitled to the income he will be liable to be assessed for any income tax due on that income since the death.

Any costs of transferring the property to a specific legatee, and the cost of any necessary insurance cover taken to safeguard the property are the responsibility of the legatee who should reimburse the PRs for the expenses incurred (subject to any contrary direction in a will indicating that such expenses should be paid from residue). If the deceased's title to the asset is disputed by a third party, the specific legatee will be responsible for the cost of litigation to establish ownership.

31.8.3 Pecuniary legacies – provision by will for payment

Set out below is an example of a clause dealing expressly with the payment of pecuniary legacies:

I GIVE all my estate both real and personal whatsoever and wheresoever not hereby or by any codicil hereto otherwise specifically disposed of (hereinafter called 'my residuary estate') unto my trustees UPON TRUST to raise and discharge thereout my debts and funeral and testamentary expenses and all legacies given hereby or by any codicil hereto and any and all taxes payable by reason of my death in respect of property given free of tax and subject thereto UPON TRUST to pay and divide the same equally between ...

There is clear intention shown by the testator to pay the pecuniary legacies from the fund of general residue described as 'my residuary estate'. The result would be the same if the clause gave the residuary estate 'subject to' or 'after payment of' the pecuniary legacies. In both cases the legacies should be paid from the fund of residue before the division of the balance between the residuary beneficiaries.

31.8.4 Pecuniary legacies – no provision by will for payment

Where the will makes no provision for the payment of pecuniary legacies, they are paid primarily from residuary personalty.

EXAMPLE

A will leaves a legacy of £5,000 to Dawn. There is no direction as to payment of the legacy. Residue consisting of personalty and realty is given by the will to 'Edward if he shall survive me by 28 days'. He does so survive the testator, and residue is, therefore, fully disposed of. The PRs should pay the legacy from the personalty, with the proceeds of the realty being used afterwards if necessary.

If a partial intestacy arises, for example where part of a gift of residue fails because one of the beneficiaries dies before the testator, it is often unclear as a matter of law which is the appropriate part of the estate for the payment of the pecuniary legacies. It is preferable, therefore, to make express provision for payment of legacies (as in **31.8.3**).

31.8.5 Time for payment of pecuniary legacies

31.8.5.1 The executor's year

The general rule is that a pecuniary legacy is payable at the end of 'the executor's year', ie one year after the testator's death. The AEA 1925, s 44 provides that PRs are not bound to distribute the estate to the beneficiaries before the expiration of one year from the death. It is often difficult to make payment within the year and, if payment is delayed beyond this date, the legatee will be entitled to interest by way of compensation. The rate of interest will either be the rate prescribed by the testator's will, or, in default of such provision, the rate payable on money paid into court. If the testator stipulates that the legacy is to be paid 'immediately following my death', or that it is payable at some future date, or on the happening of a particular contingency, then interest is payable from either the day following the date of death, the future date or the date the contingency occurs, as may be appropriate.

31.8.5.2 Interest payable from the date of death

There are four occasions when, as an exception to the normal rule, interest is payable on a pecuniary legacy from the date of the death. These occur when legacies are:

(a) payable in satisfaction of a debt owed by the testator to a creditor;

(b) charged on/and owned by the testator;

(c) payable to the testator's minor child (historically this was so that provision was made for maintenance of the child, and interest is not payable under this provision if other funds exist for the child's maintenance); or

(d) payable to any minor (not necessarily the child of the testator) where the intention is to provide for the maintenance of that minor.

31.9   COMPLETING THE ADMINISTRATION AND DISTRIBUTING THE RESIDUARY ESTATE

31.9.1   Introduction

Once the PRs have paid the deceased's funeral, testamentary expenses and debts and any legacies given by the will, they can consider distribution of the residuary estate in accordance with the will or the intestacy rules.

The PRs may have made interim distributions to the residuary beneficiaries on account of their entitlements, at the same time ensuring that they have retained sufficient assets to cover any outstanding liabilities, particularly tax.

Before drawing up the estate accounts and making the final distribution of residue, the PRs must deal with all outstanding matters. Such matters relate mostly to inheritance tax liability, but there will also be income tax and capital gains tax (CGT) to consider.

31.9.2   Adjusting the inheritance tax assessment

Adjustment to the amount of inheritance tax payable on the instalment and non-instalment option property in the estate may arise for a number of reasons, including:

(a)   discovery of additional assets or liabilities since the IHT account was submitted;

(b)   discovery of lifetime transfers made by the deceased within the seven years before death;

(c)   agreement of provisionally estimated values, for example with the shares valuation division of HMRC (in the case of shares in private companies) or the district valuer (in the case of land). The shares valuation division and the district valuer are official agencies established for the formal agreement of valuations on behalf of HMRC with PRs and others. Especially in the case of private company shares, but also in the case of land, valuations may require long negotiations and can often delay reaching a final settlement of inheritance tax liabilities;

(d)   agreement between the PRs and HMRC of a tax liability or repayment, in relation to the deceased's income and capital gains before the death;

(e)   sales made by the PRs after the deceased's death which have given rise to a claim for inheritance tax 'loss relief'.

31.9.2.1   Inheritance tax loss relief

The PRs are often forced to sell assets because they need cash to meet debts, tax liabilities or legacies. The value of quoted shares and land fluctuates depending on market conditions, and PRs may find that they sell these assets for less than their value at the date of death. Loss on sale relief can reduce the inheritance tax liability of the estate in such cases. Where 'qualifying investments' are sold within 12 months of death for less than their market value at the date of death (ie 'probate value') then the sale price may be substituted for the market value at death and the inheritance tax liability adjusted accordingly (IHTA 1984, ss 178–189). 'Qualifying investments' are shares or securities which are quoted on a recognised stock exchange at the date of death and also holdings in authorised unit trusts. The relief must be claimed; it is not automatic. It is normally available only when the PRs make the sale and not where a beneficiary to whom assets have been transferred does so.

If the PRs claim the relief, the value of the qualifying investments at death must be reduced for CGT purposes (s 187). This has the effect of preventing the PRs claiming a loss for CGT purposes where they have claimed inheritance tax loss relief. It would, therefore, be foolish to claim the relief if the estate is passing to a surviving spouse or civil partner as the inheritance tax reduction would be pointless and the estate would no longer be able to claim a CGT loss.

When claiming the relief, PRs must report all sales of qualifying investments made within the 12-month period, including those sold for more than death value, and must substitute the aggregate sale proceeds for the original values.

EXAMPLE

PRs are dealing with an estate which includes holdings in three quoted companies. They sell all the shares in the first 12 months after the death; they make a loss on two of the companies and a gain on the third.

	Value at death	Sale price
	£	£
Shares in XX plc	20,000	10,000
Shares in YY plc	20,000	5,000
Shares in ZZ plc	20,000	40,000
Total value	60,000	55,000

The aggregate sale price is £55,000 so the PRs can reduce the inheritance tax value of the shares from £60,000 to £55,000 saving the inheritance tax on £5,000. Obviously the reduction would have been greater had the PRs not sold the ZZ shares. The CGT acquisition value for the PRs of the XX and YY shares will be reduced to £10,000 and £5,000 respectively.

Loss on sale of shares relief is intended to help those who have to sell investments at a loss to raise money to pay tax, debts, administration expenses or legacies.

To stop PRs selling shares to create a loss and then either buying them back ('bed and breakfasting') or reinvesting the proceeds in other shares, s 180 restricts the relief where the appropriate person buys new qualifying investments within the period starting with death and ending two months after the date of the last sale.

There are similar, though separate, provisions allowing claims for loss relief in relation to the sale of land within four years of a death at a loss (IHTA 1984, ss 190–198).

31.9.3 PRs' continuing inheritance tax liability

31.9.3.1 Inheritance tax by instalments

The PRs may have opted to pay inheritance tax by instalments on the property in the deceased's estate attracting the instalment option. By the time they are ready to transfer the assets to those entitled, probably only one or two instalments will have been paid. The PRs continue to be liable for the remaining instalments. They would be foolish to transfer all the assets to the beneficiaries in reliance on a promise that the beneficiaries will pay the tax. If the beneficiaries become insolvent or disappear, the PRs will be liable for the unpaid tax but will have no assets of the estate to meet the liability. They should consider retaining sufficient assets in the estate. Details of the instalment option facility are discussed at **4.8.1.2**. If any instalment option property is sold, any outstanding inheritance tax on the property sold becomes due immediately.

31.9.3.2 Inheritance tax on lifetime transfers

If the deceased dies within seven years of making either a potentially exempt transfer (PET), or a chargeable transfer, inheritance tax (if a PET) or more inheritance tax (if a chargeable transfer) may become payable. Although the general rule is that the donees of lifetime transfers are primarily liable for the tax, the PRs of the donor's estate may become liable if the tax remains unpaid by the donees 12 months after the end of the month in which the donor died. However, the PRs' liability is limited to the extent of the deceased's assets which they have received, or would have received in the administration of the estate, but for their neglect or default.

In addition, if the deceased gave away property during his lifetime but reserved a benefit in that property, such property is treated as part of his estate on death (see **4.3.1.3**). The donee of the gift is primarily liable to pay the tax attributable, but if the tax remains unpaid 12 months after the end of the month of death, the PRs become liable. Again the PRs should consider how they can protect themselves in case this liability materialises.

31.9.4 Corrective account

When all variations in the extent or value of the deceased's assets and liabilities are known, and all reliefs to which the estate is entitled have been quantified, the PRs must report all outstanding matters to HMRC. This report is made by way of a corrective account on Form C4.

31.9.5 Inheritance tax clearance

31.9.5.1 Certificate or letter of clearance

The last step for the PRs to take in relation to inheritance tax is to obtain confirmation from HMRC that there is no further claim to inheritance tax. If HMRC is satisfied that inheritance tax attributable to a chargeable transfer has, or will be, paid, it can, and if the transfer is one made on death must, confirm that this is the case. The effect is to discharge all persons, thus in particular the PRs, from further liability to inheritance tax (unless there is fraud or non-disclosure of material facts). It also extinguishes any charge imposed by HMRC on the deceased's property for the inheritance tax.

31.9.6 Income tax and CGT

31.9.6.1 The deceased's liability

Immediately following the death, the PRs must make a return to HMRC of the income and capital gains of the deceased for the period starting on 6 April before the death and ending with the date of death. Even though the deceased died part way through the income tax year, the PRs, on his behalf, may claim the same reliefs and allowances as the deceased could have claimed had he lived throughout the whole year. Any liability to tax is a debt of the deceased which must be paid by the PRs during the administration. The debt will be deductible when calculating the amount of inheritance tax. Alternatively, if a refund of tax is obtained, this will represent an asset, so increasing the size of the estate for inheritance tax purposes.

31.9.6.2 The administration period

For each income tax year (or part) during the administration period, the PRs must make a return to HMRC of the income they receive on the deceased's assets, and any gains they make on disposals of chargeable assets for administration purposes, for example to raise money to pay inheritance tax or the pecuniary legacies. These returns for the estate are distinct from the PRs' returns of their own income and capital gains.

31.9.6.3 Income tax

Rate of tax

The rates at which PRs pay income tax depends on the type of income they receive.

PRs do not pay income tax at any higher rate(s) but nor do they benefit from the personal savings and dividend allowances. They do not have a personal allowance.

They will therefore pay tax at the following rates on all income received:

dividends	7.5%
other income	20%

Calculation of PRs' liability

In calculating any income tax liability on the income of the administration period, the PRs may be able to claim relief for interest paid on a bank loan to pay inheritance tax. If the PRs use this loan to pay the inheritance tax on the deceased's personal property in the UK which devolves on them in order to obtain the grant, income tax relief is generally available to them.

> **EXAMPLE**
>
> PRs' only income is gross interest of £4,000 for a tax year in the administration period. They pay £1,000 interest to the bank on a loan to pay inheritance tax to obtain their grant.
>
> | | |
> |---|---|
> | Gross income | £4,000 |
> | Less: interest paid | £1,000 |
> | Taxable income | £3,000 |
> | Less: tax (20%) | £600 |
> | Net income for the beneficiaries | £2,400 |

Beneficiary's income tax liability

Once the PRs' tax position has been settled, the remaining net income will be paid to the beneficiary. The grossed up amount of this income should be included by the beneficiary in his return of income for the income tax year to which it relates.

> **EXAMPLE**
>
> PRs have completed the administration of an estate and there is bank deposit account interest which, after payment of tax at 20% by the PRs, amounts to £800. That sum is paid by the PRs to the residuary beneficiary.
>
> When the beneficiary makes his return of income he must declare the estate income grossed up at 20%, ie
>
> $£800 \times \frac{100}{80} = £1,000.$

The PRs must supply the beneficiary with a certificate of deduction of tax, on Form R185, which the beneficiary should send to his own inspector of taxes as evidence of the payment of the tax by the PRs. Beneficiaries whose income, including the estate income, is not above the level of the personal allowance can reclaim the tax paid.

31.9.6.4   Capital gains tax

No disposal on death

On death, there is no disposal for CGT purposes, so that no liability to CGT arises. The PRs acquire all the deceased's assets at their probate value at death. This has the effect of wiping out gains which accrued during the deceased's lifetime so that these gains are not charged to tax. Although there is no disposal, the probate value becomes the PRs' 'base cost' of all the deceased's assets for future CGT purposes.

Calculation of PRs' liability

If the PRs dispose of chargeable assets during the administration of the deceased's estate to raise cash (eg, to pay inheritance tax, or other outgoings or legacies), they are liable to CGT on any chargeable gains that they make. For gains arising in 2017/18 the rate is 20% except for gains on residential property which are taxed at 28%. The rates are flat rates irrespective of the level of income and gains of the estate.

In addition to deducting their acquisition cost (probate value), the PRs may deduct from the disposal consideration the incidental costs of disposal (eg, stockbroker's commission on sale of shares). In addition, they may deduct a proportion of the cost of valuing the deceased's estate for probate purposes. Calculations may be based either on a scale published by HMRC, or on the actual expenditure incurred if this is higher.

The PRs may claim the annual exemption for disposals made in the tax year in which the deceased died and the following two tax years only (if the administration lasts this long). The exemption is the same as for an individual (ie, £11,300 for 2017/18). Maximum advantage will be taken from this exemption if the PRs plan sales of assets carefully so that gains are realised in stages in each of the three tax years for which it is available.

EXAMPLE

In May 2017 PRs realise they will need to raise £50,000 to pay administration expenses. The investments they are advised to sell will realise a net gain of £21,300. They have no unused losses.

(1) If all sales occur in the same tax year, their CGT position is as follows:

		£	
gain		21,300	
annual exemption		(11,300)	
taxable		10,000	at 20% = £2,000

(2) If the sales are spread evenly over two tax years, their CGT position is as follows:

		£
Year 1	gain	10,650
	annual exemption	(11,300)
	taxable	nil
Year 2	gain	10,650
	annual exemption	(11,100)
	taxable	nil

Sales at a loss

If the PRs sell assets for less than their value at death, an allowable loss for CGT will arise. This loss may be relieved by setting it against gains arising on other sales by the PRs in the same, or any future, tax year in the administration period. Any loss which is unrelieved at the end of the administration period cannot be transferred to the beneficiaries. In view of this limitation, the PRs should plan sales carefully to ensure they can obtain relief for all losses which they realise. If there is a possibility of losses being unused, the PRs should either plan sales of other assets, or consider transferring the assets worth less than their probate value to the beneficiaries (see below).

Transfer of assets to the legatees

If, instead of selling assets, the PRs vest them in the legatees, ie in the beneficiaries (or trustees if a trust arises), no chargeable gain or allowable loss arises. The beneficiary or trustee is assumed to acquire the asset transferred at its probate value. This 'base cost' of the asset will be relevant to the CGT calculation on a future disposal.

EXAMPLE 1

A testator by will leaves his residuary estate to Parvez. Among the assets forming residue are 1,000 shares in XYZ plc. Probate value of these was £5,200. By the time they were transferred to Parvez the value had risen to £10,000. Five years after death Parvez sells them for £18,500.

	£
Disposal consideration	18,500
Less: acquisition (probate) value	(5,200)
Gain	13,300
Less: annual exemption	(11,300)
Chargeable gain	2,000

EXAMPLE 2

If Parvez sells the shares for £3,400, ie £2,000 less than their probate value, his position would be as follows:

	£
Disposal consideration	3,400
Less: acquisition (probate) value	5,400
Loss	(2,000)

The loss of £2,000 is available to Parvez to set against chargeable gains he may have in the same, or any future, tax year.

PRACTICAL POINTS

Remember the following points on CGT and death:

(1)   No CGT is payable on death itself.

(2)   If PRs sell assets, they make a disposal. Their acquisition value is the market value at the date of death. They have an annual exemption equal to an individual's in the tax year of death and the two following tax years, so there will often be no tax liability on their disposals.

(3)   The rate of tax payable by PRs is 20% except for gains on residential property which are taxed at 28%.

(4)   If PRs transfer assets to beneficiaries, they do not make a disposal. The beneficiary acquires the asset at market value at the date of death.

31.9.7 Transferring assets to residuary beneficiaries

31.9.7.1 Interim distributions

Once the outstanding tax, legal costs and other matters have been disposed of, PRs should consider transferring any remaining assets to the residuary beneficiaries. In doing so they must remember that payments may have been made already to the beneficiaries as interim distributions on account of their entitlement. If so, these will be taken into account when determining what and how much more should be transferred to those beneficiaries. These interim distributions will also be shown in the estate accounts.

31.9.7.2 Adult beneficiaries

If the beneficiaries are adults, and have a vested entitlement to property in the residuary estate, their entitlement can be transferred to them. If they have a contingent entitlement, the property cannot be transferred to them but will instead be transferred to trustees to hold on their behalf until the contingency is satisfied.

31.9.7.3 Minor beneficiaries

If any beneficiaries are under 18 years of age, whether the interest enjoyed is vested or contingent, the property will usually be held in trust for them until the age of majority is reached or the contingency is satisfied. If a minor beneficiary has a vested interest the PRs may be able to transfer his entitlement to him (if expressly authorised in the will), or to parents and guardians on behalf of the minor.

31.9.7.4 Transferring property to the residuary beneficiaries

The manner in which the property is transferred to residuary beneficiaries, or to trustees of their behalf, will depend on the nature of the property remaining in the estate.

Personal property

The PRs indicate that they no longer require property for administration purposes when they pass title to it by means of an assent. Generally, no particular form of assent is required in the case of personalty so that often the property passes by delivery. The beneficiary's title to the property derives from the will; the assent is merely the manner of giving effect to the gift by the PRs. Company shares are transferred by share (stock) transfer form. The PRs must produce their grant to the company as proof of title to the shares. They, as transferors, transfer the shares 'as PRs of X deceased' to the beneficiary (the transferee), who then applies to be registered as a member of the company in place of the deceased member.

Freehold or leasehold land

Personal representatives vest the legal estate in land in the person entitled (whether beneficially or as trustee) by means of an assent, which will then become a document of title to the legal estate. If PRs are to continue to hold property in their changed capacity as trustees under trusts declared by the will, or arising under the intestacy law, an assent will again be appropriate. The PRs should formally vest the legal estate in themselves as trustees to hold for the beneficiaries.

By the AEA 1925, s 36(4), an assent must be in writing, it must be signed by the PRs, and it must name the person in whose favour it is made. It then operates to vest the legal estate in the named person. A deed is not necessary to pass the legal estate, but PRs may choose to use a deed, for example if they require the beneficiary to give them the benefit of an indemnity covenant. If the title to the land is registered, the assent must be in the form specified by the Land Registration Rules 2003.

Any person in whose favour the PRs make an assent or conveyance may require notice of it to be endorsed on the original grant of probate or administration. In view of this entitlement, it is good practice that the endorsement should be made by the PRs, or solicitors on their behalf, as a matter of routine at the same time as the assent is given. Indeed, if the PRs have made an assent where the title is unregistered in favour of a beneficiary, endorsement is essential for that beneficiary's protection in view of the provisions of the AEA 1925, s 36(6) benefitting any later purchaser from the PRs.

If the title to the land is registered, two options are open to the PRs:

(a)   they can apply to be registered as proprietor in place of the deceased, in which case they must produce the grant of representation when making the application; or

(b)   they can transfer the property by assent without being registered as proprietor themselves, in which case the beneficiary must be given a certified copy of the grant of representation so that he can present it with his application for registration.

As the register is conclusive as to title, the provisions in the AEA 1925 regarding endorsements on the grant are of no relevance.

31.9.8   Estate accounts

31.9.8.1   Purpose of the accounts

The final task of the PRs is usually to produce estate accounts for the residuary beneficiaries. The purpose of the accounts is to show all the assets of the estate, the payment of the debts, administration expenses and legacies, and the balance remaining for the residuary beneficiaries. The balance will normally be represented by a combination of assets transferred to the beneficiaries in specie, and some cash. The residuary beneficiaries sign the accounts to indicate that they approve them. In the absence of fraud or failure to disclose assets, their signatures will also release the PRs from further liability to account to the beneficiaries.

31.9.8.2   Presentation of the accounts

There is no prescribed form for estate accounts. Any presentation adopted should be clear and concise so that the accounts are easily understood by the residuary beneficiaries. If interim distribution payments were made to the residuary beneficiaries during the administration period, these must be taken into account and shown in the estate accounts.

Vertical presentation

Estate accounts may be presented vertically, disclosing assets less liabilities, etc, and a balance for the beneficiaries, or on a double-sided basis, disclosing receipts opposite the payments. It is customary to use the probate values of the assets for accounting purposes.

Narrative introduction

The accounts generally start with a narrative statement of the date of death, the date of the grant of representation, a summary of the will or succession under the intestacy law, and the value of the deceased's gross and net estate. All this information is provided to make the understanding of the accounts easier for the beneficiaries.

Capital and income accounts

Normally accounts show capital assets, and income produced by those assets during the administration period, in separate capital and income accounts. In small estates this may not be necessary, so that one account showing both capital and income will be sufficient. However, it is always necessary to prepare separate accounts if the will (or the intestacy rules) creates a life or minority interest, since the different interests of the beneficiaries in the capital and income need to be distinguished throughout the period of the trust, and when it ends.

SUMMARY

(1)   When PRs administer an estate, they are under a statutory duty to administer it correctly (Administration of Estates Act 1925, s 25 as substituted).

(2)   They are personally liable for any errors and so must be careful to protect themselves.

(3)   They have various statutory powers contained mainly in the Trustee Acts 1925 and 2000. These powers are sometimes extended by the will. Sections 31 and 32 of the Trustee Act 1925 are particularly important.

(4)   As well as paying inheritance tax, PRs may have to pay CGT and income tax:

    (a)   The PRs have an individual's CGT annual exemption for the tax year of death and the two following tax years.

    (b)   Death is not a disposal but the PRs are deemed to acquire the assets at market value at the date of death.

    (c)   If they sell, they make a disposal.

    (d)   If they transfer to beneficiaries, there is no disposal; the beneficiaries acquire at market value at the date of death.

    (e)   The PRs are liable to income tax on income of the administration period at basic and dividend ordinary rate.

(5)   At the end of the administration, PRs prepare estate accounts for approval by the residuary beneficiaries.

PROBATE AND ADMINISTRATION

Topic	Summary	References
What happens to property when someone dies?	People usually think that where property goes depends on whether or not there is a will. However, many assets pass independently of a will. For example, property held as beneficial joint tenants passes by survivorship; trust property passes under the terms of the trust. Money due from a pension scheme will be subject to the terms of the scheme which normally give the trustees power to choose who to pay it to. Often, the bulk of a person's wealth passes independently of any will.	See **29.2** and **29.3**.
What are the requirements of a valid will?	A testator must be at least 18 and have testamentary capacity. The testator must know and approve the contents of the will and must not have been subjected to undue influence, force, fear or fraud. The will must be signed and witnessed in accordance with s 9 of the Wills Act 1837.	See **29.4**.
How are wills revoked?	Wills can be revoked by a later will or codicil, by destruction or by a later marriage or the formation of a later civil partnership.	See **29.4.4**.
Failure of legacies	A gift in a will fails if the beneficiary predeceases the testator, witnesses the will or is a spouse or civil partner of a witness. A gift of a specific item will fail if the testator no longer owns the item at death. A gift to a spouse or civil partner fails if the marriage or civil partnership is dissolved.	See **29.5**.
What if there is no valid will?	If there is no valid will or if there is property undisposed of by the will, the undisposed of property passes under the intestacy rules. The deceased's personal representatives hold the property on trust. They pay any debts and inheritance tax due and then pay what is left to the closest members of the deceased's family following the order set out in s 46 of the Administration of Estates Act 1925.	See **29.6**.

Topic	Summary	References
What if a family member or dependant is inadequately provided for?	Family members and dependants can apply to the court under the Inheritance (Provision for Family and Dependants) Act 1975 for a redistribution of assets if they feel that the deceased did not make reasonable provision for them. The court is limited to providing for the reasonable maintenance of the applicant except in the case of spouses and civil partners who can claim a reasonable share of the deceased's assets.	See **29.7**.
Who deals with the estate of a deceased person?	Someone has to deal with the assets of the deceased. The generic name for people doing this job is 'personal representatives'. There are two types: executors and administrators. Executors are people appointed in the will. If there are no executors able and willing to act then beneficiaries of the estate will act as administrators. The order of entitlement for administrators is set out in rules 19 and 20 of the Non-contentious Probate Rules 1987. Both executors and administrators need proof that they are entitled to act. They need to apply to the Probate Registry for a grant of representation. Executors get a grant of probate; administrators get a grant of administration. Note that personal representatives deal only with assets capable of passing by will. Other assets such as property held as beneficial joint tenants pass directly to the person entitled.	
Procedure for applying for a grant of representation	This varies depending on what type of grant is involved, but all personal representatives must swear an oath and pay any inheritance tax due.	See **30.5– 30.11**.
What do the personal representatives do once they have obtained the grant of representation?	Once the grant is obtained, the personal representatives must pay the debts, finalise the inheritance tax position and distribute the assets to the people entitled. This is a burdensome task as personal representatives are personally liable for errors in payment. They can get limited protection under s 27 of the Administration of Estates Act 1925 by advertising for claimants to the estate. For full protection against later claims, they must apply to the court.	See **Chapter 31**.

Index